# THE ORGANIST'S SHORTCUT TO SERVICE MUSIC

Joy E. Lawrence
Kent State University

A Guide to Finding Intonations, Organ Compositions and Free
Accompaniments Based on Traditional Hymn Tunes

**LUDWIG MUSIC ⓛ PUBLISHING Cº**

**557 EAST 140th STREET, CLEVELAND, OHIO 44110–1999**
**(216) 851-1150**

BK-56
$29.95

# ACKNOWLEDGMENTS

This book is dedicated to the organist who devotes a major portion of his/her love, energy, and talent to serving the Lord each Sunday morning. The author is grateful to Dr. Walter Watson, Director of the School of Music, Kent State University, who inspired and nurtured the preparation of this work and who provided the title. A special thanks also to David Powers of Educators Music, Lakewood, Ohio who assisted with locating music appropriate for inclusion in this work. Others who have encouraged and sustained this long effort include The Reverend Harold F. Dicke, Pastor, and William D. Thomas, Director of Music of Grace Lutheran Church, Cleveland Heights, Ohio. A special thank you to my parents who remain a constant source of strength and perseverance.

Joy E. Lawrence
Kent State University
1986

# THE AUTHOR

JOY E. LAWRENCE is Professor of Music Education and Organ at Kent State University. She is also the organist of Grace Lutheran Church in Cleveland Heights, Ohio. Dr. Lawrence holds degrees from Mount Union College, Union Theological Seminary and Case Western Reserve University. She has performed extensively in the Cleveland area and maintains a busy schedule of recitals, workshops in church music, choral techniques and related arts, guest conducting and adjudication of choral festivals.

Dr. Lawrence is co-author of **Music and Related Arts for the Classroom**, (with William M. Anderson) **A Musician's Guide to Church Music**, (with John A. Ferguson) and **Integrating Music Into the Classroom**, (with William M. Anderson). She has had numerous articles published in the major music education and church music journals. She is a past dean of the Cleveland Chapter of the American Guild of Organists and Founder of the Church Music Conference of Cleveland, Ohio.

# INTRODUCTION

This book is for you, the busy organist, who is constantly seeking music suitable for use in services of worship: an introduction to a hymn, a prelude, music for communion, a voluntary (offertory) or a postlude. In addition, you may wish to play a varied harmony or free accompaniment to a particular hymn being sung.

One of your primary tasks is to select organ music which will contribute to **unity** in worship. **Unity** is often achieved through emphasis on music and scripture appropriate for the Church Year, e.g., Advent, Christmas, Lent, Easter; as well as special days so designated by the Biblical Scripture appointed for the day, e.g., Twenty-Third Psalm "The Lord is My Shepherd", for Good Shepherd Sunday. Unity may also be achieved through selecting organ music based on a theme, e.g., Faith, Hope, Love.

A major way that the organist can contribute to **unity** in worship is to select organ music which is based on either the hymns to be sung in the service or on other hymns related to the theme, sermon, or liturgy. The "traditional" way for the organist to find these compositions is to search through his/her own library of music, often a highly time consuming process. For example, an organist may know that a particular composer arranged a hymn tune, e.g., J. S. Bach, but may not know in which volume of a given edition it may be found. Again, if time permits, the organist may examine catalogs of organ music from different publishers, seeking appropriate music for his/her needs.

Usually an **Intonation** or brief introduction is played before the singing of the first verse of a hymn. This may take the form of all or part of a hymn, such as the first and last lines; a composed introduction containing fragments of the hymn tune; or a composed introduction in the style of the hymn.

It is often important that the key of the organ composition be the same as the key of the hymn since the organist may wish to play the organ piece as an introduction to the singing of the hymn by the congregation. A resource which enables the organist to link keys of compositions with keys of hymns and to find **Intonations** quickly can be most valuable.

Another task of the organist is to play the text of hymns expressively, so that there is always variety and interest, even when there are six or seven verses. This frequently involves playing different harmonizations and

V

arrangements of the tune from those found in the denominational hymnal. These are usually called **free accompaniments**. The same problems exist for finding these, as for finding organ compositions based on hymn tunes.

This book, **The Organist's Shortcut to Service Music**, is a guide to help the busy organist find titles, composers and publishers of intonations, organ compositions and free accompaniments based on hymn tunes found in eleven hymnals of the following major denominations: Baptist USA, Disciples of Christ, Episcopal, Lutheran, United Church of Christ, Roman Catholic, United Methodist and United Presbyterian. In it will be found 2300 hymn tunes, 2400 organ compositions based on these hymn tunes and 750 free accompaniments. Each hymnal has been given a code. For example, BA = **Baptist Hymnal** (Southern Baptist USA); 1940 = **The Hymnal of the Protestant Episcopal Church in the United States of America, 1940.** Each entry lists the tune name and the key in which it is written as found in the following hymnals:

CODE

Baptist — USA . . . . . . . . . . . . . . . . . . . . . . . . . . . . . . . . . . . . . . . . . **BA**
    **Baptist Hymnal** Nashville, Tenn.: Convention Press, 1955

Disciples of Christ . . . . . . . . . . . . . . . . . . . . . . . . . . . . . . . . . . . . . **DC**
    **Hymnbook for Christian Worship** St. Louis: Bethany Press, 1970

Episcopal . . . . . . . . . . . . . . . . . . . . . . . . . . . . . . . . . . . . . . . . . . . . **1940**
    **The Hymnal of the Protestant Episcopal Church in the United States of America** 1940 New York: The Church Pension Fund 1940

Episcopal 1982 . . . . . . . . . . . . . . . . . . . . . . . . . . . . . . . . . . . . . . . . **1982**
    **The Hymnal 1982** New York, New York: Church Hymnal Corporation 1985

Lutheran Church in America, The American Lutheran Church, The Evangelical Lutheran Church of Canada, The Lutheran Church — Missouri Synod . . . . . . . . . . . . . . . . . . . . . . . . . . . . . . . . . . . . . . . . **LBW**
    **Lutheran Book of Worship** Minneapolis: Augsburg Publishing House, 1978

The Lutheran Church — Missouri Synod ....................... **LW**
> **Lutheran Worship** St. Louis: Concordia Publishing House, 1982

United Church of Christ (Congregational) ....................... **PH**
> **Pilgrim Hymnal** Boston: The Pilgrim Press, 1958

Roman Catholic (Vatican II) .................................. **RCV**
> **Vatican II Hymnal** Seattle: The New Catholic Press of Seattle, 1975

United Church of Christ ...................................... **UCC**
> **The Hymnal of the United Church of Christ** Philadelphia: United Church Press, 1974

United Methodist ........................................... **UM**
> **The Methodist Hymnal** Nashville: The Methodist Publishing House, 1966

United Presbyterian ........................................ **WB**
> **The Worshipbook** Philadelphia: The Westminster Press, 1972

Beneath each hymn tune is a coded listing of all of the hymnals. If the hymn tune appears in the hymnal, the key is identified. Following this information is a listing, by composer, of intonations and organ compositions based on this tune, along with free accompaniments. Each entry consists of:

> Tune Name
>
> The hymnal in which it may be found (See Code)
>
> The key of the hymn if it appears in the hymnal
>
> Intonations
>
> Organ Compositions based on the hymn tune
>
>> Composer/Arranger
>>
>> Title/Collection
>>
>> Volume number/Opus number
>>
>> Editor
>>
>> Publisher

Catalog number

Key

Free Accompaniments

Composer/Arranger

Title/Collection

Volume number/Opus number

Editor

Publisher

Catalog number

Key

Example:

Duke Street
Hymnal

| Code: | BA | DC | 1940 | 1982 | LBW | LW | PH | RCV | UCC | UM | WB |
|-------|-----|-----|------|------|-----|-----|-----|-----|-----|-----|-----|
| Key: | Eb | D | D | D | D | D | D | Eb | D | D | D |

## INTONATIONS

McCormick, David **20 Organ Intonations on Hymns of Praise**
Hope Publishing Co. Key: D

## ORGAN COMPOSITIONS

Bish, Diane "Jesus Shall Reign" **The Diane Bish Organ Book**
Volume 4   Fred Bock Music Company   BG 0776   Key: D

Haan, Raymond H. **Festival Hymn Preludes** The Sacred Music
Press   KK 329-3   Key: D

Held, Wilbur "Give to Our God Immortal Praise" **Preludes and
Postludes** Volume I Augsburg Publishing House   11-9318
Key: D

Schack, David "Jesus Shall Reign" **The Concordia Hymn Prelude
Series** Volume 23 Edited: Herbert Gotsch Concordia
Publishing House   97-5738   Key: D

Wienhorst, Richard "I Know that My Redeemer Lives" **The Parish
Organist** Part One Edited: Heinrich Fleischer Concordia
Publishing House   97-1145   Key: D

VIII

## FREE ACCOMPANIMENTS

Bunjes, Paul **New Organ Accompaniments for Hymns** Concordia Publishing House  97-5348  Key: D

Cassler, G. Winston **Organ Descants for Selected Hymn Tunes** Augsburg Publishing House  11-9304  Key: D

Ferguson, John **Hymn Harmonizations** Book III  Ludwig Music Publishing Co.  Key: D

Johnson, David N. **Free Harmonizations of Twelve Hymn Tunes** Augsburg Publishing House  11-9190  Key: Db

Krapf, Gerhard **Hymn Preludes and Free Accompaniments** Volume 13  Augsburg Publishing House 11-9409  Key: D

Noble, T. Tertius **Free Organ Accompaniments to One Hundred Well-Known Hymn Tunes** J. Fischer & Bros.  #8175  Key: D

Wyton, Alec **New Shoots from Old Routes** The Sacred Music Press  KK 279  Key: D

Many hymn tunes are also known by other names. The best known of these have been cross indexed for the reader's convenience and will be found in both the Alphabetic Index of Hymn tunes and the Listing.

Example: **Ebenezer** (See also: Ton-y-botel)

Where an occasional tune name appears more than once, the particular composer's name will be found in parenthesis.

Example:
**St. Thomas** (Wade)
**St. Thomas** (Williams)

Major keys are indicated by upper case letters: **E** represents E Major; minor keys by lower case letters: **e** represents e minor; while a hymn in a mode is listed as **m:**, with the last pitch of the melody identified. Thus, the code **m:e** signifies that the hymn is written in a mode and ends on the pitch "E".

Because there is disagreement, even among scholars, in identifying modes of certain chorale preludes, and because the organist is frequently most concerned about how the final pitch of the organ composition will relate to the key of the hymn being sung, the author has simply designated such compositions as modal and identified the final pitch   e.g., Key: **m: e**.

It is suggested that the organist identify, with an appropriate symbol, those compositions which he/she owns. Other works discovered and purchased should be added by the organist to the listing, thus keeping **The Organist's Shortcut to Service Music** up to date.

A review of the literature has revealed only six works which have attempted to provide the organist with lists of organ music based on hymn tunes. Five of these were published before 1974, while **A Selected Source Index for Hymn and Chorale Tunes in Lutheran Worship Books** by Daniel J. Werning, was published by Concordia Publishing House in 1985. As its title indicates, this most recent resource is limited to tunes found in Lutheran Worship Books and does not differentiate between organ compositions, free accompaniments, intonations, or music for organ and instruments. Publishers' names and addresses are found at the end of the work which is published in the form of a loose leaf notebook.

Jean Slater Edson's **Organ Preludes: An Index to Compositions on Hymn Tunes, Chorales, Plainsong melodies, Gregorian Tunes and Carols** Volume I: Composers Index; Volume II: Tune Name Index, Metuchen: N. J.: 1974, is a comprehensive and scholarly work. To find an organ composition based on a hymn tune, the reader refers to Volume II, where there is a list of composers who have written organ compositions based on the tune. It is necessary to return to Volume I to locate the composer and work. There are no references to hymnals, keys or free accompaniments.

In 1952, Barenreiter published Fritz Muenger's **Choralbearbeitungen fuer Orgel** which listed compositions based on hymns in the German and Swiss Evangelical Hymnals. The **Companion to the 1940 Hymnal**, published in 1949 contains approximately 1400 pieces based on hymns in the **Hymnal 1940**.

In 1948, Concordia published a work by Martin Stellhorn, **Index to Hymn Preludes** which contained some 2250 pieces based mainly on hymns from the Lutheran Hymnal. Henry Coleman's **Index of Hymn Tune Preludes by English Composers** was published in 1930, but only includes 225 compositions.

While the author recognizes that there are many compositions which may not be listed in this book; every effort has been made to locate as many as possible, and it is hoped that **The Organist's Shortcut to Service Music** will provide a ready resource for finding organ intonations, organ compositions and free accompaniments based on hymn tunes used in major denominational hymnals. May its use enhance and enrich the worship of God.

x

# ALPHABETICAL INDEX

## OF

## HYMN TUNES

# A

**TUNE**

A la ru
| BA | DC | 1940 | 1982 | LBW | LW | PH | RCV | UCC | UM | WB |
|----|----|------|------|-----|----|----|-----|-----|----|----|
| BA | DC | 1940 | 1982 | LBW | LW | PH | RCV | UCC | UM | WB |
|    |    |      | D    |     |    |    |     |     |    |    |

A la venue de Noel
| BA | DC | 1940 | 1982 | LBW | LW | PH | RCV | UCC | UM | WB |
|----|----|------|------|-----|----|----|-----|-----|----|----|
| BA | DC | 1940 | 1982 | LBW | LW | PH | RCV | UCC | UM | WB |
|    |    | g    |      |     |    |    |     |     |    |    |

A solis ortus cardine
| BA | DC | 1940 | 1982 | LBW | LW | PH | RCV | UCC | UM | WB |
|----|----|------|------|-----|----|----|-----|-----|----|----|
| BA | DC | 1940 | 1982 | LBW | LW | PH | RCV | UCC | UM | WB |
|    |    |      |      | m:e |    |    |     |     |    |    |

ORGAN COMPOSITIONS

Scheidt, Samuel  "From East to West"  **The Concordia Hymn Prelude Series**  Volume 2  Edited: Herbert Gotsch  Concordia Publishing House  97-5536  Key: m:e

Titelouze, Jean  "Hymnus 'A solis ortus cardine'"  **Organ Music for Christmas**  Volume 1  Edited: C. H. Trevor  Oxford University Press  Key: m:e

A va de
| BA | DC | 1940 | 1982 | LBW | LW | PH | RCV | UCC | UM | WB |
|----|----|------|------|-----|----|----|-----|-----|----|----|
| BA | DC | 1940 | 1982 | LBW | LW | PH | RCV | UCC | UM | WB |
|    |    |      |      | F   |    |    |     |     |    |    |

ORGAN COMPOSITIONS

Skaalen, Peter  "Come, Let Us Eat"  **The Concordia Hymn Prelude Series**  Volume 16  Edited: Herbert Gotsch  Concordia Publishing House  97-5707  Key: F

Abbey
| BA | DC | 1940 | 1982 | LBW | LW | PH | RCV | UCC | UM | WB |
|----|----|------|------|-----|----|----|-----|-----|----|----|
| BA | DC | 1940 | 1982 | LBW | LW | PH | RCV | UCC | UM | WB |
| F  |    |      |      |     |    | G  |     |     |    |    |

FREE ACCOMPANIMENTS

**Free Harmonizations of Hymn Tunes by Fifty American Composers**  Edited: D. DeWitt Wasson  Hinshaw Music, Inc.  HMO-145  Key: G

Abbott's Leigh
| BA | DC | 1940 | 1982 | LBW | LW | PH | RCV | UCC | UM | WB |
|----|----|------|------|-----|----|----|-----|-----|----|----|
| BA | DC | 1940 | 1982 | LBW | LW | PH | RCV | UCC | UM | WB |
|    |    |      | C    | C   |    |    |     |     |    | C  |

# ORGAN COMPOSITIONS

Patterson, Kimberly Kondal  "Lord of Light"  **The Concordia Hymn Prelude Series**  Volume 19  Edited: Herbert Gotsch  Concordia Publishing House  97-5710  Key: C

# FREE ACCOMPANIMENTS

**Free Harmonizations of Hymn Tunes by Fifty American Composers**  Edited: D. DeWitt Wasson  Hinshaw Music, Inc.  HMO-145  Key: C

Abends

| BA | DC | 1940 | 1982 | LBW | LW | PH | RCV | UCC | UM | WB |
|----|----|------|------|-----|----|----|-----|-----|----|----|
|    | DC | F    | 1982 | LBW | LW | PH | RCV | UCC | Ab | WB |

Aberystwyth

| BA | DC | 1940 | 1982 | LBW | LW | PH | RCV | UCC | UM | WB |
|----|----|------|------|-----|----|----|-----|-----|----|----|
| d  | e  | e    | e    | d   | e  | e  |     | e   | e  | d  |

# ORGAN COMPOSITIONS

Harris, David S.  **Ten Hymn Preludes in Trio Style**  Set 2  H. W. Gray Co.  GB 643  Key: e

Held, Wilbur  "Jesus, Lover of My Soul"  **The Concordia Hymn Prelude Series**  Volume 19  Edited: Herbert Gotsch  Concordia Publishing House  97-5710  Key: e

Janson, Thomas  "Saviour, When in Dust to You"  **The Concordia Hymn Prelude Series**  Volume 7  Edited: Herbert Gotsch  Concordia Publishing House  97-5614  Key: d

Noble, T. Tertius "Chorale-Prelude on the tune 'Aberystwyth'"  **A Galaxy of Hymn Tune Preludes for Organ**  Galaxy Music Corp. GMC 2353  Key: g

Thalben-Ball, George **Variations on Hymn Tunes**  Novello & Co., Ltd.  Key: f

Willan, Healey  "Hear Our Solemn Litany"  **Ten Hymn Tune Preludes**  C.F. Peters Corp. No. 6011  Key: e

Young, Gordon **Prelude Based on "Aberystwyth"**  Carl Fischer P 2976  Key: e

# FREE ACCOMPANIMENTS

Busarow, Donald **All Praise to You Eternal God**
Augsburg Publishing House 11-9076  Key: d

Hancock, Gerre  **Organ Improvisations for Hymn-Singing**
Hinshaw Music  HMO-100  Key: e

Schack, David  **Hymn Preludes and Free Accompaniments**
Volume 11  Augsburg Publishing House  11-9407
Key: d

Acclamation

| BA | DC | 1940 | 1982 | LBW | LW | PH | RCV | UCC | UM | WB |
|----|----|------|------|-----|----|----|-----|-----|----|----|
| F |  |  |  |  |  |  |  |  |  |  |

Ach bleib' bei uns

| BA | DC | 1940 | 1982 | LBW | LW | PH | RCV | UCC | UM | WB |
|----|----|------|------|-----|----|----|-----|-----|----|----|
|  |  |  | D | | F | F |  |  |  |  |

# ORGAN COMPOSITIONS

Bach, J.S.  **Organ Works**  Volume 1  Edited:  Heinz-
Harald Löhlein  Urtext of the New Bach Edition
Bärenreiter  5171  Key: Bb

Bach, J.S.  **Six Organ Chorals** (Schübler)
Edited: Albert Riemenschneider, Oliver Ditson
Key: Bb

Bach, J.S.  **Organ Works** Volume VIII  Widor-Schweitzer
G. Schirmer  Key: Bb

Bach, J.S.  **Organ Works** Volume VI  C.F. Peters
Corporation  No. 245  Key: Bb

Engel, James  "Abide with Us, Our Savior"  **Preludes on
Six Hymn Tunes**  Augsburg Publishing House 11-9364
Key: Eb

Reger, Max  **30 Short Chorale Preludes** Op. 135a
C.F. Peters Corporation  Nr. 3980  Key:  Eb

Walcha, Helmut  **25 Chorale Preludes**  C.F. Peters
Nr. 4850  Key: Bb

Wente, Steven "Lord Jesus Christ, Will You Not Stay"
**The Concordia Hymn Prelude Series**  Volume 19
Edited: Herbert Gotsch  Concordia Publishing
House  97-5710  Key: F

Ach bleib' mit deiner Gnade
| BA | DC | 1940 | 1982 | LBW | LW | PH | RCV | UCC | UM | WB |
|----|----|------|------|-----|----|----|-----|-----|----|----|
|    |    |      |      |     | D  |    |     |     |    |    |

## ORGAN COMPOSITIONS

Karg-Elert, Sigfrid "Ah, Leave With Us Thy Grace"
**Choral Improvisations for Organ for Advent and
Christmastide** Op. 65 Volume1 Edited: Robert Leech
Bedell  Edward B. Marks Music Corp. Key: Eb

Karg-Elert, Sigfrid "Abide, O Dearest Jesus (Trio)
**Wedding Music** Part II  Concordia Publishing
House  97-1370  Key: Eb

Peeters, Flor "Abide, O Dearest Jesus" **30 Chorale
Preludes**  Opus 68  C.F. Peters Corporation
6023  Key:  F

Ach Gott und Herr
| BA | DC | 1940 | 1982 | LBW | LW | PH | RCV | UCC | UM | WB |
|----|----|------|------|-----|----|----|-----|-----|----|----|
|    |    |      |      |     | A  |    |     |     | A  |    |

## ORGAN COMPOSITIONS

Bach, J.S.  **Organ Chorales from the Neumeister
Collection**  Edited: Christopf Wolff  Yale
University Press/Bärenreiter 5181  Key: m:b

Bach, J.S.  **Organ Works**  Volume 3  "The Individually
Transmitted Organ Chorales"  Edited: Hans Klotz
Urtext of the New  Bach Edition Bärenreiter 5173
Key: m:b

Bach, J.S. **Organ Works** Volume VI  Widor-Schweitzer
G. Schirmer  Key: m:c; Key m:b

Bach, J.S. **Orgelwerke** Volume VI  C.F. Peters
Corporation  Nr. 245  Key: C

Bach, J.S. **Orgelwerke** Volume IX  C.F. Peters
Corporation  Nr. 2067 Key: m:b

Beck, Albert  **76 Offertories on Hymns & Chorales**
Concordia Publishing House 97-5207  Key: Bb

Johns, Donald "The Bridegroom Soon Will Call Us" **The
Concordia Hymn Prelude Series**  Volume 14  Edited:
Herbert Gotsch  Concordia Publishing House
97-5705  Key: G

Johnson, David N. "Strengthen for Service, Lord" **Deck Thyself My Soul with Gladness** Augsburg Publishing House 11-9157 Key: Ab

Karg-Elert, Sigfrid "Ah, God and Lord" **Choral Improvisations for Organ for Ascensiontide and Pentecost** Op. 65 Volume 4 Edited: Robert Leech Bedell Edward B. Marks Music Co., Key: Bb

Marpurg, Friedrich Wilhelm **Twenty-One Chorale Preludes** Edited: Robert M. Thompson Augsburg Publishing House 11-9506 Key: C

Walther, Johann Gottfried "Ach Gott und Herr" **80 Chorale Preludes - German Masters of the17th and18th Centuries** Edited: Hermann Keller C.F. Peters Corporation #4448 Key: Bb

Walther, Johann Gottfried "Draw Us to Thee" **The Parish Organist** Part Eight Music for Easter, Ascension, Pentecost and Trinity Edited: Erich Goldschmidt Concordia Publishing House 97-1404 Key: Bb

Walther, Johann Gottfried "Draw Us to Thee" **The Parish Organist** Part One Edited: Heinrich Fleischer Concordia Publishing House 97-1145 Key: Bb

Walther, Johann Gottfried "Draw Us to You" **The Concordia Hymn Prelude Series** Volume 12 Edited: Herbert Gotsch Concordia Publishing House 97-5619 Key: A

FREE ACCOMPANIMENTS

**Free Harmonizations of Hymn Tunes by Fifty American Composers** Edited: D. DeWitt Wasson Hinshaw Music, Inc. HMO-145 Key: A

Ach Gott vom Himmelreiche

| | BA | DC | 1940 | 1982 | LBW | LW | PH | RCV | UCC | UM | WB |
|---|----|----|------|------|-----|----|----|-----|-----|----|----|
| | | | | G | | G | | | | | |

ORGAN COMPOSITIONS

Bobb, Barry "O Living Bread from Heaven" **The Concordia Hymn Prelude Series** Volume 16 Edited: Herbert Gotsch Concordia Publishing House 97-5707 Key: G

Ach Herr, du allerhochster Gott
BA  DC  1940  1982  LBW  LW    PH    RCV   UCC   UM    WB
                      G

Ach, was soll ich Sünder machen
BA  DC  1940  1982  LBW  LW    PH    RCV   UCC   UM    WB
                      d

## ORGAN COMPOSITIONS

Bach, J.S. **Organ Works** Volume 1  Edited: Heinz-
Harald Löhlein  Urtext of the New Bach Edition
Bärenreiter  5171  Key: e

Bach, J.S. **Organ Works** Volume VIII  Widor-Schweitzer
G. Schirmer  Key: e

Bach, J.S. **Orgelwerke** Volume IX  C.F. Peters
Corporation  Nr. 2067  Key: e

Beck, Albert  **76 Offertories on Hymns & Chorales**
Concordia Publishing House  97-5297  Key: d

Marpurg, Friedrich Wilhelm  **Twenty-One Chorale Preludes**
Edited: Robert M. Thompson  Augsburg Publishing
House  11-9506  Key: d

Walther, Johann Gottfried  "Oh, How Great is Your
Compassion"  **The Concordia Hymn Prelude Series**
Volume 19  Edited: Herbert Gotsch  Concordia
Publishing House  97-5710 Key: d

Ack, bliv hos oss
BA  DC  1940  1982  LBW  LW    PH    RCV   UCC   UM    WB
             g    g

## ORGAN COMPOSITIONS

Beck, Theodore  "O God of Love, O King of Peace"
**The Concordia Hymn Prelude Series**  Volume 19
Edited: Herbert Gotsch  Concordia Publishing House
97-5710  Key: g

## FREE ACCOMPANIMENTS

Held, Wilbur  **Hymn Preludes and Free Accompaniments**
Volume 6  Augsburg Publishing House  11-9402
Key: g

Ack, saliga stunder
BA  DC  1940  1982  LBW  LW    PH    RCV   UCC   UM    WB
                     Bb

Rohlig, Harald  "With God as Our Friend"  **The Concordia Hymn Prelude Series**  Volume 19  Edited: Herbert Gotsch  Concordia Publishing House 97-5710  Key: Bb

Ack, vad är dock livet har

| BA | DC | 1940 | 1982 | LBW | LW | PH | RCV | UCC | UM | WB |
|----|----|------|------|-----|----|----|-----|-----|----|----|
|    |    |      | e    |     |    |    |     |     |    |    |

ORGAN COMPOSITIONS

Bender, Jan  "Jesus, in Thy Dying Woes"  **The Concordia Hymn Prelude Series**  Volume 7  Edited: Herbert Gotsch  Concordia Publishing House 97-5614  Key: e

Ackley

| BA | DC | 1940 | 1982 | LBW | LW | PH | RCV | UCC | UM | WB |
|----|----|------|------|-----|----|----|-----|-----|----|----|
| Bb |    |      |      |     |    |    |     |     |    |    |

Ad cenam Agni providi

| BA | DC | 1940 | 1982 | LBW | LW | PH | RCV | UCC | UM | WB |
|----|----|------|------|-----|----|----|-----|-----|----|----|
|    |    |      | m:f  |     |    |    |     |     |    |    |

Ad perennis

| BA | DC | 1940 | 1982 | LBW | LW | PH | RCV | UCC | UM | WB |
|----|----|------|------|-----|----|----|-----|-----|----|----|
|    |    | d    |      |     |    |    |     |     |    |    |

Ada

| BA | DC | 1940 | 1982 | LBW | LW | PH | RCV | UCC | UM | WB |
|----|----|------|------|-----|----|----|-----|-----|----|----|
| Eb |    |      |      |     |    |    |     |     |    |    |

Adelaide

| BA | DC | 1940 | 1982 | LBW | LW | PH | RCV | UCC | UM | WB |
|----|----|------|------|-----|----|----|-----|-----|----|----|
| Eb | Eb |      |      |     |    |    |     | Eb  | Eb |    |

Adeste fidelis
(See also: Portuguese Hymn)

| BA | DC | 1940 | 1985 | LBW | LW | PH | RCV | UCC | UM | WB |
|----|----|------|------|-----|----|----|-----|-----|----|----|
| G  | G  | G    | G    | G   | G  | G  | G   | G   | G  | G  |

INTONATIONS

Videro, Finn  **Twenty-One Hymn Intonations**  Concordia Publishing House  97-5004  Key: G

ORGAN COMPOSITIONS

Cherwien, David  "O Come, All Ye Faithful"  **Interpretations Based on Hymn-tunes**  Book II A.M.S.I.  OR-3  Key: G

Edmundson, Garth "Adeste Fideles" **Christus Advenit –
Christmas Suite No. 2** H.W. Gray Key: A

Diemer, Emma Lou "O Come All Ye Faithful" **Carols for
Organ** The Sacred Music Press Key:C

Hofland, Sigvart A. "Oh, Come, All Ye Faithful"
**The Parish Organist** Part One Edited: Heinrich
Fleischer Concordia Publishing House 97-1145
Key: G

Karg-Elert, Sigfrid "Adeste Fidelis" **Cathedral Windows**
London: Elkin & Co. Ltd. Key: B

Kreckel, Philip G. **Musica Divina** Volume I J. Fischer
& Bro. No. 6623 Key: A

Moser, Rudolf "O Come, All Ye Faithful" **The Parish
Organist** Christmas and Epiphany Music Part Six
Concordia Publishing House 97-1391 Key: G

Sensmeier, Randall "Oh, Come All Ye Faithful" **The
Concordia Hymn Prelude Series** Volume 2 Edited:
Herbert Gotsch Concordia Publishing House 97-
5536 Key: G

Shaw, Geoffrey **Fantasia on "Adeste Fideles"** Novello
and Company, Ltd. No. 159 Key: A

Walton, Kenneth **Fantasia on Four Christmas Carols**
Broadcast Music, Inc. Key: Ab

Whitford, Homer **Five Choral Paraphrases** Set I
H. W. Gray Key: A

FREE ACCOMPANIMENTS

Cassler, G. Winston **Descants for Selected Hymn Tunes**
Augsburg Publishing House 11-9304 Key: A

Goode, Jack C. **Thirty-Four Changes on Hymn Tunes**
H.W. Gray GB 644 Key: G

Noble, T. Tertius **Free Organ Accompaniments to One
Hundred Well Known Hymn Tunes** J. Fischer & Bros.
#8175 Key: G

Pasquet, Jean **Free Organ Accompaniments to Festival
Hymns** Volume I Augsburg Publishing House 11-9192
Key: A

8

Wood, Dale **New Settings of Twenty Well-Known Hymn Tunes** Augsburg Publishing House 11-9292
Key: G

Adon Olam
| BA | DC | 1940 | 1982 | LBW | LW | PH | RCV | UCC | UM | WB |
|----|----|------|------|-----|----|----|-----|-----|----|----|
|    |    |      | Eb   |     |    |    |     |     |    |    |

Adoro te devote
| BA | DC | 1940 | 1982 | LBW | LW | PH | RCV | UCC | UM | WB |
|----|----|------|------|-----|----|----|-----|-----|----|----|
| m:d | m:d | m:d | m:d | m:d | m:d | m:d | m:d | m:d | m:d |    |

## ORGAN COMPOSITIONS

Casner, Myron "Humbly I Adore Thee" **The Parish Organist** Part Eleven Edited: Willem Mudde Concordia Publishing House 97-4758 Key: D

Hutchings, Arthur **Seasonal Preludes for Organ** Novello & Company, Ltd. Key: D

Johnson, David N. "Thee We Adore" **Deck Thyself My Soul with Gladness** Augsburg Publishing House 11-9157 Key: D

Kalbfleisch, Rodger "Thee We Adore, O Hidden Savior" **The Concordia Hymn Prelude Series** Volume 16 Edited: Herbert Gotsch Concordia Publishing House 97-5707 Key: D

Kreckel, Philip G. **Musica Divina** J. Fischer & Bro. No. 6623 Key: Eb

Pelz, Walter L. "Eternal Spirit of the Living Christ" **The Concordia Hymn Prelude Series** Volume 19 Edited: Herbert Gotsch Concordia Publishing House 97-5710 Key: D

Willan, Healey "Thee We Adore, O Blessed Savior" **Organ Music for the Communion Service** Edited: Paul Bunjes Concordia Publishing House 97-1395 Key: D

## FREE ACCOMPANIMENTS

Held, Wilbur **Hymn Preludes and Free Accompaniments** Volume 6 Augsburg Publishing House 11-9402 Key: D

Aeterna Christi munera
| BA | DC | 1940 | 1982 | LBW | LW | PH | RCV | UCC | UM | WB |
|----|----|------|------|-----|----|----|-----|-----|----|----|
|    |    | m:f  |      |     |    |    |     |     |    |    |

Aeterne Rex altissime
BA   DC   1940   1982   LBW   LW   PH   RCV   UCC   UM   WB

Af himlens
BA   DC   1940   1982   LBW   LW   PH   RCV   UCC   UM   WB
                          F

## ORGAN COMPOSITIONS

Bouman, Paul   "Your Word, O Lord, is Gentle Dew"
**The Concordia Hymn Prelude Series**   Volume 19
Edited: Herbert Gotsch   Concordia Publishing
House   97-5710   Key: F

Cherwien, David   "Your Word, Oh Lord, is Gentle Dew"
**Interpretations Based on Hymn-tunes**   Book II
A.M.S.I.   OR-3   Key: F

African Work Song
BA   DC   1940   1982   LBW   LW   PH   RCV   UCC   UM   WB
                 E

Ainsworth 97
BA   DC   1940   1982   LBW   LW   PH   RCV   UCC   UM   WB
                                   F

Albano
BA   DC   1940   1985   LBW   LW   PH   RCV   UCC   UM   WB
          F

## ORGAN COMPOSITIONS

Haan, Raymond H.   "Once, only once, and once for all"
**The King of Love** The Sacred Music Press KK 277
Key: F

## FREE ACCOMPANIMENTS

Noble, T. Tertius   **Fifty Free Organ Accompaniments
to Well Known Hymn Tunes**   J. Fischer & Bros.
8430   Key: F

Albany
BA   DC   1940   1982   LBW   LW   PH   RCV   UCC   UM   WB
          C

## FREE ACCOMPANIMENTS

**Free Harmonizations of Hymn Tunes by Fifty American
Composers**   Edited: D. DeWitt Wasson   Hinshaw
Music, Inc.   HMO-145   Key: C

Noble, T. Tertius **Free Organ Accompaniments to One Hundred Well-Known Hymn Tunes** J. Fischer & Bros. #8175 Key: C

Albright
| BA | DC | 1940 | 1982 D | LBW | LW | PH | RCV | UCC | UM | WB |
|----|----|------|--------|-----|----|----|-----|-----|----|----|

Aldine
| BA | DC | 1940 | 1982 Eb | LBW | LW | PH | RCV | UCC | UM | WB |
|----|----|------|---------|-----|----|----|-----|-----|----|----|

Aletta
| BA F | DC | 1940 | 1982 | LBW | LW | PH | RCV | UCC | UM | WB |
|------|----|------|------|-----|----|----|-----|-----|----|----|

Alford
| BA | DC | 1940 Ab | 1982 | LBW | LW | PH Ab | RCV | UCC | UM | BW |
|----|----|---------|------|-----|----|-------|-----|-----|----|----|

FREE ACCOMPANIMENTS

Noble, T. Tertius **Free Organ Accompaniments to One Hundred Well-Known Hymn Tunes** J. Fischer & Bros. #8175 Key: Ab

All Ehr und Lob
| BA | DC | 1940 | 1982 | LBW G | LW G | PH | RCV G | UCC | UM | WB |
|----|----|------|------|-------|------|----|-------|-----|----|----|

ORGAN COMPOSITIONS

Barlow, Wayne **Four Chorale Voluntaries** Concordia Publishing House 97-5602 Key: G

Lenel, Ludwig "Creator Spirit, by Whose Aid" **The Parish Organist** Part Eight Music for Easter, Ascension, Pentecost, and Trinity Edited: Erich Goldschmidt Concordia Publishing House 97-1404 Key: G

Miles, George Th. "All Glory Be to God Alone" **The Parish Organist** Part One Edited: Heinrich Fleischer Concordia Publishing House 97-1145 Key: G

Rohlig, Harald "Creator Spirit, by Whose Aid" **The Concordia Hymn Prelude Series** Volume 12 Edited: Herbert Gotsch Concordia Publishing House 97-5619 Key: G

Shack, David  "All Glory Be to God Alone:  **The Concordia Hymn Prelude Series**  Volume 19  Edited: Herbert Gotsch  Concordia Publishing House  97-5710  Key: G

## FREE ACCOMPANIMENTS

Krapf, Gerhard  **Hymn Preludes and Free Accompaniments** Volume 13  Augsburg Publishing House  11-9409  Key: G

All for Jesus

| BA | DC | 1940 | 1982 | LBW | LW | PH | RCV | UCC | UM | WB |
|----|----|------|------|-----|----|----|----|-----|----|----|
| Db |    |      |      |     |    |    |     |     |    |    |

All Glory, Laud, and Honor
(See also: Valet will ich dir geben)

All Hallows

| BA | DC | 1940 | 1982 | LBW | LW | PH | RCV | UCC | UM | WB |
|----|----|------|------|-----|----|----|----|-----|----|----|
|    | Bb |      |      |     |    |    |     |     |    |    |

All is Well

| BA | DC | 1940 | 1982 | LBW | LW | PH | RCV | UCC | UM | WB |
|----|----|------|------|-----|----|----|----|-----|----|----|
| G  | G  |      |      |     |    |    |     | G   |    |    |

## ORGAN COMPOSITIONS

Jordan, Alice "Come, Come, Ye Saints"  **A Season and a Time**  Broadman Press  4570-37  Key: C

All morgan ist

| BA | DC | 1940 | 1982 | LBW | LW | PH | RCV | UCC | UM | WB |
|----|----|------|------|-----|----|----|----|-----|----|----|
|    |    |      |      |     |    | C  |     |     |    |    |

All Saints

| BA | DC | 1940 | 1982 | LBW | LW | PH | RCV | UCC | UM | WB |
|----|----|------|------|-----|----|----|----|-----|----|----|
|    | Bb |      |      |     |    |    |     |     |    |    |

## FREE ACCOMPANIMENTS

**Free Harmonizations of Hymn Tunes by Fifty American Composers**  Edited: D. DeWitt Wasson  Hinshaw Music, Inc.  HMO-145  Key: Bb

All Saints New
(See also: Zeuch mich, zeuch mich)

| BA | DC | 1940 | 1982 | LBW | LW | PH | RCV | UCC | UM | BW |
|----|----|------|------|-----|----|----|----|-----|----|----|
|    | Bb | Bb   |      | Bb  | Bb | Bb |     | Bb  | Bb |    |

## ORGAN COMPOSITIONS

Crane, Robert  "The Son of God Goes Forth to War"
**The Parish Organist** Part Eleven  Edited:  Willem
Mudde  Concordia Publishing House  97-4758
Key: Bb

Engel, James  "The Son of God Goes Forth to War"
**The Concordia Hymn Prelude Series**  Volume 14
Edited: Herbert Gotsch  Concordia Publishing House
97-5705  Key: Bb

Ferguson, John  "The Son of God Goes Forth to War"
**The Concordia Hymn Prelude Series**  Volume 19
Edited: Herbert Gotsch  Concordia Publishing House
97-5710  Key: Bb

Willan, Healey  **36 Short Preludes and Postludes on
Well-Known Hymn Tunes** Set III C.F. Peters
Corporation  No. 6163  Key: Bb

## FREE ACCOMPANIMENTS

Noble, T. Tertius **Free Organ Accompaniments to One
Hundred Well-Known Hymn Tunes**  J. Fischer & Bros.
#8175  Key: Bb

Ore, Charles  **Hymn Preludes and Free Accompaniments**
Volume 7  Augsburg Publishing House  11-9403
Key: Bb

All the Way

| BA | DC | 1940 | 1982 | LBW | LW | PH | RCV | UCC | UM | BW |
|----|----|------|------|-----|----|----|-----|-----|----|----|
| G  |    |      |      |     |    |    |     |     | Ab |    |

## FREE ACCOMPANIMENTS

**Free Harmonizations of Hymn Tunes by Fifty American
Composers** Edited: D. DeWitt Wasson  Hinshaw
Music, Inc. HMO-145  Key: Ab

All the World

| BA | DC | 1940 | 1982 | LBW | LW | PH | RCV | UCC | UM | WB |
|----|----|------|------|-----|----|----|-----|-----|----|----|
| D  | D  |      |      |     |    |    |     |     |    |    |

All to Christ

| BA | DC | 1940 | 1982 | LBW | LW | PH | RCV | UCC | UM | WB |
|----|----|------|------|-----|----|----|-----|-----|----|----|
| Eb |    |      |      |     |    |    |     |     |    |    |

Alle Jahre wieder

| BA | DC | 1940 | 1982 | LBW | LW | PH | RCV | UCC | UM | WB |
|----|----|------|------|-----|----|----|-----|-----|----|----|
|    |    |      |      |     | D  |    |     |     |    |    |

13

Beck, Thomas   "Every Year the Christ Child Comes Again to Earth"   **The Concordia Hymn Prelude Series** Volume 2   Edited: Herbert Gotsch   Concordia Publishing House   97-5536   Key: D

## Alle Menschen müssen sterben
(See also: Salzburg)

| BA | DC | 1940 | 1982 | LBW | LW | PH | RCV | UCC | UM | WB |
|----|----|------|------|-----|----|----|-----|-----|----|----|
|    | D  |      |      |     |    |    |     |     |    |    |

ORGAN COMPOSITIONS

Bach, J.S.   **Organ Works**   Volume 1   Edited: Heinz-Harald Lohlein   Urtext of the New Bach Edition   Barenreiter   5171   Key: G

Bach, J.S.   **Organ Chorales from the Neumeister Collection**   Edited: Christoph Wolff   Yale University Press/Barenreiter 5181   Key: m:Bb

Bach, J.S. **Organ Works** Volume VII   Widor-Schweitzer G. Schirmer   Key: G

Bach, J.S. **Orgelwerke** Volume V   C.F. Peters Corporation Nr. 244   Key: G

Bach, J.S. **The Liturgical Year** (Orgelbuchlein) Edited:   Albert Reimenschneider   Oliver Ditson Co. Key: G

Pachelbel, Johann **80 Chorale Preludes – German Masters of the 17th and 18th Centures** Edited: Hermann Keller   C.F. Peters Corporation #4448   Key:C

## Allein Gott in der Höh' sei Ehr'

| BA | DC | 1940 | 1982 | LBW | LW | PH | RCV | UCC | UM | WB |
|----|----|------|------|-----|----|----|-----|-----|----|----|
|    | F  |      | G    | G   | G  | F  | F   |     | G  |    |

ORGAN COMPOSITIONS

Bach, J.S.   **Organ Works**   Volume 2   Edited: Hans Klotz   Urtext of the New Bach Edition Bärenreiter   5171 (Three settings) Key: A; Key: G; Key: A

Bach, J.S.   **Organ Works**   Volume 3   "The Individually Transmitted Organ Chorales"   Edited: Hans Klotz Urtext of the New Bach Edition   Bärenreiter 5173   Key: G

Bach, J.S. **Organ Works** Volume VI Widor-Schweitzer
G. Schirmer Key: G

Bach, J.S. **Organ Works** Volume VII Widor-Schweitzer
G. Schirmer Key: F; Key: G; Key: A

Bach, J.S. **Organ Works** Volume VIII Widor-Schweitzer
G. Schirmer Key: G, A

Bach, J.S. **Orgelwerke** Volume VI C.F. Peters Corporation
No. 245 (Eleven settings) Key: G Key: G, Key: F,
Key: G, Key: A, Key: G. Key: A, Key: A, Key: G

Bach, J.S. **Orgelwerke** Volume IX C.F. Peters
Corporation Nr. 2067 Key: G

Bach, J.S. **Klavierübung, Dritter Teil** C.F. Peters
Corporation #3948 Key: F; Key: G; Key: A

Bach, J.S. "All Glory Be to God on High" **Wedding
Music** Part 2 Concordia Publishing House
97-1370 Key: G

Bach, J.S. "All Glory Be to God on High" **The Parish
Organist** Part Eight Music for Easter, Ascension,
Pentecost and Trinity Edited: Erich Goldschmidt
Concordia Publishing House 97-1404 Key: G

Boehm, Georg **Choral Preludes by Masters of the 17th
and 18th Centuries** Volume I Edited: Walter Buszin
Concordia Publishing House Key: G

Dupre, Marcel **Seventy-Nine Chorales for the Organ**
Opus 28 H. W. Gray Key: A

Haan, Raymond H. **Festival Hymn Preludes** The Sacred
Music Press KK 329-3 Key: G

Manz, Paul "All Glory Be to God on High" **Ten Chorale
Improvisations** Set V Op 14 Concordia Publishing
House 97-5257 Key: G

Manz, Paul "All Glory be to God on High" **Ten Chorale
Improvisations** Op. 5 Concordia Publishing House
97-4554 Key: G

Marpurg, Friedrich Wilhelm **Twenty-One Chorale Preludes**
Edited: Robert M. Thompson Augsburg Publishing
House 11-9506 Key: G

Pachelbel, Johann  "All Glory Be to God on High"  **The Parish Organist**  Part One  Edited: Heinrich Fleischer  Concordia Publishing House  97-1145  Key:  G

Reger, Max  **30 Short Chorale Preludes** Op. 135a C.F. Peters Corporation Nr. 3980  Key:  G

Sweelinck, Jan Pieterszoon  "Across the Sky the Shades of Night"  **The Concordia Hymn Prelude Series** Volume 14  Edited: Herbert Gotsch  Concordia Publishing House  97-5705  Key: G

Vetter, Andreas Nikolaus **80 Chorale Preludes – German Masters of the 17th and 18th Centuries** C.F. Peters Corporation #4448  Key: G

Vetter, Andreas Nicholaus  "All Glory Be to God on High"  **The Concordia Hymn Prelude Series** Volume 13  Edited: Herbert Gotsch  Concordia Publishing House  97-5620  Key: G

Walther, Johann Gottfried "Chorale Prelude on 'Allein Gott in der Hoh sei Ehr" **For Manuals Only** Edited: John Christopher  McAfee Music Corporation Key: G

Walther, Johann Gottfried  "All Glory Be to God on High" **The Concordia Hymn Prelude Series**  Volume 19 Edited: Herbert Gotsch  Concordia Publishing House 97-5710  Key: G

Walther, Johann Gottfried   **80 Chorale Preludes – German Masters of the 17th and 18th Centuries** Edited: Hermann Keller  C.F. Peters Corporation

Zachau, Friedrich W.  "Praise Be to God in the Highest" **Short Classic Organ Pieces from the 16th, 17th and 18th Centuries**  Arr. Norris L. Stephens J. Fischer & Bros.  No. 9607  Key: G

Zachau, Friedrich Wilhelm "Chorale Prelude on 'Allein Gott in der Hoh sei Ehr'' **For Manuals Only** Edited: John Christopher  McAfee Music Corporation Key: G

Zachau, Friedrich Wilhelm  "Allein Gott in der Hoh sei Ehr" **80 Chorale Preludes – German Masters of the 17th and 18th Centuries** Edited: Hermann Keller C.F. Peters Corporation #4448  Key: G

## FREE ACCOMPANIMENTS

Bunjes, Paul  **New Organ Accompaniments for Hymns**
Concordia Publishing House  97-5348  Key: G

Cassler, G. Winston **Free Organ Accompaniments to
Hymns** Volume IV - Festival Services
Augsburg Publishing House 11-9179  Key: G

Hillert, Richard  **Hymn Preludes and Free Accompaniments**
Volume 10  Augsburg Publishing House  11-9406
Key: G

Johnson, David N.  **Free Harmonizations of Twelve Hymn
Tunes**  Augsburg Publishing House  11-9190  Key: G

Wood, Dale  **New Settings of Twenty Well-Known Hymn
Tunes**  Augsburg Publishing House  11-9292
Key:  G

Allein zu dir

| BA | DC | 1940 | 1982 | LBW | LW | PH | RCV | UCC | UM | BW |
|----|----|------|------|-----|----|----|-----|-----|----|----|
|    |    |      |      | A   | A  |    |     |     |    |    |

## ORGAN COMPOSITIONS

Bach, J.S.  **Organ Chorales from the Neumeister
Collection**  Edited: Christoph Wolff  Yale
University Press/Bärenreiter 5181
Key: m:a

Pachelbel, Johann  **80 Chorale Preludes - German Masters
of the 17th and 18th Centuries** Edited: Hermann
Keller  C.F. Peters Corporation #4448  Key: g

Pepping, Ernst  **Praeludia Postludia** I  B. Schott's
Sohne  Edition 6040  Key: m:f

Zachow, Friedrich  "I Trust, O Christ, in You Alone"
**The Concordia Hymn Prelude Series**  Volume 19
Edited: Herbert Gotsch  Concordia Publishing House
97-5710  Key: f#

Alleluia

| BA | DC | 1940 | 1982 | LBW | LW | PH | RCV | UCC | UM | BW |
|----|----|------|------|-----|----|----|-----|-----|----|----|
| G  |    | F    | F    |     |    |    |     |     |    |    |

Alleluia No. 1

| BA | DC | 1940 | 1982 | LBW | LW | PH | RCV | UCC | UM | WB |
|----|----|------|------|-----|----|----|-----|-----|----|----|
|    |    |      | E    |     |    |    |     |     |    |    |

| | Alles ist an Gottes segen | | | | | | | | | |
|---|---|---|---|---|---|---|---|---|---|---|
| BA | DC | 1940 | 1982 | LBW | LW | PH | RCV | UCC | UM | WB |
| | F | | F | F | F | F | | | | |

## ORGAN COMPOSITIONS

Cherwien, David "Praise the Lord, Rise Up Rejoicing" **Interpretations Based on Hymn-tunes** Book IV A.M.S.I. OR-9 Key: F

Johnson, David "Praise the Lord, Rise Up Rejoicing" **Deck Thyself with Gladness** Augsburg Publishing House 11-9101 Key: F

Manz, Paul "Praise the Lord, Rise Up Rejoicing" **Hymn Preludes for Holy Communion** Volume II Concordia Publishing House 97-5487 Key: F

Manz, Paul "All Depends on Our Possessing" **Ten Chorale Improvisations** Set VIII Op. 20 Concordia Publishing House 97-5342 Key: F

Pelz, Walter L. "Praise the Lord, Rise Up Rejoicing" **The Concordia Hymn Prelude Series** Volume 16 Edited; Herbert Gotsch Concordia Publishing House 97-5707 Key: F

Polley, David "All Depends on Our Possessing" **The Concordia Hymn Prelude Series** Volume 19 Edited: Herbert Gotsch Concordia Publishing House 97-5710 Key: F

Reger, Max **30 Short Chorale Preludes** Op. 135a C.F. Peters Corporation Nr. 3980 Key: Ab

Reger, Max **Chorale Preludes for the Church Year from Max Reger, Op. 67** Edited: Alec Wyton Carl Fischer 0-4667 Key: G

## FREE ACCOMPANIMENTS

Gehring, Philip **Hymn Preludes and Free Accompaniments** Volume 3 Augsburg Publishing House 11-9399 Key: F

| | Allgütiger, mein Preisgesang | | | | | | | | | |
|---|---|---|---|---|---|---|---|---|---|---|
| BA | DC | 1940 | 1982 | LBW | LW | PH | RCV | UCC | UM | BW |
| | | | | | | | | | F | |

| | Almsgiving | | | | | | | | | |
|---|---|---|---|---|---|---|---|---|---|---|
| BA | DC | 1940 | 1982 | LBW | LW | PH | RCV | UCC | UM | WB |
| | | F | | | | | | | | |

### Alstone

| BA | DC | 1940 | 1982 | LBW | LW | PH | RCV | UCC | UM | WB |
|---|---|---|---|---|---|---|---|---|---|---|
|  | C |  |  |  |  |  |  |  |  |  |

### Alta Trinita beata

| BA | DC | 1940 | 1982 | LBW | LW | PH | RCV | UCC | UM | WB |
|---|---|---|---|---|---|---|---|---|---|---|
| F | Eb | Eb |  |  |  | Eb |  |  | F |  |

### Amazing Grace
(See also: New Britain)

| BA | DC | 1940 | 1982 | LBW | LW | PH | RCV | UCC | UM | WB |
|---|---|---|---|---|---|---|---|---|---|---|
| G |  |  |  |  | F |  |  |  | F | G |

## FREE ACCOMPANIMENTS

**Free Harmonizations of Hymn Tunes by Fifty American Composers** Edited: D. DeWitt Wasson Hinshaw Music, Inc. HMO-145 Key: F

Hancock, Gerre **Organ Improvisations for Hymn-Singing** Hinshaw Music Co. HMO-100 Key: G

Hebble, Robert **Robert Hebble's Hymnal Companion for Organ** Bradley Publications CE/283A/3 Key: G

### Amen

| BA | DC | 1940 | 1982 | LBW | LW | PH | RCV | UCC | UM | WB |
|---|---|---|---|---|---|---|---|---|---|---|
|  |  |  |  |  |  |  | E |  |  |  |

### Amen sjunge hvarje tunga

| BA | DC | 1940 | 1982 | LBW | LW | PH | RCV | UCC | UM | WB |
|---|---|---|---|---|---|---|---|---|---|---|
|  |  | C |  |  |  |  |  |  |  |  |

## ORGAN COMPOSITIONS

Schultz, Ralph C. "One There Is, Above All Others" **The Concordia Hymn Prelude Series** Volume 19 Edited: Herbert Gotsch Concordia Publishing House 97-5710 Key: C

### Amen, Jesus han skal raade

| BA | DC | 1940 | 1982 | LBW | LW | PH | RCV | UCC | UM | WB |
|---|---|---|---|---|---|---|---|---|---|---|
|  |  |  |  |  |  |  |  |  | C# |  |

### America

| BA | DC | 1940 | 1982 | LBW | LW | PH | RCV | UCC | UM | WB |
|---|---|---|---|---|---|---|---|---|---|---|
| F | F | F | F/G | F | F | F | F | F | F | F |

## ORGAN COMPOSITIONS

Held, Wilbur "God Bless Our Native Land" **Hymn Preludes for the Autumn Festivals** Concordia Publishing House 97-5360 Key: G

Ives, Charles **Variations on "America" for Organ**
Mercury Music Corp.  Key: F

Reger, Max  **Variations and Fugue on "God Save the King"**
**("America")** Universal Edition UE 1288 N
Joseph Boonin, Inc. Music Publications  Key: C

FREE ACCOMPANIMENTS

Goode, Jack C. **Thirty-Four Changes on Hymn Tunes**
H. W. Gray  GB 644  Key: F

Hancock, Gerre  **Organ Improvisations for Hymn-Singing**
Hinshaw Music Co.  HMO-100  Key: F

Noble, T. Tertius  **Free Organ Accompaniments to One
Hundred Well-Known Hymn Tunes**  J. Fischer & Bros.
#8175  Key: F

<u>American Hymn</u>

| BA | DC | 1940 | 1982 | LBW | LW | PH | RCV | UCC | UM | WB |
|----|----|------|------|-----|----|----|-----|-----|----|----|
|    |    |      | Eb   |     |    |    |     |     |    |    |

ORGAN COMPOSITIONS

Wienhorst, Richard  "Blessing and Honor" **The Concordia
Hymn Prelude Series**  Volume 19  Edited: Herbert
Gotsch  Concordia Publishing House  97-5710
Key: Eb

<u>Amsterdam</u>

| BA | DC | 1940 | 1982 | LBW | LW | PH | RCV | UCC | UM | WB |
|----|----|------|------|-----|----|----|-----|-----|----|----|
| F  |    |      |      |     |    |    |     |     | F  | F  |

ORGAN COMPOSITIONS

Lovelace, Austin  "Praise the Lord who reigns above"
**Eight Hymn Preludes**  Augsburg Publishing House
11-9144  Key: G

McKinley, Carl  **Ten Hymn Tune Fantasies** H.W. Gray
Key: F

FREE ACCOMPANIMENTS

**Free Harmonizations of Hymn Tunes by Fifty American
Composers**  Edited: D. DeWitt Wasson  Hinshaw
Music, Inc.  HMO-145  Key: F

Noble, T. Tertius  **Free Organ Accompaniments to One
Hundred Well-Known Hymn Tunes**  J. Fischer & Bros.
#8175  Key: F

Noble, T. Tertius **Free Organ Accompaniments to One Hundred Well-Known Hymn Tunes** J. Fischer & Bros. #8175 Key: C

<u>An die Freude</u>
BA   DC   1940 1982  LBW  LW    PH    RCV  UCC  UM   WB
                                                        F

<u>An Wasserflüssen Babylon</u>
BA   DC   1940 1982  LBW  LW    PH    RCV  UCC  UM   WB
                            F    F

ORGAN COMPOSITIONS

Bach, J. S. **Organ Works** Volume 2 Edited: Hans Klotz Urtext of the New Bach Edition Bärenreiter 5172 Key: G

Bach, J.S. **Organ Works** Volume VIII Widor-Schweitzer G. Schirmer Key: C

Bach, J.S. **Organ Works** Volume VI Widor-Schweitzer G. Schirmer Key: G

Bach, J. S. **Orgelwerke** Volume VI C.F. Peters Corporation No. 245 (Two settings) Key: G

Dupre, Marcel **Seventy-Nine Chorales for the Organ** Opus 28 H. W. Gray Key: G

Karg-Elert, Sigfrid "By the Waters of Babylon" **Choral Improvisations for Organ for Passion Week** Op. 65, Volume 2 Edward B. Marks Music Corp. Key: F

Krapf, Gerhard **Partita for Organ "Ein Lammlein geht'** Concordia Publishing House 97-4952 Key: F

Pachelbel, Johann **80 Chorale Preludes – German Masters of the 17th and 18th Centures** Edited: Hermann Keller C.F. Peters Corporation #4448 Key: G

Pachelbel, Johann "A Lamb Goes Uncomplaining Forth" **The Parish Organist** Part Seven Music for Lent, Palm Sunday and Holy Week Edited: Erich Goldschmidt Concordia Publishing House 97-1403 Key: F

Zipp, Friedrich "A Lamb Alone Bears Willingly" **The Concordia Hymn Prelude Series** Volume 7 Edited: Herbert Gotsch Concordia Publishing House 97-5614 Key: F

Ancient of Days
(See also: Albany)

| BA | DC | 1940 | 1982 | LBW | LW | PH | RCV | UCC | UM | WB |
|----|----|------|------|-----|----|----|-----|-----|----|----|
|    |    |      |      |     |    | C  |     |     | Eb |    |

## FREE ACCOMPANIMENTS

**Free Harmonizations of Hymn Tunes by Fifty American Composers** Edited: D. DeWitt Wasson Hinshaw Music, Inc. HMO-145 Key: C

Andujar

| BA | DC | 1940 | 1982 | LBW | LW | PH | RCV | UCC | UM | WB |
|----|----|------|------|-----|----|----|-----|-----|----|----|
|    |    |   C  |      |     |    |    |     |     |    |    |

Angel Voices

| BA | DC | 1940 | 1982 | LBW | LW | PH | RCV | UCC | UM | WB |
|----|----|------|------|-----|----|----|-----|-----|----|----|
|    |    |      |      |     |    |    |     |     | F  |    |

Angel's Song
(See also: Song 34)

| BA | DC | 1940 | 1982 | LBW | LW | PH | RCV | UCC | UM | WB |
|----|----|------|------|-----|----|----|-----|-----|----|----|
|    |    |  Eb  |      |     | Eb | Eb |     |     |    |    |

## ORGAN COMPOSITIONS

Thalben-Ball, George **113 Variations on Hymn Tunes for Organ** Novello Key: E

Angel's Story

| BA | DC | 1940 | 1982 | LBW | LW | PH | RCV | UCC | UM | WB |
|----|----|------|------|-----|----|----|-----|-----|----|----|
| G  | G  |      |      | F   | F  | G  |     |     | F  |    |

## ORGAN COMPOSITIONS

Krapf, Gerhard "O Savior, Precious Savior" **The Concordia Hymn Prelude Series** Volume 19 Edited: Herbert Gotsch Concordia Publishing House 97-4710 Key: F

Angelic Songs
(See also: Tidings)

| BA | DC | 1940 | 1982 | LBW | LW | PH | RCV | UCC | UM | WB |
|----|----|------|------|-----|----|----|-----|-----|----|----|
|    |    |      |      | Bb  |    |    |     |     |    |    |

## ORGAN COMPOSITIONS

Busarow, Donald "O Zion, Haste" **The Concordia Hymn Prelude Series** Volume 20 Edited: Herbert Gotsch Concordia Publishing House 97-5711 Key: Bb

22

<u>Angelorum Apostolus</u>

| BA | DC | 1940 | 1982 | LBW | LW | PH | RCV | UCC | UM | WB |
|----|----|------|------|-----|----|----|-----|-----|----|----|
|    | D  |      |      |     |    |    |     |     |    |    |

<u>Angelus</u>
(See also: Du meiner Seelen)

| BA | DC | 1940 | 1982 | LBW | LW | PH | RCV | UCC | UM | WB |
|----|----|------|------|-----|----|----|-----|-----|----|----|
|    | Eb |      | D    |     |    | Eb |     |     |    |    |

ORGAN COMPOSITIONS

Johnson, David N. "Be Still, My Soul, for God is Near" **Deck Thyself My Soul with Gladness** Augsburg Publishing House 11-9157 Key: D

Johnson, David N. "Nature with Open Volume Stands" **The Concordia Hymn Prelude Series** Volume 7 Edited: Herbert Gotsch Concordia Publishing House 97-5614 Key: D

Kreckel, Philip G. **Musica Divina** Volume I J. Fischer & Bro. No. 6623 Key: E

<u>Angelus emittitur</u>

| BA | DC | 1940 | 1982 | LBW | LW | PH | RCV | UCC | UM | WB |
|----|----|------|------|-----|----|----|-----|-----|----|----|
|    |    |      | F    |     |    |    |     |     |    |    |

<u>Anima Christi</u>

| BA | DC | 1940 | 1982 | LBW | LW | PH | RCV | UCC | UM | WB |
|----|----|------|------|-----|----|----|-----|-----|----|----|
|    | d  |      |      |     |    |    |     |     |    |    |

<u>Annunciation</u>

| BA | DC | 1940 | 1982 | LBW | LW | PH | RCV | UCC | UM | WB |
|----|----|------|------|-----|----|----|-----|-----|----|----|
|    | Ab |      |      |     |    |    |     |     |    |    |

<u>Anthes</u>

| BA | DC | 1940 | 1982 | LBW | LW | PH | RCV | UCC | UM | WB |
|----|----|------|------|-----|----|----|-----|-----|----|----|
|    |    |      |      | Ab  | Ab |    |     |     |    |    |

ORGAN COMPOSITIONS

Hildner, Victor "Come unto Me, Ye Weary" **The Parish Organist** Part One Edited: Heinrich Fleischer Concordia Publishing House 97-1145 Key: A

Kloppers, Jacobus "Come Unto Me, Ye Weary" **The Concordia Hymn Prelude Series** Volume 20 Edited: Herbert Gotsch Concordia Publishing House 97-5711 Key: Ab

<u>Antioch</u>

| BA | DC | 1940 | 1982 | LBW | LW | PH | RCV | UCC | UM | WB |
|----|----|------|------|-----|----|----|-----|-----|----|----|
| D | D | | D | D | D | D | D | D | D | D |

## INTONATIONS

McCormick, David  **20 Organ Intonations on Hymns of Praise**  Hope Publishing Co. Key: D

## ORGAN COMPOSITIONS

Gehrke, Hugo  "Joy to the World"  **The Parish Organist** Part One  Edited: Heinrich Fleischer  Concordia Publishing House  97-1145  Key: D

Gehrke, Hugo  "Joy to the World"  **The Concordia Hymn Prelude Series**  Volume 2  Edited: Herbert Gotsch  Concordia Publishing House  97-5536 Key: D

Haan, Raymond H.  **Festival Hymn Preludes**  The Sacred Music Press  KK 329-3  Key: D

Held, Wilbur  "Joy to the World" **Nativity Suite** Concordia Publishing House  Key: D

Wolz, Larry **O Little Town of Bethlehem**  Broadman Press 4570-68  Key: D

Wood, Dale **Organ Book of American Folk Hymns** The Sacred Music Press  Key: g

## FREE ACCOMPANIMENTS

Bender, Jan **Free Organ Accompaniment to Hymns** Volume II: Advent-Christmas-Epiphany Augsburg Publishing House 11-9187  Key: D

Cassler, G. Winston  **Organ Descants for Selected Hymn Tunes**  Augsburg Publishing House 11-9304 Key: D

Ferguson, John  **Hymn Harmonizations for Organ** Book II Ludwig Music Publishing Co.  0-07  Key: D

Goode, Jack C. **Thirty-Four Changes on Hymn Tunes** H. W. Gray  GB 644  Key: D

Wyton, Alec **New Shoots from Old Routes** The Sacred Music Press  KK 279  Key: D

## Ar hyd y nos

| BA | DC | 1940 | 1982 | LBW | LW | PH | RCV | UCC | UM | WB |
|----|----|------|------|-----|----|----|-----|-----|----|----|
|    |    | F    |      | G   | G  | F  |     |     | F  | F  |

### ORGAN COMPOSITIONS

Bobb, Barry L.  "God, Who Made the Earth and Heaven" **The Concordia Hymn Prelude Series**  Volume 20  Edited: Herbert Gotsch  Concordia Publishing House  97-5711  Key: G

Harris, David S. **Ten Hymn Preludes in Trio Style**  Set 2  H.W. Gray Co.  GB 643  Key: A

Jordan, Alice "Cantilena on a Traditional Welsh Melody" **Worship Service Music for the Organist**  Broadman Press  Key: F/Db

Kerr, J. Wayne  **O God Our Help in Ages Past**  Broadman Press  Key: F

### FREE ACCOMPANIMENTS

Ferguson, John  **Hymn Harmonizations for Organ**  Book II Ludwig Music Publishing Co.  0-07  Key: G

**Free Harmonizations of Hymn Tunes by Fifty American Composers**  Edited: D. DeWitt Wasson  Hinshaw Music, Inc.  HMO-145  Key: F

Hancock, Gerre **Organ Improvisations for Hymn-Singing**  Hinshaw Music Co.  HMO-100  Key: F

## Arbor Street

| BA | DC | 1940 | 1982 | LBW | LW | PH | RCV | UCC | UM | WB |
|----|----|------|------|-----|----|----|-----|-----|----|----|
|    |    |      | g    |     |    |    |     |     |    |    |

## Arfon

| BA | DC | 1940 | 1982 | LBW | LW | PH | RCV | UCC | UM | WB |
|----|----|------|------|-----|----|----|-----|-----|----|----|
|    | g  |      |      |     |    | g  |     |     | g  | g  |

### ORGAN COMPOSITIONS

Lovelace, Austin **Fourteen Hymn Preludes** Augsburg Publishing House  11-6152  Key: g

Peek, Richard "Throned Upon the Awful Tree" **Hymn Preludes for the Church Year** Carl Fischer 04266  Key: g

## Ariel

| BA | DC | 1940 | 1982 | LBW | LW | PH | RCV | UCC | UM | WB |
|----|----|------|------|-----|----|----|-----|-----|----|----|
|    |    |      |      |     |    |    |     |     | D  |    |

## Arise

| BA | DC | 1940 | 1982 | LBW | LW | PH | RCV | UCC | UM | WB |
|---|---|---|---|---|---|---|---|---|---|---|
| g |  |  |  |  |  |  |  |  |  |  |

## Arlington

| BA | DC | 1940 | 1982 | LBW | LW | PH | RCV | UCC | UM | WB |
|---|---|---|---|---|---|---|---|---|---|---|
| F | F |  |  |  |  |  |  |  | F |  |

## Armenia

| BA | DC | 1940 | 1982 | LBW | LW | PH | RCV | UCC | UM | WB |
|---|---|---|---|---|---|---|---|---|---|---|
|  |  |  |  |  |  |  |  |  | Ab |  |

## Armes

| BA | DC | 1940 | 1982 | LBW | LW | PH | RCV | UCC | UM | WB |
|---|---|---|---|---|---|---|---|---|---|---|
|  | D |  |  |  |  |  |  |  |  |  |

## Arnsberg
(See also: Gröningen; Wunderbarer König)

| BA | DC | 1940 | 1982 | LBW | LW | PH | RCV | UCC | UM | WB |
|---|---|---|---|---|---|---|---|---|---|---|
| F | G |  |  |  |  | G |  |  | G | F |

### FREE ACCOMPANIMENTS

**Free Harmonizations of Hymn Tunes by Fifty American Composers** Edited: D. DeWitt Wasson Hinshaw Music, Inc. HMO-145 Key: Ab

## Artavia

| BA | DC | 1940 | 1982 | LBW | LW | PH | RCV | UCC | UM | WB |
|---|---|---|---|---|---|---|---|---|---|---|
|  | Ab |  |  |  |  |  |  |  |  |  |

## Arthur's Seat

| BA | DC | 1940 | 1982 | LBW | LW | PH | RCV | UCC | UM | WB |
|---|---|---|---|---|---|---|---|---|---|---|
|  | A |  |  |  |  | A |  | A | Bb |  |

## Ascended Triumph

| BA | DC | 1940 | 1982 | LBW | LW | PH | RCV | UCC | UM | WB |
|---|---|---|---|---|---|---|---|---|---|---|
|  |  |  |  | d | d |  |  |  |  |  |

### ORGAN COMPOSITIONS

Polley, David  "Up Through Endless Ranks of Angels"
**The Concordia Hymn Prelude Series** Volume 12
Edited: Herbert Gotsch  Concordia Publishing House
97-5619  Key: d

## Ascension

| BA | DC | 1940 | 1982 | LBW | LW | PH | RCV | UCC | UM | WB |
|---|---|---|---|---|---|---|---|---|---|---|
|  | G | Eb |  |  |  |  |  | Eb |  |  |

Noble, T. Tertius **Fifty Free Organ Accompaniments To Well Known Hymn Tunes** J. Fischer & Bros. 8430  Key: G

### Assam

| BA | DC | 1940 | 1982 | LBW | LW | PH | RCV | UCC | UM | WB |
|----|----|------|------|-----|----|----|-----|-----|----|----|
| Db |    |      |      |     |    |    |     |     |    |    |

### Assisi

| BA | DC | 1940 | 1982 | LBW | LW | PH | RCV | UCC | UM | WB |
|----|----|------|------|-----|----|----|-----|-----|----|----|
|    |    | f    | f    |     |    |    |     |     |    |    |

### Assurance, with Refrain

| BA | DC | 1940 | 1982 | LBW | LW | PH | RCV | UCC | UM | WB |
|----|----|------|------|-----|----|----|-----|-----|----|----|
| D  |    |      |      |     |    |    |     |     | D  |    |

FREE ACCOMPANIMENTS

Hancock, Gerre **Organ Improvisations for Hymn-Singing** Hinshaw Music Co.  HMO-100  Key: D

### Atkinson

| BA | DC | 1940 | 1982 | LBW | LW | PH | RCV | UCC | UM | WB |
|----|----|------|------|-----|----|----|-----|-----|----|----|
|    |    |      |      | G   |    |    |     |     |    |    |

ORGAN COMPOSITIONS

Powell, Robert J.  "O God of Light" **The Concordia Hymn Prelude Series** Volume 20  Edited: Herbert Gotsch  Concordia Publishing House  97-5711 Key: G

### Attwood

| BA | DC | 1940 | 1982 | LBW | LW | PH | RCV | UCC | UM | WB |
|----|----|------|------|-----|----|----|-----|-----|----|----|
|    | Db |      |      |     |    |    |     |     |    |    |

### Auch jetzt macht

| BA | DC | 1940 | 1982 | LBW | LW | PH | RCV | UCC | UM | WB |
|----|----|------|------|-----|----|----|-----|-----|----|----|
|    |    |      |      |     |    |    | E   |     |    |    |

ORGAN COMPOSITIONS

Stearns, Peter Pindar **Twenty Hymn Preludes** Coburn Press (Theodore Presser Company) Key: D

### Audrey

| BA | DC | 1940 | 1982 | LBW | LW | PH | RCV | UCC | UM | WB |
|----|----|------|------|-----|----|----|-----|-----|----|----|
|    |    |      |      |     |    |    |     |     |    | F  |

Auf meinen lieben Gott
(See also: Wo soll ich fliehen hin)
    BA    DC    1940 1982  LBW  LW    PH    RCV  UCC  UM   WB
                                   e

## ORGAN COMPOSITIONS

Bach, J. S. **Organ Works** Volume 3 (Appears here as "Wo soll ich fliehen hin") "The Individually Transmitted Organ Chorales" Edited: Hans Klotz Urtext of the New Bach Edition Bärenreiter 5173 Key: g

Bach. J.S. **Orgelwerke** Volume IX C.F. Peters Corporation #2067 Key: a

Bach, J.S. **Orgelwerke** Volume VII C.F. Peters Corporation Nr. 246 Key: e

Beck, Albert **76 Offertories on Hymns & Chorales** Concordia Publishing House 97-5207 Key: d

Buxtehude, Dietrich **Orgelwerke II: Choral Preludes** #4457 Key: e

Buxtehude, Dietrich **80 Chorale Preludes – German Masters of the 17th and 18th Centures** Edited: Hermann Keller C.F. Peters Corporation #4448 Key: e

Doles, Johann Friedrich **Choral Preludes by Masters of the 17th and 18th Centuries** Volume I Edited: Walter Buszin Concordia Publishing House Key: g

Zachow, Friedrich "In God, My Faithful God" **The Concordia Hymn Prelude Series** Volume 20 Edited: Herbert Gotsch Concordia Publishing House 97-5711 Key: e

## FREE ACCOMPANIMENTS

Bunjes, Paul **New Organ Accompaniments for Hymns** Concordia Publishing House 97-5348 Key: e

Auf, auf, mein Herz
  BA   DC   1940  1982   LBW   LW    PH    RCV   UCC  UM    WB
                           D     D

ORGAN COMPOSITIONS

Haase, Hans-Heinz  "Awake, My Heart, with Gladness"
      **The Concordia Hymn Prelude Series**  Volume 10
      Edited: Herbert Gotsch  Concordia Publishing House
      97-5617  Key: D

Held, Wilbur "Awake My Heart with Gladness" **Six
      Preludes on Easter Hymns** Concordia Publishing
      House 97-5330  Key: Eb

Manz, Paul "Awake, My Heart , with Gladness"  **Ten
      Chorale Improvisations** Opus 16  Set VI  Concordia
      Publishing House 97-5305  Key: Eb

Marpurg, Friedrich Wilhelm  **Twenty-One Chorale Preludes**
      Edited: Robert M. Thompson  Augsburg Publishing
      House  11-9506  Key: F

Moser, Rudolf  "Awake, My Heart with Gladness"  **The
      Parish Organist**  Part One  Edited: Heinrich
      Fleischer  Concordia Publishing House  97-1145
      Key:  Eb

Moser, Rudolf "Awake, My Heart, with Gladness" **The
      Parish Organist**  Part Eight  Edited: Erich
      Goldschmidt  Music for Easter, Ascension,
      Pentecost and Trinity  Concordia Publishing House
      97-1404  Key:  Eb

FREE ACCOMPANIMENTS

Bunjes, Paul  **New Organ Accompaniments for Hymns**
      Concordia Publishing House 97-5348  Key: Eb

Hillert, Richard  **Hymn Preludes and Free Accompaniments**
      Volume 10  Augsburg Publishing House  11-9406
      Key: D

Aughton
      BA    DC    1940 1982  LBW  LW   PH   RCV  UCC  UM   WB
                   D

ORGAN COMPOSITIONS

Goode, Jack  **Seven Communion Meditations**  Harold
      Flammer, Inc.  HF-5084  Key: D

Augustine
      BA    DC    1940 1982  LBW  LW   PH   RCV  UCC  UM   WB
                   Bb

Aurelia
(See also: Wedlock; Llanfyllin)

| BA | DC | 1940 | 1982 | LBW | LW | PH | RCV | UCC | UM | WB |
|----|----|------|------|-----|----|----|-----|-----|----|----|
| Eb | Eb | Eb | Eb | D | Eb | Eb | Eb | Eb | Eb | D |

## ORGAN COMPOSITIONS

Beck, Albert **76 Offertories on Hymns and Chorales** Concordia Publishing House 97-5207 Key: Eb

Bunjes, Paul "The Church's One Foundation" **The Parish Organist** Part One Edited: Heinrich Fleischer Concordia Publishing House 97-1145 Key: Eb

Johns, Donald "O Living Bread from Heaven" **The Concordia Hymn Prelude Series** Volume 16 Edited: Herbert Gotsch Concordia Publishing House 97-5707 Key: D

Lovelace, Austin C. "The Church's One Foundation" **The Concordia Hymn Prelude Series** Volume 20 Edited: Herbert Gotsch Concordia Publishing House 97-5711 Key D (Second setting: Eb)

## FREE ACCOMPANIMENTS

Cassler, G. Winston **Organ Descants for Selected Hymn Tunes** Augsburg Publishing House 11-9304 Key: Eb

Hancock, Gerre **Organ Improvisations for Hymn-Singing** Hinshaw Music Co. HMO-100 Key: Eb

Hebble, Robert **Robert Hebble's Hymnal Companion for Organ** Bradley Publications CE/283A/3 Key: Eb

Hudson, Richard **Hymn Preludes and Free Accompaniments** Volume 12 Augsburg Publishing House 11-9408 Key: D

Noble, T. Tertius **Free Organ Accompaniments to One Hundred Well-Known Hymn Tunes** J. Fischer & Bros. #8175 Key: Eb

Wyton, Alex **New Shoots from Old Routes** The Sacred Music Press KK 279 Key: Eb

Aus der Tiefe ruhe ich
(See also: Heinlein)

| BA | DC | 1940 | 1982 | LBW | LW | PH | RCV | UCC | UM | WB |
|----|----|------|------|-----|----|----|-----|-----|----|----|
|  | e |  | d |  |  |  |  |  | d | d |

Bach, J.S. **Orgelwerke** Volume IX  C.F. Peters
        Corporation  #2067  Key:e

Sowerby, Leo "Forty Days and Forty Nights" **Advent to
        Whitsuntide** Volume Four  Hinrichsen  No. 743b
        Key: d

<u>Aus Gnaden soll ich</u>

| BA | DC | 1940 | 1982 | LBW | LW | PH | RCV | UCC | UM | WB |
|----|----|------|------|-----|----|----|-----|-----|----|----|
|    |    |      |      |     |    | G  |     |     |    |    |

<u>Aus meines Herzens Grunde</u>

| BA | DC | 1940 | 1982 | LBW | LW | PH | RCV | UCC | UM | WB |
|----|----|------|------|-----|----|----|-----|-----|----|----|
|    |    |      |      |     | F  |    |     |     |    |    |

ORGAN COMPOSITIONS

Bach, Johann Christoph **80 Chorale Preludes - German
        Masters of the 17th and 18th Centuries** Edited:
        Hermann Keller  C.F. Peters Corporation #4448
        Key: F

Bach, Johann Christoph  "My Inmost Heart Now Raises"
        **The Parish Organist** Part One  Edited: Heinrich
        Fleischer  Concordia Publishing House  97-1145
        Key:  F

Bach, Johann Sebastian  **The Parish Organist** Part 5
        Advent and Christmas Music  Concordia Publishing
        House  97-1382  Key: F

Karg-Elert, Sigfrid "From the depth of my Heart"
        **Choral Improvisations for Organ for Advent and
        Christmastide** Edited: Robert Leech Bedell
        Edward B. Marks Music Corp.  Key: G

Manz, Paul "Arise, Sons of the Kingdom" **Ten Chorale
        Improvisations** Set IV  Op. 10 Concordia
        Publishing House  97-4951  Key: F

Walther, Johann Gottfried **80 Chorale Preludes - German
        Masters of the 17th and 18th Centuries** Edited:
        Hermann Keller  C.F. Peters Corporation #4448
        Key:

Walther, Johann Gottfried  **Chorale Preludes by Masters
        of the 17th and 18th Centuries** Volume I  Edited:
        Walter Buszin  Concordia Publishing House  Key: G

31

Zipp, Friedrich **The Concordia Hymn Prelude Series**
Advent  Volume I  Edited: Herbert Gotsch  Concordia
Publishing House  97-5536  Key: F

Aus tiefer Not I

| BA | DC | 1940 | 1982 | LBW | LW | PH | RCV | UCC | UM | WB |
|----|----|------|------|-----|----|----|-----|-----|----|----|
|    |    |      | m:e  | m:e | m:e|    |     |     | m:e|    |

INTONATIONS

Videro, Finn  **Twenty-One Hymn Intonations**  Concordia
Publishing House  97-5004  Key: m:e

ORGAN COMPOSITIONS

Bach, J.S. **Organ Works** Volume VII  Widor-Schweitzer
G. Schirmer  Key: m:e, m:f#

Bach, J.S. **Orgelwerke** Volume VI  C.F. Peters
Corporation  No. 245 (Two settings)  Key: m:e,
m:f#

Bach, J.S. **Klavierubung, Dritter Teil** #3948
C.F. Peters  Key: e,  Key: f#

Beck, Albert  **76 Offertories on Hymns & Chorales**
Concordia Publishing House  97-5207  Key: e

Dupre, Marcel  **Seventy-Nine Chorales for the Organ**
Opus 28  H. W. Gray  Key: e

Karg-Elert, Sigfrid "Out of the Deep Have I called Unto
Thee"  **Choral Improvisations for Organ for Refor-
mation Day, Fast Days, Communion and Funeral Rites**
Op. 65  Volume 5  Edited: Robert Leech Bedell Edward
B. Marks Music Corp.  Key: e

Pepping, Ernst **Praeludia Postludia** II  B. Schott's
Sohne  Edition 6041  Key: m:d

Pepping, Ernst **Funfundzwanzig Orgelchorale**
Edition Schott  4723  B. Schott's Sohne Key: m:e

Reger, Max  **30 Short Chorale Preludes**  Op. 135a
C.F. Peters Corporation  Nr. 3980  Key: m:b

Scheidt, Samuel **80 Chorale Preludes – German Masters
of the 17th and 18th Centuries** Edited: Hermann
Keller  C.F. Peters Corporation #4448 Key: m:e

Zachau, Friedrich Wilhelm **80 Chorale Preludes – German Masters of the 17th and 18th Centuries** Edited: Hermann Keller  C.F. Peters Corporation #4448 Key: Key: m:e

Zachau, Friedrich Wilhelm  **Chorale Preludes by Masters of the 17th and 18th Centuries** Volume I  Edited: Walter Buszin  Concordia Publishing House  Key: e

Zachau, Friedrich  "From Depths of Woe I Cry to You" **The Concordia Hymn Prelude Series** Volume 20 Edited: Herbert Gotsch  Concordia Publishing House 97-5711  Key: m:e

<u>Aus tiefer Not II</u>

| BA | DC | 1940 | 1982 | LBW | LW | PH | RCV | UCC | UM | WB |
|----|----|------|------|-----|----|----|-----|-----|----|----|
|    |    |      |      |     | G  |    |     |     |    |    |

ORGAN COMPOSITIONS

Bach, J. S.  **Organ Chorales from the Neumeister Collection** Edited:  Christoph Wolff Yale University Press/Bärenreiter 5181  Key: G

Krapf, Gerhard "Lord Jesus Christ, Thou Living Bread" **Hymn Preludes for Holy Communion** Volume 3 Concordia Publishing House 97-5488  Key: G

Marpurg, Friedrich Wilhelm  **Twenty-One Chorale Preludes** Edited: Robert M. Thompson  Augsburg Publishing House  11-9506  Key: G

Micheelsen, Hans Friedrich  "Lord Jesus Christ, Life-Giving Bread" **The Concordia Hymn Prelude Series** Volume 16  Edited: Herbert Gotsch  Concordia Publishing House  97-5707  Key: G

Pachelbel, Johann  **80 Chorale Preludes – German Masters of the 17th and 18th Centuries** Edited: Hermann Keller  C.F. Peters Corporation #4448  Key: G

<u>Austria</u>

| BA | DC | 1940 | 1982 | LBW | LW | PH | RCV | UCC | UM | WB |
|----|----|------|------|-----|----|----|-----|-----|----|----|
|    | Eb | Eb   | Eb   | Eb  | Eb |    | Eb  |     | Eb |    |

ORGAN COMPOSITIONS

Barlow, Wayne  "Glorious Things of You are Spoken" **The Concordia Hymn Prelude Series** Volume 20 Edited: Herbert Gotsch  Concordia Publishing House 97-5711  Key: Eb

FREE ACCOMPANIMENTS

Gehring, Philip **Hymn Preludes and Free Accompaniments**
    Volume 3  Augsburg Publishing House  11-9399
    Key: Eb

Hancock, Gerre **Organ Improvisations for Hymn–Singing**
    Hinshaw Music Co.  HMO-100  Key: Eb

Noble, T. Tertius **Free Organ Accompaniments to One
    Hundred Well–Known Hymn Tunes**  J. Fischer & Bros.
    #8175  Key: Eb

Norris, Devin **Hymn Preludes and Free Accompaniments**
    Volume 15  Augsburg Publishing House  11-9411
    Key: Eb

Wyton, Alec **New Shoots from Old Routes**  The Sacred
    Music Press  KK 279  Key: Eb

**Austrian Hymn**

| BA | DC | 1940 | 1982 | LBW | LW | PH | RCV | UCC | UM | WB |
|----|----|------|------|-----|----|----|-----|-----|----|----|
| F  | Eb |      |      | Eb  |    | Eb |     | Eb  |    | Eb |

ORGAN COMPOSITIONS

Jordan, Alice "Word of God, Across the Ages" **A Season
    and a Time**  Broadman Press  4570-37  Key: F

Paine, John Knowles  "Concert Variations on the
    Austrian Hymn"  **19th Century American Organ
    Music**  Cleveland Chapter AGO  Key: F

FREE ACCOMPANIMENTS

Ferguson, John **Ten Hymn Tune Harmonizations**  Book I
    Ludwig Music Publishing Co.  0-05  Key: Eb

Nelson, Ronald **Free Organ Accompaniments to Festival
    Hymns**  Volume I  Augsburg Publishing House 11-9192
    Key: F

**Author of Life**

| BA | DC | 1940 | 1982 | LBW | LW | PH | RCV | UCC | UM | WB |
|----|----|------|------|-----|----|----|-----|-----|------|----|
|    |    | 1940 | 1982 | LBW | LW | PH | RCV | UCC | UM d | WB |

**Autumn**

| BA | DC | 1940 | 1982 | LBW | LW | PH | RCV | UCC | UM | WB |
|----|----|------|------|-----|----|----|-----|-----|------|----|
|    | DC | 1940 | 1982 | LBW | LW | PH | RCV | UCC | UM G | WB |

**Ave caeli janua**

| BA | DC | 1940 | 1982 | LBW | LW | PH | RCV | UCC | UM | WB |
|----|----|------|------|-----|----|----|-----|-----|----|----|
|    | DC | 1940 | 1982 m:e | LBW | LW | PH | RCV | UCC | UM | WB |

34

Ave Maria

| BA | DC | 1940 | 1982 | LBW | LW | PH | RCV | UCC | UM | WB |
|----|----|------|------|-----|----|----|-----|-----|----|----|
|    |    |      |      |     |    |    | m:d |     |    |    |

## ORGAN COMPOSITIONS

Kreckel, Philip G. **Musica Divina** Volume 2 J. Fischer
& Bro. No. 6715 Key: Bb

Ave Maria, klarer und lichter Morgenstern
(See also: Ellacombe)

| BA | DC | 1940 | 1982 | LBW | LW | PH | RCV | UCC | UM | WB |
|----|----|------|------|-----|----|----|-----|-----|----|----|
|    |    |      |      | A   |    |    |     |     |    |    |

## ORGAN COMPOSITIONS

Johns, Donald  "O Day of Rest and Gladness"  **The
Concordia Hymn Prelude Series**  Volume 20
Edited: Herbert Gotsch  Concordia Publishing House
97-5711  Key: A

Ave virgo virginum
(See also: Gaudeamus pariter)

| BA | DC | 1940 | 1982 | LBW | LW | PH | RCV | UCC | UM | WB |
|----|----|------|------|-----|----|----|-----|-----|----|----|
|    |    |      |      |     |    | F  |     |     | F  | F  |

Avison

| BA | DC | 1940 | 1982 | LBW | LW | PH | RCV | UCC | UM | WB |
|----|----|------|------|-----|----|----|-----|-----|----|----|
|    |    | F    |      |     |    |    |     |     |    |    |

Avon

| BA | DC | 1940 | 1982 | LBW | LW | PH | RCV | UCC | UM | WB |
|----|----|------|------|-----|----|----|-----|-----|----|----|
| Ab |    |      |      |     |    |    |     |     |    |    |

Away in a Manger

| BA | DC | 1940 | 1982 | LBW | LW | PH | RCV | UCC | UM | WB |
|----|----|------|------|-----|----|----|-----|-----|----|----|
|    |    |      |      |     |    | F  |     |     |    |    |

(Note: F also appears under LW)

## ORGAN COMPOSITIONS

Busarow, Donald  "Away in a Manger"  **The Concordia
Hymn Prelude Series**  Volume 2  Edited: Herbert
Gotsch  Concordia Publishing House  97-5536
Key: F

Chapman, Keith "Away in a Manger" **Christmas for Organ**
McAfee Music Corp.  Key: G

Hudson, Richard  **Hymn Preludes and Free Accompaniments**
Volume 12  Augsburg Publishing House  11-9408
Key: F

| | BA | DC | 1940 | 1982 | LBW | LW | PH | RCV | UCC | UM | WB |
|---|---|---|---|---|---|---|---|---|---|---|---|
| Aylesbury | | DC | 1940 | 1982 | LBW | LW | PH | RCV | UCC | UM | WB e |
| Ayrshire | | DC | 1940 | 1982 | LBW | LW | PH | RCV | UCC | UM G | WB |
| Azmon | G | DC Ab | 1940 | 1982 | LBW G | LW G | PH Ab | RCV | UCC G | UM G | WB Ab |

## ORGAN COMPOSITIONS

Beck, Albert **76 Offertories on Hymns and Chorales**
Concordia Publishing House  97-5207  Key: G

Jordan, Alice "Canticle of Praise on 'Azmon'" **Worship Service Music for the Organist** Broadman Press
Key: C

Lovelace, Austin "Jesus, Thine all-victorious Love"
**Eight Hymn Preludes**  Augsburg Publishing House
11-9144  Key: G

Manz, Paul "Oh, for a Thousand Tongues to Sing" **Ten Chorale Improvisations** Set IX Op. 21 Concordia Publishing House 97-5556  Key: A

## FREE ACCOMPANIMENTS

Carson, J. Bert  **Hymn Preludes and Free Accompaniments**
Volume 16  Augsburg Publishing House  11-9412
Key: F

Ferguson, John  **Hymn Harmonizations for Organ**
Book II Ludwig Music Publishing Co.  0-07  Key: G

Hancock, Gerre **Organ Improvisations for Hymn-Singing**
Hinshaw Music Co.  HMO-100  Key: G

Hillert, Richard  **Hymn Preludes and Free Accompaniments**
Volume 10  Augsburg Publishing House  11-9406
Key: G

Wyton, Alec  **New Shoots from Old Routes**  The Sacred Music Press  KK 279  Key: G

# B

**Babylon's Streams**

| BA | DC | 1940 | 1982 | LBW | LW | PH | RCV | UCC | UM | WB |
|----|----|------|------|-----|----|----|-----|-----|----|----|
|    | d  | d    |      |     |    |    |     |     |    |    |

**Baker**

| BA | DC | 1940 | 1982 | LBW | LW | PH | RCV | UCC | UM | WB |
|----|----|------|------|-----|----|----|-----|-----|----|----|
|    |    |      |      |     |    |    |     |     |    | F  |

**Balfour**

| BA | DC | 1940 | 1982 | LBW | LW | PH | RCV | UCC | UM | WB |
|----|----|------|------|-----|----|----|-----|-----|----|----|
|    |    | Bb   |      |     |    |    |     |     |    |    |

ORGAN COMPOSITIONS

Orr, Robin **Three Preludes on Scottish Psalm Tunes**
Hinrichsen   No. 720b   Key: C

**Ballad**

| BA | DC | 1940 | 1982 | LBW | LW | PH | RCV | UCC | UM | WB |
|----|----|------|------|-----|----|----|-----|-----|----|----|
|    |    |      | e    |     |    |    |     |     |    |    |

**Ballerma**

| BA | DC | 1940 | 1982 | LBW | LW | PH | RCV | UCC | UM | WB |
|----|----|------|------|-----|----|----|-----|-----|----|----|
|    |    | G    |      |     |    |    |     |     | G  |    |

FREE ACCOMPANIMENTS

**Free Harmonizations of Hymn Tunes by Fifty American Composers** Edited: D. DeWitt Wasson  Hinshaw Music, Inc.  HMO-145  Key: G

**Balm in Gilead**

| BA | DC | 1940 | 1982 | LBW | LW | PH | RCV | UCC | UM | WB |
|----|----|------|------|-----|----|----|-----|-----|----|----|
|    |    | G    |      |     |    |    |     |     | G  |    |

ORGAN COMPOSITIONS

Jordan, Alice "There is a Balm in Gilead" **A Season and a Time** Broadman Press  4570-37  Key: Eb

**Bangor**

| BA | DC | 1940 | 1982 | LBW | LW | PH | RCV | UCC | UM | WB |
|----|----|------|------|-----|----|----|-----|-----|----|----|
|    | c  | c    | c    |     |    | c  | c   | c   | c  | c  |

ORGAN COMPOSITIONS

Gieseke, Richard W. "God Moves in a Mysterious Way" **The Concordia Hymn Prelude Series** Volume 20 Edited; Herbert Gotsch  Concordia Publishing House 97-5711  Key: c

Willan, Healey  **36 Short Preludes and Postludes on Well-Known Hymn Tunes**  Set II  C. F. Peters Corp. No. 6162  Key: c

## FREE ACCOMPANIMENTS

**Free Harmonizations of Hymn Tunes by Fifty American Composers**  Edited: D. DeWitt Wasson  Hinshaw Music, Inc.  HMO-145  Key: c

Noble, T. Tertius  **Fifty Free Organ Accompaniments to Well Known Hymn Tunes**  J. Fischer & Bros. 8430  Key: c

### Barnabas

| BA | DC | 1940 | 1982 | LBW | LW | PH | RCV | UCC | UM | WB |
|----|----|------|------|-----|----|----|-----|-----|----|----|
| BA | DC | 1940 | 1982 | LBW | LW | PH | RCV | UCC | UM F | WB |

### Battle Hymn

| BA | DC | 1940 | 1982 | LBW | LW | PH | RCV | UCC | UM | WB |
|----|----|------|------|-----|----|----|-----|-----|----|----|
| BA Bb | DC | 1940 | 1982 | LBW Bb | LW | PH Bb | RCV C | UCC Bb | UM Bb | WB Bb |

## ORGAN COMPOSITIONS

Busarow, Donald  "Battle Hymn of the Republic"  **The Concordia Hymn Prelude Series**  Volume 20 Edited: Herbert Gotsch  Concordia Publishing House  97-5711  Key: Bb

## FREE ACCOMPANIMENTS

Hebble, Robert  **Robert Hebble's Hymnal Companion for Organ**  Bradley Publications  CE/283A/3  Key: Bb

### Batty
(See also: Ringe recht)

| BA | DC | 1940 | 1982 | LBW | LW | PH | RCV | UCC | UM | WB |
|----|----|------|------|-----|----|----|-----|-----|----|----|
| BA | DC | 1940 E | 1982 | LBW | LW | PH Eb | RCV | UCC | UM | WB |

## ORGAN COMPOSITIONS

Haan, Raymond H.  "Sweet the Moments, Rich in Blessing"  **The King of Love**  The Sacred Music Press  KK 277 Key: E

## FREE ACCOMPANIMENTS

**Free Harmonizations of Hymn Tunes by Fifty American Composers**  Edited: D. DeWitt Wasson  Hinshaw Music, Inc.  HMO-145  Key: E

Noble, T. Tertius  **Fifty Free Organ Accompaniments to Well Known Hymn Tunes**  J. Fischer & Bros. 8430  Key: E

Beach Spring

| BA | DC | 1940 | 1982 | LBW | LW | PH | RCV | UCC | UM | WB |
|----|----|------|------|-----|----|----|-----|-----|----|----|
| G  |    |      |      | F   |    |    |     |     |    |    |

## ORGAN COMPOSITIONS

Held, Wilbur  **7 Settings of American Folk Hymns**
Concordia Publishing House  97-5829  Key: F

Powell, Robert J.  "Lord, Whose Love in Humble Service"
**The Concordia Hymn Prelude Series**  Volume 20
Edited: Herbert Gotsch  Concordia Publishing House
97-5711  Key: F

## FREE ACCOMPANIMENTS

Busarow, Donald **All Praise to You Eternal God**
Augsburg Publishing House  11-9076  Key: F

Krapf, Gerhard  **Hymn Preludes and Free Accompaniments**
Volume 13  Augsburg Publishing House  11-9409
Key: F

Beacon Hill

| BA | DC | 1940 | 1982 | LBW | LW | PH | RCV | UCC | UM | WB |
|----|----|------|------|-----|----|----|-----|-----|-----|----|
|    |    |      |      |     |    |    |     |     | Ab |    |

Bealoth

| BA | DC | 1940 | 1982 | LBW | LW | PH | RCV | UCC | UM | WB |
|----|----|------|------|-----|----|----|-----|-----|-----|----|
|    |    |      |      |     |    |    |     |     | Ab |    |

Beata nobis gaudia

| BA | DC | 1940 | 1982 | LBW | LW | PH | RCV | UCC | UM | WB |
|----|----|------|------|-----|----|----|-----|-----|----|----|
|    |    | m:f  |      |     |    |    |     |     |    |    |

Beati

| BA | DC | 1940 | 1982 | LBW | LW | PH | RCV | UCC | UM | WB |
|----|----|------|------|-----|----|----|-----|-----|----|----|
|    |    | C    |      |     |    |    |     |     |    |    |

Beatitudes

| BA | DC | 1940 | 1982 | LBW | LW | PH | RCV | UCC | UM | WB |
|----|----|------|------|-----|----|----|-----|-----|----|----|
|    |    |      | F    |     |    |    |     |     |    |    |

Beatitudo

| BA | DC | 1940 | 1982 | LBW | LW | PH | RCV | UCC | UM | WB |
|----|----|------|------|-----|----|----|-----|-----|----|----|
|    |    | G    | G    |     | G  | Ab | Ab  |     |    |    |

## ORGAN COMPOSITIONS

Mackie, Ruth "Oh, for a Thousand Tongues to Sing"
**The Concordia Hymn Prelude Series**  Volume 20
Edited: Herbert Gotsch  Concordia Publishing House
97-5711  Key: G

# FREE ACCOMPANIMENTS

**Beck, Albert 76 Offertories on Hymn and Chorales**
Concordia Publishing House 97-5207  Key: G

**Hebble, Robert Robert Hebble's Hymnal Companion for Organ** Bradley Publications  CE/283A/3  Key: G

## Beatus vir

| BA | DC | 1940 | 1982 | LBW | LW | PH | RCV | UCC | UM | WB |
|---|---|---|---|---|---|---|---|---|---|---|
|  |  |  | D |  |  |  |  |  |  | D |

### ORGAN COMPOSITIONS

Sensmeier, Randall "Lord of All Nations, Grant Me Grace" **The Concordia Hymn Prelude Series** Volume 20  Edited: Herbert Gotsch  Concordia Publishing House  97-5711  Key: D

### FREE ACCOMPANIMENTS

Busarow, Donald **All Praise to You Eternal God** Augsburg Publishing House  11-9076  Key: D

**Free Harmonizations of Hymn Tunes by Fifty American Composers** Edited: D. DeWitt Wasson  Hinshaw Music, Inc.  HMO-145  Key: D

Gehring, Philip **Hymn Preludes and Free Accompaniments** Volume 3  Augsburg Publishing House  11-9399 Key: D

## Bedford
(See also: Edmonton)

| BA | DC | 1940 | 1982 | LBW | LW | PH | RCV | UCC | UM | WB |
|---|---|---|---|---|---|---|---|---|---|---|
|  |  | Db |  |  |  |  |  |  |  |  |

### ORGAN COMPOSITIONS

Willan, Healey **36 Short Preludes and Postludes on Well-Known Hymn Tunes** Set III C. F. Peters Corporation  No. 6163  Key: Db

Thalben-Ball, George **113 Variations on Hymn Tunes for Organ** Novello & Co., Ltd.  Key: Eb

## Beecher

| BA | DC | 1940 | 1982 | LBW | LW | PH | RCV | UCC | UM | WB |
|---|---|---|---|---|---|---|---|---|---|---|
| Bb | Bb | A | A |  |  | Bb |  | Bb | Bb |  |

Noble, T. Tertius **Free Organ Accompaniments to One Hundred Well-Known Hymn Tunes**
J. Fischer & Bros. #8175 Key: A

Behold a Host

| BA | DC | 1940 | 1982 | LBW | LW | PH | RCV | UCC | UM | WB |
|----|----|------|------|-----|----|----|-----|-----|----|----|
|    |    |      |      |     | Eb |    |     |     |    |    |

Bellwoods

| BA | DC | 1940 | 1982 | LBW | LW | PH | RCV | UCC | UM | WB |
|----|----|------|------|-----|----|----|-----|-----|----|----|
|    |    | Db   | Db   |     |    |    |     |     |    |    |

## ORGAN COMPOSITIONS

Thalben-Ball, George **113 Variations on Hymn Tunes for Organ** Novello & Co., Ltd. Key: Db

Belmont

| BA | DC | 1940 | 1982 | LBW | LW | PH | RCV | UCC | UM | WB |
|----|----|------|------|-----|----|----|-----|-----|----|----|
|    | G  | G    |      |     | G  |    |     |     |    |    |

## ORGAN COMPOSITIONS

Gerike, Henry V. "The Lord's My Shepherd" **The Concordia Hymn Prelude Series** Volume 20 Edited: Herbert Gotsch Concordia Publishing House 97-5711 Key: G

Haan, Raymond H. "By cool Siloam's shady rill" **The King of Love** The Sacred Music Press K 277 Key: G

## FREE ACCOMPANIMENTS

Beck, Albert **76 Offertories on Hymns and Chorales** Concordia Publishing House 97-5207 Key: G

Bemerton

| BA | DC | 1940 | 1982 | LBW | LW | PH | RCV | UCC | UM | WB |
|----|----|------|------|-----|----|----|-----|-----|----|----|
|    |    |      |      |     |    |    |     | F   |    |    |

Beng-Li

| BA | DC | 1940 | 1982 | LBW | LW | PH | RCV | UCC | UM | WB |
|----|----|------|------|-----|----|----|-----|-----|----|----|
|    |    |      | m:d  |     |    |    |     |     |    |    |

Benifold

| BA | DC | 1940 | 1982 | LBW | LW | PH | RCV | UCC | UM | WB |
|----|----|------|------|-----|----|----|-----|-----|----|----|
|    |    |      | E    |     |    |    |     |     |    |    |

## Benson

| BA | DC | 1940 | 1982 | LBW | LW | PH | RCV | UCC | UM | WB |
|----|----|------|------|-----|----|----|-----|-----|----|----|
| G |  |  |  |  |  |  |  |  |  |  |

## Bereden väg för Herran

| BA | DC | 1940 | 1982 | LBW | LW | PH | RCV | UCC | UM | WB |
|----|----|------|------|-----|----|----|-----|-----|----|----|
|  |  | G | G | G |  |  |  |  |  |  |

### ORGAN COMPOSITIONS

Cassler, G. Winston **The Concordia Hymn Prelude Series**
Volume I    Edited: Herbert Gotsch
Concordia Publishing House   97-5536   Key: G

Cherwien, David "Prepare the Royal Highway"
**Interpretations Based on Hymn-Tunes**
Book IV   A.M.S.I.   OR-9   Key: G

## Bernard of Cluny

| BA | DC | 1940 | 1982 | LBW | LW | PH | RCV | UCC | UM | WB |
|----|----|------|------|-----|----|----|-----|-----|----|----|
|  |  |  |  |  |  |  | Ab |  |  |  |

## Bethany

| BA | DC | 1940 | 1982 | LBW | LW | PH | RCV | UCC | UM | WB |
|----|----|------|------|-----|----|----|-----|-----|----|----|
| G | F |  |  |  | F | G | G |  | F |  |

### ORGAN COMPOSITIONS

Bingham, Seth **Twleve Hymn Preludes** Opus 38 Set 2
H.W. Gray   GB 152 Key: G

Johns, Donald   "Nearer, My God to Thee"   **The Concordia Hymn Prelude Series** Volume 21   Edited: Herbert Gotsch   Concordia Publishing House   97-5736   Key: F

Stearns, Peter Pindar   **Twenty Hymn Preludes**
Coburn Press (Theodore Presser Company) Key: A

### FREE ACCOMPANIMENTS

**Free Harmonizations of Hymn Tunes by Fifty American Composers** Edited: D. DeWitt Wasson   Hinshaw Music, Inc.   HMO-145   Key: F

Noble, T. Tertius **Free Accompaniments to One Hundred Well-Known Hymn Tunes**  J. Fischer & Bros. #8175   Key: F

## Bethlehem (Fink)

| BA | DC | 1940 | 1982 | LBW | LW | PH | RCV | UCC | UM | WB |
|----|----|------|------|-----|----|----|-----|-----|----|----|
|  | Ab |  |  |  |  |  |  | A | Bb |  |

# FREE ACCOMPANIMENTS

## Free Harmonizations of Hymn Tunes by Fifty American Composers  Edited: D. DeWitt Wasson  Hinshaw Music, Inc.  HMO-145  Key: Bb

**Bethlehem** (Johnson)

| | BA | DC | 1940 | 1982 | LBW | LW | PH | RCV | UCC | UM | WB |
|---|---|---|---|---|---|---|---|---|---|---|---|
| | BA | DC | 1940 | 1982 | LBW | LW | PH | RCV | UCC | UM | WB |
| | | | | | | | | | | | D |

**Beulah**

| | BA | DC | 1940 | 1982 | LBW | LW | PH | RCV | UCC | UM | WB |
|---|---|---|---|---|---|---|---|---|---|---|---|
| | | | A | | | | | | | | |

**Beverly**

| | BA | DC | 1940 | 1982 | LBW | LW | PH | RCV | UCC | UM | WB |
|---|---|---|---|---|---|---|---|---|---|---|---|
| | | | | | F | | | | | | |

## ORGAN COMPOSITIONS

Bouman, Paul  "Christ is the King"  **The Concordia Hymn Prelude Series**  Volume 21  Edited: Herbert Gotsch  Concordia Publishing House  97-5736  Key: F

**Bickford**

| | BA | DC | 1940 | 1982 | LBW | LW | PH | RCV | UCC | UM | WB |
|---|---|---|---|---|---|---|---|---|---|---|---|
| | | | | F | | | | | | | |

**Bingham**

| | BA | DC | 1940 | 1982 | LBW | LW | PH | RCV | UCC | UM | WB |
|---|---|---|---|---|---|---|---|---|---|---|---|
| | | | | Ab | | | | | | | |

**Birabus**

| | BA | DC | 1940 | 1982 | LBW | LW | PH | RCV | UCC | UM | WB |
|---|---|---|---|---|---|---|---|---|---|---|---|
| | | | e | e | | | | | | | |

## ORGAN COMPOSITIONS

Held, Wilbur  "All Who Love and Serve Your City"  **The Concordia Hymn Prelude Series**  Volume 21  Edited: Herbert Gotsch  Concordia Publishing House  97-5736  Key: e

**Birmingham**

| | BA | DC | 1940 | 1982 | LBW | LW | PH | RCV | UCC | UM | WB |
|---|---|---|---|---|---|---|---|---|---|---|---|
| | D | Db | D | | | | | | | | |

**Bishopgarth**

| | BA | DC | 1940 | 1982 | LBW | LW | PH | RCV | UCC | UM | WB |
|---|---|---|---|---|---|---|---|---|---|---|---|
| | | | | | | | Eb | | | | |

43

Bishopthorpe

| | | | | | | | | | | |
|---|---|---|---|---|---|---|---|---|---|---|
| BA | DC | 1940 | 1982 | LBW | LW | PH | RCV | UCC | UM | WB |
| G | F | | | | | F | | | | |

## ORGAN COMPOSITIONS

**Thalben-Ball, George** **113 Variations on Hymn Tunes for Organ** Novello & Co., Ltd. Key: G

Blackbourne

| | | | | | | | | | | |
|---|---|---|---|---|---|---|---|---|---|---|
| BA | DC | 1940 | 1982 | LBW | LW | PH | RCV | UCC | UM | WB |
| | c | | | | | | | | | |

Blaenhafren

| | | | | | | | | | | |
|---|---|---|---|---|---|---|---|---|---|---|
| BA | DC | 1940 | 1982 | LBW | LW | PH | RCV | UCC | UM | WB |
| | | | g | | | g | | | | g |

Blairgowrie

| | | | | | | | | | | |
|---|---|---|---|---|---|---|---|---|---|---|
| BA | DC | 1940 | 1982 | LBW | LW | PH | RCV | UCC | UM | WB |
| | Eb | | | | | | | | D | |

Blencathra

| | | | | | | | | | | |
|---|---|---|---|---|---|---|---|---|---|---|
| BA | DC | 1940 | 1982 | LBW | LW | PH | RCV | UCC | UM | WB |
| G | | | | | | | | | | |

Blessed Name

| | | | | | | | | | | |
|---|---|---|---|---|---|---|---|---|---|---|
| BA | DC | 1940 | 1982 | LBW | LW | PH | RCV | UCC | UM | WB |
| Ab | | | | | | | | | | |

Blessings

| | | | | | | | | | | |
|---|---|---|---|---|---|---|---|---|---|---|
| BA | DC | 1940 | 1982 | LBW | LW | PH | RCV | UCC | UM | WB |
| Eb | | | | | | | | | | |

Blomstertid

| | | | | | | | | | | |
|---|---|---|---|---|---|---|---|---|---|---|
| BA | DC | 1940 | 1982 | LBW | LW | PH | RCV | UCC | UM | WB |
| | F | | | | | | | | | |

Blott en Dag

| | | | | | | | | | | |
|---|---|---|---|---|---|---|---|---|---|---|
| BA | DC | 1940 | 1982 | LBW | LW | PH | RCV | UCC | UM | WB |
| Eb | | | | | | | | | | |

## ORGAN COMPOSITIONS

**Jordan, Alice** "Adagio on a Traditional Swedish Folk Tune" **Music Service Music for the Organist** Broadman Press Key: Eb

Bohemian Brethren
(See also: Mit Freuden zart)

| | | | | | | | | | | |
|---|---|---|---|---|---|---|---|---|---|---|
| BA | DC | 1940 | 1982 | LBW | LW | PH | RCV | UCC | UM | WB |
| | Db | | | | | | | | | |

<u>Bone</u> <u>Pastor</u>
   BA    DC    1940 1982 LBW  LW     PH    RCV   UCC   UM    WB
   D

## ORGAN COMPOSITIONS

Johnson, David "Bread of Life, Good Shepherd, Tend Us"
**Deck Thyself with Gladness** Augsburg Publishing
House 11-9101  Key: F

<u>Born</u> <u>Again</u>
   (See also: Warum sollt ich)
   BA    DC    1940 1982 LBW  LW     PH    RCV   UCC   UM    WB
   Eb

<u>Boundless</u> <u>Mercy</u>
   BA    DC    1940 1982 LBW  LW     PH    RCV   UCC   UM    WB
                                                                     F

<u>Bourbon</u>
   BA    DC    1940 1982 LBW  LW     PH    RCV   UCC   UM    WB
                  f                     f

## ORGAN COMPOSITIONS

Ore, Charles W.  "It Happened on That Fateful Night"
**The Concordia Hymn Prelude Series** Volume 7
Edited: Herbert Gotsch  Concordia Publishing
House  97-5614  Key: f

## FREE ACCOMPANIMENTS

Busarow, Donald **All Praise to You Eternal God**
Augsburg Publishing House  11-9076  Key: f

**Free Harmonizations of Hymn Tunes by Fifty American
Composers** Edited: D. DeWitt Wasson  Hinshaw
Music, Inc.  HMO-145  Key: f

<u>Bourgeois</u>
   (See also: Psalm 42)
   BA    DC    1940 1982 LBW  LW     PH    RCV   UCC   UM    WB
   F

## INTONATIONS

Hermann, David  **11 Hymn Intonations, Free
Accompaniments, Instrumental Descants for Organ**
Volume I  Advent, Christmas, Epiphany
G.I.A. Publications  G-2378  Key: F

## Bourne

| BA | DC | 1940 | 1982 | LBW | LW | PH | RCV | UCC | UM | WB |
|----|----|------|------|-----|----|----|-----|-----|----|----|
|    |    | F    |      |     |    |    |     |     |    |    |

## Bouwerie

| BA | DC | 1940 | 1982 | LBW | LW | PH | RCV | UCC | UM | WB |
|----|----|------|------|-----|----|----|-----|-----|----|----|
|    |    | Ab   |      |     |    |    |     |     |    |    |

## Boylston

| BA | DC | 1940 | 1982 | LBW | LW | PH | RCV | UCC | UM | WB |
|----|----|------|------|-----|----|----|-----|-----|----|----|
|    |    | C    |      |     | C  | C  |     |     | C  |    |

### ORGAN COMPOSITIONS

Beck, Albert **76 Offertories on Hymns and Chorales** Concordia Publishing House 97-5207  Key: C

Lenel, Ludwig  "Blest Be the Tie That Binds"  **The Parish Organist**  Part One  Edited: Heinrich Fleischer  Concordia Publishing House  97-1145  Key:  C

Patterson, Kimberly Kondal   "Blest Be the Tie That Binds"  **The Concordia Hymn Prelude Series** Volume 21  Edited: Herbert Gotsch  Concordia Publishing House  97-5736  Key: C

### FREE ACCOMPANIMENTS

**Free Harmonizations of Hymn Tunes by Fifty American Composers**  Edited: D. DeWitt Wasson  Hinshaw Music, Inc.  HMO-145  Key: C

## Bradbury

| BA | DC | 1940 | 1982 | LBW | LW | PH | RCV | UCC | UM | WB |
|----|----|------|------|-----|----|----|-----|-----|----|----|
| Db | Eb |      |      |     |    | Eb |     |     | D  |    |

### ORGAN COMPOSITIONS

Jordan, Alice "Savior, Like a Shepherd Lead Us" **A Season and A Time**  Broadman Press  4570-37 Key:Db

### FREE ACCOMPANIMENTS

**Free Harmonizations of Hymn Tunes by Fifty American Composers**  Edited: D. DeWitt Wasson  Hinshaw Music, Inc.  HMO-145  Key: Eb

Hancock, Gerre  **Organ Improvisations for Hymn-Singing** Hinshaw Music Co.  HMO-100  Key: D

## Bradford

| BA | DC | 1940 | 1982 | LBW | LW | PH | RCV | UCC | UM | WB |
|---|---|---|---|---|---|---|---|---|---|---|
| | | | | | | | Eb | | | |

## Brasted

| BA | DC | 1940 | 1982 | LBW | LW | PH | RCV | UCC | UM | WB |
|---|---|---|---|---|---|---|---|---|---|---|
| | | G | | | | | | | | |

## Bread of Heaven

| BA | DC | 1940 | 1982 | LBW | LW | PH | RCV | UCC | UM | WB |
|---|---|---|---|---|---|---|---|---|---|---|
| | | D | | | | | | | | |

## Bread of Life

| BA | DC | 1940 | 1982 | LBW | LW | PH | RCV | UCC | UM | WB |
|---|---|---|---|---|---|---|---|---|---|---|
| Eb | Eb | D | D | | | Eb | Eb | | Eb | Eb |

### ORGAN COMPOSITIONS

Bingham, Seth **Twelve Hymn Preludes** Opus 38  Set 2 H.W. Gray  GB 152  Key: Eb

Johnson, David N. "Break Thou the Bread of Life" **Deck Thyself My Soul with Gladness** Augsburg Publishing House 11-9157  Key: D

Jordan, Alice "Break Thou the Bread of Life" **Hymns of Grateful Praise** Broadman Press Key: Eb

Lovelace, Austin  "Break Now the Bread of Life"  **The Concordia Hymn Prelude Series**  Volume 21  Edited: Herbert Gotsch  Concordia Publishing House 97-5736  Key: D

Miles, Russell Hancock "Break Thou the Bread of Life" **Three Improvisations** The Arthur P. Schmidt Co. Key: Eb

### FREE ACCOMPANIMENTS

**Free Harmonizations of Hymn Tunes by Fifty American Composers** Edited: D. DeWitt Wasson  Hinshaw Music, Inc.  HMO-145  Key: Eb

## Break Bread Together
(See also: Let Us Break Bread)

| BA | DC | 1940 | 1982 | LBW | LW | PH | RCV | UCC | UM | WB |
|---|---|---|---|---|---|---|---|---|---|---|
| Eb | | | | | | | | | | |

### ORGAN COMPOSITIONS

Jordan, Alice  "Let Us Break Bread Together" **A Season and a Time** Broadman Press  4570-37  Key: Eb

47

Powell, Robert J.  "Let Us Break Bread Together"
**The Concordia Hymn Prelude Series**  Volume 17
Edited: Herbert Gotsch  Concordia Publishing House
97-5708  Key: Eb

## Bremen

| BA | DC | 1940 | 1982 | LBW | LW | PH | RCV | UCC | UM | WB |
|----|----|------|------|-----|----|----|-----|-----|----|----|
|    | DC | 1940 | 1982 | LBW | LW | PH | RCV | UCC | UM | WB |
|    |    |      |      |     |    |    | D   |     |    |    |

### FREE ACCOMPANIMENTS

**Free Harmonizations of Hymn Tunes by Fifty American
Composers**  Edited:  D. DeWitt Wasson  Hinshaw
Music, Inc.  HMO-145  Key: g

## Breslau

| BA | DC | 1940 | 1982 | LBW | LW | PH | RCV | UCC | UM | WB |
|----|----|------|------|-----|----|----|-----|-----|----|----|
|    | DC | 1940 | 1982 | LBW | LW | PH | RCV | UCC | UM | WB |
| G  | G  | G    |      |     |    | G  | G   |     |    |    |

### ORGAN COMPOSITIONS

Thalben-Ball, George  **113 Variations on Hymn Tunes
for Organ**  Novello & Co., Ltd.  Key: Ab

### FREE ACCOMPANIMENTS

Noble, T. Tertius **Free Organ Accompaniments to One
Hundred Well-Known Hymn Tunes**  J. Fischer & Bros.
#8175  Key: G

## Bridegroom

| BA | DC | 1940 | 1982 | LBW | LW | PH | RCV | UCC | UM | BW |
|----|----|------|------|-----|----|----|-----|-----|----|----|
|    | DC | 1940 | 1982 | LBW | LW | PH | RCV | UCC | UM | BW |
|    |    |      | F    |     |    |    |     | F   |    |    |

## Bring a Torch

| BA | DC | 1940 | 1982 | LBW | LW | PH | RCV | UCC | UM | BW |
|----|----|------|------|-----|----|----|-----|-----|----|----|
|    | DC | 1940 | 1982 | LBW | LW | PH | RCV | UCC | UM | BW |
|    |    |      |      |     |    | F  |     |     |    | F  |

### ORGAN COMPOSITIONS

Chapman, Keith "Bring a Torch, Jeanette Isabella"
**Christmas for Organ** McAfee Music Corp.
Key: G/Db

Diemer, Emma Lou  "Bring a Torch, Jeanette Isabella"
**Carols for Organ** The Sacred Music Press Key:Eb

Hudson, Richard "Toccata1 **Suite of Organ Carols**
Augsburg Publishing House  Key: C

Jordan, Alice "Cradle Song" **Hymns of Grateful Praise**
Broadman Press Key; F

**Bristol**

| BA | DC | 1940 | 1982 | LBW | LW | PH | RCV | UCC | UM | BW |
|----|----|------|------|-----|----|----|-----|-----|----|----|
|    |    | F    | F    |     |    |    |     |     |    |    |

### ORGAN COMPOSITIONS

Lang, C.S. **Twenty Hymn-Preludes** (First Set)
Oxford University Press  Key: G

Willan, Healey **Ten Hymn Preludes** Set II  C. F.
Peters Corporation  6012  Key: G

### FREE ACCOMPANIMENTS

Coleman, Henry **Varied Hymn Accompaniments** Oxford
University Press  Key: G

**Brocklesbury**

| BA | DC | 1940 | 1982 | LBW | LW | PH | RCV | UCC | UM | BW |
|----|----|------|------|-----|----|----|-----|-----|----|----|
|    |    | Eb   |      |     |    |    |     |     |    |    |

**Bromley**

| BA | DC | 1940 | 1982 | LBW | LW | PH | RCV | UCC | UM | BW |
|----|----|------|------|-----|----|----|-----|-----|----|----|
|    |    | F    | F    |     |    |    | F   |     |    |    |

**Bronxville**

| BA | DC | 1940 | 1982 | LBW | LW | PH | RCV | UCC | UM | BW |
|----|----|------|------|-----|----|----|-----|-----|----|----|
|    |    |      |      |     | d  |    |     |     |    |    |

### ORGAN COMPOSITIONS

Schultz, Ralph  "Lo, Judah's Lion Wins the Strife"
**The Concordia Hymn Prelude Series** Volume 10
Edited: Herbert Gotsch  Concordia Publishing House
97-5617  Key: m:d

**Brother James' Air**

| BA | DC | 1940 | 1982 | LBW | LW | PH | RCV | UCC | UM | BW |
|----|----|------|------|-----|----|----|-----|-----|----|----|
|    |    | D    | D    | D   |    |    | D   |     |    |    |

### ORGAN COMPOSITIONS

Darke, Harold **A Meditation on 'Brother James' Air**
Oxford University Press  Key: D

Kalbfleisch, Rodger  "The Lord's My Shepherd" **The
Concordia Hymn Prelude Series** Volume 21  Edited:
Herbert Gotsch  Concordia Publishing House
97-5736  Key: D

## FREE ACCOMPANIMENTS

Arnatt, Ronald **Hymn Preludes and Free Accompaniments**
Volume 9   Augsburg Publishing House   11-9405
Key: D

<u>Brother's Keeper</u>

| BA | DC | 1940 | 1982 | LBW | LW | PH | RCV | UCC | UM | BW |
|----|----|------|------|-----|-----|-----|-----|-----|-----|-----|
|    |    |      |      |     |    |    |     | a   |    |    |

<u>Bryn Calfaria</u>

| BA | DC | 1940 | 1982 | LBW | LW | PH | RCV | UCC | UM | BW |
|----|----|------|------|-----|-----|-----|-----|-----|-----|-----|
| g  |    |      |      | g   | g  | g  | g   |     | g  | g  |

## ORGAN COMPOSITIONS

Ferko, Frank "Look, the Sight is Glorious"  **The
Concordia Hymn Prelude Series**  Volume 12
Edited: Herbert Gotsch   Concordia Publishing House
97-5619   Key: g

Goode, Jack  **Seven Communion Meditations**  Harold
Flammer, Inc.   HF-5084   Key: g

Manz, Paul "Look Ye Saints, the Sight is Glorious"
**Ten Chorale Improvisations** Opus 16   Set VI
Concordia Publishing House   97-5305   Key: g

Pelz, Walter L.  "Lord Enthroned in Heavenly Splendor"
**The Concordia Hymn Prelude Series**  Volume 21
Edited; Herbert Gotsch   Concordia Publishing House
97-5736   Key: g

Powell, Robert J.  "Lord, Enthroned in Heavenly
Splendor"  **The Concordia Hymn Prelude Series**
Volume 14   Edited: Herbert Gotsch   Concordia
Publishing House   97-5705   Key: g

Vaughan William, Ralph  **Three Preludes**  Stainer
& Bell  (Galaxy Music Corp) Key: g

## FREE ACCOMPANIMENTS

Cassler, G. Winston **Organ Descants for Selected Hymn
Tunes**  Augsburg Publishing House 11-9304   Key: g

Diemer, Emma Lou  **Hymn Preludes and Free Accompaniments**
Volume 2  Augsburg Publishing House   11-9398
Key: g

**Free Harmonizations of Hymn Tunes by Fifty American
Composers**  Edited: D. DeWitt Wasson   Hinshaw
Music, Inc.  HMO-145   Key: g

**Buckland**

| BA | DC | 1940 | 1982 | LBW | LW | PH | RCV | UCC | UM | BW |
|----|----|------|------|-----|----|----|-----|-----|----|----|
|    |    | D    |      |     |    | D  |     |     |    |    |

## ORGAN COMPOSITIONS

Thalben-Ball, George **113 Variations on Hymn Tunes for Organ** Novello & Co., Ltd. Key: D

**Built on the Rock** (Kirken)

| BA | DC | 1940 | 1982 | LBW | LW | PH | RCV | UCC | UM | BW |
|----|----|------|------|-----|----|----|-----|-----|----|----|
|    |    |      |      |     |    |    |     |     |    | c  |

## INTONATIONS

McCormick, David **20 Organ Intonations on Hymns of Praise** Hope Publishing Co. Key: d

**Bullinger**

| BA | DC | 1940 | 1982 | LBW | LW | PH | RCV | UCC | UM | WB |
|----|----|------|------|-----|----|----|-----|-----|----|----|
|    | Ab |      |      |     |    |    |     |     | Ab |    |

**Bunessan**

| BA | DC | 1940 | 1982 | LBW | LW | PH | RCV | UCC | UM | WB |
|----|----|------|------|-----|----|----|-----|-----|----|----|
| C  |    |      | C    | C   | C  | C  | C   | C   |    |    |

## ORGAN COMPOSITIONS

Gieschen, Thomas "Praise and Thanksgiving" **The Concordia Hymn Prelude Series** Volume 21 Edited: Herbert Gotsch Concordia Publishing House 97-5736 Key: C

Manz, Paul "Praise and Thanksgiving" **Ten Chorale Improvisations** Set IX Op. 21 Concordia Publishing House 97-5556 Key: C

## FREE ACCOMPANIMENTS

Schack, David **Hymn Preludes and Free Accompaniments** Volume 11 Augsburg Publishing House 11-9407 Key: C

**Burford**

| BA | DC | 1940 | 1982 | LBW | LW | PH | RCV | UCC | UM | WB |
|----|----|------|------|-----|----|----|-----|-----|----|----|
|    |    | f    | f    |     |    |    |     |     |    |    |

## ORGAN COMPOSITIONS

Bouman, Paul "Prayer is the Soul's Sincere Desire" **The Parish Organist** Part Eleven Edited: Willem Mudde Concordia Publishing House 97-4758 Key: f

## By and By

| BA | DC | 1940 | 1982 | LBW | LW | PH | RCV | UCC | UM | WB |
|---|---|---|---|---|---|---|---|---|---|---|
| Eb | | | | | | | | | | |

# C

## Caelites plaudant

| BA | DC | 1940 | 1982 | LBW | LW | PH | RCV | UCC | UM | WB |
|---|---|---|---|---|---|---|---|---|---|---|
| | | | C | | | | | | | |

## Caelitum Joseph

| BA | DC | 1940 | 1982 | LBW | LW | PH | RCV | UCC | UM | WB |
|---|---|---|---|---|---|---|---|---|---|---|
| | | | m:d | | | | | | | |

## Caithness

| BA | DC | 1940 | 1982 | LBW | LW | PH | RCV | UCC | UM | WB |
|---|---|---|---|---|---|---|---|---|---|---|
| | | Eb | D | Eb | Eb | D | | | Eb | |

### ORGAN COMPOSITIONS

Johnson, David N. "O Lord, Throughout These Forty Days" **The Concordia Hymn Prelude Series** Volume 7 Edited: Herbert Gotsch Concordia Publishing House 97-5614 Key: Eb

Krapf, Gerhard "O for a Closer Walk with God" **The Parish Organist** Part Eleven Edited: Willem Mudde Concordia Publishing House 97-4758 Key: Eb

Thalben-Ball, George **113 Variations on Hymn Tunes** Novello & Co., Ltd. Key: Eb

### FREE ACCOMPANIMENTS

**Free Harmonizations of Hymn Tunes by Fifty American Composers** Edited: D. DeWitt Wasson Hinshaw Music, Inc. HMO-145 Key: Eb

## Call Street

| BA | DC | 1940 | 1982 | LBW | LW | PH | RCV | UCC | UM | WB |
|---|---|---|---|---|---|---|---|---|---|---|
| | | | C | | | | | | | |

## Calling Today

| BA | DC | 1940 | 1982 | LBW | LW | PH | RCV | UCC | UM | WB |
|---|---|---|---|---|---|---|---|---|---|---|
| C | | | | | | | | | | |

## Calvary

| BA | DC | 1940 | 1982 | LBW | LW | PH | RCV | UCC | UM | WB |
|---|---|---|---|---|---|---|---|---|---|---|
| C | | | | | | | | | | |

Camacha
  BA  DC  1940 1982  LBW  LW  PH  RCV  UCC  UM  WB
  Eb

Camano
  BA  DC  1940 1982  LBW  LW  PH  RCV  UCC  UM  WB
            F

Cambridge
  BA  DC  1940 1982  LBW  LW  PH  RCV  UCC  UM  WB
                                            G

Campian
  BA  DC  1940 1982  LBW  LW  PH  RCV  UCC  UM  WB
          g

ORGAN COMPOSITIONS

Willan, Healey **36 Short Preludes and Postludes on Well-Known Hymn Tunes** Set II  C.F. Peters Corporation  No. 6162  Key: g

Campmeeting
  BA  DC  1940 1982  LBW  LW  PH  RCV  UCC  UM  WB
                                            F

Cana
  BA  DC  1940 1982  LBW  LW  PH  RCV  UCC  UM  WB
          D

Candler
  BA  DC  1940 1982  LBW  LW  PH  RCV  UCC  UM  WB
                                            F

Cannock
  BA  DC  1940 1982  LBW  LW  PH  RCV  UCC  UM  WB
                     G

ORGAN COMPOSITIONS

Dahl, David P.  "O God of Life's Great Mystery"  **The Concordia Hymn Prelude Series** Volume 17 Edited: Herbert Gotsch  Concordia Publishing House 97-5708  Key: G

Johnson, David "O God of Life's Great Mystery" **Deck Thyself With Gladness** Volume 2  Augsburg Publishing House 11-9101  Key: G

Thalben-Ball, George **113 Variations on Hymn Tunes** Novello & Co., Ltd.  Key: A

Canonbury

| BA | DC | 1940 | 1982 | LBW | LW | PH | RCV | UCC | UM | WB |
|----|----|------|------|-----|----|----|-----|-----|----|----|
| G  | G  |      |      | G   |    | F  |     | G   | G  |    |

### ORGAN COMPOSITIONS

Jordan, Alice "Chorale on 'Canonbury'" **Worship Service Music for the Organist** Broadman Press Key: G

Pearce, Thomas R. "Lord, Speak to Us, That We May Speak" **The Concordia Hymn Prelude Series** Volume 21 Edited: Herbert Gotsch Concordia Publishing House 97-5736 Key: G

### FREE ACCOMPANIMENTS

Noble, T. Tertius **Free Organ Accompaniments to One Hundred Well-Known Hymn Tunes** J. Fischer & Bros. #8175 Key: G

Canterbury
(See also: Song)

| BA | DC | 1940 | 1982 | LBW | LW | PH | RCV | UCC | UM | WB |
|----|----|------|------|-----|----|----|-----|-----|----|----|
|    |    |      |      |     |    | D  |     |     | D  |    |

Canticum refectionis

| BA | DC | 1940 | 1982 | LBW | LW | PH | RCV | UCC | UM | WB |
|----|----|------|------|-----|----|----|-----|-----|----|----|
|    | C  | C    | C    |     |    |    |     | C   |    |    |

Cantique de Noel

| BA | DC | 1940 | 1982 | LBW | LW | PH | RCV | UCC | UM | WB |
|----|----|------|------|-----|----|----|-----|-----|----|----|
|    |    |      |      |     |    |    | Db  |     |    |    |

Capel

| BA | DC | 1940 | 1982 | LBW | LW | PH | RCV | UCC | UM | WB |
|----|----|------|------|-----|----|----|-----|-----|----|----|
|    |    | D    |      |     |    |    |     |     |    |    |

### ORGAN COMPOSITIONS

Thalben-Ball, George **113 Variations on Hymn Tunes** Novello & Co., Ltd. Key: Eb

Capetown

| BA | DC | 1940 | 1982 | LBW | LW | PH | RCV | UCC | UM | WB |
|----|----|------|------|-----|----|----|-----|-----|----|----|
|    |    | D    |      |     |    |    |     |     |    |    |

### ORGAN COMPOSITIONS

Thalben-Ball, George **113 Variations on Hymn Tunes** Novello & Co., Ltd. Key: Eb

# FREE ACCOMPANIMENTS

**Noble, T. Tertius  Fifty Free Organ Accompaniments to Well Known Hymn Tunes**  J. Fischer & Bros. 8430  Key: D

Captivity

| | BA | DC | 1940 | 1982 | LBW | LW | PH | RCV | UCC | UM | WB |
|---|---|---|---|---|---|---|---|---|---|---|---|
| | | | | | | | | | d | | |

Carey
(See also: Surrey)

| | BA | DC | 1940 | 1982 | LBW | LW | PH | RCV | UCC | UM | WB |
|---|---|---|---|---|---|---|---|---|---|---|---|
| | | | F | | | | | | | | |

Carlisle

| | BA | DC | 1940 | 1982 | LBW | LW | PH | RCV | UCC | UM | WB |
|---|---|---|---|---|---|---|---|---|---|---|---|
| | | | Eb | Eb | | | D | | | | |

# ORGAN COMPOSITIONS

**Thalben-Ball, George 113 Variations on Hymn Tunes**  Novello & Co., Ltd.  Key: Eb

**Willan, Healey 36 Short Preludes and Postludes on Well-Known Hymn Tunes**  Set II  C.F. Peters Corporation  No. 6162  Key: Eb

Carlson

| | BA | DC | 1940 | 1982 | LBW | LW | PH | RCV | UCC | UM | WB |
|---|---|---|---|---|---|---|---|---|---|---|---|
| | Db | | | | | | | | | | |

Carman

| | BA | DC | 1940 | 1982 | LBW | LW | PH | RCV | UCC | UM | WB |
|---|---|---|---|---|---|---|---|---|---|---|---|
| | D | | | | | | | | | | |

Carmichael

| | BA | DC | 1940 | 1982 | LBW | LW | PH | RCV | UCC | UM | WB |
|---|---|---|---|---|---|---|---|---|---|---|---|
| | F | | | | | | | | | | |

Carn Brea

| | BA | DC | 1940 | 1982 | LBW | LW | PH | RCV | UCC | UM | WB |
|---|---|---|---|---|---|---|---|---|---|---|---|
| | | | | | a | | | | | | |

# ORGAN COMPOSITIONS

**Johns, Donald  "God Has Spoken By His Prophets" The Concordia Hymn Prelude Series**  Volume 21  Edited: Herbert Gotsch  Concordia Publishing House  97-5736  Key: a

Carol

| | BA | DC | 1940 | 1982 | LBW | LW | PH | RCV | UCC | UM | WB |
|---|---|---|---|---|---|---|---|---|---|---|---|
| | Bb | Bb | Bb | Bb | Bb | Bb | Bb | Bb | | Bb | Bb |

Schalk, Carl   "It Came Upon the Midnight Clear"
**The Concordia Hymn Prelude Series**   Volume 2
Edited: Herbert Gotsch   Concordia Publishing
House   97-5536   Key: Bb

## FREE ACCOMPANIMENTS

Goode, Jack C. **Thirty-Four Changes on Hymn Tunes**
H.W. Gray   Key: Bb

Held, Wilbur   **Hymn Preludes and Free Accompaniments**
Volume 6   Augsburg Publishing House 11-9402
Key: Bb

<u>Carol of Advent</u>

| BA | DC | 1940 | 1982 | LBW | LW | PH | RCV | UCC | UM | WB |
|----|----|------|------|-----|----|----|-----|-----|----|----|
|    |    |      |      |     |    |    | C   |     |    |    |

<u>Carol of Hope</u>

| BA | DC | 1940 | 1982 | LBW | LW | PH | RCV | UCC | UM | WB |
|----|----|------|------|-----|----|----|-----|-----|----|----|
|    |    |      |      |     |    |    |     | e   |    |    |

<u>Carpenter 1970</u>

| BA | DC | 1940 | 1982 | LBW | LW | PH | RCV | UCC | UM | WB |
|----|----|------|------|-----|----|----|-----|-----|----|----|
| D  |    |      |      |     |    |    |     |     |    |    |

<u>Cas radosti</u>

| BA | DC | 1940 | 1982 | LBW | LW | PH | RCV | UCC | UM | WB |
|----|----|------|------|-----|----|----|-----|-----|----|----|
|    |    |      |      | F   |    |    |     |     |    |    |

ORGAN COMPOSITIONS

Weinhorst, Richard   "Come Rejoicing, Praises Voicing"
**The Concordia Hymn Prelude Series**   Volume 3
Edited:  Herbert Gotsch   Concordia Publishing
House   97-5538   Key: F

<u>Cassell</u>

| BA | DC | 1940 | 1982 | LBW | LW | PH | RCV | UCC | UM | WB |
|----|----|------|------|-----|----|----|-----|-----|----|----|
| G  |    |      |      |     |    |    |     |     |    |    |

ORGAN COMPOSITIONS

Lovelace, Austin **Fourteen Hymn Preludes**
Augsburg Publishing House 11-6152 Key: G

<u>Caswall</u>
(See also: Wem in Leidenstagen)

| BA | DC | 1940 | 1982 | LBW | LW | PH | RCV | UCC | UM | WB |
|----|----|------|------|-----|----|----|-----|-----|----|----|
|    |    |      |      | F   |    |    |     |     |    |    |

# ORGAN COMPOSITIONS

Thalben-Ball, George **113 Variations on Hymn Tunes**
Novello & Co., Ltd.  Key: G

## FREE ACCOMPANIMENTS

Noble, T. Tertius **Free Organ Accompaniments to One
Hundred Well-Known Hymn Tunes**  J. Fischer & Bros.
#8175  Key: F

Cates
| | | | | | | | | | | |
|---|---|---|---|---|---|---|---|---|---|---|
| BA | DC | 1940 | 1982 | LBW | LW | PH | RCV | UCC | UM | WB |
| C | | | | | | | | | | |

Celestia
| | | | | | | | | | | |
|---|---|---|---|---|---|---|---|---|---|---|
| BA | DC | 1940 | 1982 | LBW | LW | PH | RCV | UCC | UM | WB |
| | | | | D | | | | | | |

## FREE ACCOMPANIMENTS

Hystedt, Knut **Free Organ Accompaniment to Hymns**
Volume II  Advent-Christmas-Epiphany  Augsburg
Publishing House  Key: Eb

Noble, T. Tertius **Free Organ Accompaniments to One
Hundred Well-Known Hymn Tunes**  J. Fischer & Bros.
#8175

Centralia
| | | | | | | | | | | |
|---|---|---|---|---|---|---|---|---|---|---|
| BA | DC | 1940 | 1982 | LBW | LW | PH | RCV | UCC | UM | WB |
| | G | | | | | | | | | |

Cette odeur agreable
(See also: Fragrance)

Chalvey
| | | | | | | | | | | |
|---|---|---|---|---|---|---|---|---|---|---|
| BA | DC | 1940 | 1982 | LBW | LW | PH | RCV | UCC | UM | WB |
| | | Eb | | | | | | | | |

Chapman
| | | | | | | | | | | |
|---|---|---|---|---|---|---|---|---|---|---|
| BA | DC | 1940 | 1982 | LBW | LW | PH | RCV | UCC | UM | WB |
| Db | | | | | | | | | | |

Charles
| | | | | | | | | | | |
|---|---|---|---|---|---|---|---|---|---|---|
| BA | DC | 1940 | 1982 | LBW | LW | PH | RCV | UCC | UM | WB |
| F | | | | | | | | | | |

Charlestown
| | | | | | | | | | | |
|---|---|---|---|---|---|---|---|---|---|---|
| BA | DC | 1940 | 1982 | LBW | LW | PH | RCV | UCC | UM | WB |
| | | | D | | | | | | Db | C |

ORGAN COMPOSITIONS

Lovelace, Austin **Fourteen Hymn Preludes**
　　Augsburg Publishing House　11-6152　Key: Db

Lovelace, Austin "Cross of Jesus, Cross of Sorrow"
　　**Eight Hymn Preludes**　Augsburg Publishing House
　　11-9144　Key: D

FREE ACCOMPANIMENTS

Busarow, Donald **All Praise to You Eternal God**
　　Augsburg Publishing House　11-9076　Key: C

Charlotte

| BA | DC | 1940 | 1982 | LBW | LW | PH | RCV | UCC | UM | WB |
|----|----|------|------|-----|----|----|----|-----|----|----|
|    |    | F    |      |     |    |    |    |     |    |    |

Charlotte (Hankey)

| BA | DC | 1940 | 1982 | LBW | LW | PH | RCV | UCC | UM | WB |
|----|----|------|------|-----|----|----|----|-----|----|----|
|    |    |      |      |     |    |    |    |     |    | e  |

Charterhouse

| BA | DC | 1940 | 1982 | LBW | LW | PH | RCV | UCC | UM | WB |
|----|----|------|------|-----|----|----|----|-----|----|----|
| F  | F  | F    | G    |     |    |    |    | F   |    | F  |

Chartres

| BA | DC | 1940 | 1982 | LBW | LW | PH | RCV | UCC | UM | WB |
|----|----|------|------|-----|----|----|----|-----|----|----|
|    |    | g    |      |     |    |    |    |     |    |    |

ORGAN COMPOSITIONS

Bassett, Anita Denniston **Nine Hymn-Tune Preludes**
　　Ludwig Music Publishing Co.　0-08　Key: m:g

Chautauqua

| BA | DC | 1940 | 1982 | LBW | LW | PH | RCV | UCC | UM | WB |
|----|----|------|------|-----|----|----|----|-----|----|----|
|    | G  |      |      |     |    | G  |    |     | G  |    |

Chelsea Square

| BA | DC | 1940 | 1982 | LBW | LW | PH | RCV | UCC | UM | WB |
|----|----|------|------|-----|----|----|----|-----|----|----|
|    |    | C    | C    |     |    |    |    |     |    |    |

Chereponi (Jesu, Jesu)

| BA | DC | 1940 | 1982 | LBW | LW | PH | RCV | UCC | UM | WB |
|----|----|------|------|-----|----|----|----|-----|----|----|
|    |    |      | e    |     |    |    |    |     |    |    |

Cheshire

| BA | DC | 1940 | 1982 | LBW | LW | PH | RCV | UCC | UM | WB |
|----|----|------|------|-----|----|----|----|-----|----|----|
|    | e  |      | e    |     |    |    |    |     |    | e  |

Chester

| BA | DC | 1940 | 1982 | LBW | LW | PH | RCV | UCC | UM | WB |
|----|----|------|------|-----|-----|----|-----|-----|----|----|
|    |    | Bb   |      |     |     |    |     |     |    |    |

Chesterfield
(See also: Richmond)

| BA | DC | 1940 | 1982 | LBW | LW | PH | RCV | UCC | UM | WB |
|----|----|------|------|-----|-----|----|-----|-----|----|----|
|    |    |      |      | F   | F   |    |     |     |    |    |

ORGAN COMPOSITIONS

Beck, Albert **76 Offertories on Hymns & Chorales**
Concordia Publishing House 97-5207  Key: G

Lang, C.S.  **The Concordia Hymn Prelude Series**
Volume 1  Edited: Herbert Gotsch Concordia
Publishing House  97-5536  Key: F

FREE ACCOMPANIMENTS

Ore, Charles  **Hymn Preludes and Free Accompaniments**
Volume 7  Augsburg Publishing House  11-9403
Key: F

Chesterton

| BA | DC | 1940 | 1982 | LBW | LW | PH | RCV | UCC | UM | WB |
|----|----|------|------|-----|-----|----|-----|-----|----|----|
|    | Eb |      |      |     |     |    |     |     |    |    |

Chhattisgahr

| BA | DC | 1940 | 1982 | LBW | LW | PH | RCV | UCC | UM | WB |
|----|----|------|------|-----|-----|----|-----|-----|----|----|
|    |    |      |      |     |     |    |     | F   |    |    |

Chichester

| BA | DC | 1940 | 1982 | LBW | LW | PH | RCV | UCC | UM | WB |
|----|----|------|------|-----|-----|----|-----|-----|----|----|
|    | e  |      |      |     |     |    |     |     |    |    |

Childhood

| BA | DC | 1940 | 1982 | LBW | LW | PH | RCV | UCC | UM | WB |
|----|----|------|------|-----|-----|----|-----|-----|----|----|
|    |    |      |      |     |     | F  |     |     | F  |    |

China

| BA | DC | 1940 | 1982 | LBW | LW | PH | RCV | UCC | UM | WB |
|----|----|------|------|-----|-----|----|-----|-----|----|----|
|    | Eb |      |      |     |     |    |     |     |    |    |

Chinese Melody

| BA | DC | 1940 | 1982 | LBW | LW | PH | RCV | UCC | UM | WB |
|----|----|------|------|-----|-----|----|-----|-----|----|----|
|    |    |      |      |     |     | C  |     |     |    |    |

Chislehurst

| BA | DC | 1940 | 1982 | LBW | LW | PH | RCV | UCC | UM | WB |
|----|----|------|------|-----|-----|----|-----|-----|----|----|
| C  |    |      |      |     |     |    |     |     |    |    |

## Christ Arose

| BA | DC | 1940 | 1982 | LBW | LW | PH | RCV | UCC | UM | WB |
|----|----|------|------|-----|----|----|-----|-----|----|----|
| C  |    |      |      |     |    |    |     |     |    | C  |

## Christ is Arisen

| BA | DC | 1940 | 1982 | LBW | LW | PH | RCV | UCC | UM | WB |
|----|----|------|------|-----|----|----|-----|-----|----|----|
|    | m:a |     |      |     |    |    |     |     |    |    |

## Christ is My Life
(See also: Christus der ist mein Leben)

| BA | DC | 1940 | 1982 | LBW | LW | PH | RCV | UCC | UM | WB |
|----|----|------|------|-----|----|----|-----|-----|----|----|
|    | D  |      |      |     |    |    | D   |     |    |    |

## Christ ist erstanden

| BA | DC | 1940 | 1982 | LBW | LW | PH | RCV | UCC | UM | WB |
|----|----|------|------|-----|----|----|-----|-----|----|----|
|    | m:d |     | m:d  | m:d | m:d | m:d |   |     |    | m:d |

### ORGAN COMPOSITIONS

Ahrens, Joseph Toccata "Christus ist erstanden"
**Das Heilige Jahr** Volume II
Willy Muller - Suddeutscher Muskiverlag -
Heidelberg. C.F. Peters Corporation Key:m:d

Bach, J. S. **Organ Works** Volume 1 Edited: Heinz-Harald Löhlein Urtext of the New Bach Edition Bärenreiter 5171 Key: m:d

Bach, J.S. **Organ Works** Volume VII Widor-Schweitzer G. Schirmer Key: m:d

Bach, J.S. **Orgelwerke** Volume V C.F. Peters Corporation Nr. 244 Key: m:d

Bach, J.S. **The Liturgical Year** (Orgelbuchlein) Edited: Albert Reimenschneider Oliver Ditson Co. Key: m:d

Dupre, Marcel **Seventy-Nine Chorales for the Organ** Opus 28 H. W. Gray Key: m:d

Engel, James "Christ is Arisen" **The Concordia Hymn Prelude Series** Volume 10 Edited: Herbert Gotsch Concordia Publishing House 97-5617 Key: m:d

Fischer, Johann Kaspar Ferdinand **80 Chorale Preludes – German Masters of the 17th and 18th Centuries** Edited: Hermann Keller C.F. Peters Corporation #4448 Key:m:d

Fischer, Johann Kaspar Ferdinand "Christ is
  Arisen" **The Parish Organist** Part Eight
  Music for Easter, Ascension, Pentecost and
  Trinity Edited: Erich Goldschmidt Concordia
  Publishing House 97-1404 Key: m:d

Lenel, Ludwig "Christ is Arisen" **Three Chorale
  Fantasias on Pre-Reformation Hymns**
  Concordia Publishing House 97-4408 Key: m:d

Scheidt, Samuel "Christ is Arisen" **The Parish
  Organist** Part One Edited: Heinrich
  Fleischer Concordia Publishing House
  97-1145 Key: m:d

Walcha, Helmut **Chorale Preludes** II C.F. Peters
  Corporation Nr. 4871 Key: m:d

Wyton, Alec "Prologue" **Resurrection Suite**
  Harold Flammer, Inc. HF 5014 Key:m:a

FREE ACCOMPANIMENTS

Rohlig, Harald **Free Organ Accompaniments to Hymns**
  Volume III Palm Sunday - Easter Augsburg
  Publishing House 11-9189 Key: m:d

Christ lag in Todesbanden

| BA | DC | 1940 | 1982 | LBW | LW | PH | RCV | UCC | UM | WB |
|----|----|------|------|-----|----|----|-----|-----|----|----|
|    | m:d|      | m:d  | m:d | m:d|    | m:d |     | m:d| m:d|

ORGAN COMPOSITIONS

Bach, Heinrich "Christ lag in Todesbanden" **Festival
  Anthology for Organ** Edited and Arranged: E. Power
  Biggs Associated Music Publishers Key: d

Bach, J. S. **Organ Works** Volume 1 Edited: Heinz-
  Harald Löhlein Urtext of the New Bach Edition
  Bärenreiter 5171 Key: m:d

Bach, J. S. **Organ Works** Volume 3 "The Individually
  Transmitted Organ Chorales Edited: Hans Klotz
  Urtext of the New Bach Edition Bärenreiter
  5173 Key: m:d; m:e

Bach, J.S. **Organ Works** Volume VI Widor-Schweitzer
  G. Schirmer (#26) Key: e; (#27); Key: d

Bach, J.S. **Organ Works** Volume VII Widor-Schweitzer
  G. Schirmer Key: d

Bach, J.S. **Orgelwerke** Volume V  C.F. Peters
Corporation   No. 244  Key: d

Bach, J.S. **Orgelwerke** Volume VI  C.F. Peters
Corporation   No. 245 (Two settings) Key: e, Key: d

Bach, J.S. **The Liturgical Year** (Orgelbuchlein)
Edited: Albert Reimenschneider  Oliver Ditson Co.
Key: m:d

Bach, J.S.  "Chorale" (Arranged by Edwin Arthur Kraft)
Compiled by John Holler  **The Lutheran Organist**
H. W. Gray Co.  Key: m:e

Dupre, Marcel  **Seventy-Nine Chorales for the Organ**
Opus 28  H. W. Gray  Key: m:d

Held, Wilbur "Christ Jesus Lay in Death's Strong Bonds"
**Six Preludes on Easter Hymns** Concordia Publishing
House  97-5330  Key: d

Manz, Paul "Christ Jesus Lay in Death's Strong Bands"
**Ten Chorale Improvisations** Opus 16  Set VI
Concordia Publishing House 97-5305  Key: d

Scheidt, Samuel **80 Chorale Preludes – German Masters
of the 17th and 18th Centuries** Edited: Hermann
Keller  C.F. Peters Corporation #4448  Key:m:d

Vetter, Andreas Nicolaus "Christ Jesus Lay in Death's
Strong Bonds"  **The Concordia Hymn Prelude Series**
Volume 10  Edited: Herbert Gotsch  Concordia
Publishing House  97-5617  Key: m:d

Volckmar, Tobias  "Christ Jesus Lay in Death's Strong
Bands" **The Parish Organist** Part Eight  Music
for Easter, Ascension, Pentecost and Trinity
Edited: Erich Goldschmidt  Concordia Publishing
House  97-1404  Key: m:d

Zachau, Friedrich Wilhelm **80 Chorale Preludes – German
Masters of the 17th and 18th Centuries** Edited:
Hermann Keller  C.F. Peters Corporation #4448
Key: m:d

Zachau, Friedrich Wilhelm "Chorale Prelude on 'Christ
Lag in Todesbanden'" **For Manuals Only**  Edited:
John Christopher  McAfee Music Corp.  Key: d

Cassler, G. Winson **Organ Descants for Selected Hymn Tunes** Augsburg Publishing House 11-9304
Key: m:d

Pelz, Walter **Free Organ Accompaniments to Hymns**
Augsburg Publishing House  11-9179  Key: m:d

Christ, der du bist Tag und Licht

| BA | DC | 1940 | 1982 | LBW | LW | PH | RCV | UCC | UM | WB |
|----|----|------|------|-----|----|----|-----|-----|----|-----|
|    |    |      |  g   |     |    |    |     |     |    |     |

ORGAN COMPOSITIONS

Scheidt, Samuel  "O Christ, You are the Light and Day"
**The Concordia Hymn Prelude Series**  Volume 21
Edited: Herbert Gotsch  Concordia Publishing House
97-5736  Key g

Christ, unser Herr zum Jordan kam

| BA | DC | 1940 | 1982 | LBW | LW | PH | RCV | UCC | UM | WB |
|----|----|------|------|-----|----|----|-----|-----|----|-----|
|    |    | m:c  | m:c  | m:c |    |    |     |     |    |     |

ORGAN COMPOSITIONS

Bach, J.S. **Organ Works** Volume VII  Widor-Schweitzer
G. Schirmer  (#61) Key: g; (#62) Key: a

Bach, J.S. **Orgelwerke** Volume VI  C.F. Peters
Corporation No. 245 (Two settings) Key: g, Key:a

Bach, J.S. **Klavierubung, Dritter Teil** #3948
C.F. Peters  Key:g,  Key: a

Bender, Jan  "To Jordan Came the Christ, Our Lord"
**The Concordia Hymn Prelude Series**  Volume 5
Edited: Herbert Gotsch  Concordia Publishing
House  97-5611  Key: g

Dupre, Marcel  **Seventy-Nine Chorales for the Organ**
Opus 28  H. W. Gray  Key: c

Engel, James  "To Jordan Came the Christ, Our Lord"
**The Concordia Hymn Prelude Series** Volume 16
Edited: Herbert Gotsch  Concordia Publishing
House  97-5707 Key: g

Pepping, Ernst  **Fünfundzwanzig Orgelchorale**
Edition Schott  4723  B. Schott's Sohne Key: m:a

Christ, Whose Glory

| BA | DC | 1940 | 1982 | LBW | LW | PH | RCV | UCC | UM | WB |
|----|----|------|------|-----|----|----|-----|-----|----|-----|
|    |    | Eb   |      |     |    |    |     |     |    |     |

<u>Christe Redemptor</u>
```
     BA    DC    1940  1982   LBW   LW    PH    RCV   UCC   UM    WB
                 m:e   m:e    m:e   m:e         m:e
```

## ORGAN COMPOSITIONS

Held, Wilbur  "O Savior of Our Fallen Race"  **The
Concordia Hymn Prelude Series**  Volume 3  Edited:
Herbert Gotsch  Concordia Publishing House  97-
5538  Key: m:e

Purvis, Richard "Introit"  **An American Organ Mass**
Harold Flammer, Inc.  Key: e/G

<u>Christe sanctorum</u> (Sarum Plainsong)
```
     BA    DC    1940  1982   LBW   LW    PH    RCV   UCC   UM    WB
                 m:d
```

<u>Christe sanctorum</u>
```
     BA    DC    1940  1982   LBW   LW    PH    RCV   UCC   UM    WB
           D     D     D      D     D     D     D     D     D     D
```

## ORGAN COMPOSITIONS

Engel, James  "Father We Praise You"  **The Concordia
Hymn Prelude Series**  Volume 21  Edited: Herbert
Gotsch  Concordia Publishing House  97-5736
Key: D

Lovelace, Austin C.  "Praise and Thanksgiving be to
God"  **The Concordia Hymn Prelude Series**
Volume 21  Edited: Herbert Gotsch  Concordia
Publishing House  97-5707  Key: D

Wienhorst, Richard  "Father Most Holy"  **The Concordia
Hymn Prelude Series**  Volume 13  Edited: Herbert
Gotsch  Concordia Pubishing House  97-5620
Key: D

## FREE ACCOMPANIMENTS

**Free Harmonizations of Hymn Tunes by Fifty American
Composers**  Edited: D. DeWitt Wasson  Hinshaw
Music, Inc.  HMO-145  Key: D

Gehring, Philip  **Hymn Preludes and Free Accompaniments**
Volume 3  Augsburg Publishing House  11-9399
Key: D

<u>Christe, du Lamm Gottes</u>
```
     BA    DC    1940  1982   LBW   LW    PH    RCV   UCC   UM    WB
                 m:f                     m:f
```

# ORGAN COMPOSITIONS

Bach, J. S. **Organ Works** Volume 1 Edited: Heinz-Harald Löhlein Urtext of the New Bach Edition Bärenreiter 5171 Key: m:f

Bach, J.S. **Orgelwerke** Volume V C.F. Peters Corporation Nr. 244 Key: m:f

Bach, J.S. **The Liturgical Year** (Orgelbuchlein) Edited: Albert Reimenschneider Oliver Ditson Co. Key: m:g

Distler, Hugo **Short Chorale Arrangements** Opus 8/3 Bärenreiter 1222 Key: m:g

Dupre, Marcel **Seventy-Nine Chorales for the Organ** Opus 28 H. W. Gray Key: m:d

Gerike, Henry V. "O Christ, Thou Lamb of God" **The Concordia Hymn Prelude Series** Volume 7 Edited: Herbert Gotsch Concordia Publishing House 97-5614 Key: F

Karg-Elert, Sigfrid "Christ, Thou Lamb of Bod" **Choral Improvisations for Organ for Reformation Day, Fast Days, Communion and Funeral Rites** Op. 65, Volume 5 Edited: Robert Leech Bedell Edward B. Marks Music Corp. Key: d

Manz, Paul "O Christ, Thou Lamb of God" **Ten Chorale Improvisations** Set IV Op. 10 Concordia Publishing House 97-4951 Key: d

Mueller, Gottfried "O Christ, Thou Lamb of God" **The Parish Organist** Part Seven Music for Lent, Palm Sunday and Holy Week Edited: Erich Goldschmidt Concordia Publishing House 97-1403 Key: d

Pepping, Ernst **Praeludia Postludia I** B. Schott's Sohne Edition 6040 Key: m:c

## FREE ACCOMPANIMENTS

Shack, David **Hymn Preludes and Free Accompaniments** Volume 11 Augsburg Publishing House 11-9407 Key: F

<u>Christe, Lux mundi</u>

| BA | DC | 1940 | 1982 | LBW | LW | PH | RCV | UCC | UM | WB |
|----|----|------|------|-----|----|----|-----|-----|----|----|
|    |    | m:a  |      |     |    |    |     |     |    |    |

## Christe, qui Lux es et dies

| BA | DC | 1940 | 1982 | LBW | LW | PH | RCV | UCC | UM | WB |
|----|----|------|------|-----|----|----|-----|-----|----|----|
|    |    |      | m:g  |     |    |    |     |     |    |    |

## Christian Home

| BA | DC | 1940 | 1982 | LBW | LW | PH | RCV | UCC | UM | WB |
|----|----|------|------|-----|----|----|-----|-----|----|----|
| Eb |    |      |      |     |    |    |     |     |    |    |

## Christian Love

| BA | DC | 1940 | 1982 | LBW | LW | PH | RCV | UCC | UM | WB |
|----|----|------|------|-----|----|----|------|-----|----|-----|
| F  |    |      |      |     |    |    | m:f# |     |    | m:e |

## Christmas
(See also: Siroe)

| BA | DC | 1940 | 1982 | LBW | LW | PH | RCV | UCC | UM | WB |
|----|----|------|------|-----|----|----|-----|-----|----|----|
| D  | D  |      |      |     |    | D  |     |     | D  | D  |

ORGAN COMPOSITIONS

Barlow, Wayne   "Awake, My Soul, Stretch Every Nerve"
**The Parish Organist**  Part Eleven  Edited: Willem
Mudde  Concordia Publishing House  97-4758  Key: D

FREE ACCOMPANIMENTS

**Free Harmonizations of Hymn Tunes by Fifty American
Composers**  Edited: D. DeWitt Wasson  Hinshaw
Music, Inc.  HMO-145  Key: D

## Christmas Dawn

| BA | DC | 1940 | 1982 | LBW | LW | PH | RCV | UCC | UM | WB |
|----|----|------|------|-----|----|----|-----|-----|----|----|
|    |    |      |      | Eb  |    |    |     |     |    |    |

FREE ACCOMPANIMENTS

Ore, Charles  **Hymn Preludes and Free Accompaniments**
Volume 7  Augsburg Publishing House  11-9403
Key: Eb

## Christmas Eve

| BA | DC | 1940 | 1982 | LBW | LW | PH | RCV | UCC | UM | WB |
|----|----|------|------|-----|----|----|-----|-----|----|----|
|    |    |      |      | G   | G  |    |     |     |    |    |

FREE ACCOMPANIMENTS

Busarow, Donald  **Hymn Preludes and Free Accompaniments**
Volume 8  Augsburg Publishing House  11-9404
Key: G

## Christmas Song

| BA | DC | 1940 | 1982 | LBW | LW | PH | RCV | UCC | UM | WB |
|----|----|------|------|-----|----|----|-----|-----|----|----|
|    |    |      |      |     |    |    |     |     | G  |    |

Christum wir sollen loben schon
    BA    DC    1940 1982 LBW   LW    PH    RCV   UCC   UM    WB
                               m:e

                    ORGAN COMPOSITIONS

    Bach, J. S.  **Organ Works**  Volume 1  Edited: Heinz-
        Harald Löhlein  Urtext of the New Bach Edition
        Bärenreiter  5171  Key: m:e

    Bach, J. S.  **Organ Works**  Volume 3  "The Individually
        Transmitted Organ Chorales"  Edited: Hans Klotz
        Urtext of the New Bach Edition  Bärenreiter
        5173  Key: m:e

    Bach, J.S.  **Organ Works** Volume VI  Widor-Schweitzer
        G. Schirmer Key: m:a

    Bach, J.S.  **Organ Works** Volume VII  Widor-Schweitzer
        G. Schirmer  Key: m:a

    Bach, J.S.  **Orgelwerke** Volume V  C.F. Peters
        Corporation  Nr. 244 (#7) Key: m:a; (#8)
        Key: m:a

    Bach, J.S.  **The Liturgical Year**  (Orgelbuchlein)
        Edited: Albert Reimenschneider  Oliver Ditson Co.
        Key: m:e

    Walther, Johann Gottfried  "From East to West"
        **The Concordia Hymn Prelude Series**  Volume 3
        Edited: Herbert Gotsch  Concordia Publishing House
        97-5538  Key: m:e

    Willan, Healey  "Christum wir sollen loben schon"
        **Six Chorale Preludes** Set II  Concordia Publishing
        House 97-3905  Key: a

Christus, der ist mein Leben
    BA    DC    1940 1982 LBW   LW    PH    RCV   UCC   UM    WB
                 D         D     D           F           Eb

                    ORGAN COMPOSITIONS

    Bach, J. S.  **Organ Chorales from the Neumeister
        Collection**  Edited: Christoph Wolff  Yale
        University Press/Bärenreiter 5181  Key: F

    Beck, Albert  **76 Offertories on Hymns & Chorales**
        Concordia Publishing House  97-5207  Key: Eb

    Cherwien, David **Interprestations Based on Hymn-Tunes**
        A.M.S.I.  OR-1  Key: D

Gieschen, Thomas **Four Quiet Hymn Settings** Concordia
    Publishing House 97-5839 Key: D

Manz, Paul "Abide, O Dearest Jesus" **Ten Chorale**
    **Improvisations** Set II Op. 7 Concordia Publishing
    House 97-4656 Key: Eb

Marpurg, Friedrich Wilhelm **Twenty-One Chorale Preludes**
    Edited: Robert M. Johnson Augsburg Publishing
    House 11-9506 Key: F

Pachelbel, Johann **80 Chorale Preludes – German Masters**
    **of the 17th and 18th Centuries** Edited: Hermann
    Keller C.F. Peters Corporation #4448 Key: Eb

Pachelbel, Johann "Abide, O Dearest Jesus" **The Parish**
    **Organist** Part One Edited: Heinrich Fleischer
    Concordia Publishing House 97-1145 Key: Eb

Walther, Johann Gottfried **Chorale Preludes – German**
    **Masters of the 17th and 18th Centuries** Hermann
    Keller C.F. Peters Corporation #4448 Key: Eb

Walther, Johann Gottfried "Abide with Us, Our Savior"
    **The Concordia Hymn Prelude Series** Volume 21
    Edited: Herbert Gotsch Concordia Publishing House
    97-5736 Key: D

## FREE ACCOMPANIMENTS

Bunjes, Paul **New Organ Accompaniments for Hymns**
    Concordia Publishing House 97-5348 Key: D

| Christus Rex | | | | | | | | | | |
|---|---|---|---|---|---|---|---|---|---|---|
| BA | DC | 1940 | 1982 | LBW | LW | PH | RCV | UCC | UM | WB |
| | | D | D | | | | | | | |

| Cibavit Eos | | | | | | | | | | |
|---|---|---|---|---|---|---|---|---|---|---|
| BA | DC | 1940 | 1982 | LBW | LW | PH | RCV | UCC | UM | WB |
| | | | | | | | Ab | | | |

| City of God | | | | | | | | | | |
|---|---|---|---|---|---|---|---|---|---|---|
| BA | DC | 1940 | 1982 | LBW | LW | PH | RCV | UCC | UM | WB |
| | | | | g | | | | | | g |

## ORGAN COMPOSITIONS

Schalk, Carl "O Jesus Christ, May Grateful Hymns Be
    Rising" **The Concordia Hymn Prelude Series**
    Edited: Herbert Gotsch Concordia Publishing House
    97-5736 Key: g

Claudius
(See also: Wir pflugen)
| BA | DC | 1940 | 1982 | LBW | LW | PH | RCV | UCC | UM | WB |
|----|----|------|------|-----|----|----|-----|-----|----|----|
|    |    | A    |      |     |    |    |     |     |    |    |

Clay Court
| BA | DC | 1940 | 1982 | LBW | LW | PH | RCV | UCC | UM | WB |
|----|----|------|------|-----|----|----|-----|-----|----|----|
|    |    |      |      |     |    |    |     |     |    | e  |

Cleansing Fountain
| BA | DC | 1940 | 1982 | LBW | LW | PH | RCV | UCC | UM | WB |
|----|----|------|------|-----|----|----|-----|-----|----|----|
| C  |    |      |      |     |    |    |     |     | C  |    |

Cloisters
| BA | DC | 1940 | 1982 | LBW | LW | PH | RCV | UCC | UM | WB |
|----|----|------|------|-----|----|----|-----|-----|----|----|
|    |    | D    |      |     |    | D  |     |     |    |    |

FREE ACCOMPANIMENTS

**Free Harmonizations of Hymn Tunes by Fifty American Composers** Edited: D. DeWitt Wasson Hinshaw Music, Inc. HMO-145 Key: D

Clonmel
| BA | DC | 1940 | 1982 | LBW | LW | PH | RCV | UCC | UM | WB |
|----|----|------|------|-----|----|----|-----|-----|----|----|
| Eb |    |      |      |     |    |    |     |     | Eb |    |

Close to Thee
| BA | DC | 1940 | 1982 | LBW | LW | PH | RCV | UCC | UM | WB |
|----|----|------|------|-----|----|----|-----|-----|----|----|
|    |    |      |      |     |    |    |     |     | G  |    |

Closer Walk
| BA | DC | 1940 | 1982 | LBW | LW | PH | RCV | UCC | UM | WB |
|----|----|------|------|-----|----|----|-----|-----|----|----|
| Bb |    |      |      |     |    |    |     |     |    |    |

Cobb
| BA | DC | 1940 | 1982 | LBW | LW | PH | RCV | UCC | UM | WB |
|----|----|------|------|-----|----|----|-----|-----|----|----|
|    |    | F    |      |     |    |    |     |     |    |    |

Cobbs
| BA | DC | 1940 | 1982 | LBW | LW | PH | RCV | UCC | UM | WB |
|----|----|------|------|-----|----|----|-----|-----|----|----|
| G  |    |      |      |     |    |    |     |     |    |    |

Coblenz
| BA | DC | 1940 | 1982 | LBW | LW | PH | RCV | UCC | UM | WB |
|----|----|------|------|-----|----|----|-----|-----|----|----|
|    |    |      |      |     |    |    | d   |     |    |    |

Coburn
| BA | DC | 1940 | 1982 | LBW | LW | PH | RCV | UCC | UM | WB |
|----|----|------|------|-----|----|----|-----|-----|----|----|
|    |    |      | D    |     |    |    |     |     |    |    |

**Coelites plaudant**

| BA | DC | 1940 | 1982 | LBW | LW | PH | RCV | UCC | UM | WB |
|---|---|---|---|---|---|---|---|---|---|---|
|  |  | C |  |  |  |  |  |  |  |  |

**Coena Domini**

| BA | DC | 1940 | 1982 | LBW | LW | PH | RCV | UCC | UM | WB |
|---|---|---|---|---|---|---|---|---|---|---|
|  |  |  |  | Eb |  |  |  |  |  |  |

## ORGAN COMPOSITIONS   •

Busarow, Donald "Draw Near and Take the Body of the Lord" **the Concordia Hymn Prelude Series** Volume 17 Edited: Herbert Gotsch Concordia Publishing House 97-5708 Key: Eb

**Coleman**

| BA | DC | 1940 | 1982 | LBW | LW | PH | RCV | UCC | UM | WB |
|---|---|---|---|---|---|---|---|---|---|---|
| Ab |  |  |  |  |  |  |  |  |  |  |

**College of Preachers**

| BA | DC | 1940 | 1982 | LBW | LW | PH | RCV | UCC | UM | WB |
|---|---|---|---|---|---|---|---|---|---|---|
|  |  | D |  |  |  |  |  |  |  |  |

**Combe Martin**

| BA | DC | 1940 | 1982 | LBW | LW | PH | RCV | UCC | UM | WB |
|---|---|---|---|---|---|---|---|---|---|---|
|  |  | G |  |  |  |  |  |  |  |  |

**Come Holy Ghost**

| BA | DC | 1940 | 1982 | LBW | LW | PH | RCV | UCC | UM | WB |
|---|---|---|---|---|---|---|---|---|---|---|
|  |  | C | D |  |  |  |  |  |  |  |

**Coming Home**

| BA | DC | 1940 | 1982 | LBW | LW | PH | RCV | UCC | UM | WB |
|---|---|---|---|---|---|---|---|---|---|---|
| Ab |  |  |  |  |  |  |  |  |  |  |

**Coming to the Cross**

| BA | DC | 1940 | 1982 | LBW | LW | PH | RCV | UCC | UM | WB |
|---|---|---|---|---|---|---|---|---|---|---|
|  |  |  |  |  |  |  |  |  | G |  |

**Commandments**

| BA | DC | 1940 | 1982 | LBW | LW | PH | RCV | UCC | UM | WB |
|---|---|---|---|---|---|---|---|---|---|---|
|  |  | G |  |  |  |  |  | G | G |  |

**Commemoration**

| BA | DC | 1940 | 1982 | LBW | LW | PH | RCV | UCC | UM | WB |
|---|---|---|---|---|---|---|---|---|---|---|
|  |  | F |  |  |  |  |  |  |  |  |

**Commune**

| BA | DC | 1940 | 1982 | LBW | LW | PH | RCV | UCC | UM | WB |
|---|---|---|---|---|---|---|---|---|---|---|
|  |  |  |  |  |  |  |  | Ab |  |  |

Complainer

| BA | DC | 1940 | 1982 | LBW | LW | PH | RCV | UCC | UM | WB |
|----|----|------|------|-----|----|----|-----|-----|----|----|
|    |    | Eb   |      |     |    |    |     |     | Eb |    |

ORGAN COMPOSITIONS

Rotermund, Donald   "Jerusalem the Golden"  **The Concordia Hymn Prelude Series**  Volume 21 Edited: Herbert Gotsch  Concordia Publishing House 97-5736  Key: Eb

Busarow, Donald **All Praise to You Eternal God**  Augsburg Publishing House  11-9076  Key: Eb

Diemer, Emma Lou  **Hymn Preludes and Free Accompaniments** Volume 2  Augsburg Publishing House  11-9398 Key: Eb

Compline

| BA | DC | 1940 | 1982 | LBW | LW | PH | RCV | UCC | UM | WB |
|----|----|------|------|-----|----|----|-----|-----|----|----|
|    |    | m:f# |      |     |    |    |     |     |    |    |

Concordi laetitia

| BA | DC | 1940 | 1982 | LBW | LW | PH | RCV | UCC | UM | WB |
|----|----|------|------|-----|----|----|-----|-----|----|----|
|    |    |      |      |     |    |    | m:f |     |    |    |

Conditor alme

| BA  | DC  | 1940 | 1982 | LBW | LW  | PH  | RCV | UCC | UM  | WB  |
|-----|-----|------|------|-----|-----|-----|-----|-----|-----|-----|
| m:g | m:g | m:g  | m:g  | m:g | m:g |     |     |     | m:g | m:g |

ORGAN COMPOSITIONS

Zimmer, Dennis  "O Lord of Light, Who Made the Stars" **The Concordia Hymn Prelude Series**  Volume 21 Edited: Herbert Gotsch  Concordia Publishing House 97-5736  Key: m:g

Johnson, David N.  **The Concordia Hymn Prelude Series – Advent**  Volume 1  Edited: Herbert Gotsch  Concordia Publishing House  97-5536  Key: m:g

Conquest

| BA | DC | 1940 | 1982 | LBW | LW | PH | RCV | UCC | UM | WB |
|----|----|------|------|-----|----|----|-----|-----|----|----|
|    |    | D    |      |     |    |    |     |     |    |    |

Consecration

| BA | DC | 1940 | 1982 | LBW | LW | PH | RCV | UCC | UM | WB |
|----|----|------|------|-----|----|----|-----|-----|----|----|
|    |    | F    |      |     |    |    |     |     |    |    |

Consolation

| BA | DC | 1940 | 1982 | LBW | LW | PH | RCV | UCC | UM | WB |
|----|----|------|------|-----|----|----|-----|-----|----|----|
|    |    | C    |      |     |    |    |     |     |    |    |

Consolation (Kentucky Harmony)
(See also: Morning Song)

| BA | DC | 1940 | 1982 | LBW | LW | PH | RCV | UCC | UM | WB |
|----|----|------|------|-----|----|----|-----|-----|----|----|
|    |    | f    |      | f   | f  | f  |     |     |    |    |

ORGAN COMPOSITIONS

Beck, Theodore Beck  "The King Shall Come"  **The
Concordia Hymn Prelude Series** Volume 1
Concordia Publishing House  97-5536  Key: f

Shack, David "The King Shall Come When Morning Dawns"
**Preludes on Ten Hymntunes** Augsburg Publishing
House  11-9363  Key: f

FREE ACCOMPANIMENTS

Busarow, Donald **All Praise to You Eternal God**
Augsburg Publishing House 11-9076  Key: f

Consolation (Mendelssohn)

| BA | DC | 1940 | 1982 | LBW | LW | PH | RCV | UCC | UM | WB |
|----|----|------|------|-----|----|----|-----|-----|----|----|
|    |    |      |      |     |    | Eb |     |     | Eb |    |

Consolator

| BA | DC | 1940 | 1982 | LBW | LW | PH | RCV | UCC | UM | WB |
|----|----|------|------|-----|----|----|-----|-----|----|----|
| C  |    |      |      |     |    |    |     |     | C  |    |

ORGAN COMPOSITIONS

Stearns, Peter Pindar  **Twenty Hymn Preludes**
Coburn Press (Theodore Presser Company) Key: C

FREE ACCOMPANIMENTS

**Free Harmonizations of Hymn Tunes by Fifty American
Composers** Edited: D. DeWitt Wasson  Hinshaw
Music, Inc.  HMO-145  Key: C

Contrition

| BA | DC | 1940 | 1982 | LBW | LW | PH | RCV | UCC | UM | WB |
|----|----|------|------|-----|----|----|-----|-----|----|----|
|    |    |      |      |     |    | d  |     |     |    |    |

Converse

| BA | DC | 1940 | 1982 | LBW | LW | PH | RCV | UCC | UM | WB |
|----|----|------|------|-----|----|----|-----|-----|----|----|
| F  |    |      |      | F   | F  |    |     |     | F  |    |

ORGAN COMPOSITIONS

Gotsch, Herbert  "What a Friend We Have in Jesus"
**The Concordia Hymn Prelude Series** Volume 22
Edited: Herbert Gotsch  Concordia Publishing House
97-5737  Key: F

# FREE ACCOMPANIMENTS

Carson, J. Bert **Hymn Preludes and Free Accompaniments**
Volume 16  Augsburg Publishing House  11-9412
Key: Eb

**Free Harmonizations of Hymn Tunes by Fifty American
Composers** Edited: D. DeWitt Wasson  Hinshaw
Music, Inc.  HMO-145  Key: F

Hancock, Gerre **Organ Improvisations For Hymn-Singing**
Hinshaw Music Co.  HMO-100  Key: F

Cooling
| BA | DC | 1940 | 1982 | LBW | LW | PH | RCV | UCC | UM | BW |
|---|---|---|---|---|---|---|---|---|---|---|
|    |    |      |      |     |    |    |     |     | D  |    |

Corde natus
(See also: Divinum mysterium)

Corinth
(See also: Dulce carmen)

Cormac
| BA | DC | 1940 | 1982 | LBW | LW | PH | RCV | UCC | UM | WB |
|---|---|---|---|---|---|---|---|---|---|---|
|    |    |      |      |     |    |    |     |     | C  |    |

Corner
| BA | DC | 1940 | 1982 | LBW | LW | PH | RCV | UCC | UM | WB |
|---|---|---|---|---|---|---|---|---|---|---|
|    | F  |      |      |     |    |    |     |     |    |    |

Cornhill
| BA | DC | 1940 | 1982 | LBW | LW | PH | RCV | UCC | UM | WB |
|---|---|---|---|---|---|---|---|---|---|---|
|    |    |      | C    |     |    |    |     |     |    |    |

Cornish
| BA | DC | 1940 | 1982 | LBW | LW | PH | RCV | UCC | UM | WB |
|---|---|---|---|---|---|---|---|---|---|---|
|    |    |      | D    |     |    |    |     |     |    |    |

# ORGAN COMPOSITIONS

Purvis, Richard "Interlude" **An American Organ Mass**
Harold Flammer, Inc.  Key: G

Cornwall
| BA | DC | 1940 | 1982 | LBW | LW | PH | RCV | UCC | UM | WB |
|---|---|---|---|---|---|---|---|---|---|---|
|    | D  |      | D    |     |    |    |     |     |    |    |

Corona
| BA | DC | 1940 | 1982 | LBW | LW | PH | RCV | UCC | UM | WB |
|---|---|---|---|---|---|---|---|---|---|---|
|    |    |      |      |     |    |    |     | C   |    |    |

Coronae

| BA | DC | 1940 | 1982 | LBW | LW | PH | RCV | UCC | UM | WB |
|----|----|------|------|-----|----|----|-----|-----|----|----|
|    |    | F    |      |     |    | F  | F   |     |    |    |

Coronation

| BA | DC | 1940 | 1982 | LBW | LW | PH | RCV | UCC | UM | WB |
|----|----|------|------|-----|----|----|-----|-----|----|----|
| G  | G  | F    | F    | F   | F  | F  |     | F   | G  | F  |

## ORGAN COMPOSITIONS

Petrich, Roger T. "All Hail the Power of Jesus' Name"
**The Concordia Hymn Prelude Series** Volume 22
Edited: Herbert Gotsch Concordia Publishing House
97-5737 Key: F

## INTONATIONS

Videro, Finn **Twenty-One Hymn Intonations**
Concordia Publishing House 97-5004 Key: F

## ORGAN COMPOSITIONS

Copland, Mark **Three Variations on Hymn Tunes**
Randall M. Egan & Associates Key: F

Fleischer, Heinrich "All Hail the Power of Jesus' Name"
**The Parish Organist** Part One Edited: Heinrich
Fleischer Concordia Publishing House 97-1145
Key: G

Hopson, Hal H. **Five Preludes on Familiar Hymns**
Harold Flammer, Inc. HF-5123 Key: G

Langlais, Jean "Prelude on 'Coronation'" **Modern Organ
Music** Book 2 Edited by David Willcocks
Oxford University Press Key: G

Young, Gordon "Toccata on 'Coronation'" **Contemporary
Hymn Preludes** Hope Publishing Co. No. 328
Key: G

## FREE ACCOMPANIMENTS

Cherwien, David **Interpretations Based on Hymn-Tunes**
A.M.S.I. OR-1 Key: F

Goode, Jack C. **Thirty-Four Changes on Hymn Tunes**
H.W. Gray Co. GB 644 Key: G

Hancock, Gerre **Organ Improvisations For Hymn-Singing**
Hinshaw Music Co. HMO-100 Key: F

Hudson, Richard **Hymn Preludes and Free Accompaniments**
Volume 12   Augsburg Publishing House   11-9408
Key: F

Noble, T. Tertius **Free Organ Accompaniments to One Hundred Well-Known Hymn Tunes**   J. Fischer & Bros.
#8175   Key: F

Wyton, Alec   **New Shoots from Old Routes** The Sacred
Music Press   KK 279   Key: F

## Coutances

| BA | DC | 1940 | 1982 | LBW | LW | PH | RCV | UCC | UM | WB |
|----|----|------|------|-----|----|----|-----|-----|----|----|
|    | d  |      |      |     |    |    |     |     |    |    |

## Covenant

| BA | DC | 1940 | 1982 | LBW | LW | PH | RCV | UCC | UM | WB |
|----|----|------|------|-----|----|----|-----|-----|----|----|
|    | E  |      |      |     |    |    |     |     |    |    |

## Covenant Hymn

| BA | DC | 1940 | 1982 | LBW | LW | PH | RCV | UCC | UM | WB |
|----|----|------|------|-----|----|----|-----|-----|----|----|
|    |    |      |      |     |    |    |     |     | G  |    |

## Coventry Carol

| BA | DC | 1940 | 1982 | LBW | LW | PH | RCV | UCC | UM | WB |
|----|----|------|------|-----|----|----|-----|-----|----|----|
|    |    | g    |      |     |    |    |     |     |    |    |

## Cowley

| BA | DC | 1940 | 1982 | LBW | LW | PH | RCV | UCC | UM | WB |
|----|----|------|------|-----|----|----|-----|-----|----|----|
|    | C  |      |      |     |    |    |     |     |    |    |

## Cowper

| BA | DC | 1940 | 1982 | LBW | LW | PH | RCV | UCC | UM | WB |
|----|----|------|------|-----|----|----|-----|-----|----|----|
|    |    |      |      |     | D  |    |     |     |    |    |

## ORGAN COMPOSITIONS

Gehrke, Hugo   "There Stands a Fountain Where for Sun"
**the Concordia Hymn Prelude Series**   Volume 22
Edited: Herbert Gotsch   Concordia Publishing
House   97-5737   Key: D

## Cradle Hymn

| BA | DC | 1940 | 1982 | LBW | LW | PH | RCV | UCC | UM | WB |
|----|----|------|------|-----|----|----|-----|-----|----|----|
|    | d  |      |      |     |    |    |     |     |    |    |

## Cradle Song

| BA | DC | 1940 | 1982 | LBW | LW | PH | RCV | UCC | UM | WB |
|----|----|------|------|-----|----|----|-----|-----|----|----|
|    | F  | F    |      |     | F  |    | F   | F   |    |    |

Hermann, David **11 Hymn Intonations, Free Accompaniments, Instrumental Descants for Organ** Volume I Advent, Christmas, Epiphany G.I.A. Publications G-2378 Key: F

ORGAN COMPOSITIONS

Engle, James "Away in a Manger" **The Concordia Hymn Prelude Series** Volume 3 Edited: Herberr Gotsch Concordia Publishing House 97-5538 Key: F

### Cranham

| BA | DC | 1940 | 1982 | LBW | LW | PH | RCV | UCC | UM | WB |
|----|----|------|------|-----|----|----|-----|-----|----|----|
|    | F  | F    | F    |     |    | F  |     | F   | F  |    |

### Crasselius

(See also: Winchester New; Dir, dir Jehovah)

| BA | DC | 1940 | 1982 | LBW | LW | PH | RCV | UCC | UM | WB |
|----|----|------|------|-----|----|----|-----|-----|----|----|
|    |    | Bb   |      | Bb  |    |    |     | Bb  |    |    |

### Creation

| BA | DC | 1940 | 1982 | LBW | LW | PH | RCV | UCC | UM | WB |
|----|----|------|------|-----|----|----|-----|-----|----|----|
|    | Ab | Ab   | G    |     |    | G  |     |     | Ab | Ab |

ORGAN COMPOSITIONS

Bish, Diane "The Spacious Firmament on High" **The Diane Bish Organ Book** Volume 4 Fred Bock Music Co. BG 0776 Key: Ab

FREE ACCOMPANIMENTS

**Free Harmonizations to Hymn Tunes by Fifty American Composers** Edited: D. DeWitt Wasson Hinshaw Music, Inc. HMO-145 Key: Ab

### Crimond

| BA | DC | 1940 | 1982 | LBW | LW | PH | RCV | UCC | UM | WB |
|----|----|------|------|-----|----|----|-----|-----|----|----|
| F  | F  |      | F    |     |    | F  |     |     |    | F  |

ORGAN COMPOSITIONS

Haan, Raymond H. **A Second Book of Contemplative Hymn Tune Preludes** Harold Flammer, Inc. HF-5127 Key: F

FREE ACCOMPANIMENTS

**Free Harmonizations to Hymn Tunes by Fifty American Composers** Edited: D.DeWitt Wasson Hinshaw Music, Inc. HMO-145 Key: F

Croft's 136th

| | | | | | | | | | |
|---|---|---|---|---|---|---|---|---|---|
| BA | DC | 1940 | 1982 | LBW | LW | PH | RCV | UCC | UM | WB |
| | | | C | | | C | | | |

Cross of Jesus

| | | | | | | | | | |
|---|---|---|---|---|---|---|---|---|---|
| BA | DC | 1940 | 1982 | LBW | LW | PH | RCV | UCC | UM | WB |
| | | | F | | | | | | |

Crucifer

| | | | | | | | | | |
|---|---|---|---|---|---|---|---|---|---|
| BA | DC | 1940 | 1982 | LBW | LW | PH | RCV | UCC | UM | WB |
| | | | C | C | C | | | | |

ORGAN COMPOSITIONS

Busarow, Donald **Processional on "Lift High the Cross"** Concordia Publishing House 97-5442 Key: D

Manz, Paul "Lift High the Cross" **Ten Chorale Improvisations** Set IX Op. 21 Concordia Publishing House 97-5556 Key: G

Powell, Robert J. "Lift High the Cross" **The Concordia Hymn Prelude Series** Volume 22 Edited: Herbert Gotsch Concordia Publishing House 97-5737 Key: C

FREE ACCOMPANIMENTS

**Free Harmonizations to Hymn Tunes by Fifty American Composers** Edited: D. DeWitt Wasson Hinshaw Music, Inc. HMO-145 Key: C

Held, Wilbur **Hymn Preludes and Free Accompaniments** Volume 6 Augsburg Publishing House 11-9402 Key: C

Crueger

| | | | | | | | | | |
|---|---|---|---|---|---|---|---|---|---|
| BA | DC | 1940 | 1982 | LBW | LW | PH | RCV | UCC | UM | WB |
| | | | | | | | e | | |

ORGAN COMPOSITIONS

Thalben-Ball, George **113 Variations on Hymn Tunes** Novello & Co., Ltd. Key: F

Crusader's Hymn
(See also: Schonster Herr Jesu; St. Elizabeth)

| | | | | | | | | | |
|---|---|---|---|---|---|---|---|---|---|
| BA | DC | 1940 | 1982 | LBW | LW | PH | RCV | UCC | UM | WB |
| Eb | | | | | | | | | |

ORGAN COMPOSITIONS

Jordan, Alice "Fairest Lord Jesus" **Hymns of Grateful Praise** Broadman Press Key: C

FREE ACCOMPANIMENTS

Noble, T. Tertius **Free Organ Accompaniments to One Hundred Well-Known Hymn Tunes** J. Fischer & Bros. #8175 Key: Eb

Wyton, Alec **New Shoots from Old Routes** The Sacred Music Press KK 279 Key: Eb

| Culbach |  |  |  |  |  |  |  |  |  |  |
|---|---|---|---|---|---|---|---|---|---|---|
| BA | DC | 1940<br>D | 1982 | LBW | LW | PH | RCV | UCC | UM | WB |

| Culross |  |  |  |  |  |  |  |  |  |  |
|---|---|---|---|---|---|---|---|---|---|---|
| BA | DC | 1940 | 1982<br>D | LBW | LW | PH | RCV | UCC | UM | WB |

| Cura Dei |  |  |  |  |  |  |  |  |  |  |
|---|---|---|---|---|---|---|---|---|---|---|
| BA | DC | 1940<br>D | 1982 | LBW | LW | PH | RCV | UCC | UM | WB |

| Cushman |  |  |  |  |  |  |  |  |  |  |
|---|---|---|---|---|---|---|---|---|---|---|
| BA | DC | 1940 | 1982 | LBW | LW | PH<br>Bb | RCV | UCC | UM<br>Bb | WB |

| Cwm Rhondda |  |  |  |  |  |  |  |  |  |  |
|---|---|---|---|---|---|---|---|---|---|---|
| BA<br>G | DC<br>G | 1940 | 1982<br>G | LBW<br>G | LW<br>F | PH<br>G | RCV | UCC<br>G | UM<br>G | WB<br>G |

ORGAN COMPOSITIONS

Kerr, J. Wayne "God of Grace and God of Glory" **O God Our Help in Ages Past** Broadman Press Key: G

Lovelace, Austin **Fourteen Hymn Preludes** Augsburg Publishing House 11-6152 Key: G

Manz, Paul "God of Grace" **Ten Chorale Improvisations** Set V Op. 14 Concordia Publishing House 97-5257 Key: F

Schultz, Ralph C. "Guide Me Ever, Great Redeemer" **The Concordia Hymn Prelude Series** Volume 22 Edited: Herbert Gotsch Concordia Publishing House 97-5737 Key: F (Second setting: Key: G )

# FREE ACCOMPANIMENTS

Cassler, G. Winston **Organ Descants for Selected Hymn Tunes** Augsburg Publishing House 11-9304 Key: G

**Free Harmonizations to Hymn Tunes by Fifty American Composers** Edited: D. DeWitt Wasson Hinshaw Music, Inc. HMO-145 Key: G

Hebble, Robert **Robert Hebble's Hymnal Companion for Organ** Bradley Publications CE/283A/3 Key: G

# D

<u>Da Jesus an dem Kreuze stund</u>
| | BA | DC | 1940 | 1982 | LBW | LW | PH | RCV | UCC | UM | WB |
|---|---|---|---|---|---|---|---|---|---|---|---|
| | | | | | | m:e | | | | | |

## ORGAN COMPOSITIONS

Ahrens, Joseph "Da Jesus an dem Kreuze stund" **Das Heilige Jahr** Volume II Willy Muller, Suddeutscher Musikverlag, Heidelberg. C.F. Peters Corporation Key: m:e

Bach, J. S. **Organ Works** Volume 1 Edited: Heinz-Harald Löhlein Urtext of the New Bach Edition Bärenreiter 5171 Key: m:e

Bach, J.S. **Organ Works** Volume VII Widor-Schweitzer G. Schirmer Key: a

Bach, J.S. **Orgelwerke** Volume V C.F. Peters Corporation Nr. 244 Key: e

Bach, J.S. **The Liturgical Year** (Orgelbuchlein) Edited: Albert Reimenschneider Oliver Ditson Co. Key: m:e

Pachelbel, Johann "Our Blessed Savior Seven Times Spoke" **The Parish Organist** Part Seven Music for Lent, Palm Sunday and Holy Week Edited: Erich Goldschmidt Concordia Publishing House 97-1403 Key: m:e

Pepping, Ernst **Fünfundzwanzig Orgelchorale** Edition Schott 4723 B. Schott's Sohne Key: m:e

Scheidt, Samuel "As Jesus Stood Beside the Cross" **Historical Organ-Recitals** Volume 1 **Forerunners of Bach: Hofhaimer to DuMage** Key: e

Scheidt, Samuel **Six Chorale Preludes on "When Jesus on the Cross Was Bound"** Concordia Publishing House  OC 339  Key: e

Scheidt, Samuel "From Calvary's Cross I Heard Christ Say"  **The Concordia Hymn Prelude Series** Volume 7  Edited: Herbert Gotsch  Concordia Publishing House  97-5614  Key: m:e

## Dakota Indian Chant
(See also: Lacquiparle)

| BA | DC | 1940 | 1982 | LBW | LW | PH | RCV | UCC | UM | WB |
|----|----|------|------|-----|----|----|-----|-----|----|----|
|    |    | c    | 1982 | LBW | LW | PH | RCV | UCC | UM | WB |

## Dalehurst

| BA | DC | 1940 | 1982 | LBW | LW | PH | RCV | UCC | UM | WB |
|----|----|------|------|-----|----|----|-----|-----|----|----|
| BA | DC | 1940 | 1982 | LBW | LW | PH | RCV | UCC | UM | WB |
|    |    |      |      |     |    |    | F   |     |    |    |

## Damstadt
(See also: O Gott, du frommer Gott)

## Danby

| BA | DC | 1940 | 1982 | LBW | LW | PH | RCV | UCC | UM | WB |
|----|----|------|------|-----|----|----|-----|-----|----|----|
| BA | DC | 1940 | 1982 | m:d | m:d | m:d | RCV | UCC | UM | WB |

## Daniel

| BA | DC | 1940 | 1982 | LBW | LW | PH | RCV | UCC | UM | WB |
|----|----|------|------|-----|----|----|-----|-----|----|----|
| BA | DC | 1940 | 1982 | LBW | LW | PH | RCV | UCC | UM | WB |
|    | E  |      |      |     |    |    |     |     |    |    |

## Daniel's Tune

| BA | DC | 1940 | 1982 | LBW | LW | PH | RCV | UCC | UM | WB |
|----|----|------|------|-----|----|----|-----|-----|----|----|
| BA | DC | F    | 1982 | LBW | LW | PH | RCV | UCC | UM | WB |

## Danish Folk Song

| BA | DC | 1940 | 1982 | LBW | LW | PH | RCV | UCC | UM | WB |
|----|----|------|------|-----|----|----|-----|-----|----|----|
| BA | DC | 1940 | 1982 | LBW | LW | PH | RCV | UCC | UM | WB |
|    | d  |      |      |     |    |    |     |     |    |    |

## Darmstadt
(See also: Was frag' ich nach der Welt)

| BA | DC | 1940 | 1982 | LBW | LW | PH | RCV | UCC | UM | WB |
|----|----|------|------|-----|----|----|-----|-----|----|----|
| BA | DC | 1940 | 1982 | LBW | LW | PH | RCV | UCC | UM | WB |
| C  | D  |      |      |     |    |    |     |     |    |    |

### ORGAN COMPOSITIONS

Hillert, Richard  "What is the World to Me"  **The Parish Organist**  Part Eleven  Edited:  Willem Mudde  Concordia Publishing House  97-4758  Key: m:d

### FREE ACCOMPANIMENTS

Cassler, G. Winston  **Organ Descants for Selected Hymn Tunes**  Augsburg Publishing House  11-9304  Key: D

## Darwall

| | DC | 1940 | 1982 | LBW | LW | PH | RCV | UCC | UM | WB |
|---|---|---|---|---|---|---|---|---|---|---|
| BA | DC | 1940 | 1982 | LBW | LW | PH | RCV | UCC | UM | WB |
| C | C | | | | | | | | | |

## Darwall's 148th

| | DC | 1940 | 1982 | LBW | LW | PH | RCV | UCC | UM | WB |
|---|---|---|---|---|---|---|---|---|---|---|
| BA | DC | 1940 | 1982 | LBW | LW | PH | RCV | UCC | UM | WB |
| | C | | C | C | C | C | D | C | D | C |

## INTONATIONS

McCormick, David **20 Organ Intonations on Hymns of Praise** Hope Publishing Co. Key: D

## ORGAN COMPOSITIONS

Barlow, Wayne "Before You, Lord, We Bow" **The Concordia Hymn Prelude Series** Volume 22 Edited: Herbert Gotsch Concordia Publishing House 97-5737 Key: C

Lovelace, Austin C. "Rejoice the Lord is King" **The Concordia Hymn Prelude Series** Volume 14 Edited: Herbert Gotsch Concordia Publishing House 97-5705 Key: C

Reger, Max **Chorale Preludes for the Church Year from Max Reger, Op. 67** Edited: Alec Wyton Carl Fischer, Inc. 0-4667 Key: m:d

## FREE ACCOMPANIMENTS

Cassler, G. Winston **Organ Descants for Selected Hymn Tunes** Augsburg Publishing House 11-9304 Key: C

Gehring, Philip **Hymn Preludes and Free Accompaniments** Volume 3 Augsburg Publishing House 11-9399 Key: C

Hebble, Robert **Robert Hebble's Hymnal Companion for Organ** Bradley publications CE/283A/3 Key: C

Miles, George Th. "Christ is Our Corner-Stone" **The Parish Organist** Part One Edited: Heinrich Fleischer Concordia Publishing House 97-1145 Key: C

Thalben-Ball, George **113 Variations on Hymn Tunes** Novello & Co., Ltd. Key: D

Wyton, Alec **New Shoots from Old Routes** The Sacred Music Press KK 279 Key: C

Das neugeborne Kindelein

| BA | DC | 1940 | 1982 | LBW | LW | PH | RCV | UCC | UM | WB |
|----|----|------|------|-----|----|----|-----|-----|----|----|
|    | e  |      |      | d   |    | e  |     |     |    | d  |

ORGAN COMPOSITIONS

Johnson, David N. "Victim Divine, Thy Grace We Claim"
**Deck Thyself My Soul with Gladness** Augsburg
Publishing House 11-9157 Key: e

Rohlig, Harald "Victim Divine, Your Grace We Claim"
**The Concordia Hymn Prelude Series** Volume 17
Edited: Herbert Gotsch Concordia Publishing House
97-5708 Key: m:d

FREE ACCOMPANIMENTS

Cassler, G. Winston **Organ Descants for Selected Hymn
Tunes** Augsburg Publishing House 11-9304 Key: e

**Free Harmonizations of Hymn Tunes by Fifty American
Composers** Edited: D. DeWitt Wasson Hinshaw
Music, Inc. HMO-145 Key: d

Das walt Gott Vater

| BA | DC | 1940 | 1982 | LBW | LW | PH | RCV | UCC | UM | WB |
|----|----|------|------|-----|----|----|-----|-----|----|----|
|    |    |      |      |     | D  | D  |     |     |    |    |

ORGAN COMPOSITIONS

Beck, Theodore "Sweet Flowerets of the Martyr Band"
**The Concordia Hymn Prelude Series** Volume 14
Edited: Herbert Gotsch Concordia Publishing House
97-5705 Key: D

Daugava

| BA | DC | 1940 | 1982 | LBW | LW | PH | RCV | UCC | UM | WB |
|----|----|------|------|-----|----|----|-----|-----|----|----|
| d  |    |      |      |     |    |    |     |     |    |    |

David's Harp

| BA | DC | 1940 | 1982 | LBW | LW | PH | RCV | UCC | UM | WB |
|----|----|------|------|-----|----|----|-----|-----|----|----|
|    |    | D    |      |     |    |    |     |     |    |    |

Davis

| BA | DC | 1940 | 1982 | LBW | LW | PH | RCV | UCC | UM | WB |
|----|----|------|------|-----|----|----|-----|-----|----|----|
| D  |    |      |      |     |    |    |     |     | D  |    |

Dawn

| BA | DC | 1940 | 1982 | LBW | LW | PH | RCV | UCC | UM | WB |
|----|----|------|------|-----|----|----|-----|-----|----|----|
|    |    | F    |      |     |    | F  |     |     |    |    |

## Day of Rest

| BA | DC | 1940 | 1982 | LBW | LW | PH | RCV | UCC | UM | WB |
|----|----|------|------|-----|----|----|-----|-----|----|----|
|    | Eb |      |      |     |    |    |     |     |    |    |

## Dayton

| BA | DC | 1940 | 1982 | LBW | LW | PH | RCV | UCC | UM | WB |
|----|----|------|------|-----|----|----|-----|-----|----|----|
| G  |    |      |      |     |    |    |     |     |    |    |

## De eersten zijn de laatsten

| BA | DC | 1940 | 1982 | LBW | LW | PH | RCV | UCC | UM | WB |
|----|----|------|------|-----|----|----|-----|-----|----|----|
|    |    |      | m:g  |     |    |    |     |     |    |    |

## De Tar

| BA | DC | 1940 | 1982 | LBW | LW | PH | RCV | UCC | UM | WB |
|----|----|------|------|-----|----|----|-----|-----|----|----|
|    |    |      | m:g  |     |    |    |     | m:g |    |    |

## Dean

| BA | DC | 1940 | 1982 | LBW | LW | PH | RCV | UCC | UM | WB |
|----|----|------|------|-----|----|----|-----|-----|----|----|
|    |    |      |      |     |    |    | f   |     |    |    |

## Decatur Place

| BA | DC | 1940 | 1982 | LBW | LW | PH | RCV | UCC | UM | WB |
|----|----|------|------|-----|----|----|-----|-----|----|----|
|    |    |      | m:e  |     |    |    |     |     |    |    |

## Dedication

| BA | DC | 1940 | 1982 | LBW | LW | PH | RCV | UCC | UM | WB |
|----|----|------|------|-----|----|----|-----|-----|----|----|
|    | C  |      |      |     |    |    |     |     |    |    |

## Deirdre
(See also: St. Patrick's Breastplate)

| BA | DC | 1940 | 1982 | LBW | LW | PH | RCV | UCC | UM | WB |
|----|----|------|------|-----|----|----|-----|-----|----|----|
|    |    | g    |      |     |    |    |     |     |    | g  |

## Dejlig er den Himmel blaa

| BA | DC | 1940 | 1982 | LBW | LW | PH | RCV | UCC | UM | WB |
|----|----|------|------|-----|----|----|-----|-----|----|----|
|    |    |      | D    |     |    |    |     |     |    |    |

### ORGAN COMPOSITIONS

Cassler, G. Winston  "Bright and Glorious is the Sky" **The Concordia Hymn Prelude Series** Volume 5 Edited: Herbert Gotsch  Concordia Publishing House  97-5611  Key: D

Manz, Paul "O, How Beautiful the Sky" **Ten Chorale Improvisations** Set VII Op. 17  Concordia Publishing House 97-5308  Key: Eb

### FREE ACCOMPANIMENTS

Krapf, Gerhard  **Hymn Preludes and Free Accompaniments** Volume 13  Augsburg Publishing House  11-9409 Key: D

Delaware
| | BA | DC | 1940 | 1982 | LBW | LW | PH | RCV | UCC | UM | WB |
|---|---|---|---|---|---|---|---|---|---|---|---|
| | | | | | | | | | g | | |

Deliverance
| | BA | DC | 1940 | 1982 | LBW | LW | PH | RCV | UCC | UM | WB |
|---|---|---|---|---|---|---|---|---|---|---|---|
| | Bb | | | | | | | | | | |

Den Blomstertid nu kommer
| | BA | DC | 1940 | 1982 | LBW | LW | PH | RCV | UCC | UM | WB |
|---|---|---|---|---|---|---|---|---|---|---|---|
| | | | | F | | | | | | | |

### ORGAN COMPOSITIONS

Krapf, Gerhard   "How Marvelous God's Greatness"  **The Concordia Hymn Prelude Series**  Volume 22   Edited: Herbert Gotsch  Concordia Publishing House  97-5737  Key: F

Den des Vaters Sinn geboren
| | BA | DC | 1940 | 1982 | LBW | LW | PH | RCV | UCC | UM | WB |
|---|---|---|---|---|---|---|---|---|---|---|---|
| | | | D | | | | | | | | |

Den signede Dag
| | BA | DC | 1940 | 1982 | LBW | LW | PH | RCV | UCC | UM | WB |
|---|---|---|---|---|---|---|---|---|---|---|---|
| | | | | C | C | | | | | | |

### ORGAN COMPOSITIONS

Gehrke, Hugo   "O Day Full of Grace"  **The Concordia Hymn Prelude Series**  Volume 12   Edited: Herbert Gotsch  Concordia Publishing House  97-5619  Key: C

Patterson, Kimberly Kondal   "I Know of a Sleep in Jesus' Name"  **The Concordia Hymn Prelude Series**  Volume 22 Edited:  Herbert Gotsch  Concordia Publishing House  97-5737  Key: C

### FREE ACCOMPANIMENTS

Ferguson, John  **Hymn Tune Harmonizations**  Book III  Ludwig Music Publishing Co.  Key: C

Hillert, Richard  **Hymn Preludes and Free Accompaniments**  Volume 10  Augsburg Publishing House  11-9406  Key: C

Den store hvide Flok
| | BA | DC | 1940 | 1982 | LBW | LW | PH | RCV | UCC | UM | WB |
|---|---|---|---|---|---|---|---|---|---|---|---|
| | | | | Eb | Eb | | | | | | |

84

ORGAN COMPOSITIONS

Ferguson, John "Behold a Host" **Behold a Host**
Augsburg Publishing House   Key: Eb

Hillert, Richard   "Behold a Host Arrayed in White"
**The Concordia Hymn Prelude Series**  Volume 14
Edited: Herbert Gotsch   Concordia Publishing House
97-5705  Key: Eb

Schack, David   "Who is This Host Arrayed in White"
**The Concordia Hymn Prelude Series**  Volume 22
Edited: Herbert Gotsch   Concordia Publishing House
97-5737  Key: Eb

<u>Dennis</u>

| BA | DC | 1940 | 1982 | LBW | LW | PH | RCV | UCC | UM | WB |
|----|----|------|------|-----|----|----|-----|-----|----|----|
| F  | F  | F    |      | F   |    | F  |     |     | F  |    |

ORGAN COMPOSITIONS

Ferguson, John   "Blest Be the Tie That Binds"  **The Concordia Hymn Prelude Series**  Volume 22  Edited: Herbert Gotsch   Concordia Publishing House 97-5737   Key: F**

FREE ACCOMPANIMENTS

Noble, T. Tertius **Free Organ Accompaniments to One Hundred Well-Known Hymn Tunes**  J. Fischer & Bros. #8175  Key: F

<u>Denny</u>

| BA | DC | 1940 | 1982 | LBW | LW | PH | RCV | UCC | UM | WB |
|----|----|------|------|-----|----|----|-----|-----|----|----|
| F  |    |      |      |     |    |    |     |     |    |    |

<u>Deo gracias</u>

| BA | DC | 1940 | 1982 | LBW | LW | PH | RCV | UCC | UM | WB |
|----|----|------|------|-----|----|----|-----|-----|----|----|
| m:c |   | m:c  | m:c  | m:c | m:c |  |     |     |    | m:c |

ORGAN COMPOSITIONS

Hillert, Richard   "Oh, Love, How Deep"  **The Concordia Hymn Prelude Series**  Volume 5  Edited: Herbert Gotsch  Concordia Publishing House  97-5611 Key: m:c

Kreckel, Philip G. **Musica Divina** Volume I  J. Fischer & Bro.  No. 6623  Key:F

Kreckel, Philip G. **Musica Divina** Volume 2  J. Fischer & Bro.  No. 6715  Key: Eb

Mackie, Ruth "O Love, How Deep" **The Concordia Hymn Prelude Series** Volume 22 Edited: Herbert Gotsch Concordia Publishing House 97-5737 Key: m:c

Manz, Paul "O Love, How Deep" **Ten Chorale Improvisations** Set IX Op. 21 Concordia Publishing House 97-5556 Key: c

Willan, Healey **Ten Hymn Preludes** Set II C. F. Peters Corporation 6012 Key: m:d

FREE ACCOMPANIMENTS

**Free Harmonizations of Hymn Tunes by Fifty American Composers** Edited: D. DeWitt Wasson Hinshaw Music, Inc. HMO-145 Key: m:c

Held, Wilbur **Hymn Preludes and Free Accompaniments** Volume 6 Augsburg Publishing House 11-9402 Key: c

Der am Kreuz

| BA | DC | 1940 | 1982 | LBW | LW | PH | RCV | UCC | UM | WB |
|----|----|------|------|-----|----|----|-----|-----|----|----|
|    |    |      |      | a   | a  |    |     |     |    |    |

ORGAN COMPOSITIONS

Mackie, Ruth Garchow "Grant, Lord Jesus" **The Concordia Hymn Prelude Series** Volume 7 Edited: Herbert Gotsch Concordia Publishing House 97-5614 Key: a

Miles, George Th. "Jesus Grant that Balm and Healing" **The Parish Organist** Part Seven Music for Lent, Palm Sunday and Holy Week Edited: Erich Goldschmidt Concordia Publishing House 97-1403 Key: a

FREE ACCOMPANIMENTS

Bunjes, Paul **New Organ Accompaniments for Hymns** Concordia Publishing House 97-5348 Key: a

Der lieben Sonne Licht und Pracht

| BA | DC | 1940 | 1982 | LBW | LW | PH | RCV | UCC | UM | WB |
|----|----|------|------|-----|----|----|-----|-----|----|----|
|    |    |      |      |     | F  |    |     |     |    |    |

ORGAN COMPOSITIONS

Engel, James  "I Walk in Danger All the Way"  **The Concordia Hymn Prelude Series**  Volume 22 Edited: Herbert Gotsch  Concordia Publishing House 97-5737  Key: F

Der mange skal komme

| BA | DC | 1940 | 1982 | LBW | LW | PH | RCV | UCC | UM | WB |
|----|----|------|------|-----|----|----|-----|-----|----|----|
|    |    |      |      | D   | D  |    |     |     |    |    |

ORGAN COMPOSITIONS

Wente, Steven  "A Multitude Comes"  **The Concordia Hymn Prelude Series**  Volume 22  Edited: Herbert Gotsch  Concordia Publishing House  97-5737 Key: m:f#

Des Plaines

| BA | DC | 1940 | 1982 | LBW | LW | PH | RCV | UCC | UM | WB |
|----|----|------|------|-----|----|----|-----|-----|----|----|
|    |    |      |      | D   |    |    |     |     |    |    |

ORGAN COMPOSITIONS

Held, Wilbur  "Lord God, the Holy Ghost"  **The Concordia Hymn Prelude Series**  Volume 12 'Edited: Herbert Gotsch  Concordia Publishing House  97-5619 Key: D

Det ar ett Fast Ord

| BA | DC | 1940 | 1982 | LBW | LW | PH | RCV | UCC | UM | WB |
|----|----|------|------|-----|----|----|-----|-----|----|----|
| A  |    |      |      |     |    |    |     |     |    |    |

Det kimer nu til Julefest

| BA | DC | 1940 | 1982 | LBW | LW | PH | RCV | UCC | UM | WB |
|----|----|------|------|-----|----|----|-----|-----|----|----|
|    |    |      |      | Eb  |    |    |     |     |    |    |

ORGAN COMPOSITIONS

Bender, Jan  "The Bells of Christmas"  **The Concordia Hymn Preludes Series**  Volume 3  Edited: Herbert Gotsch  Concordia Publishing House 97-5538 Key: Eb

Detroit

| BA | DC | 1940 | 1982 | LBW | LW | PH | RCV | UCC | UM | WB |
|----|----|------|------|-----|----|----|-----|-----|----|----|
|    |    | d    | d    |     |    |    |     |     | d  |    |

ORGAN COMPOSITIONS

Held, Wilbur  **7 Settings of American Folk Hymns** Concordia Publishing House  97-5829  Key: d

Johnson, David "Shepherd of Souls, Refresh and Bless"
**Deck Thyself With Gladness** Volume 2  Augsburg
Publishing House 11-9101  Key: d

Pelz, Walter L.  "Father of Mercies, in Your Word"
**The Concordia Hymn Prelude Series** Volume 22
Edited: Herbert Gotsch  Concordia Publishing House
97-5737  Key: d

## FREE ACCOMPANIMENTS

Hillert, Richard  **Hymn Preludes and Free Accompaniments**
Volume 10  Augsburg Publishing House   11-9406
Key: d

### Deus turorum militum

| BA | DC | 1940 | 1982 | LBW | LW | PH | RCV | UCC | UM | WB |
|---|---|---|---|---|---|---|---|---|---|---|
|  | C | Bb | Bb | Bb | Bb | Bb |  |  | C |  |

## ORGAN COMPOSITIONS

Krapf, Gerhard  "O Love, How Deep, How Broad, How High"
**The Parish Organist** Part Eleven  Edited: Willem
Mudde  Concordia Publishing House  97-4758  Key: C

Schack, David  "From God the Father, Virgin-Born"
**The Concordia Hymn Prelude Series** Volume 5
Edited: Herbert Gotsch Concordia Publishing House
97-5611  Key: Bb

Stearns, Peter Pindar  **Eight Hymn Preludes for Lent**
Harold Flammer, Inc.  HF-5133  Key: Bb

### Dexter Street

| BA | DC | 1940 | 1982 | LBW | LW | PH | RCV | UCC | UM | WB |
|---|---|---|---|---|---|---|---|---|---|---|
|  |  | Bb |  |  |  |  |  |  |  |  |

### Diadem

| BA | DC | 1940 | 1982 | LBW | LW | PH | RCV | UCC | UM | WB |
|---|---|---|---|---|---|---|---|---|---|---|
| Bb |  |  |  |  |  |  |  |  | Bb |  |

### Diademata

| BA | DC | 1940 | 1982 | LBW | LW | PH | RCV | UCC | UM | WB |
|---|---|---|---|---|---|---|---|---|---|---|
| Db | D | D | D | D | D | D | D | Eb | Eb | D |

## INTONATIONS

McCormick, David  **20 Organ Intonations on Hymns of
Praise**  Hope Publishing Co.  Key: Eb

Videro, Finn  **Twenty-One Hymn Intonations**
Concordia Publishing House  95-5004  Key: Eb

ORGAN COMPOSITIONS

Busarow, Donald "Crown Him with Many Crowns" **The Concordia Hymn Prelude Series** Volume 22 Edited: Herbert Gotsch Concordia Publishing House 97-5737 Key: D

Crane, Robert "Crown Him with Many Crowns" **The Parish Organist** Part Eleven Edited: Willem Mudde Concordia Publishing House 97-4758 Key: D

Held, Wilbur "Crown Him with Many Crowns" **Hymn Preludes for the Pentecost Season** Concordia Publishing House 97-5517 Key: D

Patterson, Kim Kondal "Crown Him with Many Crowns" **The Concordia Hymn Prelude Series** Volume 14 Edited: Herbert Gotsch Concordia Publishing House 97-5705 Key: D

FREE ACCOMPANIMENTS

Cassler, G. Winston **Organ Descants for Selected Hymn Tunes** Augsburg Publishing House 11-9304 Key: D

Diemer, Emma Lou **Hymn Preludes and Free Accompaniments** Volume 2 Augsburg Publishing House 11-9398 Key: D

Ferguson, John **Ten Hymn Tune Harmonizations** Book I Ludwig Music Publishing Co. 0-05 Key: D

Hebble, Robert **Robert Hebble's Hymnal Companion for Organ** Bradley Publications CE/283A/e Key: D

Noble, T. Tertius **Free Organ Accompaniments to One Hundred Well-Known Hymn Tunes** J. Fischer & Bros. #8175 Key: D

Wood, Dale **New Settings of Twenty Well-Known Hymn Tunes** Augsburg Publishing House 11-9292 Key: D

Wyton, Alec **New Shoots from Old Routes** The Sacred Music Press KK 279 Key: D

Diana
| | | | | | | | | | | |
|---|---|---|---|---|---|---|---|---|---|---|
| BA | DC | 1940 | 1982 | LBW | LW | PH | RCV | UCC | UM | WB |
| | | G | | | | | | | | |

Dicamus laudes Domino
| | | | | | | | | | | |
|---|---|---|---|---|---|---|---|---|---|---|
| BA | DC | 1940 | 1982 | LBW | LW | PH | RCV | UCC | UM | WB |
| | | m:d | | | | | | | | |

## Dickinson College

| BA | DC | 1940 | 1982 | LBW | LW | PH | RCV | UCC | UM | WB |
|----|----|------|------|-----|----|----|-----|-----|----|----|
|    |    | Db   |      |     |    |    |     |     |    |    |

## Die gülde Sonne

| BA | DC | 1940 | 1982 | LBW | LW | PH | RCV | UCC | UM | WB |
|----|----|------|------|-----|----|----|-----|-----|----|----|
|    |    | F    |      |     | F  |    |     |     |    |    |

### ORGAN COMPOSITIONS

Cherwien, David  "Evening and Morning"  **Interpretations Based on Hymn-tunes**  Book IV  A.M.S.I.  Key: F

Rotermund, Donald  "Evening and Morning"  **The Concordia Hymn Prelude Series**  Volume 22  Edited: Herbert Gotsch  Concordia Publishing House  97-5737  Key: F

### FREE ACCOMPANIMENTS

Shack, David  **Hymn Preludes and Free Accompaniments**  Volume 11  Augsburg Publishing House  11-9407  Key: F

## Die helle Sonn leucht

| BA | DC | 1940 | 1982 | LBW | LW | PH | RCV | UCC | UM | WB |
|----|----|------|------|-----|----|----|-----|-----|----|----|
|    |    | D    | D    |     |    |    |     |     |    |    |

### ORGAN COMPOSITIONS

Beck, Theodore  "God Loved the World So that He Gave"  **The Concordia Hymn Prelude Series**  Volume 23  Edited: Herbert Gotsch  Concordia Publishing House  97-5738  Key: D

## Die Profundis

| BA | DC | 1940 | 1982 | LBW | LW | PH | RCV | UCC | UM | WB |
|----|----|------|------|-----|----|----|-----|-----|----|----|
|    |    |      |      |     |    |    | g   |     |    |    |

## Dies est laetitiae

| BA | DC | 1940 | 1982 | LBW | LW | PH | RCV | UCC | UM | WB |
|----|----|------|------|-----|----|----|-----|-----|----|----|
|    |    | F    | F    |     | F  |    |     |     |    |    |

### ORGAN COMPOSITIONS

Fischer, Johann Kaspar Ferdinand  "Hail the Day So Rich in Cheer"  **The Parish Organist**  Part 5  Advent and Christmas Music  Concordia Publishing House  97-1382  Key: G

Pachelbel, Johann   "Who Are These That Earnest Knock"
**The Concordia Hymn Prelude Series**  Volume 3
Edited: Herbert Gotsch   Concordia Publishing
House   97-5538   Key: F

## Dies irae

| BA | DC | 1940 | 1982 | LBW | LW | PH | RCV | UCC | UM | WB |
|----|----|------|------|-----|----|----|----|----|----|----|
|    |    | m:f  |      |     |    |    |    |    |    |    |

## Dir, dir, Jehova

| BA | DC | 1940 | 1982 | LBW | LW | PH | RCV | UCC | UM | WB |
|----|----|------|------|-----|----|----|----|----|----|----|
|    |    |      | Bb   | Bb  | Bb |    |    |    |    |    |

### ORGAN COMPOSITIONS

Metzger, Hans Arnold   "Jehovah, Let Me Now Adore Thee"
**The Parish Organist**  Part One   Edited: Heinrich
Fleischer   Concordia Publishing House   97-1145
Key:  Bb

Pasquet, Jean  "Awake, Thou Spirit of the Watchmen"
**Nine Chorale Preludes** Augsburg Publishing
House   11-9298   Key: Bb

Pepping, Ernst **Praeludia Postludia II**  B. Schott's
Sohne   Edition 6041   Key: Bb

Schalk, Carl   "Awake, Thou Spirit of the Watchmen"
**The Concordia Hymn Prelude Series**  Volume 23
Edited: Herbert Gotsch   Concordia Publishing House
97-5738   Key: Bb

## Dismissal
(See also: Sicilian Mariners)

| BA | DC | 1940 | 1982 | LBW | LW | PH | RCV | UCC | UM | WB |
|----|----|------|------|-----|----|----|----|----|----|----|
|    |    | Ab   |      |     |    |    |    |    |    |    |

## Distler

| BA | DC | 1940 | 1982 | LBW | LW | PH | RCV | UCC | UM | WB |
|----|----|------|------|-----|----|----|----|----|----|----|
|    |    |      | m:d  |     |    |    |    |    |    |    |

## Distress

| BA | DC | 1940 | 1982 | LBW | LW | PH | RCV | UCC | UM | WB |
|----|----|------|------|-----|----|----|----|----|----|----|
|    | d  |      |      | d   |    |    |    |    |    |    |

### ORGAN COMPOSITIONS

Engel, James   "O Christ, the Healer, We Have Come"
**The Concordia Hymn Prelude Series**  Volume 23
Edited: Herbert Gotsch Concordia Publishing House
97-5738   Key: d

Patterson, Kim Kondal   "We Place Upon Your Table, Lord"
**The Concordia Hymn Prelude Series**   Volume 17
Edited: Herbert Gotsch   Concordia Publishing House
97-5708   Key: d

Powell, Robert J. "We Place Upon Your Table, Lord"
**Hymn Preludes for Holy Communion** Volume I
Concordia Publishing House   97-5486   Key: d

## FREE ACCOMPANIMENTS

Busarow, Donald   **Hymn Preludes and Free Accompaniments**
Volume 8   Augsburg Publishing House   11-9404
Key: d

## Diva servatrix

| BA | DC | 1940 | 1982 | LBW | LW | PH | RCV | UCC | UM | WB |
|----|----|------|------|-----|----|----|-----|-----|----|----|
|    |    | F    |      |     |    | F  |     |     |    |    |

## FREE ACCOMPANIMENTS

**Free Harmonizations of Hymn Tunes by Fifty American
Composers** Edited: D. DeWitt Wasson  Hinshaw
Music, Inc.   HMO-145   Key: F

## Divine Image

| BA | DC | 1940 | 1982 | LBW | LW | PH | RCV | UCC | UM | WB |
|----|----|------|------|-----|----|----|-----|-----|----|----|
|    |    |      |      |     |    |    | F   |     |    |    |

## Divinum mysterium
(See also: Corde natus)

| BA | DC | 1940 | 1982 | LBW | LW | PH | RCV | UCC | UM | WB |
|----|----|------|------|-----|----|----|-----|-----|----|----|
| e: | m:eb | m:eb | m:eb | m:eb | m:eb | m:eb | m:eb | m:eb | m:eb | m:eb |

## INTONATIONS

Hermann, David   **11 Hymn Intonations, Free Accompani-
ments, Instrumental Descants for Organ**   Volume I
Advent, Christmas, Epiphany   G.I.A. Publications
G-2378   Key: m:eb

## ORGAN COMPOSITIONS

Blackburn, John "Prelude on 'Of the Father's Love
Begotten'" **A Galaxy of Hymn Tune Preludes for
Organ** Galaxy Music Corp. GMC 2353   Key: m:eb

Held, Wilbur "Of the Father's Love Begotten" **Six Carol
Settings**   Concordia Publishing House   Key: m:eb

Johnson, David N. **Of the Father's Love Begotten**
Augsburg Publishing House 11-841   Key: m:eb

Lenel, Ludwig  "Of the Father's Love Begotten"
    **The Parish Organist** Christmas and Epiphany
    Music  Part Six  Concordia Publishing House
    97-1391  Key:  m:f

Peeters, Flor  "Of the Father's Love Begotten"  **The
    Concordia Hymn Prelude Series** Volume 3  Edited:
    Herbert Gotsch  Concordia Publishing House
    97-5538  Key: Eb

Purvis, Richard "Divinum Mysterium" **Leeds' Organ
    Selections** Leeds Music Corp.  Key: D

Shack, David "Of the Father's Love Begotten" **Preludes
    on Ten Hymntunes** Augsburg Publishing House
    11-9363  Key:  Eb

Wolz, Larry  **O Little Town of Bethlehem** Broadman
    Press  4570-68  Key: Eb

                FREE ACCOMPANIMENTS

Cassler, G. Winston  **Organ Descants for Selected Hymn
    Tunes** Augsburg Publishing House  11-9304  Key: Eb

Johnson, David N.  **Free Harmonizations of Twelve
    Hymn Tunes** Augsburg Publishing House  11-9190
    Key: Eb

Dix

| BA | DC | 1940 | 1982 | LBW | LW | PH | RCV | UCC | UM | WB |
|----|----|------|------|-----|----|----|-----|-----|----|----|
| G  | G  | G    | G    | G   | G  | G  | G   | G   | G  | G  |

                INTONATIONS

McCormick, David  **20 Organ Intonations on Hymns
    of Praise** Hope Publishing Co.  Key: G

                ORGAN COMPOSITIONS

Beck, Albert  **76 Offertories on Hymns & Chorales**
    Concordia Publishing House 97-5207  Key: A

Bish, Diane  "For the Beauty of the Earth"  **The Diane
    Bish Organ Book** Volume 4 Fred Bock Music
    Company  BG 0776  Key: E

Bobb, Barry L.  "For the Beauty of the Earth"  **The
    Concordia Hymn Prelude Series** Volume 23  Edited:
    Herbert Gotsch  Concordia Publishing House
    97-5738  Key: G

Jordan, Alice "For the Beauty of the Earth" **A Season and a Time** Broadman Press 4570-37 Key: G

Markworth, Henry J. "As with Gladness Men of Old" **The Parish Organist** Part One Edited: Heinrich Fleischer Concordia Publishing House 97-1145 Key: A

Markworth, Henry J. "As with Gladness Men of Old" **The Concordia Hymn Prelude Series** Volume 6 Edited: Herbert Gotsch Concordia Publishing House 97-5612 Key: G

Speller, Frank N. **A Triptych of Praise and Thanksgiving** J. Fischer & Bros. FES 10052 Key: Gb

### FREE ACCOMPANIMENTS

Busarow, Donald **All Praise to You Eternal God** Augsburg Publishing House 11-9076 Key:G

Cassler, G. Winston **Organ Descants for Selected Hymn Tunes** Augsburg Publishing House 11-9304 Key: D

Hancock, Gerre **Organ Improvisations for Hymn-Singing** Hinshaw Music Co. HMO-100 Key: G

Hudson, Richard **Hymn Preludes and Free Accompaniments** Volume 12 Augsburg Publishing House 11-9408 Key: G

Moe, Daniel **Free Organ Accompaniment to Hymns** Volume II Advent-Christmas-Epiphany Augsburg Publishing House 11-9187 Key: G

Noble, T. Tertius **Free Organ Accompaniments to One Hundred Well-Known Hymn Tunes** J. Fischer & Bros. #8175 Key: G

Dominus regit me

| BA | DC | 1940 | 1982 | LBW | LW | PH | RCV | UCC | UM | WB |
|----|----|------|------|-----|----|----|-----|-----|----|----|
| G  | G  | G    | G    |     | G  |    |     |     | G  |    |

### ORGAN COMPOSITIONS

Haan, Raymond H. "Where streams of living water flow" **The King of Love** The Sacred Music Press K 277 Key: G

Jordan, Alice "The King of Love My Shepherd Is" **A Season and A Time** Broadman Press 4570-37 Key: Db

94

Lang, C. S. **Twenty Hymn-Tune Preludes** (First Set)
Oxford University Press Key: G

McKinley, Carl **Ten Hymn Tune Fantasies**
H. W. Gray Key: G

Thalben-Ball, George **113 Variations on Hymn Tunes**
Novello & Co., Ltd. Key: D

Willan, Healey **36 Short Preludes and Postludes on
Well-Known Hymn Tunes** Set II C.F. Peters
Corporation No. 6162 Key: G

## FREE ACCOMPANIMENTS

Noble, T. Tertius **Fifty Free Organ Accompaniments
to Well Known Hymn Tunes** J. Fischer & Bros.
No. 8430 Key: G

Dona nobis pacem

| BA | DC | 1940 | 1982 | LBW | LW | PH | RCV | UCC | UM | WB |
|----|----|------|------|-----|----|----|-----|-----|----|----|
|    |    |      | F    |     |    |    |     |     |    |    |

Donata

| BA | DC | 1940 | 1982 | LBW | LW | PH | RCV | UCC | UM | WB |
|----|----|------|------|-----|----|----|-----|-----|----|----|
|    |    |      | F    |     |    |    |     |     |    |    |

## ORGAN COMPOSITIONS

Krapf, Gerhard "Spirit of God, Unleashed on Earth"
**The Concordia Hymn Prelude Series** Volume 23
Edited: Herbert Gotsch Concordia Publishing House
97-5738 Key: F

Doncaster

| BA | DC | 1940 | 1982 | LBW | LW | PH | RCV | UCC | UM | WB |
|----|----|------|------|-----|----|----|-----|-----|----|----|
|    |    | D    |      |     |    |    |     |     |    |    |

Donne

| BA | DC | 1940 | 1982 | LBW | LW | PH | RCV | UCC | UM | WB |
|----|----|------|------|-----|----|----|-----|-----|----|----|
|    |    | e    |      |     |    |    |     |     |    |    |

Donne secours

| BA | DC | 1940 | 1982 | LBW | LW | PH | RCV | UCC | UM | WB |
|----|-----|------|------|-----|-----|-----|------|-----|----|-----|
|    | m:d |      | m:d  | m:d | m:d | m:d |      | m:d |    | m:d |

## ORGAN COMPOSITIONS

Busarow, Donald "Hope of the World" **The Concordia
Hymn Prelude Series** Volume 23 Edited: Herbert
Gotsch Concordia Publishing House 97-5738
Key: m:d

Diemer, Emma Lou  **Hymn Preludes and Free Accompaniments**
Volume 2  Augsburg Publishing House  11-9398
Key: d

**Free Harmonizations of Hymn Tunes by Fifty American
Composers**  Edited: D. DeWitt Wasson  Hinshaw
Music, Inc.  HMO-145  Key: m:d

<u>Dorothy</u>

| BA | DC | 1940 | 1982 | LBW | LW | PH | RCV | UCC | UM | WB |
|----|----|------|------|-----|----|----|-----|-----|----|----|
|    |    |      |      |     | Eb |    |     |     |    |    |

ORGAN COMPOSITIONS

Pearce, Thomas R.  "Love in Christ is Strong and
Living"  **The Concordia Hymn Prelude Series**
Volume 23  Edited: Herbert Gotsch  Concordia
Publishing House  97-5738  Key: Eb

<u>Dort</u>

| BA | DC | 1940 | 1982 | LBW | LW | PH | RCV | UCC | UM | WB |
|----|----|------|------|-----|----|----|-----|-----|----|----|
|    |    |      |      |     |    |    |     |     | Bb |    |

<u>Down Ampney</u>

| BA | DC | 1940 | 1982 | LBW | LW | PH | RCV | UCC | UM | WB |
|----|----|------|------|-----|----|----|-----|-----|----|----|
|    |    | D    | D    | D   | D  | D  | D   | D   | D  | D  |

ORGAN COMPOSITIONS

Alwes, Charles  **Six Organ Preludes**  Augsburg
Publishing House  11-9416  Key: D

Arnatt, Ronald  "Come Down, O Love Divine"  **The Parish
Organist**  Part Eleven  Edited: Willem Mudde
Concordia Publishing House  97-4758  Key: D

Engel, James  "Come Down, O Love Divine"  **The
Concordia Hymn Prelude Series**  Volume 12
Edited: Herbert Gotsch  Concordia Publishing House
97-5619  Key: D

Held, Wilbur  "Come Down, O Love Divine"  **Hymn Preludes
for the Pentecost Season**  Concordia Publishing
House 97-5517  Key:D

Schultz, Ralph C.  "Come Down, O Love Divine"  **The
Concordia Hymn Prelude Series**  Volume 23
Edited: Herbert Gotsch  Concordia Publishing House
97-5738  Key: D

Drakes Broughton

| BA | DC | 1940 | 1982 | LBW | LW | PH | RCV | UCC | UM | WB |
|----|----|------|------|-----|----|----|-----|-----|----|----|
|    |    |      |      |     |    |    | D   |     |    |    |

Du Friedensfürst, Herr Jesu Christ

| BA | DC | 1940 | 1982 | LBW | LW | PH | RCV | UCC | UM | WB |
|----|----|------|------|-----|----|----|-----|-----|----|----|
|    |    |      |      |     |    |    |     |     | F  |    |

ORGAN COMPOSITIONS

Bach, J. S. **Organ Chorales from the Neumeister Collection** Edited: Christoph Wolff Yale University Press/Barenreiter 5181 Key: Bb

Du Lebensbrot, Herr Jesu Christ

| BA | DC | 1940 | 1982 | LBW | LW | PH | RCV | UCC | UM | WB |
|----|----|------|------|-----|----|----|-----|-----|----|----|
|    |    | A    | Bb   | A   |    |    |     |     |    |    |

ORGAN COMPOSITIONS

Engel, James "Lord Jesus Christ, You Have Prepared" **Hymn Preludes for Holy Communion** Volume 3 Concordia Publishing House 97-5488 Key: Bb

Johnson, David "Lord Jesus Christ, You Have Prepared" **Deck Thyself With Gladness** Volume 2 Augsburg Publishing House 11-9101 Key: G

Munch, Gisela "Lord Jesus Christ, You Have Prepared" **The Concordia Hymn Prelude Series** Volume 17 Edited: Herbert Gotsch Concordia Publishing House 97-5708 Key: A

Raphael, Gunter "Lord Jesus Christ, You Have Prepared" **The Concordia Hymn Prelude Series** Volume 17 Edited: Herbert Gotsch Concordia Publishing House 97-5708 Key: Bb

Du meine Seele, singe

| BA | DC | 1940 | 1982 | LBW | LW | PH | RCV | UCC | UM | WB |
|----|----|------|------|-----|----|----|-----|-----|----|----|
|    |    |      |      |     |    | Bb |     |     |    |    |

Du meiner Seelen

| BA | DC | 1940 | 1982 | LBW | LW | PH | RCV | UCC | UM | WB |
|----|----|------|------|-----|----|----|-----|-----|----|----|
|    |    |      | Eb   |     |    |    |     |     |    |    |

Du som gaar ud

| BA | DC | 1940 | 1982 | LBW | LW | PH | RCV | UCC | UM | WB |
|----|----|------|------|-----|----|----|-----|-----|----|----|
|    |    |      | C    |     |    |    |     |     |    |    |

ORGAN COMPOSITIONS

Zimmer, Dennis  "Spirit of God, Sent from Heaven Abroad"  **The Concordia Hymn Prelude Series** Volume 23  Edited: Herbert Gotsch  Concordia Publishing House  97-5738  Key: C

<u>Du, Herr, Heisst uns Hoffen</u>

| BA | DC | 1940 | 1982 | LBW | LW | PH | RCV | UCC | UM | WB |
|----|----|------|------|-----|----|----|-----|-----|----|----|
| F  |    |      |      |     |    |    |     |     |    |    |

<u>Duke Street</u>

| BA | DC | 1940 | 1982 | LBW | LW | PH | RCV | UCC | UM | WB |
|----|----|------|------|-----|----|----|-----|-----|----|----|
| Eb | D  | D    | D    | D   | D  | D  | Eb  | D   | D  | D  |

INTONATIONS

McCormick, David  **20 Organ Intonations on Hymns of Praise**  Hope Publishing Co.  Key: D

ORGAN COMPOSITIONS

Bish, Diane  "Jesus Shall Reign"  **The Diane Bish Organ Book**  Volume 4  Fred Bock Music Company  BG 0776  Key: D

Haan, Raymond H.  **Festival Hymn Preludes**  The Sacred Music Press  KK 329-3  Key: D

Held, Wilbur  "Give to Our God Immortal Praise"  **Preludes and Postludes**  Volume I  Augsburg Publishing House  11-9318  Key: D

Schack, David  "Jesus Shall Reign"  **The Concordia Hymn Prelude Series**  Volume 23  Edited: Herbert Gotsch  Concordia Publishing House  97-5738  Key: D

Wienhorst, Richard  "I Know that My Redeemer Lives"  **The Parish Organist**  Part One  Edited: Heinrich Fleischer  Concordia Publishing House  97-1145  Key: D

FREE ACCOMPANIMENTS

Bunjes, Paul  **New Organ Accompaniments for Hymns**  Concordia Publishing House  97-5348  Key: D

Cassler, G. Winston  **Organ Descants for Selected Hymn Tunes**  Augsburg Publishing House  11-9304  Key: D

Ferguson, John  **Hymn Tune Harmonizations**  Book III  Ludwig Music Publishing Co.  0-10  Key: D

Johnson, David N. **Free Harmonizations of Twelve
Hymn Tunes** Augsburg Publishing House 11-9190
Key: Db

Krapf, Gerhard **Hymn Preludes and Free Accompaniments**
Volume 13 Augsburg Publishing House 11-9409
Key: D

Noble, T. Tertius **Free Organ Accompaniments to One
Hundred Well-Known Hymn Tunes** J. Fischer & Bros.
#8175 Key: D

Wyton, Alec **New Shoots from Old Routes** The Sacred
Music Press KK 279 Key: D

## Duke's Tune

| | BA | DC | 1940 | 1982 | LBW | LW | PH | RCV | UCC | UM | WB |
|---|---|---|---|---|---|---|---|---|---|---|---|
| | | F | | | | | F | | | | |

## Dulce carmen

| | BA | DC | 1940 | 1982 | LBW | LW | PH | RCV | UCC | UM | WB |
|---|---|---|---|---|---|---|---|---|---|---|---|
| | | G | Ab | G | | | G | Ab | | | |

ORGAN COMPOSITIONS

Harris, David S. **Ten Hymn Preludes in Trio Style**
H. W. Gray Co. GB 643 Key: G

Manz, Paul "Alleluia, Song of Gladness" **The Parish
Organist** Part Eleven Edited: Willem Mudde
Concordia Publishing House 97-4758 Key: Ab

FREE ACCOMPANIMENTS

Noble, T. Tertius **Free Organ Accompaniments to One
Hundred Well-Known Hymn Tunes** J. Fischer & Bros.
#8175 Key: G

## Dunbar

| | BA | DC | 1940 | 1982 | LBW | LW | PH | RCV | UCC | UM | WB |
|---|---|---|---|---|---|---|---|---|---|---|---|
| | F | | | | | | | | | | |

## Duncannon

| | BA | DC | 1940 | 1982 | LBW | LW | PH | RCV | UCC | UM | WB |
|---|---|---|---|---|---|---|---|---|---|---|---|
| | Eb | | | | | | | | | | |

## Dundee

| | BA | DC | 1940 | 1982 | LBW | LW | PH | RCV | UCC | UM | WB |
|---|---|---|---|---|---|---|---|---|---|---|---|
| | Eb | Eb | Eb | Eb | Eb | Eb | Eb | | Eb | Eb | Eb |

Johnson, David N. "According to Thy Gracious Word"
**Deck Thyself My Soul with Gladness** Augsburg
Publishing House 11-9157 Key: Eb

Lang, C. S. **Twenty Hymn-Tune Preludes** (First Set)
Oxford University Press Key: Eb

Lang, C. S. "God Moves in a Mysterious Way" **The
Concordia Hymn Prelude** Volume 23 Edited: Herbert
Gotsch Concordia Publishing House 97-5738
Key: Eb

Unkel, Rolf "Almighty God, Thy Word is Cast" **The
Parish Organist** Part One Edited: Heinrich
Fleischer Concordia Publishing House 97-1145
Key: Eb

### FREE ACCOMPANIMENTS

Beck, Albert **76 Offertories on Hymns & Chorales**
Concordia Publishing House 97-5207 Key: Eb

Cassler, G. Winston **Organ Descants for Selected Hymn
Tunes** Augsburg Publishing House 11-9304 Key: Eb

Noble, T. Tertius **Free Organ Accompaniments to One
Hundred Well-Known Hymn Tunes** J. Fischer & Bros.
#8175 Key: Eb

Thalben-Ball, George **113 Variations on Hymn Tunes**
Novello & Co., Ltd. Key: Eb

## Dunedin

| BA | DC | 1940 | 1982 | LBW | LW | PH | RCV | UCC | UM | WB |
|----|----|------|------|-----|----|----|-----|-----|----|----|
|    |    | F    |      |     |    |    |     |     |    |    |

## Dunfermline

| BA | DC | 1940 | 1982 | LBW | LW | PH | RCV | UCC | UM | WB |
|----|----|------|------|-----|----|----|-----|-----|----|----|
|    | Eb |      |      |     |    | Eb |     | Eb  | Eb | E  |

### ORGAN COMPOSITIONS

Thalben-Ball, George **113 Variations on Hymn Tunes**
Novello & Co., Ltd. Key: E

### FREE ACCOMPANIMENTS

**Free Harmonizations of Hymn Tunes by Fifty American
Composers** Edited: D. DeWitt Wasson Hinshaw
Music, Inc. HMO-145 Key: Eb

Dunlap's Creek
  BA  DC   1940 1982 LBW  LW   PH   RCV  UCC  UM   WB
            D

Dunstan
  BA  DC   1940 1982 LBW  LW   PH   RCV  UCC  UM   WB
                     G

ORGAN COMPOSITIONS

Gotsch, Herbert  "Drawn to the Cross, Which You Have
    Blessed"  **The Concordia Hymn Prelude Series**
    Volume 23  Edited: Herbert Gotsch  Concordia
    Publishing House  97-5738  Key: G

Dunwody
  BA  DC   1940 1982 LBW  LW   PH   RCV  UCC  UM   WB
  c

Duquesne
  BA  DC   1940 1982 LBW  LW   PH   RCV  UCC  UM   WB
                                    d

Durham
  BA  DC   1940 1982 LBW  LW   PH   RCV  UCC  UM   WB
           E    E    D

ORGAN COMPOSITIONS

Sensmeier, Randall "Breathe on Me, Breath of God"
    **The Concordia Hymn Prelude Series**  Volume 23
    Edited: Herbert Gotsch  Concordia Publishing House
    97-5738  Key: D

Willan, healey  **36 Short Preludes and Postludes on
    Well-Known Hymn Tunes**  Set II  C.F. Peters
    Corporation  No. 6162  Key: E

Durrow
  BA  DC   1940 1982 LBW  LW   PH   RCV  UCC  UM   WB
                     c    c    c         c

ORGAN COMPOSITIONS

Wienhorst, Richard  "The Clouds of Judgment Gather"
    **The Concordia Hymn Prelude Series**  Volume 23
    Edited: Herbert Gotsch  Concordia Publishing House
    97-5738  Key: Eb

**Free Harmonizations of Hymn Tunes by Fifty American Composers** Edited: D. DeWitt Wasson  Hinshaw Music, Inc.  HMO-145  Key: c

# E

Earl Avenue
| BA | DC | 1940 | 1982 | LBW | LW | PH | RCV | UCC | UM | WB |
|----|----|------|------|-----|----|----|-----|-----|----|----|
|    |    |      |      |     |    |    |     | Eb  |    |    |

Earth and all Stars
| BA | DC | 1940 | 1982 | LBW | LW | PH | RCV | UCC | UM | WB |
|----|----|------|------|-----|----|----|-----|-----|----|----|
|    |    |      | Ab   | Ab  | Ab |    |     |     |    |    |

ORGAN COMPOSITIONS

Held, Wilbur  "Earth and All Stars"  **The Concordia Hymn Prelude Series**  Volume 23  Edited: Herbert Gotsch  Concordia Publishing House  97-5738 Key: Ab

Wyton, Alec  **Variants on "Earth and All Stars"** Augsburg Publishing House 11-0849  Key: Ab

FREE ACCOMPANIMENTS

John, David N.  **Hymn Preludes and Free Accompaniments**  Volume 14  Augsburg Publishing House  11-9410  Key: Ab

East Acklam
| BA | DC | 1940 | 1982 | LBW | LW | PH | RCV | UCC | UM | WB |
|----|----|------|------|-----|----|----|-----|-----|----|----|
|    | D  |      |      |     |    |    |     |     |    |    |

East Dallas
| BA | DC | 1940 | 1982 | LBW | LW | PH | RCV | UCC | UM | WB |
|----|----|------|------|-----|----|----|-----|-----|----|----|
|    | a  |      |      |     |    |    |     |     |    |    |

Easter Glory
(See also: Fred Til Bod)
| BA | DC | 1940 | 1982 | LBW | LW | PH | RCV | UCC | UM | WB |
|----|----|------|------|-----|----|----|-----|-----|----|----|

FREE ACCOMPANIMENTS

Cassler, G. Winston **Organ Descants for Selected Hymn Tunes**  Augsburg Publishing House  11-9304  Key: D

Easter Hymn
| BA | DC | 1940 | 1982 | LBW | LW | PH | RCV | UCC | UM | WB |
|----|----|------|------|-----|----|----|-----|-----|----|----|
| C  | C  | C    | C    | C   | C  | C  | C   | C   | C  | C  |

## ORGAN COMPOSITIONS

Campbell, Edith **Paraphrase on "Jesus Christ is Risen"**
H. W. Gray Co., Inc. No. 725 Key: C

Fleischer, Heinrich "Jesus Christ is Risen Today,
Alleluia" **The Parish Organist** Part One
Edited: Heinrich Fleischer Concordia Publishing
House 97-1145 Key: C

Jordan, Alice "Exultation on 'Christ the Lord is Risen
Today'" **Hymns of Grateful Praise** Broadman
Press Key: C

Held, Wilbur "Jesus Christ is Risen Today" **Six Preludes
on Easter Hymns** Concordia Publishing House
97-5330 Key: C

Krapf, Gerhard "Jesus Christ is Risen Today" **The
Concordia Hymn Prelude Series** Volume 10
Edited: Herbert Gotsch Concordia Pubishing House
97-5617 Key: C

Lovelace, Austin **Fourteen Hymn Preludes**
Augsburg Publishing House 11-6152 Key: C

Manz, Paul "Jesus Christ is Risen Today" **Ten Chorale
Improvisations** Opus 16 Set VI Concordia Publishing House 97-5305 Key: C

McRae, William **Improvisation on 'Jesus Christ is Risen
Today'** H.W. Gray No. 738 Key: D

Willan, Healey "Jesus Christ is Risen Today, Alleluia!"
**The Parish Organist** Part Eight Music for Easter,
Ascension, Pentecost and Trinity Edited: Erich
Goldschmidt Concordia Publishing House 97-1404
Key: C

## FREE ACCOMPANIMENTS

Ferguson, John **Hymn Harmonizations for Organ** Book II
Ludwig Music Publishing Co. 0-07 Key: C

Manz, Paul **Free Organ Accompaniments to Hymns** Volume III
General-Palm Sunday- Easter Augsburg
Publishing House 11-9189 Key: C

Moe, Daniel **Free Organ Accompaniments to Festival
Hymns** Volume I Augsburg Publishing House 11-9192
Key: C

Noble, T. Tertius **Free Organ Accompaniments to One Hundred Well-Known Hymn Tunes** J. Fischer & Bros. #8175 Key: C

Wood, Dale **New Settings of Twenty Well-Known Hymn Tunes** Augsburg Publishing House 11-9292 Key: Bb

Wyton, Alec **New Shoots from Old Routes** The Sacred Music Press KK 279 Key: C

## Eastview

| BA | DC | 1940 | 1982 | LBW | LW | PH | RCV | UCC | UM | WB |
|----|----|------|------|-----|----|----|-----|-----|----|-----|
|    |    | G    |      |     |    |    |     |     |    |     |

## Ebeling
(See also: Warum sollt ich)

| BA | DC | 1940 | 1982 | LBW | LW | PH | RCV | UCC | UM | WB |
|----|----|------|------|-----|----|----|-----|-----|----|-----|
|    |    | F    |      |     |    |    |     |     |    | F   |

## Ebenezer
(See also: Ton-y-botel)

| BA | DC | 1940 | 1982 | LBW | LW | PH | RCV | UCC | UM | WB |
|----|----|------|------|-----|----|----|-----|-----|----|-----|
| e  | f  | f    |      | f   | f  | f  | f   | f   | f  | f   |

### INTONATIONS

Videro, Finn **Twenty-One Hymn Intonations** Concordia Publishing House 97-5004 Key: f

### ORGAN COMPOSITIONS

Gotsch, Herbert "Thy Strong Word" **The Concordia Hymn Prelude Series** Volume 23 Edited: Herbert Gotsch Concordia Publishing House 97-5738 Key: f

Manz, Paul "Thy Strong Word Did Cleave the Darkness" **Ten Chorale Improvisations** Set VIII Op. 20 Concordia Publishing House 97-5342 Key: f

Willan, Healey **Ten Hymn Preludes** Set II C.F. Peters Corporation 6012 Key: f

### FREE ACCOMPANIMENTS

Carson, J. Bert **Hymn Preludes and Free Accompaniments** Volume 16 Augsburg Publishing House 11-9412 Key: f

Noble, T. Tertius **Free Organ Accompaniments to One Hundred Well-Known HymnTunes** J. Fischer & Bros. #8175 Key: f

Wyton, Alec **New Shoots from Old Routes** The Sacred
Music Press  KK  279  Key: f

Ecce agnus

| BA | DC | 1940 | 1982 | LBW | LW | PH | RCV | UCC | UM | WB |
|----|----|------|------|-----|----|----|-----|-----|----|----|
|    |    |      |      |     |    |    |     | g   |    |    |

Ecce jam noctis

| BA | DC | 1940 | 1982 | LBW | LW | PH | RCV | UCC | UM | WB |
|----|----|------|------|-----|----|----|-----|-----|----|----|
|    |    | m:f# |      |     |    |    | m:f#|     |    |    |

Ecce Sacerdos

| BA | DC | 1940 | 1982 | LBW | LW | PH | RCV | UCC | UM | WB |
|----|----|------|------|-----|----|----|-----|-----|----|----|
|    |    |      |      |     |    |    | A   |     |    |    |

Ecumenical
(See also: Sursum corda)

Eden Church

| BA | DC | 1940 | 1982 | LBW | LW | PH | RCV | UCC | UM | WB |
|----|----|------|------|-----|----|----|-----|-----|----|----|
|    |    |      | c    |     |    |    |     |     |    |    |

ORGAN COMPOSITIONS

Krapf, Gerhard  **A New Song** The Sacred Music Press
Key: c

Rohlig, Harald  "Christ Is Made the Sure Foundation"
**The Concordia Hymn Prelude Series**  Volume 24
Edited: Herbert Gotsch  Concordia Publishing House
97-5739  Key: c

Edina

| BA | DC | 1940 | 1982 | LBW | LW | PH | RCV | UCC | UM | WB |
|----|----|------|------|-----|----|----|-----|-----|----|----|
|    |    | G    |      |     |    |    |     |     |    |    |

Edmonton

| BA | DC | 1940 | 1982 | LBW | LW | PH | RCV | UCC | UM | WB |
|----|----|------|------|-----|----|----|-----|-----|----|----|
|    |    |      | D    |     |    |    |     |     |    |    |

Edsall

| BA | DC | 1940 | 1982 | LBW | LW | PH | RCV | UCC | UM | WB |
|----|----|------|------|-----|----|----|-----|-----|----|----|
|    |    | e    |      |     |    |    |     |     |    |    |

Ein Lämmlein geht
(See also:  An Wasserflüssen Babylon)

| BA | DC | 1940 | 1982 | LBW | LW | PH | RCV | UCC | UM | WB |
|----|----|------|------|-----|----|----|-----|-----|----|----|
|    |    |      | F    | F   |    |    |     |     |    |    |

# FREE ACCOMPANIMENTS

Ore, Charles **Hymn Preludes and Free Accompaniments**
Volume 7  Augsburg Publishing House  11-9403
Key: F

Ein' feste Burg

| BA | DC | 1940 | 1982 | LBW | LW | PH | RCV | UCC | UM | WB |
|----|----|------|------|-----|----|----|-----|-----|----|----|
| C  | C  | C    | C    | C   | C  | C  | C   | C   | C  | C  |

# INTONATIONS

Manz, Paul **Ten Short Intonations on Well Known
Hymn Tunes** Augsburg Publishing House
11-9492 Key: D

Videro, Finn **Twenty-One Hymn Intonations** Concordia
Publishing House  97-5004  Key: C

# ORGAN COMPOSITIONS

Bach, J. S. **Organ Works** Volume 3  "The Individually
Transmitted Organ Chorales"  Edited: Hans Klotz
Urtext of the New Bach Edition  Bärenreiter
5173  Key: D

Bach, J.S. **Organ Works** Volume VI  Widor-Schweitzer
G. Schirmer  Key: D

Bach, J.S. **Orgelwerke** Volume VI  C.F. Peters
Corporation  No. 245  Key: D

Buxtehude, J.S. **Orgelwerke II: Chorale Preludes**
C.F. Peters #4457  Key: C

Bender, Jan "A Mighty Fortress is Our God" **Festival
Preludes on Six Chorales** Concordia Publishing
House  97-4608  Key: C

Buxtehude, Dietrich "Ein feste Burg" **Festival Anthology
for Organ** Edited and Arranged: E. Power Biggs
Associated Music Publishers  Key: C

Cherwien, David **Interpretations Based on Hymn-tunes**
A.M.S.I.  OR-1  Key: C

Dupre, Marcel **Seventy-Nine Chorales for the Organ**
Opus 28  H. W. Gray  Key: D

Faulkes, William **Festival Prelude on 'Ein' Feste Burg'**
Novello  Key: A

106

Held, Wilbur "A Mighty Fortress" **Hymn Preludes for the Autumn Festivals** Concordia Publishing House 97-5360 Key: C

Karg-Elert, Sigfrid "A Mighty Fortress" **Choral Improvisations for Organ for Reformation Day, Fast Days,Communion and Funeral Rites** Op. 65, Volume 5 Edited: Robert Leech Bedell Edward B. Marks Music Corp. Key: D

Krapf, Gerhard "A Mighty Fortress is Our God" (Rhythmic) **The Concordia Hymn Prelude Series** Volume 24 Edited: Herbert Gotsch Concordia Publishing House 97-5739 Key: C

Manz, Paul "A Mighty Fortress" **Ten Chorale Improvisations** Set VIII Op. 20 Concordia Publishing House 97-5342 Key: D

Marpurg, Friedrich Wilhelm **Twenty-One Chorale Preludes** Edited: Robert M. Johnson Augsburg Publishing House 11-9506 Key: C

Pachelbel, Johann **80 Chorale Preludes - German Masters of the 17th and 18th Centuries** Edited: Hermann Keller C.F. Peters Corporation #4448 Key: D

Praetorius, Michael **80 Chorale Preludes - German Masters of the 17th and 18th Centuries** Edited: Hermann Keller C.F. Peters Corporation #4448 Key: C

Praetorius, Michael **Phantasy on the Chorale "A Mighty Fortress is Our God"** Concordia Publishing House 97-1381 Key: C

Reger, Max **30 Short Chorale Preludes** Op. 135a C.F. Peters Corporation Nr. 3980 Key: D

Scheidt, Samuel "A Mighty Fortress is Our God" **The Parish Organist** Part One Edited: Heinrich Fleischer Concordia Publishing House 97-1145 Key: C

Sellers, Gatty **Rhapsody on Reformation Hymn "Ein Feste Burg"** Oxford University Press Key: Bb

Walcha, Helmut **25 Chorale Preludes** C.F. Peters Corp. Nr. 4850 Key: C

Walther, Johann Gottfried **80 Chorale Preludes - German Masters of the 17th and 18th Centuries** Edited: Hermann Keller C.F. Peters Corporation #4448 Key: D

Walther, Johann Gottfried **Chorale Preludes by Masters of the 17th and 18th Centuries** Volume I Edited: Walter Buszin Concordia Publishing House (Two settings) Key: D

Walther, Johann Gottfried **For Manuals Only** Edited: John Christopher McAfee Music Corp. Key: D

Walther, Johann Gottfried "A Mighty Fortress is Our God" (Isorhythmic) **The Concordia Hymn Prelude Series** Volume 24 Edited: Herbert Gotsch Concordia Publishing House 97-5739 (Two settings) Key: C; Key: D

Whitford, Homer **Five Choral Paraphrases** Set I H.W. Gray Co. Key: D

FREE ACCOMPANIMENTS

Bunjes, Paul **New Organ Accompaniments for Hymns** Concordia Publishing House 97-5348 Key: C

Ferguson, John **Hymn Harmonizations for Organ** Book II Ludwig Music Publishing Co. 0-07 Key: C

Hancock, Gerre **Organ Improvisations for Hymn-Singing** Hinshaw Music Co. HMO-100 Key: C

Johnson, David N. **Free Organ Accompaniments to Festival Hymns** Volume I Augsburg Publishing House 11-9192 Key: D

Noble, T. Tertius **Free Organ Accompaniments to One Hundred Well-Known Hymn Tunes** J. Fischer & Bros. #8175 Key: C

Wood, Dale **New Settings of Twenty Well-Known Hymn Tunes** Augsburg Publishing House 11-9292 Key: C

| Eins | ist | not | | | | | | | | |
|------|-----|-----|------|------|-----|----|-----|-----|----|----|
| BA | DC | | 1940 | 1982 | LBW | LW | PH | RCV | UCC | UM | WB |
| | | | | | | D | | | | |

ORGAN COMPOSITIONS

Beck, Albert **76 Offertories on Hymns & Chorales** Concordia Publishing House 97-5207 Key: m:e

Gerike, Henry V.  "One Thing's Needful"  **The Concordia Hymn Prelude Series**  Volume 24  Edited: Herbert Gotsch  Concordia Publishing House  97-5739  Key: D

Reger, Max  **30 Short Chorale Preludes**  Op. 135a C.F. Peters Corporation Nr. 3980  Key: Eb

## Eisenach
(See also: Machs mit mir, Gott)

| BA | DC | 1940 | 1982 | LBW | LW | PH | RCV | UCC | UM | WB |
|----|----|------|------|-----|----|----|-----|-----|----|----|
|    | D  |      |      |     |    | D  |     |     | D  |    |

### ORGAN COMPOSITIONS

Near, Gerald  **Preludes on Four Hymn Tunes**  Augsburg Publishing House  11-828  Key: D

Pasquet, Jean  "To Realms of Glory in the Skies"  **Nine Chorale Preludes**  Augsburg Publishing House  11-9298  Key: D

Thalben-Ball, George  **113 Variations on Hymn Tunes**  Novello & Co., Ltd.  Key: Ab

## El Dorado

| BA | DC | 1940 | 1982 | LBW | LW | PH | RCV | UCC | UM | WB |
|----|----|------|------|-----|----|----|-----|-----|----|----|
| F  |    |      |      |     |    |    |     |     |    |    |

## El Nathan

| BA | DC | 1940 | 1982 | LBW | LW | PH | RCV | UCC | UM | WB |
|----|----|------|------|-----|----|----|-----|-----|----|----|
| Eb |    |      |      |     |    |    |     |     |    |    |

## Elbing
(See also: Du Lebensbrot, Herr Jesu Christ)

| BA | DC | 1940 | 1982 | LBW | LW | PH | RCV | UCC | UM | WB |
|----|----|------|------|-----|----|----|-----|-----|----|----|
| Ab |    |      |      |     |    |    |     |     |    |    |

### ORGAN COMPOSITIONS

Mudde, Willem  "Give Praise and Glory unto God"  **The Parish Organist**  Part Eleven  Edited: Willem Mudde  Concordia Publishing House  97-4758  Key: Eb

## Elizabeth (Mahnke)

| BA | DC | 1940 | 1982 | LBW | LW | PH | RCV | UCC | UM | WB |
|----|----|------|------|-----|----|----|-----|-----|----|----|
| A  |    |      |      |     |    |    |     |     |    |    |

ORGAN COMPOSITIONS

Gieseke, Richard W.  "Oh, Gladsome Light"  **The Concordia Hymn Prelude Series**  Volume 24 Edited: Herbert Gotsch  Concordia Publishing House 97-5739  Key: G

### Elizabeth (Thompson)

| BA | DC | 1940 | 1982 | LBW | LW | PH | RCV | UCC | UM | WB |
|----|----|------|------|-----|----|-----|-----|-----|-----|----|
| Ab |    |      |      |     |    |     |     |     | Ab |    |

### Ellacombe

(See also: Ave Maria, Klarer und Lichter Morgenstern)

| BA | DC | 1940 | 1982 | LBW | LW | PH | RCV | UCC | UM | WB |
|----|----|------|------|-----|----|-----|-----|-----|-----|----|
| A  | A  | A    |      | A   | A  | A   | A   | A   |     | Bb |

INTONATIONS

McCormick, David  **20 Organ Intonations on Hymns of Praise**  Hope Publishing Co.  Key: Bb

ORGAN COMPOSITIONS

Busarow, Donald  "Hosanna, Loud Hosanna"  **The Concordia Hymn Prelude Series**  Volume 7  Edited: Herbert Gotsch  Concordia Publishing House 97-5614  Key: A

Metzger, Hans-Arnold  "Hosanna, Loud Hosanna"  **The Parish Organist**  Part Seven  Music for Lent, Palm Sunday and Holy Week  Edited: Erich Goldschmidt  Concordia Publishing House  97-1403 Key: Bb

FREE ACCOMPANIMENTS

Diemer, Emma Lou  **Hymn Preludes and Free Accompaniments** Volume 2  Augsburg Publishing House  11-9398 Key: A

Ferguson, John  **Ten Hymn Tune Harmonizations** Book I Ludwig Music Publishing Co.  0-05  Key: A

Hebble, Robert  **Robert Hebble's Hymnal Companion for Organ**  Bradley Publications  CE/283A/3  Key: Bb

Krapf, Gerhard **Free Organ Accompaniments to Hymns** Volume II  Advent-Christmas-Epiphany.  Augsburg Publishing House  11-9187  Key: Bb

### Ellers

| BA | DC | 1940 | 1982 | LBW | LW | PH | RCV | UCC | UM | WB |
|----|----|------|------|-----|----|-----|-----|-----|-----|----|
| G  | G  | G    | G    | G   | G  | G   | Eb  |     | G   |    |

ORGAN COMPOSITIONS

Harris, David S. **Ten Hymn Preludes in Trio Style**
H. W. Gray Co. GB 643 Key: Ab

Held, Wilbur "Saviour Again to Thy Dear Name we Raise"
**Preludes and Postludes** Volume I Augsburg
Publishing House Key: G

Lovelace, Austin C. "Savior, Again to Your Dear Name"
**The Concordia Hymn Prelude Series** Volume 24
Edited: Herbert Gotsch Concordia Publishing House
97-5739 Key: G

Stearns, Peter Pindar **Twenty Hymn Preludes**
Coburn Press (Theodore Presser Company) Key: C

Willan, Healey **36 Short Preludes and Postludes on
Well-Known Hymn Tunes** Set II C.F. Peters
Corporation No. 6162 Key: Eb

FREE ACCOMPANIMENTS

Hebble, Robert **Robert Hebble's Hymnal Companion for
Organ** Bradley Publications CE/283A/3 Key: G

Lovelace, Austin C. **Hymn PreludesandFree
Accompaniments** Volume 4 Augsburg Publishing
House 11-9400 Key: G

Noble, T. Tertius **Free Organ Accompaniments to One
Hundred Well-Known Hymn Tunes** J. Fischer & Bros.
#8175 Key: G

Wood, Dale **New Settings of Twenty Well-Known Hymn Tunes**
Augsburg Publishing House 11-9292 Key: G

Ellesdie
    BA    DC   1940 1982 LBW  LW   PH   RCV  UCC  UM   WB
                                                    Ab

Ellsworth
    BA    DC   1940 1982 LBW  LW   PH   RCV  UCC  UM   WB
    G

Elmhurst
    BA    DC   1940 1982 LBW  LW   PH   RCV  UCC  UM   WB
               Eb

Eltham
    BA    DC   1940 1982 LBW  LW   PH   RCV  UCC  UM   WB
               eb

## Elton

| BA | DC | 1940 | 1982 | LBW | LW | PH | RCV | UCC | UM | WB |
|----|----|------|------|-----|----|----|-----|-----|----|----|
|    | A  |      |      |     |    | A  |     |     |    | A  |

## Ely Cathedral
(See also: Manchester)

| BA | DC | 1940 | 1982 | LBW | LW | PH | RCV | UCC | UM | WB |
|----|----|------|------|-----|----|----|-----|-----|----|----|
|    |    | G    |      |     |    |    |     |     |    |    |

## Emmanuel
(See also: Det Kimer Nu Til Julefest)

| BA | DC | 1940 | 1982 | LBW | LW | PH | RCV | UCC | UM | WB |
|----|----|------|------|-----|----|----|-----|-----|----|----|
|    | E  |      |      |     |    |    |     |     |    |    |

### FREE ACCOMPANIMENTS

Post, Piet **Free Organ Accompaniments to Hymns** Volume II Advent-Christmas-Epiphany Augsburg Publishing House 11-9187 Key: E

## En clara vox

| BA | DC | 1940 | 1982 | LBW | LW | PH | RCV | UCC | UM | WB |
|----|----|------|------|-----|----|----|-----|-----|----|----|
|    |    |      |      |     |    |    | Eb  |     |    |    |

## Energy

| BA | DC | 1940 | 1982 | LBW | LW | PH | RCV | UCC | UM | WB |
|----|----|------|------|-----|----|----|-----|-----|----|----|
|    |    |      |      | G   |    |    |     |     |    |    |

### ORGAN COMPOSITIONS

Lang, C. S. "We Give You But Your Own" **The Concordia Hymn Prelude Series** Volume 24 Edited: Herbert Gotsch Concordia Publishing House 97-5739 Key: G

## Engelberg

| BA | DC | 1940 | 1982 | LBW | LW | PH | RCV | UCC | UM | WB |
|----|----|------|------|-----|----|----|-----|-----|----|----|
|    | F  | F    | G    |     |    | F  |     | F   |    |    |

### ORGAN COMPOSITIONS

Cherwien, David **Interpretations Based on Hymn-tunes** A.M.S.I. OR-1 Key: G

Schack, David "We Know that Christ is Raised" **The Concordia Hymn Prelude Series** Volume 16 Edited: Herbert Gotsch Concordia Publishing House 97-5707 Key: G

## England's Lane

| BA | DC | 1940 | 1982 | LBW | LW | PH | RCV | UCC | UM | WB |
|----|----|------|------|-----|----|----|-----|-----|----|----|
|    |    | Bb   | Bb   |     |    |    |     |     |    |    |

Casner, Myron  "For the Beauty of the Earth"  **The Parish Organist**  Part Eleven  Edited: Willem Mudde  Concordia Publishing House  97-4758  Key: Bb

**Epworth**

| BA | DC | 1940 | 1982 | LBW | LW | PH | RCV | UCC | UM | WB |
|----|----|------|------|-----|----|----|-----|-----|----|----|
|    |    |  D   |      |     |    |    |     |     |    |    |

**Epworth Church**

| BA | DC | 1940 | 1982 | LBW | LW | PH | RCV | UCC | UM | WB |
|----|----|------|------|-----|----|----|-----|-----|----|----|
|    |    |      |      |     |    |    |     |     | f  | f  |

**Erfurt**
(See also: Vom Himmel Hoch)

**Erfyniad**

| BA | DC | 1940 | 1982 | LBW | LW | PH | RCV | UCC | UM | WB |
|----|----|------|------|-----|----|----|-----|-----|----|----|
|    |    |      |      |     |    |    |     |     |    | g  |

**Erhalt' uns, Herr**

| BA | DC | 1940 | 1982 | LBW | LW | PH | RCV | UCC | UM | WB |
|----|----|------|------|-----|----|----|-----|-----|----|----|
|    | e  |      | e    | e   |    |    |     |     |    |    |

ORGAN COMPOSITIONS

Beck, Albert  **76 Offertories on Hymns & Chorales**  Concordia Publishing House  97-5207  Key: e

Bender, Jan "Lord, Keep Us Steadfast in Thy Word"  **Festival Preludes on Six Chorales**  Concordia Publishing House  97-4608  Key: e

Buxtehude, Dietrich **Orgelwerke II: Chorale Preludes**  C.F. Peters #4457  Key: g

Gieschen, Thomas  "Lord, Keep Us Steadfast in Your Word"  **The Concordia Hymn Prelude Series**  Volume 24  Edited: Herbert Gotsch  Concordia Publishing House  97-5739  Key: e

Manz, Paul "Lord, Keep Us Steadfast in Thy Word" **Ten Chorale Improvisations** Set II  Op. 7  Concordia Publishing House 97-4656  Key: e

Peeters, Flor  "Lord, Keep Us Steadfast in Thy Word"  **30 Chorale Preludes**  Op. 68  C.F. Peters Corporation  No. 6023  Key: g

Praetorius, Michael  "Lord, Keep Us Steadfast in Thy
    Word"  **The Parish Organist**  Part One  Edited:
    Heinrich Fleischer  Concordia Publishing House
    97-1145  Key:  g

Walcha, Helmut **25 Chorale Preludes**  C.F. Peters
    Corporation  Nr. 4850  Key: e

Walther, Johann Gottfried **80 Chorale Preludes – German
    Masters of the 17th and 18th Centuries** Edited:
    Hermann Keller  C.F. Peters Corporation #4448
    Key: e

Walther, Johann G.  "Lord, Keep Us Steadfast in Thy
    Word"  **Short Classic Pieces for Organ from the
    16th, 17th and 18th Centuries**  Arr. Norris L.
    Stephens  J. Fischer & Bros.  No. 9607  Key: e

FREE ACCOMPANIMENTS

Bunjes, Paul  **New Organ Accompaniments for Hymns**
    Concordia Publishing House  97-5348  Key: e

Hudson, Richard  **Hymn Preludes and Free Accompaniments**
    Volume 12  Augsburg Publishing House  11-9408
    Key: e

Erie
(See also: Converse; What a Friend We Have)

| BA | DC | 1940 | 1982 | LBW | LW | PH | RCV | UCC | UM | WB |
|----|----|------|------|-----|----|----|-----|-----|----|----|
| F  | F  |      |      | F   |    | F  |     | F   |    |    |

Erin

| BA | DC | 1940 | 1982 | LBW | LW | PH | RCV | UCC | UM | WB |
|----|----|------|------|-----|----|----|-----|-----|----|----|
| c  |    |      |      |     |    |    |     |     |    |    |

Ermuntre dich (Schop)

| BA | DC | 1940 | 1982 | LBW | LW | PH | RCV | UCC | UM | WB |
|----|----|------|------|-----|----|----|-----|-----|----|----|
| Eb |    |      | Eb   |     |    | Eb |     | Eb  | Eb | Eb |

Erschienen ist der herrlich Tag

| BA | DC | 1940 | 1982 | LBW | LW | PH | RCV | UCC | UM | WB |
|----|----|------|------|-----|----|----|-----|-----|----|----|
|    |    |      | m:d  | m:d | m:d|    |     |     |    |    |

ORGAN COMPOSITIONS

Ahrens, Joseph "Erschienen ist der herrlich' Tag"
    **Das Heilige Jahr** Volume II
    Willy Muller – Suddeutscher Musikverlag –
    Heidelberg.  C.F. Peters Corporation Key: d

Bach, J. S. **Organ Works** Volume 1   Edited: Heinz-
Harald Löhlein   Urtext of the New Bach Edition
Bärenreiter  5171  Key: m:d

Bach, J.S. **Organ Works** Volume VII   Widor-Schweitzer
G. Schirmer  Key: m:d

Bach, J.S. **Orgelwerke** Volume V   C.F. Peters
Corporation Nr. 244  Key: m:d

Bach, J.S.   **The Liturgical Year** (Orgelbuchlein)
Edited: Albert Reimenschneider  Oliver Ditson
Co.  Key: m:d

Buxtehude, Dietrich **Six Organ Preludes on Chorales**
Edited: Henry G. Ley "Ere Yet the Dawn Hath Fill'd
the Skies"  Oxford University Press  Key: d

Beyer, Michael   "That Easter Day with Joy was Bright"
**The Concordia Hymn Prelude Series**  Volume 10
Edited: Herbert Gotsch  Concordia Publishing House
97-5617  Key: m:d

Buxtehude, Dietrich **Orgelwerke II: Chorale Preludes**
#4457  C.F. Peters  Key:d

Dupre, Marcel  **Seventy-Nine Chorales for the Organ**
Opus 28  H. W. Gray  Key: m:d

Kauffman, Georg Friedrich  "Look Toward the Mountains"
**The Concordia Hymn Prelude Series**  Volume 24
Edited: Herbert Gotsch  Concordia Publishing House
97-5739  Key: m:d

Walther, Johann Gottfried **80 Chorale Preludes - German
Masters of the 17th and 18th Centuries**  Edited:
Hermann Keller  C.F. Peters Corporation #4448
Key: d

Walther, Johann Gottfried  "We Thank Thee, Jesus,
Dearest Friend" **The Parish Organist**  Part
Eight  Music for Easter, Ascension, Pentecost,
and Trinity  Edited: Erich Goldschmidt  Concordia
Publishing House  97-1404  Key: d

FREE ACCOMPANIMENTS

Ore, Charles  **Hymn Preludes and Free Accompaniments**
Volume 7  Augsburg Publishing House  11-9403
Key: F

## Es flog ein kleins Waldvogelein

| BA | DC | 1940 | 1982 | LBW | LW | PH | RCV | UCC | UM | WB |
|----|----|------|------|-----|----|----|-----|-----|----|----|
|    |    |      | G    |     |    |    |     |     |    | G  |

## Es ist das Heil uns kommen her

| BA | DC | 1940 | 1982 | LBW | LW | PH | RCV | UCC | UM | WB |
|----|----|------|------|-----|----|----|-----|-----|----|----|
|    |    |      | D    | D   | D  |    |     |     |    |    |

## INTONATIONS

Videro, Finn **Twenty-One Hymn Intonations** Concordia Publishing House 97-5004 Key: D

## ORGAN COMPOSITIONS

Bach, J. S. **Organ Works** Volume 1 Edited: Heinz-Harald Löhlein Urtext of the New Bach Edition Bärenreiter 5171 Key: D

Bach, J.S. **Organ Works** Volume VII Widor-Schweitzer G. Schirmer Key: D

Bach, J.S. **Orgelwerke** Volume V C.F. Peters Corporation Nr. 244 Key: D

Bach, J.S. **The Liturgical Year** (Orgelbuchlein) Edited: Albert Reimenschneider Oliver Ditson Co. Key: D

Buxtehude, Dietrich **Orgelwerke II: Chorale Preludes** C.F. Peters #4457 Key: D

Dupre, Marcel **Seventy-Nine Chorales for the Organ** Opus 28 H. W. Gray Key: D

Karg-Elert, Sigfrid "Salvation Has Come to Us" **Choral Improvisations for Organ for Advent and Christmastide** Op. 65, Volume I Edited: Robert Leech Bedell Edward B. Marks Music Corp. Key: Eb

Kauffman, Georg Friedrich "All Who Believe and Are Baptized" **The Concordia Hymn Prelude Series** Volume 16 Edited: Herbert Gotsch Concordia Publishing House 97-5707 Key: D

Kloppers, Jacobus "Salvation Unto Us Has Come" **The Concordia Hymn Prelude Series** Volume 24 Edited: Herbert Gotsch Concordia Publishing House 97-5739 Key: D

Walcha, Helmut **25 Chorale Preludes** C.F. Peters Nr. 4850 Key: Eb

Reger, Max **Chorale Preludes for the Church Year from Max Reger, Op. 67** Edited: Alec Wyton  Carl Fischer, Inc.  0-4667  Key: Eb

Walther, Johann Gottfried **Chorale Preludes by Masters of the 17th and 18th Centuries** Volume I  Edited: Walter Buszin  Concordia Publishing House  Key: D

FREE ACCOMPANIMENTS

Bunjes, Paul **New Organ Accompaniments for Hymns** Concordia Publishing House  97-5348  Key: D

Schack, David **Hymn Preludes and Free Accompaniments** Volume 11  Augsburg Publishing House  11-9407 Key: G

Krapf, Gerhard **Hymn Preludes and Free Accompaniments** Volume 13  Augsburg Publishing House  11-9409 Key: D

Es ist ein' Ros'

| BA | DC | 1940 | 1982 | LBW | LW | PH | RCV | UCC | UM | WB |
|----|----|------|------|-----|----|----|-----|-----|----|----|
|    |    | F    | F    | F   | F  |    |     |     |    | F  |

ORGAN COMPOSITIONS

Best, Albert **76 Offertories on Hymns & Chorales** Concordia Publishing House  97-5207  Key: G

Brahms, Johanness **Samtliche Orgelwerke** Breitkopf & Hartel No. 6062 Key:F

Brahms, Johannes "A Lovely Rose is Blooming" **The St. Cecelia Series of Christmas Music** Set 2  Compiled by John Holler H.W. Gray Co., #617  Key: F

Brahms, Johannes "Behold, a Rose Breaks Into Bloom" **Eleven Chorale Preludes** Opus 122  Edited: E. Power Biggs  Mercury Music Corporation  A-260 Key: F

Brahms, Johannes  "A Lovely Rose is Blooming"  **The Lutheran Organist** H. W. Gray Co.  Key: F

Mueller, Gottfried  "Behold, a Branch is Growing" **The Parish Organist** Part One  Edited: Heinrich Fleischer  Concordia Publishing House  97-1145 Key:  F

Stearns, Peter Pindar **Twenty Hymn Preludes** Coburn Press (Theodore Presser Company)  Key: F

117

Stephens, Norris L. (Arr.) "Lo, How a Rose" **Short Service Pieces for Organ** Arr. Norris L. Stephens J. Fischer & Bros FE 9797 Key: G

Thate, Albert "Lo How a Rose E'er Blooming" **The Parish Organist** Part 5 Advent & Christmas Music Concordia Publishing House 97-1382 Key: F

Vogel, Willem "Lo, How a Rose is Growing" **The Concordia Hymn Prelude Series** Volume 3 Edited: Herbert Gotsch Concordia Publishing House 97-5538 Key: F

Wolz, Larry **Little Town of Bethlehem** Broadman Press 5470-68 Key: G

FREE ACCOMPANIMENTS

Hillert, Richard **Hymn Preludes and Free Accompaniments** Volume 10 Augsburg Publishing House 11-9406 Key: F

Es ist genug
   BA    DC   1940 1982 LBW  LW    PH   RCV  UCC  UM    WB
                            D

ORGAN COMPOSITIONS

Held, Wilbur "I Am Content! My Jesus Ever Lives" **The Concordia Hymn Prelude Series** Volume 10 Edited: Herbert Gotsch Concordia Publishing House 97-5617 Key: G

Es ist gewisslich an der Zeit
(See also: Nun freut euch, lieben Christen g'mein)
   BA    DC   1940 1982 LBW  LW    PH   RCV  UCC  UM    WB
                      G    G

ORGAN COMPOSITIONS

Bach, J.S. **80 Chorale Preludes – German Masters of the 17th and 18th Centuries** Edited: Hermann Keller C.F. Peters Corporation #4448 Key: G

Bach, J.S. **Orgelwerke** Volume VII C.F. Peters Corporation Nr. 246 Key: G

Kauffman, Georg Friedrich "Grant, Holy Ghost, that We Behold" **The Concordia Hymn Prelude Series** Volume 24 Edited: Herbert Gotsch Concordia Publishing House 97-5739 Key: G

Krebs, Johann Ludwig **80 Chorale Preludes – German Masters of the 17th and 18th Centuries** Edited: Hermann Keller C.F. Peters Corporation #4448 Key: G

Krebs, Johann Ludwig **Chorale Preludes by Masters of the 17th and 18th Centuries** Volume I Edited: Walter Buszin Concordia Publishing House Key: F

Praetorius, Michael "The Day is Surely Drawing Near" **The Parish Organist** Part One Edited: Heinrich Fleischer Concordia Publishing House 97-1145 Key: G

Reger, Max **30 Short Choarle Preludes** Op. 135a C.F. Peters Corporation Nr. 3980 Key: G

## Es wolle Gott uns gnädig sein

| BA | DC | 1940 | 1982 | LBW | LW | PH | RCV | UCC | UM | WB |
|----|----|------|------|-----|-----|-----|-----|-----|-----|-----|
|    |    |      |      | m:e |     |     |     |     |     |     |
|    |    |      |      | m:e |     |     |     |     |     |     |

ORGAN COMPOSITIONS

Johns, Donald "May God Embrace Us with His Grace" **The Concordia Hymn Prelude Series** Volume 24 Edited: Herbert Gotsch Concordia Publishing House 97-5739 Key: a

Scheidt, Samuel **80 Chorale Preludes – German Masters of the 17th and 18th Centuries** Edited: Hermann Keller C.F. Peters Corporation #4448 Key: e

## Eternal Light

| BA | DC | 1940 | 1982 | LBW | LW | PH | RCV | UCC | UM | WB |
|----|----|------|------|-----|-----|-----|-----|-----|-----|-----|
|    | Eb |      |      |     |     |     |     |     |     |     |

## Eucharistic Hymn

| BA | DC | 1940 | 1982 | LBW | LW | PH | RCV | UCC | UM | WB |
|----|----|------|------|-----|-----|-----|-----|-----|-----|-----|
| Eb | Eb |      |      |     |     | Eb | Eb  |     | Eb  |     |

FREE ACCOMPANIMENTS

Noble, T. Tertius **Fifty Free Organ Accompaniments to Well Known Hymn Tunes** J. Fischer & Bros. No. 8430 Key: Eb

## Euclid

| BA | DC | 1940 | 1982 | LBW | LW | PH | RCV | UCC | UM | WB |
|----|----|------|------|-----|-----|-----|-----|-----|-----|-----|
| Ab |    |      |      |     |     |     |     |     | e   |     |

## Eudoxia

| BA | DC | 1940 | 1982 | LBW | LW | PH | RCV | UCC | UM | WB |
|----|----|------|------|-----|-----|-----|-----|-----|-----|-----|
|    | F  |      |      |     |     | F  | F   |     |     |     |

**Free Harmonizations of Hymn Tunes by Fifty American Composers** Edited: D. DeWitt Wasson  Hinshaw Music, Inc.  HMO-145  Key: F

<u>Evan</u>

| | BA | DC | 1940 | 1982 | LBW | LW | PH | RCV | UCC | UM | WB |
|---|----|----|------|------|-----|----|----|-----|-----|----|----|
| | G  | Ab |      |      | Ab  | Ab |    | Ab  |     | Ab | Ab |

## ORGAN COMPOSITIONS

Beck, Theodore  "Oh, that the Lord Would Guide My Ways" **The Concordia Hymn Prelude Series** Volume 24 Edited: Herbert Gotsch  Concordia Publishing House 07-5739  Key: Ab

Best, Albert  **76 Offertories on Hymns & Chorales** Concordia Publishing House  97-5207  Key: G

## FREE ACCOMPANIMENTS

Diemer, Emma Lou **Hymn Preludes and Free Accompaniments** Volume 2  Augsburg Publishing House  11-9398 Key: Ab

**Free Harmonizations of Hymn Tunes by Fifty American Composers** Edited: D. DeWitt Wasson  Hinshaw Music, Inc.  HMO-145  Key: Ab

Goode, Jack C.  **Thirty-Four Changes on Hymn Tunes** H.W. Gray Co.  GB 644  Key: Ab

Norris, Kevin  **Hymn Preludes and Free Accompaniments** Volume 15  Augsburg Publishing House  11-9411 Key: Ab

<u>Evelyn</u>

| | BA | DC | 1940 | 1982 | LBW | LW | PH | RCV | UCC | UM | WB |
|---|----|----|------|------|-----|----|----|-----|-----|----|----|
| | BA | DC | 1940 | 1982 | LBW | LW | PH | RCV | UCC | UM | WB |
| |    |    | F    |      |     |    |    |     |     |    |    |

## FREE ACCOMPANIMENTS

Noble, T. Tertius  **Fifty Free Organ Accompaniments to Well Known Hymn Tunes**  J. Fischer & Bros. No. 8430  Key: Eb

<u>Evelyns</u>

| | BA | DC | 1940 | 1982 | LBW | LW | PH | RCV | UCC | UM | WB |
|---|----|----|------|------|-----|----|----|-----|-----|----|----|
| | BA | DC | 1940 | 1982 | LBW | LW | PH | RCV | UCC | UM | WB |
| |    |    | Eb   |      |     |    |    |     |     |    |    |

| Evening Hymn | | | | | | | | | | |
|---|---|---|---|---|---|---|---|---|---|---|
| BA | DC | 1940 | 1982 | LBW | LW | PH | RCV | UCC | UM | WB |
|  |  |  | f |  |  |  |  |  |  |  |

| Evening Prayer | | | | | | | | | | |
|---|---|---|---|---|---|---|---|---|---|---|
| BA | DC | 1940 | 1982 | LBW | LW | PH | RCV | UCC | UM | WB |
|  |  | Eb |  |  |  |  |  |  |  |  |

| Eventide | | | | | | | | | | |
|---|---|---|---|---|---|---|---|---|---|---|
| BA | DC | 1940 | 1982 | LBW | LW | PH | RCV | UCC | UM | WB |
| Eb | Eb | Eb | Eb | Eb | Eb | Eb | F | Eb | Eb | Eb |

## ORGAN COMPOSITIONS

Haan, Raymond H. "Abide with me, fast falls the eventide" **The King of Love** The Sacred Music Press K 277 Key: Eb

Hofland, Sigvart A. "Abide with Me!" **The Parish Organist** Part One Edited: Heinrich Fleischer Concordia Publishing House 97-1145 Key: Eb

Johnson, Alfred H. "Eventide" **Three Pennsylvania Dutch Chorale Preludes for Organ** J. Fischer & Bro. #9628 Key: Bb

Lang, C. S. **Twenty Hymn-Tune Preludes** (First Set) Oxford University Press Key: Eb

Lang, C. S. "Abide with Me" **The Concordia Hymn Prelude Series** Volume 24 Edited: Herbert Gotsch Concordia Publishing House 97-5739 Key: Eb

Lovelace, Austin "Abide with me" **Eight Hymn Preludes** Augsburg Publishing House 11-9144 Key: Eb

Stearns, Peter Pindar **Twenty Hymn Preludes** Coburn Press (Theodore Presser Company) Key: Eb

Thalben-Ball, George **113 Variations on Hymn Tunes** Novello & Co., Ltd. Key: Eb

Willan, Healey **36 Short Preludes and Postludes on Well-Known Hymn Tunes** Set III C.F. Peters Corporation No. 6163 Key: Eb

## FREE ACCOMPANIMENTS

Hancock, Gerre **Organ Improvisations for Hymn-Singing** Hinshaw Music Co. HMO-100 Key: Eb

Noble, T. Tertius **Free Organ Accompaniments to One Hundred Well-Known Hymn Tunes** J. Fischer & Bros. #8175 Key: Eb

Wyton, Alec **New Shoots from Old Routes** The Sacred Music Press KK 279 Key: Eb

| Everett | | | | | | | | | | |
|---|---|---|---|---|---|---|---|---|---|---|
| BA | DC | 1940 | 1982 | LBW | LW | PH | RCV | UCC | UM | WB |
| F | | | | | | | | | | |

| Everlasting Love | | | | | | | | | | |
|---|---|---|---|---|---|---|---|---|---|---|
| BA | DC | 1940 | 1982 | LBW | LW | PH | RCV | UCC | UM | WB |
| D | | | | | | | | | | |

| Every Day and Hour, with Refrain | | | | | | | | | | |
|---|---|---|---|---|---|---|---|---|---|---|
| BA | DC | 1940 | 1982 | LBW | LW | PH | RCV | UCC | UM | WB |
| | | | | | | | | | Ab | |

| Every Star | | | | | | | | | | |
|---|---|---|---|---|---|---|---|---|---|---|
| BA | DC | 1940 | 1982 | LBW | LW | PH | RCV | UCC | UM | WB |
| | | | | | | | | f | | |

| Everytime | | | | | | | | | | |
|---|---|---|---|---|---|---|---|---|---|---|
| BA | DC | 1940 | 1982 | LBW | LW | PH | RCV | UCC | UM | WB |
| | | | | | | | | D | | |

| Ewing | | | | | | | | | | |
|---|---|---|---|---|---|---|---|---|---|---|
| BA | DC | 1940 | 1982 | LBW | LW | PH | RCV | UCC | UM | WB |
| | C | C | | | C | C | | | Db | |

## ORGAN COMPOSITIONS

Beck, Albert **76 Offertories on Hymns & Chorales** Concordia Publishing House 97-5207 Key: C

Beck, Theordore "Jerusalem the Golden" **The Parish Organist** Part Eleven Edited: Willem Mudde Concordia Publishing House 97-4758 Key: C

Kalbfleisch, Rodger "Jerusalem the Golden" **The Concordia Hymn Prelude Series** Volume 24 Edited: Herbert Gotsch Concordia Publishing House 97-5739 Key: C

Stearns, Peter Pindar **Twenty Hymn Preludes** Coburn Press (theodore Presser Company) Key: G

## FREE ACCOMPANIMENTS

**Free Harmonizations to Hymn Tunes by Fifty American Composers** Edited: D. DeWitt Wasson Hinshaw Music, Inc. HMO-145 Key: C

Ex more docti mystico
| BA | DC | 1940 | 1982 | LBW | LW | PH | RCV | UCC | UM | WB |
| | | m:d | | | | | | | | |

# F

Face to Face
| BA | DC | 1940 | 1982 | LBW | LW | PH | RCV | UCC | UM | WB |
| Bb | | | | | | | | | | |

Faciem ejus videtis
| BA | DC | 1940 | 1982 | LBW | LW | PH | RCV | UCC | UM | WB |
| | | a | | | | | | | | |

Fairest Lord Jesus
(See also: Schonster Herr Jesu)
| BA | DC | 1940 | 1982 | LBW | LW | PH | RCV | UCC | UM | WB |
| | | Eb | | | | | | | | |

ORGAN COMPOSITIONS

Edmundson, Garth **Fairest Lord Jesus** J. Fischer and Co. Key: F

Fairview
| BA | DC | 1940 | 1982 | LBW | LW | PH | RCV | UCC | UM | WB |
| | | | | | | | | F | | |

Faith
| BA | DC | 1940 | 1982 | LBW | LW | PH | RCV | UCC | UM | WB |
| | | d | | | | | | | | |

Faithful Guide
| BA | DC | 1940 | 1982 | LBW | LW | PH | RCV | UCC | UM | WB |
| | | | | | | | | | G | |

ORGAN COMPOSITIONS

Kerr, J. Wayne "Holy Spirit, Faithful Guide" **O God Our Help in Ages Past** Broadman Press Key: G

Faithfulness
| BA | DC | 1940 | 1982 | LBW | LW | PH | RCV | UCC | UM | WB |
| Eb | Eb | | | | | | | | | |

Falls Creek
| BA | DC | 1940 | 1982 | LBW | LW | PH | RCV | UCC | UM | WB |
| F | | | | | | | | | | |

<u>Fang</u> <u>dein</u> <u>Werk</u>
<u>BA</u>   <u>DC</u>   1940  1982 LBW   LW    PH    RCV   UCC   UM    WB
                       C     C

ORGAN COMPOSITIONS

Hornberger, Mark A.   "With the Lord Begin Your Task"
    **The Concordia Hymn Prelude Series**  Volume 25
    Edited: Herbert Gotsch  Concordia Publishing House
    97-5740  Key: C

FREE ACCOMPANIMENTS

Gehring, Philip  **Hymn Preludes and Free Accompaniments**
    Volume 3  Augsburg Publishing House  11-9399
    Key: C

<u>Far</u> <u>Off</u> <u>Lands</u>
<u>BA</u>   <u>DC</u>   1940  1982 LBW   LW    PH    RCV   UCC   UM    WB
          D                          D                 D

FREE ACCOMPANIMENTS

**Free Harmonizations of Hymn Tunes by Fifty American
Composers**  Edited: D. DeWitt Wasson  Hinshaw
Music, Inc.  HMO-145  Key: D

<u>Farley</u> <u>Castle</u>
    <u>BA</u>   <u>DC</u>   1940  1982 LBW   LW    PH    RCV   UCC   UM    WB
    C                        C     D

ORGAN COMPOSITIONS

Bender, Jan 'Here, O My Lord, I See Thee" **Hymn Preludes
    for Holy Communion** Volume 2 97-5487  Key:C

Johnson, David "Here, O My Lord, I See Thee" **Deck
    Thyself with Gladness** Volume 2  Augsburg Publishing
    House 11-9101  Key: C

Wente, Steven  "Here, O My Lord, I See Thee"  **The
    Concordia Hymn Prelude Series** Volume 17
    Edited: Herbert Gotsch  Concordia Publishing House
    97-5708  Key: C (Second setting: Key: D)

FREE ACCOMPANIMENTS

Arnatt, Ronald  **Hymn Preludes and Free Accompaniments**
    Volume 9  Augsburg Publishing House  11-9405
    Key: C

## Farnaby

| BA | DC | 1940 | 1982 | LBW | LW | PH | RCV | UCC | UM | WB |
|----|----|------|------|-----|----|----|-----|-----|----|----|
|    | D  |      |      |     |    |    |     |     |    |    |

## Farrant

| BA | DC | 1940 | 1982 | LBW | LW | PH | RCV | UCC | UM | WB |
|----|----|------|------|-----|----|----|-----|-----|----|----|
|    | G  |      |      |     |    | G  |     |     |    |    |

## Father, Hear

| BA | DC | 1940 | 1982 | LBW | LW | PH | RCV | UCC | UM | WB |
|----|----|------|------|-----|----|----|-----|-----|----|----|
|    | f# |      |      |     |    |    |     |     |    |    |

## Fealty

| BA | DC | 1940 | 1982 | LBW | LW | PH | RCV | UCC | UM | WB |
|----|----|------|------|-----|----|----|-----|-----|----|----|
|    | Db |      |      |     |    |    |     |     |    |    |

## Federal Street

| BA | DC | 1940 | 1982 | LBW | LW | PH | RCV | UCC | UM | WB |
|----|----|------|------|-----|----|----|-----|-----|----|----|
| D  | Eb |      |      |     | F  | F  |     |     | F  | F  |

ORGAN COMPOSITIONS

Gieseke, Richard W.   "Jesus! Oh, How Could It Be True"
**The Concordia Hymn Prelude Series**  Volume 25
Edited: Herbert Gotsch  Concordia Publishing House
97-5740  Key: F

FREE ACCOMPANIMENTS

**Free Harmonizations of Hymn Tunes by Fifty American
Composers**  Edited: D. DeWitt Wasson  Hinshaw
Music, Inc.  HMO-145  Key: F

## Festal Song

| BA | DC | 1940 | 1982 | LBW | LW | PH | RCV | UCC | UM | WB |
|----|----|------|------|-----|----|----|-----|-----|----|----|
| Bb | Bb | Bb   | Bb   | Bb  | Bb | Bb | Bb  |     | Bb | Bb |

ORGAN COMPOSITIONS

Barlow, Wayne  "For All Your Saints, O Lord"  **The
Concordia Hymn Prelude Series**  Volume 14
Edited: Herbert Gotsch  Concordia Publishing House
97-5705  Key: Bb

Beck, Theodore  "Rise Up, O Saints of God"  **The
Concordia Hymn Prelude Series**  Volume 25
Edited: Herbert Gotsch  Concordia Publishing
House  97-5740  Key: A

Bingham, Seth  "Rise Up O Men of God"  **Twelve Hymn
Preludes on Familiar Tunes**  Set 1  GB 151
H.W. Gray  Key: Bb

FREE ACCOMPANIMENTS

**Free Harmonizations of Hymn Tunes by Fifty American
Composers** Edited: D. DeWitt Wasson  Hinshaw
Music, Inc.  HMO-145  Key: Bb

Hancock, Gerre  **Organ Improvisations for Hymn-Singing**
Hinshaw Music Co.  HMO-100  Key: Bb

Festgesang
(See also: Mendelssohn)

Festival Canticle

| BA | DC | 1940 | 1982 | LBW | LW | PH | RCV | UCC | UM | WB |
|----|----|------|------|-----|----|----|-----|-----|----|----|
|    |    |      | D    |     |    |    |     |     |    |    |

Ffigysbren

| BA | DC | 1940 | 1982 | LBW | LW | PH | RCV | UCC | UM | WB |
|----|----|------|------|-----|----|----|-----|-----|----|----|
|    |    |      |      |     |    | F  |     |     |    |    |

Field

| BA | DC | 1940 | 1982 | LBW | LW | PH | RCV | UCC | UM | WB |
|----|----|------|------|-----|----|----|-----|-----|----|----|
|    |    |      |      |     |    | G  |     |     | F  |    |

Fillmore

| BA | DC | 1940 | 1982 | LBW | LW | PH | RCV | UCC | UM | WB |
|----|----|------|------|-----|----|----|-----|-----|----|----|
|    |    |      |      |     |    |    |     |     | Eb |    |

Finlandia

| BA | DC | 1940 | 1982 | LBW | LW | PH | RCV | UCC | UM | WB |
|----|----|------|------|-----|----|----|-----|-----|----|----|
|    |    |      |      |     | F  | Eb |     | F   | F  |    |

ORGAN COMPOSITIONS

Krapf, Gerhard  "Be Still, My Soul"  **The Concordia
Hymn Prelude Series** Volume 25  Edited: Herbert
Gotsch  Concordia Publishing House 97-5740
Key: F

Finlay

| BA | DC | 1940 | 1982 | LBW | LW | PH | RCV | UCC | UM | WB |
|----|----|------|------|-----|----|----|-----|-----|----|----|
|    | g  |      |      |     |    | g  |     |     |    |    |

Finnian

| BA | DC | 1940 | 1982 | LBW | LW | PH | RCV | UCC | UM | WB |
|----|----|------|------|-----|----|----|-----|-----|----|----|
|    |    |      | Eb   |     |    |    |     |     |    |    |

First Nowell, The
(See also: The First Nowell)

| BA | DC | 1940 | 1982 | LBW | LW | PH | RCV | UCC | UM | WB |
|----|----|------|------|-----|----|----|-----|-----|----|----|
|    |    |      | D    |     |    |    |     |     |    |    |

Held, Wilbur  "The First Noel" **Six Carol Settings**
Concordia Publishing House  Key: D

Phillips, Gordon **Six Carol Preludes for** Organ
Oxford University Press  Key:  D

Walton, Kenneth **Fantasia on Four Christmas Carols**
Broadcast Music Inc.  Key: G

<u>Fischer</u>

| BA | DC | 1940 | 1982 | LBW | LW | PH | RCV | UCC | UM | WB |
|----|----|------|------|-----|----|----|-----|-----|----|----|
| Ab |    |      |      |     |    |    |     |     |    |    |

<u>Fisher</u>

| BA | DC | 1940 | 1982 | LBW | LW | PH | RCV | UCC | UM | WB |
|----|----|------|------|-----|----|----|-----|-----|----|----|
| Bb |    |      |      |     |    |    |     |     |    |    |

<u>Fisk of Gloucester</u>

| BA | DC | 1940 | 1982 | LBW | LW | PH | RCV | UCC | UM | WB |
|----|----|------|------|-----|----|----|-----|-----|----|----|
|    |    | F    |      |     |    |    |     |     |    |    |

<u>Flemming</u>

| BA | DC | 1940 | 1982 | LBW | LW | PH | RCV | UCC | UM | WB |
|----|----|------|------|-----|----|----|-----|-----|----|----|
| Ab |    |      |      | G   |    |    |     |     | Ab |    |

ORGAN COMPOSITIONS

Petrick, Roger  "Praise to the Father"  **The Concordia Hymn Prelude Series**  Volume 25  Edited:  Herbert Gotsch  Concordia Publishing House  97-5740
Key: G

FREE ACCOMPANIMENTS

**Free Harmonizations of Hymn Tunes by Fifty American Composers**  Edited: D. DeWitt Wasson  Hinshaw Music, Inc.  HMO-145  Key: F

<u>Flentge</u>

| BA | DC | 1940 | 1982 | LBW | LW | PH | RCV | UCC | UM | WB |
|----|----|------|------|-----|----|----|-----|-----|----|----|
|    |    | D    |      |     |    |    |     |     |    |    |

<u>Fletcher</u>
(See also: Song)

<u>Folkingham</u>

| BA | DC | 1940 | 1982 | LBW | LW | PH | RCV | UCC | UM | WB |
|----|----|------|------|-----|----|----|-----|-----|----|----|
|    |    |      |      |     |    | c  |     |     |    |    |

| Follow On | | | | | | | | | | |
|---|---|---|---|---|---|---|---|---|---|---|
| BA | DC | 1940 | 1982 | LBW | LW | PH | RCV | UCC | UM | WB |
| G | | | | | | | | | | |

| Footsteps | | | | | | | | | | |
|---|---|---|---|---|---|---|---|---|---|---|
| BA | DC | 1940 | 1982 | LBW | LW | PH | RCV | UCC | UM | WB |
| Eb | | | | | | | | | | |

| For Me | | | | | | | | | | |
|---|---|---|---|---|---|---|---|---|---|---|
| BA | DC | 1940 | 1982 | LBW | LW | PH | RCV | UCC | UM | WB |
| a | | | | | | | | | | |

| Forest Green | | | | | | | | | | |
|---|---|---|---|---|---|---|---|---|---|---|
| BA | DC | 1940 | 1982 | LBW | LW | PH | RCV | UCC | UM | WB |
| F | F | F | F | | F | F | | F | F | F |

## ORGAN COMPOSITIONS

Gieschen, Thomas "O Little Town of Bethlehem" **The Concordia Hymn Prelude Series** Volume 3 Edited: Herbert Gotsch Concordia Publishing House 97-5538 Key: F

Kerr, J. Wayne "I Sing the Almighty Power of God" **O God Our Help in Ages Past** Broadman Press Key: F

Held, Wilbur "O Little Town of Bethlehem" **Six Carol Settings** Concordia Publishing House Key: F

Hudson, Richard "Trio" **Suite of Organ Carols** Augsburg Publishing House Key: G

Manz, Paul "O Little Town of Bethlehem" **Ten Chorale Improvisations** Set VII Op. 17 Concordia Publishing House 97-5308 Key: F

Phillips, Gordon **Six Carol Preludes for Organ** Oxford University Press Key: F

## FREE ACCOMPANIMENTS

Busarow, Donald **All Praise to You Eternal God** Augsburg Publishing House 11-9076 Key: F

**Free Harmonizations of Hymn Tunes by Fifty American Composers** Edited: D. DeWitt Wasson Hinshaw Music, Inc. HMO-145 Key: Ab

Hebble, Robert **Robert Hebble's Hymnal Companion for Organ** CE/283A/3 Key: F

Hancock, Gerre **Organ Improvisations for Hymn-Singing**
Hinshaw Music Co. HMO-100 Key: F

Forest Park

| BA | DC | 1940 | 1982 | LBW | LW | PH | RCV | UCC | UM | WB |
|----|----|------|------|-----|----|----|-----|-----|----|----|
| Eb |    |      |      |     |    |    |     |     |    |    |

Fortitude

| BA | DC | 1940 | 1982 | LBW | LW | PH | RCV | UCC | UM | WB |
|----|----|------|------|-----|----|----|-----|-----|----|----|
|    |    |      |      | G   |    |    |     |     |    |    |

Fortunatus

| BA | DC | 1940 | 1982 | LBW | LW | PH | RCV | UCC | UM | WB |
|----|----|------|------|-----|----|----|-----|-----|----|----|
| G  | G  | G    |      |     |    |    |     |     |    |    |

ORGAN COMPOSITIONS

Ore, Charles W. "Welcome, Happy Morning" **The
Concordia Hymn Prelude Series** Volume 10
Edited: Herbert Gotsch Concordia Publishing House
97-5617 Key: G

FREE ACCOMPANIMENTS

Noble, T. Tertius **Free Organ Accompaniments to One
Hundred Well-Known Hymn Tunes** J. Fischer & Bros.
#8175 Key: G

Ore, Charles **Hymn Preludes and Free Accompaniments**
Volume 7 Augsburg Publishing House 11-9403
Key: G

Fortunatus New

| BA | DC | 1940 | 1982 | LBW | LW | PH | RCV | UCC | UM | WB |
|----|----|------|------|-----|----|----|-----|-----|----|----|
|    |    |      |      | d   | d  |    |     |     |    |    |

ORGAN COMPOSITIONS

Johns, Donald "Sing, My Tongue" **The Concordia
Hymn Prelude Series** Volume 7 Edited:
Herbert Gotsch Concordia Publishing House
97-5614 Key: d

Foundation

| BA | DC | 1940 | 1982 | LBW | LW | PH | RCV | UCC | UM | WB |
|----|----|------|------|-----|----|----|-----|-----|----|----|
| Ab | G  |      | G    | G   | G  | A  |     | G   | Ab | G  |

ORGAN COMPOSITIONS

Bish, Diane "How Firm a Foundation" **The Diane Bish
Organ Book** Volume 4 Fred Bock Music Company
BG 0776 Key: G

Bristol, Lee Hastings Jr. "Prelude on a Southern Folk
   Hymn 'How Firm a Foundation' " **The Bristol
   Collection of Contemporary Hymn Tune Preludes for
   Organ** Volume 2  Edited: Lee Hastings Bristol, Jr.
   Harold Flammer  Key: F

Goode, Jack  **Seven Communion Meditations**  Harold
   Flammer, Inc.  HF-5084  Key: A

Held, Wilbur  **7 Settings of American Folk Hymns**
   Concordia Publishing House  97-5829  Key: G

Owens, Sam Batt  "How Firm a Foundation"  **The Concordia
   Hymn Prelude Series**  Volume 25  Edited: Herbert
   Gotsch  Concordia Publishing House  97-5740
   Key: G

FREE ACCOMPANIMENTS

Busarow, Donald **All Praise to You Eternal God**
   Augsburg Publishing House  11-9076  Key: G

Goode, Jack C. **Thirty-Four Changes on Hymn Tunes**
   H.W. Gray Co.  GB 644  Key: G

Hancock, Gerre  **Organ Improvisations for Hymn-Singing**
   Hinshaw Music Co.  HMO-100  Key: G

Norris, Kevin  **Hymn Preludes and Free Accompaniments**
   Volume 15  Augsburg Publishing House  11-9411
   Key: G

Fragrance
   (See also: Cette odeur agreable)
   BA    DC    1940 1982 LBW  LW    PH    RCV   UCC   UM    WB
                                               D

Franconia
   BA    DC    1940 1982 LBW  LW    PH    RCV   UCC   UM    WB
   D     D     D    Eb   D    D     D           D

ORGAN COMPOSITIONS

Lang, C.S.  "The Advent of Our Lord"  **The Concordia
   Hymn Prelude Series**  Volume 1 Edited: Herbert
   Gotsch Concordia Publishing  House  97-5536
   Key: Eb

Lang, C.S.  "Within the Father's House"  **The Concordia
   Hymn Prelude Series**  Volume 6  Edited:  Herbert
   Gotsch  Concordia Publishing House  97-5612
   Key:D

130

Mackie, Ruth  "Our Children Jesus Calls"  **The Concordia Hymn Prelude Series**  Volume 16  Edited: Herbert Gotsch  Concordia Publishing House  97-5707 Key: D

Thalben-Ball, George  **113 Variations on Hymn Tunes** Novello & Co., Ltd.  Key: Eb

FREE ACCOMPANIMENTS

Cassler, G. Winston  **Organ Descants for Selected Hymn Tunes**  Augsburg Publishing House  11-9304 Key: Eb

Hillert, Richard  "Within the Father's House"  **The Parish Organist**  Part Eleven  Edited: Willem Mudde Concordia Publishing House  97-4758  Key: D

Krapf, Gerhard  **Hymn Prelude and Free Accompaniments** Volume 13  Augsburg Publishing House  11-9409 Key: Eb

Noble, T. Tertius  **Fifty Free Organ Accompaniments to Well Known Hymn Tunes**  J. Fischer & Bros. No. 8430  Key: D

Frankfort
(See also: Wie schon leuchtet)

| BA | DC | 1940 | 1982 | LBW | LW | PH | RCV | UCC | UM | WB |
|----|----|------|------|-----|----|----|-----|-----|----|----|
|    |    | D    |      |     |    |    | D   |     |    | D  |

Franzen
(See also: O Jesu, An de dina)

| BA | DC | 1940 | 1982 | LBW | LW | PH | RCV | UCC | UM | WB |
|----|----|------|------|-----|----|----|-----|-----|----|----|
|    |    |      |      | Eb  |    |    |     |     |    |    |

Fred til Bod

| BA | DC | 1940 | 1982 | LBW | LW | PH | RCV | UCC | UM | WB |
|----|----|------|------|-----|----|----|-----|-----|----|----|
|    |    |      |      | D   |    |    |     |     |    |    |

ORGAN COMPOSITIONS

Cassler, G. Winston  "Hallelujah! Jesus Lives!"  **The Concordia Hymn Prelude Series**  Volume 10 Edited: Herbert Gotsch  Concordia Publishing House 97-5617  Key: D

Goode, Jack C.  "Peace, to Soothe Our Bitter Woes" **The Concordia Hymn Prelude Series**  Volume 25 Edited: Herbert Gotsch  Concordia Publishing House 97-5740  Key: D

# FREE ACCOMPANIMENTS

Gehring, Philip **Hymn Preludes and Free Accompaniments**
Volume 3  Augsburg Publishing House  11-9399
Key: D

### Fredericktown

| BA | DC | 1940 | 1982 | LBW | LW | PH | RCV | UCC | UM | WB |
|----|----|------|------|-----|----|----|-----|-----|----|----|
|    |    |      |      | C   | C  |    |     |     |    |    |

# ORGAN COMPOSITIONS

John, Donald  "When in Our Music God is Glorified"
**The Concordia Hymn Prelude Series**  Volume 25
Edited: Herbert Gotsch  Concordia Publishing House
97-5740  Key: C

### Freedom Song
(See also; We Shall Overcome)

### French
(See also: Dundee)

| BA | DC | 1940 | 1982 | LBW | LW | PH | RCV | UCC | UM | WB |
|----|----|------|------|-----|----|----|-----|-----|----|----|
|    |    |      |      |     |    |    |     |     |    | WB |
|    |    |      |      |     |    |    |     |     |    | Eb |

### French Carol

| BA | DC | 1940 | 1982 | LBW | LW | PH | RCV | UCC | UM | WB |
|----|----|------|------|-----|----|----|-----|-----|----|----|
|    |    |      |      |     |    |    |     |     | UM | WB |
|    |    |      |      |     |    |    |     |     | f  |    |

### Freu dich sehr
(See also: Psalm 42)

| BA | DC | 1940 | 1982 | LBW | LW | PH | RCV | UCC | UM | WB |
|----|----|------|------|-----|----|----|-----|-----|----|----|
|    |    |      |      | F   | F  |    |     |     |    |    |

# INTONATIONS

Manz, Paul  **Ten Short Intonations on Well Known
Hymns**  Augsburg Publishing House  11-9492
Key: F

# ORGAN COMPOSITIONS

Bohm, Georg  **80 Chorale Preludes – German Masters of
the 17th and 18th Centuries**  Edited: Hermann
Keller  C.F. Peters Corporation #4448 Key: G

Boehm, Georg "Comfort, Comfort, Ye My People" **The
Parish Organist** Part 5  Advent & Christmas Music
Concordia Publishing House  97-1382  Key: F

Bunjes, Paul **New Organ Accompaniments for Hymns**
Concordia Publishing House  97-5348  Key: F

Karg-Elert, Sigfrid "Rejoice Greatly, O My Soul"
**Choral Improvisations for Organ for Advent
and Christmastide** Op. 65, Volume I Edited: Robert
Leech Bedell  Edward B. Marks Music Corp. Key:G

Kickstat, Paul  "Praise and Thanks and Adoration"
(Isometric) **The Concordia Hymn Prelude Series**
Volume 25  Edited: Herbert Gotsch  Concordia
Publishing House  97-5740  Key: F

Manz, Paul "Comfort, Comfort Ye My People" **Ten Chorale
Improvisations** Op. 5 Concordia Publishing House
97-4554  Key: F

Pachelbel, Johann  "Comfort, Comfort These My People"
**The Concordia Hymn Preludes Series**  Volume 1
Edited: Herbert Gotsch Concordia Publishing
House  97-5536  Key: F

Pasquet, Jean "Comfort Ye, My People" **Nine Chorale
Preludes** Augsburg Publishing House  11-9298
Key: F

Rohlig, Harald **Free Organ Accompaniments to Hymns**
Volume II  Advent-Christmas-Epiphany  Augsburg
Publishing House  11-9187  Key: F

Schultz, Ralph C.  "For Jerusalem You're Weeping"
(Rhythmic) **The Concordia Hymn Prelude Series**
Volume 25  Edited: Herbert Gotsch  Concordia
Publishing House  97-5740  Key: F

FREE ACCOMPANIMENTS

Held, Wilbur  **Hymn Preludes and Free Accompaniments**
Volume 6  Augsburg Publishing House  11-9402
Key: F

Freuen wir uns all in ein

| BA | DC | 1940 | 1982 | LBW | LW | PH | RCV | UCC | UM | WB |
|----|----|------|------|-----|----|----|-----|-----|----|----|
|    |    |      |      | m:d | m:d | e |     |     |    |    |

ORGAN COMPOSITIONS

Bouman, Paul  "Hark! A Thrilling Voice is Sounding"
**The Concordia Hymn Prelude Series** Volume 1
Edited: Herbert Gotsch  Concordia Publishing House
97-5536  Key: m:d

Freuet euch,ihr Christen

| BA | DC | 1940 | 1982 | LBW | LW | PH | RCV | UCC | UM | WB |
|----|----|------|------|-----|----|----|-----|-----|----|----|
|    |    |      |      |     | d  |    |     |     |    |    |

ORGAN COMPOSITIONS

Beck, Theodore   "Oh, Rejoice, All Christians Loudly"
**The Concordia Hymn Prelude Series**   Volume 3
Edited: Herbert Gotsch   Concordia Publishing House
97-5538  Key: d

FREE ACCOMPANIMENTS

Bunjes, Paul **New Organ Accompaniments for Hymns**
Concordia Publishing House   97-5348   Key: m:d

Freut euch, ihr lieben

| BA | DC | 1940 | 1982 | LBW | LW | PH | RCV | UCC | UM | WB |
|----|----|------|------|-----|----|----|-----|-----|----|----|
|    |    |      |      | F   | F  |    |     |     |    |    |

ORGAN COMPOSITIONS

Gerike, Hanry V.   "Hail to the Lord's Anointed"  **The
Concordia Hymn Prelude Series**   Volume 6   Edited:
Herbert Gotsch   Concordia Publishing House
97-5612  Key: F

Friend

| BA | DC | 1940 | 1982 | LBW | LW | PH | RCV | UCC | UM | WB |
|----|----|------|------|-----|----|----|-----|-----|----|----|
| Ab |    |      |      |     |    |    |     |     | Ab |    |

FREE ACCOMPANIMENTS

Beck, Albert   **76 Offertories on Hymns & Chorales**
Concordia Publishing House   97-5207   Key: F

Fröhlich soll mein Herze springen

| BA | DC | 1940 | 1982 | LBW | LW | PH | RCV | UCC | UM | WB |
|----|----|------|------|-----|----|----|-----|-----|----|----|
|    |    |      |      | Eb  | D  |    |     |     |    |    |

ORGAN COMPOSITIONS

Busarow, Donald   "Once Again My Heart Rejoices"
**The Concordia Hymn Prelude Series**   Volume 3
Edited:  Herbert Gotsch   Concordia Publishing
House  97-5538  Key: D, (Second setting: Eb)

Moser, Rudolf   "All My Heart This Night Rejoices"
**The Parish Organist**  Part 5   Advent and
Christmas Music   Concordia Publishing House
97-1382  Key: Eb

Pepping, Ernst  **Fünfundzwanzig Orgelchorale**
Edition  Schott  4723  B. Schott's Sohne
Key: m:eb

Walcha, Helmut **25 Chorale Preludes** C.F. Peters
Corporation Nr. 4850 Key: Eb

Walther, Johann Gottfried "Frohlich soll mein Herze
springen" **Organ Music for Christmas** Edited: C.
F. Trevor Oxford University Press Key: F

Frohlockt mit Freud

| BA | DC | 1940 | 1982 | LBW | LW | PH | RCV | UCC | UM | WB |
|----|----|------|------|-----|----|----|-----|-----|----|----|
|    |    | F    |      |     |    |    |     |     |    |    |

From Heaven High
(See also: Vom Himmel Hoch)

| BA | DC | 1940 | 1982 | LBW | LW | PH | RCV | UCC | UM | WB |
|----|----|------|------|-----|----|----|-----|-----|----|----|
|    |    | C    |      |     |    |    |     |     |    |    |

# G

Gabriel

| BA | DC | 1940 | 1982 | LBW | LW | PH | RCV | UCC | UM | WB |
|----|----|------|------|-----|----|----|-----|-----|----|----|
| Db |    |      |      |     |    |    |     |     |    |    |

Gabriel's Message

| BA | DC | 1940 | 1982 | LBW | LW | PH | RCV | UCC | UM | WB |
|----|----|------|------|-----|----|----|-----|-----|----|----|
|    |    | a    |      |     |    |    |     |     |    |    |

Galilean

| BA | DC | 1940 | 1982 | LBW | LW | PH | RCV | UCC | UM | WB |
|----|----|------|------|-----|----|----|-----|-----|----|----|
|    |    | G    |      | G   |    |    |     |     |    |    |

ORGAN COMPOSITIONS

Dahl, David P. "Hark, the Voice of Jesus Calling"
**The Concordia Hymn Prelude Series** Volume 25
Edited: Herbert Gotsch Concordia Publishing House
97-5740 Key: G

Hofland, Sigvart A. "Hark! the Voice of Jesus Crying"
**The Parish Organist** Part One Edited: Heinrich
Fleischer Concordia Publishing House 97-1145
Key: G

Galilee
(See also: Armes)

| BA | DC | 1940 | 1982 | LBW | LW | PH | RCV | UCC | UM | WB |
|----|----|------|------|-----|----|----|-----|-----|----|----|
| Ab | Bb |      | G    |     | Ab |    |     | Ab  | Bb |    |

ORGAN COMPOSITIONS

Gotsch, Herbert  "Jesus Calls Us; O'er the Tumult"
**The Concordia Hymn Prelude Series**  Volume 25
Edited: Herbert Gotsch  Concordia Publishing House
97-5740  Key: G

Lang, C. S.  **Twenty Hymn-Tune Preludes**  (First Set)
Oxford University Press  Key: E

Lovelace, Austin "Jesus calls us, o'er the tumult"
**Eight Hymn Preludes**  Augsburg Publishing House
11-9144  Key: Bb

FREE ACCOMPANIMENTS

**Free Harmonizations to Hymn Tunes by Fifty American
Composers**  Edited: D. DeWitt Wasson  Hinshaw
Music, Inc.  HMO-145  Key: G

Hancock, Gerre  **Organ Improvisations for Hymn-Singing**
Hinshaw Music Co.  HMO-100  Key: Ab

Lovelace, Austin C.  **Hymn Preludes and Free
Accompaniments**  Volume 4  Augsburg Publishing
House  11-9400  Key: G

Gallery Carol
| BA | DC | 1940 | 1982 | LBW | LW | PH | RCV | UCC | UM | WB |
|---|---|---|---|---|---|---|---|---|---|---|
|  |  |  |  |  |  |  |  |  |  | F |

Garden
| BA | DC | 1940 | 1982 | LBW | LW | PH | RCV | UCC | UM | WB |
|---|---|---|---|---|---|---|---|---|---|---|
| Ab | Eb |  |  |  |  |  |  |  |  |  |

Garden City
| BA | DC | 1940 | 1982 | LBW | LW | PH | RCV | UCC | UM | WB |
|---|---|---|---|---|---|---|---|---|---|---|
|  | Ab |  |  |  |  |  |  |  |  |  |

FREE ACCOMPANIMENTS

Noble, T. Tertius  **Free Organ Accompaniments to One
Hundred Well-Known Hymn Tunes**  J. Fischer & Bros.
#8175  Key: Ab

Gardiner
(See also: Germany)
| BA | DC | 1940 | 1982 | LBW | LW | PH | RCV | UCC | UM | WB |
|---|---|---|---|---|---|---|---|---|---|---|
|  |  | A | Ab |  |  |  |  |  |  |  |

ORGAN COMPOSITIONS

Whitford, Homer  **Five Choral Paraphrases** Set I
H.W. Gray Co.  Key: Bb

Willan, Healey  **36 Short Preludes and Postludes on
Well-Known Hymn Tunes**  Set II  C.F. Peters
Corporation  No. 6162  Key: A

Garelochside

| BA | DC | 1940 | 1982 | LBW | LW | PH | RCV | UCC | UM | WB |
|----|----|------|------|-----|----|----|-----|-----|----|----|
|    |    |      |      |  C  |    |    |     |     |    |    |

ORGAN COMPOSITIONS

Gieschen, Thomas  "All Praise to You, O Lord"  **The
Concordia Hymn Prelude Series**  Volume 6  Edited:
Herbert Gotsch  Concordia Publishing House
97-5612  Key: C

Gartan

| BA | DC | 1940 | 1982 | LBW | LW | PH | RCV | UCC | UM | WB |
|----|----|------|------|-----|----|----|-----|-----|----|----|
|    | F  |      | F    |     | F  |    |     |     |    |    |

ORGAN COMPOSITIONS

Krapf, Gerhard  "Love Came Down at Christmas"  **The
Concordia Hymn Prelude Series**  Volume 3  Edited:
Herbert Gotsch  Concordia Publishing House
97-5538  Key: F

Garton

| BA | DC | 1940 | 1982 | LBW | LW | PH | RCV | UCC | UM | WB |
|----|----|------|------|-----|----|----|-----|-----|----|----|
|    |    |      |      |     |    |    |     |     | UM |    |
|    |    |      |      |     |    |    |     |     | F  |    |

Gaudeamus pariter
(See also: Ave virgo virginum)

| BA | DC | 1940 | 1982 | LBW | LW | PH | RCV | UCC | UM | WB |
|----|----|------|------|-----|----|----|-----|-----|----|----|
|    |    | F    | F    | F   | F  |    |     |     |    |    |

INTONATIONS

Videro, Finn  **Twenty-One Hymn Intonations**
Concordia Publishing House  97-5004  Key: F

ORGAN COMPOSITIONS

Alwes, Charles  **Six Organ Preludes**  Augsburg
Publishing House  11-9416  Key: F

Beck, Theodore "Come You Faithful, Raise the Strain"
   **The Concordia Hymn Prelude Series** Volume 10
   Edited: Herbert Gotsch   Concordia Publishing House
   97-5617  Key: F

Held, Wilbur "Come Ye Faithful, Raise the Strain"
   **Six Preludes on Easter Hymns** Concordia
   Publishing House 97-5330  Key: G

Hillert, Richard "Cradling Children in His Arm" **The
   Concordia Hymn Prelude Series** Volume 16  Edited:
   Herbert Gotsch   Concordia Publishing House
   97-5707  Key: F

## FREE ACCOMPANIMENTS

Alwes, Charles **Six Organ Preludes** Augsburg
   Publishing House  11-9416  Key: F

Hudson, Richard **Hymn Preludes and Free Accompaniments**
   Volume 12  Augsburg Publishing House  11-9408
   Key: F

Gaza

| BA | DC | 1940 | 1982 | LBW | LW | PH | RCV | UCC | UM | WB |
|----|----|------|------|-----|----|----|-----|-----|----|----|
|    |    | e    |      |     |    |    |     |     |    |    |

Geibel

| BA | DC | 1940 | 1982 | LBW | LW | PH | RCV | UCC | UM | WB |
|----|----|------|------|-----|----|----|-----|-----|----|----|
| F  |    |      |      |     |    |    |     |     |    |    |

Gelobet seist du, Jesu Christ

| BA | DC | 1940 | 1982 | LBW | LW  | PH | RCV | UCC | UM | WB |
|----|----|------|------|-----|-----|----|-----|-----|----|----|
|    |    |      |      | m:g | m:g |    |     |     |    |    |

## ORGAN COMPOSITIONS

Bach, J. S.  **Organ Works** Volume 1  Edited: Heinz-
   Harald Löhlein  Urtext of the New Bach Edition
   Bärenreiter  5171  Key: m:g

Bach,  J. S. **Organ Works** Volume 3 "The Individually
   Transmitted Organ Chorales" Edited: Hans Klotz
   Urtext of the New Bach Edition  Bärenreiter
   5173  Key: m:g

Bach, J.S. **Organ Works** Volume VI  Widor-Schweitzer
   G. Schirmer  Key: m:g (#4, 34, 35)

Bach, J.S. **Organ Works** Volume VII  Widor-Schweitzer
   G. Schirmer  Key: m:g

Bach, J.S. **Orgelwerke** Volume V  C.F. Peters
Corporation  Nr. 244  (Two settings) Key: m:g

Bach, J.S.  **Orgelwerke**  Volume VI  C.F. Peters
Corporation No. 245 Key: m:g

Bach, J.S. **The Liturgical Year** (Orgelbuchlein)
Edited: Albert Reimenschneider  Oliver Ditson Co.
Key: m:g

Bach, J.S. **Choral Fantasia on 'Gelobet seist du, Jesus
Christ'** Arr. Robert L. Bedell New York:
Edward Schuberth and Co. Key: m:g

Buttstedt, Johann Heinrich **80 Chorale Preludes - German
Masters of the 17th and 18th Centuries** Edited:
Hermann Keller  C.F. Peters Corporation #4448
Key: m:g

Buxtehude, Dietrich **Orgelwerke II: Chorale Preludes**
C.F. Peters Corporation# 4457  Key: m:c

Dupre, Marcel  **Seventy-Nine Chorales for the Organ**
Opus 28  H. W. Gray  Key: g

Karg-Elert, Sigfrid "Praised Be Thou, Jesus Christ"
**Choral Improvisations for Organ for Advent and
Christmastide** Op. 65, VolumeI  Edited: Robert
Leech Bedell  Edward B. Marks Music Corp. Key:m:g

Lenel, Ludwig "All Praise to Thee, Eternal God"
**Three Chorale Fantasias on Pre-Reformation Hymns**
Concordia Publishing House 97-4408  Key: m:g

Manz, Paul "All Praise to Thee, Eternal God" **Ten
Chorale Improvisations** Set III  Op. 9  97-4950
Key: m:f

Pachelbel, Johann  "All Praise to Thee, Eternal God"
**The Parish Organist** Part 5  Advent and
Christmas Music  Concordia Publishing House
97-1382  Key:  m:g

Scheidt, Samuel **80 Chorale Preludes - German Masters
of the 17th and 18th Centuries** Edited: Hermann
Keller  C.F. Peters Corporation #4448  Key: m:g

Scheidt, Samuel  "All Praise to Thee, Eternal God"
**The Parish Organist** Christmas and Epiphany
Music  Part Six  Concordia Publishing House
97-1391  Key: m:g

Scheidt, Samuel   "All Praise to You, Eternal Lord"
**The Concordia Hymn Prelude Series**   Volume 3
Edited: Herbert Gotsch   Concordia Publishing
House   97-5538   Key: m:g

Walcha, Helmut  **25 Chorale Preludes**   C.F. Peters
Nr. 4850   Key: m:g

FREE ACCOMPANIMENTS

Bunjes, Paul   **New Organ Accompaniments for Hymns**
Concordia Publishing House   97-5348   Key: m:g

Gehring, Philip   **Hymn Preludes and Free Accompaniments**
Volume 3   Augsburg Publishing House   11-9399
Key: G

Gelobt sei Gott

| BA | DC | 1940 | 1982 | LBW | LW | PH | RCV | UCC | UM | WB |
|----|----|------|------|-----|----|----|-----|-----|----|----|
| C  | C  |      |      | C   | C  | C  | C   |     | C  | C  |

ORGAN COMPOSITIONS

Ahrens, Joseph  **Das Heilige Jahr**  Volume II
Willy Muller - Suddeutscher Musikverlag -
Heidelberg, New York:   C.F. Peters Corporation
Key: D

Bender, Jan   "Ye Sons and Daughters of the King"
**The Parish Organist**   Part Eight   Music for
Easter, Ascension, Pentecost and Trinity
Edited: Erich Goldschmidt   Concordia Publishing
House   97-1404   Key: C

Krapf, Gerhard   "God Christian Friends, Rejoice and
Sing"   **The Concordia Hymn Prelude Series**
Volume 10   Edited: Herbert Gotsch   Concordia
Publishing House   97-5617   Key: C

Manz, Paul  "Good Christian Men, Rejoice"  **Ten Chorale
Improvisations**  Set V Op. 14   Concordia Publishing
House 97-5257   Key: C

Martin, Gilbert  "Finale on 'Gelobt Sei Gott'"  **The
Bristol Collection of Contemporary Hymn Tunes for
Organ**  Volume 2   Edited: Lee Hastings Bristol, Jr.
Harold Flammer Inc.   Key:   C

Willan, Healey   "Gelobt sei Gott" by Melchior Vulpius
**Six Chorale Preludes**   Set I   Concordia
Publishing House   OC 220   Key: C

# FREE ACCOMPANIMENTS

Ferguson, John  **Hymn Harmonizations for Organ**
Book II  Ludwig  Music Publishing Co.  0-07
Key: C

Hillert, Richard  **Hymn Preludes and Free Accompaniments**
Volume 10  Augsburg Publishing House  11-9406
Key: C

Johnson, David N.  **Free Harmonizations of Twelve**
**Hymn Tunes**  Augsburg Publishing House  11-9190
Key: C

General Seminary

| BA | DC | 1940 | 1982 | LBW | LW | PH | RCV | UCC | UM | WB |
|----|----|------|------|-----|----|----|-----|-----|----|----|
|    |    |      | Eb   |     |    |    |     |     |    |    |

Geneva

| BA | DC | 1940 | 1982 | LBW | LW | PH | RCV | UCC | UM | WB |
|----|----|------|------|-----|----|----|-----|-----|----|----|
| F  | F  | F    | F    |     |    |    |     | F   | F  | F  |

## ORGAN COMPOSITIONS

Owens, Sam Batt  "Not Alone for Mighty Empire"  **The**
**Concordia Hymn Prelude Series**  Volume 25  Edited:
Herbert Gotsch  Concordia Publishing House
97-5740  Key: F

## FREE ACCOMPANIMENTS

Cassler, G. Winston  **Organ Descants for Selected Hymn**
**Tunes**  Augsburg Publishing House  11-9304  Key: F

**Free Harmonizations to Hymn Tunes by Fifty American**
**Composers**  Edited: D. DeWitt Wasson  Hinshaw
Music, Inc.  HMO-145  Key: F

Genevan Psalm 22

| BA | DC | 1940 | 1982 | LBW | LW | PH | RCV | UCC | UM | WB |
|----|----|------|------|-----|----|----|-----|-----|----|----|
|    |    |      |      |     |    | e  |     |     |    |    |

Gentle Jesus

| BA | DC | 1940 | 1982 | LBW | LW | PH | RCV | UCC | UM | WB |
|----|----|------|------|-----|----|----|-----|-----|----|----|
|    |    | F    |      |     |    |    |     |     |    |    |

Georgetown

| BA | DC | 1940 | 1982 | LBW | LW | PH | RCV | UCC | UM | WB |
|----|----|------|------|-----|----|----|-----|-----|----|----|
|    |    | F    | F    |     |    | F  |     |     |    |    |

Gerald

| BA | DC | 1940 | 1982 | LBW | LW | PH | RCV | UCC | UM | WB |
|----|----|------|------|-----|----|----|-----|-----|----|----|
|    |    |      |      |     |    |    |     |     | D  |    |

Germany
(See also: Gardiner; Walton)
  BA   DC   1940 1982 LBW  LW    PH   RCV  UCC  UM   WB
  Bb   A                        A        A    Bb  A

ORGAN COMPOSITIONS

Jordan, Alice "Voluntary on 'Germany'" **Worship Service Music for the Organist** Broadman Press Key:Bb

FREE ACCOMPANIMENTS

**Free Harmonizations to Hymn Tunes By Fifty American Composers** Edited: D. DeWitt Wasson  Hinshaw Music, Inc.  HMO-145  Key: A

Goode, Jack C. **Thirty-Four Changes on Hymn Tunes** H.W. Gray Co.  GB 644  Key: Bb

Gerontius
  BA   DC   1940 1982 LBW  LW    PH   RCV  UCC  UM   WB
             G    G

FREE ACCOMPANIMENTS

Noble, T. Tertius **Free Organ Accompaniments to One Hundred Well-Known HymnTunes** J. Fischer & Bros. #8175  Key: G

Gethsemane
(See also: Redhead #76)
  BA   DC   1940 1982 LBW  LW    PH   RCV  UCC  UM   WB
                 Eb  Eb

ORGAN COMPOSITIONS

Beck, Albert  **76 Offertories on Hymns & Chorales** Concordia Publishing House  97-5207  Key: Eb

Bingham, Seth  "Go to Dark Gethsemane" **Twelve Hymn-Preludes on Familiar Tunes for Organ** Set 1  H. W. Gray  GB 151  Key: Eb

Lang, C. S.  "Go to Dark Gethsemane" **The Concordia Hymn Prelude Series** Volume 7  Edited: Herbert Gotsch  Concordia Publishing House  97-5614 Key: Eb

Lenel, Ludwig  "Go to Dark Gethsemane" **The Parish Organist** Part Seven  Music for Lent, Palm Sunday and Holy Week  Edited: Erich Goldschmidt Concordia Publishing House  97-1403  Key: Eb

142

Powell, Newman W. "Go to Dark Gethsemane" **The Parish
Organist** Part One Edited: Heinrich Fleischer
Concordia Publishing House 97-1145 Key: Eb

Rotermund, Melvin "Chief of Sinners Thought I Be" **The
Concordia Hymn Prelude Series** Volume 25 Edited:
Herbert Gotsch Concordia Publishing House
97-5740 Key: Eb

FREE ACCOMPANIMENTS

Hudson, Richard **Hymn Preludes and Free Accompaniments**
Volume 12 Augsburg Publishing House 11-9408
Key: Eb

Gevaert

| BA | DC | 1940 | 1982 | LBW | LW | PH | RCV | UCC | UM | WB |
|----|----|------|------|-----|----|----|-----|-----|----|----|
|    |    | d    |      |     |    |    |     |     |    |    |

ORGAN COMPOSITIONS

Purvis, Richard "Communion"**An American Organ Mass**
Harold Flammer, Inc. Key: g

Gibbons
(See also: Song 13)

Gladness
(See also: Cas Radosti)

| BA | DC | 1940 | 1982 | LBW | LW | PH | RCV | UCC | UM | WB |
|----|----|------|------|-----|----|----|-----|-----|----|----|
|    |    |      | F    |     |    |    |     |     |    |    |

Glen
(See also: Resignation)

Glenfinlas

| BA | DC | 1940 | 1982 | LBW | LW | PH | RCV | UCC | UM | WB |
|----|----|------|------|-----|----|----|-----|-----|----|----|
|    | G  |      |      |     |    |    |     |     | G  |    |

Gloria
(See also: Iris; Angels We Have Heard On High)

| BA | DC | 1940 | 1982 | LBW | LW | PH | RCV | UCC | UM | WB |
|----|----|------|------|-----|----|----|-----|-----|----|----|
| F  | F  | F    | F    | F   | F  | F  |     | F   | F  | F  |

INTONATIONS

Hermann, David **11 Hymn Intonations, Free Accompani-
ments, Instrumental Descants for Organ** Volume I
Advent, Christmas, Epiphany G.I.A. Publications
G-2378 Key: F

# ORGAN COMPOSITIONS

Chapman, Keith "Angels We Have Heard on High"
**Christmas for Organ** McAfee Music Corp. Key: F

Gehrke, Hugo "Angels We Have Heard on High" **The
Parish Organist** Christmas and Epiphany Music
Part Six Concordia Publishing House 97-1391
Key: G

Gehrke, Hugo "Angels We Have Heard on High" **The
Concordia Hymn Prelude Series** Volume 4 Edited:
Herbert Gotsch Concordia Publishing House
97-5539 Key: F

# FREE ACCOMPANIMENTS

Diemer, Emma Lou **Hymn Preludes and Free Accompaniments**
Volume 2 Augsburg Publishing House 11-9398
Key: F

Ferguson, John **Hymn Harmonizations for Organ**
Ludwig Music Publishing Co. 0-07 Key: G

Goode, Jack C. **Thirty-Four Changes on Hymn Tunes**
H. W. Gray Co. GB 644 Key: F

Noble, T. Tertius **Fifty Free Organ Accompaniments
to Well Known Hymn Tunes** J. Fischer & Bros.
No. 8430 Key: F

Gloria Patri (Greatorex)
BA   DC   1940 1982 LBW  LW   PH   RCV  UCC  UM   WB
Eb

Gloria Patri (Meineke)
BA   DC   1940 1982 LBW  LW   PH   RCV  UCC  UM   WB
A

Gloria, laus, et honor
BA   DC   1940 1982 LBW  LW   PH   RCV  UCC  UM   WB
m:d

Glorious Name
BA   DC   1940 1982 LBW  LW   PH   RCV  UCC  UM   WB
F

Glory Song
BA   DC   1940 1982 LBW  LW   PH   RCV  UCC  UM   WB
Ab

## Glory to His Name

| BA | DC | 1940 | 1982 | LBW | LW | PH | RCV | UCC | UM | WB |
|----|----|------|------|-----|----|----|-----|-----|----|----|
| Ab |    |      |      |     |    |    |     |     |    |    |

## Go Down Moses

| BA | DC | 1940 | 1982 | LBW | LW | PH | RCV | UCC | UM | WB |
|----|----|------|------|-----|----|----|-----|-----|----|----|
|    |    |      | f    |     |    | g  |     | g   |    |    |

## Go Tell It

| BA | DC | 1940 | 1982 | LBW | LW | PH | RCV | UCC | UM | WB |
|----|----|------|------|-----|----|----|-----|-----|----|----|
| G  |    |      | F    | G   | G  | G  | G   | G   | G  | G  |

### ORGAN COMPOSITIONS

Hillert, Richard  "Go Tell it On the Mountains"  **The Concordia Hymn Prelude Series** Volume 4  Edited: Herbert Gotsch  Concordia Publishing House 97-5539  Key: G

Manz, Paul "Go Tell It on the Mountain" **Ten Chorale Improvisations** Set X  Op. 22  Concordia Publishing House 97-5557  Key: G

### FREE ACCOMPANIMENTS

Ferguson, John  **Hymn Tune Harmonizations**  Book III Ludwig Music Publishing Co.    0-10  Key: G

## God be in My Head

| BA | DC | 1940 | 1982 | LBW | LW | PH | RCV | UCC | UM | WB |
|----|----|------|------|-----|----|----|-----|-----|----|----|
|    |    |      |      |     |    | A  |     |     |    |    |

## God be With You

| BA | DC | 1940 | 1982 | LBW | LW | PH | RCV | UCC | UM | WB |
|----|----|------|------|-----|----|----|-----|-----|----|----|
| C  | Db |      |      |     |    | Db |     |     | Db |    |

### ORGAN COMPOSITIONS

Held, Wilbur  "God Be With You 'Till We Meet Again" **Gospel Hymn Settings** Hinshaw Music Co., Inc. HMO-146  Key: Db

### FREE ACCOMPANIMENTS

**Free Harmonizations to Hymn Tunes By Fifty American Composers** Edited: D. DeWitt Wasson  Hinshaw Music, Inc.  HMO-145  Key: Db

## God Cares

| BA | DC | 1940 | 1982 | LBW | LW | PH | RCV | UCC | UM | WB |
|----|----|------|------|-----|----|----|-----|-----|----|----|
| Bb |    |      |      |     |    |    |     |     |    |    |

145

God is Love

| BA | DC | 1940 | 1982 | LBW | LW | PH | RCV | UCC | UM | WB |
|----|----|------|------|-----|----|----|-----|-----|----|----|
|    |    |      |      |     |    |    |     | Db  |    |    |

God of the Ages

| BA | DC | 1940 | 1982 | LBW | LW | PH | RCV | UCC | UM | WB |
|----|----|------|------|-----|----|----|-----|-----|----|----|
|    |    |      |      |     |    |    |     |     |    | F  |

God Rest You Merry

| BA | DC | 1940 | 1982 | LBW | LW | PH | RCV | UCC | UM | WB |
|----|----|------|------|-----|----|----|-----|-----|----|----|
| d  | d  |      |      |     |    | d  | e   |     | d  | d  |

### ORGAN COMPOSITIONS

Held, Wilbur  "God Rest You Merry" **Six Carol Settings**
Concordia Publishing House  Key: e

Roberts, Myron J.  **Improvisation on "God Rest Ye Merry Gentlemen"**  H. W. Gray Co., Inc.
No. 663  Key: e

Walton, Kenneth **Fantasia on Four Christmas Carols**
Broadcast Music Inc.  Key: c

### FREE ACCOMPANIMENTS

Busarow, Donald **All Praise to You Eternal God**
Augsburg Publishing House  11-9076  Key: d & e

Noble, T. Tertius **Free Organ Accompaniments to One Hundred Well-Known Hymn Tunes**  J. Fischer & Bros.
#8175  Key: d

Golden Chain

| BA | DC | 1940 | 1982 | LBW | LW | PH | RCV | UCC | UM | WB |
|----|----|------|------|-----|----|----|-----|-----|----|----|
| F  |    |      |      |     |    |    |     |     |    |    |

Golden Sequence, The

| BA | DC | 1940 | 1982 | LBW | LW | PH | RCV | UCC | UM | WB |
|----|----|------|------|-----|----|----|-----|-----|----|----|
|    | m:d |     |      |     |    |    |     |     |    |    |

Gonfalon Royal

| BA | DC | 1940 | 1982 | LBW | LW | PH | RCV | UCC | UM | WB |
|----|----|------|------|-----|----|----|-----|-----|----|----|
|    |    | G    | G    |     |    |    |     |     |    |    |

### ORGAN COMPOSITIONS

Cundick, Robert  "Look from Your Sphere of Endless Day" **The Concordia Hymn Prelude Series**  Volume 25
Edited: Herbert Gotsch  Concordia Publishing House
97-5740  Key: G

Good Shepherd,Rosemont

| BA | DC | 1940 | 1982 | LBW | LW | PH | RCV | UCC | UM | WB |
|---|---|---|---|---|---|---|---|---|---|---|
| | | C | | | | | | | | |

Goodness

| BA | DC | 1940 | 1982 | LBW | LW | PH | RCV | UCC | UM | WB |
|---|---|---|---|---|---|---|---|---|---|---|
| Eb | | | | | | | | | | |

Gopsal

| BA | DC | 1940 | 1982 | LBW | LW | PH | RCV | UCC | UM | WB |
|---|---|---|---|---|---|---|---|---|---|---|
| | | | C | | | | | | | |

Gordon

| BA | DC | 1940 | 1982 | LBW | LW | PH | RCV | UCC | UM | WB |
|---|---|---|---|---|---|---|---|---|---|---|
| F | | | | | | | | | F | |

ORGAN COMPOSITIONS

Goode, Jack **Seven Communion Meditations** Harold
Flammer, Inc. HF-5084 Key: F

Gosterwood

| BA | DC | 1940 | 1982 | LBW | LW | PH | RCV | UCC | UM | WB |
|---|---|---|---|---|---|---|---|---|---|---|
| | | | | | | | | | | F |

Gott der Vater wohn uns bei

| BA | DC | 1940 | 1982 | LBW | LW | PH | RCV | UCC | UM | WB |
|---|---|---|---|---|---|---|---|---|---|---|
| | | | | m:c | m:c | | | | | |

ORGAN COMPOSITIONS

Bach, J.S. **Orgelwerke** Volume VI C.F. Peters
Corporation Nr. 245 Key: D

Busarow, Donald "God the Father, Be Our Stay" **The
Concordia Hymn Prelude Series** Volume 25 Edited:
Herbert Gotsch Concordia Publishing House
97-5740 Key: C

Buxtehude, Dietrich **Orgelwerke II: Chorale Preludes**
C.F. Peters Corporation #4457 Key:C

Manz, Paul "God the Father, Be Our Stay" **Ten Chorale
Improvisations** Set IV Op. 10 Concordia Publishing House 97-4951 Key: C

Micheelsen, Hans Friedrich "Triune God, Oh, Be Our
Stay" **The Concordia Hymn Prelude Series**
Volume 13 Edited: Herbert Gotsch Concordia
Publishing House 97-5610 Key: C

147

Pachelbel, Johann **Chorale Preludes by Masters of the 17th and 18th Centuries** Volume I Edited: Walter Buszin Concordia Publishing House key: C

Scheidt, Samuel **80 Chorale Preludes – German Masters of the 17th and 18th Centuries** Edited: Hermann Keller C.F. Peters Corporation #4448 Key: C

Gott des Himmels

| BA | DC | 1940 | 1982 | LBW | LW | PH | RCV | UCC | UM | WB |
|----|----|------|------|-----|----|----|-----|-----|----|----|
|    |    |      |      | G   |    | G  |     |     |    |    |

ORGAN COMPOSITIONS

Heaton, Charles Huddleston "Maker of the Earth and Heaven" **The Concordia Hymn Prelude Series** Volume 25 Edited: Herbert Gotsch Concordia Publishing House 97-5740 Key: G

Karg-Elert, Sigfrid "God Of the Heavens and the Earth" **Choral Improvisations for Organ for Ascensiontide and Pentecost** Op. 65 Volume 4 Edited: Robert Leech Bedell Edward B. Marks Music Corp. Key: A

Marpurg, Friedrich Wilhelm **Twenty-One Chorale Preludes** Edited: Robert M. Johnson Augsburg Publishing House 11-9506 Key: G

Reger, Max **Chorale Preludes for the Church Year from Max Reger, Op. 67** Edited: Alec Wyton Carl Fischer, Inc. 0-4667 Key: A

Walther, Johann Gottfried **80 Chorale Preludes – German Masters of the 17th and 18th Centuries** Edited: Hermann Keller C.F. Peters Corporation #4448 Key: G

Walcha, Helmut **Chorale Preludes** II C.F. Peters Corporation Nr. 4871 Key: G

FREE ACCOMPANIMENTS

**Free Harmonizations to Hymn Tunes by Fifty American Composers** Edited: D. DeWitt Wasson Hinshaw Music, Inc. HMO-145 Key: G

Gott sei Dank

| BA | DC | 1940 | 1982 | LBW | LW | PH | RCV | UCC | UM | WB |
|----|----|------|------|-----|----|----|-----|-----|----|----|
| C  |    |      | C    | C   | C  | C  | C   |     |    | C  |

## INTONATIONS

McCormick, David  **20 Organ Intonations on Hymns of Praise**  Hope Publishing Co.  Key: G

## ORGAN COMPOSITIONS

Garske, Herbert  "Spread the Reight of God the Lord"  **The Concordia Hymn Prelude Series**  Volume 26  Edited: Herbert Gotsch  Concordia Publishing House  97-5741  Key: C

Gieseke, Richard W.  "Jesus! Name of Wondrous Love"  **The Concordia Hymn Prelude Series**  Volume 14  Edited: Herbert Gotsch  Concordia Publishing House  97-5705  Key: C

Lenel, Ludwig  "To Thy Temple I Repair"  **The Parish Organist**  Part One  Edited: Heinrich Fleischer  Concordia Publishing House  97-1145  Key:  D

Thalben-Ball, George  **113 Variations on Hymn Tunes**  Novello & Co., Ltd.  Key: D

## FREE ACCOMPANIMENTS

**Free Harmonizations to Hymn Tunes By Fifty American Composers**  Edited: D. DeWitt Wasson  Hinshaw Music, Inc.  HMO-145  Key: C

Krapf, Gerhard  **Hymn Preludes and Free Accompaniments**  Volume 13  Augsburg Publishing House  11-9409  Key: C

Post, Piet  **Free Organ Accompaniments to Hymns**  Volume II  Advent-Christmas-Epiphany  Augsburg Publishing House  11-9187  Key: D

Gott sei gelobet und gebenedeiet
| BA | DC | 1940 | 1982 | LBW | LW | PH | RCV | UCC | UM | WB |
|----|----|------|------|-----|----|----|----|-----|----|----|
|    |    | m:g  | m:g  | m:g |    |    |    |     |    |    |

## ORGAN COMPOSITIONS

Henning, Walter  "O Lord, We Praise You"  **The Concordia Hymn Prelude Series**  Volume 17  Edited: Herbert Gotsch  Concordia Publishing House  97-5708  Key: G

Orr, Charles W.  "O Lord We Praise You"  **Hymn Preludes for Holy Communion**  Volume 2  Concordia Publishing House  97-5487  Key: G

149

Pepping, Ernst **Praeludia Postludia** I  B. Schott's
Sohne  Edition 6040  Key: C

Scheidemann, Heinrich  **Chorale Preludes by Masters
of the 17th and 18th Centuries**  Volume I  Edited:
Walter Buszin  Concordia Publishing House
Key: m:g

Scheidemann, Heinrich **80 Chorale Preludes – German
Masters of the 17th and 18th Centuries**  Edited:
Hermann Keller  C.F. Peters Corporatin #4448
Key: G

Scheidt, Samuel "O Lord, We Praise Thee" **Organ
Compositions for the Communion Service** Edited:
Paul Bunjes  Concordia Publishing House
#97-1395  Key: G

## FREE ACCOMPANIMENTS

Shack, David **Hymn Preludes and Free Accompaniments**
Volume 11  Augsburg Publishing House  11-9407
Key: G

<u>Gott Vater sei gepriesen</u>

| BA | DC | 1940 | 1982 | LBW | LW | PH | RCV | UCC | UM | WB |
|----|----|------|------|-----|----|----|-----|-----|----|----|
|    |    |      |      |     |    |    | G   |     |    |    |

<u>Gott will's machen</u>

| BA | DC | 1940 | 1982 | LBW | LW | PH | RCV | UCC | UM | WB |
|----|----|------|------|-----|----|----|-----|-----|----|----|
|    |    |      |      |     |    |    | F   |     |    |    |

## ORGAN COMPOSITIONS

Thalben-Ball, George **113 Variations on Hymn Tunes**
Novello & Co., Ltd.  Key: G

<u>Gottes Sohn ist kommen</u>
(See also: Gott, durch deine Güte)

| BA | DC | 1940 | 1982 | LBW | LW | PH | RCV | UCC | UM | WB |
|----|----|------|------|-----|----|----|-----|-----|----|----|
|    |    | Eb   | Eb   | Eb  |    |    | F   |     |    |    |

## ORGAN COMPOSITIONS

Bach, J. S.  **Organ Works**  Volume 1  Edited: Heinz-
Harald Lohlein  Urtext of the New Bach Edition
Barenreiter  5171  Key: F

Bach, J. S.  **Organ Works**  Volume 3  "The Individually
Transmitted Organ Chorales"  Edited: Hans Klotz
Urtext of the New Bach Edition  Bärenreiter
5173  Key: G

Bach, J.S. **Organ Works** Volume VI   Widor-Schweitzer
    G. Schirmer   Key: F, Key: G

Bach, J.S. **Organ Works** Volume VII   Widor-Schweitzer
    G. Schirmer   Key: F

Bach, J.S. **Orgelwerke** Volume V   C.F. Peters
    Corporation Nr. 245 (Two settings) Key: F, Key: F

Bach, J. S. **Orgelwerke** Volume VI   C.F. Peters
    Corporation  Nr. 245  Key: G

Bach, J.S. **The Liturgical Year** (Orgelbuchlein)
    Edited: Albert Reimenschneider  Oliver Ditson Co.
    Key: F

Bach, J.S. "Once He Came in Blessing" **The Parish
Organist** Part Five  Advent and Christmas Music
    Concordia Publishing House  97-1382  Key:  F

Bobb, Barry L.  "Once He Came in Blessing" **The
Concordia Hymn Prelude Series** Volume 26
    Edited: Herbert Gotsch  Concordia Publishing House
    97-5741  Key: Eb

Dupre, Marcel  **Seventy-Nine Chorales for the Organ**
    Opus 28  H. W. Gray  Key: F

Manz, Paul "Once He Came in Blessing" **Ten Chorale
Improvisations** Set X  Op. 22  Concordia
    Publishing House 97-5557  Key: F

Pepping, Ernst  **Fünfundzwanzig Orgelchorale**  Edition
    Schott 4723  B. Schott's Sohne  Key: m:eb

Petzold, Johannes  "Once He Came in Blessing" **The
Concordia Hymn Prelude Series** Volume 1  Concordia
    Publishing House  97-5536  Key: Eb

Walcha, Helmut **Chorale Preludes** II  C.F. Peters
    Corporation  Nr. 4871  Key: F

FREE ACCOMPANIMENTS

Bunjes, Paul **New Organ Accompaniments for Hymns**
    Concordia Publishing House  97-5348  Key: Eb

Krapf, Gerhard  **Hymn Preludes and Free Accompaniments**
    Volume 13  Augsburg Publishing House  11-9409
    Key: Eb

151

## Gottlob, es geht nunmehr zu Ende

| BA | DC | 1940 | 1982 | LBW | LW | PH | RCV | UCC | UM | WB |
|----|----|------|------|-----|----|----|-----|-----|----|----|
|    |    |      |      | G   | F  | G  |     |     |    | F  |

### ORGAN COMPOSITIONS

Schalk, Carl  "The Death of Jesus Christ, Our Lord" **The Concordia Hymn Prelude Series**  Volume 7 Edited: Herbert Gotsch  Concordia Publishing House  97-5614  Key: e

Stearns, Peter Pindar  **Twenty Hymn Preludes** Coburn Press (Theodore Presser Company) Key: G

## Gottschalk
(See also: Mercy)

| BA | DC | 1940 | 1982 | LBW | LW | PH | RCV | UCC | UM | WB |
|----|----|------|------|-----|----|----|-----|-----|----|----|

## Grace Church

| BA | DC | 1940 | 1982 | LBW | LW | PH | RCV | UCC | UM | WB |
|----|----|------|------|-----|----|----|-----|-----|----|----|
| F  |    |      |      |     |    | F  |     |     |    |    |

### ORGAN COMPOSITIONS

Krapf, Gerhard  "Lord Jesus Christ, We Humble Pray" **The Concordia Hymn Prelude Series**  Volume 17 Edited: Herbert Gotsch  Concordia Publishing House 97-5708  Key: F

Rohlig, Harald "Lord Jesus Christ, We Humbly Pray" **Hymn Preludes for Holy Communion** Volume 2 Concordia Publishing House 97-5487  Key: F

### FREE ACCOMPANIMENTS

Busarow, Donald **All Praise to You Eternal God** Augsburg Publishing House  11-9076  Key: F

Noble, T. Tertius  **Free Organ Accompaniments to One Hundred Well-Known Hymn Tunes**  J. Fischer & Bros. #8175  Key: F

## Grace Church, Gananoque

| BA | DC | 1940 | 1982 | LBW | LW | PH | RCV | UCC | UM | WB |
|----|----|------|------|-----|----|----|-----|-----|-----|----|----|
|    |    |      |      | m:b | m:b|    |     |     | m:c |    |

### ORGAN COMPOSITIONS

Lovelace, Austin C.  "Fight the Good Fight" **The Concordia Hymn Prelude Series**  Volume 26 Edited: Herbert Gotsch  Concordia Publishing House  97-5741  Key: m:b

Gracias
| BA | DC | 1940 | 1982 | LBW | LW | PH | RCV | UCC | UM | WB |
|----|----|------|------|-----|----|----|-----|-----|----|----|
|    | F  |      |      |     |    |    |     |     |    |    |

Gräfenberg
(See also: Nun danket all')
| BA | DC | 1940 | 1982 | LBW | LW | PH | RCV | UCC | UM | WB |
|----|----|------|------|-----|----|----|-----|-----|----|----|
| F  | F  |      |      |     |    |    |     |     | F  | F  |

### FREE ACCOMPANIMENTS

**Free Harmonizations to Hymn Tunes By Fifty American Composers** Edited: D. DeWitt Wasson Hinshaw Music, Inc. HMO-145 Key: F

Grafton
| BA | DC | 1940 | 1982 | LBW | LW | PH | RCV | UCC | UM | WB |
|----|----|------|------|-----|----|----|-----|-----|----|----|
|    |    |      | Eb   |     |    |    |     |     |    |    |

Grand Isle
| BA | DC | 1940 | 1982 | LBW | LW | PH | RCV | UCC | UM | WB |
|----|----|------|------|-----|----|----|-----|-----|----|----|
|    |    | C    | C    |     |    | C  |     | C   |    |    |

### FREE ACCOMPANIMENTS

**Free Harmonizations to Hymn Tunes By Fifty American Composers** Edited: D. DeWitt Wasson Hinsaw Music, Inc. HMO-145 Key: C

Grand Prairie
| BA | DC | 1940 | 1982 | LBW | LW | PH | RCV | UCC | UM | WB |
|----|----|------|------|-----|----|----|-----|-----|----|----|
|    |    |      | Eb   |     |    |    |     |     |    |    |

Granton
| BA | DC | 1940 | 1982 | LBW | LW | PH | RCV | UCC | UM | WB |
|----|----|------|------|-----|----|----|-----|-----|----|----|
|    |    |      |      | C   | C  |    |     |     |    |    |

### ORGAN COMPOSITIONS

Hillert, Richard "Amid the World's Bleak Wilderness"
**The Concordia Hymn Prelude Series** Volume 26
Edited: Herbert Gotsch Concordia Publishing House
97-5741 Key: C

Great God, Our Source
| BA | DC | 1940 | 1982 | LBW | LW | PH | RCV | UCC | UM | WB |
|----|----|------|------|-----|----|----|-----|-----|----|----|
|    |    |      | d    |     |    |    |     |     |    |    |

Haan, Raymond H.  "Great God, Our Source" **The Concordia Hymn Prelude Series** Volume 26  Edited: Herbert Gotsch  Concordia Publishing House 97-5741  Key: d

Great Physician

| BA | DC | 1940 | 1982 | LBW | LW | PH | RCV | UCC | UM | WB |
|----|----|------|------|-----|----|----|-----|-----|----|----|
|    |    |      |      | Eb  |    |    |     |     |    |    |

Great White Host
(See also: Den Store Hvide Flok)

| BA | DC | 1940 | 1982 | LBW | LW | PH | RCV | UCC | UM | WB |
|----|----|------|------|-----|----|----|-----|-----|----|----|
|    |    |      |      | Eb  |    |    |     |     |    |    |

Greenland

| BA | DC | 1940 | 1982 | LBW | LW | PH | RCV | UCC | UM | WB |
|----|----|------|------|-----|----|----|-----|-----|----|----|
|    |    | Eb   |      |     |    | D  | Eb  |     |    |    |

## FREE ACCOMPANIMENTS

Noble, T. Tertius  **Free Organ Accompaniments to One Hundred Well-Known HymnTunes**  J. Fischer & Bros. #8175  Key: Eb

Greensleeves

| BA | DC | 1940 | 1982 | LBW | LW | PH | RCV | UCC | UM | WB |
|----|----|------|------|-----|----|----|-----|-----|----|----|
|    | e  | e    | e    | e   | e  | e  | e   |     | e  | e  |

## ORGAN COMPOSITIONS

"Christmas Prelude on Three Carols" **A Galaxy of Hymn Tune Preludes for Organ** Galaxy Music Corp. GMC 2353  (With "I Saw Three Ships - Unto Us a Child is Born")  Key: e/D/A

Cherwien, David  **Interpretations Based on Hymn-tunes** Book II  A.M.S.I.  OR-3  Key: e

Gehrke, Hugo  "What Child is This"  **The Parish Organist**  Part Five  Advent and Christmas Music Concordia Publishing House  97-1382  Key: e

Gehrke, Hugo  "What Child is This"  **The Concordia Hymn Prelude Series**  Volume 4  Edited: Herbert Gotsch  Concordia Publishing House  97-5539 Key: e

Manz, Paul "What Child is This?" **Ten Chorale Improvisations** Set VII Op. 17 Concordia Publishing House 97-5308  Key: e

Purvis, Richard "Greensleeves" **Leeds' Organ Selections**
Leeds Music Corp.  Key: e

Purvis, Richard **Greensleeves**  Leeds Music Corporation
Key: e

Vaughan Williams, Ralph  "Greensleeves"  **A Vaughan
Williams Organ Album**  Oxford University Press
Key: g

Wright, Searle **Carol-Prelude on 'Greensleeves'**  H.W.
Gray Co., Inc. No.798  Key: a

FREE ACCOMPANIMENTS

Schack, David  **Hymn Preludes and Free Accompaniments**
Volume 11  Augsburg Publishing House  11-9407
Key: e

Greenwell
| BA | DC | 1940 | 1982 | LBW | LW | PH | RCV | UCC | UM | WB |
|----|----|------|------|-----|----|----|-----|-----|----|----|
| D | | | | | | | | | | |

Gresham
| BA | DC | 1940 | 1982 | LBW | LW | PH | RCV | UCC | UM | WB |
|----|----|------|------|-----|----|----|-----|-----|----|----|
| | | F | | | | | F | | | |

Gröningen
(See also: Arnsberg; Wunderbarer Konig)

Grosser Gott
| BA | DC | 1940 | 1982 | LBW | LW | PH | RCV | UCC | UM | WB |
|----|----|------|------|-----|----|----|-----|-----|----|----|
| | F | | F | F | F | F | | F | F | F |

ORGAN COMPOSITIONS

Callahan, Charles  "Holy God, We Praise Your Name"
**The Concordia Hymn Prelude Series**  Volume 26
Edited: Herbert Gotsch  Concordia Publishing House
97-5741  Key: F

Fleischer, Heinrich  "Holy God, We Praise Thy Name"
**The Parish Organist**  Part One  Edited: Heinrich
Fleischer  Concordia Publishing House  97-1145
Key: G

Held, Wilbur "Holy God, We Praise Your Name"
**Hymn Preludes for the Pentecost Season**
Concordia Publishing House 97-5517 Key: F

Johns, Donald  "Holy God, We Praise Your Name"  **The Concordia Hymn Prelude Series** Volume 13 Edited: Herbert Gotsch  Concordia Publishing House 97-5620  Key: F

Manz, Paul "Holy God, We Praise Thy Name" **Ten Chorale Improvisations** Set VIII Op. 20  Concordia Publishing House 97-5342  Key: G

Reger, Max  **30 Short Chorale Preludes** Op. 135a C.F. Peters Corporation  Nr. 3980  Key: G

FREE ACCOMPANIMENTS

Held, Wilbur  **Hymn Preludes and Free Accompaniments** Volume 6  Augsburg Publishing House  11-9402 Key: F

Grove Street

| BA | DC | 1940 | 1982 | LBW | LW | PH | RCV | UCC | UM | WB |
|----|----|------|------|-----|----|----|-----|-----|----|----|
|    |    |      |      |     |    |    |     | C   |    |    |

Gud er Gud

| BA | DC | 1940 | 1982 | LBW | LW | PH | RCV | UCC | UM | WB |
|----|----|------|------|-----|----|----|-----|-----|----|----|
|    |    |      |      | D   |    |    |     |     |    | D  |

ORGAN COMPOSITIONS

Busarow, Donald  "Lord Our God, with Praise We Come" **The Concordia Hymn Prelude Series** Volume 26 Edited: Herbert Gotsch  Concordia Publishing House 97-5741  Key: D

Gud skal alting Mage

| BA | DC | 1940 | 1982 | LBW | LW | PH | RCV | UCC | UM | WB |
|----|----|------|------|-----|----|----|-----|-----|----|----|
|    |    |      |      | F   |    |    |     |     |    |    |

ORGAN COMPOSITIONS

Held, Wilbur  "Jesu, Priceless Treasure"  **The Concordia Hymn Prelude Series**  Volume 26  Edited: Herbert Gotsch  Concordia Publishing House  97-5741 Key: F

Guds menighed syng

| BA | DC | 1940 | 1982 | LBW | LW | PH | RCV | UCC | UM | WB |
|----|----|------|------|-----|----|----|-----|-----|----|----|
|    |    | Bb   |      | A   |    |    |     |     |    |    |

Held, Wilbur   "Oh, Sing Jubilee to the Lord"  **The Concordia Hymn Prelude Series**  Volume 26   Edited: Herbert Gotsch   Concordia Publishing House 97-5741  Key: A

<u>Guidetti</u>

| BA | DC | 1940 | 1982 | LBW | LW | PH | RCV | UCC | UM | WB |
|----|----|------|------|-----|----|----|-----|-----|----|----|
|    |    | F    |      |     |    |    |     |     |    |    |

<u>Gwalchmai</u>

| BA | DC | 1940 | 1982 | LBW | LW | PH | RCV | UCC | UM | WB |
|----|----|------|------|-----|----|----|-----|-----|----|----|
| G  | G  |      |      |     |    | G  |     |     |    |    |

ORGAN COMPOSITIONS

Purvis, Richard "Gwalchmai" **Leeds' Organ Selections** Leeds Music Corp.  Key: G

Thalben-Ball, George  **113 Variations on Hymn Tunes** Novello & Co., Ltd.  Key: G

FREE ACCOMPANIMENTS

Coleman, Henry  **Varied Hymn Accompaniments** Oxford University Press  Key: G

**Free Harmonizations to Hymn Tunes By Fifty American Composers**  Edited: D. DeWitt Wasson   Hinshaw Music, Inc.  HMO-145   Key: G

# H

<u>Haf trones lampa färdig</u>

| BA | DC | 1940 | 1982 | LBW | LW | PH | RCV | UCC | UM | WB |
|----|----|------|------|-----|----|----|-----|-----|----|----|
|    |    |      |      | Ab  |    |    |     |     |    |    |

ORGAN COMPOSITIONS

Hahn, Harvey E.  "Rejoice, Rejoice, Believers"  **The Concordia Hymn Prelude Series**  Volume 1  Concordia Publishing House  97-5536  Key: Ab

<u>Halifax</u>

| BA | DC | 1940 | 1982 | LBW | LW | PH | RCV | UCC | UM | WB |
|----|----|------|------|-----|----|----|-----|-----|----|----|
|    |    | f    | f    |     |    | f  |     |     | f  |    |

**Free Harmonizations to Hymn Tunes By Fifty American Composers** Edited: D. DeWitt Wasson  Hinshaw Music, Inc.  HMO-145  Key: f

Hall

| BA | DC | 1940 | 1982 | LBW | LW | PH | RCV | UCC | UM | WB |
|----|----|------|------|-----|----|----|-----|-----|----|----|
| Eb |    |      | F    |     |    |    |     |     |    | Eb |

Halle

| BA | DC | 1940 | 1982 | LBW | LW | PH | RCV | UCC | UM | WB |
|----|----|------|------|-----|----|----|-----|-----|----|----|
|    |    | g    |      |     |    |    |     |     |    |    |

Hallelujah! What a Savior

| BA | DC | 1940 | 1982 | LBW | LW | PH | RCV | UCC | UM | WB |
|----|----|------|------|-----|----|----|-----|-----|----|----|
| Bb |    |      |      |     |    |    |     |     |    |    |

Halton Holgate

| BA | DC | 1940 | 1982 | LBW | LW | PH | RCV | UCC | UM | WB |
|----|----|------|------|-----|----|----|-----|-----|----|----|
|    |    |      | D    |     |    |    |     |     |    |    |

Hamburg

| BA | DC | 1940 | 1982 | LBW | LW | PH | RCV | UCC | UM | WB |
|----|----|------|------|-----|----|----|-----|-----|----|----|
| F  | F  | F    |      |     | F  | F  | F   | F   | F  | F  |

ORGAN COMPOSITIONS

Bunjes, Paul  "When I Survey the Wondrous Cross" **The Parish Organist** Part Two  Edited: Heinrich Fleischer Concordia Publishing House  97-1151 Key: F

McKinley, Carl **Ten Hymn Tune Fantasies**  H.W. Gray Key: F

Miles, Russell Hancock **Three Improvisations** The Arthur P. Schmidt Co.  Key: F

Schalk, Carl  "When I Survey the Wondrous Cross" **The Concordia Hymn Prelude Series** Volume 7 Edited: Herbert Gotsch  Concordia Publishing House 97-5614  Key: F

FREE ACCOMPANIMENTS

Cassler, G. Winston **Organ Descants for Selected Hymn Tunes** Augsburg Publishing House  11-9304  Key: F

Hancock, Gerre **Organ Improvisations for Hymn-Singing** Hinshaw Music Co.  HMO-100  Key: F

Noble, T. Tertius **Free Organ Accompaniments to One Hundred Well-Known Hymn Tunes** J. Fischer & Bros. #8175 Key: F

<u>Hampton</u>

| BA | DC | 1940 | 1982 | LBW | LW | PH | RCV | UCC | UM | WB |
|----|----|------|------|-----|----|----|-----|-----|----|----|
|    |    |      | G    |     |    |    |     |     |    |    |

<u>Hampton Poyle</u>

| BA | DC | 1940 | 1982 | LBW | LW | PH | RCV | UCC | UM | WB |
|----|----|------|------|-----|----|----|-----|-----|----|----|
|    | F  |      |      |     |    |    |     |     |    |    |

<u>Hanford</u>

| BA | DC | 1940 | 1982 | LBW | LW | PH | RCV | UCC | UM | WB |
|----|----|------|------|-----|----|----|-----|-----|----|----|
|    |    | D    |      |     |    |    |     |     |    |    |

<u>Hankey</u>
(See also: I Love to Tell the Story)

| BA | DC | 1940 | 1982 | LBW | LW | PH | RCV | UCC | UM | WB |
|----|----|------|------|-----|----|----|-----|-----|----|----|
| Ab |    |      |      | Ab  |    | Ab |     | Ab  | Ab |    |

## ORGAN COMPOSITIONS

Held, Wilbur "I Love to Tell the Story" **Gospel Hymn Settings** Hinshaw Music Co., Inc. HMO-146 Key: Ab

Schack, David "I Love to Tell the Story" **The Concordia Hymn Prelude Series** Volume 26 Edited: Herbert Gotsch Concordia Publishing House 97-5741 Key: Ab

## FREE ACCOMPANIMENTS

**Free Harmonizations to Hymn Tunes By Fifty American Composers** Edited: D. DeWitt Wasson Hinshaw Music, Inc. HMO-145 Key: Ab

<u>Hannah</u>

| BA | DC | 1940 | 1982 | LBW | LW | PH | RCV | UCC | UM | WB |
|----|----|------|------|-----|----|----|-----|-----|----|----|
| C  |    |      |      |     |    |    |     |     |    |    |

<u>Hanover</u>

| BA | DC | 1940 | 1982 | LBW | LW | PH | RCV | UCC | UM | WB |
|----|----|------|------|-----|----|----|-----|-----|----|----|
| G  | G  | G    | G    | G   | G  | G  | G   | G   | Ab |    |

## INTONATIONS

McCormick, David **20 Organ Intonations on Hymns of Praise** Hope Publishing Co. Key: G

ORGAN COMPOSITIONS

Cherwien, David **Interpretations Based on Hymn-tunes**
A.M.S.I.   OR-1   Key: G

Haan, Raymond H.   **Festival Hymn Preludes**   The Sacred
Music Press   KK 329-3   Key: G

Mudde, Willem   "O Worship the King"   **The Parish
Organist**   Part Eleven   Edited: Willem Mudde
Concordia Publishing House   97-4758   Key: G

Schalk, Carl   "Oh, Worship the King"   **The Concordia
Hymn Prelude Series**   Volume 26   Edited: Herbert
Gotsch   Concordia Publishing House   97-5741
Key: G

Thalben-Ball, George   **113 Variations on Hymn Tunes**
Novello & Co., Ltd.   Key: Ab

FREE ACCOMPANIMENTS

Carson, J. Bert   **Hymn Preludes and Free Accompaniments**
Volume 16   Augsburg Publishing House   11-9412
Key: G

Cassler, G. Winston **Organ Descants for Selected Hymn
Tunes**   Augsburg Publishing House   11-9304   Key: Ab

Goode, Jack C.   **Thirty-Four Changes on Hymn Tunes**
H. W. Gray Co.   GB 644   Key: G

Noble, T. Tertius   **Free Organ Accompaniments to One
Hundred Well-Known Hymn Tunes**   J. Fischer & Bros.
#8175   Key: G

Ore, Charles   **Hymn Preludes and Free Accompaniments**
Volume 7   Augsburg Publishing House 11-9403
Key: G

Wyton, Alec   **New Shoots from Old Routes**   The Sacred
Music Press   KK  279   Key: G

<u>Hanson Place</u>
    BA   DC   1940 1982 LBW  LW    PH    RCV   UCC   UM    WB
    D

<u>Happy Day</u>
    BA   DC   1940 1982 LBW  LW    PH    RCV   UCC   UM    WB
    F

## Harewood
| BA | DC | 1940 | 1982 | LBW | LW | PH | RCV | UCC | UM | WB |
|----|----|------|------|-----|----|----|-----|-----|----|----|
|    |    |      |      |     |    | G  |     |     |    |    |

## Harlech
| BA | DC | 1940 | 1982 | LBW | LW | PH | RCV | UCC | UM | WB |
|----|----|------|------|-----|----|----|-----|-----|----|----|
|    |    |      |      |     |    |    |     | G   |    |    |

## Harper Memorial
| BA | DC | 1940 | 1982 | LBW | LW | PH | RCV | UCC | UM | WB |
|----|----|------|------|-----|----|----|-----|-----|----|----|
| F  |    |      |      |     |    |    |     |     |    |    |

## Harris
| BA | DC | 1940 | 1982 | LBW | LW | PH | RCV | UCC | UM | WB |
|----|----|------|------|-----|----|----|-----|-----|----|----|
| Bb |    |      |      |     |    |    |     |     |    |    |

## Hartford
| BA | DC | 1940 | 1982 | LBW | LW | PH | RCV | UCC | UM | WB |
|----|----|------|------|-----|----|----|-----|-----|----|----|
| G  |    |      |      |     |    |    |     |     |    |    |

## Harts
| BA | DC | 1940 | 1982 | LBW | LW | PH | RCV | UCC | UM | WB |
|----|----|------|------|-----|----|----|-----|-----|----|----|
| Ab |    |      |      |     |    |    |     |     |    |    |

## ORGAN COMPOSITIONS

Thalben-Ball, George  **113 Variations on Hymn Tunes**
Novello & Co., Ltd.  Key: Ab

## Haslemere
| BA | DC | 1940 | 1982 | LBW | LW | PH | RCV | UCC | UM | WB |
|----|----|------|------|-----|----|----|-----|-----|----|----|
|    | F  |      |      |     |    |    |     |     |    |    |

## Hastings-on-Hudson
| BA | DC | 1940 | 1982 | LBW | LW | PH | RCV | UCC | UM | WB |
|----|----|------|------|-----|----|----|-----|-----|----|----|
|    | Eb |      |      |     |    |    |     |     |    |    |

## Haven of Rest
| BA | DC | 1940 | 1982 | LBW | LW | PH | RCV | UCC | UM | WB |
|----|----|------|------|-----|----|----|-----|-----|----|----|
| Ab |    |      |      |     |    |    |     |     |    |    |

## Hayn
| BA | DC | 1940 | 1982 | LBW | LW | PH | RCV | UCC | UM | WB |
|----|----|------|------|-----|----|----|-----|-----|----|----|
| G  |    |      |      |     |    |    |     |     |    |    |

## Haydn
| BA | DC | 1940 | 1982 | LBW | LW | PH | RCV | UCC | UM | WB |
|----|----|------|------|-----|----|----|-----|-----|----|----|
|    |    |      |      |     |    |    |     |     | D  |    |

## He Leadeth Me
| BA | DC | 1940 | 1982 | LBW | LW | PH | RCV | UCC | UM | WB |
|----|----|------|------|-----|----|----|-----|-----|----|----|
| C  | D  |      |      | D   | D  |    |     |     | D  |    |

ORGAN COMPOSITIONS

Goode, Jack C.  "He Leadeth Me: Oh, Blessed Thought"
**The Concordia Hymn Prelude Series** Volume 26
Edited: Herbert Gotsch  Concordia Publishing House
97-5741  Key: D

FREE ACCOMPANIMENTS

**Free Harmonizations to Hymn Tunes By Fifty American
Composers** Edited: D. DeWitt Wasson  Hinshaw
Music, Inc.  HMO-145  Key: D

Hancock, Gerre **Organ Improvisations for Hymn-Singing**
Hinshaw Music Co.  HMO-100  Key: D

He Lifted Me
|  | BA | DC | 1940 | 1982 | LBW | LW | PH | RCV | UCC | UM | WB |
|---|----|----|------|------|-----|----|----|-----|-----|----|----|
|   |  G |    |      |      |     |    |    |     |     |    |    |

Heath
|  | BA | DC | 1940 | 1982 | LBW | LW | PH | RCV | UCC | UM | WB |
|---|----|----|------|------|-----|----|----|-----|-----|----|----|
|   |  G |    |      |   G  |     |    |    |     |     |    |    |

ORGAN COMPOSITIONS

Pearce, Thomas R.  "We Give Thee but Thine Own" **The
Concordia Hymn Prelude Series** Volume 26  Edited:
Herbert Gotsch  Concordia Publishing House
97-5741  Key: G

Heatherwood
|  | BA | DC | 1940 | 1982 | LBW | LW | PH | RCV | UCC | UM | WB |
|---|----|----|------|------|-----|----|----|-----|-----|----|----|
|   |    |    |      |      |     |    |    |     |  c  |    |    |

Heaven
|  | BA | DC | 1940 | 1982 | LBW | LW | PH | RCV | UCC | UM | WB |
|---|----|----|------|------|-----|----|----|-----|-----|----|----|
|   |  C |    |      |      |     |    |    |     |     |    |    |

Heaven Came Down
|  | BA | DC | 1940 | 1982 | LBW | LW | PH | RCV | UCC | UM | WB |
|---|----|----|------|------|-----|----|----|-----|-----|----|----|
|   |  F |    |      |      |     |    |    |     |     |    |    |

Heaven is My Home
|  | BA | DC | 1940 | 1982 | LBW | LW | PH | RCV | UCC | UM | WB |
|---|----|----|------|------|-----|----|----|-----|-----|----|----|
|   |    |    |      |      |     |  G |    |     |     |    |    |

ORGAN COMPOSITIONS

Wente, Steven  "I'm But a Stranger Here" **The Concordia
Hymn Prelude Series** Volume 26  Edited: Herbert
Gotsch  Concordia Publishing House  97-5741
Key: G

Heavy Load
<u>    BA</u>   DC    1940 1982 LBW  LW    PH    RCV   UCC   UM    WB
   F

Hebron
<u>    BA</u>   DC    1940 1982 LBW  LW    PH    RCV   UCC   UM    WB
                                                             UM — Bb

Heinlein
   (See also: Aus der Tiefe rufe ich)
<u>    BA</u>   DC    1940 1982 LBW  LW    PH    RCV   UCC   UM    WB
   d    d                         d    d

ORGAN COMPOSITIONS

Bassett, Anita Denniston **Nine Hymn-Tune Preludes**
Ludwig Music Publishing Co.  O-08  Key: d

Clokey, Joseph W. "Meditation 'Heinlein'" **Ten
Meditations on Hymn Melodies**  J. Fischer & Bro.
Key: d

Mudde, Willem  "Forty Days and Forty Nights"  **The
Parish Organist**  Part Eleven  Edited: Willem
Mudde  Concordia Publishing House  97-4758  Key: e

FREE ACCOMPANIMENTS

Noble, T. Tertius **Free Organ Accompaniments to One
Hundred Well-Known Hymn Tunes**  J. Fischer & Bros.
#8175  Key: d

Helmsley
<u>    BA</u>   DC    1940 1982 LBW  LW    PH    RCV   UCC   UM    WB
            D       G      G

ORGAN COMPOSITIONS

Held, Wilbur  "Lo, He Comes with Clouds Descending"
**The Concordia Hymn Prelude Series**  Volume 1
Concordia Publishing House  97-5536  Key: G

FREE ACCOMPANIMENTS

**Free Harmonizations to Hymn Tunes By Fifty American
Composers**  Edited: D. DeWitt Wasson  Hinshaw
Music, Inc.  HMO-145  Key: G

Hendon
<u>    BA</u>   DC    1940 1982 LBW  LW    PH    RCV   UCC   UM    WB
   F                                         F    F

ORGAN COMPOSITIONS

Jordan, Alice "Ask Ye What Great Thing I Know"
**A Season and a Time** Broadman Press 4570-37
Key: F

Lovelace, Austin "Ask ye what great thing I know"
**Eight Hymn Preludes** Augsburg Publishing House
11-9144 Key: G

Her kommer dine arme Smaa

| BA | DC | 1940 | 1982 | LBW | LW | PH | RCV | UCC | UM | WB |
|----|----|------|------|-----|----|----|-----|-----|----|----|
|    |    |      | F    |     |    |    |     |     |    |    |

ORGAN COMPOSITIONS

Cassler, G. Winston  "Your Little Ones, Dear Lord"
**The Concordia Hymn Prelude Series** Volume 4
Edited: Herbert Gotsch  Concordia Publishing
House  97-5539  Key: F

Her vil ties

| BA | DC | 1940 | 1982 | LBW | LW | PH | RCV | UCC | UM | WB |
|----|----|------|------|-----|----|----|-----|-----|----|----|
|    |    |      | G    |     |    |    |     |     |    |    |

ORGAN COMPOSITIONS

Barlow, Wayne  "Savior, Like a Shepherd Lead Us"
**The Concordia Hymn Prelude Series** Volume 26
Edited: Herbert Gotsch  Concordia Publishing House
97-5741  Key: G

Herald, Sound

| BA | DC | 1940 | 1982 | LBW | LW | PH | RCV | UCC | UM | WB |
|----|----|------|------|-----|----|----|-----|-----|----|----|
|    |    | c    |      |     |    |    |     |     |    |    |

Hereford

| BA | DC | 1940 | 1982 | LBW | LW | PH | RCV | UCC | UM | WB |
|----|----|------|------|-----|----|----|-----|-----|----|----|
|    |    | Eb   | Eb   |     |    |    |     |     | F  |    |

Hermann
(See also: Lobt Gott ihr Christen)

| BA | DC | 1940 | 1982 | LBW | LW | PH | RCV | UCC | UM | WB |
|----|----|------|------|-----|----|----|-----|-----|----|----|
|    |    | Eb   |      |     |    |    |     | Eb  |    |    |

Hermas

| BA | DC | 1940 | 1982 | LBW | LW | PH | RCV | UCC | UM | WB |
|----|----|------|------|-----|----|----|-----|-----|----|----|
|    |    | G    | G    |     |    |    |     |     | A  |    |

ORGAN COMPOSITIONS

Ferguson, John "On Our Way Rejoicing" **The Concordia Hymn Prelude Series** Volume 26 Edited: Herbert Gotsch Concordia Publishing House 97-5741 Key: G

FREE ACCOMPANIMENTS

**Free Harmonizations to Hymn Tunes By Fifty American Composers** Edited: D. DeWitt Wasson Hinshaw Music, Inc. HMO-145 Key: G

Hermon

| BA | DC | 1940 | 1982 | LBW | LW | PH | RCV | UCC | UM | WB |
|----|----|------|------|-----|----|----|-----|-----|----|----|
|    |    |      |      |     | f  |    |     |     |    |    |

Herr Christ, der einig Gottes Sohn

| BA | DC | 1940 | 1982 | LBW | LW | PH | RCV | UCC | UM | WB |
|----|----|------|------|-----|----|----|-----|-----|----|----|
|    |    |      |      | F   | F  |    |     |     |    |    |

ORGAN COMPOSITIONS

Bach, J. S. **Organ Works** Volume 1 Edited: Heinz-Harald Löhlein Urtext of the New Bach Edition Bärenreiter 5171 Key: A

Bach, J. S. **Organ Works** Volume 3 "The Individually Transmitted Organ Chorales" Edited: Hans Klotz Urtext of the New Bach Edition Bärenreiter 5173 Key: G

Bach, J.S. **Organ Works** Volume VI Widor-Schweitzer G. Schirmer Key: G

Bach, J.S. **Organ Works** Volume VII Widor-Schweitzer G. Schirmer Key: A

Bach, J.S. **Orgelwerke** Volume V C.F. Peters Corporation Nr. 244 (Two settings) Key: A; Key: G

Bach, J.S. **The Liturgical Year** (Orgelbuchlein) Edited: Albert Reimenschneider Oliver Ditson Co. Key: A

Buxtehude, Dietrich **Orgelwerke II: Chorale Preludes** C.F. Peters #4457 Key: G

Dupre, Marcel **Seventy-Nine Chorales for the Organ** Opus 28 H. W. Gray Key: A

Scheidemann, Heinrich "The Only Son From Heaven" **The Concordia Hymn Prelude Series** Volume 6 Edited: Herbert Gotsch Concordia Publishing House 97-5612 Key: F

Walcha, Helmut **Chorale Preludes** II C.F. Peters Corporation Nr. 4871 Key: G

Walther, Johann Gottfried **80 Chorale Preludes - German Masters of the 17th and 18th Centuries** Edited: Hermann Keller C.F. Peters Corporation #4448 Key:G

Walther, Johann Gottfried **For Manuals Only** Edited: John Christopher McAfee Music Corp. Key: G

Walther, Johann Gottfried "When over Sin I Sorrow" **The Concordia Hymn Prelude Series** Volume 26 Edited: Herbert Gotsch Concordia Publishing House 97-5741 Key: F

### FREE ACCOMPANIMENTS

Hillert, Richard **Hymn Preludes and Free Accompaniments** Volume 10 Augsburg Publishing House 11-9406 Key: F

Herr Jesu Christ, dich zu uns wend

| BA | DC | 1940 | 1982 | LBW | LW | PH | RCV | UCC | UM | WB |
|----|----|------|------|-----|----|----|-----|-----|----|----|
| F  | F  | F    | F    | F   | F  | F  |     | F   | F  |    |

### ORGAN COMPOSITIONS

Armsdorf, Andreas **Chorale Preludes by Masters of the 17th and 18th Centuries** Volume I Edited: Walter Buszin Concordia Publishing House Key: F

Bach, J. S. **Organ Works** Volume 1 Edited: Heinz-Harald Löhlein Urtext of the New Bach Edition Bärenreiter 5171 Key: F

Bach, J.S. **Organ Works** Volume 2 Edited: Hans Kloz Urtext of the New Bach Edition Bärenreiter 5172 Key: G

Bach, J. S. **Organ Works** Volume 3 "The Individually Transmitted Organ Chorales" Edited: Hans Klotz Urtext of the New Bach Edition Bärenreiter 5173 Key: G

Bach, J.S. **Organ Works** Volume VI Widor-Schweitzer G. Schirmer (Two settings) Key: G

Bach, J.S. **Organ Works** Volume VII  Widor-Schweitzer
G. Schirmer  Key: F

Bach. J.S. **Organ Works** Volume VIII  Widor-Schweitzer
G. Schirmer  (Two settings) Key: G

Bach, J.S. **Orgelwerke** Volume V  C.F. Peters
Corporation  Nr. 244 (Two settings) Key: F; Key: G

Bach, J.S. **Orgelwerke** Volume VI  C.F. Peters
Corporation Nr. 245  Key: G

Bach, J.S. **Orgelwerke** Volume IX C.F. Peters
Corporation #2067  Key: G

Bach, J.S. "Lord Jesus Christ, We Humbly Pray"
**Organ Music for the Communion Service**
Edited: Paul Bunjes  Concordia Publishing House
#97-1395  Key: F

Bach, J.S. **The Liturgical Year** (Orgelbuchlein)
Edited: Albert Reimenschneider  Oliver Ditson Co.
Key: F

Bohm, Georg **80 Chorale Preludes – German Masters of
the 17th and 18th Centuries** Edited: Hermann
Keller  C.F. Peters Corporation #4448  Key: F

Dupre, Marcel **Seventy-Nine Chorales for the Organ**
Opus 28  H. W. Gray  Key: G

Karg-Elert, Sigfrid "Lord Jesus Christ Be With Us Now"
**Choral Improvisations for Organ for Passion
Week** Op. 65, Volume 2  Edward B. Marks Music Corp.
Key: G

Manz, Paul "Lord Jesus Christ, Be Present Now" **Ten
Chorale Improvisations** Set II  Op. 7  Concordia
Publishing House 97-4656  Key: F

Manz, Paul "Lord Jesus Christ, Be Present Now" **Ten
Chorale Improvisations** Set III Op. 9  97-4950
Key: F

Reger, Max **30 Short Chorale Preludes** Op. 135a
C.F. Peters Corporation  Nr. 3980  Key: F

Rotermund, Donald "Lord Jesus Christ, Be Present Now"
**The Concordia Hymn Prelude Series** Volume 27
Edited: Herbert Gotsch  Concordia Publishing House
97-5742  Key: E  (Second setting: Key: F)

Skaalen, Peter A. **Lord Jesus Christ, Be Present Now**
    Augsburg Publishing House  11-0834  Key: C/A

Walther, Johann Gottfried "Lord Jesus Christ, Be
    Present Now" **Wedding Music** Part 2  Concordia
    Publishing House 97-1370  Key: G

Walther, Johann Gottfried "Lord Jesus Christ, Be
    Present Now" **The Parish Organist** Part Two
    Edited: Heinrich Fleischer  Concordia Publishing
    House  97-1151  Key: F

Walther, Johann Gottfried  "Lord Jesus Christ, We
    Humbly Pray" **The Concordia Hymn Prelude Series**
    Volume 17  Edited: Herbert Gotsch  Concordia
    Publishing House  97-5708  Key: F

FREE ACCOMPANIMENTS

Bender, Jan  **Hymn Preludes and Free Accompaniments**
    Volume 1  Augsburg Publishing House  11-9397
    Key: F

Bunjes, Paul  **New Organ Accompaniments for Hymns**
    Concordia Publishing House  97-5348  Key: F

Cassler, G. Winston  **Organ Descants for Selected Hymn
    Tunes** Augsburg Publishing House  11-9304  Key: F

Herr Jesu Christ, du hast bereit
    BA    DC    1940 1982 LBW  LW    PH    RCV   UCC   UM    WB

ORGAN COMPOSITIONS

Wienhorst, Richard "Lord Jesus Christ, Thou Hast
    Prepared" **Organ Music for the Communion Service**
    Edited: Paul Bunjes  Concordia Publishing House
    #97-1395  Key: Bb

Herr Jesu Christ, meins
    (See also: Breslau)
    BA    DC    1940 1982 LBW  LW    PH    RCV   UCC   UM    WB
                         A    A    A                Ab

ORGAN COMPOSITIONS

Gieschen, Thomas  "Bow Down Your Ear, Almighty Lord"
    **The Concordia Hymn Prelude Series** Volume 27
    Edited: Herbert Gotsch  Concordia Publishing House
    97-5742  Key: Ab

168

Gieschen, Thomas  "Lord, Help Us Ever to Retain"  **The Concordia Hymn Prelude Series** Volume 27  Edited: Herbert Gotsch  Concordia Publishing House 97-5742  Key: A

Manz, Paul "Renew Me, O Eternal Light" **Ten Chorale Improvisations** Op. 5 Concordia Publishing House 97-4554  Key: Bb

Walther, Johann Gottfried  "Renew Me, O Eternal Light" **The Parish Organist** Part Two  Edited: Heinrich Fleischer  Concordia Publishing House 97-1151 Key: Bb

FREE ACCOMPANIMENTS

Bender, Jan  **Hymn Preludes and Free Accompaniments** Volume 1  Augsburg Publishing House  11-9397 Key: A

Bunjes, Paul  **New Organ Accompaniments for Hymns** Concordia Publishing House  97-5348  Key: Bb

Herr Jesu Christ, wahr Mensch und Gott
   BA   DC  1940 1982 LBW  LW   PH   RCV   UCC   UM   WB
                      F    d

ORGAN COMPOSITIONS

Gieschen, Thomas  "The Royal Banners Forward Go" **The Concordia Hymn Prelude Series** Volume 7 Edited: Herbert Gotsch  Concordia Publishing House  97-5614  Key: d

Herr, ich habe missgehandelt
   BA   DC  1940 1982 LBW  LW   PH   RCV   UCC   UM   WB
                      e    f

ORGAN COMPOSITIONS

Gieseke, Richard W.  "Glory be to God the Father" **The Concordia Hymn Prelude Series** Volume 13 Edited: Herbert Gotsch  Concordia Publishing House 97-5620  Key: e

Marpurg, Friedrich Wilhelm  **Twenty-One Chorale Preludes** Edited: Robert M. Thompson  Augsburg Publishing House  11-9506  Key: g

Patterson, Kimberly Kondal  "Lord, to You I Make Confession"  **The Concordia Hymn Prelude Series** Volume 26  Edited: Herbert Gotsch  Concordia Publishing House  97-5741  Key: f

Herrnhut

| BA | DC | 1940 | 1982 | LBW | LW | PH | RCV | UCC | UM | WB |
|----|----|------|------|-----|----|----|-----|-----|----|----|
|    | g  |      |      |     |    |    |     | g   |    |    |

Hervey's Litany

| BA | DC | 1940 | 1982 | LBW | LW | PH | RCV | UCC | UM | WB |
|----|----|------|------|-----|----|----|-----|-----|----|----|
|    | Ab |      |      |     |    |    |     |     |    |    |

Herzlich lieb

| BA | DC | 1940 | 1982 | LBW | LW | PH | RCV | UCC | UM | WB |
|----|----|------|------|-----|----|----|-----|-----|----|----|
|    |    |      |      | Bb  | A  |    |     |     |    |    |

## ORGAN COMPOSITIONS

Alberti, Johann Friedrich **80 Chorale Preludes – German Masters of the 17th and 18th Centuries** Edited: Hermann Keller  C.F. Peters Corporation #4448 Key: Bb

Bach, J. S.  **Organ Chorales from the Neumeister Collection** Edited: Christoph Wolff  Yale University Press/Bärenreiter 5181  Key: C

Engel, James  "Lord, You I Love with All My Heart" **The Concordia Hymn Prelude Series** Volume 27 Edited: Herbert Gotsch  Concordia Publishing House 97-5742  Key: A (Second setting: Bb)

Karg-Elert, Sigfrid "Heart-Felt Love Have I for Thee, O Lord" **Choral Improvisations for Organ for Passion Week** Op. 65, Volume 2 Edward B. Marks Music Corp.  Key: Bb

Herzlich tut mich erfreuen

| BA | DC | 1940 | 1982 | LBW | LW | PH | RCV | UCC | UM | WB |
|----|----|------|------|-----|----|----|-----|-----|----|----|
|    |    | D    | D    |     |    |    |     | D   |    |    |

## ORGAN COMPOSITIONS

Brahms, Johannes  "My Heart Abounds with Pleasure" **Eleven Chorale Preludes** Opus 122  Edited: E. Power Biggs  Mercury Music Corporation  A-260 Key: D

Brahms, Johannes **Santliche Orgelwerke** Breitkoph & Hartel  Key: D

Kalbfleisch, Roger  "The Day of Resurrection" **The Concordia Hymn Prelude Series** Volume 10 Edited: Herbert Gotsch  Concordia Publishing House 97-5617  Key: D

Stearns, Peter Pindar **Twenty Hymn Preludes**
Coburn Press (Theodore Presser Company) Key: C

Wienhorst, Richard "Entrust Your Days and Burdens"
**The Concordia Hymn Prelude Series** Volume 27
Edited: Herbert Gotsch Concordia Publishing House
97-5742 Key: C

Herzlich tut mich verlangen
(See also: Passion Chorale; O Sacred Head Now Wounded;
Ach Herr, mich armen Sunder)
BA   DC   1940 1982 LBW  LW   PH   RCV  UCC  UM   WB
              m:e  m:e  m:e

ORGAN COMPOSITIONS

Alwes, Charles **Six Organ Preludes** Augsburg Publishing
House   11-9416  Key: a

Bach, J. S. **Organ Works** Volume 3  "The Individually
Transmitted Organ Chorales"  Edited: Hans Klotz
Urtext of the New Bach Edition  Bärenreiter
5173  Key: m:f#

Bach, J. S. **Organ Chorales from the Neumeister
Collection** Edited: Christoph Wolff  Yale
University Press/Bärenreiter  5181  Key: m:f#

Bach, J.S. "O Sacred Head, Now Wounded" **The Parish
Organist** Part Seven  Music for Lent, Palm Sunday
and Holy Week  Edited: Erich Goldschmidt
Concordia Publishing House 97-1403  Key: m:e

Bach, J.S. "O Sacred Head, Surrounded" **The Lutheran
Organist** Compiled by John Holler  H. W. Gray Co.
Key: m:f#

Bach, J.S. **Orgelwerke** Volume V  C.F. Peters
Corporation  Nr. 244  Key: b

Bach, J.S. **Organ Works** Volume VI  Widor-Schweitzer
G. Schirmer  Key: b

Beck, Albert **76 Offertories on Hymns & Chorales**
Concordia Publishing House  97-5207  Key: m:e

Brahms, Johnnes **Samtliche Orgelwerke**
Breitkoph and Hartel No. 6062 (Two choral
preludes) Keys: a

171

Brahms, Johannes   "My Heart is Ever Yearning"
   **Eleven Chorale Preludes**  Opus 122  Edited:
   E. Power Biggs  Mercury Music Corporation  A-260
   Key: m:e

Buxtehude, Dietrich **Six Organ Preludes on Chorales**
   Edited: Henry G. Ley  Oxford University Press
   Key: e

Buxtehude, Dietrich **80 Chorale Preludes - German
   Masters of the 17th and 18th Centuries**  Edited:
   Hermann Keller  C.F. Peters Corporation Key: e

Buxtehude, Dietrich  "O Lord, to Me, Poor Sinner"
   **Anthologia Antiqua**  Book Five  **Six Chorale
   Preludes**  J. Fischer & Bros.  No. 8090  Key: m:e

Douglas, Winfred "Two Chorale Preludes" **The St. Cecilia
   Series of Lent and Easter Music** Compiled: John
   Holler  H.W. Gray  Key: b

Dupre, Marcel  **Seventy-Nine Chorales for the Organ**
   Opus 28  H. W. Gray  Key: b

Karg-Elert, Sigfrid "My Heart is Filled with Longing"
   **Choral Improvisations for Organ for Passion
   Week** Op. 65, Volume 2 Edward B. Marks Music Corp.
   Key: a

Kuhnau, Johann "O Sacred Head Now Wounded" Joseph
   Bonnet **Historical Organ-Recital**  Volume I
   **Forerunners of Bach: Hofhaimer to DuMage**
   G. Schirmer  Key: c

Manz, Paul "O Sacred Head, Now Wounded" **Ten Chorale
   Improvisations** Opus 16 Set VI 97-5305  Key: a

Marpurg, Friedrich Wilhelm **Twenty-One Chorale Preludes**
   Edited: Robert M. Thompson  Augsburg Publishing
   House  11-9506  Key: g

Pachelbel, Johann "O Sacred Head Now Wounded"  **The
   Parish Organist** Part Two  Edited: Heinrich
   Fleischer  Concordia Publishing House  97-1151
   Key: m:e

Pepping, Ernst  "O Sacred Head, Now Wounded" (rhythmic)
   **The Concordia Hymn Prelude Series**  Volume 7
   Edited: Herbert Gotsch  Concordia Publishing House
   97-5614  Key: m:e

Reger, Max "Passion Chorale 'O Sacred Head Now Wounded'" **Selected Festival Music for the Organ – Lent and Easter Services** Edited: William C. Carl Boston Music Company  Key: e

Reger, Max **30 Short Chorale Preludes** Op. 135a C.F. Peters Corporation  Nr. 3980  Key: b

Reger, Max  **Chorale Preludes for the Church Year from Max Reger, Op. 67** Edited: Alec Wyton  Carl Fischer, Inc.  0-4667  Key: m:e

Stearns, Peter Pindar **Eight Hymn Preludes for Lent** Harold Flammer, Inc.  HF-5133  Key: m:e

Walther, Johann Gottfried  **80 Chorale Preludes – German Masters of the 17th and 18th Centuries** Edited: Hermann Keller  C.F. Peters Corporation #4448 Key: e

Walther, Johann Gottfried **For Manuals Only** Edited: John Christopher McAfee Corp. Key: g Key: g;  Key: e

Walther, Johann Gottfried  "O Sacred Head Now Wounded" (Isorhythmic) **The Concordia Hymn Prelude Series** Volume 7  Edited: Herbert Gotsch  Concordia Publishing House  97-5614  Key: m:e

FREE ACCOMPANIMENTS

Carson, J. Bert  **Hymn Preludes and Free Accompaniments** Volume 16  Augsburg Publishing House  11-9412 Key: e

Herzliebster Jesu

| BA | DC | 1940 | 1982 | LBW | LW | PH | RCV | UCC | UM | WB |
|----|----|------|------|-----|-----|-----|-----|-----|-----|-----|
|    | f  | f    | f    | g   | g   | f   | f   | f   | f   | g   |

INTONATIONS

Manz, Paul  **Ten Short Intonations on Well Known Hymn Tunes** Augsburg Publishing House 11-9492  Key: g

Videro, Finn **Twenty-One Hymn Intonations** Concordia Publishing House 97-5004  Key: g

ORGAN COMPOSITIONS

Bach, J. S.  **Organ Chorales from the Neumeister Collection** Edited: Christoph Wolff  Yale University Press/Bärenreiter  5181  Key: m:g

Beck, Albert   **76 Offertories on Hymns & Chorales**
Concordia Publishing House   97-5207   Key: g

Brahms, Johannes **Samtliche Orgelwerke**
Breitkoph & Hartel   Key:g

Brahms, Johannes "Ah, Jesus, Dear" **Eleven Chorale
Preludes** Opus 122   Edited: E. Power Biggs
Mercury Music Corporation   A-260   Key: g

Brahms, Johannes   "O Dearest Jesus"   **The Parish
Organist**   Part Seven   Music for Lent, Palm Sunday
and Holy Week   Edited:   Erich Goldschmidt
Concordia Publishing House   97-1403   Key: g

Haase, Hans-Heinz   "O Dearest Jesus"   **The Concordia
Hymn Prelude Series** Volume 8   Edited: Herbert
Gotsch   Concordia Publishing House   97-5615
Key: g

Held, Wilbur "Ah, Dearest Jesu"   **A Suite of Passion
Hymn Settings** Concordia Publishing House
97-4843 Key: g

Karg-Elert, Sigfrid "O Blessed Jesu" **Choral Improvisations for Organ for Passion Week** Op. 65, Volume 2
Edward B. Marks Music Corp.   Key: g

Oley, Johann Christoph "O Dearest Jesus" **The Parish
Organist** Part Two   Edited:   Heinrich Fleischer
Concordia Publishing House   97-1151   Key: g

Stearns, Peter Pindar **Eight Hymn Preludes for Lent**
Harold Flammer, Inc.   HF-5133   Key: f

Walcha, Helmut **25 Chorale Preludes**   C.F. Peters
Nr. 4850   Key: g

FREE ACCOMPANIMENTS

Busarow, Donald **All Praise To You Eternal God**
Augsburg Publishing House   11-9076   Key: g & f

Carson, J. Bert   **Hymn Preludes and Free Accompaniments**
Volume 16   Augsburg Publishing House   11-9412
Key: g

Ferguson, John **Hymn Harmonizations for Organ**   Book II
Ludwig Music Publishing Co.   0-07   Key: g

Hebble, Robert   **Robert Hebble's Hymnal Companion for
Organ** Bradley Publications   CE/283A/3   Key: f

174

Ore, Charles **Hymn Preludes and Free Accompaniments**
Volume 7   Augsburg Publishing House   11-9403
Key: g

<u>Hesperus</u>

| BA | DC | 1940 | 1982 | LBW | LW | PH | RCV | UCC | UM | WB |
|----|----|------|------|-----|----|----|-----|-----|----|----|
| Eb | F  |      |      |     |    | F  |     | F   | F  |    |

FREE ACCOMPANIMENTS

**Free Harmonizations to Hymn Tunes By Fifty American
Composers** Edited: D. DeWitt Wasson  Hinshaw
Music, Inc.  HMO-145  Key: F

<u>Heut triumphiret Gottes Sohn</u>

| BA | DC | 1940 | 1982 | LBW | LW | PH | RCV | UCC | UM | WB |
|----|----|------|------|-----|----|----|-----|-----|----|----|
|    |    |      |      |     | e  |    |     |     |    |    |

ORGAN COMPOSITIONS

Bach, J. S.  **Organ Works**  Volume 1  Edited: Heinz-
Harald Löhlein  Urtext of the New Bach Edition
Bärenreiter  5171  Key: d

Bach,J.S. **Organ Works** Volume VII  Widor-Schweitzer
G. Schirmer  Key: g

Bach, J.S. **Orgelwerke** Volume V  C.F. Peters
Corporation  Nr. 244  Key: a

Bach, J.S. **The Liturgical Year** (Orgelbuchlein)
Edited: Albert Reimenschneider  Oliver Ditson Co.
Key: m:d

Johns, Donald  "Today in Triumph Christ Arose"  **The
Concordia Hymn Prelude Series**  Volume 10
Edited: Herbert Gotsch  Concordia Publishing House
97-5617  Key: m:b

<u>Hiding Place</u>

| BA | DC | 1940 | 1982 | LBW | LW | PH | RCV | UCC | UM | WB |
|----|----|------|------|-----|----|----|-----|-----|----|----|
|    |    |      |      | G   | G  |    |     |     |    |    |

ORGAN COMPOSITIONS

Busarow, Donald  "O Jesus, King Most Wonderful" (minor)
**The Concordia Hymn Prelude Series**  Volume 27
Edited: Herbert Gotsch  Concordia Publishing House
97-5742  Key: g

Zimmer, Dennis   "O Jesus, King Most Wonderful" (major)
**The Concordia Hymn Prelude Series**  Volume 27
Edited: Herbert Gotsch   Concordia Publishing House
97-5742  Key: G

### High Popples

| BA | DC | 1940 | 1982 | LBW | LW | PH | RCV | UCC | UM | WB |
|----|----|------|------|-----|----|----|-----|-----|----|----|
|    |    |      |      |     |    |    |     |     | g  | g  |

### High Road

| BA | DC | 1940 | 1982 | LBW | LW | PH | RCV | UCC | UM | WB |
|----|----|------|------|-----|----|----|-----|-----|----|----|
|    |    | C    |      |     |    |    | C   |     |    |    |

### Higher Ground

| BA | DC | 1940 | 1982 | LBW | LW | PH | RCV | UCC | UM | WB |
|----|----|------|------|-----|----|----|-----|-----|----|----|
| G  |    |      |      |     |    |    |     |     |    |    |

### Hilariter (Dirksen)

| BA | DC | 1940 | 1982 | LBW | LW | PH | RCV | UCC | UM | WB |
|----|----|------|------|-----|----|----|-----|-----|----|----|
|    |    |      | F    |     |    |    |     |     |    |    |

### Hilariter (Shaw)

| BA | DC | 1940 | 1982 | LBW | LW | PH | RCV | UCC | UM | WB |
|----|----|------|------|-----|----|----|-----|-----|----|----|
|    |    |      |      |     |    | f  |     |     |    |    |

### Hinman

| BA | DC | 1940 | 1982 | LBW | LW | PH | RCV | UCC | UM | WB |
|----|----|------|------|-----|----|----|-----|-----|----|----|
|    |    |      |      |     |    |    |     |     | F  |    |

### Hoff
(See also: Guds menighed, syng)

| BA | DC | 1940 | 1982 | LBW | LW | PH | RCV | UCC | UM | WB |
|----|----|------|------|-----|----|----|-----|-----|----|----|
|    |    |      |      | A   |    |    |     |     |    |    |

## FREE ACCOMPANIMENTS

Busraow, Donald **Hymn Preludes and Free Accompaniments**
Volume 8  Augsburg Publishing House   11-9404
Key: A

### Holborn

| BA | DC | 1940 | 1982 | LBW | LW | PH | RCV | UCC | UM | WB |
|----|----|------|------|-----|----|----|-----|-----|----|----|
|    | F  |      |      |     |    |    |     |     |    |    |

### Holcomb

| BA | DC | 1940 | 1982 | LBW | LW | PH | RCV | UCC | UM | WB |
|----|----|------|------|-----|----|----|-----|-----|----|----|
| F  |    |      |      |     |    |    |     |     |    |    |

### Holiness

| BA | DC | 1940 | 1982 | LBW | LW | PH | RCV | UCC | UM | WB |
|----|----|------|------|-----|----|----|-----|-----|----|----|
| F  |    |      |      |     |    |    |     |     | F  |    |

## Holley

| BA | DC | 1940 | 1982 | LBW | LW | PH | RCV | UCC | UM | WB |
|----|----|------|------|-----|----|----|----|----|----|----|
| | Eb | Eb | | | | | | | | |

## Hollingside

| BA | DC | 1940 | 1982 | LBW | LW | PH | RCV | UCC | UM | WB |
|----|----|------|------|-----|----|----|----|----|----|----|
| | | D | D | | | | D | | | |

### ORGAN COMPOSITIONS

Rowley, Alec  "Jesu, Lover of My Soul" **Choral Preludes based on Famous Hymn Tunes**  Volume 1 Edwin Ashdown Ltd.  Key:  Eb

### FREE ACCOMPANIMENTS

Noble, T. Tertius  **Free Organ Accompaniments to One Hundred Well-Known Hymn Tunes**  J. Fischer & Bros. #8175  Key:  D

## Holy Ghost

| BA | DC | 1940 | 1982 | LBW | LW | PH | RCV | UCC | UM | WB |
|----|----|------|------|-----|----|----|----|----|----|----|
| | | e | | | | | e | | | |

## Holy Innocents

| BA | DC | 1940 | 1982 | LBW | LW | PH | RCV | UCC | UM | WB |
|----|----|------|------|-----|----|----|----|----|----|----|
| | | e | | | | | | | | |

## Holy Manna

| BA | DC | 1940 | 1982 | LBW | LW | PH | RCV | UCC | UM | WB |
|----|----|------|------|-----|----|----|----|----|----|----|
| G | | | G | F | | | | | | |

### ORGAN COMPOSITIONS

Held, Wilbur "God Who Stretched the Spangled Heavens" **Preludes and Postludes** Volume I  Augsburg Publishing House  Key: G

Powell, Robert J.  "God, Who Stretched the Spangled Heavens" **The Concordia Hymn Prelude Series** Volume 27  Edited: Herbert Gotsch  Concordia Publishing House  97-5742  Key: F

Young, Gordon "Pastorale on 'Holy Manna'" **Contemporary Hymn Preludes** Hope Publishing Co. No. 328  Key: G

### FREE ACCOMPANIMENTS

Busarow, Donald  **All Praise to You Eternal God** Augsburg Publishing House  11-9076  Key: F

Diemer, Emma Lou **Hymn Preludes and Free Accompaniments**
Volume 2  Augsburg Publishing House  11-9398
Key: F

## Holy Mountain
(See also: Naar mit oie)

| BA | DC | 1940 | 1982 | LBW | LW | PH | RCV | UCC | UM | WB |
|----|----|------|------|-----|----|----|-----|-----|----|----|
|    |    | Ab   |      |     |    |    |     |     |    |    |

FREE ACCOMPANIMENTS

Busarow, Donald **Hymn Preludes and Free Accompaniments**
Volume 8  Augsburg Publishing House  11-9404
Key: Ab

## Holy Name
(See also: Louez Dieu)

| BA | DC | 1940 | 1982 | LBW | LW | PH | RCV | UCC | UM | WB |
|----|----|------|------|-----|----|----|-----|-----|----|----|
|    |    | G    |      |     |    |    |     |     |    |    |

## Holy Night
(See also: Stille Nacht)

| BA | DC | 1940 | 1982 | LBW | LW | PH | RCV | UCC | UM | WB |
|----|----|------|------|-----|----|----|-----|-----|----|----|
|    |    | Bb   |      |     |    |    |     |     |    |    |

FREE ACCOMPANIMENTS

Noble, T. Tertius **Free Organ Accompaniments to One
Hundred Well-Known Hymn Tunes**  J. Fischer & Bros.
#8175  Key: Bb

## Holy Offerings

| BA | DC | 1940 | 1982 | LBW | LW | PH | RCV | UCC | UM | WB |
|----|----|------|------|-----|----|----|-----|-----|----|----|
|    |    | F    |      |     |    |    |     |     |    |    |

## Homeland

| BA | DC | 1940 | 1982 | LBW | LW | PH | RCV | UCC | UM | WB |
|----|----|------|------|-----|----|----|-----|-----|----|----|
|    |    | G    |      |     |    |    |     |     |    |    |

## Horning Road

| BA | DC | 1940 | 1982 | LBW | LW | PH | RCV | UCC | UM | WB |
|----|----|------|------|-----|----|----|-----|-----|----|----|
|    |    |      |      |     |    |    |     | G   |    |    |

## Horsley

| BA | DC | 1940 | 1982 | LBW | LW | PH | RCV | UCC | UM | WB |
|----|----|------|------|-----|----|----|-----|-----|----|----|
|    |    | E    | D    |     |    | D  | Eb  |     | D  |    |

ORGAN COMPOSITIONS

Lang, C. S. **Twenty Hymn-Tune Preludes**  (First Set)
Oxford University Press  Key: Eb

Willan, Healey  "There is a Green Hill Far Away"
**The Parish Organist**  Part Eleven  Edited: Willem
Mudde  Concordia Publishing House  97-4758 Key: Eb

## FREE ACCOMPANIMENTS

Noble, T. Tertius **Fifty Free Organ Accompaniments
to Well Known Hymn Tunes**  J. Fischer & Bros.
No. 8430  Key: D

### Hosanna

| BA | DC | 1940 | 1982 | LBW | LW | PH | RCV | UCC | UM | WB |
|----|----|------|------|-----|----|----|-----|-----|----|----|
|    |    | Ab   | Ab   |     |    |    |     |     |    |    |

### Hosmer

| BA | DC | 1940 | 1982 | LBW | LW | PH | RCV | UCC | UM | WB |
|----|----|------|------|-----|----|----|-----|-----|----|----|
|    |    | G    |      |     |    |    |     |     |    |    |

### Houston

| BA | DC | 1940 | 1982 | LBW | LW | PH | RCV | UCC | UM | WB |
|----|----|------|------|-----|----|----|-----|-----|----|----|
|    |    |      | Db   |     |    |    |     |     |    |    |

### Hsuan p'ing

| BA | DC | 1940 | 1982 | LBW | LW | PH | RCV | UCC | UM | WB |
|----|----|------|------|-----|----|----|-----|-----|----|----|
|    |    |      |      |     |    | c  |     |     |    |    |

### Hudson

| BA | DC | 1940 | 1982 | LBW | LW | PH | RCV | UCC | UM | WB |
|----|----|------|------|-----|----|----|-----|-----|----|----|
| Eb |    |      |      |     |    |    |     |     |    |    |

### Humility

| BA | DC | 1940 | 1982 | LBW | LW | PH | RCV | UCC | UM | WB |
|----|----|------|------|-----|----|----|-----|-----|----|----|
|    |    |      |      |     |    |    | G   |     |    |    |

### Hummel

| BA | DC | 1940 | 1982 | LBW | LW | PH | RCV | UCC | UM | WB |
|----|----|------|------|-----|----|----|-----|-----|----|----|
|    |    |      |      |     |    | G  |     |     |    |    |

### Hungarian Mass Song

| BA | DC | 1940 | 1982 | LBW | LW | PH | RCV | UCC | UM | WB |
|----|----|------|------|-----|----|----|-----|-----|----|----|
|    |    |      |      |     |    |    | G   |     |    |    |

### Hunter's Glen

| BA | DC | 1940 | 1982 | LBW | LW | PH | RCV | UCC | UM | WB |
|----|----|------|------|-----|----|----|-----|-----|----|----|
| d  |    |      |      |     |    |    |     |     |    |    |

### Hursley

| BA | DC | 1940 | 1982 | LBW | LW | PH | RCV | UCC | UM | WB |
|----|----|------|------|-----|----|----|-----|-----|----|----|
|    |    | F    |      |     | F  | F  | F   |     | F  |    |

ORGAN COMPOSITIONS

Beck, Theodore  "Sun of My Soul, O Savior Dear"
**The Concordia Hymn Prelude Series** Volume 27
Edited: Herbert Gotsch  Concordia Publishing House
97-5742  Key: F

FREE ACCOMPANIMENTS

Cassler, G. Winston  **Organ Descants for Selected Hymn
Tunes** Augsburg Publishing House  11-9304  Key: F

Noble, T. Tertius  **Fifty Free Organ Accompaniments to
Well Known Hymn Tunes**  J. Fischer & Bros.
No. 8430  Key: F

Hyfrydol

| BA | DC | 1940 | 1982 | LBW | LW | PH | RCV | UCC | UM | WB |
|----|----|------|------|-----|----|----|-----|-----|----|----|
| F  | F  | F    | F    | F   | F  | F  | F   | F   | F  | F  |

ORGAN COMPOSITIONS

Bouman, Paul  "Lord of Glory, You Have Bought Us"
**The Concordia Hymn Prelude Series** Volume 27
Edited: Herbert Gotsch  Concordia Publishing House
97-5742  Key: F

Coleman, Henry  "Alleluia! Sing to Jesus"  **The
Concordia Hymn Prelude Series** Volume 12  Edited:
Herbert Gotsch  Concordia Publishing House
97-5619  Key: F

Harris, David S. **Ten Hymn Preludes in Trio Style**
H. W. Gray Co.  GB 643  Key: F

Held, Wilbur "Alleluia! Sing to Jesus" **Preludes and
Postludes** Augsburg Publishing House  Key:F

Manz, Paul "Lord of Glory, Who Hast Bought Us" **Ten
Chorale Improvisations** Op. 5  Concordia Publishing
House  97-4554  Key: F

Near, Gerald **Preludes on Four Hymn Tunes** Augsburg
Publishing House 11-828  Key: F

Thalben-Ball, George  **113 Variations on Hymn Tunes**
Novello & Co., Ltd.  Key: F

Vaughan Williams, Ralph **A Galaxy of Hymn Tune Preludes
for Organ** Galaxy Music Corp. GMC 2353  Key:C

Vaughan Williams, Ralph **Three Preludes**  Stainer & Bell
(Galaxy Music Corp.)  Key: C

Wienhorst, Richard  "Alleluia! Sing to Jesus"  **The Parish Organist** Part Eleven  Edited: Willem Mudde  Concordia Publishing House  97-4758  Key: F

Willan, Healey  "Hark the Songs"  **Ten Hymn Preludes** Set I  C.F. Peters Corp.  Key: D

FREE ACCOMPANIMENTS

Bunjes, Paul  **New Organ Accompaniments for Hymns** Concordia Publishing House 97-5348  Key: F

Cassler, G. Winston  **Organ Descants for Selected Hymn Tunes**  Augsburg Publishing House  11-9304  Key: F

Coleman, Henry  **Varied Hymn Accompaniments** Oxford University Press  Key: F

Ferguson, John  **Ten Hymn Tune Harmonizations** Book I Ludwig Music Publishing Co.  0-05  Key: F

**Free Harmonizations to Hymn Tunes By Fifty American Composers**  Edited: D. DeWitt Wasson  Hinshaw Music, Inc.  HMO-145  Key: F

Hancock, Gerre  **Organ Improvisations for Hymn-Singing** Hinshaw Music Co.  HMO-100  Key:  F

Hillert, Richard  **Hymn Preludes and Free Accompaniments** Volume 10  Augsburg Publishing House  11-9406 Key: F

Wetzler, Robert  **Free Organ Accompaniments to Festival Hymns**  Volume I  Augsburg Publishing House  11-9192 Key: F

Wyton, Alec  **New Shoots from Old Routes**  The Sacred Music Press  KK  279  Key: F

Hymn of Thanksgiving

| BA | DC | 1940 | 1982 | LBW | LW | PH | RCV | UCC | UM | WB |
|----|----|------|------|-----|----|----|-----|-----|----|----|
|    |    |      |      |     |    |    | G   |     |    |    |

Hymn to Joy

| BA | DC | 1940 | 1982 | LBW | LW | PH | RCV | UCC | UM | WB |
|----|----|------|------|-----|----|----|-----|-----|----|----|
| F  | G  |      | G    | G   |    | G  |     | G   | G  | G  |

ORGAN COMPOSITIONS

Engel, James  "Joyful, Joyful We Adore Thee"  **The Concordia Hymn Prelude Series**  Volume 27 Edited: Herbert Gotsch  Concordia Publishing House  97-5742  Key: G

## FREE ACCOMPANIMENTS

Diemer, Emma Lou **Hymn Preludes and Free Accompaniments**
Volume 2  Augsburg Publishing House  11-9398
Key: G

Ferguson, John  **Hymn Harmonizations for Organ**  Book II
Ludwig Music Publishing Co.  0-07  Key: G

Goode, Jack C.  **Thirty-Four Changes on Hymn Tunes**
H. W. Gray Co.  GB 644  Key: G

Wyton, Alec  **New Shoots from Old Routes**  The Sacred
Music Press  KK  279  Key: G

# I

I Am the Bread of Life

| BA | DC | 1940 | 1982 | LBW | LW | PH | RCV | UCC | UM | WB |
|----|----|------|------|-----|----|----|-----|-----|----|----|
|    |    |      | A    |     |    |    |     |     |    |    |

I am Thine

| BA | DC | 1940 | 1982 | LBW | LW | PH | RCV | UCC | UM | WB |
|----|----|------|------|-----|----|----|-----|-----|----|----|
| Ab |    |      |      |     |    |    |     |     | Ab |    |

I Himmelen, I Himmelen

| BA | DC | 1940 | 1982 | LBW | LW | PH | RCV | UCC | UM | WB |
|----|----|------|------|-----|----|----|-----|-----|----|----|
|    |    |      | A    |     |    |    |     |     |    |    |

### ORGAN COMPOSITIONS

Ferguson, John "In Heaven Above" **Behold a Host**
Augsburg Publishing House  Key: A

Heaton, Charles Huddleston  "In Heaven Above"  **The
Concordia Hymn Prelude Series**  Volume 27
Edited: Herbert Gotsch  Concordia Publishing House
97-5742  Key: A

I Love Thee

| BA | DC | 1940 | 1982 | LBW | LW | PH | RCV | UCC | UM | WB |
|----|----|------|------|-----|----|----|-----|-----|----|----|
| Eb |    |      |      |     |    |    |     |     |    |    |

### ORGAN COMPOSITIONS

Johnson, David "I Love Thee, My Lord" **Deck Thyself
with Gladness** Volume 2  Augsburg Publishing House
11-9101  Key: Eb

I Love to Tell the Story
  (See also: Hankey)

I Want to be Ready
   BA    DC    1940 1982 LBW  LW    PH    RCV   UCC   UM    WB
                                                E

I Want to be a Christian
   BA    DC    1940 1982 LBW  LW    PH    RCV   UCC   UM    WB
   Eb                               Eb          Eb    Eb

I Wonder as I Wander
   BA    DC    1940 1982 LBW  LW    PH    RCV   UCC   UM    WB
                                                g

ORGAN COMPOSITIONS

Niles, John Jacob (Arranged and adapted) **Four American
Carols for Organ** G. Schirmer, Inc.  Key: g

Ich dank dir, lieber Herre
   BA    DC    1940 1982 LBW  LW    PH    RCV   UCC   UM    WB
                                          G

ORGAN COMPOSITIONS

Bach, Johann Christoph  "Let Me Be Thine Forever"
**The Parish Organist** Part Two  Edited: Heinrich
Fleischer  Concordia Publishing House 97-1151
Key: G

Karg-Elert, Sigfrid "I thank Thee, Dear Lord"
**Choral Improvisations for Organ for Ascensiontide
and Pentecost** Op. 65 Volume 4  Edited: Robert Leech
Bedell  Edward B. Marks Music Corp.  Key: A

Karg-Elert, Sigfrid "I Thank Thee, Lord Through Thy
Dear Son" **Choral Improvisations for Organ for
Passion Week** Op. 65, Volume 2  Edward B. Marks
Music Corp.  Key: Eb

FREE ACCOMPANIMENTS

Bunjes, Paul **New Organ Accompaniments for Hymns**
Concordia Publishing House 97-5348  Key: G

Ich halte treulich still
   BA    DC    1940 1982 LBW  LW    PH    RCV   UCC   UM    WB
                                    D                       D

183

Ich heb mein Augen sehnlich auf
   BA    DC    1940 1982 LBW   LW     PH    RCV   UCC   UM    WB
                          m:c

                    ORGAN COMPOSITIONS

      Kloppers, Jacobus  "My Soul Now Magnified the Lord"
          **The Concordia Hymn Prelude Series**  Volume 14
          Edited: Herbert Gotsch  Concordia Publishing House
          97-5705  Key: m:c

Ich ruf zu dir
   BA    DC    1940 1982 LBW   LW     PH    RCV   UCC   UM    WB
                          d

                    ORGAN COMPOSITIONS

      Bach, J. S.  **Organ Works**  Volume 1  Edited: Heinz-
          Harald Löhlein  Urtext of the New Bach Edition
          Bärenreiter  5171  Key: f

Ich singe dir
   BA    DC    1940 1982 LBW   LW     PH    RCV   UCC   UM    WB
                          A

                    ORGAN COMPOSITIONS

      Hofland, Sigvart A.  "Rejoice, My Heart, Be Glad and
          Sing"  **The Parish Organist**  Part Two
          Edited: Heinrich Fleischer  Concordia Publishing
          House  97-1151  Key: Bb

      Hofland, Sigvart A.  "O Christ, Our Hope"  **The
          Concordia Hymn Prelude Series**  Volume 12  Edited:
          Herbert Gotsch  Concordia Publishing House
          97-5619  Key: A

      Polley, David  "Rejoice, My Heart, Be Glad"  **The
          Concordia Hymn Prelude Series**  Volume 27
          Edited: Herbert Gotsch  Concordia Publishing House
          97-5742  Key: A

Ich sterbe täglich
   BA    DC    1940 1982 LBW   LW     PH    RCV   UCC   UM    WB
                          C     C

                    ORGAN COMPOSITIONS

      Gehrke, Hugo "I Come, O Savior, to Thy Table"
          **Hymn Preludes for Holy Communion** Volume I
          Concordia Publishing House 97-5486 Key: C

Johnson, David "I Come, O Savior, to Your Table"
**Deck Thyself, My Soul, with Gladness**
Volume 2  Augsburg Publishing House 11-9101 Key: C

Kretzschmar, Paul  "I Come, O Savior, to Thy Table"
**The Parish Organist** Part Two  Edited:
Heinrich Fleischer  Concordia Publishing House
97-1151  Key: C

Schultz, Ralph C.  "I Come, O Saviour, to Your Table"
**The Concordia Hymn Prelude Series** Volume 17
Edited: Herbert Gotsch  Concordia Publishing House
97-5708  Key: C

FREE ACCOMPANIMENTS

Bunjes, Paul **New Organ Accompaniments for Hymns**
Concordia Publishing House  97-5348  Key: C

Ich will dich lieben
| BA | DC | 1940 | 1982 | LBW | LW | PH | RCV | UCC | UM | WB |
|----|----|------|------|-----|----|----|-----|-----|----|----|
|    |    |      |      | D   | D  |    | D   |     |    |    |

ORGAN COMPOSITIONS

Karg-Elert, Sigfrid "Thee Will I Love, My Strength and
Tower" **Choral Improvisations for Organ for Passion
Week** Op. 65, Volume 2  Edward B. Marks Music Corp.
Key: c

Kickstat, Paul  "You Will I Love, My Strength"  **The
Concordia Hymn Prelude Series** Volume 27
Edited: Herbert Gotsch  Concordia Publishing House
97-5742  Key: D

FREE ACCOMPANIMENTS

Krapf, Gerhard  **Hymn Preludes and Free Accompaniments**
Volume 13  Augsburg Publishing House  11-9409
Key: D

Ihr kinderlein kommet
| BA | DC | 1940 | 1982 | LBW | LW | PH | RCV | UCC | UM | WB |
|----|----|------|------|-----|----|----|-----|-----|----|----|
|    | Eb |      |      |     |    |    |     |     |    |    |

Immense caeli Conditor
| BA | DC | 1940 | 1982 | LBW | LW | PH | RCV | UCC | UM | WB |
|----|----|------|------|-----|----|----|-----|-----|----|----|
|    |    |      | m:e  |     |    |    |     |     |    |    |

In Babilone
| BA | DC | 1940 | 1982 | LBW | LW | PH | RCV | UCC | UM | WB |
|----|----|------|------|-----|----|----|-----|-----|----|----|
|    | G  | G    | G    | G   | G  | G  |     | G   | G  | G  |

ORGAN COMPOSITIONS

Cherwien, David  "Holy Spirit, Ever Dwelling"
  **Interpretations Based on Hymn-Tunes** Book IV
  A.M.S.I.  OR-9  Key: G

Haan, Raymond H.  "Son of God, Eternal Savior"  **The
  Concordia Hymn Prelude Series**  Volume 28
  Edited: Herbert Gotsch  Concordia Publishing House
  97-5753  Key: G

Held, Wilbur "Holy Spirit, Ever Dwelling" **Hymn Preludes
  for the Pentecost Season** Concordia Publishing
  House  97-5517  Key: G

Manz, Paul "Holy Spirit, Ever Dwelling" **Ten Chorale
  Improvisations** Set VIII Op. 20 Concordia
  Publishing House 97-5342  Key: G

Weiss, Ewald  "See the Conqueror Mounts in Triumph"
  **The Parish Organist** Part Eleven  Edited:  Willem
  Mudde  Concordia Publishing House  97-4758  Key: G

Wienhorst, Richard  "Holy Spirit, Ever Dwelling"
  **The Concordia Hymn Prelude Series**  Volume 12
  Edited: Herbert Gotsch  Concordia Publishing House
  97-5619  Key: G

FREE ACCOMPANIMENTS

Hancock, Gerre  **Organ Improvisations for Hymn-Singing**
  Hinshaw Music Co.  HMO-100  Key: G

Johnson, David N.  **Hymn Preludes and Free
  Accompaniments**  Volume 14  Augsburg Publishing
  House  11-9410  Key: G

Noble, T. Tertius  **Free Organ Accompaniments to One
  Hundred Well-Known Hymn Tunes**  J. Fischer & Bros.
  #1875  Key: G

| In Bethlehem | | | | | | | | | |
|----|----|------|------|-----|----|----|-----|-----|----|----|
| BA | DC | 1940 | 1982 | LBW | LW | PH | RCV | UCC | UM | WB |
| | | | a | | | | | | | |

| In dich hab ich gehoffet | | | | | | | | | |
|----|----|------|------|-----|----|----|-----|-----|----|----|
| BA | DC | 1940 | 1982 | LBW | LW | PH | RCV | UCC | UM | WB |
| | | | | | F | | | | | |

Bach, J. S. **Organ Works** Volume 1  Edited: Heinz-Harald Löhlein  Urtext of the New Bach Edition Bärenreiter  5171  Key: e

Bach, J. S. **Organ Works** Volume 3  "The Individually Transmitted Organ Chorales"  Edited: Hans Klotz Urtext of the New Bach Edition  Bärenreiter 5173  Key: A

Bach, Johann Christoph **Chorale Preludes by Masters of the 17th and 18th Centuries** Volume I  Edited: Walter Buszin  Concordia Publishing House  Key: F

Bach, Johann Michael  "In You, Lord, I Have Put My Trust" **The Concordia Hymn Prelude Series** Volume 28  Edited: Herbert Gotsch  Concordia Publishing House  97-5743  Key: F

Bach, J.S. **Organ Works** Volume VI  Widor-Schweitzer G. Schirmer  Key: A

Bach, J.S. **Organ Works** Volume VII  Widor-Schweitzer G. Schirmer  Key:e

Bach, Johann Christoph **80 Chorale Preludes – German Masters of the 17th and 18th Centuries**  Edited: Hermann Keller  C.F. Peters Corporation #4448 Key: f

Bach, J.S. **Orgelwerke** Volume V  C.F. Peters Corporation  Nr. 244  Key:e

Bach, J.S. **The Liturgical Year** (Orgelbuchlein) Edited: Albert Reimenschneider  Oliver Ditson Co. Key: m:e

Pepping, Ernst **Praeludia Postludia** II B. Schott's Sohne  Edition 6041  Key: m:d

In dir ist Freude
       BA    DC    1940 1982 LBW   LW    PH    RCV   UCC   UM    WB
                             F     F

Bach, J. S. **Organ Works** Volume 1  Edited: Heinz-Harald Löhlein  Urtext of the New Bach Edition Bärenreiter  5171  Key: G

Bach, J.S. **Organ Works** Volume VII  Widor-Schweitzer G. Schirmer  Key: G

Bach, J.S. **Orgelwerke** Volume V  C.F. Peters Corporation  Nr. 244  Key: G

Bach. J.S. **The Liturgical Year** (Orgelbuchlein) Edited: Albert Reimenschneider  Oliver Ditson Co. Key: G

Beck, Theodore  "In You is Gladness"  **The Concordia Hymn Prelude Series** Volume 28  Edited: Herbert Gotsch  Concordia Publishing House  97-5753 Key: F

Dupre, Marcel  **Seventy-Nine Chorales for the Organ** Opus 28  H. W. Gray  Key: G

Manz, Paul "In Thee is Gladness" **Ten Chorale Improvisations** Set IX Op. 21 Concordia Publishing House 97-5556  Key: F

Manz, Paul "In Thee is Gladness" **Ten Chorale Improvisations** Set VIII Op. 20  Concordia Publishing House 97-5342  Key: F

FREE ACCOMPANIMENTS

Schack, David  **Hymn Preludes and Free Accompaniments** Volume 11  Augsburg Publishing House  11-9407 Key: F

<u>In</u> <u>dulci</u> <u>jubilo</u>

| BA | DC | 1940 | 1982 | LBW | LW | PH | RCV | UCC | UM | WB |
|----|----|------|------|-----|----|----|-----|-----|----|----|
| F  | F  | F    | F    | F   | F  | F  | F   | F   | F  | F  |

ORGAN COMPOSITIONS

Bach, J. S.  **Organ Works**  Volume 1  Edited: Heinz-Harald Löhlein  Urtext of the New Bach Edition Bärenreiter  5171  Key: A

Bach, J. S.  **Organ Works**  Volume 3 "The Individually Transmitted Organ Chorales"  Edited: Hans Klotz Urtext of the New Bach Edition  Bärenreiter 5173  Key: A

Bach, J.S. **Organ Works** Volume VI  Widor-Schweitzer G. Schirmer (#9, 10)  Key: A; Key: G

Bach, J.S. **Organ Works** Volume VII  Widor-Schweitzer G. Schirmer  Key: A

Bach, J.S. **Orgelwerke** Volume V  C.F. Peters Corporation Nr. 244  Key: A

Bach, J.S. **Orgelwerke** Volume IX   C.F. Peters
    Corporation #2067   Key: G

Bach, J.S. **In Dulci Jubilo**   Three Preludes
    arranged in the form of a suite by John Huston.
    Galleon Press    Key: A

Bach, J.S. "Now Sing We, Now Rejoice" **The Parish
    Organist**   Christmas and Epiphany Music   Part Six
    Concordia Publishing House   97-1391   Key: G

Bach, J.S. **The Liturgical Year** (Orgelbuchlein)
    Edited: Albert Reimenschneider   Oliver Ditson Co.
    (2 settings)  Key: A

Bach, J. S.   "Chorale prelude 'In dulci jubilo'"
    (canon)  **Christmas Music for Organ**   Volume I
    Edited: C. H. Trevor   Oxford University Press
    Key: A

Bach, J. S.   "Chorale prelude 'In dulci jubilo'"
    (fantasia)  **Christmas Music for Organ**   Volume 1
    Edited: C. H. Trevor   Oxford University Press
    Key: A

Beck, Albert  **76 Offertories on Hymns & Chorales**
    Concordia Publishing House   97-5207   Key: G

Buxtehude, Dietrich **Six Organ Preludes on Chorales**
    Edited by Henry G. Ley   Oxford University Press
    Key: G

Buxtehude, Dietrich **Orgelwerke II: Chorale Preludes**
    C.F. Peters Corporation #4457   Key: G

Buxtehude, Dietrich "Chorale prelude 'In dulci
    jubilo'" **Organ Music for Christmas**   Volume 1
    Edited: C. H. Trevor   Oxford University Press
    Key: G

Dupre, Marcel  **Seventy-Nine Chorales for the Organ**
    Opus 28   H. W. Gray   Key: A

Edmundson, Garth "In Dulci Jubilo" **Christus Advenit –
    Christmas Suite No. 2**   H.W. Gray   Key: F

Held, Wilbur "Good Christian Men, Rejoice" **Six Carol
    Settings** Concordia Publishing House   Key: F

Karg-Elert, Sigfrid  **Choral Improvisation on 'In
    Dulci Jubilo'**   H.W. Gray   #27 G

Lubeck, Vincent "Good Christian Friends, Rejoice"
**The Concordia Hymn Prelude Series** Volume 4
Edited: Herbert Gotsch  Concordia Publishing
House  97-5539  Key: F

Manz, Paul "Now Sing We, Now Rejoice" **Ten Chorale
Improvisations** Set III  Op. 9  Concordia
Publishing House 97-4950  Key: F

Manz, Paul "Now Sing We, Now Rejoice" **Ten Chorale
Improvisations** Set VII Op. 17 Concordia
Publishing  House 97-5308  Key: F

Sicher, Fridolin "Now Sing We, Now Rejoice"  **The Parish
Organist**  Part Five  Advent and Christmas Music
Concordia Publishing House  97-1382  Key: G

Sowerby, Leo "Good Christian Men, Rejoice" **Advent to
Whitsuntide** Volume Four  Hinrichsen  No. 743b
Key: F

Walther, Johann Gottfried  "Chorale prelude 'In dulci
jubilo'" **Organ Music for Christmas** Volume 1
Edited: C. H. Trevor  Oxford University Press
Key: F

Zachau, Friedrich Wilhelm **80 Chorale Preludes – German
Masters of the 17th and 18th Centuries** Edited:
Hermann Keller  C.F. Peters Corporation #4448
Key: G

Zachau, Friedrich Wilhelm "Chorale Prelude on 'In dulci
jubilo'" **For Manuals Only** Edited: John Christopher
McAfee Music Corp.  Key: G

Zachau, Friedrich W.  "In Dulci Jubilo" **Short Classic
Pieces for Organ from the 16th, 17th, and 18th
Centuries** Arr.  Norris L. Stephens  J. Fischer
& Bros.  No. 9607  Key: G

FREE ACCOMPANIMENTS

Arnatt, Ronald  **Hymn Preludes and Free Accompaniments**
Volume 9  Augsburg Publishing House  11-9405
Key: F

Cassler, G. Winston  **Organ Descants for Selected Hymn
Tunes**  Augsburg Publishing House  11-9304  Key: F

Goode, Jack C.  **Thirty-Four Changes on Hymn Tunes**
H. W. Gray Co.  GB 644  Key: F

Wetzler, Robert **Free Organ Accompaniments to Festival Hymns** Volume I Augsburg Publishing House 11-9192 Key: F

Wood, Dale **New Settings of Twenty Well-Known Hymn Tunes** Augsburg Publishing House 11-9292 Key: F

<u>In Gottes Namen</u> fahren wir

| BA | DC | 1940 | 1982 | LBW | LW | PH | RCV | UCC | UM | WB |
|----|----|------|------|-----|----|----|-----|-----|----|----|
|    |    |      |      | m:g |    |    |     |     |    |    |

ORGAN COMPOSITIONS

Rotermund, Donald "Here is the Tenfold Sure Command" **The Concordia Hymn Prelude Series** Volume 28 Edited: Herbert Gotsch Concordia Publishing House 97-5743 Key: C

<u>In manus tuas</u>

| BA | DC | 1940 | 1982 | LBW | LW | PH | RCV | UCC | UM | WB |
|----|----|------|------|-----|----|----|-----|-----|----|----|
|    |    |      |      | F   |    |    |     |     |    |    |

ORGAN COMPOSITIONS

Cundick, Robert "O God, I Love Thee" **The Concordia Hymn Prelude Series** Volume 28 Edited: Herbert Gotsch Concordia Publishing House 97-5743 Key: F

<u>In paradisum</u>

| BA | DC | 1940 | 1982 | LBW  | LW | PH | RCV | UCC | UM | WB |
|----|----|------|------|------|----|----|-----|-----|----|----|
|    |    |      |      | m:eb |    |    |     |     |    |    |

<u>Indonesian Folk Tune</u>

| BA | DC | 1940 | 1982 | LBW | LW | PH | RCV | UCC | UM | WB |
|----|----|------|------|-----|----|----|-----|-----|----|----|
|    | G  |      |      |     |    |    |     |     |    |    |

<u>Infant Holy, Infant Lowly</u>
   (See also: W Zlobie Lezy)

<u>Ingredient</u>

| BA | DC | 1940 | 1982 | LBW | LW | PH | RCV | UCC | UM | WB |
|----|----|------|------|-----|----|----|-----|-----|----|----|
|    |    |      |      |     |    |    | C   |     |    |    |

<u>Innisfree Farm</u>

| BA | DC | 1940 | 1982 | LBW  | LW | PH | RCV | UCC | UM | WB |
|----|----|------|------|------|----|----|-----|-----|----|----|
|    |    |      |      | m:eb |    |    |     |     |    |    |

<u>Innocents</u>

| BA | DC | 1940 | 1982 | LBW | LW | PH | RCV | UCC | UM | WB |
|----|----|------|------|-----|----|----|-----|-----|----|----|
| D  | D  | D    |      |     | D  | D  |     |     | D  |    |

ORGAN COMPOSITIONS

Arnatt, Ronald  "Songs of Praise the Angels Sang"
**The Parish Organist** Part Eleven  Edited:
Willem Mudde  Concordia Publishing House  97-4758
Key: D

Haan, Raymond H.  "Songs of Praise the Angels Sang"
**The Concordia Hymn Prelude Series** Volume 28
Edited: Herbert Gotsch  Concordia Publishing House
97-5743  Key: D

Kerr, J. Wayne  "Saviour, Teach Me Day by Day"  **O God
Our Help in Ages Past** Broadman Press  Key: F

FREE ACCOMPANIMENTS

Noble, T. Tertius  **Fifty Free Organ Accompaniments
to Well Known Hymn Tunes**  J. Fischer & Bros.
No. 8430  Key: D

Innsbruck
(See also: O Welt, ich muss dich lassen)

| BA | DC | 1940 | 1982 | LBW | LW | PH | RCV | UCC | UM | WB |
|----|----|------|------|-----|----|----|-----|-----|----|----|
|    |    | F    |      |     |    | F  |     | F   |    |    |

ORGAN COMPOSITIONS

Johnson, David N.  "O Bread of Life from Heaven"
**Deck Thyself My Soul with Gladness** Augsburg
Publishing House 11-9157  Key: F

FREE ACCOMPANIMENTS

Cassler, G. Winston  **Organ Descants for Selected
Hymn Tunes** Augsburg Publishing House  11-9304
Key: G

Integer vitae

| BA | DC | 1940 | 1982 | LBW | LW | PH | RCV | UCC | UM | WB |
|----|----|------|------|-----|----|----|-----|-----|----|----|
|    |    |      |      |     |    | Ab |     |     |    |    |

Intercession

| BA | DC | 1940 | 1982 | LBW | LW | PH | RCV | UCC | UM | WB |
|----|----|------|------|-----|----|----|-----|-----|----|----|
|    | G  |      |      |     |    |    |     |     |    |    |

Intercessor

| BA | DC | 1940 | 1982 | LBW | LW | PH | RCV | UCC | UM | WB |
|----|----|------|------|-----|----|----|-----|-----|----|----|
|    | a  | a    | a    |     |    | a  |     |     |    |    |

ORGAN COMPOSITIONS

Sensmeier, Randall  "O God, Send Heralds"  **The Concordia Hymn Prelude Series** Volume 28 Edited: Herbert Gotsch  Concordia Publishing House  97-5743  Key: a

Thalben-Ball, George  **113 Variations on Hymn Tunes** Novello & Co., Ltd.  Key: a

Invocation
```
    BA   DC   1940 1982 LBW  LW   PH   RCV  UCC  UM   WB
                         G
```

ORGAN COMPOSITIONS

Powell, Robert J.  "Eternal God, before Your Throne" **The Concordia Hymn Prelude Series** Volume 28 Edited: Herbert Gotsch  Concordia Publishing House 97-5743  Key: G

Irby
```
    BA   DC   1940 1982 LBW  LW   PH   RCV  UCC  UM   WB
    F    F    F         F              F    G         F
```

ORGAN COMPOSITIONS

Hutchings, Arthur  **Seasonal Preludes for Organ** Novello & Company, Ltd.  Key: F

Johns, Donald  "Once in Royal David's City"  **The Concordia Hymn Prelude Series** Volume 4 Edited: Herbert Gotsch  Concordia Publishing House  97-5539  Key: F

Jordan, Alice "Procession on 'Once in Royal David's City'" **Hymns of Grateful Praise** Broadman Press  Key: F

Kerr, J. Wayne  "Once in Royal David's City"  **O God Our Help in Ages Past** Broadman Press  Key: F

Thalben-Ball, George  **113 Variations on Hymn Tunes** Novello & Co., Ltd.  Key: F

FREE ACCOMPANIMENTS

Carson, J. Bert  **Hymn Preludes and Free Accompaniments** Volume 16  Augsburg Publishing House  11-9412 Key: Eb

**Free Harmonizations to Hymn Tunes By Fifty American Composers** Edited: D. DeWitt Wasson  Hinshaw Music, Inc.  HMO-145  Key: F

## Iris
See also: Gloria

## Irish

| BA | DC | 1940 | 1982 | LBW | LW | PH | RCV | UCC | UM | WB |
|----|----|------|------|-----|----|----|-----|-----|----|----|
| Eb | Eb | D | D | | | | | | Eb | Eb |

ORGAN COMPOSITIONS

Willan, Healey **36 Short Preludes and Postludes on Well-Known Hymn Tunes** Set II  C.F. Peters Corporation  No. 6162  Key: D

## Irondale

| BA | DC | 1940 | 1982 | LBW | LW | PH | RCV | UCC | UM | WB |
|----|----|------|------|-----|----|----|-----|-----|----|----|
| F | | | | | | | | | | |

## Irons (St. Columba Irons)

| BA | DC | 1940 | 1982 | LBW | LW | PH | RCV | UCC | UM | WB |
|----|----|------|------|-----|----|----|-----|-----|----|----|
| | | F | | | | | | | | |

## Isleworth

| BA | DC | 1940 | 1982 | LBW | LW | PH | RCV | UCC | UM | WB |
|----|----|------|------|-----|----|----|-----|-----|----|----|
| | d | d | | | d | | | | | |

ORGAN COMPOSITIONS

Sensmeier, Randall "O God, Send Heralds" **The Concordia Hymn Prelude Series** Volume 28  Edited: Herbert Gotsch  Concordia Publishing House  97-5743  Key: a

## Israeli Round

| BA | DC | 1940 | 1982 | LBW | LW | PH | RCV | UCC | UM | WB |
|----|----|------|------|-----|----|----|-----|-----|----|----|
| | | 1940 | 1982 | LBW | LW | PH | RCV | m:d | UM | WB |

## Ist Gott für mich

| BA | DC | 1940 | 1982 | LBW | LW | PH | RCV | UCC | UM | WB |
|----|----|------|------|-----|----|----|-----|-----|----|----|
| | | 1940 | m:d | m:d | | | | | | |

ORGAN COMPOSITIONS

Kickstat, Paul  "If God Himself Be for Me" **The Concordia Hymn Prelude Series** Volume 28 Edited: Herbert Gotsch  Concordia Publishing House  97-5743  Key: m:d

Walcha, Helmut **25 Chorale Preludes** C.F. Peters Corporation   Nr. 4850  Key: d

Iste confessor

| BA | DC | 1940 | 1982 | LBW | LW | PH | RCV | UCC | UM | WB |
|----|----|------|------|-----|----|----|-----|-----|----|----|
| m:d | m:d | | | m:d | m:d | m:d | | | | |

INTONATIONS

Videro, Finn **Twenty-One Hymn Intonations**
Concordia Publishing House 97-5004 Key: m:d

FREE ACCOMPANIMENTS

Busarow, Donald **Hymn Preludes and Free Accompaniments**
Volume 8 Augsburg Publishing House 11-9404
Key: d

Petrich, Roger "Lord of Our Life" **The Concordia Hymn
Prelude Series** Volume 28 Edited: Herbert Gotsch
Concordia Publishing House 97-5743 Key: d

It is Well

| BA | DC | 1940 | 1982 | LBW | LW | PH | RCV | UCC | UM | WB |
|----|----|------|------|-----|----|----|-----|-----|----|----|
| | | | | Db | | | | | | |

ORGAN COMPOSITIONS

Gotsch, Herbert "When Peace, Like a River" **The
Concordia Hymn Prelude Series** Volume 28 Edited:
Herbert Gotsch Concordia Publishing House
97-5743 Key" Db

Italian Hymn
(See also: Moscow; Trinity)

| BA | DC | 1940 | 1982 | LBW | LW | PH | RCV | UCC | UM | WB |
|----|----|------|------|-----|----|----|-----|-----|----|----|
| F | F | | | F | F | G | G | F | F | F |

ORGAN COMPOSITIONS

Jordan, Alice "Hymn of Praise on 'Come Thou Almighty
King'" **Hymns of Grateful Praise** Broadman
Press Key: G

McKinley, Carl **Ten Hymn Tune Fantasies** H.W. Gray
Key: G

Pearce, Thomas R. "God Whose Almighty Word" **The
Concordia Hymn Prelude Series** Volume 28
Edited: Herbert Gotsch Concordia Publishing House
97-5743 Key: F

Stellhorn, Martin "Come, Thou Almighty Kind" **The
Parish Organist** Part Two Edited: Heinrich
Fleischer Concordia Publishing House 97-1151
Key: G

Wente, Steven   "Come, O Almighty King"   **The Concordia Hymn Prelude Series**   Volume 13   Edited: Herbert Gotsch   Concordia Publishing House   97-5620   Key: F

Willan, Healey   "Come, Thou Almighty King"   **The Parish Organist**   Part Eight   Music for Easter, Ascension, Pentecost and Trinity   Edited: Erich Goldschmidt   Concordia Publishing House 97-1404   Key: G

### FREE ACCOMPANIMENTS

Beck, Albert   **76 Offertories on Hymns & Chorales**   Concordia Publishing House   97-5207   Key: G

Gehring, Philip   **Hymn Preludes and Free Accompaniments**   Volume 3   Augsburg Publishing House   11-9399   Key: F

Goode, Jack C.   **Thirty-Four Changes on Hymn Tunes**   H. W. Gray Co.   GB 644   Key: F

Hancock, Gerre   **Organ Improvisations for Hymn-Singing**   Hinshaw Music Co.   HMO-100   Key: F

Wyton, Alec   **New Shoots from Old Routes**   The Sacred Music Press   KK 279   Key: F

**Iverson**

| | | | | | | | | | | |
|---|---|---|---|---|---|---|---|---|---|---|
| BA | DC | 1940 | 1982 | LBW | LW | PH | RCV | UCC | UM | WB |
| G | | | | | | | | | | |

**Ives**

| | | | | | | | | | | |
|---|---|---|---|---|---|---|---|---|---|---|
| BA | DC | 1940 | 1982 | LBW | LW | PH | RCV | UCC | UM | WB |
| | | | | | | C | | | | |

# J

**Jacob**

| | | | | | | | | | | |
|---|---|---|---|---|---|---|---|---|---|---|
| BA | DC | 1940 | 1982 | LBW | LW | PH | RCV | UCC | UM | WB |
| | | | Eb | | | | | | | |

**Jacob's Ladder**

| | | | | | | | | | | |
|---|---|---|---|---|---|---|---|---|---|---|
| BA | DC | 1940 | 1982 | LBW | LW | PH | RCV | UCC | UM | WB |
| D | | | F | | | Db | | | D | |

**Jacob's Vision**

| | | | | | | | | | | |
|---|---|---|---|---|---|---|---|---|---|---|
| BA | DC | 1940 | 1982 | LBW | LW | PH | RCV | UCC | UM | WB |
| F | | | | | | | | | | |

Jalan
  BA    DC    1940 1982 LBW   LW    PH    RCV   UCC   UM    WB
  F

Jam lucis
  BA    DC    1940 1982 LBW   LW    PH    RCV   UCC   UM    WB
  m:g   m:g               m:g       m:g         m:g

### ORGAN COMPOSITIONS

Barlow, Wayne  "Before the Ending of the Day"  **The Concordia Hymn Prelude Series** Volume 28  Edited: Herbert Gotsch  Concordia Publishing House 97-5743  Key: m:g

Jam lucis orto sidere
  BA    DC    1940 1982 LBW   LW    PH    RCV   UCC   UM    WB
  m:g   m:d   m:g             m:g

Jefferson
  BA    DC    1940 1982 LBW   LW    PH    RCV   UCC   UM    WB
              g     g                     g

### INTONATIONS

Hermann, David  **11 Hymn Intonations, Free Accompaniments, Instrumental Descants for Organ** Volume I Advent, Christmas, Epiphany  G.I.A. Publications G-2378  Key: m:g

### ORGAN COMPOSITIONS

Cherwien, David  "Come, Thou Long-Expected Jesus" **Interpretations Based on Hymn-tunes** Book IV A.M.S.I.  OR-9  Key: g

Powell, Robert  "Come, O Long-Expected Jesus"  **The Concordia Hymn Prelude Series** Volume 1  Edited: Herbert Gotsch  Concordia Publishing House 97-5536  Key: g

### FREE ACCOMPANIMENTS

Held, Wilbur  **Hymn Preludes and Free Accompaniments** Volume 6  Augsburg Publishing House  11-9402 Key: g

Jeg er saa glad
  BA    DC    1940 1982 LBW   LW    PH    RCV   UCC   UM    WB
              G     G

ORGAN COMPOSITIONS

Ore, Charles  "I Am So Glad When Christmas Comes"
**The Concordia Hymn Prelude Series** Volume 4
Edited: Herbert Gotsch  Concordia Publishing
House  97-5539  Key: G

Jeg vil mig Herren love
     BA   DC   1940 1982 LBW   LW    PH    RCV   UCC   UM    WB
                          A

ORGAN COMPOSITIONS

Mackie, Ruth  "I Pray You, Dear Lord Jesus"  **The
Concordia Hymn Prelude Series** Volume 28  Edited:
Herbert Gotsch  Concordia Publishing House
97-5743  Key: A

Jena
(See also: Das neugeborne Kindelein)

Jerusalem
     BA   DC   1940 1982 LBW   LW    PH    RCV   UCC   UM    WB
                     C

Jerusalem, du hochgebaute Stadt
     BA   DC   1940 1982 LBW   LW    PH    RCV   UCC   UM    WB
                     D    D

ORGAN COMPOSITIONS

Karg-Elert, Sigfrid "Jerusalem, Thou High Built City"
**Choral Improvisations for Organ for Reformation
Day, Fast Days, Communion and Funeral Rites**
Op. 65, Volume 5  Edited: Robert Leech Bedell
Edward B. Marks Music Corp.  Key: D

Kickstat, Paul  "Jerusalem, O City Fair and High"
**The Concordia Hymn Prelude Series** Volume 28
Edited: Herbert Gotsch  97-5743  Key: D

Reger, Max  **30 Short Chorale Preludes**  Op. 135a
C.F. Peters Corporation  Nr. 3980  Key: D

Jervaulx Abbey
     BA   DC   1940 1982 LBW   LW    PH    RCV   UCC   UM    WB
          D

Jesaia, dem Propheten
     BA   DC   1940 1982 LBW   LW    PH    RCV   UCC   UM    WB
                     D    D

ORGAN COMPOSITIONS

Krapf, Gerhard  "Isaiah, Mighty Seer, in Spirit
    Soared"  **The Concordia Hymn Prelude Series**
    Volume 29  Edited: Herbert Gotsch  Concordia
    Publishing House  97-5744  Key: D

Scheidt, Samuel "The Sanctus"  **Organ Music for the
    Communion Service**  Edited: Paul Bunjes
    Concordia Publishing House #97-1395  Key: D

Zachow, Freidrich Wilhelm  **Chorale Preludes by
    Masters of the 17th and 18th Centuries**
    Volume I Edited: Walter Buszin  Concordia
    Publishing House  Key: D

FREE ACCOMPANIMENTS

Bunjes, Paul  **New Organ Accompaniments for Hymns**
    Concordia Publishing House 97-5348  Key: D

Jesu dulcis memoria

| BA | DC | 1940 | 1982 | LBW | LW | PH | RCV | UCC | UM | WB |
|----|----|------|------|-----|----|----|-----|-----|----|----|
|    |    | m:g  | m:a  |     |    |    | m:a |     |    |    |

ORGAN COMPOSITIONS

Kreckel. Philip G.  **Musica Divina** Volume 1 J. Fischer
    & Bro. No. 6623  Key:  D

Jesu Kreuz, Leiden und Pein

| BA | DC | 1940 | 1982 | LBW | LW | PH | RCV | UCC | UM | WB |
|----|----|------|------|-----|----|----|-----|-----|----|----|
|    |    |      |      | Eb  | Eb |    |     |     |    |    |

ORGAN COMPOSITIONS

Bach, J.S.  "Jesus, I Will Ponder Now"  **The Parish
    Organist**  Part Seven  Music for Lent, Palm
    Sunday and Holy Week  Edited:  Erich Goldschmidt
    Concordia Publishing House  97-1403  Key: Eb

Beck, Albert  **76 Offertories on Hymns & Chorales**
    Concordia Publishing House  97-5207  Key: Eb

Held, Wilbur "Jesus, I Will Ponder Now" **A Suite of
    Passion Hymn Settings** Concordia Publishing House
    97-4843  Key: F

Manz, Paul  "Jesus, I Will Ponder Now"  **Ten Chorale
    Improvisations** Opus 16  Set VI  Concordia
    Publishing House 97-5305  Key: Eb

Reger, Max **Chorale Preludes for the Church Year from Max Reger, Op. 67** Edited: Alec Wyton Carl Fischer, Inc. o-4667 Key: F

Walther, Johann Gottfried "Jesus, I Will Ponder Now" **The Parish Organist** Part Two Edited: Heinrich Fleischer Concordia Publishing House 97-1151 Key: Eb

Wienhorst, Richard "Jesus, I Will Ponder Now" **The Concordia Hymn Prelude Series** Volume 8 Edited: Herbert Gotsch Concordia Publishing House 97-5615 Key: Eb

Jesu, Jesu, du mein Hirt

| BA | DC | 1940 | 1982 | LBW | LW | PH | RCV | UCC | UM | WB |
|----|----|------|------|-----|----|----|-----|-----|----|----|
|    |    |      | d    |     |    |    |     |     |    |    |

Jesu, joy of man's desiring
(See also: Werde munter)

| BA | DC | 1940 | 1982 | LBW | LW | PH | RCV | UCC | UM | WB |
|----|----|------|------|-----|----|----|-----|-----|----|----|
|    |    | F    | F    |     |    |    | F   |     |    |    |

ORGAN COMPOSITIONS

Bach, J.S. **Jesu, Joy of Man's Desiring** Chorale from Cantata #147 Arr. Harvey Grace Oxford University Press Key: G

Walther, Johann Gottfried "Come with Us, O Blessed Jesus" **The Concordia Hymn Prelude Series** Volume 17 Edited: Herbert Gotsch Concordia Publishing House 97-5708 Key: F

FREE ACCOMPANIMENTS

Johnson, David N. **Hymn Preludes and Free Accompaniments** Volume 14 Augsburg Publishing House 11-9410 Key: F

Jesu, meine Freude

| BA | DC | 1940 | 1982 | LBW | LW | PH | RCV | UCC | UM | WB |
|----|----|------|------|-----|----|----|-----|-----|----|----|
| m:c |   | m:c  |      | m:c | m:c | m:c |    | m:c | m:c | m:c |

ORGAN COMPOSITIONS

Bach, J. S. **Organ Works** Volume 1 Edited: Heinz-Harald Löhlein Urtext of the New Bach Edition Bärenreiter 5171 Key: m:c

Bach, J. S. **Organ Works** Volume 3 "The Individually
   Transmitted Organ Chorales" Edited: Hans Klotz
   Urtext of the New Bach Edition Bärenreiter
   5173 Key: m:e

Bach, J. S. **Organ Chorales from the Neumeister
   Collection** Edited: Chistoph Wolff Yale
   University Press/Bärenreiter 5181 Key: m:d

Bach,J.S. **Organ Works** Volume VI Widor-Schweitzer
   G. Schirmer Key: e

Bach, J.S. **Organ Works** Volume VII Widor-Schweitzer
   G. Schirmer Key c

Bach, J.S. "Jesu, meine Freude" **Festival Anthology for
   Organ** Edited and Arranged: E. Power Biggs
   Associated Music Publishers Key: d

Bach, J.S. **The Liturgical Year** (Orgelbuchlein)
   Edited: Albert Reimenschneider Oliver Ditson Co.
   Key: c

Bach, J. S. "Jesu, Priceless Treasure" **Wedding Music**
   Part II Concordia Publishing House 97-1370
   Key: d

Bach, J. S. "Jesus Priceless Treasure" **Short Classic
   Pieces for Organ from the 16th, 17th and 18th
   Centuries** Arr. Norris L. Stephens J. Fischer
   & Bros. No. 9607 Key: d

Beck, Albert **76 Offertories on Hymns & Chorales**
   Concordia Publishing House 97-5207 Key: c

Bouman, Paul "Jesu, Priceless Treasure"
   **The Concordia Hymn Prelude Series** Volume 29
   Edited: Herbert Gotsch Concordia Publishing
   House 97-5744 Key: c

Dupre, Marcel **Seventy-Nine Chorales for the Organ**
   Opus 28 H. W. Gray Key: c

Marpurg, Friedrich Wilhelm **Twenty-One Chorale Preludes**
   Edited: Robert M. Thompson Augsburg Publishing
   House 11-9506 Key: d

Pepping, Ernst **Fünfundzwanzig Orgelchorale** Edition
   Schott 4723 B. Schott's Sohne Key: m:c

Reger, Max **Chorale Preludes for the Church Year from
   Max Reger, Op. 67** Edited: Alec Wyton Carl
   Fischer, Inc. 0-4667 Key: m:d

Zachau, Friedrich Wilhelm  **80 Chorale Preludes – German Masters of the 17th and 18th Centuries**  Edited: Hermann Keller  C.F. Peters Corporation #4448  Key: m:g

Zachau, Friedrich Wilhelm  "Jesu, meine Freude"  **Organ Music for Christmas**  Edited: C.F. Trevor  Oxford Press  Key: m:d

FREE ACCOMPANIMENTS

Bender, Jan  **Hymn Preludes and Free Accompaniments**  Volume 1  Augsburg Publishing House  11-9397  Key: g

Jesu, meines Lebens Leben

| BA | DC | 1940 | 1982 | LBW | LW | PH | RCV | UCC | UM | WB |
|----|----|------|------|-----|----|----|-----|-----|----|----|
|    |    |      |      | G   | G  |    |     |     |    |    |

ORGAN COMPOSITIONS

Bach, Johann Christoph  "Christ, the Life of All the Living"  **The Concordia Hymn Prelude Series**  Volume 8  Edited: Herbert Gotsch  Concordia Publishing House  97-5615  Key: G

Bach, J. S.  **Organ Chorales from the Neumeister Collection**  Edited: Christoph Wolff  Yale University Press/Bärenreiter 5181  Key: D

Zachow, Friedrich Wilhelm  "Christ, the Life of All the Living"  **The Parish Organist**  Part Seven  Music for Lent, Palm Sunday and Holy Week  Edited: Erich Goldschmidt  Concordia Publishing House  97-1403  Key:  G

FREE ACCOMPANIMENTS

Busarow, Donald  **Hymn Preludes and Free Accompaniments**  Volume 8  Augsburg Publishing House  11-9404  Key: G

Jesu, nostra redemptio

| BA | DC | 1940 | 1982 | LBW | LW | PH | RCV | UCC | UM | WB |
|----|----|------|------|-----|----|----|-----|-----|----|----|
|    |    |      | m:g  |     |    |    |     |     |    |    |

Jesus, all my gladness
(See also: Jesu, meine Freude)

| BA | DC | 1940 | 1982 | LBW | LW | PH | RCV | UCC | UM | WB |
|----|----|------|------|-----|----|----|-----|-----|----|----|
|    |    | c    |      |     |    |    |     |     |    |    |

Jesus Christus unser Heiland (Erfurt)
```
BA   DC   1940 1982 LBW   LW    PH    RCV   UCC   UM    WB
     m:d                  m:d
```

ORGAN COMPOSITIONS

Bach, J. S. **Organ Works** Volume 1 Edited: Heinz-
Harald Löhlein  Urtext of the New Bach Edition
Bärenreiter 5171  Key: m:a

Bach, J.S. **Organ Works** Volume 2  Edited: Hans Klotz
Urtext of the New Bach Edition  Bärenreiter 5172
Key: m:e

Bach, J.S. **Organ Works** Volume VII  Widor-Schweitzer
G. Schirmer  Key: a; Key: d; Key: f

Bach, J.S. **Organ Works** Volume VIII Widor-Schweitzer
G. Schirmer  (2 settings) Key: e

Bach, J.S. **Klavierbung, Dritter Teil** C.F. Peters
Corporation #3948 (Two settings) Key d;  Key: f

Bach, J.S. **The Liturgical Year** (Orgelbuchlein)
Edited: Albert Reimenschneider  Oliver Ditson Co.
Key: m:a

Beck, Theodore  "Jesus Christ, Our Blessed Savior"
**The Concordia Hymn Prelude Series** Volume 17
Edited: Herbert Gotsch  Concordia Publishing
House  97-5708  Key: d

Bender, Jan "Jesus Christ, Our Blessed Savior" **Organ
Music for the Communion Service** Edited: Paul
Bunjes   Concordia Publishing House   Key: F

Buxtehude, Dietrich  **Orgelwerke II: Chorale Preludes**
C.F. Peters Corporation  #4457  Key: g

Distler, Hugo  **Short Chorale Arrangements** Opus 8/3
Barenreiter 1222  Key: m:d

Hennig, Theodore  "Jesus Christ, Our Blessed Savior"
**The Concordia Hymn Prelude Series** Volume 17
Edited: Herbert Gotsch  Concordia Publishing
House 97-5708  Key: d

Pepping, Ernst **Praeludia Postludia** Volume I
B. Schott's Sohne  Edition 6040  Key: m:d

Pepping, Ernst  **Fünfundzwanzig Orgelchorale** Edition
Schott 4723  B. Schott's Sohne  Key: m:d

Jesus I Come
<u>BA</u>   DC   1940 1982 LBW   LW   PH   RCV   UCC   UM   WB
Ab

Jesus is Calling
<u>BA</u>   DC   1940 1982 LBW   LW   PH   RCV   UCC   UM   WB
                                                      C

Jesus ist kommen, Grund ewiger Freude
<u>BA</u>   DC   1940 1982 LBW   LW   PH   RCV   UCC   UM   WB
                         Eb

ORGAN COMPOSITIONS

Brod, Karl   "Jesus Has Come and Brings Pleasure"
**The Concordia Hymn Prelude Series**   Volume 6
Edited: Herbert Gotsch   Concordia Publishing
House   97-5612   Key: Eb

Jesus Saves
<u>BA</u>   DC   1940 1982 LBW   LW   PH   RCV   UCC   UM   WB
G

Jesus, meine Zuversicht
<u>BA</u>   DC   1940 1982 LBW   LW   PH   RCV   UCC   UM   WB
           Bb    C     C

ORGAN COMPOSITIONS

Bach, J. S.   **Organ Works**   Volume 3   "The Individually
Transmitted Organ Chorales"   Edited: Hans Klotz
Urtext of the New Bach Edition   Bärenreiter
5173   Key: C

Bach, J.S.   "Jesus Christ, My Sure Defense"   **The
Parish Organist**   Part Two   Edited: Heinrich
Fleischer   Concordia Publishing House   97-1151
Key: C

Dupre, Marcel   **Seventh-Nine Chorales for the Organ**
Opus 28   H. W. Gray   Key: C

Lovelace, Austin   "Jesus Christ, My Sure Defense"
**The Concordia Hymn Prelude Series**   Volume 29
Edited: Herbert Gotsch   Concordia Publishing House
9705744   Key: C

Micheelsen, Hans Friedrich   "Jesus Lives! The Victory's
Won"   **The Concordia Hymn Prelude Series**
Volume 10   Edited: Herbert Gotsch   Concordia
Publishing House   97-5617   Key: C

Reger, Max **Chorale Preludes for the Church Year from Max Reger, Op. 67** Edited: Alec Wyton  Carl Fischer, Inc.  0-4667  Key: C

Walther, Johann Gottfried **80 Chorale Preludes - German Masters of the 17th and 18th Centuries** Edited: Hermann Keller  C.F. Peters Corporation #4448  Key: C

Walther, Johann Gottfried  "Jesus Christ, My Sure Defense" **The Parish Organist** Part Eight  Music for Easter, Ascension, Pentecost and Trinity Edited: Erich Goldschmidt  Concordia Publishing House  97-1404  Key: C

FREE ACCOMPANIMENTS

Krapf, Gerhard **Hymn Preludes and Free Accompaniments** Volume 13  Augsburg Publishing House  11-9409 Key: C

Joanna
(See also: St. Denio)

| BA | DC | 1940 | 1982 | LBW | LW | PH | RCV | UCC | UM | WB |
|----|----|------|------|-----|----|----|-----|-----|----|----|
|    |    |      |      |     |    |    | Ab  |     |    |    |

Jordan

| BA | DC | 1940 | 1982 | LBW | LW | PH | RCV | UCC | UM | WB |
|----|----|------|------|-----|----|----|-----|-----|----|----|
|    | D  |      |      |     |    |    |     |     |    |    |

Joseph and the Angel

| BA | DC | 1940 | 1982 | LBW | LW | PH | RCV | UCC | UM | WB |
|----|----|------|------|-----|----|----|-----|-----|----|----|
|    |    |      |      |     |    |    | A   |     |    |    |

Joyful Song

| BA | DC | 1940 | 1982 | LBW | LW | PH | RCV | UCC | UM | WB |
|----|----|------|------|-----|----|----|-----|-----|----|----|
| G  |    |      |      |     |    |    |     |     |    |    |

Jubilate

| BA | DC | 1940 | 1982 | LBW | LW | PH | RCV | UCC | UM | WB |
|----|----|------|------|-----|----|----|-----|-----|----|----|
|    | D  |      |      |     |    |    | C   |     |    |    |

FREE ACCOMPANIMENTS

Noble, T. Tertius **Fifty Free Organ Accompaniments to Well Known Hymn Tunes** J. Fischer & Bros. No. 8430  Key: C

Judas Maccabaeus

| BA | DC | 1940 | 1982 | LBW | LW | PH | RCV | UCC | UM | WB |
|----|----|------|------|-----|----|----|-----|-----|----|----|
|    |    | Eb   |      |     |    | Eb |     | Eb  | Eb |    |

ORGAN COMPOSITIONS

Johns, Donald  "Thine is the Glory"  **The Concordia Hymn Prelude Series**  Volume 10  Edited: Herbert Gotsch  Concordia Publishing House  97-5617  Key: Eb

FREE ACCOMPANIMENTS

Krapf, Gerhard  **Hymn Preludes and Free Accompaniments**  Volume 13  Augsburg Publishing House  11-9409  Key: Eb

Julion

| BA | DC | 1940 | 1982 | LBW | LW | PH | RCV | UCC | UM | WB |
|----|----|------|------|-----|----|----|-----|-----|----|----|
|    |    | F    |      |     |    |    |     |     |    |    |

Just as I Am

| BA | DC | 1940 | 1982 | LBW | LW | PH | RCV | UCC | UM | WB |
|----|----|------|------|-----|----|----|-----|-----|----|----|
| Ab |    |      |      | Ab  | G  |    |     |     | Ab |    |

ORGAN COMPOSITIONS

Bouman, Paul  "O God of Mercy, God of Light"  **The Concordia Hymn Prelude Series**  Volume 29  Edited: Herbert Gotsch  Concordia Publishing House  97-5744  Key: G (Second Setting: Ab)

Cherwien, David  **Interpretations Based on Hymn-tunes**  A.M.S.I.  OR-1  Key: Ab

FREE ACCOMPANIMENTS

Lovelace, Austin C.  **Hymn Preludes and Free Accompaniments**  Volume 4  Augsburg Publishing House  11-9400  Key: Ab

# K

Keble

| BA | DC | 1940 | 1982 | LBW | LW | PH | RCV | UCC | UM | WB |
|----|----|------|------|-----|----|----|-----|-----|----|----|
|    |    |      |      |     |    |    |     |     | G  |    |

Kedron

| BA | DC | 1940 | 1982 | LBW | LW | PH | RCV | UCC | UM | WB |
|----|----|------|------|-----|----|----|-----|-----|----|----|
| Eb |    |      |      |     |    |    |     |     |    |    |

Kedron (Southern Harmony)

| BA | DC | 1940 | 1982 | LBW | LW | PH | RCV | UCC | UM | WB |
|----|----|------|------|-----|----|----|-----|-----|----|----|
| c  | c  | c    | c    |     |    | c  |     |     | c  |    |

Gieseke, Richard W.   "Lord, Save Your World"  **The Concordia Hymn Prelude Series**  Volume 29
Edited: Herbert Gotsch   Concordia Publishing House  97-5744  Key: c

Held, Wilbur  **7 Settings on American Folk Hymns**
Concordia Publishing House  97-5829  Key: c

FREE ACCOMPANIMENTS

**Free Harmonizations to Hymn Tunes By Fifty American Composers**  Edited: D. DeWitt Wasson  Hinshaw Music, Inc.  HMO-145  Key: c

| Keegan | | | | | | | | | | |
|---|---|---|---|---|---|---|---|---|---|---|
| BA | DC | 1940 | 1982 | LBW | LW | PH | RCV | UCC | UM | WB |
| Ab | | | | | | | | | | |

| Kemper | | | | | | | | | | |
|---|---|---|---|---|---|---|---|---|---|---|
| BA | DC | 1940 | 1982 | LBW | LW | PH | RCV | UCC | UM | WB |
| | | E | | | | | | | | |

| Kendal | | | | | | | | | | |
|---|---|---|---|---|---|---|---|---|---|---|
| BA | DC | 1940 | 1982 | LBW | LW | PH | RCV | UCC | UM | WB |
| | | F | | | | | | | | |

| Kenosis | | | | | | | | | | |
|---|---|---|---|---|---|---|---|---|---|---|
| BA | DC | 1940 | 1982 | LBW | LW | PH | RCV̇ | UCC | UM | WB |
| Bb | | | | | | | | | | |

| Kent | | | | | | | | | | |
|---|---|---|---|---|---|---|---|---|---|---|
| BA | DC | 1940 | 1982 | LBW | LW | PH | RCV | UCC | UM | WB |
| | | | | | | | | | D | |

| Kentucky | 93rd | | | | | | | | | |
|---|---|---|---|---|---|---|---|---|---|---|
| BA | DC | 1940 | 1982 | LBW | LW | PH | RCV | UCC | UM | WB |
| | | | | G | | | | G | | |

ORGAN COMPOSITIONS

Zimmer, Dennis  "The First Day of the Week"  **The Concordia Hymn Prelude Series**  Volume 29
Edited: Herbert Gotsch   Concordia Publishing House  97-5744  Key:G

| Ketchum | | | | | | | | | | |
|---|---|---|---|---|---|---|---|---|---|---|
| BA | DC | 1940 | 1982 | LBW | LW | PH | RCV | UCC | UM | WB |
| Ab | | | | | | | | | | |

## Kilmarnock

| BA | DC | 1940 | 1982 | LBW | LW | PH | RCV | UCC | UM | WB |
|----|----|------|------|-----|----|----|-----|-----|----|----|
|    | D  |      |      |     |    |    |     |     |    |    |

## King

| BA | DC | 1940 | 1982 | LBW | LW | PH | RCV | UCC | UM | WB |
|----|----|------|------|-----|----|----|-----|-----|----|----|
|    |    |      | m:bb |     |    |    |     |     |    |    |

## King's Highway

| BA | DC | 1940 | 1982 | LBW | LW | PH | RCV | UCC | UM | WB |
|----|----|------|------|-----|----|----|-----|-----|----|----|
|    |    |      |      |     |    |    |     | b   |    |    |

## King's Lynn

| BA | DC | 1940 | 1982 | LBW | LW | PH | RCV | UCC | UM | WB |
|----|----|------|------|-----|----|----|-----|-----|----|----|
|    |    | d    | d    | d   | d  |    |     |     | d  |    |

### ORGAN COMPOSITIONS

Schalk, Carl "By All Your Saints in Warfare" **The Concordia Hymn Prelude Series** Volume 15 Edited: Herbert Gotsch  Concordia Publishing House  97-5706  Key: d

Shack, David "By All Your Saints in Warfare" **Preludes on Ten Hymntunes** Augsburg Publishing House 11-9363  Key: d

Thalben-Ball, George  **113 Variations on Hymn Tunes** Novello & Co., Ltd.  Key: d

### FREE ACCOMPANIMENTS

Arnatt, Ronald  **Hymn Preludes and Free Accompaniments** Volume 9  Augsburg Publishing House 11-9405

**Free Harmonizations to Hymn Tunes By Fifty American Composers** Edited: D. DeWitt Wasson  Hinshaw Music, Inc.  HMO-145  Key: d

## King's Majesty, The

| BA | DC | 1940 | 1982 | LBW | LW | PH | RCV | UCC | UM | WB |
|----|----|------|------|-----|----|----|-----|-----|----|----|
|    |    | f    |      |     |    |    |     |     |    |    |

### ORGAN COMPOSITIONS

Shack, David "Ride On, Ride On in Majesty" **Preludes on Ten Hymntunes** Augsburg Publishing House 11-9363  Key: e

## King's Weston

| BA | DC | 1940 | 1982 | LBW | LW | PH | RCV | UCC | UM | WB |
|----|----|------|------|-----|----|----|-----|-----|----|----|
| d  | d  | d    | d    | d   | d  | d  |     | d   | d  | d  |

ORGAN COMPOSITIONS

Bassett, Anita Denniston  **Nine Hymn-Tune Preludes**
Ludwig Music Publishing Co.  0-08  Key: d

Johnson, David N.  "At the Name of Jesus"  **The Concordia Hymn Prelude Series**  Volume 14
Edited: Herbert Gotsch  Concordia Publishing House
97-5705  Key: d

Wienhorst, Richard  "At the Name of Jesus"  **The Concordia Hymn Prelude Series**  Volume 15
Edited: Herbert Gotsch  Concordia Publishing
House  97-5706  Key: d

FREE ACCOMPANIMENTS

**Free Harmonizations to Hymn Tunes By Fifty American Composers**  Edited: D. DeWitt Wasson  Hinshaw
Music, Inc.  HMO-145  Key: d

Kingdom

| | BA | DC | 1940 | 1982 | LBW | LW | PH | RCV | UCC | UM | WB |
|---|---|---|---|---|---|---|---|---|---|---|---|
| | G | | | G | | | | | G | G | |

ORGAN COMPOSITIONS

Schalk, Carl  "In the Quiet Consecration"  **The Concordia Hymn Prelude Series**  Volume 17
Edited: Herbert Gotsch  Concordia Publishing
House  97-5708  Key: G

White, Louie L. "In the Quiet Consecration"  **Hymn Preludes for Holy Communion** Volume 3 Concordia
Publishing House 97-5488  Key: G

FREE ACCOMPANIMENTS

Hillert, Richard  **Hymn Preludes and Free Accompaniments**
Volume 10  Augsburg Publishing House 11-9406
Key: G

Kingly Love

| | BA | DC | 1940 | 1982 | LBW | LW | PH | RCV | UCC | UM | WB |
|---|---|---|---|---|---|---|---|---|---|---|---|
| | | | | | | g | | | | | |

ORGAN COMPOSITIONS

Hillert, Richard  "O Kingly Love, That Faithfully"
**The Concordia Hymn Prelude Series**  Volume 29
Edited: Herbert Gotsch  Concordia Publishing House
97-5744  Key: g

<u>Kingsfold</u>

| BA | DC | 1940 | 1982 | LBW | LW | PH | RCV | UCC | UM | WB |
|----|----|------|------|-----|----|----|-----|-----|----|----|
| e | e | e | e | e | | e | | e | | e |

## ORGAN COMPOSITIONS

Johns, Donald  "And Have the Bright Immensities"
**The Concordia Hymn Prelude Series**  Volume 29
Edited: Herbert Gotsch  Concordia Publishing House
97-5744  Key: e

## FREE ACCOMPANIMENTS

**Free Harmonizations of Hymn Tunes By Fifty American
Composers**  Edited: D. DeWitt Wasson  Hinshaw
Music, Inc.  HMO-145  Key: e

<u>Kingswood</u>

| BA | DC | 1940 | 1982 | LBW | LW | PH | RCV | UCC | UM | WN |
|----|----|------|------|-----|----|----|-----|-----|----|----|
| | | | | | | | a | | | |

<u>Kings of the Orient</u>

| BA | DC | 1940 | 1982 | LBW | LW | PH | RCV | UCC | UM | WB |
|----|----|------|------|-----|----|----|-----|-----|----|----|
| | | | | | | G | G | | G | |

## FREE ACCOMPANIMENTS

**Free Harmonizations to Hymn Tunes By Fifty American
Composers**  Edited: D. DeWitt Wasson  Hinshaw
Music, Inc.  HMO-145  Key: G

<u>Kirken den er et gammelt Hus</u>
(See also: Kirchen)

| BA | DC | 1940 | 1982 | LBW | LW | PH | RCV | UCC | UM | WB |
|----|----|------|------|-----|----|----|-----|-----|----|----|
| c | c | | | c | c | c | d | c | c | c |

## INTONATIONS

Manz. Paul  **Ten Short Intonations on Well Known
Hymns**  Augsburg Publishing House  11-9492
Key: d

## ORGAN COMPOSITIONS

Hoelty-Nickel, Theodore  "Built on the Rock the Church
doth Stand"  **The Parish Organist**  Part Two
Edited: Heinrich Fleischer  Concordia Publishing
House  97-1151  Key:  d

Manz, Paul "Built on a Rock" **Ten Chorale Improvisations**
Set VIII Op. 20  Concordia Publishing House 97-5342
Key: d

Powell, Robert J. "Built on the Rock" **The Concordia Hymn Prelude Series** Volume 29 Edited: Herbert Gotsch Concordia Publishing House 97-5744 Key: c

## FREE ACCOMPANIMENTS

Bunjes, Paul **New Organ Accompaniments for Hymns** Concordia Publishing House 97-5348 Key: d

Diemer, Emma Lou **Hymn Preludes and Free Accompaniments** Volume 2 11-9398 Key: c

**Free Harmonizations to Hymn Tunes By Fifty American Composers** Edited: D. DeWitt Wasson Hinshaw Music, Inc. HMO-145 Key: c

Johnson, David N. **Free Harmonizations of Twelve Hymn Tunes** Augsburg Publishing House 11-9190 Key: c

Wood, Dale **New Settings of Twenty Well-Known Hymn Tunes** Augsburg Publishing House 11-9292 Key: c

## Kirkpatrick

| BA | DC | 1940 | 1982 | LBW | LW | PH | RCV | UCC | UM | WB |
|----|----|------|------|-----|----|----|-----|-----|----|----|
| D  |    |      |      |     |    |    |     |     |    |    |

## Kit Smart

| BA | DC | 1940 | 1982 | LBW | LW | PH | RCV | UCC | UM | WB |
|----|----|------|------|-----|----|----|-----|-----|----|----|
|    |    |      | m:f  |     |    |    |     |     |    |    |

## Knickerbocker

| BA | DC | 1940 | 1982 | LBW | LW | PH | RCV | UCC | UM | WB |
|----|----|------|------|-----|----|----|-----|-----|----|----|
| Ab |    |      | G    |     |    |    |     |     |    |    |

## ORGAN COMPOSITIONS

Barlow, Wayne "Come, Risen Lord" **The Concordia Hymn Prelude Series** Volume 17 Edited: Herbert Gotsch Concordia Publishing House 97-5708 Key: G

Held, Wilbur "Come, Risen Lord" **Hymn Preludes for Holy Communion** Volume 3 Concordia Publishing House 97-5488 Key: G

## Kohoutek

| BA | DC | 1940 | 1982 | LBW | LW | PH | RCV | UCC | UM | WB |
|----|----|------|------|-----|----|----|-----|-----|----|----|
| d  |    |      |      |     |    |    |     |     |    |    |

<u>Komm, Gott, Schöpfer, heiliger Geist</u>
(See also: Komm, Gott, Schopfer)
   BA   DC   1940 1982 LBW  LW    PH   RCV  UCC  UM    WB
               m:f  m:f  m:f

## ORGAN COMPOSITIONS

Ahrens, Joseph **Das Heilige Jahr** Volume II
    Willy Muller - Suddeutscher Musikverlag -
    Heidelberg, New York:  C.F. Peters Corporation
    Key: m:f

Ahrens, Joseph "Fantasie 'Komm, Schopfer Geist'"
    **Das Heilige Jahr** Willy Muller - Suddeutscher
    Musikverlag - Heidelberg, New York: C.F. Peters
    Key: m:g

Bach, J. S. **Organ Works** Volume 1  Edited: Heinz-
    Harald Löhlein  Urtext of the New Bach Edition
    Bärenreiter  5171  Key: m:g

Bach, J.S.  **Organ Works**  Volume 2  Edited: Hans
    Kloz  Urtext of the New Bach Edition  Bärenreiter
    5172  Key: m:g

Bach, J.S. **Organ Works** Volume VIII Widor-Schweitzer
    G. Schirmer  Key: C

Bach, J.S. **Organ Works**Volume VII  Widor-Schweitzer
    G. Schirmer  Key:  C

Bach, J.S. **Orgelwerke** Volume VII  C.F. Peters
    Corporation Nr. 246  Key: C

Bach, J.S. **The Liturgical Year**  (Orgelbuchlein)
    Edited: Albert Reimenschneider  Oliver Ditson Co.
    Key: m:g

Dupre, Marcel  **Seventy-Nine Chorales for the Organ**
    Opus 28  H. W. Gray  Key: C

Manz, Paul "Come Holy Ghost, Creator Blest" **Ten Chorale
    Improvisations** Set IV  Op. 10 Concordia Publish-
    ing House 97-4951  Key: Bb

Pachelbel, Johann  **Chorale Preludes by Masters of the
    17th and 18th Centuries** Volume I Edited: Walter
    Buszin  Concordia Publishing House  Key: m:f

Schack, David  "Come, Holy Ghost, Our Souls Inspire"
    **The Concordia Hymn Prelude Series**  Volume 29
    Edited: Herbert Gotsch  Concordia Publishing
    House  97-5744  Key: m:f

Titelouze, Jean  "Come, Holy Ghost, Creator Blest"
**the Parish Organist**  Part Eight  Music for
Easter, Ascension, Pentecost and Trinity  Edited:
Erich Goldschmidt  Concordia Publishing House
97-1404  Key:  f

Walcha, Helmut **Chorale Preludes** II  C.F. Peters
Corporation Nr. 4871  Key: Bb

Zachow, Friedrich "Come Holy Ghost, Our Souls Inspire"
**The Concordia Hymn Prelude Series**  Volume 12
Edited: Herbert Gotsch  Concordia Publishing House
97-5619  Key: m:f

## FREE ACCOMPANIMENTS

Schack, David  **Hymn Preludes and Free Accompaniments**
Volume 11  Augsburg Publishing House  11-9407
Key: F

Komm, heiliger Geist, Herre Gott

| BA | DC | 1940 | 1982 | LBW | LW | PH | RCV | UCC | UM | WB |
|----|----|------|------|-----|-----|----|-----|-----|----|----|
|    |    |      |      | m:f | m:f |    |     |     |    |    |

## INTONATIONS

Manz, Paul  **Ten Short Intonations on Well Known
Hymn Tunes**  Augsburg Publishing House  11-9492
Key: m:f

## ORGAN COMPOSITIONS

Ahrens, Joseph **Das Heilige Jahr** Volume II
Willy Müller - Süddeutscher Musikverlag -
Heidelberg, New York: C.F. Peters Corporation
Key: m:f

Armsdorf, Andreas **80 Chorale Preludes - German Masters
of the 17th and 18th Centuries** Edited: Hermann
Keller  C.F. Peters Corporation #4448  Key: G

Armsdorf, Andreas "Come Holy Ghost, God and Lord"
**Wedding Music** Part 2  Concordia Publishing
House  97-1370  Key: F

Bach, J.S. **Organ Works**  Volume 2  Edited: Hans
Kloz  Urtext of the New Bach Edition  Bärenreiter
5172  Key: F

Bach, J.S. **Organ Works**  Volume VIII
Widor-Schweitzer  G. Schirmer  Key: F; Key: G

Bach, J.S. **Orgelwerke** Volume VII C.F. Peters
    Corporation Nr. 246 #36 Key: F;  #37  Key: G

Buxtehude, Dietrich **Six Organ Preludes on Chorales**
    Edited: Henry G. Ley  Oxford University Press
    Key: F

Buxtehude, Dietrich **Orgelwerke II: Chorale Preludes**
    C.F. Peters Corporation #4457  Key: F

Dupre, Marcel  **Seventy-Nine Chorales for the Organ**
    Opus 28  H. W. Gray  Key: F

Karg-Elert, Sigfrid "Come Holy Ghost, Lord God" **Choral
    Improvisations for Organ for Ascensiontide and
    Pentecost** Op. 65 Volume 4 Edited: Robert Leech
    Bedell Edward B. Marks Music Corp.  Key: G

Metzler, Friedrich  "Lord God, to You We All Give
    Praise"  **The Concordia Hymn Prelude Series**
    Volume 15  Edited: Herbert Gotsch  Concordia
    Publishing House  97-5706  Key: m:f

Telemann, Georg Philipp  "Come, Holy Ghost, God and
    Lord"  **The Parish Organist**  Part Two  Edited:
    Heinrich Fleischer  Concordia Publishing House
    97-1151  Key:  F

Telemann, Georg Philipp  "Come Holy Ghost, God and
    Lord"  **The Concordia Hymn Prelude Series**
    Volume 12  Edited: Herbert Gotsch  Concordia
    Publishing House  97-5619  Key: F

Vetter, Andreas Nicolaus  **Chorale Preludes by Masters
    of the 17th and 18th Centuries**  Volume I  Edited:
    Walter Buszin  Concordia Publishing House   Key: F

Weckmann, Matthias  "Come, Holy Ghost, God and Lord"
    **The Parish Organist**  Part Eight Music for
    Easter, Ascension, Pentecost and Trinity  Edited:
    Erich Goldschmidt  Concordia Publishing House  97-
    1404  Key: F

Zachau, Friedrich Wilhelm  **80 Chorale Preludes – German
    Masters of the 17th and 18th Centuries**  Edited:
    Hermann Keller  C.F. Peters Corporation #4448
    Key: F

Zachau, Friedrich Wilhelm "Chorale Prelude on 'Komm,
    heiliger Geist, Herre Gott'"  **For Manuals Only**
    Edited: John Christopher  McAfee Music Corp.
    Key: F

Cassler, G. Winston **Free Organ Accompaniments to Hymns**
Augsburg Publishing House 11-9179 Key: F

Cassler, G. Winston **Free Organ Accompaniments to
Festival Hymns** Volume I Augsburg Publishing House
11-9192 Key: F

Komm, o komm, du Geist des Lebens
| BA | DC | 1940 | 1982 | LBW | LW | PH | RCV | UCC | UM | WB |
|----|----|------|------|-----|----|----|-----|-----|----|----|
|    |    | F    | F    |     |    |    |     |     |    | F  |

ORGAN COMPOSITIONS

Beck, Albert **76 Offertories on Hymns & Chorales**
Concordia Publishing House 97-5207 Key: G

Drews, Claudia "Come, Oh, Come, O Quickening Spirit"
**The Concordia Hymn Prelude Series** Volume 29
Edited: Herbert Gotsch Concordia Publishing
House 97-5744 Key: F

Klotz, Hans "Come, Oh, Come, O Quickening Spirit"
**The Concordia Hymn Prelude Series** Volume 12
Edited: Herbert Gotsch Concordia Publishing House
97-5619 Key: F

Raphael, Guenter "Come, Oh, Come, Thou Quickening
Spirit" **The Parish Organist** Part Eight
Music for Easter, Ascension, Pentecost and
Trinity Edited: Erich Goldschmidt Concordia
Publishing House 97-1404 Key: G

FREE ACCOMPANIMENTS

Cassler, G. Winston **Organ Descants for Selected Hymn
Tunes** Augsburg Publishing House 11-9304 Key: G

Kommt her zu mir
| BA | DC | 1940 | 1982 | LBW | LW   | PH | RCV | UCC | UM | WB |
|----|----|------|------|-----|------|----|-----|-----|----|----|
|    |    |      |      | m:f | m:f# |    |     |     |    |    |

ORGAN COMPOSITIONS

Gerike, Henry V. "Do Not Despair, O Little Flock"
**The Concordia Hymn Prelude Series** Volume 29
Edited: Herbert Gotsch Concordia Publishing
House 97-5744 Key: f (Second setting: f#)

König
| BA | DC | 1940 | 1982 | LBW | LW | PH | RCV | UCC | UM | WB |
|----|----|------|------|-----|----|----|-----|-----|----|----|
| Eb |    |      |      |     |    |    |     |     |    |    |

Kontakion(Kievan Chant)

| BA | DC | 1940 | 1982 | LBW | LW | PH | RCV | UCC | UM | WB |
|----|----|------|------|-----|----|----|-----|-----|----|----|
|    |    |      | g    |     |    |    |     |     |    |    |

Korea

| BA | DC | 1940 | 1982 | LBW | LW | PH | RCV | UCC | UM | WB |
|----|----|------|------|-----|----|----|-----|-----|----|----|
|    | Eb |      |      |     |    |    |     | C   |    |    |

Kremser

| BA | DC | 1940 | 1982 | LBW | LW | PH | RCV | UCC | UM | WB |
|----|----|------|------|-----|----|----|-----|-----|----|----|
| D  | D  | D    | D    | D   | D  | C  | D   | C   | D  | C  |

## ORGAN COMPOSITIONS

Beck, Albert **76 Offertories on Hymns & Chorales**
Concordia Publishing House  97-5207  Key: D

Engel, James  "We Praise You, O God"  **The Concordia Hymn Prelude Series**  Volume 29  Edited: Herbert Gotsch  Concordia Publishing House  97-5744
Key: D

Fisk, Beatrice Hatton "Prelude on 'Netherlands'"
**Thanksgiving Music**  H.W. Gray  Key: D

Fisk, Beatrice Hatton  "Prelude on 'Netherlands'"
**The Lutheran Organist**  Compiled by John Holler
H. W. Gray Co.  Key: D

Willan, healey  "We Praise Thee, O God Our Redeemer"
**The Parish Organist**  Part Two  Edited: Heinrich Fleischer  Concordia Publishing House  97-1151
Key:  D

## FREE ACCOMPANIMENTS

Busarow, Donald  **Hymn Preludes and Free Accompaniments**
Volume 8  Augsburg Publishing House  11-9404
Key: D

Carson, J. Bert  **Hymn Preludes and Free Accompaniments**
Volume 16  Augsburg Publishing House  11-9412
Key: D

Cassler, G. Winston  **Organ Descants for Selected Hymn Tunes**  Augsburg Publishing House  11-9304  Key: D

Hancock, Gerre  **Organ Improvisations for Hymn-Singing**
Hinshaw Music Co.  HMO-100  Key: D

Noble, T. Tertius **Free Organ Accompaniments to One Hundred Well-Known Hymn Tunes**  J. Fischer & Bros.
#8175  Key: D

Wyton, Alec **New Shoots From Old Routes**
Sacred Music Press   KK 279   Key: D

Kum bah Yah

| BA | DC | 1940 | 1982 | LBW | LW | PH | RCV | UCC | UM | WB |
|----|----|------|------|-----|----|----|-----|-----|----|----|
|    |    |      |      |     |    |    | D   |     |    |    |

Kuortane

| BA | DC | 1940 | 1982 | LBW | LW | PH | RCV | UCC | UM | WB |
|----|----|------|------|-----|----|----|-----|-----|----|----|
|    |    |      |      | Eb  |    |    |     |     |    |    |

ORGAN COMPOSITIONS

Held, Wilbur   "O Lord, Now Let Your Servant"   **The Concordia Hymn Prelude Series**   Volume 29 Edited: Herbert Gotsch   Concordia Publishing House   97-5744   Key: Eb

Kyrie, Gott Vater in Ewigkeit

| BA  | DC  | 1940 | 1982 | LBW | LW  | PH | RCV | UCC | UM | WB |
|-----|-----|------|------|-----|-----|----|-----|-----|----|----|
| m:d |     |      |      |     | m:e | m:e|     |     |    |    |

ORGAN COMPOSITIONS

Bach, J. S.   **Organ Works** Vol VII   Widor-Schweitzer G. Schirmer   (#46) Key: m:c; Key: m:a

Bach, J. S.   **Klavierübung, Dritter Teil**   C.F. Peters Corporation #3948   Key: m:a

Bach, J.S.   **Klavierubung, Dritter Teil**   C.F. Peters Corporation #3948   Key: m:e

Dupre, Marcel   **Seventy-Nine Chorales for the Organ** Opus 28   H. W. Gray   Key: m:eb

Krapf, Gerhard   "Kyrie, God Father"   **The Concordia Hymn Prelude Series**   Volume 13   Edited: Herbert Gotsch   Concordia Publishing House   97-5620 Key: m:e

Volckmar, Nobias   **Chorale Preludes by Masters of the 17th and 18th Centuries**   Volume I   Edited: Walter Buszin   Concordia Publishing House   Key: e

Wente, Steven   "Kyrie, God Father"   **The Concordia Hymn Prelude Series**   Volume 29   Edited: Herbert Gotsch   Concordia Publishing House 97-5744   Key: m:e

# L

L'Omnipotent

| | BA | DC | 1940 | 1982 | LBW | LW | PH | RCV | UCC | UM | WB |
|---|----|----|------|------|-----|----|----|-----|-----|----|----|
| | | | | | | | g | | | | g |

Laban

| | BA | DC | 1940 | 1982 | LBW | LW | PH | RCV | UCC | UM | WB |
|---|----|----|------|------|-----|----|----|-----|-----|----|----|
| | | | | | | | | | | Bb | |

Labor

| | BA | DC | 1940 | 1982 | LBW | LW | PH | RCV | UCC | UM | WB |
|---|----|----|------|------|-----|----|----|-----|-----|----|----|
| | | | d | | | | | | | | |

Lacquiparle
(See also: Dakota Indian Chant)

| | BA | DC | 1940 | 1982 | LBW | LW | PH | RCV | UCC | UM | WB |
|---|----|----|------|------|-----|----|----|-----|-----|----|----|
| | | | | | | | | | | c | |

LaDue Chapel

| | BA | DC | 1940 | 1982 | LBW | LW | PH | RCV | UCC | UM | WB |
|---|----|----|------|------|-----|----|----|-----|-----|----|----|
| | | | | | | | | | G | | G |

ORGAN COMPOSITIONS

Arnatt, Ronald "LaDue Chapel" **The Bristol Collection of Contemporary Hymn Tune Preludes for Organ** Volume One  Edited: Lee Hastings Bristol, Jr. Harold Flammer, Inc.  Key: D

Lake Enon

| | BA | DC | 1940 | 1982 | LBW | LW | PH | RCV | UCC | UM | WB |
|---|----|----|------|------|-----|----|----|-----|-----|----|----|
| | | | | | | | | | G | | |

ORGAN COMPOSITIONS

Lovelace, Austin **Fourteen Hymn Preludes** Augsburg Publishing House  11-6152  Key: G

Lakewood

| | BA | DC | 1940 | 1982 | LBW | LW | PH | RCV | UCC | UM | WB |
|---|----|----|------|------|-----|----|----|-----|-----|----|----|
| | | | | | | Ab | | | | | |

ORGAN COMPOSITIONS

Bobb, Barry L.  "Forth in Your Name, O Lord, I Go" **The Concordia Hymn Prelude Series** Volume 30  Edited: Herbert Gotsch  Concordia Publishing House  97-5745  Key: Ab

Lammas

| | BA | DC | 1940 | 1982 | LBW | LW | PH | RCV | UCC | UM | WB |
|---|----|----|------|------|-----|----|----|-----|-----|----|----|
| | | | Eb | | | | | | | | |

Lancashire

| BA | DC | 1940 | 1982 | LBW | LW | PH | RCV | UCC | UM | WB |
|----|----|------|------|-----|----|----|-----|-----|----|----|
| C | Db | Db | Db | C | | C | Db | C | Db | D |

### ORGAN COMPOSITIONS

Arnatt, Ronald  "Lead On, O King Eternal"  **The Parish Organist**  Part Eleven  Edited: Willem Mudde  Concordia Publishing House  97-4758  Key: C

Gerike, Henry V.  "Lead On, O King Eternal"  **The Concordia Hymn Prelude Series**  Volume 30  Edited: Herbert Gotsch  Concordia Publishing House  97-5745  Key: C

### FREE ACCOMPANIMENTS

Hudson, Richard  **Hymn Preludes and Free Accompaniments**  Volume 12  Augsburg Publishing House  11-9408  Key: C

Noble, T. Tertius  **Free Organ Accompaniments to One Hundred Well-Known Hymn Tunes**  J. Fischer & Bros.  #8175  Key: Db

Land of Rest

| BA | DC | 1940 | 1982 | LBW | LW | PH | RCV | UCC | UM | WB |
|----|----|------|------|-----|----|----|-----|-----|----|----|
| F | F | F | F | F | F | F | | | | F |

### ORGAN COMPOSITIONS

Gieschen, Thomas  "Jesusalem, My Happy Home"  **The Concordia Hymn Prelude Series**  Volume 30  Edited: Herbert Gotsch  Concordia Publishing House  97-5745  Key: F

Held, Wilbur  **7 Settings of American Folk Hymns**  Concordia Publishing House  97-5829  Key: F

### FREE ACCOMPANIMENTS

Busarow, Donald  **All Praise to You Eternal God**  Augsburg Publishing House  11-9076  Key: F

**Free Harmonizations to Hymn Tunes By Fifty American Composers**  Edited: D. DeWitt Wasson  Hinshaw Music, Inc.  HMO-145  Key: F

Gehring, Philip  **Hymn Preludes and Free Accompaniments**  Volume 3  Augsburg Publishing House  11-9399  Key: F

## Landås
| BA | DC | 1940 | 1982 | LBW | LW | PH | RCV | UCC | UM | WB |
|----|----|------|------|-----|----|----|-----|-----|----|----|
| Ab |    |      |      |     |    |    |     |     |    |    |

## Langham
| BA | DC | 1940 | 1982 | LBW | LW | PH | RCV | UCC | UM | WB |
|----|----|------|------|-----|----|----|-----|-----|----|----|
| c  | c  | c    | c    |     |    | c  |     | c   |    | c  |

### ORGAN COMPOSITIONS

Wienhorst, Richard  "Father Eternal, Ruler of Creation"
**The Concordia Hymn Prelude Series**  Volume 30
Edited: Herbert Gotsch  Concordia Publishing
House  97-5745  Key: c

### FREE ACCOMPANIMENTS

**Free Harmonizations to Hymn Tunes By Fifty American
Composers**  Edited: D. DeWitt Wasson  Hinshaw
Music, Inc.  HMO-145  Key: c

## Langley
| BA | DC | 1940 | 1982 | LBW | LW | PH | RCV | UCC | UM | WB |
|----|----|------|------|-----|----|----|-----|-----|----|----|
| Db |    |      |      |     |    |    |     |     |    |    |

## Langran
| BA | DC | 1940 | 1982 | LBW | LW | PH | RCV | UCC | UM | WB |
|----|----|------|------|-----|----|----|-----|-----|----|----|
|    |    | F    |      |     | F  |    |     |     | F  |    |

### ORGAN COMPOSITIONS

Bingham, Seth **Twelve Hymn Preludes**  Opus 38 Set 2
H.W. Gray GB 152  Key: F

### FREE ACCOMPANIMENTS

Noble, T. Tertius  **Free Organ Accompaniments to One
Hundred Well-Known Hymn Tunes**  J. Fischer & Bros.
#8175  Key: F

## Laramie
| BA | DC | 1940 | 1982 | LBW | LW | PH | RCV | UCC | UM | WB |
|----|----|------|------|-----|----|----|-----|-----|----|----|
|    |    | F    | F    |     |    |    |     |     |    |    |

## Lasset uns mit Jesu ziehen
| BA | DC | 1940 | 1982 | LBW | LW | PH | RCV | UCC | UM | WB |
|----|----|------|------|-----|----|----|-----|-----|----|----|
|    |    |      |      | D   | D  |    |     |     |    |    |

### ORGAN COMPOSITIONS

Beck, Albert  **76 Offertories on Hymns & Chorales**
Concordia Publishing House  97-5207  Key: D

Buszin, Walter "Let Us Ever Walk with Jesus" **Wedding Music** Part 2   Concordia Publishing House 97-1370 Key: D

Kretzschmar, Paul   "Let Us Ever Walk with Jesus"   **The Parish Organist**   Part Two   Edited: Heinrich Fleischer   Concordia Publishing House 97-1151 Key:  D

Manz, Paul "Let Us Ever Walk with Jesus" **Ten Chorale Improvisations** Set IX Op. 21 Concordia Publishing House 97-5556   Key: D

Rotermund, Melvin   "Let Us Ever Walk With Jesus" **The Concordia Hymn Prelude Series**   Volume 30 Edited: Herbert Gotsch   Concordia Publishing House 97-5745   Key: D

ORGAN COMPOSITIONS? 

FREE ACCOMPANIMENTS

Busarow, Donald   **Hymn Preludes and Free Accompaniments** Volume 8   Augsburg Publishing House   11-9404 Key: D

## Lasst uns alle

| BA | DC | 1940 | 1982 | LBW | LW | PH | RCV | UCC | UM | WB |
|----|----|------|------|-----|----|----|-----|-----|----|----|
|    |    |      |      |     | F  |    |     |     |    |    |

ORGAN COMPOSITIONS

Held, Wilbur   "Let Us All with Gladsome Voice"   **The Concordia Hymn Preludes Series**   Volume 4 Edited: Herbert Gotsch   Concordia Publishing House 97-5539   Key: F

Metzger, Hans Arnold "Let Us All with Gladsome Voice" **The Parish Organist** Part Five   Advent and Christmas Music   Concordia Publishing House 97-1382   Key: F

## Lasst uns erfreuen
(See also: Vigili et sancti)

| BA | DC | 1940 | 1982 | LBW | LW | PH | RCV | UCC | UM | WB |
|----|----|------|------|-----|----|----|-----|-----|----|----|
| Eb | D  |      | Eb   | Eb  | Eb | Eb | Eb  | D   | Eb | d  |

INTONATIONS

McCormick, David   **20 Organ Intonations on Hymns of Praise**   Hope Publishing Co.   Key: D

ORGAN COMPOSITIONS

Bender, Jan  "Now All the Vault of Heaven Resounds"
    **The Concordia Hymn Prelude Series**  Volume 10
    Edited: Herbert Gotsch  Concordia Publishing House
    97-5617  Key: D (Second setting: Key: Eb)

Ferguson, John  "All Creatures of Our God and King"
    **The Concordia Hymn Prelude Series**  Volume 30
    Edited: Herbert Gotsch  Concordia Publishing
    House  97-5745  Key: D (Second setting: Eb)

Gieschen, Thomas  "A Hymn of Glory Let Us Sing"  **The
    Concordia Hymn Prelude Series**  Volume 12  Edited:
    Herbert Gotsch  Concordia Publishing House
    97-5619  Key: Eb

Hopson, Hal H.  **Five Preludes on Familiar Hymns**
    Harold Flammer, Inc.  HF-5123  Key: D

Johnson, David N.  "Ye Watchers and Ye Holy Ones"
    **The Concordia Hymn Prelude Series**  Volume 15
    Edited: Herbert Gotsch  Concordia Publishing House
    97-5706  Key: Eb

Martin, Miles  "Postlude on 'Ye Watchers and Ye
    Holy Ones'"  **The Lutheran Organist**  Compiled by
    John Holler  H. W. Gray Co.  Key:  Eb

Moser, Rudolf  "Ye Watchers and Ye Holy Ones"  **The
    Parish Organist**  Part Two  Edited: Heinrich
    Fleischer  Concordia Publishing House  97-1151
    Key:  Eb

Reidel, Bernard "A Hymn of Glory Let Us Sing" p.26 Pro Easter

Thalben-Ball, George  **113 Variations on Hymn Tunes**
    Novello & Co., Ltd.  Key: Eb

FREE ACCOMPANIMENTS

Coleman, Henry  **Varied Hymn Accompaniments**
    Oxford University Press  Key: Eb

Ferguson, John  **Hymn Tune Harmonizations**  Book III
    Ludwig Music Publishing Co.  0-10 Key: D

Gehring, Philip  **Hymn Preludes and Free Accompaniments**
    Volume 3  Augsburg Publishing House  11-9399
    Key: Eb

Goode, Jack C.  **Thirty-Four Changes on Hymn Tunes**
    H. W. Gray Co.  GB 644  Key: D

Hancock, Gerre **Organ Improvisations for Hymn-Singing**
Hinshaw Music Co. HMO-100 Key: Eb

Hebble, Robert **Robert Hebble's Hymnal Companion for
Organ** Bradley Publications CE/283A/3 Key: Eb

Johnson, David N. **Free Harmonizations of Twelve Hymn
Tunes** Augsburg Publishing House 11-9190 Key:D

Norris, Kevin **Hymn Preludes and Free Accompaniments**
Volume 15 Augsburg Publishing House 11-9411
Key: Eb

Wyton, Alex **New Shoots from Old Routes** Sacred Music
Press KK 279 Key: Eb

Latvian Melody
(See also: Captivity)

Lauda anima (Andrews)
(See also: Praise my Soul)

| BA | DC | 1940 | 1982 | LBW | LW | PH | RCV | UCC | UM | WB |
|----|----|------|------|-----|----|----|-----|-----|----|----|
| D  |    | D    | D    |     |    |    | D   |     | D  | D  |

INTONATIONS

McCormick, David **20 Organ Intonations on Hymns of
Praise** Hope Publishing Co. Key: D

ORGAN COMPOSITIONS

Adam, Johann Ludwig "Praise My Soul, the King of
Heaven" **The Parish Organist** Part Eleven
Edited: Willem Mudde Concordia Publishing House
97-4758 Key: D

Bassett, Anita Denniston **Nine Hymn-Tune Preludes**
Ludwig Music Publishing Co. 0-08 Key: D

Lauda anima (Goss)

| BA | DC | 1940 | 1982 | LBW | LW | PH | RCV | UCC | UM | WB |
|----|----|------|------|-----|----|----|-----|-----|----|----|
| D  |    |      |      |     |    |    |     |     |    |    |

FREE ACCOMPANIMENTS

Noble, T. Tertius **Fifty Free Organ Accompaniments
to Well Known Hymn Tunes** J. Fischer & Bros.
No. 8430 Key: D

Lauda Sion

| BA | DC | 1940 | 1982 | LBW | LW | PH | RCV | UCC | UM | WB |
|----|----|------|------|-----|----|----|-----|-----|----|----|
|    |    | m:f  | m:f  |     |    |    |     |     |    |    |

## Laudate Dominum

| BA | DC | 1940 | 1982 | LBW | LW | PH | RCV | UCC | UM | WB |
|----|----|------|------|-----|----|----|-----|-----|----|----|
|    |    |      | Bb   |     |    |    |     |     |    |    |

## Laudes Domini

| BA | DC | 1940 | 1982 | LBW | LW | PH | RCV | UCC | UM | WB |
|----|----|------|------|-----|----|----|-----|-----|----|----|
| Bb | C  | C    | C    | C   | C  | C  | C   |     | C  | Bb |

### INTONATIONS

McCormick, David  **20 Organ Intonations on Hymns of Praise**  Hope Publishing Co.   Key: C

### ORGAN COMPOSITIONS

Saxton, Stanley E.   "Prelude on 'When Morning Gilds the Skies'"  **A Galaxy of Hymn Tunes Preludes for Organ**  Galaxy Music Corp.   GMC 2353   Key: C

Wyble, Richard   "When Morning Gilds the Skies"  **The Concordia Hymn Prelude Series**  Volume 30   Edited: Herbert Gotsch   Concordia Publishing House   97-5745   Key: C

### FREE ACCOMPANIMENTS

Noble, T. Tertius  **Free Organ Accompaniments to One Hundred Well-Known Hymn Tunes**   J. Fischer & Bros.   #8175   Key: C

## Laurel

| BA | DC | 1940 | 1982 | LBW | LW | PH | RCV | UCC | UM | WB |
|----|----|------|------|-----|----|----|-----|-----|----|----|
|    |    |      | D    |     |    |    |     |     |    |    |

### ORGAN COMPOSITIONS

Schalk, Carl   "Now that the Daylight Fills the Sky"  **The Concordia Hymn Prelude Series**  Volume 30   Edited: Herbert Gotsch   Concordia Publishing House   97-5745   Key: D

## Laus Deo

| BA | DC | 1940 | 1982 | LBW | LW | PH | RCV | UCC | UM | WB |
|----|----|------|------|-----|----|----|-----|-----|----|----|
|    |    |      | G    |     |    |    | G   |     |    |    |

## Laus Regis

| BA | DC | 1940 | 1982 | LBW | LW | PH | RCV | UCC | UM | WB |
|----|----|------|------|-----|----|----|-----|-----|----|----|
|    |    |      | D    |     |    |    |     |     |    |    |

Schack, David   "Rejoice, the Lord is King"   **The Concordia Hymn Prelude Series**   Volume 14
Edited: Herbert Gotsch   Concordia Publishing House   97-5705   Key: D

<u>Laus</u> <u>Tibi</u> <u>Christe</u>

| BA | DC | 1940 | 1982 | LBW | LW | PH | RCV | UCC | UM | WB |
|----|----|------|------|-----|----|----|-----|-----|----|----|
|    |    |      |      |     |    |    | D   |     |    |    |

<u>Le</u> <u>Cenacle</u>

| BA | DC | 1940 | 1982 | LBW | LW | PH | RCV | UCC | UM | WB |
|----|----|------|------|-----|----|----|-----|-----|----|----|
|    |    |      | m:d  |     |    |    |     |     |    |    |

<u>Le</u> <u>Cantique</u> <u>de</u> <u>Simeon</u>

| BA | DC | 1940 | 1982 | LBW | LW | PH | RCV | UCC | UM | WB |
|----|----|------|------|-----|----|----|-----|-----|----|----|
|    |    |      | F    |     |    |    |     |     |    |    |

<u>Le</u> <u>P'ing</u>

| BA | DC  | 1940 | 1982 | LBW | LW | PH  | RCV | UCC | UM  | WB |
|----|-----|------|------|-----|----|-----|-----|-----|-----|----|
|    | m:d |      |      |     |    | m:d |     |     | m:d |    |

<u>Leach</u>

| BA | DC | 1940 | 1982 | LBW | LW | PH | RCV | UCC | UM | WB |
|----|----|------|------|-----|----|----|-----|-----|----|----|
| D  |    |      |      |     |    |    |     |     |    |    |

<u>Leaning</u>

| BA | DC | 1940 | 1982 | LBW | LW | PH | RCV | UCC | UM | WB |
|----|----|------|------|-----|----|----|-----|-----|----|----|
|    |    |      |      |     |    |    |     | A   |    |    |

<u>Lebbaeus</u>

| BA | DC | 1940 | 1982 | LBW | LW | PH | RCV | UCC | UM | WB |
|----|----|------|------|-----|----|----|-----|-----|----|----|
|    |    | G    |      |     |    |    |     |     |    |    |

<u>Lee</u>

| BA | DC | 1940 | 1982 | LBW | LW | PH | RCV | UCC | UM | WB |
|----|----|------|------|-----|----|----|-----|-----|----|----|
| C  |    |      |      |     |    |    |     |     |    |    |

<u>Leicester</u>

| BA | DC | 1940 | 1982 | LBW | LW | PH | RCV | UCC | UM | WB |
|----|----|------|------|-----|----|----|-----|-----|----|----|
|    | a  |      |      |     |    |    |     |     |    | g  |

<u>Leila</u>

| BA | DC | 1940 | 1982 | LBW | LW | PH | RCV | UCC | UM | WB |
|----|----|------|------|-----|----|----|-----|-----|----|----|
| F  |    |      |      |     |    |    |     |     |    |    |

<u>Leisentritt</u>

| BA | DC | 1940 | 1982 | LBW | LW | PH | RCV | UCC | UM | WB |
|----|----|------|------|-----|----|----|-----|-----|----|----|
|    |    |      |      |     |    |    | Eb  |     |    |    |

Lemmel

| BA | DC | 1940 | 1982 | LBW | LW | PH | RCV | UCC | UM | WB |
|---|---|---|---|---|---|---|---|---|---|---|
| F |  |  |  |  |  |  |  |  |  |  |

Lenox

| BA | DC | 1940 | 1982 | LBW | LW | PH | RCV | UCC | UM | WB |
|---|---|---|---|---|---|---|---|---|---|---|
|  |  |  |  |  |  |  |  |  | Bb |  |

Leominster

| BA | DC | 1940 | 1982 | LBW | LW | PH | RCV | UCC | UM | WB |
|---|---|---|---|---|---|---|---|---|---|---|
|  |  |  | D |  |  |  |  | D |  |  |

## ORGAN COMPOSITIONS

Johns, Donald "Wide Open Are Your Hands" **The Concordia Hymn Prelude Series** Volume 30 Edited: Herbert Gotsch Concordia Publishing House 97-5745 Key: D

Leoni
(See also: Yigdal)

| BA | DC | 1940 | 1982 | LBW | LW | PH | RCV | UCC | UM | WB |
|---|---|---|---|---|---|---|---|---|---|---|
| e | f | f | f |  |  | f | f | f | f | f |

## INTONATIONS

Videro, Finn **Twenty-One Hymn Intonations** Concordia Publishing House 97-5004 Key: e

## ORGAN COMPOSITIONS

Childs, Edwin T. **Fantasia on "Leoni"** Harold Flammer, Inc. HH-5031 Key: f/C

Hopson, Hal H. **Five Preludes on Familiar Hymns** Harold Flammer, Inc. Hf-5123 Key: f

Lubrich, Fritz "The God of Abraham Praise" **The Parish Organist** Part Eleven Edited: Willem Mudde Concordia Publishing House 97-4758 Key: f

## FREE ACCOMPANIMENTS

Cassler, G. Winston **Organ Descants for Selected Hymn Tunes** Augsburg Publishing House 11-9304 Key: f

Hancock, Gerre **Organ Improvisations for Hymn-Singing** Hinshaw Music Co. HMO-100 Key: f

Noble, T. Tertius **Free Orban Accompaniments to One Hundred Well-Known Hymn Tunes** J. Fischer & Bros. #8175 Key: f

Wyton, Alec **New Shoots from Old Routes** Sacred
Music Press  KK 279  Key: f

Les Commandemens de Dieu
| BA | DC | 1940 | 1982 | LBW | LW | PH | RCV | UCC | UM | WB |
| G | | | | | G | | | | | |

ORGAN COMPOSITIONS

Thalben-Ball, George  **113 Variations on Hymn Tunes**
Novello & Co., Ltd.  Key: b

Let Us Break Bread
| BA | DC | 1940 | 1982 | LBW | LW | PH | RCV | UCC | UM | WB |
| Eb | | Eb | | Eb | | | | Eb | Eb | |

ORGAN COMPOSITIONS

Bristol, Lee Hastings Jr. "Prelude on Two Traditional
Tunes" **The Bristol Collection of Contemporary Hymn
Tune Preludes for Organ** Volume 2  Edited: Lee Hasting
Bristol Jr. Harold Flammer, Inc.  Key: Eb

FREE ACCOMPANIMENTS

**Free Harmonizations to Hymn Tunes By Fifty American
Composers** Edited: D. DeWitt Wasson  Hinshaw
Music, Inc.  HMO-145  Key: F

Hancock, Gerre **Organ Improvisations for Hymn-Singing**
Hinshaw Music Co.  HMO-100  Key: Eb

Leupold
| BA | DC | 1940 | 1982 | LBW | LW | PH | RCV | UCC | UM | WB |
| | | | | c | c | | | | | |

ORGAN COMPOSTIONS

Schalk, Carl  "O God, Whose Will is Life and Good"
**The Concordia Hymn Prelude Series** Volume 30
Edited: Herbert Gotsch  Concordia Publishing
House  97-5745  Key: c

Lew Trenchard
| BA | DC | 1940 | 1982 | LBW | LW | PH | RCV | UCC | UM | WB |
| | C | | | | | | C | | | |

Lewis-Town
| BA | DC | 1940 | 1982 | LBW | LW | PH | RCV | UCC | UM | WB |
| | | | | g | | | | | | |

## ORGAN COMPOSITIONS

Fedak, Alfred   "O Son of God, in Galilee"   **The Concordia Hymn Prelude Series**   Volume 30   Edited: Herbert Gotsch   Concordia Publishing House   97-5745   Key: g

<u>Liberty</u>

| BA | DC | 1940 | 1982 | LBW | LW | PH | RCV | UCC | UM | WB |
|----|----|------|------|-----|----|----|-----|-----|----|----|
| e  |    |      |      |     |    |    |     |     |    |    |

<u>Lieben ist mein leben</u>

| BA | DC | 1940 | 1982 | LBW | LW | PH | RCV | UCC | UM | WB |
|----|----|------|------|-----|----|----|-----|-----|----|----|
|    | A  |      |      |     |    |    |     |     |    |    |

<u>Liebster Jesu, wir sind hier</u>

| BA | DC | 1940 | 1982 | LBW | LW | PH | RCV | UCC | UM | WB |
|----|----|------|------|-----|----|----|-----|-----|----|----|
| G  | G  | G    | G    | G   | G  | G  | G   |     | G  | G  |

## INTONATIONS

Manz, Paul   **Ten Short Intonations on Well Known Hymn Tunes**   Augsburg Publishing House   11-9492   Key: G

## ORGAN COMPOSITIONS

Bach, J. S.   **Organ Works**   Volume 1   Edited: Heinz Harald Löhlein   Urtext of the New Bach Edition   Bärenreiter   5171   Key: A

Bach, J. S.   **Organ Works**   Volume 3   "The Individually Transmitted Organ Chorales"   Edited: Hans Klotz   Urtext of the New Bach Edition   Bärenreiter   5173   Key: G; Key: A

Bach, J.S.   **Organ Works**   Volume VI   Widor-Schweitzer   G. Schirmer   (#47, 48)   Key: G; Key: A

Bach, J.S.   **Organ Works**   Volume VII   Widor-Schweitzer   G. Schirmer   (35.a , 35.b)   Key: A

Bach, J.S.   **Orgelwerke**   Volume V   C.F. Peters Corporation   Nr. 244   #36   Key: A   #37   Key: A

Bach, J.S.   **The Liturgical Year**   (Orgelbuchlein)   Edited: Albert Reimenschneider   Oliver Ditson Co.   Key: A

Bach, J.S.   "Blessed Jesus, at Thy Word"   **The Parish Organist**   Part Two   Edited: Heinrich Fleischer   Concordia Publishing House   97-1151   Key: G

Beck, Albert  **76 Offertories on Hymns & Chorales**
Concordia Publishing House  97-5207  Key: G

Bender, Jan  "Dearest Jesus, We Are Here"  **The
Concordia Hymn Prelude Series**  Volume 16
Edited: Herbert Gotsch  Concordia Publishing House
97-5707  Key: G

Cherwien, David  **Interpretations Based on Hymn-tunes**
A.M.S.I.  OR-1  Key: G

Clokey, Joseph W.  "Meditation on 'Liebster Jesu'"
**Ten Meditations on Hymn Melodies** J. Fischer
and Bro. #8824  Key: G

Dupre, Marcel  **Seventy-Nine Chorales for Organ**
Opus 28  H. W. Gray  Key: A

Gieschen, Thomas  **Four Quiet Hymn Settings**  Concordia
Publishing House  97-5839  Key: G

Karg-Elert, Sigfrid  "Dearest Jesu, We are Here"
**Choral Improvisations for Organ** Key: G

Kerr, J. Wayne  "Blessed Jesus at Thy Word"  **O God
Our Help in Ages Past**  Broadman Press  Key: G

Kickstat, Paul  "Dearest Jesus, at Your Word"  **The
Concordia Hymn Prelude Series**  Volume 30
Edited: Herbert Gotsch  Concordia Publishing House
97-5745  Key: G

Stearns, Peter Pindar  **Twenty Hymn Preludes**
Coburn Press (Theodore Presser Company) Key: G

Thalben-Ball, George  **113 Variations on Hymn Tunes**
Novello & Co., Ltd.  Key: G

Walther, Johann Gottfried "Choral Prelude on 'Liebster
Jesu, wir sind hier'" **For Manuals Only**
Edited: John Christopher  McAfee Music Corporation
Key: G

Walther, Johann Gottfried **80 Chorale Preludes – German
Masters of the 17th and 18th Centuries**  Edited:
Hermann Keller  C.F. Peters Corporation #4448
Key: G

Walther, Johann Gottfried **Chorale Preludes by Masters
of the 17th and 18th Centuries**  Volume I  Edited:
Walter Buszin  Concordia Publishing House  Key: G

FREE ACCOMPANIMENTS

Bunjes, Paul  **New Organ Accompaniments for Hymns**
Concordia Publishing House   97-5348   Key: G

Hillert, Richard  **Hymn Preludes and Free Accompaniments**
Volume 10   Augsburg Publishing House   11-9406
Key: G

## Lift Every Voice and Sing

| BA | DC | 1940 | 1982 | LBW | LW | PH | RCV | UCC | UM | WB |
|----|----|------|------|-----|----|----|-----|-----|----|----|
|    |    | Ab   | G    |     |    |    |     |     |    |    |

ORGAN COMPOSITIONS

Busarow, Donald  "Lift Every Voice and Sing"  **The Concordia Hymn Prelude Series**  Volume 30
Edited: Herbert Gotsch   Concordia Publishing House
97-5745   Key: G

## Light

| BA | DC | 1940 | 1982 | LBW | LW | PH | RCV | UCC | UM | WB |
|----|----|------|------|-----|----|----|-----|-----|----|----|
|    |    | g    | g    |     |    |    |     |     |    |    |

## Light Divine
(See also: Song 13)

ORGAN COMPOSITIONS

Noehren, Robert  "Holy Ghost, with Light Divine"
**The Parish Organist**  Part Eight   Music for
Easter, Ascension, Pentecost and Trinity
Edited: Erich Goldschmidt   Concordia Publishing
House   97-1404   Key: Eb

## Light of the World

| BA | DC | 1940 | 1982 | LBW | LW | PH | RCV | UCC | UM | WB |
|----|----|------|------|-----|----|----|-----|-----|----|----|
|    |    |      |      |     |    |    |     | F   |    |    |

## Limpsfield

| BA | DC | 1940 | 1982 | LBW | LW | PH | RCV | UCC | UM | WB |
|----|----|------|------|-----|----|----|-----|-----|----|----|
| D  |    |      |      |     |    |    |     |     |    |    |

## Lindemann

| BA | DC | 1940 | 1982 | LBW | LW | PH | RCV | UCC | UM | WB |
|----|----|------|------|-----|----|----|-----|-----|----|----|
|    |    |      |      |     |    |    |     | F   |    |    |

FREE ACCOMPANIMENTS

Cassler, G. Winston  **Organ Descants for Selected Hymn
Tunes**  Augsburg Publishing House   11-9304   Key: F

## Lindens

| BA | DC | 1940 | 1982 | LBW | LW | PH | RCV | UCC | UM | WB |
|----|----|------|------|-----|----|----|-----|-----|----|----|
|    |    |      |      |     |    |    | f   |     |    |    |

## Lindsborg

| BA | DC | 1940 | 1982 | LBW | LW | PH | RCV | UCC | UM | WB |
|----|----|------|------|-----|----|----|-----|-----|----|----|
|    |    |      |      | m:d |    |    |     |     |    |    |

### ORGAN COMPOSITIONS

Rohlig, Harald  "In His Temple Now Behold Him"  **The Concordia Hymn Prelude Series**  Volume 15 Edited: Herbert Gotsch  Concordia Publishing House 97-5706  Key: m:d

## Litany of the Passion

| BA | DC | 1940 | 1982 | LBW | LW | PH | RCV | UCC | UM | WB |
|----|----|------|------|-----|----|----|-----|-----|----|----|
|    |    | D    |      |     |    |    |     |     |    |    |

## Little Cornard

| BA | DC | 1940 | 1982 | LBW | LW | PH | RCV | UCC | UM | WB |
|----|----|------|------|-----|----|----|-----|-----|----|----|
|    |    | D    |      |     |    | Eb |     |     |    |    |

## Little Flock

| BA | DC | 1940 | 1982 | LBW | LW | PH | RCV | UCC | UM | WB |
|----|----|------|------|-----|----|----|-----|-----|----|----|
| Eb |    |      |      | Eb  | Eb |    |     |     |    |    |

### ORGAN COMPOSITIONS

Schultz, Ralph C.  "Have No Fear, Little Flock" **The Concordia Hymn Prelude Series**  Volume 30 Edited: Herbert Gotsch  Concordia Publishing House 97-5745  Key: Eb

## Litton

| BA | DC | 1940 | 1982 | LBW | LW | PH | RCV | UCC | UM | WB |
|----|----|------|------|-----|----|----|-----|-----|----|----|
|    |    |      | Eb   |     |    |    |     |     |    |    |

## Living

| BA | DC | 1940 | 1982 | LBW | LW | PH | RCV | UCC | UM | WB |
|----|----|------|------|-----|----|----|-----|-----|----|----|
| F  |    |      |      |     |    |    |     |     |    |    |

## Llanfair

| BA | DC | 1940 | 1982 | LBW | LW | PH | RCV | UCC | UM | WB |
|----|----|------|------|-----|----|----|-----|-----|----|----|
| F  | F  | F    | G    | F   | F  | F  | F   | F   | G  | F  |

### INTONATIONS

McCormick, David  **20 Organ Intonations on Hymns of Praise**  Hope Publishing Co.  Key: G

## ORGAN COMPOSITIONS

Geiseke, Richard W. "Christ the Lord is Risen Today: Alleluia" **The Concordia Hymn Prelude Series** Volume 10 Edited: Herbert Gotsch Concordia Publishing House 97-5617 Key: F

Schroeder, Hermann "Christ the Lord is Risen Today, Alleluia!" **The Parish Organist** Part Eight Music for Easter, Ascension, Pentecost and Trinity Concordia Publishing House 97-1404 Key: G

Thalben-Ball, George **113 Variations on Hymn Tunes** Novello & Co., Ltd. Key: G

## FREE ACCOMPANIMENTS

Cassler, G. Winston **Organ Descants for Selected Hymn Tunes** Augsburg Publishing House 11-9304 Key:G

Ferguson, John **Ten Hymn Tune Harmonizations** Book I Ludwig Music Publishing Co. 0-05 Key: F

Gehrke, Hugo **Hymn Preludes and Free Accompaniments** Volume 5 Augsburg Publishing House 11-9401 Key: F

Lovelace, Austin C. **Hymn Preludes and Free Accompaniments** Volume 4 Augsburg Publishing House 11-9400 Key: F

Post, Piet **Free Organ Accompaniments to Hymns** Volume III General-Palm Sunday-Easter Augsburg Publishing House 11-9189 Key: G

Wyton, Alec **New Shoots From Old Routes** Sacred Music Press KK 279 Key: F

### Llanfyllin

| BA | DC | 1940 | 1982 | LBW | LW | PH | RCV | UCC | UM | WB |
|----|----|------|------|-----|----|----|-----|-----|----|----|
| G  | G  |      |      |     |    |    |     |     | G  |    |

## ORGAN COMPOSITIONS

Goode, Jack **Seven Communion Meditations** Harold Flammer, Inc. HF-5084 Key: D

### Llangloffan

| BA | DC | 1940 | 1982 | LBW | LW | PH | RCV | UCC | UM | WB |
|----|----|------|------|-----|----|----|-----|-----|----|----|
|    | g  | g    | g    |     |    | g  |     | g   | g  | g  |

232

## ORGAN COMPOSITIONS

Dahl, David P.   "Where Restless Crowds are Thronging"
**The Concordia Hymn Prelude Series**  Volume 30
Edited: Herbert Gotsch  Concordia Publishing House
97-5745  Key: Bb

## FREE ACCOMPANIMENTS

**Free Harmonizations to Hymn Tunes By Fifty American
Composers**  Edited: D. DeWitt Wasson  Hinshaw
Music, Inc.  HMO-145  Key: g

Goode, Jack C.  **Thirty-Four Changes on Hymn Tunes**
H. W. Gray Co.  GB 644  Key: g

Llanherne

| BA | DC | 1940 | 1982 | LBW | LW | PH | RCV | UCC | UM | WB |
|----|----|------|------|-----|----|----|-----|-----|----|----|
|    |    |      |      |     |    | G  |     |     |    |    |

Llanllyfni

| BA | DC | 1940 | 1982 | LBW | LW | PH | RCV | UCC | UM | WB |
|----|----|------|------|-----|----|----|-----|-----|----|----|
|    | d  |      |      |     |    | d  |     |     |    |    |

Llansannan

| BA | DC | 1940 | 1982 | LBW | LW | PH | RCV | UCC | UM | WB |
|----|----|------|------|-----|----|----|-----|-----|----|----|
|    |    |      |      |     |    | c  |     | c   |    |    |

Lledrod

| BA | DC | 1940 | 1982 | LBW | LW | PH | RCV | UCC | UM | WB |
|----|----|------|------|-----|----|----|-----|-----|----|----|
|    |    | Ab   | Ab   |     | Ab | PH |     |     |    |    |

## ORGAN COMPOSITIONS

Patterson, Kim Kondal   "Forth in the Peace of Christ"
**The Concordia Hymn Prelude Series**  Volume 30
Edited: Herbert Gotsch  Concordia Publishing House
97-5745  Key: Ab

Llef

| BA | DC | 1940 | 1982 | LBW | LW | PH | RCV | UCC | UM | WB |
|----|----|------|------|-----|----|----|-----|-----|----|----|
|    |    |      |      |     |    |    |     |     |    | d  |

Lo desembre congelat

| BA | DC | 1940 | 1982 | LBW | LW | PH | RCV | UCC | UM | WB |
|----|----|------|------|-----|----|----|-----|-----|----|----|
|    |    |      |      | D   |    |    |     |     |    |    |

## ORGAN COMPOSITIONS

Busarow, Donald   "Cold December Flies Away"  **The
Concordia Hymn Prelude Series**  Volume 4  Edited:
Herbert Gotsch  Concordia Publishing House
97-5539  Key: D

Lob Gott getrost mit Singen
| BA | DC | 1940 | 1982 | LBW | LW | PH | RCV | UCC | UM | WB |
|----|----|------|------|-----|----|----|-----|-----|----|----|
|    |    |      |      | G   | G  |    |     |     |    |    |

## FREE ACCOMPANIMENTS

Ore, Charles **Hymn Preludes and Free Accompaniments**
Volume 7  Augsburg Publishing House  11-9403
Key: G

Lob sei dem allmächtigen Gott
| BA | DC | 1940 | 1982 | LBW | LW | PH | RCV | UCC | UM | WB |
|----|----|------|------|-----|----|----|-----|-----|----|----|
|    |    |      |      | D   |    |    |     |     |    |    |

## ORGAN COMPOSITIONS

Bach, J. S. **Organ Works** Volume 1 Edited: Heinz-
Harald Löhlein  Urtext of the New Bach Edition
Bärenreiter  5171  Key: m:a

Bach, J. S. **Organ Works** Volume 3  "The Individually
Transmitted Organ Chorales"  Edited: Hans Klotz
Urtext of the New Bach Edition  Bärenreiter
5173  Key: m:a

Bach, J. S. **Organ Works** Volume VI  Widor-Schweitzer
G. Schirmer  Key: F

Bach, J. S. **Organ Works** Volume VII Widor-Schweitzer
G. Schirmer  Key: F

Bach, J.S. **The Liturgical Year** (Orgelbuchlein)
Edited: Albert Reimenschneider  Oliver Ditson
Key: m:a

Dupre, Marcel **Seventy-Nine Chorales for Organ**
Opus 28  H. W. Gray  Key: F

Kosche, Kenneth T.  "Great God, a Blessing From Your
Throne" **The Concordia Hymn Prelude Series**
Volume 15  Edited: Herbert Gotsch  Concordia
Publishing House  97-5706  Key D

Lobe den Herren
(See also: Kommst du nun, Jesu, Vom Himmel herrunter)
| BA | DC | 1940 | 1982 | LBW | LW | PH | RCV | UCC | UM | WB |
|----|----|------|------|-----|----|----|-----|-----|----|----|
| F  | G  |      | F    | F   | F  | G  |     | G   | G  | F  |

## INTONATIONS

McCormick, David **20 Organ Intonations on Hymns of
Praise** Hope Publishing Co.  Key: F

# ORGAN COMPOSITIONS

Bach, J. S. **Six Organ Chorales** (Schubler)
  Edited: Albert Riemenschneider  Oliver
  Ditson Co.  Key: G

Bach, J.S.  **Organ Works** Col. VIII  Widor-
  Schweitzer  G. Schirmer  Key: G

Bender, Jan  "Praise to the Lord, the Almighty,
  the King of Creation" **Festival Preludes on
  Six Chorales** Concordia Publishing House
  97-4608  Key: G

Cherwien, David **Interpretations Based on Hymn-
  tunes** Book II  A.M.S.I.  OR-3  Key: G

Walther, Johann Gottfried 80 **Chorale Preludes –
  German Masters of the 17th and 18th Centuries**
  Edited:  Hermann  Keller   C.F.  Peters
  Corporation  #4448  Key: G

Walther, Johann Gottfried  **Chorale Preludes by
  Masters of the 17th and 18th Centuries** Volume
  I  Edited:  Walter  Buszin   Concordia
  Publishing House  Key: G

Zipp, Friedrich  "Praise to the Lord, the Almighty"
  **The Parish Organist** Part Twelve  Edited: Willem
  Mudde  Concordia Publishing House  97-4759  Key: G

# FREE ACCOMPANIMENTS

Alwes, Charles  **Six Organ Preludes**  Augsburg Publishing
  House  11-9416  Key: G

Bunjes, Paul  **New Organ Accompaniments for Hymns**
  Concordia Publishing House  97-5348  Key: G

Busarow, Donald  **Hymn Preludes and Free Accompaniments**
  Volume 8  Augsburg Publishing House  11-9404
  Key: F

Cassler, G. Winston **Organ Descants for Selected Hymn
  Tunes** Augsburg Publishing House  11-9304  Key: G

Coleman, Henry  **Varied Hymn Accompaniments**
  Oxford University Press  Key: G

Ferguson, John  **Ten Hymn Tune Harmonizations**  Book I
  Ludwig Music Publishing Co.  0-05  Key: G

Goode, Jack C. **Thirty-Four Changes on Hymn Tunes**
H. W. Gray Co. GB 644 Key: F

Hancock, Gerre **Organ Improvisations for Hymn-Singing**
Hinshaw Music Co. HMO-100 Key: G

Hebble, Robert **Robert Hebble's Hymnal Companion for
Organ** Bradley Publications CE/283A/3 Key: G

Moe, Daniel **Free Organ Accompaniments to Festival
Hymns** Volume I Augsburg Publishing House 11-9192
Key: G

Noble, T. Tertius **Free Organ Cccompaniments to One
Hundred Well-Known Hymn Tunes** J. Fischer & Bros.
#8175 Key: G

Ore, Charles **Hymn Preludes and Free Accompaniments**
Volume 7 Augsburg Publishing House 11-9403
Key: F

Schack, David **Hymn Preludes and Free Accompaniments**
Volume 11 Augsburg Publishing House 11-9407
Key: G

Wood, Dale **New Settings of Twenty Well-Known Hymn
Tunes** Augsburg Publishing House 11-9292 Key: F

Wyton, Alec **New Shoots From Old Routes** Sacred Music
Press KK 279 Key: F

<u>Lobe den Herren, o meine Seele</u>

| BA | DC | 1940 | 1982 | LBW | LW | PH | RCV | UCC | UM | WB |
|----|----|------|------|-----|----|----|-----|-----|----|----|
|    |    |      |      | G   | G  | G  |     |     |    |    |

ORGAN COMPOSITIONS

Bender, Jan "Praise the Almighty, My Soul, Adore Him"
**Festival Preludes on Six Chorales** Concordia
Publishing House 97-4608 Key: G

FREE ACCOMPANIMENTS

Bunjes, Paul **New Organ Accompaniments for Hymns**
Concordia Publishing House 97-5348 Key: G

<u>Lobet den Herren</u>

| BA | DC | 1940 | 1982 | LBW | LW | PH | RCV | UCC | UM | WB |
|----|----|------|------|-----|----|----|-----|-----|----|----|
|    |    |      | C    |     |    |    |     |     |    |    |

Lobt Gott den Herren, ihr
(See also: Sing Praise to God, the Highest Good)
    BA    DC    1940 1982 LBW  LW    PH    RCV   UCC   UM    WB
                          F    F                             E

ORGAN COMPOSITIONS

Barlow, Wayne **Four Chorale Voluntaries**
    Concordia Publishing House 97-5602  Key: F

Dupre, Marcel  **Seventy-Nine Chorales for Organ**
    Opus 28  H. W. Gray  Key: G

Walther, Johann Gottfried  "Praise God the Lord, Ye
    Sons of Men:  **The Parish Organist**  Part Two
    Edited: Heinrich Fleischer  Concordia Publishing
    House  97-1151  Key:  F

Walther, Johann Gottfried  "Praise God the Lord, Ye
    Sons of Men" **The Parish Organist**  Part Five
    Advent and Christmas Music  Concordia Publishing
    House  97-1382   Key: F

Walther, Johann Gottfried  "Chorale prelude 'Lobt Gott,
    ihr Christen, allzugleich'" **Organ Music for
    Christmas** Volume 1  Edited: C. H. Trevor
    Oxford University Press  Key: G

FREE ACCOMPANIMENTS

Bunjes, Paul  **New Organ Accompaniments for Hymns**
    Concordia Publishing House  97-5348  Key: F

Lobt Gott, ihr Christen allzugleich
(See also: Hermann)
    BA    DC    1940 1982 LBW  LW    PH    RCV   UCC   UM    WB
    F                     F    F    F           F     Eb

ORGAN COMPOSITIONS

Bach, J. S.  **Organ Works**  Volume 1  Edited: Heinz
    Harald Löhlein  Urtext of the New Bach Edition
    Bärenreiter  5171  Key: G

Bach, J. S.  **Organ Works**  Volume 3  "The Individually
    Transmitted Organ Chorales" Edited: Hans Klotz
    Urtext of the New Bach Edition  Bärenreiter
    5173  Key: E

Buxtehude, Dietrich "Choralvorspiel: Lobt Gott, ihr
    Christen, allzugleich" **Alte Meister** Edited:
    Karl Straube  Book I  C.F. Peters Corporation
    No. 4301  Key: G

Buxtehude, Dietrich  "Praise God, Ye Christians"
   **Anthologia Antiqua**  Book Five  **Six Chorale**
   **Preludes**  Edited: Seth Bingham  J. Fischer & Bros.
   No. 8090  Key: G

Bach, J. S.  **Organ Works** Volume VI  Widor-Schweitzer
   G. Schirmer  Key: E

Bach, J. S.  **Organ Works** Volume VII  Widor-Schweitzer
   G. Schirmer  Key: G

Bach, J. S.  "Chorale Prelude on 'Lobt Gott, ihr
   Christen allzugleich"  **For Manuals Only**  Edited:
   John Christopher  McAfee Music Corporation  Key: E

Bach, J.S.  **The Liturgical Year**  (Orgelbuchlein)
   Edited: Albert Reimenschneider  Oliver Ditson Co.
   Key: G

Buxtehude, Dietrich  **Orgelwerke II: Chorale Preludes**
   C.F. Peters Corporation  #4457  Key: G

Walther, Johann Gottfried "Chorale Prelude on 'Lobt
   Gott, ihr Christien, allzugleich'"  **For Manuals**
   **Only**  Edited: John Christopher  McAfee Music
   Corporation  Key: G

Walther, Johann Gottfried  **80 Chorale Preludes – German**
   **Masters of the 17th and 18th Centuries**  Edited:
   Hermann Keller  C.F. Peters Corporation #4448
   Key: F

Walther, Johann Gottfried  "Praise God the Lord, Ye
   Sons of Men"  **The Parish Organist** Part Five
   Advent and Christmas Music  Concordia Publishing
   House  97-1382  Key: F

Walther, Johann Gottfried  "Lobt Gott, ihr Christen"
   **Organ Music for Christmas**  Edited:  C. H. Trevor
   Oxford University Press  Key: G

Walther, Johann Gottfried  "Let All Together Praise Our
   God"  **The Concordia Hymn Prelude Series**  Volume 4
   Edited:  Herbert Gotsch  Concordia Publishing
   House  97-5539  Key: F

Willan, Healey  **Six Chorale Preludes**  Concordia
   Publishing House  97-3905  Key: F

FREE ACCOMPANIMENTS

Bender, Jan **Hymn Preludes and Free Accompaniments**
Volume 1  Augsburg Publishing House  11-9397
Key: F

## Locust Grove

| BA | DC | 1940 | 1982 | LBW | LW | PH | RCV | UCC | UM | WB |
|----|----|------|------|-----|----|----|-----|-----|----|----|
|    |    | 1940 | 1982 | LBW | LW | PH | RCV | UCC c | UM | WB |

## Lombard Street

| BA | DC | 1940 | 1982 | LBW | LW | PH | RCV | UCC | UM | WB |
|----|----|------|------|-----|----|----|-----|-----|----|----|
|    | d  | 1940 | 1982 | LBW | LW | PH d | RCV | UCC d | UM | WB d |

## London New

| BA | DC | 1940 | 1982 | LBW | LW | PH | RCV | UCC | UM | WB |
|----|----|------|------|-----|----|----|-----|-----|----|----|
|    |    | 1940 D | 1982 D | LBW | LW | PH | RCV | UCC | UM | WB |

ORGAN COMPOSITIONS

Thalben-Ball, George **113 Variations on Hymn Tunes**
Novello & Co., Ltd.  Key: D

FREE ACCOMPANIMENTS

Lang, C. S. **Twenty Hymn-Tune Preludes**  (First Set)
Oxford University Press    (Two Settings) Key: D
Key: Eb

Noble, T. Tertius  **Fifty Free Organ Accompaniments
to Well Known Hymn Tunes**  J. Fischer & Bros.
No. 8430  Key: D

Willan, Healey  **36 Short Preludes and Postludes** on
**Well-Known Hymn Tunes**  Set II  C.F. Peters
Corporation  No. 6162  Key: D

## Lonesome Valley

| BA | DC | 1940 | 1982 | LBW | LW | PH | RCV | UCC | UM | WB |
|----|----|------|------|-----|----|----|-----|-----|----|----|
|    |    | 1940 | 1982 | LBW | LW | PH | RCV | UCC F | UM | WB |

ORGAN COMPOSITIONS

Jackson, Francis "Prelude on a Folk Hymn 'Lonesome
Valley'" **The Bristol Collection of Contemporary
Hymn Tune Preludes for Organ**  Volume 2 Editor:
Lee Hastings Bristol  Harold Flammer  Key: d/D

## Lord Revive Us

| BA | DC | 1940 | 1982 | LBW | LW | PH | RCV | UCC | UM | WB |
|----|----|------|------|-----|----|----|-----|-----|----|----|
|    |    | 1940 F | 1982 | LBW | LW | PH | RCV | UCC | UM | WB |

Busarow, Donald **All Praise to You Eternal God**
Augsburg Publishing House  11-9076  Key: F

Lordship of Christ

| BA | DC | 1940 | 1982 | LBW | LW | PH | RCV | UCC | UM | WB |
|----|----|------|------|-----|----|----|-----|-----|----|----|
| Db |    |      |      |     |    |    |     |     |    |    |

Loriann

| BA | DC | 1940 | 1982 | LBW | LW | PH | RCV | UCC | UM | WB |
|----|----|------|------|-----|----|----|-----|-----|----|----|
| F  |    |      |      |     |    |    |     |     |    |    |

Lost in the Night

| BA | DC | 1940 | 1982 | LBW | LW | PH | RCV | UCC | UM | WB |
|----|----|------|------|-----|----|----|-----|-----|----|----|
|    |    | c    |      |     |    |    |     |     |    |    |

Louez Dieu

| BA | DC | 1940 | 1982 | LBW | LW | PH | RCV | UCC | UM | WB |
|----|----|------|------|-----|----|----|-----|-----|----|----|
|    |    | G    |      |     |    |    |     |     |    |    |

Lourdes Hymn

| BA | DC | 1940 | 1982 | LBW | LW | PH | RCV | UCC | UM | WB |
|----|----|------|------|-----|----|----|-----|-----|----|----|
|    |    |      |      |     |    |    | G   |     |    |    |

Louvan

| BA | DC | 1940 | 1982 | LBW | LW | PH | RCV | UCC | UM | WB |
|----|----|------|------|-----|----|----|-----|-----|----|----|
|    |    |      |      |     |    | G  |     |     | G  | G  |

FREE ACCOMPANIMENTS

Noble, T. Tertius **Free Organ Accompaniments to One Hundred Well-Known Hymn Tunes** J. Fischer & Bros. #8175  Key: Ab

Love Divine

| BA | DC | 1940 | 1982 | LBW | LW | PH | RCV | UCC | UM | WB |
|----|----|------|------|-----|----|----|-----|-----|----|----|
|    |    | Eb   |      |     |    |    | Eb  |     |    |    |

ORGAN COMPOSITIONS

Hopkins, Douglas  "Postlude on 'Love Divine'"
**Canterbury Organ Album**  Edited: Allan Wicks
Novello  Key: G

Thalben-Ball, George  **113 Variations on Hymn Tunes**
Novello & Co., Ltd.  Key: G

Love Unknown
(See also: Rhosymedre; Lovely)

| BA | DC | 1940 | 1982 | LBW | LW | PH | RCV | UCC | UM | WB |
|----|----|------|------|-----|----|----|-----|-----|----|----|
|    |    | D    |      |     | D  |    |     | Eb  |    |    |

Held, Wilbur  "My Song is Love Unknown" **The Concordia Hymn Prelude Series** Volume 8  Edited: Herbert Gotsch  Concordia Publishing House  97-5615 Key: D

Stearns, Peter Pindar **Eight Hymn Preludes for Lent** Harold Flammer, Inc.  HF-5133  Key: Eb

Love's Offering

| BA | DC | 1940 | 1982 | LBW | LW | PH | RCV | UCC | UM | WB |
|----|----|------|------|-----|----|----|-----|-----|----|----|
|    |    |      |      |     |    | Ab |     |     |    |    |

Lovely
(See a~~ls~~. Rhosymedre; Love Unknown)

Lower Lights

| BA | DC | 1940 | 1982 | LBW | LW | PH | RCV | UCC | UM | WB |
|----|----|------|------|-----|----|----|-----|-----|----|----|
|    |    |      |      |     |    |    |     |     | Bb |    |

Lowry

| BA | DC | 1940 | 1982 | LBW | LW | PH | RCV | UCC | UM | WB |
|----|----|------|------|-----|----|----|-----|-----|----|----|
|    |    |      | F    |     |    |    |     |     |    |    |

Lubbock

| BA | DC | 1940 | 1982 | LBW | LW | PH | RCV | UCC | UM | WB |
|----|----|------|------|-----|----|----|-----|-----|----|----|
| F  |    |      |      |     |    |    |     |     |    |    |

Lübeck
(See also: Gott sei Dank)

| BA | DC | 1940 | 1982 | LBW | LW | PH | RCV | UCC | UM | WB |
|----|----|------|------|-----|----|----|-----|-----|----|----|
|    |    | C    |      |     |    |    |     |     |    |    |

Lucerna Laudoniae

| BA | DC | 1940 | 1982 | LBW | LW | PH | RCV | UCC | UM | WB |
|----|----|------|------|-----|----|----|-----|-----|----|----|
|    |    |      | Ab   |     |    |    |     |     |    |    |

Lucis Creator

| BA | DC | 1940 | 1982 | LBW | LW | PH | RCV | UCC | UM | WB |
|----|----|------|------|-----|----|----|-----|-----|----|----|
|    |    | m:f  | m:f  |     |    |    | m:f |     |    |    |

Luise
(See also: Jesus, meine Zuversicht)

| BA | DC | 1940 | 1982 | LBW | LW | PH | RCV | UCC | UM | WB |
|----|----|------|------|-----|----|----|-----|-----|----|----|
|    |    | Bb   |      |     |    |    |     |     |    |    |

Luke

| BA | DC | 1940 | 1982 | LBW | LW | PH | RCV | UCC | UM | WB |
|----|----|------|------|-----|----|----|-----|-----|----|----|
|    |    | D    |      |     |    |    |     |     |    |    |

Lukkason

| BA | DC | 1940 | 1982 | LBW | LW | PH | RCV | UCC | UM | WB |
|----|----|------|------|-----|----|----|-----|-----|----|----|
|    |    |      | Ab   |     |    |    |     |     |    |    |

<u>Luther's Hymn</u>
(See also: Nun freut euch)

<u>Lux benigna</u>

| BA | DC | 1940 | 1982 | LBW | LW | PH | RCV | UCC | UM | WB |
|----|----|------|------|-----|----|----|-----|-----|----|----|
|    |    | Ab   |      |     |    | Ab | Ab  | Ab  | Ab |    |

FREE ACCOMPANIMENTS

**Free Harmonizations to Hymn Tunes By Fifty American Composers** Edited: D. DeWitt Wasson Hinshaw Music, Inc. HMO-145 Key: Ab

<u>Lux eoi</u>

| BA | DC | 1940 | 1982 | LBW | LW | PH | RCV | UCC | UM | WB |
|----|----|------|------|-----|----|----|-----|-----|----|----|
|    | C  | C    |      |     |    |    | C   |     |    |    |

<u>Lux prima</u>

| BA | DC | 1940 | 1982 | LBW | LW | PH | RCV | UCC | UM | WB |
|----|----|------|------|-----|----|----|-----|-----|----|----|
|    | G  |      |      |     |    |    |     |     |    |    |

<u>Lynchburg</u>

| BA | DC | 1940 | 1982 | LBW | LW | PH | RCV | UCC | UM | WB |
|----|----|------|------|-----|----|----|-----|-----|----|----|
|    | Eb |      |      |     |    |    |     |     |    |    |

<u>Lynne</u>

| BA | DC | 1940 | 1982 | LBW | LW | PH | RCV | UCC | UM | WB |
|----|----|------|------|-----|----|----|-----|-----|----|----|
|    | D  |      |      | D   |    | D  |     |     |    |    |

FREE ACCOMPANIMENTS

**Free Harmonizations to Hymn Tunes By Fifty American Composers** Edited: D. DeWitt Wasson Hinshaw Music, Inc. HMO-145 Key: D

<u>Lyons</u>

| BA | DC | 1940 | 1982 | LBW | LW | PH | RCV | UCC | UM | WB |
|----|----|------|------|-----|----|----|-----|-----|----|----|
| Ab | Ab | G    | G    | G   |    | G  |     | G   | A  | Ab |

INTONATIONS

McCormick, David **20 Organ Intonations on Hymns of Praise** Hope Publishing Co. Key: G

Videro, Finn **Twenty-One Hymn Intonations** Concordia Publishing House 97-5004 Key: G

ORGAN COMPOSITIONS

Cherwien, David **Interpretations Based on Hymn-tunes** A.M.S.I. OR-1 Key: G

242

Cobb, Nancy Hill **O Worship the King** Van Ness Press
4180-02 Key: A

Johnson, David "How Wondrous and Great" **The Parish
Organist** Part Eleven Edited: Willem Mudde
Concordia Publishing House 97-4758 Key: G

Thalben-Ball, George **113 Variations on Hymn Tunes**
H.W. Gray Co. Key: G

FREE ACCOMPANIMENTS

Cassler, G. Winston **Organ Descants for Selected Hymn
Tunes** Augsburg Publishing House 11-9304 Key: A

Goode, Jack C. **Thirty-Four Changes on Hymn Tunes**
H. W. Gray Co. GB 644 Key: A

Hebble, Robert **Robert Hebble's Hymnal Companion for
Organ** Bradley Publications CE/283A/3 Key: G

Noble, T. Tertius **Free Organ Accompaniments to One
Hundred Well-Known Hymn Tunes** J. Fischer & Bros.
#8175 Key: G

Wyton, Alec **New Shoots From Old Routes** Sacred Music
Press KK 279 Key: G

Lystra

| BA | DC | 1940 | 1982 | LBW | LW | PH | RCV | UCC | UM | WB |
|----|----|------|------|-----|----|----|-----|-----|----|----|
|    |    | Eb   |      |     |    |    |     |     |    |    |

Lytlington

| BA | DC | 1940 | 1982 | LBW | LW | PH | RCV | UCC | UM | WB |
|----|----|------|------|-----|----|----|-----|-----|----|----|
|    | D  | D    | D    |     |    | D  |     |     |    |    |

# M

Mabune

| BA | DC | 1940 | 1982 | LBW | LW | PH | RCV | UCC | UM | WB |
|----|----|------|------|-----|----|----|-----|-----|----|----|
|    |    |      |      | F   |    |    |     |     |    |    |

Maccabeus

| BA | DC | 1940 | 1982 | LBW | LW | PH | RCV | UCC | UM | WB |
|----|----|------|------|-----|----|----|-----|-----|----|----|
|    | E  |      |      |     |    |    |     |     |    |    |

MacDougall

| BA | DC | 1940 | 1982 | LBW | LW | PH | RCV | UCC | UM | WB |
|----|----|------|------|-----|----|----|-----|-----|----|----|
|    |    |      | Eb   |     |    |    |     |     |    |    |

<u>Machs mit mir, Gott</u>
  (See also: Come, Follow Me, the Savior Spake)
    BA    DC    1940 1982 LBW   LW    PH    RCV   UCC   UM    WB
                     D    D     D     D

ORGAN COMPOSITIONS

    Bach, J. S. **Organ Chorales from the Neumeister
        Collection** Edited: Christoph Wolff  Yale
        University Press/Bärenreiter 5181  Key: G

    Barlow, Wayne **Four Chorale Voluntaries**
        Concordia Publishing House 97-5602  Key: Eb

    Karg-Elert, Sigfrid "Do With Me Lord, After Thy
        Goodness" **Choral Improvisations for Organ for
        New Year, Easter and other Church Festivals**
        Op. 65, Volume 3 Edited: Robert Leech Bedell
        Edward B. Marks Music Corp.  Key: Eb

    Reger, Max **Chorale Preludes for the Church Year from
        Max Reger** Op. 67  Edited: Alec Wyton  Carl
        Fischer, Inc.  0-4667  Key: Eb

    Walther, Johann Gottfried **80 Chorale Preludes –
        German Masters of the 17th and 18th Centuries**
        Edited: Hermann Keller  C.F. Peters Corporation
        #4448  Key: Eb

    Walther, Johann Gottfried **For Manuals Only**  Edited:
        John Christopher  McAfee Music Corp. Key: Eb

    Walther, Johann Gottfried "Partita on 'Machs mit mir,
        Gott, nach deiner Gut'" **For Manuals Only**
        Edited: John Christopher  McAfee Music Corp.
        Key: D

<u>Macht hoch die Tur</u>
    BA    DC    1940 1982 LBW   LW    PH    RCV   UCC   UM    WB
                     F     F

ORGAN COMPOSITIONS

    Beck, Albert  **76 Offertories on Hymns & Chorales**
        Concordia Publishing House  97-5207  Key: Ab

    Bender, Jan  "Lift Up Your Heads, Ye Mighty Gates"
        **The Parish Organist** Part Five  Advent and
        Christmas Music  Concordia Publishing House
        97-1382  Key: F

244

Johnson, David N. **Free Organ Accompaniments to Hymns**
Advent-Christmas-Epiphany  Augsburg Publishing
House  11-9187  Key: F

Johnson, David N.  "Lift Up Your Heads, You Mighty
Gates" **The Concordia Hymn Prelude Series**  Volume 1
Edited: Herbert Gotsch  Concordia Publishing House
97-5536  Key: F

Walcha, Helmut **25 Chorale Preludes** C.F. Peters
Corporation  Nr. 4850  Key: F

FREE ACCOMPANIMENTS

Cassler, G. Winston  **Organ Descants for Selected Hymn
Tunes**  Augsburg Publishing House  11-9304  Key: F

Krapf, Gerhard  **Hymn Preludes and Free Accompaniments**
Volume 13  Augsburg Publishing House  11-9409
Key: F

| | | | | | | | | | |
|---|---|---|---|---|---|---|---|---|---|
| **Maddermarket** | | | | | | | | | |
| BA | DC C | 1940 | 1982 LBW | LW | PH | RCV | UCC | UM | WB |
| **Madill** | | | | | | | | | |
| BA F | DC | 1940 | 1982 LBW | LW | PH | RCV | UCC | UM | WB |
| **Madrid** | | | | | | | | | |
| BA Ab | DC A | 1940 | 1982 LBW | LW | PH | RCV | UCC | UM | WB A |
| **Magda** | | | | | | | | | |
| BA | DC D | 1940 | 1982 LBW | LW | PH | RCV | UCC | UM | WB |
| **Magdalen** | | | | | | | | | |
| BA | DC | 1940 | 1982 LBW | LW Bb | PH | RCV | UCC | UM | WB |

ORGAN COMPOSITIONS

Van Hulse, Camil "My Hope is Built on Nothing Less"
**The Parish Organist**  Part Two  Edited:
Heinrich Fleischer  Concordia Publishing House
97-1151  Key:  C

FREE ACCOMPANIMENTS

Beck, Albert  **76 Offertories on Hymns and Chorales**
Concordia Publishing House  97-5207  Key: C

## Magdalen College

| BA | DC | 1940 | 1982 | LBW | LW | PH | RCV | UCC | UM | WB |
|----|----|------|------|-----|----|----|-----|-----|----|----|
|    |    | C    | C    |     |    |    |     |     |    |    |

## Magyar

| BA | DC | 1940 | 1982 | LBW | LW | PH | RCV | UCC | UM | WB |
|----|----|------|------|-----|----|----|-----|-----|----|----|
|    |    |      |      |     |    | f  |     | f   |    |    |

### ORGAN COMPOSITIONS

Lovelace, Austin **Fourteen Hymn Preludes** Augsburg Publishing House 11-6152   Key: F

## Maidstone

| BA | DC | 1940 | 1982 | LBW | LW | PH | RCV | UCC | UM | WB |
|----|----|------|------|-----|----|----|-----|-----|----|----|
|    |    | F    |      |     |    |    |     |     |    |    |

## Mainz
(See also: Stabat Mater dolorosa)

| BA | DC | 1940 | 1982 | LBW | LW | PH | RCV | UCC | UM | WB |
|----|----|------|------|-----|----|----|-----|-----|----|----|
|    |    | F    |      |     |    |    | F   |     |    |    |

## Mainzer

| BA | DC | 1940 | 1982 | LBW | LW | PH | RCV | UCC | UM | WB |
|----|----|------|------|-----|----|----|-----|-----|----|----|
|    | Bb |      |      |     |    |    |     |     | Ab |    |

## Maitland

| BA | DC | 1940 | 1982 | LBW | LW | PH | RCV | UCC | UM | WB |
|----|----|------|------|-----|----|----|-----|-----|----|----|
| Ab |    |      |      |     |    |    |     |     | Ab |    |

## Malabar

| BA | DC | 1940 | 1982 | LBW | LW | PH | RCV | UCC | UM | WB |
|----|----|------|------|-----|----|----|-----|-----|----|----|
|    |    | Bb   | Bb   |     |    |    |     |     |    |    |

### ORGAN COMPOSITIONS

Arnatt, Ronald  "Strengthen for Service, Lord" **The Parish Organist** Part Eleven  Edited: Willem Mudde  Concordia Publishing House  97-4758 Key: Bb

## Maldwyn

| BA | DC | 1940 | 1982 | LBW | LW | PH | RCV | UCC | UM | WB |
|----|----|------|------|-----|----|----|-----|-----|----|----|
|    |    |      |      |     | g  |    |     |     |    |    |

## Malvern

| BA | DC | 1940 | 1982 | LBW | LW | PH | RCV | UCC | UM | WB |
|----|----|------|------|-----|----|----|-----|-----|----|----|
|    |    |      |      |     |    |    |     |     | D  |    |

## Manchester

| BA | DC | 1940 | 1982 | IBW | LW | PH | RCV | UCC | UM | WB |
|----|----|------|------|-----|----|----|-----|-----|----|----|
|    |    |      | e    |     |    |    |     |     |    |    |

## Mandatum

| BA | DC | 1940 | 1982 | LBW | LW | PH | RCV | UCC | UM | WB |
|----|----|------|------|-----|----|----|-----|-----|----|----|
|    |    | Eb   |      |     |    |    |     |     |    |    |

## Manna

| BA | DC | 1940 | 1982 | LBW | LW | PH | RCV | UCC | UM | WB |
|----|----|------|------|-----|----|----|-----|-----|----|----|
| G  |    |      |      |     |    |    |     |     |    |    |

## Mannheim

| BA | DC | 1940 | 1982 | LBW | LW | PH | RCV | UCC | UM | WB |
|----|----|------|------|-----|----|----|-----|-----|----|----|
|    |    | E    | E    |     |    |    |     |     |    |    |

ORGAN COMPOSITIONS

Schwarz, Gerhard   "God of Grace and God of Glory" **The Parish Organist**   Part Eleven   Edited: Willem Mudde   Concordia Publishing House   97-4758   Key: E

## Mannitto

| BA | DC | 1940 | 1982 | LBW | LW | PH | RCV | UCC | UM | WB |
|----|----|------|------|-----|----|----|-----|-----|----|----|
|    |    |      |      |     |    |    |     |     |    | C  |

## Manoah

| BA | DC | 1940 | 1982 | LBW | LW | PH | RCV | UCC | UM | WB |
|----|----|------|------|-----|----|----|-----|-----|-----|----|----|
|    |    |      |      |     |    |    |     |     | F   |    |

## Maoz Tsur
(See also: Rock of Ages)

| BA | DC | 1940 | 1982 | LBW | LW | PH | RCV | UCC | UM | WB |
|----|----|------|------|-----|----|----|-----|-----|----|----|
|    |    | Eb   |      |     |    |    |     |     |    |    |

## Marching to Zion

| BA | DC | 1940 | 1982 | LBW | LW | PH | RCV | UCC | UM | WB |
|----|----|------|------|-----|----|----|-----|-----|----|----|
| G  |    |      |      |     |    |    |     |     |    |    |

ORGAN COMPOSITIONS

Held, Wilbur   "We're Marching to Zion"   **Gospel Hymn Settings**   Hinshaw Music Co., Inc.   HMO-146   Key: Ab

Young, Gordon   "Marching to Zion"   **Contemporary Hymn Preludes**   Hope Publishing Co.   No. 328   Key: G

## Margaret

| BA | DC | 1940 | 1982 | LBW | LW | PH | RCV | UCC | UM | WB |
|----|----|------|------|-----|----|----|-----|-----|----|----|
| D  | D  |      |      |     |    | D  |     |     |    |    |

ORGAN COMPOSITIONS

Jordan, Alice "Entreaty on 'Thou Didst Leave Thy Throne'" **Worship Service Music for the Organist** Broadman Press   Key: Db

## FREE ACCOMPANIMENTS

Noble, T. Tertius  **Fifty Free Organ Accompaniments to Well Known Hymn Tunes**  J. Fischer & Bros. No. 8430  Key: Ab

Maria ist geboren

| BA | DC | 1940 | 1982 | LBW | LW | PH | RCV | UCC | UM | WB |
|----|----|------|------|-----|----|----|-----|-----|----|----|
|    |    |      |      |     | e  |    |     |     |    |    |

## ORGAN COMPOSITIONS

Busarow, Donald  "Hosanna Now Through Advent"  **The Concordia Hymn Prelude Series**  Volume 1  Edited: Harbert Gotsch  Concordia Publishing House 97-5536  Key: e

Maria, Mater

| BA | DC | 1940 | 1982 | LBW | LW | PH | RCV | UCC | UM | WB |
|----|----|------|------|-----|----|----|-----|-----|----|----|
|    |    |      |      |     |    |    | m:g |     |    |    |

Marion

| BA | DC | 1940 | 1982 | LBW | LW | PH | RCV | UCC | UM | WB |
|----|----|------|------|-----|----|----|-----|-----|----|----|
| F  | G  | G    | F    | G   | F  | G  |     | G   | G  | G  |

## FREE ACCOMPANIMENTS

Cassler, G. Winston  **Organ Descants for Selected Hymn Tunes**  Augsburg Publishing House  11-9304  Key: F

**Free Harmoniztions to Hymn Tunes By Fifty American Composers**  Edited: D. DeWitt Wasson  Hinshaw Music, Inc.  HMO-145  Key: G

Goode, Jack C.  **Thirty-Four Changes on Hymn Tunes** H.W. Gray Co.  GB 644  Key: G

Noble, T. Tertius  **Free Accompaniments to One Hundred Well-Known Hymn Tunes**  J. Fischer & Bros. #8175  Key: G

Schack, David  **Hymn Preludes and Free Accompaniments** Volume 11  Augsburg Publishing House  11-9407 Key: G

Marlee

| BA | DC | 1940 | 1982 | LBW | LW | PH | RCV | UCC | UM | WB |
|----|----|------|------|-----|----|----|-----|-----|----|----|
|    | g  |      |      | g   |    |    |     |     |    |    |

ORGAN COMPOSITIONS

Busarow, Donald  "Deep Were His Wounds"  **The Concordia Hymn Prelude Series**  Volume 8  Edited: Herbert Gotsch  Concordia Publishing House  97-5615  Key: g

Johnson, David N. "Deep Were His Wounds" **Deck Thyself My Soul with Gladness** Augsburg Publishing House 11-9157 Key: c

## Marlow

| BA | DC | 1940 | 1982 | LBW | LW | PH | RCV | UCC | UM | WB |
|----|----|------|------|-----|----|----|-----|-----|----|----|
|    |    | F    |      |     |    |    |     |     |    |    |

## Marsh Chapel

| BA | DC | 1940 | 1982 | LBW | LW | PH | RCV | UCC | UM | WB |
|----|----|------|------|-----|----|----|-----|-----|----|----|
|    |    |      | F    |     |    |    |     |     |    |    |

## Martin

| BA | DC | 1940 | 1982 | LBW | LW | PH | RCV | UCC | UM | WB |
|----|----|------|------|-----|----|----|-----|-----|----|----|
|    |    |      |      |     |    |    |     |     | Bb |    |

## Martins

| BA | DC | 1940 | 1982 | LBW | LW | PH | RCV | UCC | UM | WB |
|----|----|------|------|-----|----|----|-----|-----|----|----|
|    |    | C    | C    |     |    |    |     |     |    |    |

## Martyn

| BA | DC | 1940 | 1982 | LBW | LW | PH | RCV | UCC | UM | WB |
|----|----|------|------|-----|----|----|-----|-----|----|----|
| F  |    | F    |      |     |    | F  |     |     | F  |    |

ORGAN COMPOSITIONS

Beck, Albert  **76 Offertories on Hymns & Chorales** Concordia Publishing House  97-5207  Key: F

Bingham, Seth  **Twelve Hymn Preludes for Organ** Opus 38  Set 1  H. W. Gray GB 151  Key: F

## Martyr Dei

| BA | DC | 1940 | 1982 | LBW | LW | PH | RCV | UCC | UM | WB |
|----|----|------|------|-----|----|----|-----|-----|----|----|
|    |    | m:f  |      |     |    |    |     |     |    |    |

## Martyrdom

| BA | DC | 1940 | 1982 | LBW | LW | PH | RCV | UCC | UM | WB |
|----|----|------|------|-----|----|----|-----|-----|----|----|
|    |    | G    | G    | G   | G  | G  | G   |     | G  |    |

ORGAN COMPOSITIONS

Kroeger, William  "Alas, and Did My Saviour Bleed" **The Parish Organist** Part Eleven  Edited: Willem Mudde  Concordia Publishing House  97-4758 Key:  G

Lang, C.S. **Twenty Hymn-Tune Preludes** (First Set)
   Oxford University Press   Key: G

Lang, C. S. "Alas! and Did My Savior Bleed" **The
   Concordia Hymn Prelude Series** Volume 8  Edited:
   Herbert Gotsch  Concordia Publishing House
   97-5615  Key: G

Powell, Newman "As Pants the Hart for Cooling Streams"
   **The Parish Organist** Part Eleven  Edited: Willem
   Mudde  Concordia Publishing House  97-4758 Key: G

Thalben-Ball, George **113 Variations on Hymn Tunes**
   Novello & Co., Ltd.  Key: Ab

Willan, Healey **Ten Hymn Preludes** Set II  C. F.
   Peters Corporation  6012  Key: G

### FREE ACCOMPANIMENTS

Coleman, Henry **Varied Hymn Accompaniments**
   Oxford University Press  Key: G

Goode, Jack C. **Thirty-Four Changes on Hymn Tunes**
   H. W. Gray Co.  GB 644  Key: G

Held, Wilbur **Hymn Preludes and Free Accompaniments**
   Volume 6  Augsburg Publishing House  11-9402
   Key: G

Johnson, David N. **Hymn Preludes and Free
   Accompaniments** Volume 14  Augsburg Publishing
   House  11-9410  Key: G

Martyrs
| BA | DC | 1940 | 1982 | LBW | LW | PH | RCV | UCC | UM | WB |
|----|----|------|------|-----|----|----|-----|-----|----|-----|
|    |    | m:d  |      |     |    |    |     |     |    |     |

### ORGAN COMPOSITIONS

Johnson, David N. "O God of Truth" **Deck Thyself My
   Soul with Gladness** Augsburg Publishing House
   11-9157  Key: d

Thalben-Ball, George **113 Variations on Hymn Tunes**
   Novello & Co., Ltd.  Key: m:d

Maryton
| BA | DC | 1940 | 1982 | LBW | LW | PH | RCV | UCC | UM | WB |
|----|----|------|------|-----|----|----|-----|-----|----|-----|
| Eb | Eb | Eb   | Eb   | Eb  |    | Eb | Eb  | Eb  | Eb | Eb  |

## ORGAN COMPOSITIONS

Jordan, Alice "Meditation on 'Maryton'" **Worship Service Music for the Organist** Broadman Press  Key:Db/F

| Massachusetts | | | | | | | | | | |
|---|---|---|---|---|---|---|---|---|---|---|
| BA | DC | 1940 | 1982 | LBW | LW | PH | RCV | UCC | UM | WB |
| e | | | | | | | | | e | |

| Mater Dolorosa | | | | | | | | | | |
|---|---|---|---|---|---|---|---|---|---|---|
| BA | DC | 1940 | 1982 | LBW | LW | PH | RCV | UCC | UM | WB |
| | | | | | | | a | | | |

| Materna | | | | | | | | | | |
|---|---|---|---|---|---|---|---|---|---|---|
| BA | DC | 1940 | 1982 | LBW | LW | PH | RCV | UCC | UM | WB |
| Bb | Bb | C | C | | | Bb | C | Bb | Bb | Bb |

## ORGAN COMPOSITIONS

Beck, Albert **76 Offertories on Hymns & Chorales** Concordia Publishing House  97-5207  Key: C

## FREE ACCOMPANIMENTS

Noble, T. Tertius  **Free Organ Accompaniments to One Hundred Well-Known Hymn Tunes**  J. Fischer & Bros. #8175  Key: C

Wyton, Alec  **New Shoots From Old Routes**  Sacred Music Press  KK 279  Key: C

| Matthews | | | | | | | | | | |
|---|---|---|---|---|---|---|---|---|---|---|
| BA | DC | 1940 | 1982 | LBW | LW | PH | RCV | UCC | UM | WB |
| Ab | | | | | | | | | | |

| Mauburn | | | | | | | | | | |
|---|---|---|---|---|---|---|---|---|---|---|
| BA | DC | 1940 | 1982 | LBW | LW | PH | RCV | UCC | UM | WB |
| | | Eb | | | | | | | | |

| Maxon | | | | | | | | | | |
|---|---|---|---|---|---|---|---|---|---|---|
| BA | DC | 1940 | 1982 | LBW | LW | PH | RCV | UCC | UM | WB |
| | | C | | | | | | | | |

| McAfee | | | | | | | | | | |
|---|---|---|---|---|---|---|---|---|---|---|
| BA | DC | 1940 | 1982 | LBW | LW | PH | RCV | UCC | UM | WB |
| Db | | | | | | | | | | |

| McCabe | | | | | | | | | | |
|---|---|---|---|---|---|---|---|---|---|---|
| BA | DC | 1940 | 1982 | LBW | LW | PH | RCV | UCC | UM | WB |
| G | | | | | | | | | | |

| McClard | | | | | | | | | | |
|---|---|---|---|---|---|---|---|---|---|---|
| BA | DC | 1940 | 1982 | LBW | LW | PH | RCV | UCC | UM | WB |
| F | | | | | | | | | | |

| McConnell | | | | | | | | | | |
|---|---|---|---|---|---|---|---|---|---|---|
| BA | DC | 1940 | 1982 | LBW | LW | PH | RCV | UCC | UM | WB |
| Ab | | | | | | | | | | |

| McConnelsville | | | | | | | | | | |
|---|---|---|---|---|---|---|---|---|---|---|
| BA | DC | 1940 | 1982 | LBW | LW | PH | RCV | UCC | UM | WB |
| Ab | | | | | | | | | | |

| McCray | | | | | | | | | | |
|---|---|---|---|---|---|---|---|---|---|---|
| BA | DC | 1940 | 1982 | LBW | LW | PH | RCV | UCC | UM | WB |
| F | | | | | | | | | | |

| McDaniel | | | | | | | | | | |
|---|---|---|---|---|---|---|---|---|---|---|
| BA | DC | 1940 | 1982 | LBW | LW | PH | RCV | UCC | UM | WB |
| Ab | | | | | | | | | | |

| McIntosh | | | | | | | | | | |
|---|---|---|---|---|---|---|---|---|---|---|
| BA | DC | 1940 | 1982 | LBW | LW | PH | RCV | UCC | UM | WB |
| | | | | | | | G | | | |

| McKee | | | | | | | | | | |
|---|---|---|---|---|---|---|---|---|---|---|
| BA | DC | 1940 | 1982 | LBW | LW | PH | RCV | UCC | UM | WB |
| Bb | | C | C | C | | C | C | C | | C |

ORGAN COMPOSITIONS

Lovelace, Austin **Fourteen Hymn Preludes** Augsburg Publishing House 11-6152 Key: C

FREE ACCOMPANIMENTS

**Free Harmonizations to Hymn Tunes By Fifty American Composers** Edited: D. DeWitt Wasson Hinshaw Music, Inc. HMO-145 Key: C

| McNeely | | | | | | | | | | |
|---|---|---|---|---|---|---|---|---|---|---|
| BA | DC | 1940 | 1982 | LBW | LW | PH | RCV | UCC | UM | WB |
| Ab | | | | | | | | | | |

| Meadville | | | | | | | | | | |
|---|---|---|---|---|---|---|---|---|---|---|
| BA | DC | 1940 | 1982 | LBW | LW | PH | RCV | UCC | UM | WB |
| | | | G | | | | | | | |

| Mear | | | | | | | | | | |
|---|---|---|---|---|---|---|---|---|---|---|
| BA | DC | 1940 | 1982 | LBW | LW | PH | RCV | UCC | UM | WB |
| F | | | | | | | | | | |

Meditation

| BA | DC | 1940 | 1982 | LBW | LW | PH | RCV | UCC | UM | WB |
|----|----|------|------|-----|----|----|-----|-----|----|----|
|    |    | E    |      |     |    | E  |     |     | Eb |    |

Mein Leben (Vulpius)

| BA | DC | 1940 | 1982 | LBW | LW | PH | RCV | UCC | UM | WB |
|----|----|------|------|-----|----|----|-----|-----|----|----|
|    |    |      |      |     |    | D  |     |     |    |    |

Mein Schöpfer, steh mir bei

| BA | DC | 1940 | 1982 | LBW | LW | PH | RCV | UCC | UM | WB |
|----|----|------|------|-----|----|----|-----|-----|----|----|
|    |    |      |      |     | D  |    |     |     |    |    |

ORGAN COMPOSITIONS

Beck, Albert  **76 Offertories on Hymns & Chorales**
Concordia Publishing House  97-5207  Key: D

Meine Armuth

| BA | DC | 1940 | 1982 | LBW | LW | PH | RCV | UCC | UM | WB |
|----|----|------|------|-----|----|----|-----|-----|----|----|
|    |    |      |      |     |    |    |     |     |    | WB |
|    |    |      |      |     |    |    |     |     |    | F  |

Meine Hoffnung

| BA | DC | 1940 | 1982 | LBW | LW | PH | RCV | UCC | UM | WB |
|----|----|------|------|-----|----|----|-----|-----|----|----|
|    |    |      |      |     |    | a  |     |     |    |    |

ORGAN COMPOSITIONS

Thalben-Ball, George  **113 Variations on Hymn Tunes**
Novello & Co., Ltd.  Key: b

Meinen Jesum lass ich nicht (Darmstadt)

| BA | DC | 1940 | 1982 | LBW | LW | PH | RCV | UCC | UM | WB |
|----|----|------|------|-----|----|----|-----|-----|----|----|
|    |    | G    |      |     | G  |    |     |     |    |    |

ORGAN COMPOSITIONS

Gehrke, Hugo  "Come, O Precious Ransom" **The Concordia Hymn Prelude Series**  Volume 1 Edited: Herbert Gotsch  Concordia Publishing House  97-5536 Key: G

Karg-Elert, Sigfrid "My Jesu I Will not Leave" **Choral Improvisations for Organ for Reformation Day, Fast Days, Communion and Funeral Rites** Op. 65, Volume 5  Edited: Robert Leech Bedell Edward B. Marks Music Corp.  Key: G

Lenel, Ludwig  "Jesus, I Will Never Leave"  **The Parish Organist** Part Two  Edited: Heinrich Fleischer  Concordia Publishing House  97-1151 Key:  G

Marpurg, Friedrich Wilhelm **Twenty-One Chorale Preludes**
Edited: Robert M. Thompson  Augsburg Publishing
House  11-9506  Key: D

Walther, Johann Gottfried "Partita on 'Meinen Jesum
Lass' ich Nicht'" **For Manuals Only** Edited:
John Christopher  McAfee Music Corp. Key: D

Meinen Jesum ich nicht (Ulich)

| BA | DC | 1940 | 1982 | LBW | LW | PH | RCV | UCC | UM | WB |
|----|----|------|------|-----|----|----|-----|-----|----|----|
|    |    |      |      | F   | F  |    |     |     |    |    |

Meirionydd

| BA | DC | 1940 | 1982 | LBW | LW | PH | RCV | UCC | UM | WB |
|----|----|------|------|-----|----|----|-----|-----|----|----|
| D  | D  |      |      |     |    | D  | Eb  | D   | Eb |    |

Melchior

| BA | DC | 1940 | 1982 | LBW | LW | PH | RCV | UCC | UM | WB |
|----|----|------|------|-----|----|----|-----|-----|----|----|
|    | D  |      |      |     |    |    |     |     |    |    |

Melcombe

| BA | DC | 1940 | 1982 | LBW | LW | PH | RCV | UCC | UM | WB |
|----|----|------|------|-----|----|----|-----|-----|----|----|
|    | D  | D    | D    |     |    | D  | D   |     | D  |    |

## ORGAN COMPOSITIONS

Canning, Thomas  "O Spirit of the Living God" **The
Parish Organist** Part Eleven  Edited: Willem
Mudde  Concordia Publishing House  97-4758 Key: Eb

Haan, Raymond H. **A Second Book of Contemplative Hymn
Tune Preludes** Harold Flammer, Inc.  HF-5127
Key: Eb

Lang, C.S. **Twenty Hymn-Tune Preludes** (First Set)
Oxford University Press  (Two Settings)  Key: D
Key: Eb

McKinley, Carl **Ten Hymn Tune Fantasies** H.W. Gray
Key: Eb

Thalben-Ball, George **113 Variations on Hymn Tunes**
Novello & Co., Ltd.  Key: Eb

## FREE ACCOMPANIMENTS

Noble, T. Tertius **Free Organ Accompaniments to One
Hundred Well-Known Hymn Tunes** J. Fischer & Bros.
#8175  Key: D

Melita

| BA | DC | 1940 | 1982 | LBW | LW | PH | RCV | UCC | UM | WB |
|----|----|------|------|-----|----|----|-----|-----|----|----|
| C  | C  | C    | C    | C   |    | C  | C   | C   | C  |    |

Johnson, David N. **Free Harmonizations of Twelve Hymn Tunes** Augsburg Publishing House 11-9190 Key: D

Noble, T. Tertius **Free Organ Accompaniments to One Hundred Well-Known Hymn Tunes** J. Fischer & Bros. #8175 Key: C

Wyton, Alec **New Shoots From Old Routes** Sacred Music Press KK 279 Key: C

## Melrose

| BA | DC | 1940 | 1982 | LBW | LW | PH | RCV | UCC | UM | WB |
|----|----|------|------|-----|----|----|-----|-----|----|----|
|    |    |      |      |     |    | C  |     |     |    |    |

## Mendebras

| BA | DC | 1940 | 1982 | LBW | LW | PH | RCV | UCC | UM | WB |
|----|----|------|------|-----|----|----|-----|-----|----|----|
|    |    |      |      |     |    |    |     |     | F  |    |

FREE ACCOMPANIMENTS

Noble, T. Tertius **Free Organ Accompaniments to One Hundred Well-Known Hymn Tunes** J. Fischer & Bros. #8175 Key: F

## Mendelssohn (Festgesang)

| BA | DC | 1940 | 1982 | LBW | LW | PH | RCV | UCC | UM | WB |
|----|----|------|------|-----|----|----|-----|-----|----|----|
| F  | F  | F    | F    | F   | F  | F  | F   | F   | F  | F  |

ORGAN COMPOSITIONS

Diemer, Emma Lou "Hark the Herald Angels Sing" **Carols for Organ** The Sacred Music Press Key:G

Gehrke, Hugo "Hark! the Herald Angels Sing" **The Parish Organist** Part Two Edited: Heinrich Fleischer Concordia Publishing House 97-1151 Key: G

Goode, Jack C. **Thirty-Four Changes on Hymn Tunes** H. W. Gray Co. GB 644 Key: F

Schack, David "Hark! The Herald Angels Sing" **The Concordia Hymn Prelude Series** Volume 4 Edited: Herbert Gotsch Concordia Publishing House 97-5539 Key: F

Wyton, Alec "Fanfare on 'Hark the Herald Angels Sing'" **Preludes, Fanfares and a March for the Liturgical Year** Harold Flammer 3947 Key: G

Johnson, David N. **Free Harmonizations of Twelve Hymn
Tunes** Augsburg Publishing House 11-9190 Key: F

Noble, T. Tertius **Free Organ Accompaniments to One
Hundred Well-Known Hymn Tunes** J. Fischer & Bros.
#8175 Key: F

Wyton, Alec **New Shoots From Old Routes** Sacred Music
Press KK 279 Key: F

**Mendon**

| BA | DC | 1940 | 1982 | LBW | LW | PH | RCV | UCC | UM | WB |
|----|----|------|------|-----|----|----|-----|-----|----|----|
| Ab | Ab | Ab | A | Bb | | Bb | | Bb | | |

## ORGAN COMPOSITIONS

Gehrke, Hugo "Fight the Good Fight with All Thy Might"
**The Parish Organist** Part Eleven Edited: Willem
Mudde Concordia Publishing House 97-4758 Key: Bb

McKinley, Carl **Ten Hymn Tune Fantasies** H.W. Gray
Key: Bb

## FREE ACCOMPANIMENTS

Noble, T. Tertius **Free Organ Accompaniments to One
Hundred Well-Known Hymn Tunes** J. Fischer & Bros.
#8175 Key: A

**Mentzer**

| BA | DC | 1940 | 1982 | LBW | LW | PH | RCV | UCC | UM | WB |
|----|----|------|------|-----|----|----|-----|-----|----|----|
| | | Eb | | | | | | | | |

**Mercer Street**

| BA | DC | 1940 | 1982 | LBW | LW | PH | RCV | UCC | UM | WB |
|----|----|------|------|-----|----|----|-----|-----|----|----|
| | | | D | | | | | | | |

**Mercy** (Gottschalk)

| BA | DC | 1940 | 1982 | LBW | LW | PH | RCV | UCC | UM | WB |
|----|----|------|------|-----|----|----|-----|-----|----|----|
| Bb | Bb | | | | | Bb | | | Bb | |

**Meribah**

| BA | DC | 1940 | 1982 | LBW | LW | PH | RCV | UCC | UM | WB |
|----|----|------|------|-----|----|----|-----|-----|----|----|
| | | | | D | D | | | | | |

## FREE ACCOMPANIMENTS

Beck, Albert **76 Offertories on Hymns and Chorales**
Concordia Publishing House 97-5207 Key: Eb

Carson, J. Bert  **Hymn Preludes and Free Accompaniments**
Volume 16  Augusburg Publishing House  11-9412
Key: D

## Merrial

| BA | DC | 1940 | 1982 | LBW | LW | PH | RCV | UCC | UM | WB |
|---|---|---|---|---|---|---|---|---|---|---|
|  | A | A | A | A | A |  |  |  | A |  |

### FREE ACCOMPANIMENTS

Noble, T. Tertius  **Free Organ Accompaniments to One Hundred Well-Known Hymn Tunes**  J. Fischer & Bros. #8175  Key:  A

## Merton

| BA | DC | 1940 | 1982 | LBW | LW | PH | RCV | UCC | UM | WB |
|---|---|---|---|---|---|---|---|---|---|---|
| E | E | E |  |  |  |  |  | E |  |  |

### ORGAN COMPOSITIONS

Bassett, Anita Denniston  **Nine Hymn-Tune Preludes**
Ludwig Music Publishing Co.  0-08  Key: E

### FREE ACCOMPANIMENTS

Noble, T. Tertius  **Free Organ Accompaniments to One Hundred Well-Known Hymn Tunes**  J. Fischer & Bros. #8175  Key: Eb

Wood, Dale  **New Settings of Twenty Well-Known Hymn Tunes**  Augsburg Publishing House  11-9292  Key: Eb

## Message

| BA | DC | 1940 | 1982 | LBW | LW | PH | RCV | UCC | UM | WB |
|---|---|---|---|---|---|---|---|---|---|---|
| Eb |  |  |  |  |  |  |  |  | F |  |

## Messiah

(See also: Bereden vag for Herran)

| BA | DC | 1940 | 1982 | LBW | LW | PH | RCV | UCC | UM | WB |
|---|---|---|---|---|---|---|---|---|---|---|
|  |  |  |  |  |  |  | F |  | F |  |

## Methfessel

| BA | DC | 1940 | 1982 | LBW | LW | PH | RCV | UCC | UM | WB |
|---|---|---|---|---|---|---|---|---|---|---|
| Ab |  |  |  |  |  |  |  |  |  |  |

## Michael (Anders)

| BA | DC | 1940 | 1982 | LBW | LW | PH | RCV | UCC | UM | WB |
|---|---|---|---|---|---|---|---|---|---|---|
|  |  |  | c |  |  |  |  |  |  |  |

## Michael (Folk tune)

| BA | DC | 1940 | 1982 | LBW | LW | PH | RCV | UCC | UM | WB |
|---|---|---|---|---|---|---|---|---|---|---|
| D |  |  |  |  |  |  |  |  |  |  |

## Michael (Howells)

| BA | DC | 1940 | 1982 | LBW | LW | PH | RCV | UCC | UM | WB |
|----|----|------|------|-----|----|----|-----|-----|----|----|
|    |    |      | F    |     |    |    |     | F   |    |    |

## Midden in de Dood

| BA | DC | 1940 | 1982 | LBW | LW | PH | RCV | UCC | UM | WB |
|----|----|------|------|-----|----|----|-----|-----|----|----|
|    |    |      | A    |     |    |    |     |     |    |    |

## Middlebury

| BA | DC | 1940 | 1982 | LBW | LW | PH | RCV | UCC | UM | WB |
|----|----|------|------|-----|----|----|-----|-----|----|----|
|    |    |      | Eb   |     |    |    |     |     |    |    |

### ORGAN COMPOSITIONS

Bouman, Paul  "We Who Once Were Dead"  **The Concordia Hymn Prelude Series**  Volume 17  Edited: Herbert Gotsch  Concordia Publishing House  97-5708  Key: A

## Mieir

| BA | DC | 1940 | 1982 | LBW | LW | PH | RCV | UCC | UM | WB |
|----|----|------|------|-----|----|----|-----|-----|----|----|
| F  |    |      |      |     |    |    |     |     |    |    |

## Mighty Savior

| BA | DC | 1940 | 1982 | LBW | LW | PH | RCV | UCC | UM | WB |
|----|----|------|------|-----|----|----|-----|-----|----|----|
|    |    |      | d    |     |    |    |     |     |    |    |

## Miles Lane

| BA | DC | 1940 | 1982 | LBW | LW | PH | RCV | UCC | UM | WB |
|----|----|------|------|-----|----|----|-----|-----|----|----|
| Bb |    |      |      |     |    |    |     |     |    |    |
|    |    | A    | A    | Ab  |    | A  |     | A   | Bb | A  |

### ORGAN COMPOSITIONS

Thalben-Ball, George  **113 Variations on Hymn Tunes**  Novello & Co., Ltd.  Key: A

### FREE ACCOMPANIMENTS

**Free Harmonizations to Hymn Tunes By Fifty American Composers**  Edited: D. DeWitt Wasson  Hinshaw Music, Inc.  HMO-145  Key: A

Hebble, Robert  **Robert Hebble's Hymnal Companion for Organ**  Bradley Publications  CE/283A/3  Key: A

Norris, Kevin  **Hymn Preludes and Free Accompaniments**  Volume 15  Augsburg Publishing House  11-9411  Key: Ab

Shrubsole, William  **Free Organ Accompaniments to Festival Hymns**  Volume I  Augsburg Publishing House  11-9192  Key: A

Wood, Dale **New Settings of Twenty Well-Known Hymn Tunes** Augsburg Publishing House 11-9292 Key: L

## Millennium

| BA | DC | 1940 | 1982 | LBW | LW | PH | RCV | UCC | UM | WB |
|----|----|------|------|-----|-----|-----|-----|-----|-----|-----|
|    |    |      |      |     |     |     |     |     | A   |     |

## Milwaukee

| BA | DC | 1940 | 1982 | LBW | LW | PH | RCV | UCC | UM | WB |
|----|----|------|------|-----|-----|-----|-----|-----|-----|-----|
|    |    |      |      |     | Ab  |     |     |     |     |     |

ORGAN COMPOSITIONS

Bender, Jan "Lift Up Your Heads, You Mighty Gates"
**The Concordia Hymn Prelude Series** Volume 1
Edited: Herbert Gotsch 97-5536 Key: Ab

## Minterne

| BA | DC | 1940 | 1982 | LBW | LW | PH | RCV | UCC | UM | WB |
|----|----|------|------|-----|-----|-----|-----|-----|-----|-----|
|    |    |      |      |     |     |     |     | F   |     |     |

## Mission

| BA | DC | 1940 | 1982 | LBW | LW | PH | RCV | UCC | UM | WB |
|----|----|------|------|-----|-----|-----|-----|-----|-----|-----|
| G  |    |      |      |     |     |     |     |     |     |     |

## Missionary Chant

| BA | DC | 1940 | 1982 | LBW | LW | PH | RCV | UCC | UM | WB |
|----|----|------|------|-----|-----|-----|-----|-----|-----|-----|
| G  |    |      |      |     |     |     |     |     |     |     |

## Missionary Hymn

| BA | DC | 1940 | 1982 | LBW | LW | PH | RCV | UCC | UM | WB |
|----|----|------|------|-----|-----|-----|-----|-----|-----|-----|
| Eb |    |      |      |     | Eb  |     |     |     |     |     |

ORGAN COMPOSITIONS

Beck, Albert **76 Offertories on Hymns & Chorales**
Concordia Publishing House 97-5207 Key: Eb

Stearns, Peter Pindar **Twenty Hymn Preludes**
Coburn Press (Theodore Presser Company) Key: Eb

Stelzer, Theodore G. "From Greenland's Icy Mountains"
**The Parish Organist** Part Two Edited: Heinrich
Fleischer Concordia Publishing House 97-1151
Key: Eb

## Mit Freuden zart
(See also: Bohemian Brethren)

| BA | DC | 1940 | 1982 | LBW | LW | PH | RCV | UCC | UM | WB |
|----|----|------|------|-----|-----|-----|-----|-----|-----|-----|
| Eb | D  |      | Db   | D   | D   | D   | D   | D   |     | D   |

## INTONATIONS

Videro, Finn  **Twenty-One Hymn Intonations**
Concordia Publishing House  97-5004  Key: D

## ORGAN COMPOSITIONS

Distler, Hugo  **Short Chorale Arrangements**  Opus 8/3
Bärenreiter 1222  Key: Eb

Haase, Hans-Heinz  "Lord Christ, When First Thou Cam'st
to Men"  **The Parish Organist**  Part Eleven
Edited: Willem Mudde  Concordia Publishing House
97-4758  Key:  D

Micheelsen, Hans Friedrich  "With High Delight Let Us
Unite"  **The Concordia Hymn Prelude Series**
Volume 11  Edited: Herbert Gotsch  Concordia
Publishing House  97-5618  Key: D

## FREE ACCOMPANIMENTS

Bender, Jan  **Hymn Preludes and Free Accompaniments**
Volume 1  Augsburg Publishing House  11-9397
Key: D

Lovelace, Austin C.  **Hymn Preludes and Free
Accompaniments**  Volume 4  Augsburg Publishing
House  11-9400  Key: D

Norris, Kevin  **Hymn Preludes and Free Accompaniments**
Volume 15  Augusburg Publishing House  11-9411
Key: D

Wyton, Alec  **New Shoots From Old Routes**  Sacred
Music Press  KK 279  Key: D

## Mit Fried und Freud

| BA | DC | 1940 | 1982 | LBW | LW | PH | RCV | UCC | UM | WB |
|----|----|------|------|-----|----|----|-----|-----|----|----|
|    |    |      |      | m:d | m:d |   |     |     |    |    |

## ORGAN COMPOSITIONS

Bach, Johann Christoph  **Chorale Preludes by Masters
of the 17th and 18th Centuries**  Volume I  Edited:
Walter Buszin  Concordia Publishing House
Key: m:d

Bach, J. S.  **Organ Works**  Volume 1  Edited: Heinz-
Harald Löhlein  Urtext of the New Bach Edition
Bärenreiter 5171  Key: m:d

260

Bach, J.S. **Organ Works** Volume VII  Widor-Schweitzer
G. Schirmer  Key: d

Bach, Johann Christoph  **80 Chorale Preludes – German
Masters of the 17th and 18th Centuries** Edited:
Hermann Keller  C.F. Peters Corporation #4448
Key: d

Bach, J.S. **Orgelwerke** Volume V  C.F. Peters
Corporation  Nr. 244  Key: d

Bach, J.S. **The Liturgical Year**  (Orgelbuchlein)
Edited: Albert Reimenschneider  Oliver Ditson Co.
Key: m:d

Henning, Walter  "In Peace and Joy I Now Depart"  **The
Concordia Hymn Prelude Series** Volume 15  Edited:
Herbert Gotsch  Concordia Publishing House
97-5706  Key: m:d

Pepping, Ernst  **Fünfundzwanzig Orgelchorale**  Edition
Schott 4723  B. Schott's Sohne  Key: m:d

Walcha, Helmut **25 Chorale Preludes** C.F. Peters
Nr. 4850  Key: d

Willan, Healey "Mit Fried' und Freud'" **Six Chorale
Preludes** Set II  Concordia Publishing House
97-3905  Key: d

Buxtehude, Dietrich **Orgelwerke II: Chorale Preludes**
C.F. Peters Corporation #4457  Key: d

<u>Mitten wir im Leben sind</u>

| BA | DC | 1940 | 1982 | LBW | LW | PH | RCV | UCC | UM | WB |
|----|----|------|------|-----|----|----|-----|-----|----|----|
|    |    |      |      | m:e | m:e |    |     |     |    |    |

ORGAN COMPOSITIONS

Scheidt, Samuel  **80 Chorale Preludes – German Masters
of the 17th and 18th Centuries**  Edited: Hermann
Keller  C.F. Peters Corporation #4448  Key: E

Walcha, Helmut **25 Chorale Preludes**  C.F. Peters
Corporation Nr. 4850  Key: e

<u>Mon Dieu, prête-moi l'oreille</u>
(See also : Psalm 86)

| BA | DC | 1940 | 1982 | LBW | LW | PH | RCV | UCC | UM | WB |
|----|----|------|------|-----|----|----|-----|-----|----|----|
|    | g  |      |      |     |    | g  |     | g   |    |    |

### Monks Gate

| BA | DC | 1940 | 1982 | LBW | LW | PH | RCV | UCC | UM | WB |
|----|----|------|------|-----|----|----|-----|-----|----|----|
|    |    | D    | D    |     | D  |    |     |     |    |    |

### Monkland

| BA | DC | 1940 | 1982 | LBW | LW | PH | RCV | UCC | UM | WB |
|----|----|------|------|-----|----|----|-----|-----|----|----|
| Bb |    | Bb   | Bb   |     |    | Bb | Bb  | Bb  |    | Bb |

## ORGAN COMPOSTIONS

Copeland, Mark **Three Variations on Hymn-Tunes**
Randall M. Egan & Associates  Key: C

Lang, C.S. **Twenty Hymn-Tune Preludes**  (First Set)
Oxford University Press  Key: C

Thalben-Ball, George **113 Variations on Hymn Tunes**
Novello & Co., Ltd.  Key: Bb

## FREE ACCOMPANIMENTS

**Free Harmonizations to Hymn Tunes By Fifty American Composers**  Edited: D. DeWitt Wasson  Hinshaw Music, Inc.  HMO-145  Key: Bb

### Monsell

| BA | DC | 1940 | 1982 | LBW | LW | PH | RCV | UCC | UM | WB |
|----|----|------|------|-----|----|----|-----|-----|----|----|
|    |    |      |      |     |    | Bb |     |     |    |    |

### Mont Richard

| BA  | DC | 1940 | 1982 | LBW | LW | PH | RCV | UCC | UM | WB |
|-----|----|------|------|-----|----|----|-----|-----|----|----|
| Bbm |    |      |      |     |    |    |     |     |    |    |

### Moody

| BA | DC | 1940 | 1982 | LBW | LW | PH | RCV | UCC | UM | WB |
|----|----|------|------|-----|----|----|-----|-----|----|----|
| G  |    |      |      |     |    |    |     |     |    |    |

### Mooz Zu
(See also: Moaz Tsur; Rock of Ages)

| BA | DC | 1940 | 1982 | LBW | LW | PH | RCV | UCC | UM | WB |
|----|----|------|------|-----|----|----|-----|-----|----|----|
|    |    |      |      |     |    |    | Eb  |     |    | Eb |

### Mora Proctor

| BA | DC | 1940 | 1982 | LBW | LW | PH | RCV | UCC | UM | WB |
|----|----|------|------|-----|----|----|-----|-----|----|----|
| G  |    |      |      |     |    |    |     |     |    |    |

### More About Jesus

| BA | DC | 1940 | 1982 | LBW | LW | PH | RCV | UCC | UM | WB |
|----|----|------|------|-----|----|----|-----|-----|----|----|
|    | Ab |      |      |     |    |    |     |     |    |    |

### More Love to Thee

| BA | DC | 1940 | 1982 | LBW | LW | PH | RCV | UCC | UM | WB |
|----|----|------|------|-----|----|----|-----|-----|----|----|
| G  |    |      |      |     |    | Ab |     |     | Ab |    |

**Free Harmonizations to Hymn Tunes By Fifty American Composers** Edited: D. DeWitt Wasson Hinshaw Music, Inc. HMO-145 Key: Ab

Morecambe

| BA | DC | 1940 | 1982 | LBW | LW | PH | RCV | UCC | UM | WB |
|----|----|------|------|-----|----|----|-----|-----|----|----|
| C | C | | | Bb | | C | C | C | C | Bb |

**Free Harmonizations to Hymn Tunes By Fifty American Composers** Edited: D. DeWitt Wasson Hinshaw Music, Inc. HMO-145 Key: C

Morestead

| BA | DC | 1940 | 1982 | LBW | LW | PH | RCV | UCC | UM | WB |
|----|----|------|------|-----|----|----|-----|-----|----|----|
| BA | DC | 1940 | 1982 | LBW | LW | PH | RCV | UCC | UM | WB |
| | | D | D | | | | | | | |

Morgenlied

| BA | DC | 1940 | 1982 | LBW | LW | PH | RCV | UCC | UM | WB |
|----|----|------|------|-----|----|----|-----|-----|----|----|
| BA | DC | 1940 | 1982 | LBW | LW | PH | RCV | UCC | UM | WB |
| | | | Bb | | | | | | | |

ORGAN COMPOSITIONS

Busarow, Donald "Christ is Risen! Alleluia!" **The Concordia Hymn Prelude Series** Volume 11 Edited: Herbert Gotsch Concordia Publishing House 97-5618 Key: Bb

Morning Hymn

| BA | DC | 1940 | 1982 | LBW | LW | PH | RCV | UCC | UM | WB |
|----|----|------|------|-----|----|----|-----|-----|----|----|
| BA | DC | 1940 | 1982 | LBW | LW | PH | RCV | UCC | UM | WB |
| | | G | G | G | G | G | | | | |

ORGAN COMPOSITIONS

Thalben-Ball, George **113 Variations on Hymn Tunes** Novello & Co., Ltd. Key: G

Diemer, Emma Lou **Hymn Preludes and Free Accompaniments** Volume 2 Augsburg Publishing House 11-9398 Key: G

**Free Harmonizations to Hymn Tunes By Fifty American Composers** Edited: D. DeWitt Wasson Hinshaw Music, Inc. HMO-145 Key: G

Morning Light
(See also: Webb)

| BA | DC | 1940 | 1982 | LBW | LW | PH | RCV | UCC | UM | WB |
|----|----|------|------|-----|----|----|-----|-----|----|----|
|    |    |      | A    |     |    |    |     |     |    |    |

Morning Song

| BA | DC | 1940 | 1982 | LBW | LW | PH | RCV | UCC | UM | WB |
|----|----|------|------|-----|----|----|-----|-----|----|----|
| f  | f  | f    |      |     |    | f  |     | f   | f  | f  |

## INTONATIONS

Hermann, David **11 Hymn Intonations, Free Accompaniments, Instrumental Descants for Organ** Volume I  Advent, Christmas, Epiphany  G.I.A. Publications  G-2378  Key: f

## ORGAN COMPOSITIONS

Held, Wilbur "Awake, Awake to Love and Work" **Hymn Preludes for the Autumn Festivals** Concordia Publishing House  97-5360  Key: f

## FREE ACCOMPANIMENTS

**Free Harmonizations to Hymn Tunes By Fifty American Composers** Edited: D. DeWitt Wasson  Hinshaw Music, Inc.  HMO-145  Key: f

Morning Star

| BA | DC | 1940 | 1982 | LBW | LW | PH | RCV | UCC | UM | WB |
|----|----|------|------|-----|----|----|-----|-----|----|----|
| Ab | Ab | G    | G    | G   |    |    | Ab  |     | G  |    |

## ORGAN COMPOSITIONS

Bender, Jan "Brightest and Best of the Sons of the Morning" **The Parish Organist** Part Eleven Edited: Willem Mudde  Concordia Publishing House 97-4758  Key: Ab

Bender, Jan  "Brightest and Best of the Stars of the Morning" **The Concordia Hymn Prelude Series** Volume 6  Edited: Hebert Gotsch  Concordia Publishing House  97-5612  Key: G

Held, Wilbur  **Hymn Preludes and Free Accompaniments** Volume 6  Augsburg Publishing House  11-9402 Key: G

Pinkham, Daniel "Pastorale on 'The Morning Star'" **A Galaxy of Hymn Tune Preludes for Organ** Galaxy Music Corp.  GMC 2353  Key: a

**Free Harmonizations to Hymn Tunes By Fifty American Composers** Edited: D. DeWitt Wasson  Hinshaw Music, Inc.  HMO-145  Key: G

Mornington

| BA | DC | 1940 | 1982 | LBW | LW | PH | RCV | UCC | UM | WB |
|----|----|------|------|-----|----|----|-----|-----|----|----|
|    | D  |      |      |     |    | D  |     |     | D  |    |

**Free Harmonizations to Hymn Tunes By Fifty American Composers** Edited: D. DeWitt Wasson  Hinshaw Music, Inc.  HMO-145  Key: D

Moscow
(See also: Italian Hymn; Trinity)

| BA | DC | 1940 | 1982 | LBW | LW | PH | RCV | UCC | UM | WB |
|----|----|------|------|-----|----|----|-----|-----|----|----|
|    |    | F    | G    |     |    |    |     |     |    |    |

ORGAN COMPOSITIONS

Lang, C.S. **Twenty Hymn-Tune Preludes**  (First Set) Oxford University Press  Key: G

Noble, T. Tertius  **Fifty Free Organ Accompaniments to Well Known Hymn Tunes**  J. Fischer & Bros. No. 8430  Key: F

Moseley

| BA | DC | 1940 | 1982 | LBW | LW | PH | RCV | UCC | UM | WB |
|----|----|------|------|-----|----|----|-----|-----|----|----|
|    |    | D    | D    |     |    |    |     |     |    |    |

Moultrie

| BA | DC | 1940 | 1982 | LBW | LW | PH | RCV | UCC | UM | WB |
|----|----|------|------|-----|----|----|-----|-----|----|----|
|    |    | F    | F    |     |    |    |     |     |    |    |

Mt. St. Alban NCA

| BA | DC | 1940 | 1982 | LBW | LW | PH | RCV | UCC | UM | WB |
|----|----|------|------|-----|----|----|-----|-----|----|----|
|    |    |      | f#   |     |    |    |     |     |    |    |

Mount Sion

| BA | DC | 1940 | 1982 | LBW | LW | PH | RCV | UCC | UM | WB |
|----|----|------|------|-----|----|----|-----|-----|----|----|
|    |    | C    |      |     |    |    |     |     |    |    |

Mourning

| BA | DC | 1940 | 1982 | LBW | LW | PH | RCV | UCC | UM | WB |
|----|----|------|------|-----|----|----|-----|-----|----|----|
|    |    |      |      |     |    |    |     | D   |    |    |

## Moville

| BA | DC | 1940 | 1982 | LBW | LW | PH | RCV | UCC | UM | WB |
|----|----|------|------|-----|----|----|-----|-----|----|----|
|    |    |      |      |     | c  |    |     |     |    |    |

## Mowsley

| BA | DC | 1940 | 1982 | LBW | LW | PH | RCV | UCC | UM | WB |
|----|----|------|------|-----|----|----|-----|-----|----|----|
|    |    |      | G    |     |    |    |     |     |    |    |

## Mude bin ich

| BA | DC | 1940 | 1982 | LBW | LW | PH | RCV | UCC | UM | WB |
|----|----|------|------|-----|----|----|-----|-----|----|----|
|    |    |      |      |     | LW<br>F |    |     |     |    |    |

## Mueller

| BA | DC | 1940 | 1982 | LBW | LW | PH | RCV | UCC | UM | WB |
|----|----|------|------|-----|----|----|-----|-----|----|----|
| F  |    |      |      |     |    |    | F   |     |    |    |

## Munich

| BA | DC | 1940 | 1982 | LBW | LW | PH | RCV | UCC | UM | WB |
|----|----|------|------|-----|----|----|-----|-----|----|----|
| F  | Eb | Eb   | Eb   | D   | D  | Eb | Eb  | Eb  | Eb | Eb |

### INTONATIONS

Videro, Finn **Twenty-One Hymn Intonations**
Concordia Publishing House 97-5004   Key: Eb

### ORGAN COMPOSITIONS

McKinley, Carl **Ten Hymn Tune Fantasies**  H.W. Gray
Key: Eb

McKinley, Carl **The Lutheran Organist**  Compiled by
John Holler  H.W. Gray Co.  Key:  Eb

### FREE ACCOMPANIMENTS

Cassler, G. Winston  **Organ Descants for Selected
Hymns**  Augsburg Publishing House  11-9304  Key: D

Noble, T. Tertius  **Free Organ Accompaniments to One
Hundred Well-Known Hymn Tunes**  J. Fischer & Bros.
#8175  Key: D

Norris, Kevin  **Hymn Preludes and Free Accompaniments**
Volume 15  Augsburg Publishing House  11-9411
Key: D

## Munster

| BA | DC | 1940 | 1982 | LBW | LW | PH | RCV | UCC | UM | WB |
|----|----|------|------|-----|----|----|-----|-----|----|----|
|    |    |      |      |     |    |    | f#  |     |    |    |

## Muskogee

| BA | DC | 1940 | 1982 | LBW | LW | PH | RCV | UCC | UM | WB |
|----|----|------|------|-----|----|----|-----|-----|----|----|
| C  |    |      |      |     |    |    |     |     |    |    |

My Country Tis of Thee
(See also: National Hymn)

My Redeemer

| | | | | | | | | | |
|---|---|---|---|---|---|---|---|---|---|
| BA | DC | 1940 | 1982 | LBW | LW | PH | RCV | UCC | UM | WB |
| Ab | | | | | | | | | | |

My Saviour's Love

| | | | | | | | | | |
|---|---|---|---|---|---|---|---|---|---|
| BA | DC | 1940 | 1982 | LBW | LW | PH | RCV | UCC | UM | WB |
| Ab | | | | | | | | | | |

# N

Naar mit Öie

| | | | | | | | | | |
|---|---|---|---|---|---|---|---|---|---|
| BA | DC | 1940 | 1982 | LBW | LW | PH | RCV | UCC | UM | WB |
| | | | | Ab | G | | | | | |

ORGAN COMPOSITIONS

Johns, Donald "Come to Calvary's Holy Mountain" **The Concordia Hymn Prelude Series** Volume 8 Edited: Herbert Gotsch Concordia Publishing House 97-5615 Key: G

Name of Jesus

| | | | | | | | | | |
|---|---|---|---|---|---|---|---|---|---|
| BA | DC | 1940 | 1982 | LBW | LW | PH | RCV | UCC | UM | WB |
| | | | | Eb | | | | | | |

ORGAN COMPOSITIONS

Cherwien, David **Interpretations Based on Hymn Tunes** Book II A.M.S.I. OR-3 Key: Eb

Naomi

| | | | | | | | | | |
|---|---|---|---|---|---|---|---|---|---|
| BA | DC | 1940 | 1982 | LBW | LW | PH | RCV | UCC | UM | WB |
| | Eb | | | | | | | | D | |

Narodil se Kristus Pán

| | | | | | | | | | |
|---|---|---|---|---|---|---|---|---|---|
| BA | DC | 1940 | 1982 | LBW | LW | PH | RCV | UCC | UM | WB |
| | | | | F | F | | | | | |

ORGAN COMPOSITIONS

Beck, Theodore "Let Our Gladness Have No End" **The Concordia Hymn Prelude Series** Volume 4 Edited: Herbert Gotsch Concordia Publishing House 97-5539 Key: F

Cherwien, David  "Let Our Gladness Have No End"
**Interpretations Based on Hymn-tunes**  A.M.S.I.
OR-9  Key:  F

Nassau

| BA | DC | 1940 | 1982 | LBW | LW | PH | RCV | UCC | UM | WB |
|----|----|------|------|-----|----|----|-----|-----|----|----|
|    | D  |      |      |     |    |    |     |     |    |    |

National Anthem
(See also: My Country 'tis of Thee; National Hymn; America)

| BA | DC | 1940 | 1982 | LBW | LW | PH | RCV | UCC | UM | WB |
|----|----|------|------|-----|----|----|-----|-----|----|----|
|    |    |      |      | F   | F  |    |     |     |    |    |

### FREE ACCOMPANIMENTS

Arnatt, Ronald  **Hymn Preludes and Free Accompaniments**
Volume 9  Augusburg Publishing House  11-9405
Key: F

Ore, Charles  **Hymn Preludes and Free Accompaniments**
Volume 7  Augusburg Publishing House  11-9403
Key: F

National Anthem
(See also: Star Spangled Banner)

| BA | DC | 1940 | 1982 | LBW | LW | PH | RCV | UCC | UM | WB |
|----|----|------|------|-----|----|----|-----|-----|----|----|
| Ab |    | Bb   | Bb   |     |    |    | Bb  |     |    |    |

National City

| BA | DC | 1940 | 1982 | LBW | LW | PH | RCV | UCC | UM | WB |
|----|----|------|------|-----|----|----|-----|-----|----|----|
|    | C  |      |      |     |    |    |     |     |    | C  |

National Hymn

| BA | DC | 1940 | 1982 | LBW | LW | PH | RCV | UCC | UM | WB |
|----|----|------|------|-----|----|----|-----|-----|----|----|
| Eb | Eb | Eb   | Eb   | Eb  | Eb | Eb | F   | Eb  | Eb | Eb |

### FREE ACCOMPANIMENTS

Goode, Jack C.  **Thirty-Four Changes on Hymn Tunes**
H.W. Gray Co.  GB 644  Key: Eb

Nativity

| BA | DC | 1940 | 1982 | LBW | LW | PH | RCV | UCC | UM | WB |
|----|----|------|------|-----|----|----|-----|-----|----|----|
| Bb |    |      |      |     |    |    |     |     |    |    |

### ORGAN COMPOSITIONS

Thalben-Ball, George  **113 Variations on Hymn Tunes**
Novello & Co. Ltd.  Key: Bb

Neander
(See also: Unser Herrscher)
| BA | DC | 1940 | 1982 | LBW | LW | PH | RCV | UCC | UM | WB |
|---|---|---|---|---|---|---|---|---|---|---|
| | C | C | | | | | | | | C |

ORGAN COMPOSITIONS

Cassler, G. Winston **Organ Descants for Selected Hymn Tunes** Augsburg Publishing House 11-9304  Key: C

Fleischer, Heinrich  "Open Now Thy Gates of Beauty" **The Parish Organist** Part Two  Edited: Heinrich Fleischer  Concordia Publishing House  97-1151 Key:  C

Goode, Jack  **Seven Communion Meditations**  Harold Flammer, Inc.  HF-5084  Key: Bb

Hiltscher, Wolfgang  "Hark, Ten Thousand Harps and Voices" **The Parish Organist** Part Eight  Music for Easter, Ascension, Pentecost and Trinity Edited: Erich Goldschmidt  Concordia Publishing House  97-1404  Key: C

Manz, Paul  "Open Now Thy Gates of Beauty" **Ten Chorale Improvisations**  Op. 5  Concordia Publishing House 97-4554  Key: C

Thalben-Ball, George  **113 Variations on Hymn Tunes** Novello & Co. Ltd.  Key: Bb

FREE ACCOMPANIMENTS

Bunjes, Paul  **New Organ Accompaniments for Hymns** Concordia Publishing House  97-5348  Key: C

Hudson, Richard  **Hymn Preludes and Free Accompaniments** Volume 12  Augsburg Publishing House  11-9408  Key: Bb

Wood, Dale **New Settings of Twenty Well-Known Hymn Tunes** Augsburg Publishing House  11-9292  Key: Bb

Near the Cross
| BA | DC | 1940 | 1982 | LBW | LW | PH | RCV | UCC | UM | WB |
|---|---|---|---|---|---|---|---|---|---|---|
| F | | | | | | | | | F | |

Need
(See also: I Need Thee Every Hour)
| BA | DC | 1940 | 1982 | LBW | LW | PH | RCV | UCC | UM | WB |
|---|---|---|---|---|---|---|---|---|---|---|
| Ab | G | G | | | | G | | | Ab | |

Bingham, Seth **Twelve Hymn Preludes** Opus 38 Set 2
H.W. Gray GB 152  Key: Ab

FREE ACCOMPANIMENTS

**Free Harmonizations to Hymn Tunes By Fifty American Composers** Edited: D. DeWitt Wasson  Hinshaw Music, Inc.  HMO-145  Key: G

### Neighbor

| BA | DC | 1940 | 1982 | LBW | LW | PH | RCV | UCC | UM | WB |
|----|----|------|------|-----|----|----|-----|-----|----|----|
|    |    |      |      |     |    |    |     | e   |    |    |

### Nettleton

(See also: Sinners Call; Good Shepherd)

| BA | DC | 1940 | 1982 | LBW | LW | PH | RCV | UCC | UM | WB |
|----|----|------|------|-----|----|----|-----|-----|----|----|
| Eb | DC | 1940 | 1982 | LBW | LW | PH | RCV | UCC | UM | WB |
| Eb |    | D    | D    |     |    |    |     | Eb  | Eb | Eb |

ORGAN COMPOSITIONS

Bish, Diane  "Come, Thou Fount of Every Blessing"
**The Diane Bish Organ Book**  Volume 4
Fred Bock Music Company  Key: Eb

Harris, David S. **Ten Hymn Preludes in Trio Style**
H. W. Gray Co.  GB 643  Key: Eb

Hancock, Gerre "Nettleton" **The Bristol Collection of Contemporary Hymn Tune Preludes for Organ**
Volume One Edited: Lee Hastings Bristol, Jr.
Harold Flammer  Key: D

Manz, Paul "Come, Thou Fount of Every Blessing"
**Ten Chorale Improvisations** Set IX Op. 21
Concordia Publishing House 97-5556  Key: Eb

FREE ACCOMPANIMENTS

Gehrke, Hugo  **Hymn Preludes and Free Accompaniments**
Volume 5  Augusburg Publishing House  11-9401
Key: D

### Neumark

| BA | DC | 1940 | 1982 | LBW | LW | PH | RCV | UCC | UM | WB |
|----|----|------|------|-----|----|----|-----|-----|----|----|
| g  | DC | 1940 | 1982 | LBW | LW | PH | RCV | UCC | UM | WB |
| g  |    |      |      |     |    | g  |     | g   |    | g  |

McKinney, Mathilde "Neumark" (Wer nur den Lieben Gott)
**The Bristol Collection of Contemporary Hymn Tune
Preludes for Organ** Volume One   Key: D
Harold Flammer,.

Neumeister
  BA  DC   1940  1982  LBW   LW    PH    RCV   UCC   UM    WB
  D

New Born Again
  BA  DC   1940  1982  LBW   LW    PH    RCV   UCC   UM    WB
  G

New Britain
  (See also: Amazing Grace)
  BA    DC   1940  1982  LBW   LW    PH    RCV   UCC   UM    WB
              F     F    F

ORGAN COMPOSITIONS

Cherwien, David  "Amazing Grace"  **Interpretations
Based on Hymn-tunes** A.M.S.I.   OR-9  Key: F

Haan, Raymond H. "Amazing grace, how sweet the sound"
**The King of Love**  The Sacred Music Press
K 277  Key: G

Held, Wilbur "Amazing Grace" **Preludes and Postludes**
Volume I  Augsburg Publishing House 11-9318
Key:F

Hopson, Hal H.  **Five Preludes on Familiar Hymns**
Harold Flammer, Inc.   HF-5123  Key: G

FREE ACCOMPANIMENTS

Busarow, Donald  **All Praise to You Eternal God**
Augsburg Publishing House   11-9076   (Two
settings )  Key: F; Key: G

New Dance
  BA  DC   1940  1982  LBW   LW    PH    RCV   UCC   UM    WB
              f                                          f

New England
  BA  DC   1940  1982  LBW   LW    PH    RCV   UCC   UM    WB
        F

New Malden
  BA  DC   1940  1982  LBW   LW    PH    RCV   UCC   UM    WB
                 d

**New Orleans**

| BA | DC | 1940 | 1982 | LBW | LW | PH | RCV | UCC | UM | WB |
|----|----|------|------|-----|----|----|-----|-----|----|----|
| Ab |    |      |      |     |    |    |     |     |    |    |

**New River**

| BA | DC | 1940 | 1982 | LBW | LW | PH | RCV | UCC | UM | WB |
|----|----|------|------|-----|----|----|-----|-----|----|----|
|    |    |      |      |     |    |    | Db  |     |    |    |

**New Song**

| BA | DC | 1940 | 1982 | LBW | LW | PH | RCV | UCC | UM | WB |
|----|----|------|------|-----|----|----|-----|-----|----|----|
|    |    |      |      |     |    |    |     | m:f# |   |    |

**Newman**

| BA | DC | 1940 | 1982 | LBW | LW | PH | RCV | UCC | UM | WB |
|----|----|------|------|-----|----|----|-----|-----|----|----|
|    |    | D    | D    |     |    |    |     |     |    |    |

**Nicaea**

| BA | DC | 1940 | 1982 | LBW | LW | PH | RCV | UCC | UM | WB |
|----|----|------|------|-----|----|----|-----|-----|----|----|
| D  | Eb | D    | D    | D   | D  | Eb | E   | Eb  | Eb | D  |

## INTONATIONS

McCormick, David **20 Organ Intonations on Hymns of Praise** Hope Publishing Co. Key: D

## ORGAN COMPOSITIONS

Busarow, Donald "Holy, Holy, Holy" **The Concordia Hymn Prelude Series** Volume 13 Edited: Herbert Gotsch Concordia Publishing House 97-5620 Key: D

Canning, Thomas "Holy, Holy, Holy" **The Parish Organist** Part Two Edited: Heinrich Fleischer Concordia Publishing House 97-1151 Key: Eb

Cherwien, David "Holy, Holy, Holy" **Interpretations Based on Hymn Tunes** Book IV A.M.S.I. OR-9 Key: D

## FREE ACCOMPANIMENTS

Cassler, G. Winston **Organ Descants for Selected Hymn Tunes** Augsburg Publishing House 11-9304 Key: E

Hancock, Gerre **Organ Improvisations for Hymn-Singing** Hinsaw Music Co. HMO-100 Key: D

Hebble, Robert **Robert Hebble's Hymnal Companion for Organ** Bradley Publications CE/283A/3 Key: Eb

Noble, T. Tertius **Free Organ Accompaniments to One Hundred Well-Known Hymn Tunes** J. Fischer & Bros. #8175 Key: D

Pasquet, Jean **Free Organ Accompaniments to Festival Hymns** Volume I Augsburg Publishing House 11-9192 Key: E

Wyton, Alex **New Shoots from Old Routes** Sacred Music Press KK 279 Key: D

Nicht so traurig

| BA | DC | 1940 | 1982 | LBW | LW | PH | RCV | UCC | UM | WB |
|---|---|---|---|---|---|---|---|---|---|---|
| | F | | | | | g | | | | |

Nicolaus

| BA | DC | 1940 | 1982 | LBW | LW | PH | RCV | UCC | UM | WB |
|---|---|---|---|---|---|---|---|---|---|---|
| Eb | | | | | | | | | | |

Nigeria

| BA | DC | 1940 | 1982 | LBW | LW | PH | RCV | UCC | UM | WB |
|---|---|---|---|---|---|---|---|---|---|---|
| | | | | | | | | | F | |

Nilsson

| BA | DC | 1940 | 1982 | LBW | LW | PH | RCV | UCC | UM | WB |
|---|---|---|---|---|---|---|---|---|---|---|
| | | | d | | | | | | | |

Nobody Knows

| BA | DC | 1940 | 1982 | LBW | LW | PH | RCV | UCC | UM | WB |
|---|---|---|---|---|---|---|---|---|---|---|
| | | | | | | | F | | | |

Nocte surgentes

| BA | DC | 1940 | 1982 | LBW | LW | PH | RCV | UCC | UM | WB |
|---|---|---|---|---|---|---|---|---|---|---|
| | | m:a | m:f# | | | | | | | |

Noel

| BA | DC | 1940 | 1982 | LBW | LW | PH | RCV | UCC | UM | WB |
|---|---|---|---|---|---|---|---|---|---|---|
| | | F | F | | | | | | | |

FREE ACCOMPANIMENTS

Noble, T. Tertius **Fifty Free Organ Accompaniments to Well Known Hymn Tunes** J. Fischer & Bros. No. 8430 Key: F

Noël Nouvelet

| BA | DC | 1940 | 1982 | LBW | LW | PH | RCV | UCC | UM | WB |
|---|---|---|---|---|---|---|---|---|---|---|
| | | e | f | | | | | | | |

ORGAN COMPOSITIONS

Cherwien, David **Interpretations Based on Hymn-tunes** A.M.S.I. OR-1 Key: f

Haan, Raymond H. **Fanfare and Variations on 'Noel Nouvelet'** for Two trumpets and organ Concordia Publishing House 97-5635  Key: g

Haan, Raymond H.  **Festival Hymn Preludes**  The Sacred Music Press  KK 329-3  Key: g

Hudson, Richard "Fugue" **Suite of Organ Carols** Augsburg Publishing House  Key: d

Manz, Paul "Now the Green Blade Rises" **Ten Chorale Improvisations** Set IX Op. 21 Concordia Publishing House 97-5556 Key: f

Schalk, Carl  "Now the Green Blade Riseth"  **The Concordia Hymn Prelude Series**  Volume 11 Edited: Herbert Gotsch  Concordia Publishing House 97-5618  Key: m:f

FREE ACCOMPANIMENTS

Gehrke, Hugo  **Hymn Preludes and Free Accompaniments** Volume 5  Augsburg Publishing House  11-9401 Key: f

<u>Non nobis Domine</u>

| BA | DC | 1940 g | 1982 | LBW | LW | PH | RCV | UCC | UM | WB |
|----|----|----|----|----|----|----|----|----|----|----|

<u>None Other Lamb</u>

| BA | DC | 1940 | 1982 | LBW | LW | PH | RCV | UCC a | UM | WB |
|----|----|----|----|----|----|----|----|----|----|----|

<u>Noormarkku</u>

| BA | DC | 1940 | 1982 | LBW C | LW | PH | RCV | UCC | UM | WB |
|----|----|----|----|----|----|----|----|----|----|----|

<u>Norris</u>

| BA F | DC | 1940 | 1982 | LBW | LW | PH | RCV | UCC | UM | WB |
|----|----|----|----|----|----|----|----|----|----|----|

<u>Norse Air</u>

| BA | DC | 1940 | 1982 | LBW | LW | PH | RCV | UCC | UM Ab | WB |
|----|----|----|----|----|----|----|----|----|----|----|

<u>North Phoenix</u>

| BA D | DC | 1940 | 1982 | LBW | LW | PH | RCV | UCC | UM | WB |
|----|----|----|----|----|----|----|----|----|----|----|

<u>Northampton</u>

| BA | DC | 1940 G | 1982 | LBW | LW | PH | RCV | UCC | UM | WB |
|----|----|----|----|----|----|----|----|----|----|----|

| Northaven | | | | | | | | | | |
|---|---|---|---|---|---|---|---|---|---|---|
| BA | DC | 1940 | 1982 | LBW | LW | PH | RCV | UCC | UM | WB |
| G | | | | | | | | | | |

| Nottingham | | | | | | | | | | |
|---|---|---|---|---|---|---|---|---|---|---|
| BA | DC | 1940 | 1982 | LBW | LW | PH | RCV | UCC | UM | WB |

| Nous allons | | | | | | | | | | |
|---|---|---|---|---|---|---|---|---|---|---|
| BA | DC | 1940 | 1982 | LBW | LW | PH | RCV | UCC | UM | WB |
| | | | F | | | | | | | |

| Nova, nova | | | | | | | | | | |
|---|---|---|---|---|---|---|---|---|---|---|
| BA | DC | 1940 | 1982 | LBW | LW | PH | RCV | UCC | UM | WB |
| | | | m:e | | | | | | | |

| Nova Vita | | | | | | | | | | |
|---|---|---|---|---|---|---|---|---|---|---|
| BA | DC | 1940 | 1982 | LBW | LW | PH | RCV | UCC | UM | WB |
| | | D | D | | | | | | | |

| Now | | | | | | | | | | |
|---|---|---|---|---|---|---|---|---|---|---|
| BA | DC | 1940 | 1982 | LBW | LW | PH | RCV | UCC | UM | WB |
| | | m:g | m:g | | | | | m:g | | |

ORGAN COMPOSITIONS

Busarow, Donald  "Now the Silence" **The Concordia Hymn Prelude Series**  Volume 18  Edited: Herbert Gotsch  Concordia Publishing House  97-5709 Key: F

Pelz, Walter  "Now the Silence" **Hymn Preludes for Holy Communion** Volume 3  Concordia Publishing House 97-5488  Key: F

| Nun bitten wir den heiligen Geist | | | | | | | | | | |
|---|---|---|---|---|---|---|---|---|---|---|
| BA | DC | 1940 | 1982 | LBW | LW | PH | RCV | UCC | UM | WB |
| | | | | F | F | | | | | |

ORGAN COMPOSITIONS

Beck, Albert **76 Offertories on Hymns & Chorales** Concordia Publishing House  97-5207  Key: F

Buxtehude, Dietrich **Orgelwerke II: Chorale Preludes** C.F. Peters Corporation #4457  Key:G

Buxtehude, Dietrich **Chorale Preludes by Masters of the 17th & 18th Centuries** Volume I  Edited: Walter Buszin  Concordia Publishing House Key: G

Buxtehude, Dietrich  "We Pray Now to the Holy Spirit" **Anthologia Antiqua** Book Five **Six Chorale Preludes** Edited: Seth Bingham J. Fischer & Bros.  No. 8090  Key: G

Engel, James "To God the Holy Spirit Let Us Pray" **Preludes on Six Hymn Tunes** Augsburg Publishing House  11-9364  Key: F

Lenel, Ludwig "We Now Implore God the Holy Ghost" **Three Chorale Fantasies on Pre-Reformation Hymns** Concordia Publishing House  97-4408 Key: d

Pepping, Ernst  **Fünfundzwanzig Orgelchorale** Edition Schott 4723  B. Schott's Sohne  Key: m:f

Pepping, Ernst  "To God the Holy Spirit Let Us Pray" **The Concordia Hymn Prelude Series** Volume 12 Edited: Herbert Gotsch  Concordia Publishing House 97-5619  Key: F

Scheidemann, Heinrich  "We Now Implore God the Holy Ghost" **The Parish Organist** Part Eight  Music for Easter, Ascension, Pentecost and Trinity Edited: Erich Goldschmidt  Concordia Publishing House  97-1404  Key: F

Walther, Johann Gottfried **80 Chorale Preludes – German Masters of the 17th and 18th Centuries** Edited:  Hermann  Keller    C.F. Peters Corporation  #4448  Key: G

Nun danket

| BA | DC | 1940 | 1982 | LBW | LW | PH | RCV | UCC | UM | WB |
|----|----|------|------|-----|----|----|-----|-----|----|----|
|    |    |      |      |     |    | F  | Eb  | F   | Eb | F  |

Nun danket all'

| BA | DC | 1940 | 1982 | LBW | LW | PH | RCV | UCC | UM | WB |
|----|----|------|------|-----|----|----|-----|-----|----|----|
|    | F  | Eb   | F    | F   | F  | F  | G   | F   |    | F  |

## ORGAN COMPOSITIONS

Hark, Friedrich  "This is the Day the Lord Hath Made" **The Parish Organist** Part Two  Edited: Heinrich Fleischer  Concordia Publishing House  97-1151 Key:  G

Held, Wilbur "Spirit Divine, Attend Our Prayers" **Hymn Preludes for the Pentecost Season** Concordia Publishing House 97-5517  Key: F

276

Kauffman, Georg F. "Now Thank We All Our God" **Short Service Pieces for Organ** Arr. Norris L. Stephens J. Fischer & Bros. FE 9797 Key: F

Nun danket alle Gott

| BA | DC | 1940 | 1982 | LBW | LW | PH | RCV | UCC | UM | WB |
|----|----|------|------|-----|----|----|-----|-----|----|----|
| F | F | | Eb | F | F | | | | | |

INTONATIONS

McCormick, David W. **20 Organ Intonations on Hymns of Praise** Hope Publishing Co. Key: F

ORGAN COMPOSITIONS

Alwes, Charles **Six Organ Preludes** Concordia Publishing House 11-9416 Key: F

Bach, J.S. **Organ Works** Volume 2 Edited: Hans Kloz Urtext of the New Bach Edition Bärenreiter 5172 Key: G

Bach, J.S. **Organ Works** Volume VIII Widor - Schweitzer G. Schirmer Key: G

Bach, J.S. **Orgelwerke** Volume VII C.F. Peters Corporation Nr. 246 Key: G

Bach, J.S. "Now Thank We All Our God" Arr. Claude Means **A Collection of Thanksgiving Music** Compiled by John Holler H.W. Gray St. Cecilia #648 Key: G

Bristol, Lee Hastings Jr. "Prelude on TwoTraditional Tunes, 'Nun Danket' and 'Let Us Break Bread Together'" **The Bristol Collection of Contemporary Hymn Tune Preludesfor Organ** Volume 2 Edited: Lee Hastings Bristol, Jr. Harold Flammer Inc. Key: Eb

Dupre, Marcel **Seventy-Nine Chorales for Organ** Opus 28 H. W. Gray Key: G

Held, Wilbur "Now Thank We All Our God" **Hymn Preludes for the Autumn Festivals** Concordia Publishing House 97-5360 Key: G

Hillert, Richard "The Lord, My God, Be Praised" **The Concordia Hymn Prelude Series** Volume 13 Edited: Herbert Gotsch Concordia Publishing House 97-5620 Key: F

Karg-Elert, Sigfrid   "Choral Improvisation on 'Now
     Thank We All'"  **The Lutheran Organist**  Compiled
     by John Holler  H. W. Gray Co.   Key:  G

Karg-Elert, Sigfrid   "Now Thank We All Our God"
     **Wedding Music**  Part II  Concordia Publishing
     House  97-1370  Key: G

Karg-Elert, Sigfrid  "Now Thank We All Our God"  **Choral
     Improvisations for Organ for Confirmation,
     Marriage, Christening and Harvest Festival**  Op. 65,
     Volume 6  Edited: Robert Leech Bedell   Edward B.
     Marks Music Corp.  Key: G

Karg-Elert, Sigfrid  "Now Thank We All Our God"  **Wedding
     Music**  Part 2   Concordia Publishing House   OC 226
     Key: G

Kaufmann, Georg Frederich   "Chorale Prelude on 'Nun danket
     alle Gott'"  **For Manuals Only**  Edited: John Christopher
     McAfee Music Corporation  Key: F

Kaufmann, Georg Friedrich   "Now Thank We All Our God"
     **The Parish Organist**  Part Two  Edited: Heinrich
     Fleischer  Concordia Publishing House  97-1151
     Key:  F

Kaufmann, George Friedrich  **80 Chorale Preludes – German
     Masters of the 17th and 18th Centuries**  Edited:
     Hermann Keller  C.F. Peters Corporation #4448
     Key:  F

Manz, Paul "Now Thank We All Our God"  **Ten Chorale
     Improvisations** Set II  Op. 7  Concordia Publishing
     House 97-4656 Key: F

Manz, Paul "Now Than& We All Our God"  **Ten Chorale
     Improvisations** Set VIII  Op. 20  Concordia
     Publishing House 97-5342  Key: F

Post, Piet "Now Thank We All Our God"  **Triptych for
     Organ** Concordia Publishing House 11-835   Key:  F

Whitford, Homer  **Five Choral Paraphrases** Set I
     H.W. Gray Co.,  Key: F

## FREE ACCOMPANIMENTS

Alwes, Charles  **Six Organ Preludes** Augsburg
     Publishing  House  11-9416  Key: F

Bunjes, Paul  **New Organ Accompaniments for Hymns**
     Concordia Publishing House  97-5348  Key: F

Cassler, G. Winston **Free Organ Accompaniments to Festival Hymns** Volume I Augsburg Publishing House 11-9192 Key: F

Ferguson, John **Hymn Harmonizations for Organ** Book II Ludwig Music Publishing Co. 0-07 Key: F

Hancock, Gerre **Organ Improvisations for Hymn-Singing** Hinshaw Music Co. HMO-100 Key: F

Noble, T. Tertius **Free Organ Accompaniments to One Hundred Well-Known Hymn Tunes** J. Fischer & Bros. #8175 Key: Eb

Ore, Charles **Hymn Preludes and Free Accompaniments** Volume 7 Augsburg Publishing House 11-9403 Key: F

<u>Nun freut euch, lieben Christen gmein</u>
(See also: Es ist gewisslich an der Zeit; Luther's Hymn)

| BA | DC | 1940 | 1982 | LBW | LW | PH | RCV | UCC | UM | WB |
|----|----|------|------|-----|----|----|-----|-----|----|----|
| G  |    |      |      | F   | F  |    |     | G   | G  | G  |

ORGAN COMPOSITIONS

Bach, J. S. **Organ Works** Volume 3. "The Individually Transmitted Organ Chorales" Edited: Hans Klotz Urtext of the New Bach Edition Bärenreiter 5173 Key: G

Bach, J.S. **Organ Works** Volume VI Widor-Schweitzer G. Schirmer Key: G (#51, 52)

Bach, J.S. **Orgelwerke** Volume IX C.F. Peters Corporation #2067 Key: G

Bach, J.S. **Orgelwerke** Volume VII C.F. Peters Corporation Nr. 246 Key: G

Bender, Jan "Dear Christians, One and All, Rejoice" **Festival Preludes on Six Chorales** Concordia Publishing House 97-4608 Key: F

Bieske, 9erner "On Christ's Ascension I Now Build" **The Concordia Hymn Prelude Series** Volume 12 Edited: Herbert Gotsch Concordia Publishing House 97-5619 Key: F

Dupre, Marcel **Seventh-Nine Chorales for Organ** Opus 28 H. W. Gray Key: G

Manz, Paul "Dear Christians, One and All, Rejoice" **Ten
Chorale Improvisations** Set IV  Op. 10 Concordia
Publishing House 97-4951  Key: F

Praetorius, Michael  "Dear Christians, One and All,
Rejoice"  **The Parish Organist**  Part Two
Edited:  Heinrich Fleischer  Concordia Publishing
House  97-1151  Key:  F

Walcha, Helmut **25 Chorale Preludes** C.F. Peters
Nr. 4850  Key: F

Weckmann, Matthias **80 Chorale Preludes – German Masters
of the 17th and 18th Centuries**  Edited: Hermann
Keller  C.F. Peters Corporation #4448  Key:G

Weckman, Matthias **Chorale Preludes by Masters of the
17th & 18th Centuries**  Volume I  Edited:  Walter
Buszin  Concordia Publishing House  Key: m:f

FREE ACCOMPANIMENTS

Bunjes, Paul  **New Organ Accompaniments for Hymns**
Concordia Publishing House  97-5348  Key: F

| <u>Nun komm, der Heiden Heiland</u> | | | | | | | | | |
|------|----|------|------|-----|----|-----|-----|----|----|
| BA | DC | 1940 | 1982 LBW | LW | PH | RCV | UCC | UM | WB |
|    |    | g    | g   g    | g   |    |     |     |    | g  |

INTONATIONS

Hermann, David  **11 Hymn Intonations, Free Accompani-
ments, Instrumental Descants for Organ**  Volume I
Advent, Christmas, Epiphany  G.I.A. Publications
G-2378  Key: m:g

ORGAN COMPOSITIONS

Bach, J. S. **Organ Works**  Volume 1  Edited: Heinz-
Harald Löhlein  Urtext of the New Bach Edition
Bärenreiter  5171  Key: m:a

Bach, J.S.  **Organ Works**  Volume 2  Edited: Hans Kloz
Urtext of the New Bach Edition  Bärenreiter 5172
Key: m:g

Bach, J. S.  **Organ Works**  Volume 3  "The
Individually Transmitted Organ Chorales"
Edited: Hans Klotz  Urtext of the New Bach Edition
Bärenreiter  5173  Key: m:g

Bach, J.S. **Orgelwerke** Volume V  C.F. Peters
Corporation Nr. 244 #42  Key:a;  #43 Key: g

Bach, J.S. **Orgelwerke** Volume VII  C.F. Peters
Corporation Nr. 246  #45 Key: g; #46 Key: g
#47 Key: g

Bach, J.S. **The Liturgical Year** (Orgelbuchlein)
Edited: Albert Reimenschneider  Oliver Ditson Co.
Key: a

Bach, J.S. **Organ Works** Volume VI  Widor-Schweitzer
G. Schirmer  Key: g

Bach, J.S. **Organ Works** Volume VII Widor-Schweitzer
G. Schirmer  Key: a

Bach, J.S. **Organ Works** Volume VIII Widor-Schweitzer
G. Schirmer (#15, 16, 17, 34) Key: g

Beck, Albert  **76 Offertories on Hymns & Chorales**
Concordia Publishing House  97-5207  Key: g

Bruhns, Nikolaus "Phantasie uber den Choral: Nun komm
der Heiden Heiland" **Alte Meister** Edited: Karl
Straube, Book I  C.F. Peters Corporation
No. 4301  Key: g

Buttstedt, Johann Heinrich "Saviour of the Nations,
Come" **The Parish Organist** Part Three
Edited: Heinrich Fleischer  Concordia Publishing
House  97-1154  Key: g

Buxtehude, Dietrich **Six Organ Preludes on Chorales**
Edited: Henry G. Ley "Now Come, Redeemer of
Our Race" Oxford University Press  Key: g

Buxtehude, Dietrich **Orgelwerke II: Chorale Preludes**
C.F. Peters #4457  Key: g

Distler, Hugo  **The Parish Organist** Part Five  Advent
and Christmas Music  Edited:  Fleischer
Goldschmidt  Concordia Publishing House 97-1382
Key: m:g

Distler, Hugo  "Nun komm der Heiden Heiland"  **Organ
Partita** Opus 8(1)  Bärenreiter  637  Key: m:g

Dupre, Marcel  **Seventh-Nine Chorales for Organ**
Opus 28  H. W. Gray  Key: m:a

Kauffman, Georg Friedrich  "Saviour of the Nations,
Come"  **The Concordia Hymn Prelude Series**
Volume 2  Edited: Herbert Gotsch  Concordia
Publishing House  97-5537  Key: m:g

Kaufmann, Georg F. "Come Now, Savior of the Gentiles" **Short Classic Pieces for Organ from the 16th, 17th and 18th Centuries** Arr. Norris L. Stephens J. Fischer & Bros. No. 9607 Key: m:g

Manz, Paul "Savior of the Nations, Come" **Ten Chorale Improvisations** Set III Op. 9 Concordia Publishing House 97-4950 Key: g

Manz, Paul "Let the Earth Now Praise the Lord" **Ten Chorale Improvisations** Set VII Op. 17 Concordia Publishing House 97-5308 Key: g

Reger, Max **Chorale Preludes for the Church Year from Max Reger Op. 67** Edited: Alex Wyton Carl Fischer, Inc. O 4667 Key: g

Walcha, Helmut **25 Chorale Preludes** C.F. Peters Nr. 4850 Key: g

Vetter, Andreas Nikolaus **80 Chorale Preludes – German Masters of the 17th and 18th Centuries** Edited: Hermann Keller C.F. Peters Corporation #4448 Key: g

Vetter, Andreas N. "Come Now, Savior of the Gentiles" **Short Service Pieces for Organ** Arr. Norris L. Stephens J. Fischer & Bros. FE 9797 Key: m:g

### FREE ACCOMPANIMENTS

Bender, Jan **Hymn Preludes and Free Accompaniments** Volume 1 Augsburg Publishing House 11-9397 Key: g

Bunjes, Paul **New Organ Accompaniments for Hymns** Concordia Publishing House 97-5348 Key: m:g

| Nun | lasst | uns | den | Leib | begraben | | | | | |
|-----|-------|-----|-----|------|----------|-----|-----|-----|-----|-----|
| BA | DC | 1940 | 1982 | LBW | LW | PH | RCV | UCC | UM | WB |
| | | | | G | G | | | | | |

### ORGAN COMPOSITIONS

Bach, J. S. **Organ Chorales from the Neumeister Collection** Edited: Christoph Wolff Yale University Press/Bärenreiter 5181 Key: G

| Nun | lasst | uns | Gott | dem | Herren | | | | | |
|-----|-------|-----|------|-----|--------|-----|-----|-----|-----|-----|
| BA | DC | 1940 | 1982 | LBW | LW | PH | RCV | UCC | UM | WB |
| | | | | A | | | | | | |

Bach, Johann Christoph **Chorale Preludes by Masters of the 17th & 18th Centuries** Volume I  Edited: Walter Buszin  Concordia Publishing House  Key: G

Karg-Elert, Sigfrid "Now Let Us, Lord God" **Choral Improvisations for Organ for New Year, Easter and other Church Festivals** Op. 65, Volume 3  Edited: Robert Leech Bedell  Edward B. Marks Music Corp. Key: Bb

Pachelbel, Johann **80 Chorale Preludes – German Masters of the 17th and 18th Centures** Edited: Hermann Keller  C.F. Peters Corporation #4448  Key: A

Walther, Johann Gottfried  "Now Let Us Come Before Him" **The Concordia Hymn Prelude Series** Volume 15 Edited: Herbert Gotsch  Concordia Publishing House 97-5706  Key: A

Nun lob, mein Seel, den Herren
    (See also: My Soul, Now Praise Your Maker)
    BA    DC    1940 1982 LBW  LW    PH    RCV   UCC   UM    WB
                        G    G

ORGAN COMPOSITIONS

Barlow, Wayne **Four Chorale Voluntaries**
    Concordia Publishing House 97-5602  Key: G

Beck, Albert  **76 Offertories on Hymns & Chorales**
    Concordia Publishing House  97-5207  Key: G

Busarow, Donald "O Living Bread from Heaven" **Hymn Preludes for Holy Communion** Volume 2 97-5487 Key:e

Buxtehude, Dietrich **Orgelwerke II: Chorale Preludes**
    C.F. Peters Corporation  #4457  Key:  G

Bender, Jan "My Soul, Now Bless Thy Maker" **Festival Preludes on Six Chorales**
    Concordia Publishing House  97-4608  Key: G

Hassler,Hans Leo "O Living Bread From Heaven" **Organ Music for the Communion Service** Edited: Paul Bunjes Concordia Publishing House #97-1395  Key: G

Pachelbel, Johann  **Chorale Preludes by Masters of the 17th & 18th Centuries** Volume I  Edited:  Walter Buszin  Concordia Publishing House  Key: C

283

Pepping, Ernst **Praeludia Postludia II**  B. Schott's
Sohne Edition 6041  Key: m:g

Walther, Johann Gottfried  **80 Chorale Preludes – German
Masters of the 17th and 18th Centuries**  Edited:
Hermann Keller C.F. Peters Corporation #4448 Key:G

Nun <u>freut</u> <u>euch</u>

| BA | DC | 1940 | 1982 | LBW | LW | PH | RCV | UCC | UM | WB |
|----|----|------|------|-----|----|----|-----|-----|----|----|
|    |    |      |      |     |    | G  |     |     |    |    |

Nun <u>ruhen</u> <u>alle</u> <u>Walder</u>
(See also: Innsbruck)

| BA | DC | 1940 | 1982 | LBW | LW | PH | RCV | UCC | UM | WB |
|----|----|------|------|-----|----|----|-----|-----|----|----|

ORGAN COMPOSITIONS

Walther, Johann Gottfried  **Chorale Preludes by Masters
of the 17th & 18th Centuries**  Volume I  Edited:
Walter Buszin  Concordia Publishing House  Key: F

Nunc <u>angelorum</u>

| BA | DC | 1940 | 1982 | LBW | LW | PH | RCV | UCC | UM | WB |
|----|----|------|------|-----|----|----|-----|-----|----|----|
|    |    |      |      | F   | F  |    |     |     |    |    |

Nunc <u>dimittis</u>
(See also: Le Cantique de Simeon)

| BA | DC | 1940 | 1982 | LBW | LW | PH | RCV | UCC | UM | WB |
|----|----|------|------|-----|----|----|-----|-----|----|----|
| F  | F  |      |      |     | F  | F  |     |     |    | F  |

FREE ACCOMPANIMENTS

**Free Harmonizations to Hymn Tunes By Fifty American
Composers**  Edited: D. DeWitt Wasson  Hinshaw
Music, Inc.  HMO-145  Key: F

Nunc <u>Sancte</u> <u>nobis</u> <u>Spiritus</u>

| BA | DC | 1940 | 1982 | LBW | LW | PH | RCV | UCC | UM | WB |
|----|----|------|------|-----|----|----|-----|-----|----|----|
|    |    | m:d  |      |     |    |    |     |     |    |    |

<u>Nutfield</u>

| BA | DC | 1940 | 1982 | LBW | LW | PH | RCV | UCC | UM | WB |
|----|----|------|------|-----|----|----|-----|-----|----|----|
|    |    | D    |      |     |    |    |     |     |    |    |

<u>Nyack</u>

| BA | DC | 194t | 1982 | LBW | LW | PH | RCV | UCC | UM | WB |
|----|----|------|------|-----|----|----|-----|-----|----|----|
|    |    | D    |      |     |    |    |     |     |    |    |

<u>Nyland</u>

| BA | DC | 1940 | 1982 | LBW | LW | PH | RCV | UCC | UM | WB |
|----|----|------|------|-----|----|----|-----|-----|----|----|
| Eb | Eb | Eb   | Eb   |     |    | Eb | Eb  |     | Eb |    |

ORGAN COMPOSITIONS

Hayton, Russell  "In Heavenly Love Abiding"
    **Prelude on 'Nyland'** H.W. Gray No. 951
    Key: Eb

FREE ACCOMPANIMENTS

Ferguson, John  **Hymn Tune Harmonizations**  Book III
    Ludwig Music Publishing Co.  Key: Eb

**Free Harmonizations to Hymn Tunes By Fifty American
    Composers** Edited: D. DeWitt Wasson  Hinshaw
    Music, Inc.  HMO-145  Key: Eb

Nyt ylös, sieluni
    BA    DC    1940 1982 LBW  LW    PH    RCV   UCC   UM    WB
                          e

# O

O dass ich tausend Zungen hätte (Dretzel)
    BA    DC    1940 1982 LBW  LW    PH    RCV   UCC   UM    WB
                          F

ORGAN COMPOSITIONS

Busarow, Donald  "Baptized into Your Name Most Holy"
    **The Concordia Hymn Prelude Series** Volume 16
    Edited: Herbert Gotsch  Concordia Publishing House
    97-5707  Key: F

Manz, Paul "O That I Had a Thousand Voices" **Ten Chorale
    Improvisations** Set II  Op. 7  Concordia Publishing
    House 97-4656  Key: F

Manz, Paul "Oh, that I Had a Thousand Voices"**Ten
    Chorale Improvisations** Set II  Op. 9  Concordia
    Publishing House 97-4950  (17) Key: F (22) Key: F

Peeters, Flor  "Oh, that I had a Thousand Voices"
    **30 Chorale Preludes**  Op. 68  C.F. Peters
    Corporation  No. 6023  Key:  F

Reger, Max  **30 Short Chorale Preludes** Op. 135a
    C.F. Peters Corporation Nr. 3980  Key: F

Metzger, Hans Arnold "Oh, that I Had a Thousand Voices"
    **The Parish Organist**  Part Three  Edited:
    Heinrich Fleischer  Concordia Publishing House
    97-1154  Key: F

O dass ich tausend Zungen hätte (König)
  BA    DC    1940 1982 LBW  LW    PH    RCV   UCC   UM    WB
                         F    F

### ORGAN COMPOSITIONS

Karg-Elert, Sigfrid "O that I had a thousand tongues" **Choral Improvisations for Organ for Ascensiontide and Pentecost** Op. 65 Vo. 4 Edited: Robert Leech Bedell  Edwards B. Marks Music Corp. Key: G

Reger, Max  "Oh, that I Had a Thousand Voices" **The Parish Organist** Part Three  Edited: Heinrich Fleischer  Concordia Publishing House 97-1154  Key: F

### FREE ACCOMPANIMENTS

Bunjes, Paul  **New Organ Accompaniments for Hymns** Concordia Publishing House  97-5348  Key: F

Gehrke, Hugo  **Hymn Preludes and Free Accompaniments** Volume 5  Augsburg Publishing House  11-9401 Key: F

O du Liebe meiner Liebe
  BA    DC    1940 1982 LBW  LW    PH    RCV   UCC   UM    WB
                         G    G

### ORGAN COMPOSITIONS

Engel, James  "Jesus, Refuge of the Weary"  **Preludes on Six Hymn Tunes** Augsburg Publishing House 11-9364  Key: F

Karg-Elert, Sigfrid "O Thou Love, of My Love" **Choral Improvisations for Organ for Confirmation, Marriage, Christening and Harvest Festival** Op. 65, Volume 6  Edited: Robert Leech Bedell Edward B. Marks Music Corp.  Key: g

Klotz, Hans  "Love, Divine, All Love Excelling" **The Parish Organist** Part Three Edited: Heinrich Fleischer  Concordia Publishing House  97-1154 Key: G

Schack, David  "Jesus, Refuge of the Weary"  **The Concordia Hymn Prelude Series** Volume 8  Edited: Herbert Gotsch  Concordia Publishing House 97-5615  Key: G

O Durchbrecher

| | BA | DC | 1940 | 1982 | LBW | LW | PH | RCV | UCC | UM | WB |
|---|---|---|---|---|---|---|---|---|---|---|---|
| | | | | | | D | | | | | |

## ORGAN COMPOSITIONS

Abel, Otto "Hail, O Source of Every Blessing" **The Concordia Hymn Prelude Series** Volume 6 Edited: Herbert Gotsch Concordia Publishing House 97-5612 Key: D

Karg-Elert, Sigfrid "O break loose all chains" **Choral Improvisations for Organ for Ascension-tide and Pentecost** Op. 65 Volume 4 Edited: Robert Leech Bedell Edward B. Marks Music Corp. Key: Eb

O Esca viatorum
(See also: Psalm 6)

| | BA | DC | 1940 | 1982 | LBW | LW | PH | RCV | UCC | UM | WB |
|---|---|---|---|---|---|---|---|---|---|---|---|
| | | | | | | e | | | | | |

O filii et filiae

| | BA | DC | 1940 | 1982 | LBW | LW | PH | RCV | UCC | UM | WB |
|---|---|---|---|---|---|---|---|---|---|---|---|
| | m:f | m:f | m:g | m:g | m:g | m:g | m:g | m:g | m:g | m:g | |

## ORGAN COMPOSITIONS

Dandrieu, Jean Francois "O Sons and Daughters, Let Us Sing" **The Parish Organist** Part Eight Music for Easter, Ascension, Pentecost and Trinity Edited: Erich Goldschmidt Concordia Publishing House 97-1404 Key: d

Deshayes, Henri "Easter Offertory 'O Sons and Daughters of the Lord'" **Selected Festival Music for the Organ – Lent and Easter Services** Edited: William C. Carl Boston Music Company Key: a

Held, Wilbur **Partita on "O Sons and Daughters"** Augsburg Publishing House 11-0819 Key: a

Held, Wilbur "O Sons and Daughters of the King" **The Concordia Hymn Prelude Series** Volume 11 Edited: Herbert Gotsch Concordia Publishing House 97-5618 Key: m:g

Hutchings, Arthur **Seasonal Preludes for Organ** Novello & Company, Ltd. Key: g

Loret, Clement "Easter Day 'O Filii et Filae'" **Selected Festival Music for the Organ – Lent and Easter Services** Edited: William C. Carl   Boston Music Company   Key: a

Sowerby, Leo "O Sons and Daughters" **Advent to Whitsuntide** Volume Four   Hinrichsen   No. 743b Key: g

Verrees Leon **Chorale Improvisation on 'O Filii Et Filiae'** H.W. Gray Co., Inc. No. 673 Key: g

Willan, Healey "On This Most Holy Day" **Ten Hymn Preludes** Set I   C.F. Peters Corp.   No. 6011 Key: g

Wyton, Alec "Epilogue" **Resurrection Suite** Harold Flammer, Inc.   HF 5014   Key: g

### FREE ACCOMPANIMENTS

Cassler, G. Winston **Free Organ Accompaniments to Festival Hymns** Volume I   Augsburg Publishing House   11-9192   Key: g

Goode, Jack **Thirty-Four Changes on Hymn Tunes** H.W. Gray Co.   GB 644   Key: f

Noble, T. Tertius **Free Organ Accompaniments to One Hundred Well-Known Hymn Tunes** J. Fischer & Bros. #8175   Key: f

O God Our Help in Ages Past
(See also: St. Anne)

O Gott, du frommer Gott (1646)

| BA | DC | 1940 | 1982 | LBW | LW | PH | RCV | UCC | UM | WB |
|----|----|------|------|-----|----|----|-----|-----|----|----|
|    |    |      | m:a  |     |    |    |     |     |    |    |

O Gott, du frommer Gott (1693)

| BA | DC | 1940 | 1982 | LBW | LW | PH | RCV | UCC | UM | WB |
|----|----|------|------|-----|----|----|-----|-----|----|----|
|    |    |      |      |     | F  | D  | F   | D   |    | C  |

### ORGAN COMPOSITIONS

Bach, J. S. **Organ Works** Volume 1   Edited: Heinz-Harald Löhlein   Urtext of the New Bach Edition Bärenreiter   5171   Key: m:c

Brahms, Johannes **Samtliche Orgelwerke** Breitkopf & Hartel   Key: a

Brahms, Johannes  "O God Thou Faithful God"
**Eleven Chorale Preludes** Opus 122  Edited:
E. Power Biggs  Mercury Music Corporation
A-260  Key: a

Bach, J.S. **Organ Works** Volume VIII Widor-Schweitzer
G. Schirmer  Key: c

Bach, J.S. **Orgelwerke** Volume V C.F. Peters
Corporation Nr. 244  Key: c

Karg-Elert, Sigfrid "O God Thou Good God" **Choral
Improvisations for Organ for Ascensiontide and
Pentecost** Op. 65 Volume 4 Edited: Robert Leech
Bedell  Edward B. Marks Music Corp. Key: F

Karg-Elert, Sigfrid "O God, Thou Good God" **Choral
Improvisations for Organ for Reformation Day, Fast
Days, Communion and Funeral Rites** Op. 65, Volume 5
Edited: Robert Leech Bedell  Edward B. Marks Music
Corp.  Key: Db

Manz, Paul "O God, Thou Faithful God" **Ten Chorale
Improvisations** Set III  Op. 9  97-4950 Key: F

Peeters, Flor  "O God, Thou Faithful God" **30 Chorale
Preludes** Op. 68 C.F. Peters Corporation
No. 6023  Key: E

Reger, Max  **30 Short Chorale Preludes** Op. 135a
C.F. Peters Corporation Nr. 3980  Key: F

Walther, Johann Gottfried  "O God, Thou Faithful God"
**The Parish Organist** Part Three  Edited:
Heinrich Fleischer  Concordia Publishing House
97-1154  Key: F

FREE ACCOMPANIMTNTS

Bunjes, Paul **New Organ Accompaniments for Hymns**
Concordia Publishing House  97-5348  Key: F

O grosser Gott
  BA   DC   1940 1982 LBW  LW    PH   RCV  UCC  UM   WB
                            Bb   C

ORGAN COMPOSITIONS

Schalk, Carl  "O God of God, O Light of Light" **The
Concordia Hymn Prelude Series** Volume 6  Edited:
Herbert Gotsch  Concordia Publishing House
97-5612  Key: Bb

O Haupt voll Blut und Wunden
   (See also: Herzlich tut mich verlangen; Passion Chorale;
    O Sacred Head Now Wounded)

ORGAN COMPOSITIONS
Pepping, Ernst **Funfundzwanzig Orgelchorale**  Edition
      Schott  4723  B. Schott's Sohne  Key: m:e

O Heiland reiss die Himmel auf
      BA    DC   1940 1982 LBW  LW      PH   RCV  UCC  UM    WB
                 m:d  m:d  m:d

ORGAN COMPOSITIONS

Walcha, Helmut **25 Chorale Preludes**  C.F. Peters
   Nr. 4850  Key: d

Zipp, Friedrich  "O Saviour, Rend the Heavens Wide"
   **The Concordia Hymn Prelude Series**  Volume 2
   Edited: Herbert Gotsch  Concordia Publishing
   House  97-5537  Key: m:d

FREE ACCOMPANIMENTS

Gehrke, Hugo  **Hymn Preludes and Free Accompaniments**
   Volume 5  Augsburg Publishing House  11-9401
   Key: d

O heilige Dreifaltigkeit
      BA    DC   1940 1982 LBW  LW      PH   RCV  UCC  UM    WB
                           D

ORGAN COMPOSITIONS

Bender, Jan  "O Blessed Holy Trinity"  **The Parish
   Organist**  Part Three Edited: Heinrich Fleischer
   Concordia Publishing House  97-1154  Key: D

FREE ACCOMPANIMENTS

Bender, Jan  **Hymn Preludes and Free Accompaniments**
   Volume 1  Augsburg Publishing House  11-9397
   Key: D

O heiliger Geist
      BA    DC   1940 1982 LBW  LW      PH   RCV  UCC  UM    WB
                           A

O Herre Gott
      BA    DC   1940 1982 LBW  LW      PH   RCV  UCC  UM    WB
                           G

ORGAN COMPOSITIONS

Bach, J. S. **Organ Chorales from the Neumeister Collection** Edited: Christoph Wolff Yale University Press/Bärenreiter 5181 Key: m:bb

<u>O How I Love Jesus</u>

| BA | DC | 1940 | 1982 LBW | LW | PH | RCV | UCC | UM | WB |
|----|----|------|----------|----|----|-----|-----|----|----|
| Ab |    |      |          |    |    |     |     |    |    |

<u>O Jesu</u>

| BA | DC | 1940 | 1982 LBW | LW | PH | RCV | UCC | UM | WB |
|----|----|------|----------|----|----|-----|-----|----|----|
| F  |    |      |          |    | F  |     | F   | F  |    |

ORGAN COMPOSITIONS

Bach, J. S. **Organ Chorales from the Neumeister Collection** Edited: Christoph Wolff Yale University Press/Bärenreiter 5181 Key: m:g

FREE ACCOMPANIMENTS

**Free Harmonizations to Hymn Tunes By Fifty American Composers** Edited: D. DeWitt Wasson Hinshaw Music, Inc. HMO-145 Key: F

<u>O Jesu Christ, mein's Lebens Licht</u>

| BA | DC | 1940 | 1982 LBW | LW | PH | RCV | UCC | UM | WB |
|----|----|------|----------|----|----|-----|-----|----|----|
|    |    |      |          |    |    | C   |     |    |    |

ORGAN COMPOSITIONS

Bach, J.S. "Lord Jesus Christ, My Life, My Light" **The Parish Organist** Part Three Edited: Heinrich Fleischer Concordia Publishing House 97-1154 Key: G

Manz, Paul "Jesus, Thy Church with Longing Eyes" **Ten Chorale Improvisations** Set V Op. 14 Concordia Publishing House 97-5257 Key: G

Moser, Rudolf "Lord Jesus Christ, My Life, My Light" **The Parish Organist** Part Seven Music for Lent, Palm Sunday and Holy Week Edited: Erich Goldschmidt Concordia Publishing House 97-1403 Key: G

Walcha, Helmut **25 Chorale Preludes** C.F. Peters Corporation Nr. 4850 Key: Bb

<u>O Jesu Christe, wahres Licht</u>

| BA | DC | 1940 | 1982 LBW | LW | PH | RCV | UCC | UM | WB |
|----|----|------|----------|----|----|-----|-----|----|----|
|    |    |      | G        | G  | G  |     |     |    |    |

291

ORGAN COMPOSITIONS

Walcha, Helmut **Chorale Preludes** II   C.F. Peters
Corporation Nr. 4871   Key: G

FREE ACCOMPANIMENTS

Diemer, Emma Lou   **Hymn Preludes and Free Accompaniments**
Volume 2   Augsburg Publishing House   11-9398
Key: G

<u>O Jesu än de dina</u>
        BA     DC     1940 1982 LBW   LW     PH     RCV   UCC   UM     WB
                                Eb

<u>O Jesulein süss</u>
        BA     DC     1940 1982 LBW   LW     PH     RCV   UCC   UM     WB
                                Ab

ORGAN COMPOSITIONS

Fischer, Michael Gotthardt   "Prelude on 'O Jesulein
süss, O Jesulein mild'"   **Organ Music for Christmas**
Volume 1 Edited: C. H. Trevor   Oxford University
Press   Key: A

Kauffmann, Georg Friedrich "O Jesus So Sweet, O Jesus
So Mild"   **The Parish Organist** Christmas and
Epiphany Music   Part Six   Concordia Publishing
House   97-1391   Key: Bb

Kauffman, Georg Friedrich "O Jesulein süss"   **Organ
Music for Christmas**   Edited: C.F. Trevor
Oxford University Press   Key: A

Scheidt, Samuel  "O Jesus So Sweet, O Jesus So Mild"
**The Parish Organist**  Christmas and Epiphany
Music   Part Six   Concordia Publishing House
97-1391   Key: Bb

<u>O Lamm Gottes unschuldig</u>
        BA     DC     1940 1982 LBW   LW     PH     RCV   UCC   UM     WB
                                D      D

ORGAN COMPOSITIONS

Ahrens, Joseph **Das Heilige Jahr** VolumeII
Willy Muller - Suddeutscher Musikverlag -
Heidelberg, New York: C.F. Peters   Key: F

Bach, J. S.   **Organ Works**   Volume 1   Edited: Heinz-
Harald Löhlein   Urtext of the New Bach Edition
Bärenreiter   5171   Key: F

Bach, J. S. **Organ Works** Volume 1 Edited: Heinz-Harald Lohlein Urtext of the New Bach Edition Bärenreiter 5171 Key: F

Bach, J.S. **Organ Works** Volume 2 Edited: Hans Kloz Urtext of the New Bach Edition Bärenreiter 5172 Key: A

Bach, J. S. **Organ Works** Volume 3 "The Individually Transmitted Organ Chorales" Edited: Hans Klotz Urtext of the New Bach Edition Bärenreiter 5173 Key: F

Bach, J. S. **Organ Chorales from the Neumeister Collection** Edited: Christoph Wolff Yale University Press/Bärenreiter 5181 Key: F

Bach, J.S. **Organ Works** Volume VII Widor-Schweitzer G. Schirmer Key: F

Bach, J.S. **Organ Works** Volume VIII Widor-Schweitzer G. Schirmer Key: A

Bach, J.S. **Orgelwerke** Volume V C.F. Peters Corporation Nr. 244 Key: F

Bach, J.S. **Orgelwerke** Volume VII C.F. Peters Corporation Nr. 246 Key: A

Bach, J.S. **The Liturgical Year** (Orgelbuchlein) Edited: Albert Reimenschneider Oliver Ditson Co. Key: F

Dupre, Marcel **Seventy-Nine Chorales for Organ** Opus 28 H. W. Gray Key: F

Hillert, Richard "Lamb of God, Pure and Sinless" **The Concordia Hymn Prelude Series** Volume 8 Edited: Herbert Gotsch Concordia Publishing House 97-5615 Key: D

Karg-Elert, Sigfrid "O Lamb of God, Most Holy" **Choral Improvisations for Organ for Passion Week** Op. 65, Volume 2 Edward B. Marks Music Corp. Key: F

Pachelbel, Johann **80 Chorale Preludes – German Masters of the 17th and 18th Centuries** Edited: Hermann Keller C.F. Peters Corporation #4448 Key: F

Pachelbel, Johann "Lamb of God, Pure and Holy" **The Parish Organist** Part Seven Music for Lent, Palm Sunday and Holy Week Edited: Erich Goldschmidt Concordia Publishing House 97-1403 Key: Eb

Reger, Max **Chorale Preludes for the Church Year from Max Reger, Op. 67** Edited: Alec Wyton  Carl Fischer, Inc.  0-4667  Key: F

O lux beata Trinitas

| BA | DC | 1940 | 1982 | LBW | LW | PH | RCV | UCC | UM | WB |
|----|----|------|------|-----|----|----|-----|-----|----|----|
| m:a | m:a | | | | | | | | | |

O mein Jesu, ich muss sterben

| BA | DC | 1940 | 1982 | LBW | LW | PH | RCV | UCC | UM | WB |
|----|----|------|------|-----|----|----|-----|-----|----|----|
| | | | | | f | | | | | |

ORGAN COMPOSITIONS

Schroeder Hermann  "Stricken, Smitten, and Afflicted" **The Parish Organist** Part Seven  Music for Lent, Palm Sunday and Holy Week  Edited: Erich Goldschmidt  Concordia Publishing House  97-1403 Key:  g

Wienhorst, Richard  "Stricken, Smitten, and Afflicted" **The Concordia Hymn Prelude Series** Volume 8 Edited: Herbert Gotsch  Concordia Publishing House 97-5615  Key: f

O mensch sieh

| BA | DC | 1940 | 1982 | LBW | LW | PH | RCV | UCC | UM | WB |
|----|----|------|------|-----|----|----|-----|-----|----|----|
| | | | | | | d | | | | |

O Perfect Love

| BA | DC | 1940 | 1982 | LBW | LW | PH | RCV | UCC | UM | WB |
|----|----|------|------|-----|----|----|-----|-----|----|----|
| Eb | Eb | | | D | D | Eb | | | | |

ORGAN COMPOSITIONS

Jordan, Alice  "Dolcemente on 'O Perfect Love'" **Hymns of Grateful Praise** Broadman Press Key: Eb

FREE ACCOMPANIMENTS

**Free Harmonizations of Hymn Tunes by Fifty American Composers** Edited: D. DeWitt Wasson  Hinshaw Music, Inc.  HMO-145  Key: Eb

O quanta qualia

| BA | DC | 1940 | 1982 | LBW | LW | PH | RCV | UCC | UM | WB |
|----|----|------|------|-----|----|----|-----|-----|----|----|
| G | F | D | F | F | G | | G | | | G |

ORGAN COMPOSITIONS

Hillert, Richard  "O What Their Joy and Their Glory
    Must Be"  **The Parish Organist** Part Eleven
    Edited: Willem Mudde  Concordia Publishing House
    97-4758  Key:  F

Wente, Steven  "Stars of the Morning, So Gloriously
    Bright"  **The Concordia Hymn Prelude Series**
    Volume 15  Edited: Herbert Gotsch  Concordia
    Publishing House  97-5706  Key: F

FREE ACCOMPANIMENTS

Noble, T.Tertius  **Free Organ Accompaniments to One
    Hundred Well-Known Hymn Tunes**  J. Fischer & Bros.
    #8175  Key: F

O Sacred Head Now Wounded
    (See also: Herzlich tut mich verlangen; Passion Chorale)

O Salutaris

| BA | DC | 1940 | 1982 | LBW | LW | PH | RCV | UCC | UM | WB |
|----|----|------|------|-----|----|----|-----|-----|----|----|
|    |    |      |      |     |    |    | F   |     |    |    |

O Sanctissima

| BA | DC | 1940 | 1982 | LBW | LW | PH | RCV | UCC | UM | WB |
|----|----|------|------|-----|----|----|-----|-----|----|----|
|    |    |      |      |     |    |    | D   |     |    |    |

O Seigneur

| BA | DC | 1940 | 1982 | LBW | LW | PH | RCV | UCC | UM | WB |
|----|----|------|------|-----|----|----|-----|-----|----|----|
|    |    |      | D    |     |    |    |     |     |    |    |

O store Gud

| BA | DC | 1940 | 1982 | LBW | LW | PH | RCV | UCC | UM | WB |
|----|----|------|------|-----|----|----|-----|-----|----|----|
| Bb |    |      |      | Bb  | Bb |    |     | C   | Bb |    |

ORGAN COMPOSITIONS

Held, Wilbur "How Great Thou Art" **Preludes and
    Postludes** Volume I  Augsburg Publishing House
    11-9318 Key: d

O Traurigkeit

| BA | DC | 1940 | 1982 | LBW | LW | PH | RCV | UCC | UM | WB |
|----|----|------|------|-----|----|----|-----|-----|----|----|
|    |    | f    | e    |     | e  |    |     |     |    |    |

ORGAN COMPOSITIONS

Ahrens, Joseph **Das Heilige Jahr** Volume II
    Willy Muller - Suddeutscher Musikverlag -
    Heidelberg, New York: C.F. Peters Corporation
    Key: e

Beck, Albert **76 Offertories on Hymns & Chorales**
Concordia Publishing House 97-5207 Key: f

Brahms, Johannes **Samtliche Orgelwerke**
"Choralvorspiel und Fuge über 'O Traurigkeit,O
Herzeleid'" Breitkopf & Hartel Key: a

Engel, James "O Darkest Woe" **The Concordia Hymn
Prelude Series** Volume 8 Edited: Herbert Gotsch
Concordia Publishing House 97-5615 Key: e

Held, Wilbur "O Darkest Woe" **A Suite of Passion Hymn
Settings** Concordia Publishing House 97-4843
Key: d

Pepping, Ernst **Fünfundzwanzig Orgelchorale** Edition
Schott 4723 B. Schott's Sohne Key: m:e

Thalben-Ball, George **113 Variations on Hymn Tunes**
Novello & Co., Ltd. Key: f

Weisman, Wilhelm "O Darkest Woe" **The Parish Organist**
Part Seven Music for Lent, Palm Sunday and Holy
Week Edited: Erich Goldschmidt Concordia
Publishing House 97-1403 Key: f

Willan, Healey "O Traurigkeit" **Six Chorale Preludes**
Set II Concordia Publishing House 97-3905 Key: f

O Welt, ich muss dich lassen
 BA   DC   1940 1982 LBW   LW   PH   RCV   UCC   UM   WB
               F    F    F

ORGAN COMPOSITIONS

Bach, J.S. "Now Rest Beneath Night's Shadow" **The
Parish Organist** Part Three Edited: Heinrich
Fleischer Concordia Publishing House 97-1154
Key:F

Beck, Albert **76 Offertories on Hymns & Chorales**
Concordia Publishing House 97-5207 Key: F

Brahms, Johannes **Samtliche Orgelwerke**
Breitkopf & Hartel (Two chorale Preludes)
Keys: F

Brahms, Johannes "Arise and Shine in Splendor"
**The Parish Organist** Christmas and Epiphany
Music Part Six Concordia Publishing House
97-1391 Key: F

296

Haan, Raymond H. "O Bread of Life from Heaven"
**Hymn Preludes for Holy Communion** Volume 2
Concordia Publishing House 97-5487 Key: G

Isaac, Heinrich "Upon the Cross Extended" **The
Concordia Hymn Prelude Series** Volume 8 Edited:
Herbert Gotsch  Concordia Publishing House
97-5615  Key: F

Karg-Elert, Sigfrid "O World I E'en Must Leave Thee"
**Choral Improvisations for Organ for Passion Week**
Op. 65, Volume 2  Edward B. Marks Music Corp. Key:G

Kauffman, Georg Friedrich  "O Bread of Life from
Heaven"  **The Concordia Hymn Prelude Series**
Volume 18  Edited: Herbert Gotsch  Concordia
Publishing House  97-5709  Key: G

Manz, Paul  "Now Rest Beneath Night's Shadows"  **Ten
Chorale Improvisations** Op. 16 Set VI Concordia
Publishing House 97-5305  Key: F

Ochsenkuhn, Sebastian  "Arise and Shine in Splendor"
**The Concordia Hymn Prelude Series** Volume 6
Edited: Herbert Gotsch  Concordia Publishing
House  97-5612  Key: F

Reger, Max  **30 Short Chorale Preludes** Op. 135a
C.F. Peters Corporation Nr. 3980  Key:  G

Walther, Johann Gottfried **80 Chorale Preludes – German
Masters of the 17th and 18th Centuries** Edited:
Hermann Keller  C.F. Peters Corporation #4448
Key: F

Walther, Johann Gottfried  "Upon the Cross Extended"
**The Parish Organist** Part Seven Music for Lent,
Palm SundayandHoly Week Edited: Erich
Goldschmidt  Concordia Publishing House  97-1403
Key: F

## FREE ACCOMPANIMENTS

Hillert, Richard  **Hymn Preludes and Free
Accompaniments** Volume 10  Augsburg Publishing
House  11-9406  Key: F

Johnson, David N.  **Hymn Preludes and Free
Accompaniments**  Volume 14  Augsburg Publishing
House  11-9410  Key: F

<u>O Welt, sieh hier</u>
    BA    DC    1940  1982  LBW    LW      PH     RCV   UCC   UM     WB
                                         d

## ORGAN COMPOSITIONS

Krapf, Gerhard "Upon the Cross Extended" **The Concordia Hymn Prelude Series** Volume 8 Edited: Herbert Gotsch Concordia Publishing House 97-5615 Key: m:d

<u>O wie selig</u>
    BA    DC    1940  1982  LBW    LW      PH     RCV   UCC   UM     WB
                                       Eb

## ORGAN COMPOSITIONS

Brahms, Johannes **Sämtliche Orgelwerke** Breitkopf & Hartel Key: d

Brahms, Johannes "Blessed Ye Who Live in Faith Unswerving" **Eleven Chorale Preludes** Opus 122 Edited: E. Power Biggs Mercury Music Corporation A-260 Key: d

Pepping, Ernst **Fünfundzwanzig Orgelchorale** Edition: Schott B. Schott's Sohne 4723 Key: m:c

Willan, Healey "O wie selig" **Six Chorale Preludes** Set I Concordia Publishing House OC 220 Key: Eb

<u>Oakley</u>
    BA    DC    1940  1982  LBW    LW      PH     RCV   UCC   UM     WB
                                       e

## ORGAN COMPOSITIONS

Sensmeier, Randall "O Christ, Our King, Creator Lord" **The Concordia Hymn Prelude Series** Volume 8 Edited: Herbert Gotsch Concordia Publishing House 97-5615 Key: e

<u>Oakwood</u>
    BA    DC    1940  1982  LBW    LW      PH     RCV   UCC   UM     WB
                                                 UCC                       G

<u>Oblation</u>
   (See also: Lobet den Herren)
    BA    DC    1940  1982  LBW    LW      PH     RCV   UCC   UM     WB
                                       C

## ORGAN COMPOSITIONS

Johnson, David N. "Wherefore, O Father, We Thy Humble Servants" **Deck Thyself My Soul with Gladness** Augsburg Publishing House 11-9157  Key: C

<u>Oi Herra, jos mä matkamies maan</u>

| BA | DC | 1940 | 1982 | LBW | LW | PH | RCV | UCC | UM | WB |
|----|----|------|------|-----|----|----|-----|-----|----|----|
|    |    |      |      | c   |    |    |     |     |    |    |

<u>Oikoumene</u>

| BA | DC | 1940 | 1982 | LBW | LW | PH | RCV | UCC | UM | WB |
|----|----|------|------|-----|----|----|-----|-----|----|----|
|    |    |      |      |     |    |    |     | C   |    |    |

<u>Old 22nd</u>

| BA | DC | 1940 | 1982 | LBW | LW | PH | RCV | UCC | UM | WB |
|----|----|------|------|-----|----|----|-----|-----|----|----|
|    |    |      |      |     |    | D  |     |     |    |    |

<u>Old 100th</u>

| BA | DC | 1940 | 1982 | LBW | LW | PH | RCV | UCC | UM | WB |
|----|----|------|------|-----|----|----|-----|-----|----|----|
| G  | G  | G    | G    | G   | G  | G  | G   | G   | G  | G  |

## INTONATIONS

McCormick, David W.  **20 Organ Intonations on Hymns of Praise**  Hope Publishing Co.  Key: G

## ORGAN COMPOSITIONS

Bach, Johann Christoph "Praise God, from Whom All Blessings Flow" **The Parish Organist**  Part Three Edited: Heinrich Fleischer  Concordia Publishing House  97-1154  G

Blow, John  "O Jesus, Blessed Lord, My Praise"  **The Concordia Hymn Prelude Series**  Volume 18  Edited: Herbert Gotsch  Concordia Publishing House 97-5709  Key: G

Bristol, Lee Hastings, Jr. **"Variations on 'Old Hundredth'"**  J. Fischer & Bros.  #8635  Key: G

Hurford, Peter  "Fanfare on 'Old 100th'" **Ceremonial Music for Organ**  Oxford University Press  Key: A

Jordan, Alice "Improvisation on 'Old Hundredth'" **Worship Service Music for the Organ**  Broadman Press  Key: G/C

Lovelace, Austin **Fourteen Hymn Preludes**  Augsburg Publishing House 11-6152  Key: G

Manz, Paul "Praise God, from Whom All Blessings Flow"
**Ten Chorale Improvisations** Set IV Op. 10
Concordia Publishing House 97-4951  Key: G

Post, Piet "Praise God From Whom All Blessings Flow"
**Triptych for Organ**  Concordia Publishing
House 11-835  Key: G

Purcell, Henry "Voluntary on the 100th Psalm Tune"
Arr. John West **A Collection of Thanksgiving
Music** Compiled by John Holler  H.W. Gray
St. Cecilia #648  Key: A

Purcell, Henry **Ceremonial Music for Organ** Edited:
E. Power Biggs  Mercury Music Corporation  W90
Key: A

Thalben-Ball, George  **113 Variations on Hymn Tunes**
Novello & Co., Ltd.  Key: Ab

Willan, Healey "O Enter Then His Gates"  **Ten Hymn
Preludes**  Set I  C.F. Peters Corp. No. 6011
Key: A

Young, Gordon  "Fantasia on Old Hundredth"
**Impressions for Organ**  The Sacred Music Press
KK 328  Key: G

FREE ACCOMPANIMENTS

Bunjes, Paul  **New Organ Accompaniments for Hymns**
Concordia Publishing House  97-5348  Key: G

Busarow, Donald **Hymn Preludes and Free Accompaniments**
Volume 8  Augsburg Publishing House  11-9404
Key: G

Coleman, Henry **Varied Hymn Accompaniments**  Oxford
University Press  Key: G

Hancock, Gerre  **Organ Improvisations for Hymn-Singing**
Hinshaw Music Co.  HMO-100  Key: G

Johnson, David N. **Free Organ Accompaniments to
Festival Hymns** Volume I  Augsburg Publishing House
11-9192  Key: G/A

Noble, T. Tertius  **Free Organ Accompaniments to One
Hundred Well-Known Hymn Tunes**  J. Fischer & Bros.
#8175  Key: G

Old 104th

| | BA | DC | 1940 | 1982 | LBW | LW | PH | RCV | UCC | UM | WB |
|---|----|----|------|------|-----|-----|-----|-----|-----|-----|-----|
| | | | d | d | | | | | | | |

## ORGAN COMPOSITIONS

Thalben-Ball, George **113 Variations on Hymn Tunes**
Novello & Co., Ltd.  Key: e

Willan, Healey  **Ten Hymn Preludes**  Set II  C.F.
Peters Corporation  6012  Key: d

Old 107th

| | BA | DC | 1940 | 1982 | LBW | LW | PH | RCV | UCC | UM | WB |
|---|----|----|------|------|-----|-----|-----|-----|-----|-----|-----|
| | | | | | m:d | m:d | | | | m:d | m:d |

### FREE ACCOMPANIMENTS
**Free Harmonizations of Hymn Tunes By Fifty American Composers**  Edited: D. DeWitt Wasson  Hinshaw
Music, Inc.  HMO-145  Key: m:d

Old 112th
See also: Vater unser im Himmelreich)

| | BA | DC | 1940 | 1982 | LBW | LW | PH | RCV | UCC | UM | WB |
|---|----|----|------|------|-----|-----|-----|-----|-----|-----|-----|
| | | | c | | | | | | | | |

Old 113th

| | BA | DC | 1940 | 1982 | LBW | LW | PH | RCV | UCC | UM | WB |
|---|----|----|------|------|-----|-----|-----|-----|-----|-----|-----|
| | | D | | D | | | | D | | D | D |

## ORGAN COMPOSITIONS

Near, Gerald **Preludes on Four Hymn Tunes** Augsburg
Publishing House 11-828  Key: Eb

Old 120th

| | BA | DC | 1940 | 1982 | LBW | LW | PH | RCV | UCC | UM | WB |
|---|----|----|------|------|-----|-----|-----|-----|-----|-----|-----|
| | | D | D | | | | | | | | |

Old 124th

| | BA | DC | 1940 | 1982 | LBW | LW | PH | RCV | UCC | UM | WB |
|---|----|----|------|------|-----|-----|-----|-----|-----|-----|-----|
| | F | F | F | F | F | F | F | F | | | |

## ORGAN COMPOSITIONS

Gieschen, Thomas **Four Quiet Hymn Settings**  Concordia
Publishing House  97-5839  Key: F

Moser, Rudolph  "Draw Nigh and Take the Body of the
Lord" **The Parish Organist** Part Three  Edited:
Heinrich Fleischer  Concordia Publishing House
97-1154  Key: F

Schack, David "Draw Nigh and Take the Body of the Lord" **Hymn Preludes for Holy Communion** Volume I Concordia Publishing House 97-5486  Key: F

Schultz, Ralph C.  "Draw Near and Take the Body of the Lord" **The Concordia Hymn Prelude Series** Volume 18  Edited: Herbert Gotsch  Concordia Publishing House  97-5709  Key: F

Stearns, Peter Pindar **Eight Hymn Preludes for Lent** Harold Flammer, Inc.  HF-5133  Key: F

Warner, Richard "Draw Nigh and Take the Body of the Lord" **Organ Music for the Communion Service** Edited: Paul Bunjes  Concordia Publishing House #97-1395  Key: F

Willan, Healey  **Ten Hymn Preludes** Set II  C.F. Peters Corporation  6012  Key: F

FREE ACCOMPANIMENTS

Bunjes, Paul  **New Organ Accompaniments for Hymns** Concordia Publishing House  97-5348  Key: F

Goode, Jack C.  **Thirty-Four Changes on Hymn Tunes** H. W. Gray Co.  GB 644  Key: F

Noble, T. Tertius  **Free Organ Accompaniments to One Hundred Well-Known Hymn Tunes**  J. Fischer & Bros. #8175  Key: F

Wyton, Alec  **New Shoots from Old Routes**  Sacred Music Press  KK 279  Key: F

Old 134th
(See also: St. Michael)
    BA    DC    1940 1982 LBW  LW    PH    RCV   UCC   UM    WB
    G

Old Rugged Cross
    BA    DC    1940 1982 LBW  LW    PH    RCV   UCC   UM    WB
    Bb

Old-Time Power
    BA    DC    1940 1982 LBW  LW    PH    RCV   UCC   UM    WB
    Ab

Oldbridge
    BA    DC    1940 1982 LBW  LW    PH    RCV   UCC   UM    WB
                                                        F

Olive's Brow

| BA | DC | 1940 | 1982 | LBW | LW | PH | RCV | UCC | UM | WB |
|----|----|------|------|-----|----|----|-----|-----|----|----|
|    | Ab |      |      |     |    | Ab | Ab  |     | Ab |    |

ORGAN COMPOSITIONS

Miles, Russell Hancock **Three Improvisations**
The Arthur P. Schmidt Co. Key: Ab

FREE ACCOMPANIMENTS

**Free Harmonizations of Hymn Tunes By Fifty American
Composers** Edited: D. DeWitt Wasson Hinshaw
Music, Inc. HMO-145 Key: Ab

Olivet

| BA | DC | 1940 | 1982 | LBW | LW | PH | RCV | UCC | UM | WB |
|----|----|------|------|-----|----|----|-----|-----|----|----|
| Eb | Eb | D    | D    | D   | D  | Eb | Eb  | Eb  | Eb |    |

ORGAN COMPOSITIONS

Arbatsky, Yury "My Faith Looks Up to Thee" **The Parish
Organist** Part Three Edited: Heinrich Fleischer
Concordia Publishing House 97-1154 Key: Eb

Beck, Albert **76 Offertories on Hymns & Chorales**
Concordia Publishing House 97-5207 Key: Eb

Bingham, Seth **Twelve Hymn Preludes** Opus 38 Set 2
H. W. Gray GB 152 Key: Eb

FREE ACCOMPANIMENTS

Hancock, Gerre **Organ Improvisations for Hymn-Singing**
Hinshaw Music Co. HMO-100 Key: D

Hudson, Richard **Hymn Preludes and Free Accompaniments**
Volume 12 Augsburg Publishing House 11-9408
Key: D

Noble, T. Tertius **Free Organ Accompaniments to One
Hundred Well-Known Hymn Tunes** J. Fischer & Bros.
#8175 Key: D

Norris, Kevin **Hymn Preludes and Free Accompaniments**
Volume 15 Augsburg Publishing House 11-9411
Key: D

Olwen

| BA | DC | 1940 | 1982 | LBW | LW | PH | RCV | UCC | UM | WB |
|----|----|------|------|-----|----|----|-----|-----|----|----|
|    |    |      |      |     |    |    |     |     |    | A  |

## Om Himmeriges Rige

| BA | DC | 1940 | 1982 | LBW | LW | PH | RCV | UCC | UM | WB |
|---|---|---|---|---|---|---|---|---|---|---|
|  |  |  |  | m:e | m:e |  |  |  |  |  |

## Omni Die

| BA | DC | 1940 | 1982 | LBW | LW | PH | RCV | UCC | UM | WB |
|---|---|---|---|---|---|---|---|---|---|---|
| F |  |  | F | F |  | F |  | G |  |  |

## ORGAN COMPOSITIONS

Arnatt, Ronald "For the Bread Which You Have Broken"
**Hymn Preludes for Holy Communion** Volume 2
Concordia Publishing House 97-5487  Key: F

Gerike, Henry V.  "For the Bread Which You Have Broken"
**The Concordia Hymn Prelude Series**  Volume 18
Edited: Herbert Gotsch  Concordia Publishing House
97-5709  Key: F

Kreckel, Philip G. **Musica Divina** Volume 2  J. Fischer
& Bro. No. 6715 Key: F

## FREE ACCOMPANIMENTS

Arnatt, Ronald  **Hymn Preludes and Free Accompaniments**
Volume 9  Augsburg Publishing House  11-9505
Key: F

**Free Harmonizations of Hymn Tunes By Fifty American
Composers**  Edited: D. DeWitt Wasson  Hinshaw
Music, Inc.  HMO-145  Key: F

## Omnom Kayn

| BA | DC | 1940 | 1982 | LBW | LW | PH | RCV | UCC | UM | WB |
|---|---|---|---|---|---|---|---|---|---|---|
|  | C |  |  |  |  |  |  |  |  |  |

## Once for All

| BA | DC | 1940 | 1982 | LBW | LW | PH | RCV | UCC | UM | WB |
|---|---|---|---|---|---|---|---|---|---|---|
| Eb |  |  |  |  |  |  |  |  |  |  |

## One Table Spread

| BA | DC | 1940 | 1982 | LBW | LW | PH | RCV | UCC | UM | WB |
|---|---|---|---|---|---|---|---|---|---|---|
|  |  |  |  |  |  |  |  | F |  |  |

## Oneonta

| BA | DC | 1940 | 1982 | LBW | LW | PH | RCV | UCC | UM | WB |
|---|---|---|---|---|---|---|---|---|---|---|
|  |  | D |  |  |  |  |  |  |  |  |

## Onslow

| BA | DC | 1940 | 1982 | LBW | LW | PH | RCV | UCC | UM | WB |
|---|---|---|---|---|---|---|---|---|---|---|
|  |  |  |  |  |  | G |  |  |  |  |

## FREE ACCOMPANIMENTS

Noble, T. Tertius **Free Organ Accompaniments to One Hundred Well-Known Hymn Tunes** J. Fischer & Bros. #8175 Key: Ab

## ORGAN COMPOSITIONS

Thalben-Ball, George **113 Variations on Hymn Tunes** Novello & Co., Ltd. Key: A

## FREE ACCOMPANIMENTS

Noble, T. Tertius **Fifty Free Organ Accompaniments to Well Known Hymn Tunes** J. Fischer & Bros. No. 8430 Key: Ab

## ORGAN COMPOSITIONS

Hillert, Richard "Christ the Lord is Risen Today" **The Concordia Hymn Prelude Series** Volume 11 Edited: Herbert Gotsch Concordia Publishing House 97-5618 Key: F

Markworth, Henry J. "Christ the Lord is Risen Today" **The Parish Organist** Part Three Edited: Heinrich Fleischer Concordia Publishing House 97-1154 Key: G

Matthews, Thomas "Prelude on 'Orientis Partibus'"
   **The Bristol Collection** Volume 3
      Edited: Lee Hastings Bristol, Jr. Harold
      Flammer  Key:G

Wills, Arthur "Carillon on 'Orientis Partibus'"
   **The Bristol Collection**  Volume 3
      Edited: Lee Hastings Bristol, Jr.  Harold
      Flammer  Key: F

FREE ACCOMPANIMENTS

Noble, T. Tertius  **Fifty Free Organ Accompaniments
to Well Known Hymn Tunes**  J. Fischer & Bros.
No. 8430  Key: F

Ortonville

| BA | DC | 1940 | 1982 | LBW | LW | PH | RCV | UCC | UM | WB |
|----|----|------|------|-----|----|----|-----|-----|----|----|
| Ab |    |      |      |     |    |    |     |     | Ab |    |

Oslo

| BA | DC | 1940 | 1982 | LBW | LW | PH | RCV | UCC | UM | WB |
|----|----|------|------|-----|----|----|-----|-----|----|----|
|    |    | e    |      |     |    |    |     |     |    |    |

Ostergaard

| BA | DC | 1940 | 1982 | LBW | LW | PH | RCV | UCC | UM | WB |
|----|----|------|------|-----|----|----|-----|-----|----|----|
|    | Eb |      |      |     |    |    |     |     |    |    |

Othello

| BA | DC | 1940 | 1982 | LBW | LW | PH | RCV | UCC | UM | WB |
|----|----|------|------|-----|----|----|-----|-----|----|----|
| G  |    |      |      |     |    |    |     |     |    |    |

# P

Paderborn

| BA | DC | 1940 | 1982 | LBW | LW | PH | RCV | UCC | UM | WB |
|----|----|------|------|-----|----|----|-----|-----|----|----|
|    |    |      | G    |     |    |    |     |     |    |    |

Paedia

| BA | DC | 1940 | 1982 | LBW | LW | PH | RCV | UCC | UM | WB |
|----|----|------|------|-----|----|----|-----|-----|----|----|

Palestrina
(See also: Victory)

| BA | DC | 1940 | 1982 | LBW | LW | PH | RCV | UCC | UM | WB |
|----|----|------|------|-----|----|----|-----|-----|----|----|
|    |    |      |      |     |    |    |     |     |    | D  |

Miles, George Theophilus "The Strife is O'er, the
Battle Done" **The Parish Organist** Part Eight
Music for Easter, Ascension, Pentecost and Trinity
Edited: Erich Goldschmidt  Concordia Publishing
House  97-1404  Key: Eb

<u>Palisades</u>

| BA | DC | 1940 | 1982 | LBW | LW | PH | RCV | UCC | UM | WB |
|----|----|------|------|-----|----|----|-----|-----|----|----|
|    |    | G    |      |     |    |    |     |     |    |    |

<u>Palmarum</u>

| BA | DC | 1940 | 1982 | LBW | LW | PH | RCV | UCC | UM | WB |
|----|----|------|------|-----|----|----|-----|-----|----|----|
|    |    | d    |      |     |    |    |     |     |    |    |

<u>Palmer Church</u>

| BA | DC | 1940 | 1982 | LBW | LW | PH | RCV | UCC | UM | WB |
|----|----|------|------|-----|----|----|-----|-----|----|----|
|    |    |      | e    |     |    |    |     |     |    |    |

<u>Pán Bůh</u>

| BA | DC | 1940 | 1982 | LBW | LW | PH | RCV | UCC | UM | WB |
|----|----|------|------|-----|----|----|-----|-----|----|----|
|    |    |      |      | c   |    |    |     |     |    |    |

<u>Pange lingua</u>

| BA | DC | 1940 | 1982 | LBW | LW | PH | RCV | UCC | UM | WB |
|----|----|------|------|-----|----|----|-----|-----|----|----|
|    |    | m:e  | m:e  | m:e |    |    | m:e |     |    |    |

ORGAN COMPOSITIONS

Barlow, Wayne  "Of the Glorious Body Telling"  **The
Concordia Hymn Prelude Series** Volume 8
Edited: Herbert Gotsch  Concordia Publishing House
97-5615  Key: m:e

Hampton, Calvin "Of the Glorious Body Telling"
**Hymn Preludes for Holy Communion** Volume I
Concordia Publishing House 97-5486 Key: e

Sowerby, Leo  **Meditations on Communion Hymns**
H.W. Gray Co., Inc.  Key: a/e

Stearns, Peter Pindar **Eight Hymn Preludes for Lent**
Harold Flammer, Inc.  HF-5133  Key: m:d

<u>Panis Angelicus</u>

| BA | DC | 1940 | 1982 | LBW | LW | PH | RCV | UCC | UM | WB |
|----|----|------|------|-----|----|----|-----|-----|----|----|
|    |    |      |      |     |    |    | Eb  |     |    |    |

<u>Paradise</u>

| BA | DC | 1940 | 1982 | LBW | LW | PH | RCV | UCC | UM | WB |
|----|----|------|------|-----|----|----|-----|-----|----|----|
|    |    | Db   |      |     |    |    |     |     |    |    |

## Paris

| BA | DC | 1940 | 1982 | LBW | LW | PH | RCV | UCC | UM | WB |
|----|----|------|------|-----|----|----|-----|-----|----|----|
|    | F  |      |      |     |    |    |     |     |    |    |

## Park Street

| BA | DC | 1940 | 1982 | LBW | LW | PH | RCV | UCC | UM | WB |
|----|----|------|------|-----|----|----|-----|-----|----|----|
|    |    |      |      |     |    | G  |     |     | G  | G  |

INTONATIONS

McCormick, David W. **20 Organ Intonations on Hymns of Praise** Hope Publishing Co.  Key: G

## Parker

| BA | DC | 1940 | 1982 | LBW | LW | PH | RCV | UCC | UM | WB |
|----|----|------|------|-----|----|----|-----|-----|----|----|
|    |    | Db   | C    |     |    |    |     |     |    |    |

## Parratt

| BA | DC | 1940 | 1982 | LBW | LW | PH | RCV | UCC | UM | WB |
|----|----|------|------|-----|----|----|-----|-----|----|----|
|    |    | D    |      |     |    |    |     |     |    |    |

## Parsons

| BA | DC | 1940 | 1982 | LBW | LW | PH | RCV | UCC | UM | WB |
|----|----|------|------|-----|----|----|-----|-----|----|----|
|    |    |      | g    |     |    |    |     |     |    |    |

ORGAN COMPOSITIONS

Bouman, Paul  "Look, Now He Stands"  **The Concordia Hymn Prelude Series**  Volume 11  Edited: Herbert Gotsch  Concordia Publishing House  97-5618 Key: g

## Paschall

| BA | DC | 1940 | 1985 | LBW | LW | PH | RCV | UCC | UM | WB |
|----|----|------|------|-----|----|----|-----|-----|----|----|
| D  |    |      |      |     |    |    |     |     |    |    |

## Pass It On

| BA | DC | 1940 | 1985 | LBW | LW | PH | RCV | UCC | UM | WB |
|----|----|------|------|-----|----|----|-----|-----|----|----|
| D  |    |      |      |     |    |    |     |     |    |    |

## Pass Me Not

| BA | DC | 1940 | 1982 | LBW | LW | PH | RCV | UCC | UM | WB |
|----|----|------|------|-----|----|----|-----|-----|----|----|
| Ab |    |      |      |     |    |    |     |     | Ab |    |

## Passion Chorale
(See also: Herzlich tut mich verlangen; O Sacred Head Now Wounded)

| BA | DC | 1940 | 1982 | LBW | LW | PH | RCV | UCC | UM | WB |
|----|----|------|------|-----|----|----|-----|-----|----|----|
| C  | C  | C    |      |     |    | C  | C   | D   | C  | C  |

ORGAN COMPOSITIONS

Reger, Max **Passion** Op. 145 Nr. 4  Breitkopf &
      Hartel  Wiesbaden, Germany  E.B. 4160  Key: g

Sowerby, Leo "O Sacred Head Now Wounded" **Advent to
      Whitsuntide** Volume Four  Hinrichsen  No. 743b
      Key: d

FREE ACCOMPANIMENTS

Noble, T. Tertius **Fifty Free Accompaniments to
      Well Known Hymn Tunes**  J. Fischer & Bros.
      No. 8430  Key: m:e

<u>Pater omnipotens</u>

| BA | DC | 1940 | 1982 | LBW | LW | PH | RCV | UCC | UM | WB |
|----|----|------|------|-----|----|----|-----|-----|----|----|
|    | Eb |      |      |     |    |    |     |     |    |    |

<u>Patmos</u> (Havergal)

| BA | DC | 1940 | 1982 | LBW | LW | PH | RCV | UCC | UM | WB |
|----|----|------|------|-----|----|----|-----|-----|----|----|
|    | D  |      |      | D   | D  |    |     |     |    |    |

ORGAN COMPOSITIONS

Beck, Albert **76 Offertories on Hymns & Chorales**
      Concordia Publishing House  97-5207  Key: D

Van Hulse "Take My Life and Let It Be" **The Parish
      Organist** Part Three  Edited: Heinrich Fleischer
      Concordia Publishing House  97-1154  Key:  D

<u>Patmos</u> (Storer)

| BA | DC | 1940 | 1982 | LBW | LW | PH | RCV | UCC | UM | WB |
|----|----|------|------|-----|----|----|-----|-----|----|----|
|    | G  |      |      |     |    |    |     |     |    |    |

<u>Pax</u>

| BA | DC | 1940 | 1982 | LBW | LW | PH | RCV | UCC | UM | WB |
|----|----|------|------|-----|----|----|-----|-----|----|----|
|    | a  |      |      |     |    |    | a   |     |    |    |

<u>Pax Iam</u>

| BA | DC | 1940 | 1985 | LBW | LW | PH | RCV | UCC | UM | WB |
|----|----|------|------|-----|----|----|-----|-----|----|----|
| d  |    |      |      |     |    |    |     |     |    |    |

<u>Pax tecum</u>

| BA | DC | 1940 | 1982 | LBW | LW | PH | RCV | UCC | UM | WB |
|----|----|------|------|-----|----|----|-----|-----|----|----|
|    | C  |      |      |     |    |    |     |     |    |    |

<u>Peace</u>

| BA | DC | 1940 | 1982 | LBW | LW | PH | RCV | UCC | UM | WB |
|----|----|------|------|-----|----|----|-----|-----|----|----|
|    | f  |      |      |     |    | f  |     |     |    |    |

## Peace Like a River
| BA | DC | 1940 | 1985 | LBW | LW | PH | RCV | UCC | UM | WB |
|----|----|------|------|-----|----|----|-----|-----|----|----|
| G  |    |      |      |     |    |    |     |     |    |    |

## Peace of God
| BA | DC | 1940 | 1982 | LBW | LW | PH | RCV | UCC | UM | WB |
|----|----|------|------|-----|----|----|-----|-----|----|----|
|    |    |      |      | G   |    |    |     |     |    |    |

## Peacefield
| BA | DC | 1940 | 1982 | LBW | LW | PH | RCV | UCC | UM | WB |
|----|----|------|------|-----|----|----|-----|-----|----|----|
|    |    | EB   |      |     |    |    |     |     |    |    |

## Pearsall
| BA | DC | 1940 | 1982 | LBW | LW | PH | RCV | UCC | UM | WB |
|----|----|------|------|-----|----|----|-----|-----|----|----|
|    | Db | Db   |      |     |    |    |     |     |    |    |

## Peek
| BA | DC | 1940 | 1982 | LBW | LW | PH | RCV | UCC | UM | WB |
|----|----|------|------|-----|----|----|-----|-----|----|----|
|    |    |      |      |     |    | F  |     |     | F  |    |

## Peel Castle
| BA | DC | 1940 | 1982 | LBW | LW | PH | RCV | UCC | UM | WB |
|----|----|------|------|-----|----|----|-----|-----|----|----|
|    |    | D    |      |     |    |    | D   |     |    |    |

## Penina Moise
| BA | DC | 1940 | 1982 | LBW | LW | PH | RCV | UCC | UM | WB |
|----|----|------|------|-----|----|----|-----|-----|----|----|
|    |    |      |      |     |    |    | C   |     |    |    |

## Penitence
| BA | DC | 1940 | 1982 | LBW | LW | PH | RCV | UCC | UM | WB |
|----|----|------|------|-----|----|----|-----|-----|----|----|
|    |    | C    |      | C   |    | C  |     |     | C  |    |

ORGAN COMPOSITIONS

Rohlig, Harald   "In the Hour of Trial"   **The Concordia Hymn Prelude Series**   Volume 8   Edited: Herbert Gotsch   Concordia Publishing House   97-5615   Key: C

FREE ACCOMPANIMENTS

Noble, T. Tertius   **Free Organ Accompaniments to One Hundred Well-Known Hymn Tunes**   J. Fischer & Bros.   #8175   Key: C

## Penitentia
| BA | DC | 1940 | 1982 | LBW | LW | PH | RCV | UCC | UM | WB |
|----|----|------|------|-----|----|----|-----|-----|----|----|
|    |    | Eb   |      |     |    |    | Eb  |     | Eb |    |

# FREE ACCOMPANIMENTS

Noble, T. Tertius **Fifty Free Organ Accompaniments to Well Known Hymn Tunes** J. Fischer & Bros.
No. 8430  Key: Eb

**Pentecost**

| BA | DC | 1940 | 1982 | LBW | LW | PH | RCV | UCC | UM | WB |
|----|----|------|------|-----|----|----|-----|-----|----|----|
| G |  | G | G |  |  | G |  | G | G |  |

# FREE ACCOMPANIMENTS

Noble, T. Tertius **Free Organ Accompaniments to One Hundred Well-Known Hymn Tunes** J. Fischer & Bros.
#8175  Key: G

**Perfect Love**
(See also: Sandringham)

| BA | DC | 1940 | 1982 | LBW | LW | PH | RCV | UCC | UM | WB |
|----|----|------|------|-----|----|----|-----|-----|----|----|
|  |  |  |  |  |  |  |  |  | Eb |  |

**Perry**

| BA | DC | 1940 | 1982 | LBW | LW | PH | RCV | UCC | UM | WB |
|----|----|------|------|-----|----|----|-----|-----|----|----|
|  | E |  | Eb | Eb |  |  |  |  | E |  |

# ORGAN COMPOSITIONS

Johnson, David N.  "This is the Spirit's Entry Now"
**The Concordia Hymn Prelude Series** Volume 16
Edited: Herbert Gotsch  Concordia Publishing House
97-5707  Key: Eb

**Personent hodie**

| BA | DC | 1940 | 1982 | LBW | LW | PH | RCV | UCC | UM | WB |
|----|----|------|------|-----|----|----|-----|-----|----|----|
|  | e |  | e |  |  | e |  | e |  | d |

**Petersen**

| BA | DC | 1940 | 1982 | LBW | LW | PH | RCV | UCC | UM | WB |
|----|----|------|------|-----|----|----|-----|-----|----|----|
|  |  | F |  |  |  |  | G |  |  |  |

**Petra**
(See also: Redhead No. 76)

| BA | DC | 1940 | 1982 | LBW | LW | PH | RCV | UCC | UM | WB |
|----|----|------|------|-----|----|----|-----|-----|----|----|
|  |  | D | D |  |  |  | D |  |  |  |

# ORGAN COMPOSITIONS

Held, Wilbur "Go to Dark Gethsemane" **A Suite of Passion Hymn Settings** Concordia Publishing House
97-4843  Key: Eb

# FREE ACCOMPANIMENTS

Noble, T. Tertius **Fifty Free Organ Accompaniments to Well Known Hymn Tunes** J. Fischer & Bros. No. 8430  Key: E

<u>Petrus</u>
    BA     DC     1940   1982   LBW    LW     PH     RCV    UCC    UM     WB
                         Eb

<u>Picardy</u>
    BA     DC     1940   1982   LBW    LW     PH     RCV    UCC    UM     WB
    d      d      d      d      d      d      d      d      d      d

# INTONATIONS

Hermann, David  **11 Hymn Intonations, Free Accompaniments, Instrumental Descants for Organ** Volume I Advent, Christmas, Epiphany  G.I.A. Publications G-2378  Key: d

# ORGAN COMPOSITIONS

Casner, Myron  "Let All Mortal Flesh Keep Silence" **The Parish Organist** Part Twelve  Edited: Willem Mudde  Concordia Publishing House:  97-4759 Key: m:d

Gehrke, Hugo  "Lo! He Comes with Clouds Descending" **The Concordia Hymn Prelude Series** Volume 2 Edited:  Herbert Gotsch  Concordia Publishing House  97-5536  Key: d

Hillert, Richart "Let All Mortal Flesh Keep Silence" **Hymn Preludes for Holy Communion** Volume I Concordia Publishing House 97-5486  Key: d

Johnson, David N. "Let All Mortal Flesh Keep Silence" **Deck Thyself My Soul with Gladness** Augsburg Publishing House 11-9157  Key: d

Manz, Paul "Let All Mortal Flesh" **Ten Chorale Improvisations** Set V Op. 14 Concordia Publishing House 97-5257  Key: d

Sensmeier, Randall "Let All Mortal Flesh Keep Silence" **The Concordia Hymn Prelude Series** Volume 18 Edited: Herbert Gotsch  Concordia Publishing House  97-5709  Key: d

Shack, David "Let All Mortal Flesh Keep Silence" **Preludes on Ten Hymntunes** Augsburg Publishing House  11-9363  Key: d

Sowerby, Leo **Meditations on Communion Hymns**
H. W. Gray Co., Inc.  Key: d

Thalben-Ball, George **113 Variations on Hymn Tunes**
Novello & Co., Ltd.  Key: d

Thiman, Eric H.  "Prelude on a French Traditional
Carol" **Four Miniatures for Organ**  G. Schirmer
Key: d

Warner, Richard  "Let All Mortal Flesh Keep Silence"
**Organ Music for the Communion Service**
Edited: Paul Bunjes  Concordia Publishing House
#97-1395  Key: d

FREE ACCOMPANIMENTS

Arnatt, Ronald  **Hymn Preludes and Free Accompaniments**
Volume 9  Augsburg Publishing House  11-9405
Key: d

Noble, T. Tertius **Free Organ Accompaniments to One
Hundred Well-Known Hymn Tunes**  J. Fischer & Bros.
#8175  Key: d

Wyton, Alec  **New Shoots from Old Routes**  Sacred Music
Press  KK 279  Key: d

Pilgrimage

| BA | DC | 1940 | 1982 | LBW | LW | PH | RCV | UCC | UM | WB |
|----|----|------|------|-----|----|----|-----|-----|----|----|
|    |    |      |      |     |    |    |     | F   |    |    |

Pilgrims

| BA | DC | 1940 | 1982 | LBW | LW | PH | RCV | UCC | UM | WB |
|----|----|------|------|-----|----|----|-----|-----|----|----|
|    | D  |      |      |     |    |    |     |     |    |    |

FREE ACCOMPANIMENTS

Hebble, Robert **Robert Hebble's Hymnal Companion for
Organ**  Bradley Publications  CE/283A/3  Key: D

Noble, T. Tertius  **Free Organ Accompaniments to One
Hundred Well-Known Hymn Tunes**  J. Fischer & Bros.
#8175  Key: D

Pilot

| BA | DC | 1940 | 1982 | LBW | LW | PH | RCV | UCC | UM | WB |
|----|----|------|------|-----|----|----|-----|-----|----|----|
|    |    |      |      | Bb  | Ab | Ab |     | Ab  | Bb |    |

313

# FREE ACCOMPANIMENTS

**Free Harmonizations on Hymn Tunes By Fifty American Composers**  Edited: D. DeWitt Wasson  Hinshaw Music, Inc.  HMO-145  Key: Ab

<u>Pisgah</u>

| BA | DC | 1940 | 1982 | LBW | LW | PH | RCV | UCC | UM | WB |
|----|----|------|------|-----|----|----|-----|-----|----|----|
|    |    |      |      |     |    |    |     |     | G  |    |

# ORGAN COMPOSITIONS

Wood, Dale  **Organ Book of American Folk Hymns**  The Sacred Music Press  Key: Bb

<u>Pittsburgh</u>

| BA | DC | 1940 | 1982 | LBW | LW | PH | RCV | UCC | UM | WB |
|----|----|------|------|-----|----|----|-----|-----|----|----|
|    |    |      |      |     |    |    |     |     |    | e  |

<u>Pixham</u>

| BA | DC | 1940 | 1982 | LBW | LW | PH | RCV | UCC | UM | WB |
|----|----|------|------|-----|----|----|-----|-----|----|----|
|    |    | Eb   |      |     |    |    |     |     |    |    |

<u>Plainfield</u>

| BA | DC | 1940 | 1985 | LBW | LW | PH | RCV | UCC | UM | WB |
|----|----|------|------|-----|----|----|-----|-----|----|----|
| G  |    |      |      |     |    |    |     |     |    |    |

<u>Platten</u>

| BA | DC | 1940 | 1982 | LBW | LW | PH | RCV | UCC | UM | WB |
|----|----|------|------|-----|----|----|-----|-----|----|----|
|    | D  |      |      |     |    |    |     |     |    |    |

<u>Pleading Saviour</u>

| BA | DC | 1940 | 1982 | LBW | LW | PH | RCV | UCC | UM | WB |
|----|----|------|------|-----|----|----|-----|-----|----|----|
|    | F  | F    | Eb   | F   |    | F  | F   | F   | F  |    |

# ORGAN COMPOSITIONS

Harris, David S.  **Ten Hymn Preludes in Trio Style**  H. W. Gray Co.  GB 643  Key: F

# FREE ACCOMPANIMENTS

**Free Harmonizations of Hymn Tunes By Fifty American Composers**  Edited: D. DeWitt Wasson  Hinshaw Music, Inc.  HMO-145  Key: F

<u>Pleyel's Hymn</u>

| BA | DC | 1940 | 1982 | LBW | LW | PH | RCV | UCC | UM | WB |
|----|----|------|------|-----|----|----|-----|-----|----|----|
| G  | G  |      |      |     |    |    |     |     | G  |    |

<u>Point Loma</u>

| BA | DC | 1940 | 1982 | LBW | LW | PH | RCV | UCC | UM | WB |
|----|----|------|------|-----|----|----|-----|-----|----|----|
|    |    |      | f    |     |    |    |     |     |    |    |

## Poland

| BA | DC | 1940 | 1982 | LBW | LW | PH | RCV | UCC | UM | WB |
|----|----|------|------|-----|----|----|-----|-----|----|----|
|    |    |      |      |     |    |    | F   |     |    |    |

## Ponden Cote

| BA | DC | 1940 | 1982 | LBW | LW | PH | RCV | UCC | UM | WB |
|----|----|------|------|-----|----|----|-----|-----|----|----|
| F  |    |      |      |     |    |    |     |     |    |    |

## Poor Little Jesus

| BA | DC | 1940 | 1982 | LBW | LW | PH | RCV | UCC | UM | WB |
|----|----|------|------|-----|----|----|-----|-----|----|----|
|    |    | e    |      |     |    |    |     |     |    |    |

## Portuguese Hymn
(See also: Adeste Fidelis)

## Potsdam

| BA | DC | 1940 | 1982 | LBW | LW | PH | RCV | UCC | UM | WB |
|----|----|------|------|-----|----|----|-----|-----|----|----|
| Eb |    |      |      | D   | D  | Eb |     |     |    |    |

### INTONATIONS

Videro, Finn **Twenty-One Hymn Intonations**  Concordia Publishing House  97-5004  Key: Eb

### ORGAN COMPOSITIONS

Held, Wilbur  "How Good, Lord, to Be Here"  **The Concordia Hyme Prelude Series**  Volume 6  Edited: Herbert Gotsch  Concordia Publishing House 97-5612  Key: D

### FREE ACCOMPANIMENTS

Gehrke, Hugo  **Hymn Preludes and Free Accompaniments** Volume 5  Augsburg Publishing House  11-9401 Key: D

## Power in the Blood

| BA | DC | 1940 | 1985 | LBW | LW | PH | RCV | UCC | UM | WB |
|----|----|------|------|-----|----|----|-----|-----|----|----|
| Bb |    |      |      |     |    |    |     |     |    |    |

## Praetorius
(See also: Puer nobis; Ach Gott, vom Himmelreiche)

| BA | DC | 1940 | 1982 | LBW | LW | PH | RCV | UCC | UM | WB |
|----|----|------|------|-----|----|----|-----|-----|----|----|
|    | G  |      |      |     |    |    | G   |     |    | D  |

## Praise My Soul
(See also: Lauda anima)

| BA | DC | 1940 | 1982 | LBW | LW | PH | RCV | UCC | UM | WB |
|----|----|------|------|-----|----|----|-----|-----|----|----|
|    | D  |      |      | D   |    | D  |     | D   |    | D  |

Haan, Raymond H. **Festival Hymn Preludes** The Sacred Music Press  KK 329-3  Key: D

## Praise to the Lord
(See also: Lobe den Herren)

| BA | DC | 1940 | 1982 | LBW | LW | PH | RCV | UCC | UM | WB |
|----|----|------|------|-----|----|----|-----|-----|----|----|
| BA | DC | 1940 | 1982 | LBW | LW | PH | RCV | UCC | UM | WB |

## Precious Name

| BA | DC | 1940 | 1982 | LBW | LW | PH | RCV | UCC | UM | WB |
|----|----|------|------|-----|----|----|-----|-----|----|----|
| BA | DC | 1940 | 1982 | LBW | LW | PH | RCV | UCC | UM | WB |
| Ab |    |      |      |     |    |    |     |     | Ab |    |

## Precious to Me

| BA | DC | 1940 | 1985 | LBW | LW | PH | RCV | UCC | UM | WB |
|----|----|------|------|-----|----|----|-----|-----|----|----|
| BA | DC | 1940 | 1985 | LBW | LW | PH | RCV | UCC | UM | WB |
| G  |    |      |      |     |    |    |     |     |    |    |

## Prince Rupert

| BA | DC | 1940 | 1982 | LBW | LW | PH | RCV | UCC | UM | WB |
|----|----|------|------|-----|----|----|-----|-----|----|----|
| BA | DC | 1940 | 1982 | LBW | LW | PH | RCV | UCC | UM | WB |
| Bb |    |      |      |     | Bb |    |     |     |    |    |

Hillert, Richard  "Welcome, Happy Morning" **The Concordia Hymn Prelude Series** Volume 11 Edited: Herbert Gotsch  Concordia Publishing House  97-5618  Key: Bb

## Princess Eugenie

| BA | DC | 1940 | 1982 | LBW | LW | PH | RCV | UCC | UM | WB |
|----|----|------|------|-----|----|----|-----|-----|----|----|
| BA | DC | 1940 | 1982 | LBW | LW | PH | RCV | UCC | UM | WB |
|    |    |      | g    |     |    |    |     |     |    |    |

Ferguson, John "My Heart is Longing" **Behold a Host** Augsburg Publishing House  Key: g

## Promised Land

| BA | DC | 1940 | 1982 | LBW | LW | PH | RCV | UCC | UM | WB |
|----|----|------|------|-----|----|----|-----|-----|----|----|
| BA | DC | 1940 | 1982 | LBW | LW | PH | RCV | UCC | UM | WB |
| F  |    |      |      |     |    |    |     |     | Eb |    |

## Promised One

| BA | DC | 1940 | 1982 | LBW | LW | PH | RCV | UCC | UM | WB |
|----|----|------|------|-----|----|----|-----|-----|----|----|
| BA | DC | 1940 | 1982 | LBW | LW | PH | RCV | UCC | UM | WB |
|    |    |      |      |     |    |    |     | G   |    |    |

## Promises

| BA | DC | 1940 | 1982 | LBW | LW | PH | RCV | UCC | UM | WB |
|----|----|------|------|-----|----|----|-----|-----|----|----|
| BA | DC | 1940 | 1982 | LBW | LW | PH | RCV | UCC | UM | WB |
| Bb |    |      |      |     |    |    |     |     | Bb |    |

## Propior Deo

| BA | DC | 1940 | 1982 | LBW | LW | PH | RCV | UCC | UM | WB |
|----|----|------|------|-----|----|----|-----|-----|----|----|
| BA | DC | 1940 | 1982 | LBW | LW | PH | RCV | UCC | UM | WB |
|    |    | F    |      |     |    |    |     |     |    |    |

Prospect

| BA | DC | 1940 | 1982 | LBW | LW | PH | RCV | UCC | UM | WB |
|----|----|------|------|-----|----|----|-----|-----|----|----|
|    |    |      | F    |     |    |    |     |     |    | F  |

## ORGAN COMPOSITIONS

Johnson, David  "The Hills are Bare at Bethlehem"
**The Concordia Hymn Prelude Series**  Volume 4
Edited: Herbert Gotsch  Concordia Publishing
House  97-5539  Key: F

## FREE ACCOMPANIMENTS

Busarow, Donald **All Praise to You Eternal God**
Augsburg Publishing House 11-9076  Key: F

Johnson, David N.  **Hymn Preludes and Free
Accompaniments**  Volume 14  Augsburg Publishing
House  11-9410  Key: F

Psalm 6

| BA | DC | 1940 | 1982 | LBW | LW | PH | RCV | UCC | UM | WB |
|----|----|------|------|-----|----|----|-----|-----|----|----|
|    |    |      | e    |     |    |    |     |     |    |    |

Psalm 22

| BA | DC | 1940 | 1982 | LBW | LW | PH | RCV | UCC | UM | WB |
|----|----|------|------|-----|----|----|-----|-----|----|----|
|    |    |      |      |     |    |    |     |     |    | e  |

Psalm 36

| BA | DC | 1940 | 1982 | LBW | LW | PH | RCV | UCC | UM | WB |
|----|----|------|------|-----|----|----|-----|-----|----|----|
|    |    |      |      |     |    | D  |     |     |    |    |

Psalm 42
(See also: Freu dich sehr, O meine Seele)

| BA | DC | 1940 | 1982 | LBW | LW | PH | RCV | UCC | UM | WB |
|----|----|------|------|-----|----|----|-----|-----|----|----|
| F  | F  | F    |      |     |    | F  |     | F   |    | F  |

Psalm 80

| BA | DC | 1940 | 1982 | LBW | LW | PH | RCV | UCC | UM | WB |
|----|----|------|------|-----|----|----|-----|-----|----|----|
|    |    |      |      |     |    | d  |     |     |    |    |

Psalm 86

| BA | DC | 1940 | 1982 | LBW | LW | PH | RCV | UCC | UM | WB |
|----|----|------|------|-----|----|----|-----|-----|----|----|
|    |    |      | m:g  |     |    |    |     |     |    |    |

Puer natus in Bethlehem

| BA | DC | 1940 | 1982 | LBW | LW | PH | RCV | UCC | UM | WB |
|----|----|------|------|-----|----|----|-----|-----|----|----|
|    |    |      | m:e  |     |    |    | m:e |     |    |    |

Bach, J. S. **Organ Works** Volume 1 Edited: Heinz Harald Löhlein Urtext of the New Bach Edition Bärenreiter 5171 Key: m:g

Bach, J.S. **Organ Works** Volume VII Widor-Schweitzer G. Schirmer Key: g

Bach, J.S. **Orgelwerke** Volume V C.F. Peters Corporation Nr. 244 Key: g

Bach, J.S. **The Liturgical Year** (Orgelbuchlein) Edited: Albert Reimenschneider Oliver Ditson Co. Key: g

Buxtehude, Dietrich **Orgelwerke II: Choral Preludes** C.F. Peters Corporation #4457 Key: a

Buxtehude, Dietrich "A Babe is Born in Bethlehem" **Anthologia Antiqua** Book Five **Six Chorale Preludes** Edited: Seth Bingham J. Fischer & Bros. No. 8090 Key: m:a

Walther, Johann Gottfried "A Boy Was Born in Bethlehem" **The Parish Organist** Christmas and Epiphany Music Part Six Concordia Publishing House 97-1391 Key: a

Puer nobis (Praetorius)

| BA | DC | 1940 | 1982 | LBW | LW | PH | RCV | UCC | UM | WB |
|----|----|------|------|-----|----|----|-----|-----|----|----|
|    | D  | D    | D    | D   | D  |    |     |     |    |    |

Cassler, G. Winston **Organ Descants for Selected Hymn Tunes** Augsburg Publishing House 11-9304 Key: D

Gieschen, Thomas "On Jordan's Banks the Baptist's Cry" **The Concordia Hymn Prelude Series** Volume 2 Edited Herbert Gotsch Concordia Publishing House 97-5536 Key: D

FREE ACCOMPANIMENTS

Wyton, Alex **New Shoots from Old Routes** Sacred Music Press KK 279 Key: D

Puer nobis nascitur

| BA | DC | 1940 | 1982 | LBW | LW | PH | RCV | UCC | UM | WB |
|----|----|------|------|-----|----|----|-----|-----|----|----|
|    | D  | D    | D    |     |    | D  | D   | D   | D  | D  |

## INTONATIONS

Hermann, David **11 Hymn Intonations, Free Accompaniments, Instrumental Descants for Organ** Volume I Advent, Christmas, Epiphany G.I.A. Publications G-2378 Key: D

## ORGAN COMPOSITIONS

le Begue, Nicolas "To Shepherds as They Watched By Night" **The Parish Organist** Part Five Advent and Christmas Music Concordia Publishing House 97-1382 Key Eb

le Begue, Nicholas "Noel 'Puer nobis nascitur'" **Organ Music for Christmas** Edited C. H. Trevor Oxford University Press Key: F

Manz, Paul "To Shepherds as They Watched by Night" **Ten Chorale Improvisations** Set II Op. 7 Concordia Publishing House 97-4656 Key: Eb

Purvis, Richard "Carillon" **An American Organ Mass** Harold Flammer, Inc. Key: D

Willan, Healey **Chorale Prelude No. 1 "Puer Nobis Nascitur"** Oxford University Press Key: D

## FREE ACCOMPANIMENTS

Bunjes, Paul **New Organ Accompaniments for Hymns** Concordia Publishing House 97-5348 Key: D

Busarow, Donald **All Praise to You Eternal God** Augsburg Publishing House 11-9076 Key: D

Ferguson, John **Ten Hymn Tune Harmonizations** Book I Ludwig Music Publishing Co. 0-05 Key: D

Goode, Jack C. **Thirty-Four Changes on Hymn Tunes** H. W. Gray Co. GB 644 Key: D

Purer in Heart

| BA | DC | 1940 | 1985 | LBW | LW | PH | RCV | UCC | UM | WB |
|----|----|------|------|-----|----|----|-----|-----|----|----|
| G  |    |      |      |     |    |    |     |     |    |    |

Purpose

| BA | DC | 1940 | 1982 | LBW | LW | PH | RCV | UCC | UM | WB |
|----|----|------|------|-----|----|----|-----|-----|----|----|
| f  | f  | f    | f    |     |    | f  |     | f   |    | f  |

# Q

Quam dilecta
| BA | DC | 1940 | 1982 | LBW | LW | PH | RCV | UCC | UM | WB |
|----|----|------|------|-----|----|----|----|----|----|----|
|    |    | E    | E    |     |    |    |    |    |    |    |

## FREE ACCOMPANIMENTS

Coleman, Henry **Varied Hymn Accompaniments**
Oxford University Press  Key: F

**Free Harmonizations to Hymn Tunes By Fifty American
Composers**  Edited: D. DeWitt Wasson  Hinshaw
Music, Inc.  HMO-145  Key: E

Quebec
(See also: Hesperus)
| BA | DC | 1940 | 1982 | LBW | LW | PH | RCV | UCC | UM | WB |
|----|----|------|------|-----|----|----|----|----|----|----|
| Eb |    |      |      |     |    |    |    |    |    |    |

Quem pastores
| BA | DC | 1940 | 1982 | LBW | LW | PH | RCV | UCC | UM | WB |
|----|----|------|------|-----|----|----|----|----|----|----|
|    |    | F    |      | F   | F  |    |    |    |    |    |

## ORGAN COMPOSITIONS

Kickstat, Paul "Come, Your Hearts and Voices Raising"
**The Parish Organist** Christmas and Epiphany
Music  Part Six  Concordia Publishing House
97-1391  Key: F

Kousemaker, Adr. "He Whom Shepherds Once Came
Praising" **The Concordia Hymn Prelude Series**
Volume 4  Edited: Herbert Gotsch  Concordia
Publishing House  97-5539  Key: F

Manz, Paul "He Whom Shepherd Men Came Praising" **Ten
Chorale Improvisations** Set VII Op. 17 Concordia
Publishing House 97-8305  Key: F

Willan, Healey "Quem Pastores"  **Six Chorale Preludes**
Set I  Concordia Publishing House  OC 220  Key: F

Quem terra, pontus, aethera
| BA | DC | 1940 | 1982 | LBW | LW | PH | RCV | UCC | UM | WB |
|----|----|------|------|-----|----|----|----|----|----|----|
|    |    |      | m:g  |     |    |    |    |    |    |    |

Quittez, Pasteurs
| BA | DC | 1940 | 1982 | LBW | LW | PH | RCV | UCC | UM | WB |
|----|----|------|------|-----|----|----|----|----|----|----|
|    |    |      | Eb   |     |    |    |    |    |    |    |

# R

| | BA | DC | 1940 | 1982 | LBW | LW | PH | RCV | UCC | UM | WB |
|---|---|---|---|---|---|---|---|---|---|---|---|
| **Racine** | BA | DC | 1940 Eb | 1982 | LBW | LW | PH | RCV | UCC | UM | WB |
| **Ramwold** | BA | DC | 1940 | 1982 | LBW | LW | PH C | RCV | UCC C | UM | WB |
| **Randolph** | BA D | DC D | 1940 | 1982 | LBW | LW | PH D | RCV | UCC | UM D | WB |
| **Ranshaw** | BA | DC | 1940 | 1982 | LBW | LW | PH | RCV | UCC a | UM | WB |
| **Rapture** | BA Bb | DC | 1940 | 1982 | LBW | LW | PH | RCV | UCC | UM | WB |
| **Raquel** | BA | DC | 1940 | 1982 E | LBW | LW | PH | RCV | UCC | UM | WB |
| **Rathbun** | BA Bb | DC C | 1940 C | 1982 C | LBW Bb | LW Bb | PH Bb | RCV C | UCC Bb | UM C | WB Bb |

ORGAN COMPOSITIONS

Bingham, Seth **Twelve Hymn Preludes** Opus 38 Set 2 H.W. Gray GB 152   Key: C

Engel, James   "In the Cross of Christ I Glory"   **The Concordia Hymn Prelude Series**   Volume 9   Edited: Herbert Gotsch   Concordia Publishing House 97-5616   Key: Bb

Held, Wilbur "In the Cross of Christ I Glory" **A Suite of Passion Hymn Settings**   Concordia Publishing House 97-4843   Key: Bb

Lubrich, Fritz   "In the Cross of Christ I Glory"   **The Parish Organist**   Part Twelve   Edited:   Willem Mudde   Concordia Publishing House   97-4759   Key: C

FREE ACCOMPANIMENTS

Lovelace, Austin C.   **Hymn Preludes and Free Accompaniments**   Volume 4   Augsburg Publishing House   11-9400   Key: Bb

Noble, T. Tertius  **Free Organ Accompaniments to One Hundred Well-Known Hymn Tunes**  J. Fischer & Bros. #8175  Key: Bb

## Ratisbon

| BA | DC | 1940 | 1982 | LBW | LW | PH | RCV | UCC | UM | WB |
|----|----|------|------|-----|----|----|-----|-----|----|----|
|    | D  | D    | D    | D   | D  | D  | D   | D   | D  |    |

ORGAN COMPOSITIONS

Metzger, Hans Arnold  "Christ, Whose Glory Fills the Skies"  **The Parish Organist**  Part Twelve
Edited:  Willem Mudde  Concordia Publishing House
97-4759  Key:  D

Thalben-Ball, George  **113 Variations on Hymn Tunes**
Novello & Co., Ltd.  Key: D

FREE ACCOMPANIMENTS

Hudson, Richard  **Hymn Preludes and Free Accompaniments**
Volume 12  Augsburg Publishing House  11-9408
Key: D

Noble, T. Tertius  **Free Organ Accompaniments to One Hundred Well-Known Hymn Tunes**  J. Fischer & Bros. #8175  Key:  D

## Ravenshaw

| BA | DC | 1940 | 1982 | LBW | LW | PH | RCV | UCC | UM | WB |
|----|----|------|------|-----|----|----|-----|-----|----|----|
|    |    | Eb   |      |     |    | Eb |     |     |    |    |

## Raymer

| BA | DC | 1940 | 1982 | LBW | LW | PH | RCV | UCC | UM | WB |
|----|----|------|------|-----|----|----|-----|-----|----|----|
| F  |    |      |      |     |    |    |     |     |    |    |

## Raymond

| BA | DC | 1940 | 1982 | LBW | LW | PH | RCV | UCC | UM | WB |
|----|----|------|------|-----|----|----|-----|-----|----|----|
|    |    |      | C    |     |    |    |     |     |    |    |

## Reach Out

| BA | DC | 1940 | 1982 | LBW | LW | PH | RCV | UCC | UM | WB |
|----|----|------|------|-----|----|----|-----|-----|----|----|
| Ab |    |      |      |     |    |    |     |     |    |    |

## Rector potens, verax Deus

| BA | DC | 1940 | 1982 | LBW | LW | PH | RCV | UCC | UM | WB |
|----|----|------|------|-----|----|----|-----|-----|----|----|
|    |    |      | m:d  |     |    |    |     |     |    |    |

## Redeemed

| BA | DC | 1940 | 1982 | LBW | LW | PH | RCV | UCC | UM | WB |
|----|----|------|------|-----|----|----|-----|-----|----|----|
| Ab |    |      |      |     |    |    |     |     |    |    |

## Redeemer

| BA | DC | 1940 | 1982 | LBW | LW | PH | RCV | UCC | UM | WB |
|----|----|------|------|-----|----|----|-----|-----|----|----|
| Eb |    |      |      |     |    |    |     |     |    |    |

## Redeeming Love

| BA | DC | 1940 | 1982 | LBW | LW | PH | RCV | UCC | UM | WB |
|----|----|------|------|-----|----|----|-----|-----|----|----|
| Bb |    |      |      |     |    |    |     |     |    |    |

## Redentore

| BA | DC | 1940 | 1982 | LBW | LW | PH | RCV | UCC | UM | WB |
|----|----|------|------|-----|----|----|-----|-----|----|----|
| Eb |    |      |      |     |    |    |     |     |    |    |

## Redhead 76

(See also: Gethsemane; Petra; St. Prisca)

| BA | DC | 1940 | 1985 | LBW | LW | PH | RCV | UCC | UM | WB |
|----|----|------|------|-----|----|----|-----|-----|----|----|
| Eb | Eb |      |      |     |    | Eb |     | Eb  | Eb |    |

### ORGAN COMPOSITIONS

Haan, Raymond H. **A Second Book of Contemplative Hymn Tune Preludes** Harold Flammer, Inc. HF-5127 Key: C

Rowley, Alec "Rock of Ages" **Choral Preludes Based on Famous Hymn Tunes** Volume 1 Edwin Ashdown Ltd. Key: D

## Regensburg

| BA | DC | 1940 | 1982 | LBW | LW | PH | RCV | UCC | UM | WB |
|----|----|------|------|-----|----|----|-----|-----|----|----|
|    | e  |      |      |     |    | e  |     |     |    |    |

## Regent Square

| BA | DC | 1940 | 1982 | LBW | LW | PH | RCV | UCC | UM | WB |
|----|----|------|------|-----|----|----|-----|-----|----|----|
| Bb | Bb | Bb   | A    | Bb  | Bb | Bb | Bb  | Bb  | Bb | Bb |

### INTONATIONS

Hermann, David **11 Hymn Intonations, Free Accompaniments, Instrumental Descants for Organ** Volume I Advent, Christmas, Epiphany G.I.A. Publications G-2378 Key: Bb

Videro, Finn **Twenty-One Hymn Intonations** Concordia Publishing House 87-5004 Key: Bb

### ORGAN COMPOSITIONS

Lang, C. S. **Twenty Hymn-Tune Preludes** (First Set) Oxford University Press Key: Bb

Lang, C. S.  "Angels From the Realms of Glory"  **The Concordia Hymn Prelude Series**  Volume 4  Edited: Herbert Gotsch  Concordia Publishing House  97-5539  Key: Bb

Thalben-Ball, George  **113 Variations on Hymn Tunes**  Novello & Co., Ltd.  Key: Bb

Unkel, Rolf  "Angels from the Realms of Glory"  **The Parish Organist**  Part Three  Edited: Heinrich Fleischer  Concordia Publishing House  97-1154  Key:  Bb

## FREE ACCOMPANIMENTS

Carson, J. Bert  **Hymn Preludes and Free Accompaniments**  Volume 16  Augsburg Publishing House  11-9412  Key: Bb

Ferguson, John  **Ten Hymn Tune Harmonizations**  Book I  Ludwig Music Publishing Co.  0-05  Key: Bb

Goode, Jack C.  **Thirty-Four Changes on Hymn Tunes**  H. W. Gray Co.  GB 644  Key: Bb

Hancock, Gerre  **Organ Improvisations for Hymn-Singing**  Hinshaw Music Co.  HMO-100  Key: Bb

Noble, T. Tertius  **Free Organ Accompaniments to One Hundred Well-Known Hymn Tunes**  J. Fischer & Bros.  #8175  Key: Bb

Norris, Kevin  **Hymn Preludes and Free Accompaniments**  Volume 15  Augsburg Publishing House  11-9411  Key: Bb

Wyton, Alec  **New Shoots from Old Routes**  Sacred Music Press  KK 279  Key: Bb

Regnator orbis
(See also: O quanta qualia)

| Regwal | | | | | | | | | | |
|---|---|---|---|---|---|---|---|---|---|---|
| BA | DC | 1940 | 1982 | LBW | LW | PH | RCV | UCC | UM | WB |
| | | | | F | | | | | | |

| Reitz | | | | | | | | | | |
|---|---|---|---|---|---|---|---|---|---|---|
| BA | DC | 1940 | 1985 | LBW | LW | PH | RCV | UCC | UM | WB |
| Db | | | | | | | | | | |

| Remember the Poor | | | | | | | | | | |
|---|---|---|---|---|---|---|---|---|---|---|
| BA | DC | 1940 | 1982 | LBW | LW | PH | RCV | UCC | UM | WB |
| | | | | | | G | | | | |

Rendez à Dieu

| BA | DC | 1940 | 1982 | LBW | LW | PH | RCV | UCC | UM | WB |
|----|----|------|------|-----|----|----|-----|-----|----|----|
|    | G  | G    | G    |     |    | G  | G   | G   | G  | G  |

## ORGAN COMPOSITIONS

Bassett, Anita Denniston  **Nine Hymn-Tune Preludes**
Ludwig Music Publishing Co.  0-08  Key: G

Beyer, Michael  "Bread of the World, in Mercy Broken"
**The Parish Organist** Part Twelve  Edited: Willem
Mudde  Concordia Publishing House  97-4759  Key: G

Clokey, Joseph W. "Meditation on 'Rendez à Dieu' by
Louis Bourgeois  **Ten Meditations on Hymn Melodies**
J. Fischer & Bro. #8824  Key: A

Johnson, David N. "Father, We thank Thee" **Deck Thyself
My Soul with Gladness** Augsburg Publishing House
11-9157  Key: G

Peek, Richard "Father, We Thank Thee" **Hymn Preludes for
the Church Year** Carl Fischer, Inc. Key: G

Repton

| BA | DC | 1940 | 1982 | LBW | LW | PH | RCV | UCC | UM | WB |
|----|----|------|------|-----|----|----|-----|-----|----|----|
|    |    |      | Eb   |     |    |    |     |     |    |    |

Requiescat

| BA | DC | 1940 | 1982 | LBW | LW | PH | RCV | UCC | UM | WB |
|----|----|------|------|-----|----|----|-----|-----|----|----|
|    |    | C    |      |     |    |    |     |     |    |    |

Rescue

| BA | DC | 1940 | 1982 | LBW | LW | PH | RCV | UCC | UM | WB |
|----|----|------|------|-----|----|----|-----|-----|----|----|
| Bb |    |      |      |     |    |    |     |     | Bb |    |

Resignation

| BA | DC | 1940 | 1982 | LBW | LW | PH | RCV | UCC | UM | WB |
|----|----|------|------|-----|----|----|-----|-----|----|----|
|    | C  |      | C    |     | C  |    |     | C   |    | C  |

## INTONATIONS

Videro, Finn  **Twenty-One Hymn Intonations**  Concordia
Publishing House  97-5004  Key: C

## ORGAN COMPOSITIONS

Bristol, Lee Hastings Jr. "Prelude on Two Folk Hymns"
**The Bristol Collection of Contemporary Hymn
Tune Preludes for the Organ** Volume 3 Edited:
Lee Hastings Bristol, Jr.  Harold Flammer Key: C

Martin, Gilbert "Interlude on 'Resignation'" **The Bristol Collection of Contemporary Hymn Tune Preludes for the Organ** Volume 2   Edited: Lee Hastings Bristol, Jr.,   Harold Flammer   Key: C

FREE ACCOMPANIMENTS

Busarow, Donald **All Praise to You Eternal God** Augsburg Publishing House   11-9076   Key: C

Resolution

| BA | DC | 1940 | 1982 | LBW | LW | PH | RCV | UCC | UM | WB |
|----|----|------|------|-----|----|----|-----|-----|----|----|
| Bb |    |      |      |     |    |    |     |     |    |    |

Resonet in laudibus

| BA | DC | 1940 | 1982 | LBW | LW | PH | RCV | UCC | UM | WB |
|----|----|------|------|-----|----|----|-----|-----|----|----|
|    |    | Eb   |      |     | F  | F  | F   |     |    |    |

ORGAN COMPOSITIONS

Hoegner, Friedrich "Joseph, Dearest, Joseph Mine" **The Parish Organist** Christmas and Epiphany Music   Part Six   Concordia Publishing House 97-1391   Key:  F

Karg-Elert, Sigfrid "Resonet in Laudibus" **Cathedral Windows** London: Elkin & Co. Ltd.   Key: A

Purvis, Richard "Offertory" **An American Organ Mass** Harold Flammer, Inc.   Key: Eb

FREE ACCOMPANIMENTS

Cassler, G. Winston **Free Organ Accompaniments to Hymns** Volume II   Advent-Christmas-Epiphany   Augsburg Publishing House   11-9187   Key: Eb

Rest

| BA | DC | 1940 | 1982 | LBW | LW | PH | RCV | UCC | UM | WB |
|----|----|------|------|-----|----|----|-----|-----|----|----|
| D  | D  | D    | D    | D   |    | D  |     | D   | D  | D  |

ORGAN COMPOSITIONS

Stearns, Peter Pindar **Eight Hymn Preludes for Lent** Harold Flammer, Inc.   HF-5133   Key: D

FREE ACCOMPANIMENTS

Noble, T. Tertius  **Free Organ Accompaniments to One Hundred Well-Known Hymn Tunes**   J. Fischer & Bros. #8175   Key: D

## Restoration

| BA | DC | 1940 | 1982 | LBW | LW | PH | RCV | UCC | UM | WB |
|----|----|------|------|-----|----|----|-----|-----|----|----|
|    |    | f    |      |     |    |    |     |     |    |    |

## Resurrection (Gaither)

| BA | DC | 1940 | 1982 | LBW | LW | PH | RCV | UCC | UM | WB |
|----|----|------|------|-----|----|----|-----|-----|----|----|
| Ab |    |      |      |     |    |    |     |     |    |    |

## Resurrection (Harmonia Sacra)

| BA | DC | 1940 | 1982 | LBW | LW | PH | RCV | UCC | UM | WB |
|----|----|------|------|-----|----|----|-----|-----|----|----|
|    |    | D    |      |     |    |    |     |     |    |    |

## Resurrexit

| BA | DC | 1940 | 1982 | LBW | LW | PH | RCV | UCC | UM | WB |
|----|----|------|------|-----|----|----|-----|-----|----|----|
|    |    |      | D    |     |    |    |     |     |    |    |

## Retreat

| BA | DC | 1940 | 1982 | LBW | LW | PH | RCV | UCC | UM | WB |
|----|----|------|------|-----|----|----|-----|-----|----|----|
| Ab | Bb |      |      |     |    |    |     |     | Bb |    |

## Reuter

| BA | DC | 1940 | 1982 | LBW | LW | PH | RCV | UCC | UM | WB |
|----|----|------|------|-----|----|----|-----|-----|----|----|
|    |    |      |      |     | Eb |    |     |     |    |    |

## Revive Us Again

| BA | DC | 1940 | 1982 | LBW | LW | PH | RCV | UCC | UM | WB |
|----|----|------|------|-----|----|----|-----|-----|----|----|
| G  |    |      |      |     |    |    | ʼRCV |    |    |    |

## Rex gloriae

| BA | DC | 1940 | 1982 | LBW | LW | PH | RCV | UCC | UM | WB |
|----|----|------|------|-----|----|----|-----|-----|----|----|
|    | G  | G    |      |     | G  |    |     |     |    |    |

ORGAN COMPOSITIONS

Niblock, James  "See, the Conqueror Mounts in Triumph"
**The Parish Organist**  Part Twelve  Edited:
Willem Mudde  Concordia Publishing House
97-4759  Key: G

## Rex gloriose

| BA | DC | 1940 | 1982 | LBW | LW | PH | RCV | UCC | UM | WB |
|----|----|------|------|-----|----|----|-----|-----|----|----|
|    |    | C    |      |     |    |    |     |     |    |    |

## Rex Summae Majestatis

| BA | DC | 1940 | 1982 | LBW | LW | PH | RCV | UCC | UM | WB |
|----|----|------|------|-----|----|----|-----|-----|----|----|
|    | a  |      |      |     |    |    | a   |     |    |    |

## Reynolds

| BA | DC | 1940 | 1982 | LBW | LW | PH | RCV | UCC | UM | WB |
|----|----|------|------|-----|----|----|-----|-----|----|----|
| G  |    |      |      |     |    |    |     |     |    |    |

Rhea

| BA | DC | 1940 | 1982 | LBW | LW | PH | RCV | UCC | UM | WB |
|----|----|------|------|-----|----|----|-----|-----|----|----|
| F |  |  |  |  |  |  |  |  |  |  |

Rhosymedre
(See also: Lovely)

| BA | DC | 1940 | 1982 | LBW | LW | PH | RCV | UCC | UM | WB |
|----|----|------|------|-----|----|----|-----|-----|----|----|
| G | F | F | F | F | F | F |  | F |  | F |

## ORGAN COMPOSITION

Powell, Robert J.  "My Song is Love Unknown" **The Concordia Hymn Prelude Series** Volume 9  Edited: Herbert Gotsch  Concordia Publishing House 97-5616  Key: F

Vaughan Williams, Ralph **Three Preludes** Stainer & Bell (Galaxy Music Corp.)  Key: G

## FREE ACCOMPANIMENTS

Bender, Jan  **Hymn Preludes and Free Accompaniments** Volume 1  Augsburg Publishing House  11-9397 Key: F

Cassler, G. Winston  **Organ Descants for Selected Hymn Tunes** Augsburg Publishing House 11-9304  Key: G

Coleman, Henry **Varied Hymn Accompaniments**  Oxford University Press Key: G

**Free Harmonizations of Hymn Tunes By Fifty American Composers** Edited: D. DeWitt Wasson  Hinshaw Music, Inc.  HMO-145  Key: F

Manz, Paul O. "My song is love unknown" **Free Organ Accompaniments to Hymns** Vol III  General - Palm Sunday - Easter  Augsburg Publishing House 11-9189  Key: G

Rhuddlan

| BA | DC | 1940 | 1982 | LBW | LW | PH | RCV | UCC | UM | WB |
|----|----|------|------|-----|----|----|-----|-----|----|----|
|  |  | G | G |  |  | G |  | G |  | G |

Richmond

| BA | DC | 1940 | 1982 | LBW | LW | PH | RCV | UCC | UM | WB |
|----|----|------|------|-----|----|----|-----|-----|----|----|
| F | F |  | G |  |  | F |  |  | F | F |

## ORGAN COMPOSITIONS

Willan, Healey  "One Holy Church" **Ten Hymn Preludes** C.F. Peters Corp. No. 6011  Key: G

Lang, C. S. **Twenty Hymn-Tune Preludes** (First Set)
Oxford University Press  Key: G

## FREE ACCOMPANIMENTS

Coleman, Henry **Varied Hymn Accompaniments** Oxford
University Press  Key: G

Noble, T. Tertius **Fifty Free Organ Accompaniments to
Well Known Hymn Tunes** J. Fischer & Bros.
No. 8430  Key: F

Richter
| BA | DC | 1940 | 1982 | LBW | LW | PH | RCV | UCC | UM | WB |
|----|----|------|------|-----|----|----|-----|-----|----|----|
| F | F | | | | | | | | | |

Ridgefield
| BA | DC | 1940 | 1982 | LBW | LW | PH | RCV | UCC | UM | WB |
|----|----|------|------|-----|----|----|-----|-----|----|----|
| | g | | | | | | | | | |

Riley
| BA | DC | 1940 | 1982 | LBW | LW | PH | RCV | UCC | UM | WB |
|----|----|------|------|-----|----|----|-----|-----|----|----|
| | G | | | | | | | | | |

Ring the Bells
| BA | DC | 1940 | 1982 | LBW | LW | PH | RCV | UCC | UM | WB |
|----|----|------|------|-----|----|----|-----|-----|----|----|
| Bb | | | | | | | | | | |

Ringe recht
(See also: Batty)
| BA | DC | 1940 | 1982 | LBW | LW | PH | RCV | UCC | UM | WB |
|----|----|------|------|-----|----|----|-----|-----|----|----|
| | | | | | | Eb | | Eb | | |

## ORGAN COMPOSITIONS

Karg-Elert, Sigfrid "Strive for the Right" **Choral
Improvisations for Organ for New Year, Easter and
Other Church Festivals** Op. 65, Volume 3  Edited:
Robert Leech Bedell  Edward B. Marks Music Corp.
Key: F

Markworth, Henry J.  "Lamb of God, We Fall Before Thee"
**The Parish Organist** Part Three  Edited:
Heinrich Fleischer  Coincordia Publishing House
97-1154  Key:  F

Moser, Rudolf  "Sweet the Moments, Rich in Blessing"
**The Parish Organist** Part Seven  Music for
Lent, Palm Sunday and Holy Week  Edited: Erich
Goldschmidt  Concordia Publishing House  97-1403
Key:  F

## Rise and Shine
| BA | DC | 1940 | 1982 | LBW | LW | PH | RCV | UCC | UM | WB |
|---|---|---|---|---|---|---|---|---|---|---|
|  |  | 1940 | 1982 | LBW | LW | PH | RCV | UCC<br>D | UM | WB |

## River Forest
| BA | DC | 1940 | 1982 | LBW | LW | PH | RCV | UCC | UM | WB |
|---|---|---|---|---|---|---|---|---|---|---|
|  |  | 1940 | 1982 | LBW | LW<br>d | PH | RCV | UCC | UM | WB |

## Robertson
| BA | DC | 1940 | 1982 | LBW | LW | PH | RCV | UCC | UM | WB |
|---|---|---|---|---|---|---|---|---|---|---|
| C |  | 1940 | 1982 | LBW | LW | PH | RCV | UCC | UM | WB |

## Robin
| BA | DC | 1940 | 1982 | LBW | LW | PH | RCV | UCC | UM | WB |
|---|---|---|---|---|---|---|---|---|---|---|
| F |  | 1940 | 1982 | LBW | LW | PH | RCV | UCC | UM | WB |

## Rochelle
| BA | DC | 1940 | 1982 | LBW | LW | PH | RCV | UCC | UM | WB |
|---|---|---|---|---|---|---|---|---|---|---|
| G | G | 1940 | 1982 | LBW | LW | PH | RCV | UCC | UM | WB |

### ORGAN COMPOSITIONS

Clokey, Joseph W. "Meditation on 'Rochelle' by Adam Drese" **Ten Meditations on Hymn Melodies** J. Fischer & Bro. #8824 Key: G

## Rock of Ages
(See also: Moaz Tsur)
| BA | DC | 1940 | 1982 | LBW | LW | PH | RCV | UCC | UM | WB |
|---|---|---|---|---|---|---|---|---|---|---|
|  | Eb | 1940 | 1982 | LBW | LW | PH<br>Eb | RCV | UCC<br>Eb | UM<br>Eb | WB<br>Eb |

### ORGAN COMPOSITIONS

Young, Gordon "Rocky of Ages" **Contemporary Hymn Preludes** Hope Publishing Co. No. 328 Key: Bb

### FREE ACCOMPANIMENTS

**Free Harmonizations to Hymn Tunes By Fifty American Composers** Edited: D. DeWitt Wasson Hinshaw Music, Inc. HMO-145 Key: Eb

Goode, Jack C. **Thirty-Four Changes on Hymn Tunes** H. W. Gray Co. GB 644 Key: Eb

## Rocking
| BA | DC | 1940 | 1982 | LBW | LW | PH | RCV | UCC | UM | WB |
|---|---|---|---|---|---|---|---|---|---|---|
|  |  | 1940 | 1982 | LBW | LW | PH<br>F | RCV | UCC | UM | WB |

## Rockingham (Mason)
| BA | DC | 1940 | 1982 | LBW | LW | PH | RCV | UCC | UM | WB |
|---|---|---|---|---|---|---|---|---|---|---|
|  |  | 1940 | 1982 | LBW | LW | PH | RCV | U`C | UM<br>F | WB |

Rockingham (Old)

| BA | DC | 1940 | 1982 | LBW | LW | PH | RCV | UCC | UM | WB |
|----|----|------|------|-----|----|----|-----|-----|----|----|
|    | D  | D    | D    | D   | D  | D  | D   |     |    | D  |

## ORGAN COMPOSITIONS

Harris, David S. **Ten Hymn Preludes in Trio Style**
H. W. Gray Co.   GB 643   Key: D

Lang, C. S.   "When I Survey the Wondrous Cross"   **The
Concordia Hymn Prelude Series**   Volume 9   Edited:
Herbert Gotsch   Concordia Publishing House
97-5616   Key: D

Lang, C.S.   **Twenty Hymn-Tune Preludes**   (First Set)
Oxford University Press   Key: Eb

Raphael, Guenter   "When I Survey the Wondrous Cross"
**The Parish Organist**   Part Seven   Music for
Lent, Palm Sunday and Holy Week   Edited: Erich
Goldschmidt   Concordia Publishing House   97-1403
Key:  Eb

Thalben-Ball, George   **113 Variations on Hymn Tunes**
Novello & Co., Ltd.   Key: Eb

## FREE ACCOMPANIMENTS

Coleman, Henry   **Varied Hymn Accompaniments**   Oxford
University Press   Key: Eb

Noble, T. Tertius   **Free Organ Accompaniments to One
Hundred Well-Known Hymn Tunes**   J. Fischer & Bros.
#8175   Key: D

Wyton, Alec   **New Shoots from Old Routes**   Sacred Music
Press   KK   279   Key: D

Rockport

| BA | DC | 1940 | 1982 | LBW | LW | PH | RCV | UCC | UM | WB |
|----|----|------|------|-----|----|----|-----|-----|----|----|
|    | f  |      |      |     |    | f  |     |     |    |    |

Rok novy

| BA | DC | 1940 | 1982 | LBW | LW | PH | RCV | UCC | UM | WB |
|----|----|------|------|-----|----|----|-----|-----|----|----|
|    |    |      |      | g   | g  |    |     |     |    |    |

## ORGAN COMPOSITIONS

Wienhorst, Richard   "Greet Now the Swiftly Changing
Year"   **The Concordia Hymn Prelude Series**
Volume 15   Edited: Herbert Gotsch   Concordia
Publishing House   97-5706   Key: g

Roll Call

| BA | DC | 1940 | 1982 | LBW | LW | PH | RCV | UCC | UM | WB |
|---|---|---|---|---|---|---|---|---|---|---|
| Ab | | | | | | | | | | |

Rosa mystica
  (See also: Es ist ein' Ros)

| BA | DC | 1940 | 1982 | LBW | LW | PH | RCV | UCC | UM | WB |
|---|---|---|---|---|---|---|---|---|---|---|
| | | F | | | | | | | | |

ORGAN COMPOSITIONS

Thate, Albert "Lo How a Rose E'er Blooming" **The Parish Organist** Part Five Advent and Christmas Music Edited: Fleischer Goldschmidt Concordia Publishing House 97-1382 Key: F

Roseate Hues

| BA | DC | 1940 | 1982 | LBW | LW | PH | RCV | UCC | UM | WB |
|---|---|---|---|---|---|---|---|---|---|---|
| | E | | | | | | | | | |

Rosedale

| BA | DC | 1940 | 1982 | LBW | LW | PH | RCV | UCC | UM | WB |
|---|---|---|---|---|---|---|---|---|---|---|
| | | Bb | | | | | | Bb | | |

ORGAN COMPOSITIONS

Arnatt, Ronald "Prelude on 'Rosedale'" **The Bristol Collection of Contemporary Hymn Tune Preludes for Organ** Volume 2 Edited: Lee Hastings Bristol, Jr. Harold Flammer, Inc. Key: F

Rouen
  (See also: Iste Confessor)

| BA | DC | 1940 | 1982 | LBW | LW | PH | RCV | UCC | UM | WB |
|---|---|---|---|---|---|---|---|---|---|---|
| | | d | d | | | | | | | |

Routh

| BA | DC | 1940 | 1982 | LBW | LW | PH | RCV | UCC | UM | WB |
|---|---|---|---|---|---|---|---|---|---|---|
| Eb | | | | | | | | | | |

Rowthorn

| BA | DC | 1940 | 1982 | LBW | LW | PH | RCV | UCC | UM | WB |
|---|---|---|---|---|---|---|---|---|---|---|
| | | | Eb | | | | | | | |

Royal Banner

| BA | DC | 1940 | 1982 | LBW | LW | PH | RCV | UCC | UM | WB |
|---|---|---|---|---|---|---|---|---|---|---|
| Bb | | | | | | | | | | |

Royal Oak

| BA | DC | 1940 | 1982 | LBW | LW | PH | RCV | UCC | UM | WB |
|---|---|---|---|---|---|---|---|---|---|---|
| | G | G | G | | | G | | | Ab | |

**Free Harmonizations of Hymn Tunes By Fifty American Composers** Edited: D. DeWitt Wasson  Hinshaw Music, Inc.  HMO-145  Key: G

<u>Rushford</u>

| | BA | DC | 1940 | 1982 | LBW | LW | PH | RCV | UCC | UM | WB |
|---|----|----|------|------|-----|----|----|-----|-----|----|----|
| | | | Db | C | | | | | | | |

<u>Russia</u>

| | BA | DC | 1940 | 1982 | LBW | LW | PH | RCV | UCC | UM | WB |
|---|----|----|------|------|-----|----|----|-----|-----|----|----|
| | | | D | D | | | | | | | |

Noble, T. Tertius  **Free Organ Accompaniments to One Hundred Well-Known Hymn Tunes**  J. Fischer & Bros. #8175  Key: D

<u>Russian Hymn</u>

| | BA | DC | 1940 | 1982 | LBW | LW | PH | RCV | UCC | UM | WB |
|---|----|----|------|------|-----|----|----|-----|-----|----|----|
| | | D | | | D | | D | | D | D | |

Wyton, Alec  **New Shoots from Old Routes**  Sacred Music Press  KK 279  Key: D

<u>Rustington</u>

| | BA | DC | 1940 | 1982 | LBW | LW | PH | RCV | UCC | UM | WB |
|---|----|----|------|------|-----|----|----|-----|-----|----|----|
| | | | F | F | | | | | | | |

<u>Ryburn</u>

| | BA | DC | 1940 | 1982 | LBW | LW | PH | RCV | UCC | UM | WB |
|---|----|----|------|------|-----|----|----|-----|-----|----|----|
| | | | | D | | | | | | | |

# S

<u>Sabbath</u>

| | BA | DC | 1940 | 1982 | LBW | LW | PH | RCV | UCC | UM | WB |
|---|----|----|------|------|-----|----|----|-----|-----|----|----|
| | | | | | | | | | | G | |

<u>Sacramentum unitatis</u>

| | BA | DC | 1940 | 1982 | LBW | LW | PH | RCV | UCC | UM | WB |
|---|----|----|------|------|-----|----|----|-----|-----|----|----|
| | | | Eb | | | | | | | | |

Sowerby, Leo **Meditations on Communion Hymns**
H. W. Gray Co., Inc.  Key: Eb

Safety

| BA | DC | 1940 | 1982 | LBW | LW | PH | RCV | UCC | UM | WB |
|----|----|------|------|-----|----|----|-----|-----|----|----|
| Bb |    |      |      |     |    |    |     |     |    |    |

Saffron Walden

| BA | DC | 1940 | 1982 | LBW | LW | PH | RCV | UCC | UM | WB |
|----|----|------|------|-----|----|----|-----|-----|----|----|
| D  | D  |      |      |     |    |    |     |     |    |    |

Sagina

| BA | DC | 1940 | 1982 | LBW | LW | PH | RCV | UCC | UM | WB |
|----|----|------|------|-----|----|----|-----|-----|----|----|
|    | G  |      |      |     |    |    |     |     |    |    |

St. Agnes

| BA | DC | 1940 | 1982 | LBW | LW | PH | RCV | UCC | UM | WB |
|----|----|------|------|-----|----|----|-----|-----|----|----|
| F  | G  | G    | G    | G   |    | G  | G   | G   | G  |    |

ORGAN COMPOSITIONS

Held, Wilbur "Come Holy Spirit, Heavenly Dove"
**Hymn Preludes for the Pentecost Season**
Concordia Publishing House 97-5517  Key: G

FREE ACCOMPANIMENTS

Hancock, Gerre **Organ Improvisations for Hymn-Singing**
Hinshaw  Music Co.  HMO-100  Key: G

Hudson, Richard **Hymn Preludes and Free Accompaniments**
Volume 12  Augsburg Publishing House  11-9408
Key: G

Noble, T. Tertius **Free Organ Accompaniments to One
Hundred Well-Known Hymn Tunes**  J. Fischer & Bros.
#8175  Key: G

St. Alban's

| BA | DC | 1940 | 1982 | LBW | LW | PH | RCV | UCC | UM | WB |
|----|----|------|------|-----|----|----|-----|-----|----|----|
|    | F  |      |      |     |    |    |     |     |    |    |

St. Albinus

| BA | DC | 1940 | 1982 | LBW | LW | PH | RCV | UCC | UM | WB |
|----|----|------|------|-----|----|----|-----|-----|----|----|
| Bb | Bb |      |      |     |    |    |     |     |    |    |

FREE ACCOMPANIMENTS

Noble, T. Tertius **Fifty Free Organ Accompaniments to
Well Known Hymn Tunes**  J. Fischer & Bros.
No. 8430  Key: Bb

## St. Alphege

| BA | DC | 1940 | 1982 | LBW | LW | PH | RCV | UCC | UM | WB |
|----|----|------|------|-----|----|----|-----|-----|----|----|
|    |    | F    |      |     |    |    |     |     |    |    |

## St. Anatolius

| BA | DC | 1940 | 1982 | LBW | LW | PH | RCV | UCC | UM | WB |
|----|----|------|------|-----|----|----|-----|-----|----|----|
|    |    | D    |      |     |    |    |     |     |    |    |

## St. Andrew

| BA | DC | 1940 | 1982 | LBW | LW | PH | RCV | UCC | UM | WB |
|----|----|------|------|-----|----|----|-----|-----|----|----|
|    | Eb |      | F    |     |    |    |     |     |    |    |

## St. Andrew of Crete

| BA | DC | 1940 | 1982 | LBW | LW | PH | RCV | UCC | UM | WB |
|----|----|------|------|-----|----|----|-----|-----|----|----|
|    |    | C    |      |     |    | C  |     |     |    |    |

## St. Anne
(See also: O God Our Help in Ages Past)

| BA | DC | 1940 | 1982 | LBW | LW | PH | RCV | UCC | UM | WB |
|----|----|------|------|-----|----|----|-----|-----|----|----|
| C  | C  | Bb   | C    | C   | C  | C  | Bb  | C   | C  | C  |

## ORGAN COMPOSITIONS

Bender, Jan **O God, Our Help in Ages Past**
Augsburg Publishing House   Key: C

Fleischer, Heinrich "O God Our Help in Ages Past"
**Wedding Music** Part 2   Concordia Publishing
House   97-1370   Key: C

Lang, C.S. **Twenty Hymn Tune Preludes** (First Set)
Oxford University Press   Key: C

Lang, C. S.   "Our God, Our Help in Ages Past"   **The
Concordia Hymn Prelude Series** Volume 15   Edited:
Herbert Gotsch   Concordia Publishing House
97-5706   Key: C

Manz, Paul **Partita on 'St. Anne'** Concordia Publishing
House 97-5307   Key: C

Miles, George Th.   "Our God, Our Help in Ages Past"
**The Parish Organist** Part Three   Edited: Heinrich
Fleischer   Concordia Publishing House   97-1154
Key: C

Thalben-Ball, George **113 Variations on Hymn Tunes**
Novello & Co., Ltd.   Key: C

Arnatt, Ronald **Hymn Preludes and Free Accompaniments**
Volume 9  Augsburg Publishing House  11-9405
Key: C

Cassler, G. Winston  **Organ Descants for Selected Hymn
Tunes**  Augsburg Publishing House  11-9304  Key: C

Coleman, Henry  **Varied Hymn Accompaniments**  Oxford
University Press  Key: C

Ferguson, John **Ten Hymn Tune Harmonizations** Book I
Ludwig Music Publishing Co.  0-05  Key: C

Goode, Jack  **Thirty-Four Changes on Hymn Tunes**
H. W. Gray Co.  GB 644  Key: C

Hancock, Gerre  **Organ Improvisations for Hymn-Singing**
Hinshaw Music Co.  HMO-100  Key: Bb

Hebble, Robert  **Robert Hebble's Hymnal Companion for
Organ**  Bradley Publications  CE/283A/3  Key: C

Johnson, David N.  **Free Organ Accompaniments to
Festival Hymns**  Volume I  Augsburg Publishing
House  11-9192  Key: C/D

Noble, T. Tertius  **Free Organ Accompaniments to One
Hundred Well-Known Hymn Tunes**  J. Fischer & Bros.
#8175  Key: C

Wyton, Alec  **New Shoots from Old Routes**  Sacred
Music Press  KK 279  Key: Bb

St. Anthony's Chorale

| BA | DC | 1940 | 1982 | LBW | LW | PH | RCV | UCC | UM | WB |
|----|----|------|------|-----|----|----|-----|-----|----|----|
|    |    |      |      |     |    |    |     |     | G  |    |

St. Asaph

| BA | DC | 1940 | 1982 | LBW | LW | PH | RCV | UCC | UM | WB |
|----|----|------|------|-----|----|----|-----|-----|----|----|
| Db |    |      |      |     |    | D  |     |     | D  |    |

Noble, T. Tertius  **Free Organ Accompaniments to One
Hundred Well-Known Hymn Tunes**  J. Fischer & Bros.
#8175  Key: Db

St. Athanasius

| BA | DC | 1940 | 1982 | LBW | LW | PH | RCV | UCC | UM | WB |
|----|----|------|------|-----|----|----|-----|-----|----|----|
| Ab |    |      |      |     |    |    |     |     |    |    |

336

## St. Augustine

| BA | DC | 1940 | 1982 | LBW | LW | PH | RCV | UCC | UM | WB |
|----|----|------|------|-----|----|----|-----|-----|----|----|
|    | G  |      |      |     |    |    |     |     |    |    |

## St. Bartholomew's

| BA | DC | 1940 | 1982 | LBW | LW | PH | RCV | UCC | UM | WB |
|----|----|------|------|-----|----|----|-----|-----|----|----|
|    |    | C    |      |     |    |    |     |     |    |    |

## St. Bavon

| BA | DC | 1940 | 1982 | LBW | LW | PH | RCV | UCC | UM | WB |
|----|----|------|------|-----|----|----|-----|-----|----|----|
|    | D  |      |      |     |    |    |     |     |    |    |

## St. Bees

| BA | DC | 1940 | 1982 | LBW | LW | PH | RCV | UCC | UM | WB |
|----|----|------|------|-----|----|----|-----|-----|----|----|
|    | G  | G    |      |     |    |    |     |     |    |    |

### FREE ACCOMPANIMENTS

Noble, T. Tertius **Fifty Free Organ Accompaniments to Well-Known Hymn Tunes** J. Fischer & Bros. No. 8430 Key: G

## St. Bernard

| BA | DC | 1940 | 1982 | LBW | LW | PH | RCV | UCC | UM | WB |
|----|----|------|------|-----|----|----|-----|-----|----|----|
|    | D  |      |      |     |    | D  |     |     | Eb | D  |

### ORGAN COMPOSITIONS

Busarow, Donald "Lord, as to Thy Dear Cross We Flee" **The Parish Organist** Part Twelve Edited: Willem Mudde Concordia Publishing House 97-4759 Key: D

Thalben-Ball, George **113 Variations on Hymn Tunes** Novello & Co., Ltd. Key: D

### FREE ACCOMPANIMENTS

Noble, T. Tertius **Fifty Free Organ Accompaniments to Well-Known Hymn Tunes** J. Fischer & Bros. No. 8430 Key: D

## St. Boniface

| BA | DC | 1940 | 1982 | LBW | LW | PH | RCV | UCC | UM | WB |
|----|----|------|------|-----|----|----|-----|-----|----|----|
|    | F  |      |      |     |    |    |     |     |    |    |

## St. Botolph

| BA | DC | 1940 | 1982 | LBW | LW | PH | RCV | UCC | UM | WB |
|----|----|------|------|-----|----|----|-----|-----|----|----|
|    |    | D    |      |     |    |    |     |     |    |    |

## St. Bride

| BA | DC | 1940 | 1982 | LBW | LW | PH | RCV | UCC | UM | WB |
|----|----|------|------|-----|----|----|-----|-----|----|----|
| g  | g  | g    |      |     |    | g  | g   |     | g  | g  |

Beck, Albert **76 Offertories on Hymns & Chorales**
Concordia Publishing House 97-5207 Key: g

Beck, Theodore "And Wilt Thou Pardon, Lord" **The
Parish Organist** Part Twelve Edited: Willem
Mudde Concordia Publishing House 97-4759 Key: g

Rowley, Alec "Have Mercy, Lord, on me" **Choral Preludes
Based on Famous Hymn Tunes** Volume 1 Edwin
Ashdown Ltd. Key: g

Willan, Healey **36 Short Preludes and Postludes on
Well-Known Hymn Tunes** Set II C. F. Peters
Corporation No. 6162 Key: g

## FREE ACCOMPANIMENTS

**Free Harmonizations of Hymn Tunes By Fifty American
Composers** Edited: D. DeWitt Wasson Hinshaw
Music, Inc. HMO-145 Key: g

St. Casimer

| BA | DC | 1940 | 1982 | LBW | LW | PH | RCV | UCC | UM | WB |
|----|----|------|------|-----|----|----|-----|-----|-----|-----|
|    |    |      |      |     |    |    | F   |     |     |     |

St. Catherine
(See also: St. Finbar)

| BA | DC | 1940 | 1982 | LBW | LW | PH | RCV | UCC | UM | WB |
|----|----|------|------|-----|----|----|-----|-----|-----|-----|
| F  | Ab | G    | G    | G   |    | G  | Ab  | G   | Ab  | G   |

## ORGAN COMPOSITIONS

McKinley, Carl "Fantasia on 'St. Catherine'"
**A Collection of Thanksgiving Music**
Compiled by John Holler H.W. Gray St. Cecilia
#648 Key: G

McKinley, Carl **Ten Hymn Tune Fantasies** H.W. Gray
Key: G

## FREE ACCOMPANIMENTS

Hancock, Gerre **Organ Improvisations for Hymn-Singing**
Hinshaw Music Co. HMO-100 Key: G

Noble, T. Tertius **Free Organ Accompaniments to One
Hundred Well-Known Hymn Tunes** J. Fischer & Bros.
#8175 Key: G

Wyton, Alex **New Shoots from Old Routes** Sacred
Music Press KK 279 Key: G

St. Cecilia

| BA | DC | 1940 | 1982 | LBW | LW | PH | RCV | UCC | UM | WB |
|----|----|------|------|-----|----|----|-----|-----|----|----|
| G  | G  |      |      |     |    | G  |     |     |    |    |

## ORGAN COMPOSITIONS

Boda, John "Thy Kingdom Come, O God" **The Parish Organist** Part Twelve Edited: Willem Mudde Concordia Publishing House 97-4759 Key: m:g

## FREE ACCOMPANIMENTS

**Free Harmonizations to Hymn Tunes By Fifty American Composers** Edited: D. DeWitt Wasson Hinshaw Music, Inc. HMO-145 Key: G

St. Chad

| BA | DC | 1940 | 1982 | LBW | LW | PH | RCV | UCC | UM | WB |
|----|----|------|------|-----|----|----|-----|-----|----|----|
|    | D  |      |      |     |    |    |     |     |    |    |

St. Christopher

| BA | DC | 1940 | 1982 | LBW | LW | PH | RCV | UCC | UM | WB |
|----|----|------|------|-----|----|----|-----|-----|----|----|
| Db | Db | Db   | Db   | D   |    | Db | Db  | Db  | Db | Db |

## ORGAN COMPOSITIONS

Schalk, Carl "Beneath the Cross of Jesus" **The Concordia Hymn Prelude Series** Volume 9 Edited: Herbert Gotsch Concordia Publishing House 97-5616 Key: D

## FREE ACCOMPANIMENTS

Noble, T. Tertius **Free Organ Accompaniments to One Hundred Well-Known Hymn Tunes** J. Fischer & Bros. #8175 Key: Db

St. Chrysostom

| BA | DC | 1940 | 1982 | LBW | LW | PH | RCV | UCC | UM | WB |
|----|----|------|------|-----|----|----|-----|-----|----|----|
| Eb | Eb |      |      |     |    |    |     |     |    |    |

St. Clement

| BA | DC | 1940 | 1982 | LBW | LW | PH | RCV | UCC | UM | WB |
|----|----|------|------|-----|----|----|-----|-----|----|----|
| G  | G  | Ab   | G    |     |    | Ab |     |     |    |    |

## ORGAN COMPOSITIONS

Cherwien, David "The Day You Gave Us, Lord, Has Ended" **Interpretations Based on Hymn-tunes** Book IV A.M.S.I. OR-9 Key: G

McKinley, Carl **Ten Hymn Tune Fantasies** H.W. Gray Key: Ab

Thalben-Ball, George **113 Variations on Hymn Tunes**
Novello & Co., Ltd.  Key: Ab

FREE ACCOMPANIMENTS

Noble, T. Tertius **Fifty Free Organ Accompaniments to
Well Known Hymn Tunes**  J. Fischer & Bros.
Noo 8430  Key: G

St. Columba
(See also: Irons)

| BA | DC | 1940 | 1982 | LBW | LW | PH | RCV | UCC | UM | WB |
|----|----|------|------|-----|----|----|-----|-----|----|----|
| D | D | D | Eb | Eb | D | | | | | D |

ORGAN COMPOSITIONS

Goode, Jack **Seven Communion Meditations**  Harold
Flammer, Inc.  HF-5084  Key: E

Groves, Robert **A Galaxy of Hymn Tune Preludes for
Organ** Galaxy Music Corp. GMC 2353  Key: Eb

Haan, Raymond H. "Prelude on 'The King of love my
shepherd is'" **The King of Love**  The Sacred Music
Press  Key: Eb

Krapf, Gerhard  "The King of Love My Shepherd Is"  **The
Parish Organist**  Part Twelve  Edited: Willem Mudde
Concordia Publishing House  97-4759  Key: D

Milford, Robin **Two Choral Preludes II on 'St. Columba'**
Oxford University Press Key: Ab

Milford, Robin "The King of Love My Shepherd Is"
**Wedding Music**  Part 2  Concordia Publishing House
97-1370  Key: Ab

Willan, Healey  "The King of Love" **Ten Hymn Preludes**
Set I  C. F. Peters Corp. No. 6011  Key: Eb

FREE ACCOMPANIMENTS

Arnatt, Ronald  **Hymn Preludes and Free Accompaniments**
Volume 9  Augsburg Publishing House  11-9405
Key: Eb

Busarow, Donald **All Praise to You Eternal God**
Augsburg Publishing House 11-9076  Key: D

Cassler, G. Winston  **Organ Descants for Selected Hymn
Tunes**  Augsburg Publishing House 11-9304  Key: Eb

340

Noble, T. Tertius **Fifty Free Organ Accompaniments to Well Known Hymn Tunes** J. Fischer & Bros. No. 8430  Key: D

St. Constantine

| BA | DC | 1940 | 1982 | LBW | LW | PH | RCV | UCC | UM | WB |
|----|----|------|------|-----|----|----|-----|-----|----|----|
|    |    | D    | 1982 | LBW | LW | PH | RCV | UCC | UM | WB |

St. Crispin

| BA | DC | 1940 | 1982 | LBW | LW | PH | RCV | UCC | UM | WB |
|----|----|------|------|-----|----|----|-----|-----|----|----|
| D  |    | D    | 1982 | LBW | D  | D  | RCV | UCC | UM | WB |

## ORGAN COMPOSITIONS

Beck, Albert **76 Offertories on Hymns & Chorales** Concordia Publishing House 97-5207  Key: E

Bouman, Paul  "Jesus, Thy Blood and Righteousness" **The Parish Organist** Part Three  Edited: Heinrich Fleischer  Concordia Publishing House 97-1154  Key: Eb

Willan, Healey **36 Short Preludes and Postludes on Well-Known Hymn Tunes** Set III C. F. Peters Corporation  No. 6163  Key: E

## FREE ACCOMPANIMENTS

Noble, T. Tertius **Free Organ Accompaniments to One Hundred Well-Known Hymn Tunes** J. Fischer & Bros. #8175  Key: D

St. Cross

| BA | DC | 1940 | 1982 | LBW | LW | PH | RCV | UCC | UM | WB |
|----|----|------|------|-----|----|----|-----|-----|----|----|
|    | DC | d    | 1982 | LBW | LW | d  | d   | UCC | UM | WB |

## ORGAN COMPOSITIONS

Beck, Albert **76 Offertories on Hymns & Chorales** Concordia Publishing House  97-5207  Key: d

Willan, Healey **36 Short Preludes and Postludes on Well-Known Hymn Tunes** Set III  C. F. Peters Corporation  No. 6163  Key: d

## FREE ACCOMPANIMENTS

Noble, T. Tertius **Fifty Free Organ Accompaniments to Well Known Hymn Tunes** J. Fischer & Bros. No. 8430  Key: d

St. Cuthbert

| BA | DC | 1940 | 1982 | LBW | LW | PH | RCV | UCC | UM | WB |
|----|----|------|------|-----|----|----|-----|-----|----|----|
|    |    |      |      |  D  |    |    |     |     |    |    |

### ORGAN COMPOSITIONS

Willan, Healey **36 Short Preludes and Postludes on Well-Known Hymn Tunes** Set III C. F. Peters Corporation No. 6163 Key: D

St. Denio

(See also: Joanna)

| BA | DC | 1940 | 1982 | LBW | LW | PH | RCV | UCC | UM | WB |
|----|----|------|------|-----|----|----|-----|-----|----|----|
| Ab | Ab | G    | G    | G   | G  | G  |     | G   | G  | G  |

### INTONATIONS

McCormick, David W. **20 Organ Intonations on Hymns of Praise** Hope Publishing Co. #342 Key: G

### ORGAN COMPOSITIONS

Rohlig, Harald "Immortal, Invisible, God Only Wise" **The Parish Organist** Part Twelve Edited: Willem Mudde Concordia Publishing House 97-4759 Key: G

Speller, Frank N. **A Triptych of Praise and Thanksgiving** J. Fischer & Bros. FEs 10052 Key: Ab

Thalben-Ball, George **113 Variations on Hymn Tunes** Novello & Co., Ltd. Key: Ab

Young, Gordon "Postlude on 'St. Denio'" **Contemporary Hymn Preludes** Hope Publishing Co. No. 328 Key: G

### FREE ACCOMPANIMENTS

Goode, Jack C. **Thirty-Four Changes on Hymn Tunes** H. W. Gray Co. GB 644 Key: Ab

Hancock, Gerre **Organ Improvisations for Hymn-Singing** Hinshaw Music Co. HMO-100 Key: G

Johnson, David N. **Free Organ Accompaniments to Festival Hymns** Volume I Augsburg Publishing House 11-9192 Key: Ab

Lovelace, Austin **Hymn Preludes and Free Accompaniments** Volume 4 Augsburg Publishing House 11-9400 Key: G

Wyton, Alec **New Shoots from Old Routes** Sacred Music
Press KK 279 Key: G

St. Drostane

| BA | DC | 1940 | 1982 | LBW | LW | PH | RCV | UCC | UM | WB |
|----|----|------|------|-----|----|----|-----|-----|----|----|
| Bb |    |      |      |     |    | A  |     |     |    | Bb |

St. Dunstan's

| BA | DC | 1940 | 1982 | LBW | LW | PH | RCV | UCC | UM | WB |
|----|----|------|------|-----|----|----|-----|-----|----|----|
| F  | F  | G    | G    | G   | G  | F  |     | F   | G  | F  |

## ORGAN COMPOSITIONS

Boda, John "Who Would Valiant Be" **The Parish
Organist** Part Twelve Edited: Willem Mudde
Concordia Publishing House 97-4759 Key: C

## FREE ACCOMPANIMENTS

**Free Harmonizations to Hymn Tunes By Fifty American
Composers** Edited: D. DeWitt Wasson Hinshaw
Music, Inc. HMO-145 Key: G

St. Edith
(See also: St. Hilda)

| BA | DC | 1940 | 1982 | LBW | LW | PH | RCV | UCC | UM | WB |
|----|----|------|------|-----|----|----|-----|-----|----|----|
|    |    |      |      |     |    |    |     |     |    |    |

## ORGAN COMPOSITIONS

Young, Gordon **A Galaxy of Hymn Tune Preludes for
Organ** Galaxy Music Corp. GMC 2353 Key: Eb

St. Edmund

| BA | DC | 1940 | 1982 | LBW | LW | PH | RCV | UCC | UM | WB |
|----|----|------|------|-----|----|----|-----|-----|----|----|
| G  | G  |      |      |     |    | G  |     |     | G  |    |

St. Elizabeth
(See also: Crusader's Hymn)

| BA | DC | 1940 | 1982 | LBW | LW | PH | RCV | UCC | UM | WB |
|----|----|------|------|-----|----|----|-----|-----|----|----|
|    | Eb | Eb   | Eb   |     |    |    | D   |     | Eb |    |

## ORGAN COMPOSITIONS

Harris, David S. **Ten Hymn Preludes in Trio Style**
H.W. Gray Co. GB 643 Key: F

## FREE ACCOMPANIMENTS

Goode, Jack C. **Thirty-Four Changes on Hymn Tunes**
H.W. Gray Co. GB 644 Key: Eb

Hancock, Gerre  **Organ Improvisations for Hymn-Singing**
Hinshaw Music Co.  HMO-100  Key: Eb

Noble, T. Tertius  **Free Organ Accompaniments to One
Hundred Well-Known Hymn Tunes**  J. Fischer & Bros.
#8175  Key: Eb

Wyton, Alec  **New Shoots from Old Routes**  Sacred
Music Press  KK  279  Key: Eb

## St. Ethelwald

| BA | DC | 1940 | 1982 | LBW | LW | PH | RCV | UCC | UM | WB |
|----|----|------|------|-----|----|----|-----|-----|----|----|
|    |    |      | G    |     |    |    |     |     |    |    |

## St. Finbar
(See also: St. Catherine)

## St. Flavian

| BA | DC | 1940 | 1982 | LBW | LW | PH | RCV | UCC | UM | WB |
|----|----|------|------|-----|----|----|-----|-----|----|----|
| F  | F  | F    | F    | F   | F  | F  | F   | F   | F  | F  |

### ORGAN COMPOSITIONS

Canning, Thomas  "Lord, when We Bend Before Thy Throne"
**The Parish Organist**  Part Twelve  Edited: Willem
Mudde  Concordia Publishing House  97-4759  Key: F

Haan, Raymond H.  **A Second Book of Contemplative Hymn
Tune Preludes**  Harold Flammer, Inc.  HF-5127
Key: F

Johnson, David  "O God, Unseen, Yet Ever Near" **Deck
Thyself with Gladness** Volume 2 Augsburg
Publishing House 11-9101  Key: F

Lang, C.S.  **Twenty Hymn-Tune Preludes** (First Set)
Oxford University Press  Key: F

Willan, Healey  **Ten Hymn Preludes** Set I  C. F.
Peters Corp.  No. 6011  Key: F

### FREE ACCOMPANIMENTS

Cassler, G. Winston  **Organ Descants for Selected Hymn
Tunes**  Augsburg Publishing House  11-9304  Key: D

Johnson, DavidN. **Hymn Preludes andFree
Accompaniments** Volume 14  Augsburg Publishing
House  11-9410  Key: F

Noble, T. Tertius  **Fifty Free Organ Accompaniments to
Well Known Hymn Tunes**  J. Fischer & Bros.
No. 8430  Key: F

Wyton, Alec **New Shoots from Old Routes** Sacred Music
Press  KK  279  Key: F

## St. Fulbert

| BA | DC | 1940 | 1982 | LBW | LW | PH | RCV | UCC | UM | WB |
|----|----|------|------|-----|----|----|-----|-----|----|----|
|    |    | Db   | Db   |     |    |    | Eb  |     |    |    |

## St. Gabriel

| BA | DC | 1940 | 1982 | LBW | LW | PH | RCV | UCC | UM | WB |
|----|----|------|------|-----|----|----|-----|-----|----|----|
|    |    | Eb   |      |     |    |    |     |     |    |    |

ORGAN COMPOSITIONS

Willan, Healey  **36 Short Preludes and Postludes on
Well-Known Hymn Tunes**  Set III  C. F. Peters
Corporation  No. 6163  Key: Eb

## St. George

| BA | DC | 1940 | 1982 | LBW | LW | PH | RCV | UCC | UM | WB |
|----|----|------|------|-----|----|----|-----|-----|----|----|
|    |    | Bb   | Bb   |     |    |    | Bb  |     |    |    |

ORGAN COMPOSITIONS

Gehrke, Hugo  "Come, Ye Thankful People, Come"
**The Parish Organist**  Part Three  Edited:
Heinrich Fleischer  Concordia Publishing House
97-1154  Key:  F

Woods, F. Cunningham "Variations on Elvey's Tune 'St.
George'"  **A Collection of Thanksgiving Music**
Compiled by John Holler  St. Cecilia #648
H.W. Gray  Key: G

FREE ACCOMPANIMENTS

Noble, T. Tertius  **Fifty Free Organ Accompaniments to
Well Known Hymn Tunes**  J. Fischer & Bros.
No. 8430  Key: Bb

## St. George's Windsor

| BA | DC | 1940 | 1982 | LBW | LW | PH | RCV | UCC | UM | WB |
|----|----|------|------|-----|----|----|-----|-----|----|----|
| F  | F  | F    | F    | F   | F  | F  | F   | F   | F  | F  |

ORGAN COMPOSITIONS

Engel, James  "Songs of Thankfulness and Praise"
**The Concordia Hymn Prelude Series**  Volume 6
Edited: Herbert Gotsch  Concordia Publishing
House  97-5612  Key: F

Speller, Frank N.  **A Triptych of Praise and
Thanksgiving**  J. Fischer & Bros.  FES 10052
Key: G

Cassler, G. Winston **Organ Descants for Selected Hymn Tunes** Augsburg Publishing House 11-9304 Key: G

Noble, T. Tertius **Fifty Free Organ Accompaniments to Well Known Hymn Tunes** J. Fischer & Bros. No. 8430 Key: F

St. Gertrude

| BA | DC | 1940 | 1982 | LBW | LW | PH | RCV | UCC | UM | WB |
|----|----|------|------|-----|----|----|-----|-----|----|----|
| Eb |    | Eb | Eb | Eb | Eb | Eb |    | Eb | Eb | Eb |

FREE ACCOMPANIMENTS

Noble, T. Tertius **Free Organ Accompaniments to One Hundred Well-Known Hymn Tunes** J. Fischer & Bros. #8175 Key: Eb

St. Helena

| BA | DC | 1940 | 1982 | LBW | LW | PH | RCV | UCC | UM | WB |
|----|----|------|------|-----|----|----|-----|-----|----|----|
|    |    | E |    |    |    |    |    |    |    |    |

St. Hilda
(See also: St. Edith)

| BA | DC | 1940 | 1982 | LBW | LW | PH | RCV | UCC | UM | WB |
|----|----|------|------|-----|----|----|-----|-----|----|----|
| D | D |    |    |    |    | D |    |    | Eb |    |

FREE ACCOMPANIMENTS

**Free Harmonizations to Hymn Tunes By Fifty American Composers** Edited: D. DeWitt Wasson Hinshaw Music, Inc. HMO-145 Key: D

Noble, T. Tertius **Free Organ Accompaniments to One Hundred Well-Known Hymn Tunes** J. Fischer & Bros. #8175 Key: D

St. James

| BA | DC | 1940 | 1982 | LBW | LW | PH | RCV | UCC | UM | WB |
|----|----|------|------|-----|----|----|-----|-----|----|----|
|    |    | A | A |    |    | G |    |    |    |    |

ORGAN COMPOSITIONS

Krapf, Gerhard "Thou Art the Way, to Thee Alone" **The Parish Organist** Part Twelve Edited: Willem Mudde Concordia Publishing House 97-4759 Key: A

Thalben-Ball, George **113 Variations on Hymn Tunes** Novello & Co., Ltd. Key: A

Willan, Healey **36 Short Preludes and Postludes on Well-Known Hymn Tunes** Set III  C. F. Peters Corporation  No. 6163  Key: A

### FREE ACCOMPANIMENTS

Noble, T. Tertius **Free Organ Accompaniments to One Hundred Well-Known Hymn Tunes**  J. Fischer & Bros. #8175  Key: A

### St. Joan

| BA | DC | 1940 | 1982 | LBW | LW | PH | RCV | UCC | UM | WB |
|----|----|------|------|-----|----|----|-----|-----|----|----|
|    | C  | C    |      |     |    |    |     |     |    | C  |

### St. Katrine

| BA | DC | 1940 | 1982 | LBW | LW | PH | RCV | UCC | UM | WB |
|----|----|------|------|-----|----|----|-----|-----|----|----|
|    | Eb |      |      |     |    |    |     |     |    |    |

### St. Keverne

| BA | DC | 1940 | 1982 | LBW | LW | PH | RCV | UCC | UM | WB |
|----|----|------|------|-----|----|----|-----|-----|----|----|
|    |    | e    | e    |     |    |    |     |     |    |    |

### St. Kevin

| BA | DC | 1940 | 1982 | LBW | LW | PH | RCV | UCC | UM | WB |
|----|----|------|------|-----|----|----|-----|-----|----|----|
| F  | F  | F    |      |     |    | F  | F   |     | G  |    |

### ORGAN COMPOSITIONS

Bingham, Seth "Prelude and Fughetta on 'St. Kevin'" **A Galaxy of Hymn Tune Preludes for Organ** Galaxy Music Corp. GMC 2353  Key: A

Jordan, Alice "Come, Ye Faithful, Raise the Strain" **A Season and a Time**  Broadman Press 4570-37 Key: G

Miles, Russell Hancock "Paraphrase on the Easter Hymn 'St. Kevin'" **The St. Cecilia Series of Lent and Easter Music** H.W. Gray  Key: G

Whitford, Homer **Five Choral Paraphrases**  Set I H.W. Gray Co.  Key: G

### FREE ACCOMPANIMENTS

**Free Harmonizations to Hymn Tunes By Fifty American Composers**  Edited: D. DeWitt Wasson  Hinshaw Music, Inc. HMO-145  Key: F

Goode, Jack C. **Thirty-Four Changes on Hymn Tunes** H. W. Gray Co.  GB 644  Key: F

Noble, T. Tertius **Fifty Free Organ Accompaniments to Well Known Hymn Tunes** J. Fischer & Bros. No. 8430  Key: F

St. Leonard
(See also: Komm, o komm, du Geist des Lebens)

| BA | DC | 1940 | 1982 | LBW | LW | PH | RCV | UCC | UM | WB |
|----|----|------|------|-----|----|----|-----|-----|----|----|
| Eb |    | F    |      |     |    |    |     |     |    |    |

ORGAN COMPOSITIONS

Thalben-Ball, George **113 Variations on Hymn Tunes** Novello & Co., Ltd.  Key: F

St. Louis

| BA | DC | 1940 | 1982 | LBW | LW | PH | RCV | UCC | UM | WB |
|----|----|------|------|-----|----|----|-----|-----|----|----|
| F  | F  | F    | F    | F   | F  | F  | F   | F   | F  | G  |

ORGAN COMPOSITIONS

Schalk, Carl  "O Little Town of Bethlehem"  **The Concordia Hymn Prelude Series** Volume 5  Edited: Herbert Gotsch  Concordia Publishing House 97-5611  Key: F

Wolz, Larry  "O Little Town of Bethlehem"  **O Little Town of Bethlehem** Broadman Press  4570-68 Key:  F

FREE ACCOMPANIMENTS

Noble, T. Tertius  **Free Organ Accompaniments to One Hundred Well-Known Hymn Tunes**  J. Fischer & Bros. #8175  Key: F

St. Luke

| BA | DC | 1940 | 1982 | LBW | LW | PH | RCV | UCC | UM | WB |
|----|----|------|------|-----|----|----|-----|-----|----|----|
|    |    |      |      |     | f  |    |     |     |    |    |

ORGAN COMPOSITIONS

Beck, Albert **76 Offertories on Hymns & Chorales** Concordia Publishing House  97-5207  Key: f

St. Magnus

| BA | DC | 1940 | 1982 | LBW | LW | PH | RCV | UCC | UM | WB |
|----|----|------|------|-----|----|----|-----|-----|----|----|
| G  |    | G    | G    | G   |    | F  | G   | G   | G  | G  |

INTONATIONS

Videro, Finn  **Twenty-One Hymn Intonations**  Concordia Publishing House  97-5004  Key: G

348

## ORGAN COMPOSITIONS

Barlow, Wayne  "The Head That Once Was Crowned with Thorns" **The Parish Organist** Part Twelve Edited: Willem Mudde  Concordia Publishing House 97-4759  Key: G

Busarow, Donald  "The Head That Once Was Crowned" **The Concordia Hymn Prelude Series** Volume 14  Edited: Herbert Gotsch  Concordia Publishing House 97-5705  Key: G

Lang, C.S.  **Twenty Hymn-Tune Preludes** (First Set) Oxford University Press (Two Settings): Key: A; Key: G

Thalben-Ball, George  **113 Variations on Hymn Tunes** Novello & Co., Ltd.  Key: G

## FREE ACCOMPANIMENTS

Noble, T. Tertius  **Fifty Free Organ Accompaniments to Well Known Hymn Tunes**  J. Fischer & Bros. No. 8430  Key: G

St. Margaret

| BA | DC | 1940 | 1982 | LBW | LW | PH | RCV | UCC | UM | WB |
|----|----|------|------|-----|----|----|-----|-----|----|----|
| Ab | Ab | Ab   |      | G   |    | Ab |     |     | Ab | Ab |

## ORGAN COMPOSITIONS

Jordan, Alice  "Introduction and Chorale on 'St. Margaret'" **Worship Service Music for the Organist** Broadman Press  Key: Db

Lovelace, Austin  "O Love that will not let me go" **Eight Hymn Preludes**  Augsburg Publishing House 11-9144  Key: Ab

## FREE ACCOMPANIMENTS

**Free Harmonizations to Hymn Tunes By Fifty American Composers**  Edited: D. DeWitt Wasson  Hinshaw Music, Inc.  HMO-145  Key: Ab

St. Maria

| BA | DC | 1940 | 1982 | LBW | LW | PH | RCV | UCC | UM | WB |
|----|----|------|------|-----|----|----|-----|-----|----|----|
|    | F  |      |      |     |    |    |     |     |    |    |

St. Mark's, Berkeley

| BA | DC | 1940 | 1982 | LBW | LW | PH | RCV | UCC | UM | WB |
|----|----|------|------|-----|----|----|-----|-----|----|----|
|    |    | g    |      |     |    |    |     |     |    |    |

St. Martin's

| BA | DC | 1940 | 1982 | LBW | LW | PH | RCV | UCC | UM | WB |
|----|----|------|------|-----|----|----|-----|-----|----|----|
|    |    |      |      |     |    |    |     |     | G  |    |

St. Mary

| BA | DC | 1940 | 1982 | LBW | LW | PH | RCV | UCC | UM | WB |
|----|----|------|------|-----|----|----|-----|-----|----|----|
|    | d  |      |      |     |    | d  |     |     |    |    |

## ORGAN COMPOSITIONS

Rowley, Alec "O Lord, Turn Not Thy Face From Me"
**Choral Preludes based on Famous Hymn Tunes**
Volume 1   Edwin Ashdown Ltd.   Key: d

St. Mary Magdalene

| BA | DC | 1940 | 1982 | LBW | LW | PH | RCV | UCC | UM | WB |
|----|----|------|------|-----|----|----|-----|-----|----|----|
|    |    | F    |      |     | F  |    |     |     |    |    |

St. Matthew

| BA | DC | 1940 | 1982 | LBW | LW | PH | RCV | UCC | UM | WB |
|----|----|------|------|-----|----|----|-----|-----|----|----|
|    |    | A    | A    |     |    |    |     | Bb  | Bb |    |

## ORGAN COMPOSITIONS

Thalben-Ball, George   **113 Variations on Hymn Tunes**
Novello & Co., Ltd.   Key: C

St. Matthias
(See also: Song 67)

| BA | DC | 1940 | 1982 | LBW | LW | PH | RCV | UCC | UM | WB |
|----|----|------|------|-----|----|----|-----|-----|----|----|
|    |    | F    |      |     |    |    |     |     |    |    |

## FREE ACCOMPANIMENTS

Noble, T. Tertius   **Fifty Free Organ Accompaniments to
Well Known Hymn Tunes**   J. Fischer & Bros.
No. 8430   Key: F

St. Michael (Old 134th)

| BA | DC | 1940 | 1982 | LBW | LW | PH | RCV | UCC | UM | WB |
|----|----|------|------|-----|----|----|-----|-----|----|----|
| G  | G  | G    |      | G   | G  |    |     | G   | G  | G  |

## INTONATIONS

Videro, Finn   **Twenty-One Hymn Intonations**   Concordia
Publishing House   97-5004   Key: G

## ORGAN COMPOSITIONS

Bender, Jan   "Thy Table I Approach"   **The Parish
Organist**   Part Three   Edited: Heinrich Fleischer
Concordia Publishing House   97-1154   Key: G

Manz, Paul "Prelude on 'St. Michael'" **Ten Chorale**
**Improvisations** Set V  Op. 14 Concordia Publishing
House 97-5257  Key: G

Rotermund, Donald  "Your Table I Approach"  **The**
**Concordia Hymn Prelude Series** Volume 18  Edited:
Herbert Gotsch  Concordia Publishing House
97-5709  Key: G

Thalben-Ball, George  **113 Variations on Hymn Tunes**
Novello & Co., Ltd.  Key: Ab

St. Michael

| BA | DC | 1940 | 1982 | LBW | LW | PH | RCV | UCC | UM | WB |
|----|----|------|------|-----|----|----|-----|-----|----|----|
|    |    |      |      |     |    |    |     |     | F  |    |

St. Nicholas

| BA | DC | 1940 | 1982 | LBW | LW | PH | RCV | UCC | UM | WB |
|----|----|------|------|-----|----|----|-----|-----|----|----|
|    |    | Eb   |      |     |    |    |     |     |    |    |

FREE ACCOMPANIMENTS

Cassler, G. Winson  **Organ Descants for Selected Hymn**
**Tunes** Augsburg Publishing House  11-9304  Key:e

St. Oswald

| BA | DC | 1940 | 1982 | LBW | LW | PH | RCV | UCC | UM | WB |
|----|----|------|------|-----|----|----|-----|-----|----|----|
|    |    | D    |      |     |    |    |     |     |    |    |

St. Osyth

| BA | DC | 1940 | 1982 | LBW | LW | PH | RCV | UCC | UM | WB |
|----|----|------|------|-----|----|----|-----|-----|----|----|
|    |    | C    |      |     |    |    |     |     |    |    |

St. Patrick
(See also: St. Patrick's Breastplate)

| BA | DC | 1940 | 1982 | LBW | LW | PH | RCV | UCC | UM | WB |
|----|----|------|------|-----|----|----|-----|-----|----|----|
|    |    | g    |      |     |    |    |     | g   |    | g  |

ORGAN COMPOSITIONS

Fetler, Paul "I Bind unto Myself Today"  **The Parish**
**Organist** Part Twelve  Edited: Willem Mudde
Concordia Publishing House  97-4759  Key: m:g

St. Patrick's Breastplate

| BA | DC | 1940 | 1982 | LBW | LW | PH | RCV | UCC | UM | WB |
|----|----|------|------|-----|----|----|-----|-----|----|----|
|    |    | g    | g    | g   |    |    |     |     |    |    |

ORGAN COMPOSITIONS

Held, Wilbur  "I Bind unto Myself Today"  **The
Concordia Hymn Prelude Series** Volume 13
Edited; Herbert Gotsch  Concordia Publishing
House  97-5620  Key: g

Krapf, Gerhard  "I Bind Unto Myself Today"  **The
Concordia Hymn Prelude Series** Volume 16
Edited: Herbert Gotsch  Concordia Publishing House
97-5707  Key: g

Wyton, Alec  "March on 'St. Patrick's Breastplate'"
**Preludes, Fanfares and a March for the Liturgical
Year** Harold Flammer  3947  Key: g

St. Peter

| BA | DC | 1940 | 1982 | LBW | LW | PH | RCV | UCC | UM | WB |
|----|----|------|------|-----|----|----|-----|-----|----|----|
| D | Eb | Eb | Eb | D | D | Eb | Eb | | Eb | Eb |

ORGAN COMPOSITIONS

Beck, Albert **76 Offertories on Hymns & Chorales**
Concordia Publishing House  97-5207  Key: Eb

Bouman, Paul  "How Sweet the Name of Jesus Sounds"
**The Parish Organist** Part Three  Edited:
Heinrich Fleischer  Concordia Publishing House
97-1154  Key: Eb

Engel, James  "How Sweet the Name of Jesus Sounds"
**Preludes on Six Hymn Tunes** Augsburg Publishing
House  11-9364  Key: Eb

Lang, C. S.  **Twenty Hymn-Tune Preludes** (First Set)
Oxford University Press  Key: Eb

FREE ACCOMPANIMENTS

Coleman, Henry **Varied Hymn Accompaniments**
Oxford University Press  Key: Eb

Johnson, David N.  **Hymn Preludes and Free
Accompaniments** Volume 14  Augsburg Publishing
House  11-9410  Key: D

Noble, T. Tertius  **Free Organ Accompaniments to One
Hundred Well-Known Hymn Tunes** J. Fischer & Bros.
#8175  Key: Eb

St. Petersburg

| BA | DC | 1940 | 1982 | LBW | LW | PH | RCV | UCC | UM | WB |
|----|----|------|------|-----|----|----|-----|-----|----|----|
| Bb | Bb | Bb | Bb | | | | | C | C | |

Beck, Albert **76 Offertories on Hymns & Chorales**
Concordia Publishing House  97-5207  Key: C

Wienhorst, Richard  "Before Thy Throne, O God, We
Kneel" **The Parish Organist**  Part Twelve  Edited:
Willem Mudde  Concordia Publishing House  97-4759
Key:  m:a

St. Philip

| BA | DC | 1940 | 1982 | LBW | LW | PH | RCV | UCC | UM | WB |
|----|----|------|------|-----|----|----|-----|-----|----|----|
|    |    | Eb   |      |     |    |    |     |     |    |    |

ORGAN COMPOSITIONS

Willan, Healey **Ten Hymn Preludes**  Set II  C. F.
Peters Corporation  6012  Key: Eb

FREE ACCOMPANIMENTS

Noble, T. Tertius  **Fifty Free Organ Accompaniments to
Well Known Hymn Tunes**  J. Fischer & Bros.
No. 8430  Key: Eb

St. Prisca
  (See also: Redhead No. 76)

| BA | DC | 1940 | 1982 | LBW | LW | PH | RCV | UCC | UM | WB |
|----|----|------|------|-----|----|----|-----|-----|----|----|
|    |    | C    |      |     |    |    |     |     |    |    |

St. Stephen

| BA | DC | 1940 | 1982 | LBW | LW | PH | RCV | UCC | UM | WB |
|----|----|------|------|-----|----|----|-----|-----|----|----|
|    |    | G    | G    |     |    | G  | G   |     | G  |    |

ORGAN COMPOSITIONS

Manz, Paul  "The King Shall Come when Morning Dawns"
**The Parish Organist**  Part Twelve  Edited:
Willem Mudde  Concordia Publishing House  97-4759
Key:  G

Thalben-Ball, George  **113 Variations on Hymn Tunes**
Novello & Co., Ltd.  Key: G

Willan, Healey  **36 Short Preludes and Postludes on
Well-Known Hymn Tunes**  Set III  C. F. Peters
Corporation  No. 6163  Key: G

FREE ACCOMPANIMENTS

Noble, T. Tertius  **Fifty Free Organ Accompaniments to
Well Known Hymn Tunes**  J. Fischer & Bros.
No. 8430  key: G

| St. Teilo | | | | | | | | | | |
|---|---|---|---|---|---|---|---|---|---|---|
| BA | DC | 1940 | 1982 | LBW | LW | PH | RCV | UCC | UM | WB |
| | | | | | | | | D | | |

| St. Theoctistus | | | | | | | | | | |
|---|---|---|---|---|---|---|---|---|---|---|
| BA | DC | 1940 | 1982 | LBW | LW | PH | RCV | UCC | UM | WB |
| | F | | | | | | | | | |

St. Theodulph
(See also: Valet will ich dir geben)

| BA | DC | 1940 | 1982 | LBW | LW | PH | RCV | UCC | UM | WB |
|---|---|---|---|---|---|---|---|---|---|---|
| Bb | C | Bb | | | | Bb | Bb | Bb | C | Bb |

ORGAN COMPOSITIONS

McKinley, Carl **Ten Hymn Tune Fantasies** H.W. Gray
Key: C

FREE ACCOMPANIMENTS

Cassler, G. Winston **Organ Descants for Selected Hymn Tunes** Augsburg Publishing House 11-9304 Key: C

Goode, Jack C. **Thirty-Four Changes on Hymn Tunes** H. W. Gray Co. GB 644 Key: C

Nelson, Ronald A. **Free Organ Accompaniments to Festival Hymns** Volume I Augsburg Publishing House 11-9192 Key: C

Noble, T. Tertius **Fifty Free Organ Accompaniments to Well Known Hymn Tunes** J. Fischer & Bros. No. 8430 Key: Bb

Rohlig, Harald **Free Organ Accompaniments to Hymns** Augsburg Publishing House 11-9179 Key: C

Vogel, William "All Glory Laud, and Honor" **Free Organ Accompaniments to Hymns** Volume III General - Palm Sunday - Easter Augsburg Publishing House 11-9189 Key: C

| St. Theresa | | | | | | | | | | |
|---|---|---|---|---|---|---|---|---|---|---|
| BA | DC | 1940 | 1982 | LBW | LW | PH | RCV | UCC | UM | WB |
| | | Eb | | | | | | | | |

| St. Thomas (Wade) | | | | | | | | | | |
|---|---|---|---|---|---|---|---|---|---|---|
| BA | DC | 1940 | 1982 | LBW | LW | PH | RCV | UCC | UM | WB |
| | | D | D | | | | G | | | |

## INTONATIONS

Videro, Finn **Twenty-One Hymn Intonations** Concordia
Publishing House 97-5004 Key: G

## FREE ACCOMPANIMENTS

Noble, T. Tertius **Free Organ Accompaniments to One
Hundred Well-Known Hymn Tunes** J. Fischer & Bros.
#8175 Key: D

St. Thomas (Williams)

| BA | DC | 1940 | 1982 | LBW | LW | PH | RCV | UCC | UM | WB |
|----|----|------|------|-----|----|----|-----|-----|----|----|
| F  | G  | F    | G    | F   |    | F  | F   |     | F  | F  |

## ORGAN COMPOSITIONS

Bassett, Anita Denniston **Nine Hymn-Tune Preludes**
Ludwig Music Publishing Co. 0-08 Key: D

Brandon, George "The Advent of Our God" **The
Concordia Hymn Prelude Series** Volume 2 Edited:
Herbert Gotsch Concordia Publishing House
97-5536 Key: F

Johnson, David "Now My Tongue, the Mystery Telling"
**Deck Thyself with Gladness** Volume 2 Augsburg
Publishing House 11-9101 Key: D

Manz, Paul "Lo! He Comes with Clouds Descending"
**The Parish Organist** Part Twelve Edited: Willem
Mudde Concordia Publishing House 97-4759 Key: D

Beck, Albert **76 Offertories on Hymns & Chorales**
Concordia Publishing House 97-5207 Key: G

Thalben-Ball, George **113 Variations on Hymn Tunes**
Novello & Co., Ltd. Key: Eb

Willan, Healey "Oh, Bless the Lord, My Soul" **The
Parish Organist** Part Three Edited: Heinrich
Fleischer Concordia Publishing House 97-1154
Key: G

## FREE ACCOMPANIMENTS

Hancock, Gerre **Organ Improvisations for Hymn-Singing**
Hinshaw Music Co. HMN-100 Key: F

Noble, T. Tertius **Free Organ Accompaniments to One
Hundred Well-Known Hymn Tunes** J. Fischer & Bros.
#8175 Key: F

St. Vincent

| BA | DC | 1940 | 1982 | LBW | LW | PH | RCV | UCC | UM | WB |
|----|----|------|------|-----|----|----|-----|-----|----|----|
| D  |    |      |      |     |    |    | D   |     |    |    |

## ORGAN COMPOSITIONS

Sowerby, Leo **Meditations on Communion Hymns**
H.W. Gray Co., Inc.  Key: Eb

Salem Harbor

| BA | DC | 1940 | 1982 | LBW | LW | PH | RCV | UCC | UM | WB |
|----|----|------|------|-----|----|----|-----|-----|----|----|
|    |    | g    |      |     |    |    |     |     |    |    |

Salvation

| BA | DC | 1940 | 1982 | LBW | LW | PH | RCV | UCC | UM | WB |
|----|----|------|------|-----|----|----|-----|-----|----|----|
| d  | d  | d    |      |     |    |    |     |     |    | d  |

Salvationist

| BA | DC | 1940 | 1982 | LBW | LW | PH | RCV | UCC | UM | WB |
|----|----|------|------|-----|----|----|-----|-----|----|----|
| F  |    |      |      |     |    |    |     |     |    |    |

Salvator natus

| BA | DC | 1940 | 1982 | LBW | LW | PH | RCV | UCC | UM | WB |
|----|----|------|------|-----|----|----|-----|-----|----|----|
|    |    |      |      |     |    |    |     |     |    |    |

Salve festa dies

| BA | DC | 1940 | 1982 | LBW | LW | PH | RCV | UCC | UM | WB |
|----|----|------|------|-----|----|----|-----|-----|----|----|
|    |    | F    | F    | G   | F  |    | F   |     |    |    |

## ORGAN COMPOSITIONS

Kosche, Kenneth  "Hail Thee, Festival Day"  **The Concordia Hymn Prelude Series**  Volume 11
Edited: Herbert Gotsch  Concordia Publishing House
97-5618  (Two settings) Key: F; Key: G

Wienhorst, Richard  "We Praise You, Lord"  **The Concordia Hymn Prelude Series**  Volume 16  Edited: Herbert Gotsch  Concordia Publishing House
97-5707  Key: G

Salve Regina Coelitum

| BA | DC | 1940 | 1982 | LBW | LW | PH | RCV | UCC | UM | WB |
|----|----|------|------|-----|----|----|-----|-----|----|----|
|    |    |      |      |     |    |    | C   |     |    |    |

## ORGAN COMPOSITIONS

Kreckel, Philip G. **Musica Divina** Volume I  J. Fischer & Bro. #6623  Key: F

Kreckel, Philip G. **Musica Divina** Volume 2  J. Fischer & Bro.  #6715

Salzburg

| | BA | DC | 1940 | 1982 | LBW | LW | PH | RCV | UCC | UM | WB |
|---|---|---|---|---|---|---|---|---|---|---|---|
| | | D | D | D | | | D | D | D | Eb | |

## ORGAN COMPOSITIONS

Pachelbel, Johann   "Songs of Thankfuless and Praise"
**The Concordia Hymn Prelude Series** Volume 6
Edited: Herbert Gotsch   Concordia Publishing
House   97-5612   Key: D

Pasquet, Jean "At the Lamb's High Feast" **Nine Chorale
Preludes** Augsburg Publishing House   11-9298
Key: D

Schultz, Ralph C.   "At the Lamb's High Feast"   **The
Parish Organist** Part Twelve   Edited: Willem
Mudde   Concordia Publishing House   9704759   Key: C

## FREE ACCOMPANIMENTS

Cassler, G. Winson **Organ Descants for Selected Hymn
Tunes** Augsburg Publishing House   11-9304   Key: D

Held, Wilbur **Hymn Preludes and Free Accompaniments**
Volume 6   Augsburg Publishing House   11-9402
Key: D

Johnson, David N.   "At the lamb's high feast" **Free
Organ Accompaniments to Hymns** Volume III General-
Palm Sunday - Easter   Augsburg Publishing House
11-9189   Key: D

Noble, T. Tertius **Fifty Free Organ Accompaniments to
Well Known Hymn Tunes** J. Fischer & Bros.
No. 8430   Key: D

San Rocco

| | BA | DC | 1940 | 1982 | LBW | LW | PH | RCV | UCC | UM | WB |
|---|---|---|---|---|---|---|---|---|---|---|---|
| | | | | C | | | | | | | |

Sancta Civitas

| | BA | DC | 1940 | 1982 | LBW | LW | PH | RCV | UCC | UM | WB |
|---|---|---|---|---|---|---|---|---|---|---|---|
| | | | | F | | | | | F | | |

Sandell

| | BA | DC | 1940 | 1982 | LBW | LW | PH | RCV | UCC | UM | WB |
|---|---|---|---|---|---|---|---|---|---|---|---|
| | | D | | | | | | | | | |

Sandon

| | BA | DC | 1940 | 1982 | LBW | LW | PH | RCV | UCC | UM | WB |
|---|---|---|---|---|---|---|---|---|---|---|---|
| | | F | Eb | | F | | F | | F | F | |

357

# FREE ACCOMPANIMENTS

**Free Harmonizations to Hymn Tunes By Fifty American Composers** Edited: D. DeWitt Wasson  Hinshaw Music, Inc.  HMO-145  Key: G

Sandringham
(See also: Perfect Love)

| | BA | DC | 1940 | 1982 | LBW | LW | PH | RCV | UCC | UM | WB |
|---|---|---|---|---|---|---|---|---|---|---|---|
| | | | Eb | | | | | Eb | | | |

Sandys

| | BA | DC | 1940 | 1982 | LBW | LW | PH | RCV | UCC | UM | WB |
|---|---|---|---|---|---|---|---|---|---|---|---|
| | | | C | | | | | | | | |

# ORGAN COMPOSITIONS

Willan, Healey  **36 Short Preludes and Postludes on Well-Known Hymn Tunes** Set II  C. F. Peters Corporation  No. 6162  Key: C

Sankey

| | BA | DC | 1940 | 1982 | LBW | LW | PH | RCV | UCC | UM | WB |
|---|---|---|---|---|---|---|---|---|---|---|---|
| Eb | | | | | | | | | | Ab | |

Santa Barbara

| | BA | DC | 1940 | 1982 | LBW | LW | PH | RCV | UCC | UM | WB |
|---|---|---|---|---|---|---|---|---|---|---|---|
| | | | | m:d | | | | | | | |

Sarum

| | BA | DC | 1940 | 1982 | LBW | LW | PH | RCV | UCC | UM | WB |
|---|---|---|---|---|---|---|---|---|---|---|---|
| | | | D | | | | Eb | | | Eb | |

# ORGAN COMPOSITIONS

Held, Wilbur "For All the Saints" **Hymn Preludes for the Autumn Festivals** Concordia Publishing House 97-5360  Key: D

Satisfied

| | BA | DC | 1940 | 1982 | LBW | LW | PH | RCV | UCC | UM | WB |
|---|---|---|---|---|---|---|---|---|---|---|---|
| Eb | | | | | | | | | | | |

Savannah

| | BA | DC | 1940 | 1982 | LBW | LW | PH | RCV | UCC | UM | WB |
|---|---|---|---|---|---|---|---|---|---|---|---|
| | D | D | D | D | | | D | | | D | Eb |

# ORGAN COMPOSITIONS

Bouman, Paul  "Thine Forever! God of Love"  **The Parish Organist** Part Twelve  Edited: Willem Mudde Concordia Publishing House  97-4759  Key: Eb

358

## Sawley

| BA | DC | 1940 | 1982 | LBW | LW | PH | RCV | UCC | UM | WB |
|---|---|---|---|---|---|---|---|---|---|---|
| | g | | | | | | | | | |
| BA | DC | 1940 | 1982 | LBW | LW | PH | RCV | UCC | UM | WB |

## Saxby

| BA | DC | 1940 | 1982 | LBW | LW | PH | RCV | UCC | UM | WB |
|---|---|---|---|---|---|---|---|---|---|---|
| | | | | | | Eb | | | | |
| BA | DC | 1940 | 1982 | LBW | LW | PH | RCV | UCC | UM | WB |

## Scales

| BA | DC | 1940 | 1982 | LBW | LW | PH | RCV | UCC | UM | WB |
|---|---|---|---|---|---|---|---|---|---|---|
| F | | | | | | | | | | |
| BA | DC | 1940 | 1982 | LBW | LW | PH | RCV | UCC | UM | WB |

## Scarborough

| BA | DC | 1940 | 1982 | LBW | LW | PH | RCV | UCC | UM | WB |
|---|---|---|---|---|---|---|---|---|---|---|
| | | m:d | | | | | | | | |
| BA | DC | 1940 | 1982 | LBW | LW | PH | RCV | UCC | UM | WB |

## Scheffler

| BA | DC | 1940 | 1982 | LBW | LW | PH | RCV | UCC | UM | WB |
|---|---|---|---|---|---|---|---|---|---|---|
| | | F | | | | | | | | |
| BA | DC | 1940 | 1982 | LBW | LW | PH | RCV | UCC | UM | WB |

## Schmücke dich, o liebe Seele
(See also: Berlin)

| BA | DC | 1940 | 1982 | LBW | LW | PH | RCV | UCC | UM | WB |
|---|---|---|---|---|---|---|---|---|---|---|
| D | Eb | Eb | D | D | | | | Eb | D | D |

## INTONATIONS

Manz, Paul  **Ten Short Intonations on Well Known Hymns**  Augsburg Publishing House  11-9492
Key: D

## ORGAN COMPOSITIONS

Bach, J.S.  **Organ Works**  Volume 2  Edited: Hans Kloz
Urtext of the New Bach Edition  Bärenreiter 5172
Key: Eb

Bach, J.S.  **Orgelwerke** Volume VII  C.F. Peters
Corporation  Nr. 246  Key: Eb

Brahms, Johannes  **Samtliche Orgelwerke**
Breitkopf & Hartel, Key: E

Brahms, Johannes  "Soul Adorn Thyself with Gladness"
**The Parish Organist**  Part Three  Edited:
Heinrich Fleischer  Concordia Publishing House
97-1154  Key:  D

Bach, J.S.  **Organ Works** Volume VIII  Widor-Schweitzer
G. Schirmer  Key: Eb

Bach, J.S.  **Organ Works** Volume VI  Widor-Schweitzer
G. Schirmer  Key: F

Brahms, Johannes "Deck Thyself, My Soul, with Gladness" **Eleven Chorale Preludes** Opus 122 Edited: E. Power Biggs Mercury Music Corporation A-260 Key: E

Dupre, Marcel **Seventy-Nine Chorales for Organ** Opus 28 H. W. Gray Key: Eb

Hessenberg, Kurt "Soul, Adorn Yourself with Gladness" **The Concordia Hymn Prelude Series** Volume 18 Edited: Herbert Gotsch Concordia Publishing House 97-5709 Key: D

Johnson, David N. "Deck Thyself with Joy and Gladness" **Deck Thyself My Soul with Gladness** Augsburg Publishing House 11-9157 Key: D

Johnson, David N. "Soul, Adorn Yourself with Gladness" **Deck Thyself with Gladness** Volume 2 Augsburg Publishing House 11-9101 Key: D

Karg-Elert, Sigfrid "Deck Thyself O Dear Soul" **Choral Improvisations for Organ for Reformation Day, Fast Days, Communion and Funeral Rites** Op. 65, Volume 5 Edited: Robert Leech Bedell Edward B. Marks Music Corp. Key: Eb

Manz, Paul "Soul, Adorn Thyself with Gladness" **Ten Chorale Improvisations** Set III Op. 9 Key: D

Marpurg, Friedrich Wilhelm **Twenty-One Chorale Preludes** Edited: Robert M. Thompson Augsburg Publishing House 11-9506 Key: Eb

Reger, Max **Chorale Preludes for the Church Year from Max Reger, Op. 67** Edited: Alec Wyton Carl Fischer, Inc. 0-4667 Key: Eb

Walther, Johann Gottfried "Chorale Prelude on 'Schmücke dich, o liebe Seele'" **For Manuals Only** Edited: John Christopher McAfee Music Corp. Key: D

FREE ACCOMPANIMENTS

Bunjes, Paul **New Organ Accompaniments for Hymns** Concordia Publishing House 97-5348 Key: D

Held, Wilbur **Hymn Preludes and Free Accompaniments** Volume 6 Augsburg Publishing House 11-9402 Key: D

Schönster Herr Jesu (Münster Gesangbuch)
```
BA   DC   1940 1982 LBW  LW   PH   RCV  UCC  UM   WB
               f
```

Schönster Herr Jesu
(See also: Crusader's Hymn)
```
BA   DC   1940 1982 LBW  LW   PH   RCV  UCC  UM   WB
               Eb   Eb   Eb        Eb
```

ORGAN COMPOSITIONS

Arbatsky, Yury  "Beautiful Saviour"  **The Parish Organist**  Part Three  Edited: Heinrich Fleischer  Concordia Publishing House  97-1154  Key: F

Beck.Albert  **76 Offertories on Hymns & Chorales**  Concordia Publishing House  97-5207  Key: F

Johnson, David N. "Fairest Lord Jesus" **Deck Thyself My Soul with Gladness**  Augsburg Publishing House  11-9157  Key: f

Kreckel, Philip G. **Musica Divina** Volume I J. Fischer & Bro. No. 6623  Key: f

FREE ACCOMPANIMENTS

Bender, Jan **Free Organ Accompaniments to Festival Hymns** Volume I  Augsburg Publishing House  11-9192  Key: Eb

Carson, J. Bert  **Hymn Preludes and Free Accompaniments** Volume 16  Augsburg Publishing House  11-9412  Key: Eb

Cassler, G. Winson  **Organ Descants for Selected Hymn Tunes** Augsburg Publishing House  11-9304 Key: Eb

Norris, Devin  **Hymn Preludes and Free Accompaniments** Volume 15  Augsburg Publishing House. 11-9411  Key: Eb

Schop
(See also: Ermuntre dich)
```
BA   DC   1940 1982 LBW  LW   PH   RCV  UCC  UM   WB
               Eb
```

Schuler
```
BA   DC   1940 1982 LBW  LW   PH   RCV  UCC  UM   WB
C
```

Schumann
| BA | DC | 1940 | 1982 | LBW | LW | PH | RCV | UCC | UM | WB |
|----|----|------|------|-----|----|----|-----|-----|----|----|
| Ab |    |      |      |     |    |    |     | Ab  | Ab |    |

## FREE ACCOMPANIMENTS

**Free Harmonizations to Hymn Tunes By Fifty American Composers** Edited: D. DeWitt Wasson Hinshaw Music, Inc. HMO-145 Key: G

Schütz 19
| BA | DC | 1940 | 1982 | LBW | LW | PH | RCV | UCC | UM | WB |
|----|----|------|------|-----|----|----|-----|-----|----|----|
|    | C  |      |      |     |    |    |     |     |    |    |

Schütz 81
| BA | DC | 1940 | 1982 | LBW | LW | PH | RCV | UCC | UM | WB |
|----|----|------|------|-----|----|----|-----|-----|----|----|
|    | Bb |      |      |     |    |    |     |     |    |    |

Scott
| BA | DC | 1940 | 1982 | LBW | LW | PH | RCV | UCC | UM | WB |
|----|----|------|------|-----|----|----|-----|-----|----|----|
| Ab |    |      |      |     |    |    |     |     |    |    |

Seabury
| BA | DC | 1940 | 1982 | LBW | LW | PH | RCV | UCC | UM | WB |
|----|----|------|------|-----|----|----|-----|-----|----|----|
|    | D  |      |      |     |    |    |     |     |    |    |

Sebastian
| BA | DC | 1940 | 1982 | LBW | LW | PH | RCV | UCC | UM | WB |
|----|----|------|------|-----|----|----|-----|-----|----|----|
|    | F  |      |      |     |    |    |     |     |    |    |

Second Coming
| BA | DC | 1940 | 1982 | LBW | LW | PH | RCV | UCC | UM | WB |
|----|----|------|------|-----|----|----|-----|-----|----|----|
| C  |    |      |      |     |    |    |     |     |    |    |

Seek Ye First
| BA | DC | 1940 | 1982 | LBW | LW | PH | RCV | UCC | UM | WB |
|----|----|------|------|-----|----|----|-----|-----|----|----|
|    |    | D    |      |     |    |    |     |     |    |    |

Seelenbräutigam
| BA | DC | 1940 | 1982 | LBW | LW | PH | RCV | UCC | UM | WB |
|----|----|------|------|-----|----|----|-----|-----|----|----|
| G  |    |      |      | G   | G  |    |     |     |    | G  |

## ORGAN COMPOSITIONS

Bach, J.S. "Jesus, Lead Thou On" **The Parish Organist** Part Three Edited: Heinrich Fleischer Concordia Publishing House 97-1154 Key: G

Beck, Albert **76 Offertories on Hymns & Chorales** Concordia Publishing House 97-5207 Key: G

Blackburn, John  "Bridegroom of Our Soul"  **Wedding Music**  Part II  Concordia Publishing House  97-1370  Key: G

Near, Gerald **Preludes on Four Hymn Tunes**
Augsburg Publishing House  11-828  Key: G

Reger, Max  **Chorale Preludes for the Church Year from Max Reger, Op. 67**  Edited: Alec Wyton  Carl Fischer, Inc.  0-4667  Key: A

Selena

| BA | DC | 1940 | 1982 | LBW | LW | PH | RCV | UCC | UM | WB |
|----|----|------|------|-----|----|----|-----|-----|----|----|
| BA | DC | 1940 | 1982 | LBW | LW | PH | RCV | UCC | UM | WB |
|    |    |      |      |     |    |    |     |     | Ab |    |

Selnecker

| BA | DC | 1940 | 1982 | LBW | LW | PH | RCV | UCC | UM | WB |
|----|----|------|------|-----|----|----|-----|-----|----|----|
| BA | DC | 1940 | 1982 | LBW | LW | PH | RCV | UCC | UM | WB |
| A  |    |      |      |     |    |    |     |     |    |    |

Seminary

| BA | DC | 1940 | 1982 | LBW | LW | PH | RCV | UCC | UM | WB |
|----|----|------|------|-----|----|----|-----|-----|----|----|
| BA | DC | 1940 | 1982 | LBW | LW | PH | RCV | UCC | UM | WB |
| Ab |    |      |      |     |    |    |     |     |    |    |

Septem verba

| BA | DC | 1940 | 1982 | LBW | LW | PH | RCV | UCC | UM | WB |
|----|----|------|------|-----|----|----|-----|-----|----|----|
| BA | DC | 1940 | 1982 | LBW | LW | PH | RCV | UCC | UM | WB |
|    |    |      |      |     | d  |    |     |     |    |    |

ORGAN COMPOSITIONS

Gehrke, Hugo  "Jesus, in Your Dying Woes"  **The Concordia Hymn Prelude Series**  Volume 9  Edited: Herbert Gotsch  Concordia Publishing House  97-5616  Key: d

Seraph
(See also: Bethlehem)

| BA | DC | 1940 | 1982 | LBW | LW | PH | RCV | UCC | UM | WB |
|----|----|------|------|-----|----|----|-----|-----|----|----|
| BA | DC | 1940 | 1982 | LBW | LW | PH | RCV | UCC | UM | WB |

Serenity

| BA | DC | 1940 | 1982 | LBW | LW | PH | RCV | UCC | UM | WB |
|----|----|------|------|-----|----|----|-----|-----|----|----|
| BA | DC | 1940 | 1982 | LBW | LW | PH | RCV | UCC | UM | WB |
| Eb |    |      |      |     |    | D  |     |     | Eb | Eb |

ORGAN COMPOSITIONS

Stearns, Peter Pindar  **Twenty Hymn Preludes**
Coburn Press (Theodore Presser Company) Key: A

FREE ACCOMPANIMENTS

**Free Harmonizations to Hymn Tunes By Fifty American Composers**  Edited: D. DeWitt Wasson  Hinshaw Music, Inc.  HMO-145  Key: Eb

363

## Serug

| BA | DC | 1940 | 1982 | LBW | LW | PH | RCV | UCC | UM | WB |
|---|---|---|---|---|---|---|---|---|---|---|
| A |  |  |  |  |  | Ab |  |  |  |  |

## Seven Joys

| BA | DC | 1940 | 1982 | LBW | LW | PH | RCV | UCC | UM | WB |
|---|---|---|---|---|---|---|---|---|---|---|
|  |  |  |  |  |  |  | G |  |  |  |

## Seventh and James

| BA | DC | 1940 | 1982 | LBW | LW | PH | RCV | UCC | UM | WB |
|---|---|---|---|---|---|---|---|---|---|---|
| Eb |  |  |  |  |  |  |  |  |  |  |

## Sewell

| BA | DC | 1940 | 1982 | LBW | LW | PH | RCV | UCC | UM | WB |
|---|---|---|---|---|---|---|---|---|---|---|
| Bb |  |  |  |  |  |  |  |  |  |  |

## Seymour

| BA | DC | 1940 | 1982 | LBW | LW | PH | RCV | UCC | UM | WB |
|---|---|---|---|---|---|---|---|---|---|---|
| F | F |  |  |  |  |  |  |  | F |  |

## FREE ACCOMPANIMENTS

Noble, T. Tertius **Fifty Free Organ Accompaniments to Well Known Hymn Tunes** J. Fischer & Bros. No. 8430  Key: F

## Shaddick

| BA | DC | 1940 | 1982 | LBW | LW | PH | RCV | UCC | UM | WB |
|---|---|---|---|---|---|---|---|---|---|---|
| D |  |  |  |  |  |  |  |  | D |  |

## Shalom chaverim

| BA | DC | 1940 | 1982 | IBW | LW | PH | RCV | UCC | UM | WB |
|---|---|---|---|---|---|---|---|---|---|---|
|  |  |  | d |  |  |  |  |  |  |  |

## Sharpthorne

| BA | DC | 1940 | 1982 | LBW | LW | PH | RCV | UCC | UM | WB |
|---|---|---|---|---|---|---|---|---|---|---|
|  |  |  | d |  |  |  |  | d |  |  |

## ORGAN COMPOSITIONS

McKinney, Mathilde "Prelude on 'Sharpthorne'" **The Bristol Collection of Contemporary Hymn Tune Preludes for Organ** Vol 3 (edited by Lee Hastings Bristol, Jr.) Key: g

## Sheldonian

| BA | DC | 1940 | 1982 | LBW | LW | PH | RCV | UCC | UM | WB |
|---|---|---|---|---|---|---|---|---|---|---|
|  |  |  | D |  |  |  |  |  |  |  |

Patterson, Kim Kondal   "Filled with the Spirit's Power"
**The Concordia Hymn Prelude Series**  Volume 13
Edited: Herbert Gotsch  Concordia Publishing House
97-5620  Key: D

Sheltering Rock

| BA | DC | 1940 | 1982 | LBW | LW | PH | RCV | UCC | UM | WB |
|----|----|------|------|-----|----|----|-----|-----|----|----|
| Ab |    |      |      |     |    |    |     |     |    |    |

Sheng En

| BA | DC | 1940 | 1982 | LBW | LW | PH | RCV | UCC | UM | WB |
|----|----|------|------|-----|----|----|-----|-----|----|----|
| m:d |   | m:d  |      |     |    |    |     |     | m:d |    |

Shepherds' Hymn

| BA | DC | 1940 | 1982 | LBW | LW | PH | RCV | UCC | UM | WB |
|----|----|------|------|-----|----|----|-----|-----|----|----|
|    |    |      |      |     |    |    | D   |     |    |    |

Shepherds' Pipes

| BA | DC | 1940 | 1982 | LBW | LW | PH | RCV | UCC | UM | WB |
|----|----|------|------|-----|----|----|-----|-----|----|----|
|    |    |      |      |     |    | g  |     |     | g  | g  |

Shepherding

| BA | DC | 1940 | 1982 | LBW | LW | PH | RCV | UCC | UM | WB |
|----|----|------|------|-----|----|----|-----|-----|----|----|
|    |    |      |      | m:f | m:f |   |     |     |    | m:f |

Hillert, Richard  "From Shepherding of Stars" **The
Concordia Hymn Prelude Series**  Volume 5
Edited: Herbert Gotsch  Concordia Publishing
House  97-5611  Key: m:f

Shere

| BA | DC | 1940 | 1982 | LBW | LW | PH | RCV | UCC | UM | WB |
|----|----|------|------|-----|----|----|-----|-----|----|----|
| Bb |    |      |      |     |    |    |     |     |    |    |

Shillingford

| BA | DC | 1940 | 1982 | LBW | LW | PH | RCV | UCC | UM | WB |
|----|----|------|------|-----|----|----|-----|-----|----|----|
|    |    | Ab   |      |     |    |    |     |     |    |    |

Shining Day (Abendlied)

| BA | DC | 1940 | 1982 | LBW | LW | PH | RCV | UCC | UM | WB |
|----|----|------|------|-----|----|----|-----|-----|----|----|
|    |    | F    |      |     |    |    |     |     |    |    |

Shirleyn

| BA | DC | 1940 | 1982 | LBW | LW | PH | RCV | UCC | UM | WB |
|----|----|------|------|-----|----|----|-----|-----|----|----|
|    |    |      |      |     |    |    |     |     | Ab |    |

Shorney

| BA | DC | 1940 | 1982 | LBW | LW | PH | RCV | UCC | UM | WB |
|----|----|------|------|-----|----|----|-----|-----|----|----|
|    |    | c    |      |     |    |    |     |     |    |    |

Shout On
<pre>
Shout On
  BA     DC     1940 1982 LBW   LW     PH     RCV    UCC    UM     WB
  Ab
</pre>

Showalter
<pre>
Showalter
  BA     DC     1940 1982 LBW   LW     PH     RCV    UCC    UM     WB
  Ab
</pre>

Showers of Blessing
<pre>
Showers of Blessing
  BA     DC     1940 1982 LBW   LW     PH     RCV    UCC    UM     WB
  Bb
</pre>

Sicilian Mariners
(See also: Dismissal)
<pre>
  BA     DC     1940 1982 LBW   LW     PH     RCV    UCC    UM     WB
         D      D    D                D      Eb     D      D      D
</pre>

## ORGAN COMPOSITIONS

Johnson, David "Lord, Dismiss Us with Thy Blessing"
**The Parish Organist** Part Twelve  Edited: Willem
Mudde  Concordia Publishing House  97-4759  Key: D

Jordan, Alice "Intrada on Two Hymn Tunes" **Worship
Service Music for the Organist**  Broadman Press
Key: D

## FREE ACCOMPANIMENTS

Gehrke, Hugo  **Hymn Preludes and Free Accompaniments**
Volume 5  Augsburg Publishing House  11-9401
Key: D

Noble, T. Tertius  **Free Organ Accompaniments to One
Hundred Well-Known Hymn Tunes**  J. Fischer & Bros.
#8175  Key: D

Wyton, Alec  **New Shoots from Old Routes**  Sacred
Music Press  KK  279  Key: D

Sieh, hier bin ich
<pre>
Sieh, hier bin ich
  BA     DC     1940 1982 LBW   LW     PH     RCV    UCC    UM     WB
                            c           b
</pre>

Silver Street
<pre>
Silver Street
  BA     DC     1940 1982 LBW   LW     PH     RCV    UCC    UM     WB
         Bb     Bb   Bb
</pre>

Simple Gifts
<pre>
Simple Gifts
  BA     DC     1940 1982 LBW   LW     PH     RCV    UCC    UM     WB
                G
</pre>

## Sims

| BA | DC | 1940 | 1982 | LBW | LW | PH | RCV | UCC | UM | WB |
|----|----|------|------|-----|----|----|-----|-----|----|----|
| F  |    |      |      |     |    |    |     |     | F  |    |

## Sine nomine

| BA | DC | 1940 | 1982 | LBW | LW | PH | RCV | UCC | UM | WB |
|----|----|------|------|-----|----|----|-----|-----|----|----|
| G  | G  | G    | G    | G   | G  | G  | G   | G   | G  | G  |

INTONATIONS

Manz, Paul **Ten Short Intonations on Well Known Hymns** Augsburg Publishing House 11-9492 Key: G

ORGAN COMPOSITIONS

Bouman, Paul "For All the Saints" **The Concordia Hymn Prelude Series** Volume 15 Edited: Herbert Gotsch Concordia Publishing House 97-5706 Key: G

Hutchings, Arthur **Seasonal Preludes for Organ** Novello & Company, Ltd. Key: G

FREE ACCOMPANIMENTS

Bunjes, Paul **New Organ Accompaniments for Hymns** Concordia Publishing House 97-5348 Key: G

Gehrke, Hugo "For All the Saints" **The Parish Organist** Edited: Willem Mudde Concordia Publishing House 97-4759 Key: G

Johnson, David N. **Free Harmonizations of Twelve Hymn Tunes** Augsburg Publishing House 11-9190 Key:G

## Singt dem Herren

| BA | DC | 1940 | 1982 | LBW | LW | PH | RCV | UCC | UM | WB |
|----|----|------|------|-----|----|----|-----|-----|----|----|
|    |    |      | F    |     |    |    |     |     |    |    |

## Sion

| BA | DC | 1940 | 1982 | LBW | LW | PH | RCV | UCC | UM | WB |
|----|----|------|------|-----|----|----|-----|-----|----|----|
|    |    | F    |      |     |    |    |     |     |    |    |

## Siroe

| BA | DC | 1940 | 1982 | LBW | LW | PH | RCV | UCC | UM | WB |
|----|----|------|------|-----|----|----|-----|-----|----|----|
|    |    |      | D    |     |    |    |     |     |    |    |

## Sixth Night

| BA | DC | 1940 | 1982 | LBW | LW | PH | RCV | UCC | UM | WB |
|----|----|------|------|-----|----|----|-----|-----|----|----|
|    |    |      | D    |     |    |    |     |     |    |    |

## Skillings

| BA | DC | 1940 | 1982 | LBW | LW | PH | RCV | UCC | UM | WB |
|----|----|------|------|-----|----|----|-----|-----|----|----|
| Bb |    |      |      |     |    |    |     |     |    |    |

## Slane

| BA | DC | 1940 | 1982 | LBW | LW | PH | RCV | UCC | UM | WB |
|----|----|------|------|-----|----|----|-----|-----|----|----|
| Eb | Eb | Eb   | Eb   | Eb  | Eb | Eb | Eb  | Eb  | Eb | Eb |

### ORGAN COMPOSITIONS

Arnatt, Ronald "Lord of all Hopefulness" **The Parish Organist** Part Twelve Edited: Willem Mudde Concordia Publishing House 97-4759 Key: Eb

Bassett, Anita Denniston **Nine Hymn-Tune Preludes** Ludwig Music Publishing Co. 0-08 Key: G

Bristol, Lee Hastings, Jr. "Prelude on Two Folk Hymns" **The Bristol Collection of Contemporary Hymn Tune Preludes for Organ** Volume 3 (edited by Lee Hastings Bristol, Jr.) Harold Flammer, Key:C

Hopson, Hal H. **Five Preludes on Familiar Hymns** Harold Flammer, Inc. HF-5123 Key: G

Lovelace, Austin **Fourteen Hymn Preludes** Augsburg Publishing House 11-6152 Key: E

Manz, Paul "Be Thou My Vision" **Ten Chorale Improvisations** Set IX Op. 21 Concordia Publishing House 97-5556 Key: Eb

### FREE ACCOMPANIMENTS

Arnatt, Ronald **Hymn Preludes and Free Accompaniments** Volume 9 Augsburg Publishing House 11-9405 Key: Eb

**Free Harmonizations to Hymn Tunes By Fifty American Composers** Edited: D. DeWitt Wasson Hinshaw Music, Inc. HMO-145 Key: Eb

Hancock, Gerre **Organ Improvisations for Hymn-Singing** Hinshaw Music Co. HMO-100 Key: Eb

Wyton, Alec **New Shoots from Old Routes** Sacred Music Press KK 279 Key: Eb

## Sleepers Wake
(See also: Wachet auf)

| BA | DC | 1940 | 1982 | LBW | LW | PH | RCV | UCC | UM | WB |
|----|----|------|------|-----|----|----|-----|-----|----|----|
|    |    | C    |      |     |    |    | C   |     |    |    |

So giebst du nun
| BA | DC | 1940 | 1982 | LBW | LW | PH | RCV | UCC | UM | WB |
|----|----|------|------|-----|----|----|-----|-----|----|----|
|    |    | f    |      |     |    |    |     |     |    |    |

So nimm denn meine Hände
| BA | DC | 1940 | 1982 | LBW | LW | PH | RCV | UCC | UM | WB |
|----|----|------|------|-----|----|----|-----|-----|----|----|
|    |    | D    |      |     | D  |    |     |     |    |    |

Sohren
| BA | DC | 1940 | 1982 | LBW | LW | PH | RCV | UCC | UM | WB |
|----|----|------|------|-----|----|----|-----|-----|----|----|
|    | EB |      |      |     |    |    |     |     |    |    |

Solemnis haec festivitas
| BA | DC | 1940 | 1982 | LBW | LW | PH | RCV | UCC | UM | WB |
|----|----|------|------|-----|----|----|-----|-----|----|----|
|    | F  | D    |      |     |    |    | D   |     |    |    |

Solid Rock
| BA | DC | 1940 | 1982 | LBW | LW | PH | RCV | UCC | UM | WB |
|----|----|------|------|-----|----|----|-----|-----|----|----|
| F  |    |      |      |     |    |    |     |     |    |    |

Sollt ich meinem Gott
(See also: Stuttgart)
| BA | DC | 1940 | 1982 | LBW | LW | PH | RCV | UCC | UM | WB |
|----|----|------|------|-----|----|----|-----|-----|----|----|
|    |    |      |      |     | D  |    |     |     |    |    |

## ORGAN COMPOSITIONS

Doles, Johann Friedrich **Chorale Preludes by Masters of the 18th & 19th Centuries** Volume I Edited: Walter Buszin Concordia Publishing House Key: c

Karg-Elert, Sigfrid "Shall I Not Sing Unto My Lord?" **Choral Improvisations for Organ for Passion Week** Op. 65, Volume 2 Edward B. Marks Music Corp. Key: d

Manz, Paul "I Will Sing My Maker's Praises" **Ten Chorale Improvisations** Set V Op. 14 Concordia Publishing House 97-5257 Key: c

## FREE ACCOMPANIMENTS

Bunjes, Paul **New Organ Accompaniments for Hymns** Concordia Publishing House 97-5348 Key: g

Solothurn
| BA | DC | 1940 | 1982 | LBW | LW | PH | RCV | UCC | UM | WB |
|----|----|------|------|-----|----|----|-----|-----|----|----|
|    |    | D    |      |     |    |    |     |     |    |    |

ORGAN COMPOSITIONS

Janson, Thomas "How Blessed Is This Place, O Lord" **The Concordia Hymn Prelude Series** Volume 15 Edited: Herbert Gotsch Concordia Publishing House 97-5706 Key: D

Somebody's Knockin'

| BA | DC | 1940 | 1982 | LBW | LW | PH | RCV | UCC | UM | WB |
|----|----|----|----|----|----|----|----|----|----|----|
| Eb |    |      |      |     |    |    |     | Eb  |    |    |

Something for Jesus

| BA | DC | 1940 | 1982 | LBW | LW | PH | RCV | UCC | UM | WB |
|----|----|----|----|----|----|----|----|----|----|----|
| G  | G  |      |      |     |    | G  |     |     | G  |    |

Song 1 (Gibbons)

| BA | DC | 1940 | 1982 | LBW | LW | PH | RCV | UCC | UM | WB |
|----|----|----|----|----|----|----|----|----|----|----|
|    |    | F    | F    | F   |    | F  |     |     |    | F  |

ORGAN COMPOSITIONS

Gieschen, Thomas "Lord, Who the Night You Were Betrayed" **The Concordia Hymn Prelude Series** Volume 18 Edited: Herbert Gotsch Concordia Publishing House 97-5709 Key: F

Willan, Healey **36 Short Preludes and Postludes on Well-Known Hymn Tunes** Set II C. F. Peters Corporation No. 6162 Key: F

Song 2

| BA | DC | 1940 | 1982 | LBW | LW | PH | RCV | UCC | UM | WB |
|----|----|----|----|----|----|----|----|----|----|----|
|    |    |      | b    |     |    |    |     |     |    |    |

Song 5

| BA | DC | 1940 | 1982 | LBW | LW | PH | RCV | UCC | UM | WB |
|----|----|----|----|----|----|----|----|----|----|----|
|    |    |      |      |     |    | e  |     | e   |    |    |

FREE ACCOMPANIMENTS

**Free Harmonizations to Hymn Tunes By Fifty American Composers** Edited: D. DeWitt Wasson Hinshaw Music, Inc. HMO-145 Key: e

Song 13 (Canterbury)

| BA | DC | 1940 | 1982 | LBW | LW | PH | RCV | UCC | UM | WB |
|----|----|----|----|----|----|----|----|----|----|----|
|    |    |      |      |     |    | D  |     |     |    |    |

Song 13 (Gibbons)

| BA | DC | 1940 | 1982 | LBW | LW | PH | RCV | UCC | UM | WB |
|----|----|----|----|----|----|----|----|----|----|----|
| D  | D  | EB   | D    | D   | D  |    |     |     |    | D  |

# INTONATIONS

Videro, Finn **Twenty-One Hymn Intonations** Concordia
Publishing House 97-5004 Key: Eb

## ORGAN COMPOSITIONS

Beechey, Gwilym **Chorale Prelude on Gibbons' Song 13**
Harold Flammer, Inc. HH-5032 Key: Eb

Coleman, Henry "Holy Spirit, Light Divine" **The
Concordia Hymn Prelude Series** Volume 13
Edited: Herbert Gotsch Concordia Publishing House
97-5620 Key: Eb

Willan, Healey "Song 13" or "Light Divine", by Orlando
Gibbons **Six Chorale Preludes** Set I Concordia
Publishing House OC 220 Key: Eb

## FREE ACCOMPANIMENTS

**Free Harmonizations to Hymn Tunes By Fifty American
Composers** Edited: D. DeWitt Wasson Hinshaw
Music, Inc. HMO-145 Key: Eb

Song 22

| BA | DC | 1940 | 1982 | LBW | LW | PH | RCV | UCC | UM | WB |
|----|----|------|------|-----|----|----|-----|-----|----|----|
|    |    | Eb   | F    |     |    |    |     |     |    |    |

Song 24 (Gibbons)

| BA | DC | 1940 | 1982 | LBW | LW | PH | RCV | UCC | UM | WB |
|----|----|------|------|-----|----|----|-----|-----|----|----|
|    |    |      |      |     |    | e  |     | e   |    |    |

## ORGAN COMPOSITIONS

Willan, Healey "Song 24. Gibbons: Lighten the
Darkness" **Ten Hymn Preludes** Set I
C. F. Peters Corporation No. 6011 Key: e

Song 34 (Fletcher)
(See also: Angel's Song)

| BA | DC | 1940 | 1982 | LBW | LW | PH | RCV | UCC | UM | WB |
|----|----|------|------|-----|----|----|-----|-----|----|----|
|    |    | Eb   | Eb   | Eb  |    |    |     |     |    |    |

Song 46 (Fletcher)

| BA | DC | 1940 | 1982 | LBW | LW | PH | RCV | UCC | UM | WB |
|----|----|------|------|-----|----|----|-----|-----|----|----|
|    |    | F    | F    |     |    |    | F   |     | F  |    |

Song 67 (Gibbons)

| BA | DC | 1940 | 1982 | LBW | LW | PH | RCV | UCC | UM | WB |
|----|----|------|------|-----|----|----|-----|-----|----|----|
|    |    | D    | D    | D   | D  |    |     |     |    | D  |

ORGAN COMPOSITIONS

Thalben-Ball, George **113 Variations on Hymn Tunes**
Novello & Co., Ltd. Key: D

Willan, Healey **36 Short Preludes and Postludes on**
**Well-Known Hymn Tunes** Set III C. F. Peters
Corporation No. 6163 Key: D

FREE ACCOMPANIMENTS

Noble, T. Tertius **Fifty Free Organ Accompaniments to**
**Well Known Hymn Tunes** J. Fischer & Bros.
No. 8430 Key: D

<u>Song 67</u> (St. Matthias)
BA   DC   1940 1982 LBW  LW   PH    RCV   UCC   UM    WB
                                 D

<u>Song of the Holy Spirit</u>
BA   DC   1940 1982 LBW  LW   PH    RCV   UCC   UM    WB
                               D

<u>Song of the Yangtze Boatman</u>
BA   DC   1940 1982 LBW  LW   PH    RCV   UCC   UM    WB
g

<u>Sonne der Gerechtigkeit</u>
BA   DC   1940 1982 LBW  LW   PH    RCV   UCC   UM    WB
               D    D    D

ORGAN COMPOSITIONS

Beck, Theodore "At the Lamb's High Feast We Sing"
**Hymn Preludes for Holy Communion** Volume I
Concordia Publishing House 97-5486 Key: D

Bender, Jan "At the Lamb's High Feast" **The Concordia**
**Hymn Prelude Series** Volume 18 Edited: Herbert
Gotsch Concordia Publishing House 97-5709
Key: D

Gehrke, Hugo "At the Lamb's High Feast We Sing" **The**
**Concordia Hymn Prelude Series** Volume 11
Edited: Herbert Gotsch Concordia Publishing House
97-5618 Key: D

Johnson, David "At the Lamb's High Feast We Sing"
**Deck Thyself with Gladness** Volume 2 Augsburg
Publishing House 11-9101 Key: D

Manz, Paul "At the Lamb's High Feast" **Ten Chorale Improvisations** Opus 16 Set VI  Concordia Publishing House 97-5305  Key: D

Shack, David "At the Lamb's High Feast We Sing" **Preludes on Ten Hymntunes** Augsburg Publishing House  11-9363  Key: D

FREE ACCOMPANIMENTS

Bender, Jan  **Hymn Preludes and Free Accompaniments** Volume 1  Augsburg Publishing House  11-9397 Key: D

**South Gore**

| BA | DC | 1940 | 1982 | LBW | LW | PH | RCV | UCC | UM | WB |
|----|----|------|------|-----|----|----|-----|-----|----|----|
|    | F  |      |      |     |    |    |     |     |    |    |

**Southwell** (Damon's Psalmes, 1579)

| BA | DC | 1940 | 1982 | LBW | LW | PH | RCV | UCC | UM | WB |
|----|----|------|------|-----|----|----|-----|-----|----|----|
| e  |    | e    | e    | e   |    | e  | e   |     | e  |    |

ORGAN COMPOSITIONS

Beck, Theodore  "Not All the Blood of Beasts"  **The Concordia Hymn Prelude Series** Volume 9  Edited: Herbert Gotsch  Concordia Publishing House 97-5616  Key: e

FREE ACCOMPANIMENTS

Busarow, Donald **All Praise to You Eternal God** Augsburg Publishing House 11-9076  Key: e

Canning, Thomas "O Perfect Life of Love"  **The Parish Organist** Part Three  Edited: Heinrich Fleischer Concordia Publishing House  97-1154  Key: e

Miles, George Th.  "O Perfect Life of love"  **The Parish Organist** Part Seven  Music for Lent, Palm Sunday and Holy Week  Edited:  Erich Goldschmidt  Concordia Publishing House  97-1403 Key:  e

Willan, Healey  **36 Short Preludes and Postludes on Well-Known Hymn Tunes** Set III  C. F. Peters Corporation  No. 6163  Key:  e

**Southwell** (Irons)

| BA | DC | 1940 | 1982 | LBW | LW | PH | RCV | UCC | UM | WB |
|----|----|------|------|-----|----|----|-----|-----|----|----|
|    | Eb |      |      |     |    |    |     |     |    |    |

Spanish Chant

| BA | DC | 1940 | 1982 | LBW | LW | PH | RCV | UCC | UM | WB |
|----|----|------|------|-----|----|----|-----|-----|----|----|
|    |    | Ab   |      |     |    |    |     |     |    |    |

ORGAN COMPOSITIONS

Bunjes, Paul  "Saviour, When in Dust to Thee"  **The Parish Organist**  Part Three  Edited: Heinrich Fleischer  Concordia Publishing House  97-1154 Key: Ab

FREE ACCOMPANIMENTS

Noble, T. Tertius  **Fifty Free Organ Accompaniments to Well Known Hymn Tunes**  J. Fischer & Bros. No. 8430  Key: Ab

Spanish Hymn

| BA | DC | 1940 | 1982 | LBW | LW | PH | RCV | UCC | UM | WB |
|----|----|------|------|-----|----|----|-----|-----|----|----|
| Ab |    |      |      |     |    |    |     | Ab  | A  |    |

Spires
(See also: Erhalt uns, Herr)

| BA | DC | 1940 | 1982 | LBW | LW | PH | RCV | UCC | UM | WB |
|----|----|------|------|-----|----|----|-----|-----|----|----|
|    |    | e    |      |     |    |    | e   |     |    |    |

Splendor Paternae

| BA | DC | 1940 | 1982 | LBW | LW | PH | RCV | UCC | UM | WB |
|----|----|------|------|-----|----|----|-----|-----|----|----|
|    |    | m:d  | m:d  | m:d | m:d | m:d |     |     |    |    |

Springbrook

| BA | DC | 1940 | 1982 | LBW | LW | PH | RCV | UCC | UM | WB |
|----|----|------|------|-----|----|----|-----|-----|----|----|
| F  |    |      |      |     |    |    |     |     |    |    |

Sri Lampang

| BA | DC | 1940 | 1982 | LBW | LW | PH | RCV | UCC | UM | WB |
|----|----|------|------|-----|----|----|-----|-----|----|----|
|    |    |      |      |     |    |    |     |     | m:d |   |

Stabat Mater (Gesangbuch)

| BA | DC | 1940 | 1982 | LBW | LW | PH | RCV | UCC | UM | WB |
|----|----|------|------|-----|----|----|-----|-----|----|----|
|    |    |      |      | F   |    |    | F   |     |    |    |

FREE ACCOMPANIMENTS

Bobb, Barry L.  "At the Cross, Her Station Keeping"  **The Concordia Hymn Prelude Series**  Volume 9 Edited: Herbert Gotsch  Concordia Publishing House 97-5616  Key: F

Gehrke, Hugo  **Hymn Preludes and Free Accompaniments** Volume 5  Augsburg Publishing House  11-9401 Key: F

Stabat Mater (Plainsong)
BA  DC  1940 1982 LBW  LW  PH  RCV  UCC  UM  WB
m:g  m:g

## ORGAN COMPOSITIONS

Kreckel, Philip G. **Musica Divina** Volume I  J. Fischer
& Bro. No. 6623  Key: Ab

Stabat Mater dolorosa
BA  DC  1940 1982 LBW  LW  PH  RCV  UCC  UM  WB
m:f

Stamphill
BA  DC  1940 1982 LBW  LW  PH  RCV  UCC  UM  WB
G

Stand by Me
BA  DC  1940 1982 LBW  LW  PH  RCV  UCC  UM  WB
Eb

Star in the East
BA  DC  1940 1982 LBW  LW  PH  RCV  UCC  UM  WB
e

Star Spangled Banner, The
(See also: National Anthem)
BA  DC  1940 1982 LBW  LW  PH  RCV  UCC  UM  WB
Bb

## ORGAN COMPOSITIONS

Buck, Dudley  "Concert Variations on 'The Star Spangled
Banner'"  **19th Century American Organ Music**
Cleveland Chapter AGO  Key: Bb

Steadfast
(See also: O Gott, du frommer Gott)
BA  DC  1940 1982 LBW  LW  PH  RCV  UCC  UM  WB
a               a

Stecht auf, ihr lieben Kinderlein
BA  DC  1940 1982 LBW  LW  PH  RCV  UCC  UM  WB
D

Steiner
BA  DC  1940 1982 LBW  LW  PH  RCV  UCC  UM  WB
F

Stella
BA  DC  1940 1982 LBW  LW  PH  RCV  UCC  UM  WB
Eb

## Stephanos

| BA | DC | 1940 | 1982 | LBW | LW | PH | RCV | UCC | UM | WB |
|----|----|------|------|-----|----|----|-----|-----|----|----|
| G | G | | | G | F | | | | G | |

### ORGAN COMPOSITIONS

Beck, Albert **76 Offertories on Hymns & Chorales** Concordia Publishing House 97-5207 Key: G

Engle, James "I Am Trusting You, Lord Jesus" **Preludes on Six Hymn Tunes** Augsburg Publishing House 11-9364 Key: F

Lenel, Ludwig "I Am Trusting Thee, Lord Jesus" **The Parish Organist** Part Three Edited: Heinrich Fleischer Concordia Publishing House 97-1154 Key: G

## Stevens

| BA | DC | 1940 | 1982 | LBW | LW | PH | RCV | UCC | UM | WB |
|----|----|------|------|-----|----|----|-----|-----|----|----|
| Eb | | | | | | | | | | |

## Stewart

| BA | DC | 1940 | 1982 | LBW | LW | PH | RCV | UCC | UM | WB |
|----|----|------|------|-----|----|----|-----|-----|----|----|
| | Eb | | | | | | | | | |

## Stille Nacht
(See also: Holy Night)

| BA | DC | 1940 | 1982 | LBW | LW | PH | RCV | UCC | UM | WB |
|----|----|------|------|-----|----|----|-----|-----|----|----|
| Bb | Bb | | Bb | Bb | Bb | Bb | C | Bb | Bb | Bb |

### ORGAN COMPOSITIONS

Beck, Albert **76 Offertories on Hymns & Chorales** Concordia Publishing House 97-5207 Key: C

Black, Charles "Silent Night" **The Lutheran Organist** H.W. Gray Co. Key: Bb

Bouman, Paul "Silent Night, Holy Night" **The Concordia Hymn Prelude Series** Volume 5 Edited: Herbert Gotsch 97-5611 Key: Bb

Cherwien, David "Silent Night,HolyNight" **Interpretations Based on Hymn-tunes** Book IV A.M.S.I. OR-9 Key: Bb

Diemer, Emma Lou "Silent Night, Holy Night" **Carols for Organ** The Sacred Music Press Key: C

Held, Wilbur "Silent Night" **A Nativity Suite** Concordia Publishing House 97-4461 Key: C

Kreckel, Philip G. **Musica Divina** Volume I   J. Fischer & Bro.  No. 6623  Key: Db

Walton, Kenneth **Fantasia on Four Christmas Carols** Broadcast Music Inc. Key: F

FREE ACCOMPANIMENTS

Bender, Jan  **Hymn Preludes and Free Accompaniments** Volume 1  Augsburg Publishing House 11-9397 Key: Bb

Cassler, G. Winston  **Organ Descants for Selected Hymn Tunes** Augsburg Publishing House  11-9304  Key: Bb

Goode, Jack C.  **Thirty-Four Changes on Hymn Tunes** H. W. Gray Co.  GB  644  Key: Bb

## Stockport
(See also: Yorkshire)

## Stockton

| BA | DC | 1940 | 1982 | LBW | LW | PH | RCV | UCC | UM | WB |
|----|----|------|------|-----|----|----|-----|-----|----|----|
| G |  |  |  |  |  |  |  |  | G |  |

ORGAN COMPOSITIONS

Thalben-Ball, George  **113 Variations on Hymn Tunes** Novello & Co., Ltd.  Key: Eb

## Stories of Jesus

| BA | DC | 1940 | 1982 | LBW | LW | PH | RCV | UCC | UM | WB |
|----|----|------|------|-----|----|----|-----|-----|----|----|
|  |  |  |  |  |  |  |  |  | C |  |

## Störl

| BA | DC | 1940 | 1982 | LBW | LW | PH | RCV | UCC | UM | WB |
|----|----|------|------|-----|----|----|-----|-----|----|----|
|  |  |  |  |  |  |  |  |  |  | Db |
| D |  |  |  |  |  |  |  |  |  |  |

## Story of Jesus

| BA | DC | 1940 | 1982 | LBW | LW | PH | RCV | UCC | UM | WB |
|----|----|------|------|-----|----|----|-----|-----|----|----|
| Eb |  |  |  |  |  |  |  |  |  |  |

## Stracathro

| BA | DC | 1940 | 1982 | LBW | LW | PH | RCV | UCC | UM | WB |
|----|----|------|------|-----|----|----|-----|-----|----|----|
| Db |  |  |  |  | D |  |  |  |  |  |

ORGAN COMPOSITIONS

Thalben-Ball, George  **113 Variations on Hymn Tunes** Novello & Co., Ltd.  Key: Db

# FREE ACCOMPANIMENTS

Noble, T. Tertius **Fifty Free Organ Accompaniments to Well Known Hymn Tunes** J. Fischer & Bros. No. 8430  Key: Db

**Straf mich nicht**

| BA | DC | 1940 | 1982 | LBW | LW | PH | RCV | UCC | UM | WB |
|----|----|------|------|-----|----|----|-----|-----|----|----|
|    |    |      | C    | D   | D  |    |     |     |    |    |

**Sturges**

| BA | DC | 1940 | 1982 | LBW | LW | PH | RCV | UCC | UM | WB |
|----|----|------|------|-----|----|----|-----|-----|----|----|
|    |    | f    |      |     |    |    |     |     |    |    |

**Stuttgart**

| BA | DC | 1940 | 1982 | LBW | LW | PH | RCV | UCC | UM | WB |
|----|----|------|------|-----|----|----|-----|-----|----|----|
| G  | F  | F    | F    |     |    | F  | F   | F   | G  | F  |

## ORGAN COMPOSITIONS

Bender, Jan  "Come, Thou Long-Expected Jesus"  **The Parish Organist**  Part Twelve  Edited: Willem Mudde  Concordia Publishing House  97-4759  Key:  F

Bristol, Lee Hastings "Chorale Prelude on 'Stuttgart'" **The Bristol Collection of Contemporary Hymn Tune Preludes for Organ** Volume One  Key: G Harold Flammer, Inc.

Pasquet, Jean "Earth Has Many a Noble City" **Nine Chorale Preludes** Augsburg Publishing House 11-9298  Key: F

Thalben-Ball, George  **113 Variations on Hymn Tunes** Novello & Co., Ltd.  Key: G

## FREE ACCOMPANIMENTS

Goode, Jack C.  **Thirty-Four Changes on Hymn Tunes** H. W. Gray Co.  GB  644  Key: F

Hancock, Gerre  **Organ Improvisations for Hymn-Singing** Hinshaw Music Co.  HMO-100  Key: F

Noble, T. Tertius  **Free Organ Accompaniments to One Hundred Well-Known Hymn Tunes**  J. Fischer & Bros. #8175  Key: F

Wyton, Alec  **New Shoots from Old Routes**  Sacred Music Press KK  279  Key: F

Such, wer da will

| BA | DC | 1940 | 1982 | LBW | LW | PH | RCV | UCC | UM | WB |
|---|---|---|---|---|---|---|---|---|---|---|
|  |  |  |  |  | D |  |  |  |  |  |

## ORGAN COMPOSITIONS

Walcha, Helmut **Chorale Preludes** II   C.F. Peters
Corporation   Nr. 4871  Key: D

Sullivan

| BA | DC | 1940 | 1982 | LBW | LW | PH | RCV | UCC | UM | WB |
|---|---|---|---|---|---|---|---|---|---|---|
| G |  |  |  |  |  |  |  |  |  |  |

Sumner

| BA | DC | 1940 | 1982 | LBW | LW | PH | RCV | UCC | UM | WB |
|---|---|---|---|---|---|---|---|---|---|---|
|  |  | D | D |  |  |  |  |  |  |  |

Sunlight

| BA | DC | 1940 | 1982 | LBW | LW | PH | RCV | UCC | UM | WB |
|---|---|---|---|---|---|---|---|---|---|---|
| F |  |  |  |  |  |  |  |  |  |  |

Sunshine

| BA | DC | 1940 | 1982 | LBW | LW | PH | RCV | UCC | UM | WB |
|---|---|---|---|---|---|---|---|---|---|---|
| Ab |  |  |  |  |  |  |  |  |  |  |

Suomi

| BA | DC | 1940 | 1982 | LBW | LW | PH | RCV | UCC | UM | WB |
|---|---|---|---|---|---|---|---|---|---|---|
|  |  |  |  |  |  |  |  |  |  |  |

Supplication

| BA | DC | 1940 | 1982 | LBW | LW | PH | RCV | UCC | UM | WB |
|---|---|---|---|---|---|---|---|---|---|---|
|  |  | d |  |  |  |  |  |  |  |  |

Surabaja

| BA | DC | 1940 | 1982 | LBW | LW | PH | RCV | UCC | UM | WB |
|---|---|---|---|---|---|---|---|---|---|---|
| G |  |  |  |  |  |  |  |  |  |  |

Surette

| BA | DC | 1940 | 1982 | LBW | LW | PH | RCV | UCC | UM | WB |
|---|---|---|---|---|---|---|---|---|---|---|
|  |  |  |  |  |  |  |  |  | Eb |  |

Surrender

| BA | DC | 1940 | 1982 | LBW | LW | PH | RCV | UCC | UM | WB |
|---|---|---|---|---|---|---|---|---|---|---|
| D |  |  |  |  |  |  |  |  |  |  |

Surrey

| BA | DC | 1940 | 1982 | LBW | LW | PH | RCV | UCC | UM | WB |
|---|---|---|---|---|---|---|---|---|---|---|
|  |  |  | F |  |  |  |  |  |  |  |

Sursum corda (Smith)

| BA | DC | 1940 | 1982 | LBW | LW | PH | RCV | UCC | UM | WB |
|---|---|---|---|---|---|---|---|---|---|---|
|  |  | D |  |  | D | D | D |  |  | D |

**Sussex Carol**

| BA | DC | 1940 | 1982 | LBW | LW | PH | RCV | UCC | UM | WB |
|----|----|------|------|-----|----|----|-----|-----|----|----|
|    |    |      |      |     | F  |    |     | G   |    |    |

## ORGAN COMPOSITIONS

Engel, James  "On Christmas Night All Christians Sing"
**The Concordia Hymn Prelude Series**  Volume 5
Edited: Herbert Gotsch  97-5611  Key: F

Haan, Raymond H. "Invention 'On Christmas Night'"
**Suite of Organ Carols**  Augsburg Publishing
House  Key: F

Haan, Raymond H.  **Variations on Sussex Carol**
Concordia Publishing House  97-5871  Key: G

Miles,  George  Theophilus "On  Christmas  Night  All
Christians Sing"  **The Parish Organist**  Part Five
Advent and Christmas  Concordia Publishing House
97-1382  Key: G

**Swabia**

| BA | DC | 1940 | 1982 | LBW | LW | PH | RCV | UCC | UM | WB |
|----|----|------|------|-----|----|----|-----|-----|----|----|
|    |    | D    |      |     |    |    | D   |     |    |    |

## FREE ACCOMPANIMENTS

Busarow, Donald **All Praise to You Eternal God**
Augsburg Publishing House  11-9076  Key: D

**Swedish Litany**

| BA | DC | 1940 | 1982 | LBW | LW | PH | RCV | UCC | UM | WB |
|----|----|------|------|-----|----|----|-----|-----|----|----|
|    |    | e    |      |     |    | e  |     |     |    |    |

**Sweet By and By**

| BA | DC | 1940 | 1982 | LBW | LW | PH | RCV | UCC | UM | WB |
|----|----|------|------|-----|----|----|-----|-----|----|----|
| G  |    |      |      |     |    |    |     |     |    |    |

**Sweet Hour**

| BA | DC | 1940 | 1982 | LBW | LW | PH | RCV | UCC | UM | WB |
|----|----|------|------|-----|----|----|-----|-----|----|----|
| C  |    |      |      |     |    |    |     |     | D  |    |

## ORGAN COMPOSITIONS

Jordan, Alice "Sweet Hour of Prayer" **A Season and
A Time**  Broadman Press 4570-37  Key: C

**Sweet Story**

| BA | DC | 1940 | 1982 | LBW | LW | PH | RCV | UCC | UM | WB |
|----|----|------|------|-----|----|----|-----|-----|----|----|
|    |    |      |      |     |    | D  |     |     |    |    |

Sweetest Name
    BA   DC   1940 1982 LBW  LW    PH    RCV   UCC   UM    WB
    Ab

Sweney
    BA   DC   1940 1982 LBW  LW    PH    RCV   UCC   UM    WB
    Ab

# T

Tabernacle
    BA   DC   1940 1982 LBW  LW    PH    RCV   UCC   UM    WB
    Eb

Tabor
    BA   DC   1940 1982 LBW  LW    PH    RCV   UCC   UM    WB
    Ab

Tallis' Canon
  (See also: The Eighth Tune)
    BA   DC   1940 1982 LBW  LW    PH    RCV   UCC   UM    WB
    G    G    G           G    G    G    G    G    G     G

ORGAN COMPOSITIONS

Bristol, Lee Hastings Jr. "Partita on 'Tallis Canon'"
**The Bristol Collection of Contemporary Hymn Tune
Preludes for Organ** Volume 3 Edited:  Lee
Hastings Bristol Jr.,  Harold Flammer  Key: A

Manz, Paul **Ten Chorale Improvisations** Op. 5
Concordia Publishing House 97-4554  Key: Ab

FREE ACCOMPANIMENTS

Bender, Jan  **Hymn Preludes and Free Accompaniments**
Volume 1  Augsburg Publishing House  11-9397
Key: G

Busarow, Donald  **All Praise to You Eternal God**
Augsburg Publishing House  11-9076  Key: G

Cassler, G. Winston **Organ Descants for Selected Hymn
Tunes** Augsburg Publishing House  11-9304  Key: G

Johnson, David N.  **Free Harmonizations of Twelve Hymn
Tunes** Augsburg Publishing House  11-9190  Key: G

Noble, T. Tertius  **Free Organ Accompaniments to 100
Well-Known Hymn Tunes**  J. Fischer & Bros.
#8175  Key: G

Rohlig, Harald **Free Organ Accompaniments to Hymns**
Augsburg Publishing House 11-7179 Key: G

Wetzler, Robert **Free Organ Accompaniment to Hymns**
Volume II Advent-Christmas- Epiphany Augsburg
Publishing House 11-9187 Key: G

<u>Tallis' Ordinal</u>

| BA | DC | 1940 | 1982 | LBW | LW | PH | RCV | UCC | UM | WB |
|----|----|------|------|-----|----|----|-----|-----|----|----|
| Eb | Eb | D    | D    |     |    | D  | D   |     | Eb | D  |

## ORGAN COMPOSITIONS

Haan, Raymond H. **A Second Book of Contemplative Hymn
Tune Preludes** Harold Flammer, Inc. HG-5127
Key: D

Rohlig, Harald "O Where are Kings and Empires Now"
**The Parish Organist** Part Twelve Edited: Willem
Mudde Concordia Publishing House 97-4759 Key: D

Thalben-Ball, George **113 Variations on Hymn Tunes**
Novello & Co., Ltd. Key: D

Willan, Healey **Ten Hymn Preludes** Set II C. F.
Peters Corporation 6012 Key: D

## FREE ACCOMPANIMENTS

Noble, T. Tertius **Fifty Free Organ Accompaniments to
Well Known Hymn Tunes** J. Fischer & Bros.
No. 8430 Key: D

<u>Tana mana dhana</u>

| BA | DC | 1940 | 1982 | LBW | LW | PH | RCV | UCC | UM | WB |
|----|----|------|------|-----|----|----|-----|-----|----|----|
|    |    |      |      |     |    | m:d|     |     |    |    |

<u>Tandanei</u>

| BA | DC | 1940 | 1982 | LBW | LW | PH | RCV | UCC | UM | WB |
|----|----|------|------|-----|----|----|-----|-----|----|----|
|    |    |      | F    |     |    |    |     |     |    |    |

<u>Tantum ergo</u>
(See also: Dulce carmen)

| BA | DC | 1940 | 1982 | LBW | LW | PH | RCV | UCC | UM | WB |
|----|----|------|------|-----|----|----|-----|-----|----|----|
|    |    | m:eb | m:eb |     |    |    |     |     | G  |    |

## INTONATIONS

Manz, Paul **Ten Short Intonations on Well Known
Hymns** Augsburg Publishing House 11-9492
Key: G

Taylor Hall

| BA | DC | 1940 | 1982 | LBW | LW | PH | RCV | UCC | UM | WB |
|---|---|---|---|---|---|---|---|---|---|---|
|   |   | D |   |   |   |   |   |   |   |   |

Te Deum

(See also: Grosser Gott)

| BA | DC | 1940 | 1982 | LBW | LW | PH | RCV | UCC | UM | WB |
|---|---|---|---|---|---|---|---|---|---|---|
|   |   | F |   |   |   |   | F |   |   |   |

INTONATIONS

Manz, Paul **Ten Short Intonations on Well Known Hymns** Augsburg Publishing House 11-9492 Key: F

FREE ACCOMPANIMENTS

Cassler, G. Winston **Organ Descants for Selected Hymn Tunes** Augsburg Publishing House 11-9304 Key: F

Te lucis ante terminum (Sarum)

| BA | DC | 1940 | 1982 | LBW | LW | PH | RCV | UCC | UM | WB |
|---|---|---|---|---|---|---|---|---|---|---|
| m:f | m:f |   |   |   |   |   | m:f |   |   |   |

Te lucis ante terminum (Sarum ferial)

| BA | DC | 1940 | 1982 | LBW | LW | PH | RCV | UCC | UM | WB |
|---|---|---|---|---|---|---|---|---|---|---|
|   |   | m:f |   |   |   |   |   |   |   |   |

Temple

| BA | DC | 1940 | 1982 | LBW | LW | PH | RCV | UCC | UM | WB |
|---|---|---|---|---|---|---|---|---|---|---|
|   |   | D |   |   |   |   |   |   |   |   |

Tempus adest floridum

| BA | DC | 1940 | 1982 | LBW | LW | PH | RCV | UCC | UM | WB |
|---|---|---|---|---|---|---|---|---|---|---|
|   |   | G |   |   | G |   |   |   | A | Ab |

ORGAN COMPOSITIONS

Johns, Donald "Gentle Mary Laid Her Child" **The Concordia Hymn Prelude Series** Volume 5 Edited: Herbert Gotsch Concordia Publishing House 97-6511 Key: G

Manz, Paul "Gentle Mary Laid Her Child" **Ten Chorale Improvisations** Set VII Op. 17 Concordia Publishing House 97-5308 Key: G

FREE ACCOMPANIMENTS

Busarow, Donald **All Praise to You Eternal God** Augsburg Publishing House 11-9076 (Two settings) Key: G; Key: Ab

## Tender Thought

| BA | DC | 1940 | 1982 | LBW | LW | PH | RCV | UCC | UM | WB |
|----|----|------|------|-----|----|----|-----|-----|----|----|
|    |    | m:f  | m:e  |     |    | m:f |    |     |    |    |

### ORGAN COMPOSITIONS

Janson, Thomas "O Jesu, Blessed Lord" **The Concordia Hymn Prelude Series** Volume 18 Edited: Herbert Gotsch Concordia Publishing House 97-5709 Key: m:e

## Terra beata
(See also: Terra patris)

| BA | DC | 1940 | 1982 | LBW | LW | PH | RCV | UCC | UM | WB |
|----|----|------|------|-----|----|----|-----|-----|----|----|
|    | Eb |      |      |     |    | Eb |     | Eb  | Eb | Eb |

## Terra patris

| BA | DC | 1940 | 1982 | LBW | LW | PH | RCV | UCC | UM | WB |
|----|----|------|------|-----|----|----|-----|-----|----|----|
| Eb |    |      |      | D   |    |    | E   |     |    |    |

### ORGAN COMPOSITIONS

Jordan, Alice "This is My Father's World" **A Season and a Time** Broadman Press 4570-37 Key: Eb

### FREE ACCOMPANIMENTS

Norris, Kevin **Hymn Preludes and Free Accompaniments** Volume 15 Augsburg Publishing House 11-9411 Key: D

## The Agincourt Song
(See also: Deo Gracias)

## The Ash Grove

| BA | DC | 1940 | 1982 | LBW | LW | PH | RCV | UCC | UM | WB |
|----|----|------|------|-----|----|----|-----|-----|----|----|
|    |    |      |      | G   | G  |    |     |     |    |    |

### ORGAN COMPOSITIONS

Cherwien, David **Interpretations Based on Hymn-tunes** Book II A.M.S.I. OR-3 Key: G

Johnson, David "Sent Forth by God's Blessing" **Deck Thyself with Gladness** Volume 2 Augsburg Publishing House 11-9101 Key: G

Schack, David "Sent Forth by God's Blessing" **The Concordia Hymn Prelude Series** Volume 18 Edited: Herbert Gotsch Concordia Publishing House 97-5709 Key: G

Ferguson, John **Hymn Tune Harmonizations** Book III
Ludwig Music Publishing Co.  Key: G

The Babe of Bethlehem

| BA | DC | 1940 | 1982 | LBW | LW | PH | RCV | UCC | UM | WB |
|----|----|------|------|-----|----|----|-----|-----|----|----|
|    |    |      |      |     |    |    |     |     |    | f  |

The Call

| BA | DC | 1940 | 1982 | LBW | LW | PH | RCV | UCC | UM | WB |
|----|----|------|------|-----|----|----|-----|-----|----|----|
|    |    | Eb   | Eb   |     |    |    |     |     |    |    |

The Church's Desolation

| BA | DC | 1940 | 1982 | LBW | LW | PH | RCV | UCC | UM | WB |
|----|----|------|------|-----|----|----|-----|-----|----|----|
|    |    |      | G    |     |    |    |     |     |    |    |

The Eighth Tune

| BA | DC | 1940 | 1982 | LBW | LW | PH | RCV | UCC | UM | WB |
|----|----|------|------|-----|----|----|-----|-----|----|----|
|    |    |      | G    |     |    |    |     |     |    |    |

The First Nowell (Noel)

| BA | DC | 1940 | 1982 | LBW | LW | PH | RCV | UCC | UM | WB |
|----|----|------|------|-----|----|----|-----|-----|----|----|
| D  | D  | D    |      | D   |    | D  | D   | D   | D  | D  |

## ORGAN COMPOSITIONS

Gehrke, Hugo  "The First Nowell"  **The Parish Organist**
Part Five  Advent and Christmas Music  Concordia
Publishing House  97-1382  Key: D

Gehrke, Hugo  "The First Nowell"  **The Concordia Hymn
Prelude Series**  Volume 5  Edited: Herbert Gotsch
Concordia Publishing House  97-5611  Key: D

Wolz, Larry  **O Little Town of Bethlehem**  Broadman
Press  4570-68  Key: D

## FREE ACCOMPANIMENTS

Lovelace, Austin C.  **Hymn Preludes and Free
Accompaniments**  Volume 4  Augsburg Publishing
House  11-9400  Key: D

Noble, T. Tertius  **Free Organ Accompaniments to One
Hundred Well-Known Hymn Tunes**  J. Fischer & Bros.
#8175  Key: D

The King's Majesty

| BA | DC | 1940 | 1982 | LBW | LW | PH | RCV | UCC | UM | WB |
|----|----|------|------|-----|----|----|-----|-----|----|----|
| f  |    | f    | e    | e   |    | f  |     | f   | f  |    |

ORGAN COMPOSITIONS

Drews, Claudia  "Ride On, Ride On in Majesty"  **The Concordia Hymn Prelude Series**  Volume 9  Edited: Herbert Gotsch  Concordia Publishing House  97-5616  Key: e

The Old Rugged Cross

| BA | DC | 1940 | 1982 | LBW | LW | PH | RCV | UCC | UM | WB |
|----|----|------|------|-----|----|----|-----|-----|----|-----|
|    |    |      |      |     |    |    |     |     | Bb |    |

The Rock of Refuge

| BA | DC | 1940 | 1982 | LBW | LW | PH | RCV | UCC | UM | WB |
|----|----|------|------|-----|----|----|-----|-----|----|-----|
|    |    |      |      |     |    |    |     |     | Ab |    |

The Saints' Delight

| BA | DC | 1940 | 1982 | LBW | LW | PH | RCV | UCC | UM | WB |
|----|----|------|------|-----|----|----|-----|-----|----|-----|
|    |    |      |      | e   | e  |    |     |     |    |    |

ORGAN COMPOSITIONS

Cherwien, David  **Interpretations Based on Hymn-tunes**  Book II  A.M.S.I.  OR-3  Key: e

Shack, David  "In Adam We Have All Been One"  **Preludes on Ten Hymntunes**  Augsburg Publishing House  11-9363  Key: e

FREE ACCOMPANIMENTS

Busarow, Donald  **All Praise to You Eternal God**  Augsburg Publishing House  11-9076  Key: e

The Solid Rock

| BA | DC | 1940 | 1982 | LBW | LW | PH | RCV | UCC | UM | WB |
|----|----|------|------|-----|----|----|-----|-----|----|-----|
|    |    |      |      | F   |    |    |     |     | F  |    |

The Staff of Faith

| BA | DC | 1940 | 1982 | LBW | LW | PH | RCV | UCC | UM | WB |
|----|----|------|------|-----|----|----|-----|-----|----|-----|
|    |    |      |      |     |    | Eb |     |     |    |    |

The Third Tune
(See also: Third Mode Melody)

| BA | DC | 1940 | 1982 | LBW | LW | PH | RCV | UCC | UM | WB |
|----|----|------|------|-----|----|----|-----|-----|----|-----|
|    |    | e    |      |     |    |    |     |     |    |    |

The Truth from Above

| BA | DC | 1940 | 1982 | LBW | LW | PH | RCV | UCC | UM | WB |
|----|----|------|------|-----|----|----|-----|-----|----|-----|
|    |    | f    |      |     |    |    |     |     |    |    |

Theodoric
(See also: Personent hodie)

There is a Balm

| BA | DC | 1940 | 1982 | LBW | LW | PH | RCV | UCC | UM | WB |
|----|----|------|------|-----|----|----|-----|-----|----|----|
|    |    |      |      |     |    |    |     | G   |    |    |

FREE ACCOMPANIMENTS

Hancock, Gerre **Organ Improvisations for Hymn-Singing**
Hinshaw Music Co. HMO-100 Key: F

Third Mode Melody
(See also: The Third Tune)

| BA | DC | 1940 | 1982 | LBW | LW  | PH  | RCV | RCV | UCC | UM | WB  |
|----|----|------|------|-----|-----|-----|-----|-----|-----|----|-----|
|    |    | m:e  |      | m:e | m:e |     | m:e |     |     |    | m:e |

FREE ACCOMPANIMENTS

Arnatt, Ronald **Hymn Preludes and Free Accompaniments**
Volume 9 Augsburg Publishing House 11-9405
Key: e

This Endris Night

| BA | DC | 1940 | 1982 | LBW | LW | PH | RCV | UCC | UM | WB |
|----|----|------|------|-----|----|----|-----|-----|----|----|
|    |    |      | D    |     |    |    |     |     |    |    |

Thomas Circle

| BA | DC | 1940 | 1982 | LBW | LW | PH | RCV | UCC | UM | WB |
|----|----|------|------|-----|----|----|-----|-----|----|----|
|    | D  |      |      |     |    |    |     |     |    |    |

Thomas Merton

| BA | DC | 1940 | 1982 | LBW | LW | PH | RCV | UCC | UM | WB |
|----|----|------|------|-----|----|----|-----|-----|----|----|
|    |    |      | E    |     |    |    |     |     |    |    |

Thompson

| BA | DC | 1940 | 1982 | LBW | LW | PH | RCV | UCC | UM | WB |
|----|----|------|------|-----|----|----|-----|-----|----|----|
| Ab |    |      |      |     |    |    |     |     |    |    |

ORGAN COMPOSITIONS

Held, Wilbur "Softly and Tenderly Jesus is Calling"
**Gospel Hymn Settings** Hinshaw Music Co. Inc.
HMO-146 Key: Ab

Thornbury

| BA | DC | 1940 | 1982 | LBW | LW | PH | RCV | UCC | UM | WB |
|----|----|------|------|-----|----|----|-----|-----|----|----|
|    |    | D    | D    |     |    |    |     |     |    |    |

ORGAN COMPOSITIONS

Beck, Theodore  "O One With God the Father"
**The Concordia Hymn Prelude Series** Volume 6
Edited: Herbert Gotsch  Concordia Publishing
House  97-5612  Key: D

Three Kings of Orient

| BA | DC | 1940 | 1982 | LBW | LW | PH | RCV | UCC | UM | WB |
|----|----|------|------|-----|----|----|-----|-----|----|----|
|    |    | e    | e    |     |    |    |     |     |    |    |

Tibi, Christe, splendor Patris

| BA | DC | 1940 | 1982 | LBW | LW | PH | RCV | UCC | UM | WB |
|----|----|------|------|-----|----|----|-----|-----|----|----|
|    |    | m:f# |      |     |    |    |     |     |    |    |

Tidings
(See also: Angelic Songs)

| BA | DC | 1940 | 1982 | LBW | LW | PH | RCV | UCC | UM | WB |
|----|----|------|------|-----|----|----|-----|-----|----|----|
| Bb | Bb | Bb   | Bb   |     |    | Bb |     | Bb  | Bb |    |

ORGAN COMPOSITIONS

Olsen, A. Loran  "O Sion, Haste, Thy Mission High
Fulfilling" **The Parish Organist** Part Twelve
Edited: Willem Mudde  Concordia Publishing House
97-4759  Key:  Bb

Tillman

| BA | DC | 1940 | 1982 | LBW | LW | PH | RCV | UCC | UM | WB |
|----|----|------|------|-----|----|----|-----|-----|----|----|
| F  |    |      |      |     |    |    |     |     |    |    |

Times Like These

| BA | DC | 1940 | 1982 | LBW | LW | PH | RCV | UCC | UM | WB |
|----|----|------|------|-----|----|----|-----|-----|----|----|
| Ab |    |      |      |     |    |    |     |     |    |    |

To God Be the Glory

| BA | DC | 1940 | 1982 | LBW | LW | PH | RCV | UCC | UM | WB |
|----|----|------|------|-----|----|----|-----|-----|----|----|
| Ab |    |      |      |     |    |    |     |     |    |    |

To God on high

| BA | DC | 1940 | 1982 | LBW | LW | PH | RCV | UCC | UM | WB |
|----|----|------|------|-----|----|----|-----|-----|----|----|
|    | F  |      |      |     |    |    |     |     |    |    |

Tōkyō

| BA | DC | 1940 | 1982 | LBW | LW | PH | RCV | UCC | UM | WB |
|----|----|------|------|-----|----|----|-----|-----|----|----|
|    |    |      |      |     |    |    |     |     |    | m:d |

Tollefson

| BA | DC | 1940 | 1982 | LBW | LW | PH | RCV | UCC | UM | WB |
|----|----|------|------|-----|----|----|-----|-----|----|----|
|    |    | e    |      |     |    |    |     |     |    |    |

ORGAN COMPOSITIONS

Powell, Robert J.  "A Stable Lamp is Lighted"
**The Concordia Hymn Prelude Series**  Volume 5
Concordia Publishing House  97-5611  Key: e

Tomter
| BA | DC | 1940 | 1982 | LBW | LW | PH | RCV | UCC | UM | WB |
|----|----|------|------|-----|----|----|-----|-----|----|----|
|    |    |      | A    |     |    |    |     |     |    |    |

Ton-Mân
| BA | DC | 1940 | 1982 | LBW | LW | PH | RCV | UCC | UM | WB |
|----|----|------|------|-----|----|----|-----|-----|----|----|
| e  | e  |      |      |     |    | e  |     |     |    |    |

Ton-y-botel
(See also: Ebenezer)
| BA | DC | 1940 | 1982 | LBW | LW | PH | RCV | UCC | UM | WB |
|----|----|------|------|-----|----|----|-----|-----|----|----|
|    |    |      | f    |     |    |    |     |     |    | f  |

ORGAN COMPOSITIONS

Thalben-Ball, George **113 Variations on Hymn Tunes**
Novello & Co., Ltd.  Key: f

FREE ACCOMPANIMENTS

Noble, T. Tertius  **Free Organ Accompaniments to One
Hundred Well-Known Hymn Tunes**  J. Fischer & Bros.
#8175  Key: f

Wyton, Alec **New Shoots from Old Routes**  Sacred
Music Press  KK 279  Key: f

Tonus peregrinus
| BA | DC | 1940 | 1982 | LBW | LW | PH | RCV | UCC | UM | WB |
|----|----|------|------|-----|----|----|-----|-----|----|----|
|    |    |      |      |     |    |    |     | G   |    |    |

Toplady
| BA | DC | 1940 | 1982 | LBW | LW | PH | RCV | UCC | UM | WB |
|----|----|------|------|-----|----|----|-----|-----|----|----|
| Bb | Bb | Bb   | Bb   | Bb  | Bb | Bb |     |     | Bb |    |

ORGAN COMPOSITIONS

Beck, Albert "Rock of Ages"  **76 Offertories on Hymns
& Chorales**  Concordia Publishing House  97-5207
Key: Bb

Bristol, Lee Hastings Jr. "Prelude on 'Toplady'"
**The Bristol Collection of Contemporary Hymn
Tune Preludes for Organ** Volume One
Harold  Flammer, Inc.  Key: Bb

Lovelace, Austin "Rock of Ages, cleft for me"
   **Eight Hymn Preludes**  Augsburg Publishing House
   11-9144  Key: Bb

FREE ACCOMPANIMENTS

Carson, J. Bert **Hymn Preludes and Free Accompaniments**
   Volume 16  Augsburg Publishing House  11-9412
   Key: Bb

Hancock, Gerre  **Organ Improvisations for Hymn-Singing**
   Hinshaw Music Co.  HMO-100  Key: Bb

Torah Song (Yisrael V'oraita)

| BA | DC | 1940 | 1982 | LBW | LW | PH | RCV | UCC | UM | WB |
|----|----|------|------|-----|----|----|-----|-----|-----|-----|
|    |    |      | a    |     |    |    |     |     |     |     |

Toronto

| BA | DC | 1940 | 1982 | LBW | LW | PH | RCV | UCC | UM | WB |
|----|----|------|------|-----|----|----|-----|-----|-----|-----|
| F  |    |      |      |     |    |    |     |     |     |     |

Torshov

| BA | DC | 1940 | 1982 | LBW | LW | PH | RCV | UCC | UM | WB |
|----|----|------|------|-----|----|----|-----|-----|-----|-----|
|    |    |      | m:f  |     |    |    |     |     |     |     |

ORGAN COMPOSITIONS

Gieseke, Richard W.  "Cup of Blessing That We Share"
   **The Concordia Hymn Prelude Series**  Volume 18
   Edited: Herbert Gotsch  Concordia Publishing House
   97-5709  Key: m:f

Toulon

| BA | DC | 1940 | 1982 | LBW | LW | PH | RCV | UCC | UM | WB |
|----|----|------|------|-----|----|----|-----|-----|-----|-----|
| F  | F  | F    |      |     |    | F  | F   | F   |     | F   |

FREE ACCOMPANIMENTS

Noble, T. Tertius  **Free Organ Accompaniments to One
   Hundred Well-Known Hymn Tunes**  J. Fischer & Bros.
   #8175  Key: F

Travis Avenue

| BA | DC | 1940 | 1982 | LBW | LW | PH | RCV | UCC | UM | WB |
|----|----|------|------|-----|----|----|-----|-----|-----|-----|
| C  |    |      |      |     |    |    |     |     |     |     |

Tregaron

| BA | DC | 1940 | 1982 | LBW | LW | PH | RCV | UCC | UM | WB |
|----|----|------|------|-----|----|----|-----|-----|-----|-----|
|    |    |      | a    |     |    |    |     |     |     |     |

Trentham

| BA | DC | 1940 | 1982 | LBW | LW | PH | RCV | UCC | UM | WB |
|----|----|------|------|-----|----|----|-----|-----|-----|-----|
| F  | F  |      |      |     |    | F  |     |     | F   |     |

Trinity
(See also: Italian Hymn)

| BA | DC | 1940 | 1982 | LBW | LW | PH | RCV | UVV | UM | WB |
|----|----|------|------|-----|----|----|-----|-----|----|----|
|    |    |      |      |     |    |    |     |     |    | F  |

Trisagion

| BA | DC | 1940 | 1982 | LBW | LW | PH | RCV | UCC | UM | WB |
|----|----|------|------|-----|----|----|-----|-----|----|----|
|    | F  |      |      |     |    |    |     |     |    |    |

Triumph

| BA | DC | 1940 | 1982 | LBW | LW | PH | RCV | UCC | UM | WB |
|----|----|------|------|-----|----|----|-----|-----|----|----|
|    |    |      |      |     | m:d |   |     |     |    |    |

ORGAN COMPOSITIONS

Engel, James "Triumphant from the Grave" **The Concordia Hymn Prelude Series** Volume 11 Edited: Herbert Gotsch  Concordia Publishing House 97-5618  Key: m:d

Troen

| BA | DC | 1940 | 1982 | LBW | LW | PH | RCV | UCC | UM | WB |
|----|----|------|------|-----|----|----|-----|-----|----|----|
|    |    |      | m:d  |     |    |    |     |     |    |    |

"Trostet, trostet", spricht der Herr

| BA | DC | 1940 | 1982 | LBW | LW | PH | RCV | UCC | UM | WB |
|----|----|------|------|-----|----|----|-----|-----|----|----|
|    |    |      | m:d  |     |    |    |     |     |    |    |

ORGAN COMPOSITIONS

Micheelsen, Hans Friedrich  "'Comfort, Comfort' Says the Voice" **The Concordia Hymn Prelude Series** Volume 2  Edited: Herbert Gotsch  Concordia Publishing House  97-5536  Key: m:d

True Happiness

| BA | DC | 1940 | 1982 | LBW | LW | PH | RCV | UCC | UM | WB |
|----|----|------|------|-----|----|----|-----|-----|----|----|
|    |    |      |      |     |    |    |     |     | Ab |    |

Truehearted

| BA | DC | 1940 | 1982 | LBW | LW | PH | RCV | UCC | UM | WB |
|----|----|------|------|-----|----|----|-----|-----|----|----|
|    |    |      |      |     |    |    |     |     | F  |    |

Truett

| BA | DC | 1940 | 1982 | LBW | LW | PH | RCV | UCC | UM | WB |
|----|----|------|------|-----|----|----|-----|-----|----|----|
| Eb |    |      |      |     |    |    |     |     |    |    |

Truro

| BA | DC | 1940 | 1982 | LBW | LW | PH | RCV | UCC | UM | WB |
|----|----|------|------|-----|----|----|-----|-----|----|----|
| C  | C  | C    | D    |     | D  | C  | C   | D   |    | C  |

ORGAN COMPOSITIONS

Weiss, Ewald  "Lift Up Your Heads" **The Parish Organist** Part Twelve  Edited: Willem Mudde  Concordia  Publishing House  97-4759  Key: C

FREE ACCOMPANIMENTS

Busarow, Donald **All Prasie to You Eternal God** Augsburg Publishing House  11-9076 (two settings) Key: D; Key: C

Cassler, G. Winston **Organ Descants for Selected Hymn Tunes** Augsburg Publishing House  11-9304 Key: D

Hancock, Gerre **Organ Improvisations for Hymn-Singing** Hinshaw Music Co.  HMO-100  Key: C

Johnson, David N. **Free Harmonizations of Twelve Hymn Tunes** Augsburg Publishing House  11-9190  Key: C

Wyton, Alec **New Shoots from Old Routes** Sacred Music Press  KK 279  Key: C

Trust

| | BA | DC | 1940 | 1982 | LBW | LW | PH | RCV | UCC | UM | WB |
|---|---|---|---|---|---|---|---|---|---|---|---|
| | | | Ab | | | | | | | | |

Trust and Obey

| | BA | DC | 1940 | 1982 | LBW | LW | PH | RCV | UCC | UM | WB |
|---|---|---|---|---|---|---|---|---|---|---|---|
| | F | | | | | | | | | F | |

Trust in Jesus

| | BA | DC | 1940 | 1982 | LBW | LW | PH | RCV | UCC | UM | WB |
|---|---|---|---|---|---|---|---|---|---|---|---|
| | G | | | | | | | | | Aa | |

Trusting Jesus

| | BA | DC | 1940 | 1982 | LBW | LW | PH | RCV | UCC | UM | WB |
|---|---|---|---|---|---|---|---|---|---|---|---|
| | G | | | | | | | | | | |

Truth from Above

| | BA | DC | 1940 | 1982 | LBW | LW | PH | RCV | UCC | UM | WB |
|---|---|---|---|---|---|---|---|---|---|---|---|
| | | | | | g | g | | | | | |

ORGAN COMPOSITIONS

Wienhorst, Richard "O Chief of Cities, Bethlehem" **The Concordia Hymn Prelude Series** Volume 6 Edited: Herbert Gotsch  Concordia Publishing House  97-5612  Key: g

Tryggare kan ingen vara

| BA | DC | 1940 | 1982 | LBW | LW | PH | RCV | UCC | UM | WB |
|---|---|---|---|---|---|---|---|---|---|---|
| D | | | | D | | | | | D | |

## ORGAN COMPOSTIONS

Bish, Diane  "Children of the Heavenly Father"
**The Diane Bish Organ Book**  Volume 4
Alfred Bock Music Company  BG 0776  Key: G

Cherwien, David **Interpretations Based on Hymn-tunes**
Book II  A.M.S.I.  OR-3  Key: A

Jordan, Alice "Amabile on a Swedith Folk Tune" **Worship
Service Music for the Organist**  Broadman Press
Key: D/F

Tucker

| BA | DC | 1940 | 1982 | LBW | LW | PH | RCV | UCC | UM | WB |
|---|---|---|---|---|---|---|---|---|---|---|
| | | | m:f | | | | | | | |

Tuolumne

| BA | DC | 1940 | 1982 | LBW | LW | PH | RCV | UCC | UM | WB |
|---|---|---|---|---|---|---|---|---|---|---|
| | | | m:d | | | | | | | |

## ORGAN COMPOSITIONS

Krapf, Gerhard **A New Song** The Sacred Music Press
Key: d

Twenty-fourth

| BA | DC | 1940 | 1982 | LBW | LW | PH | RCV | UCC | UM | WB |
|---|---|---|---|---|---|---|---|---|---|---|
| F | F | | | | G | | | F | F | |
| | | | | F | | | | | | |

## ORGAN COMPOSITIONS

Coe, James F.  "Love Consecrates the Humblest Act"
**The Concordia Hymn Prelude Series**  Volume 9
Edited: Herbert Gotsch  Concordia Publishing House
97-5616  Key: G

Coe, James F.  "Where Charity and Love Prevail"  **The
Concordia Hymn Prelude Series**  Volume 9  Edited:
Herbert Gotsch  Concordia Publishing House
97-5616  Key: F

## FREE ACCOMPANIMENTS

Gehrke, Hugo  **Hymn Preludes and Free Accompaniments**
Volume 5  Augsburg Publishing House  11-9401
Key: F

Lovelace, Austin C.  **Hymn Preludes and Free Accompaniments**  Volume 4  Augsburg Publishing House  11-9400  Key: G

Twinkling Stars
| BA | DC | 1940 | 1982 | LBW | LW | PH | RCV | UCC | UM | WB |
|----|----|------|------|-----|----|----|-----|-----|----|----|
|    | D  | 1940 | 1982 | LBW | LW | PH | RCV | UCC | UM | WB |

Tyholland
| BA | DC | 1940 | 1982 | LBW | LW | PH | RCV | UCC | UM | WB |
|----|----|------|------|-----|----|----|-----|-----|----|----|
|    | Eb | 1940 | 1982 | LBW | LW | PH | RCV | UCC | UM | WB |

Tysk
| BA | DC | 1940 | 1982 | LBW | LW | PH | RCV | UCC | UM | WB |
|----|----|------|------|-----|----|----|-----|-----|----|----|
|    |    | Bb   | Bb   |     |    |    |     |     |    |    |

ORGAN COMPOSITIONS

Bencriscutto, Frank  "God Himself is with Us"  **The Parish Organist**  Part Twelve  Edited: Willem Mudde  Concordia Publishing House  97-4759  Key: Bb

# U

Ubi Caritas
| BA | DC | 1940 | 1982 | LBW | LW | PH | RCV | UCC | UM | WB |
|----|----|------|------|-----|----|----|-----|-----|----|----|
|    |    |      | m:f  |     |    |    | m:f# |    |    |    |

Ubi caritas (Murray)
| BA | DC | 1940 | 1982 | LBW | LW | PH | RCV | UCC | UM | WB |
|----|----|------|------|-----|----|----|-----|-----|----|----|
|    |    |      | C    |     |    |    |     |     |    |    |

Uffingham
| BA | DC | 1940 | 1982 | LBW | LW | PH | RCV | UCC | UM | WB |
|----|----|------|------|-----|----|----|-----|-----|----|----|
|    |    |      | e    |     |    | f  |     |     |    |    |

ORGAN COMPOSITIONS

Thalben-Ball, George  **113 Variations on Hymn Tunes**  Novello & Co., Ltd.  Key: f

Unafraid
| BA | DC | 1940 | 1982 | LBW | LW | PH | RCV | UCC | UM | WB |
|----|----|------|------|-----|----|----|-----|-----|----|----|
| Ab |    | 1940 | 1982 | LBW | LW | PH | RCV | UCC | UM | WB |

Unde et memores
| BA | DC | 1940 | 1982 | LBW | LW | PH | RCV | UCC | UM | WB |
|----|----|------|------|-----|----|----|-----|-----|----|----|
|    |    | D    | D    |     |    |    | D   |     |    |    |

## Une jeune pucelle

| BA | DC | 1940 | 1982 | LBW | LW | PH | RCV | UCC | UM | WB |
|----|----|------|------|-----|----|----|----|-----|----|----|
|    |    | g    | g    |     |    |    |     |     |    |    |

ORGAN COMPOSITIONS

Cherwien, David **Interpretations Based on Hymn-tunes** Book II  A.M.S.I.  OR-3  Key: g

Manz, Paul  "'Twas in the Moon of Wintertime'" **Ten Chorale Improvisations** Set X  Op. 22  Concordia Publishing House  97-5557  Key: g

Schalk, Carl  "'Twas in the Moon of Wintertime'" **The Concordia Hymn Prelude Series** Volume 5  Edited: Herbert Gotsch  Concordia Publishing House 97-5611   Key: g

FREE ACCOMPANIMENTS

Lovelace, Austin C.  **Hymn Preludes and Free Accompaniments** Volume 4  Augsburg Publishing House  11-9400  Key: g

## Une vaine crainte

| BA | DC | 1940 | 1982 | LBW | LW | PH | RCV | UCC | UM | WB |
|----|----|------|------|-----|----|----|----|-----|----|----|
|    |    |      |      |     |    |    | Bb  |     |    |    |

## Union

| BA | DC | 1940 | 1982 | LBW | LW | PH | RCV | UCC | UM | WB |
|----|----|------|------|-----|----|----|----|-----|----|----|
|    |    |      | C    |     |    |    |     |     |    |    |

## Union Seminary

| BA | DC | 1940 | 1982 | LBW | LW | PH | RCV | UCC | UM | WB |
|----|----|------|------|-----|----|----|----|-----|----|----|
| Ab |    |      |      |     |    |    |     | Ab  |    |    |

## Unitas Fratrum

| BA | DC | 1940 | 1982 | LBW | LW | PH | RCV | UCC | UM | WB |
|----|----|------|------|-----|----|----|----|-----|----|----|
|    |    | D    |      |     |    |    |     |     |    |    |

## Universal Praise

| BA | DC | 1940 | 1982 | LBW | LW | PH | RCV | UCC | UM | WB |
|----|----|------|------|-----|----|----|----|-----|----|----|
|    |    | D    |      |     |    |    |     |     |    |    |

## University College

| BA | DC | 1940 | 1982 | LBW | LW | PH | RCV | UCC | UM | WB |
|----|----|------|------|-----|----|----|----|-----|----|----|
|    |    | F    |      |     |    |    |     |     |    |    |

ORGAN COMPOSITIONS

Fetler, Paul  "Oft in Danger, Oft in Woe" **The Parish Organist** Part Twelve  Edited: Willam Mudde  Concordia Publishing House  97-4759  Key: F

John, David N. "Jesus, Name of Wondrous Love" **Deck Thyself My Soul with Gladness** Augsburg Publishing House 11-9157  Key: F

Thalben-Ball, George  **113 Variations on Hymn Tunes** Novello & Co., Ltd.  Key: F

**Unser Herrscher**

| BA | DC | 1940 | 1982 | LBW | LW | PH | RCV | UCC | UM | WB |
|----|----|------|------|-----|----|----|-----|-----|----|----|
|    | C  |      | Bb   | C   | Bb | C  | Bb  |     | Bb | C  |

ORGAN COMPOSITIONS

Beck, Theodore  "Rise, O Children of Salvation"  **The Concordia Hymn Prelude Series** Volume 15  Edited: Herbert Gotsch  Concordia Publishing House 97-5706  Key: Bb

Cherwien, David  **Interpretations Based on Hymn-tunes** Book II  A.M.S.I.  OR-3  Key: C

**Upp, min tunga**

| BA | DC | 1940 | 1982 | LBW | LW | PH | RCV | UCC | UM | WB |
|----|----|------|------|-----|----|----|-----|-----|----|----|
|    |    |      |      | D   |    |    |     |     |    |    |

ORGAN COMPOSITIONS

Lohmeyer, Lisa Shoemaker  "Praise the Savior, Now and Ever"  **The Concordia Hymn Prelude Series** Volume 11  Edited: Herbert Gotsch  Concordia Publishing House  97-5618  Key: D

**Urbs beata**

| BA | DC | 1940 | 1982 | LBW | LW | PH | RCV | UCC | UM | WB |
|----|----|------|------|-----|----|----|-----|-----|----|----|
|    | DC | m:f  | m:f  |     |    |    |     |     |    |    |

**Urbs Zion aurea**

| BA | DC | 1940 | 1982 | LBW | LW | PH | RCV | UCC | UM | WB |
|----|----|------|------|-----|----|----|-----|-----|----|----|
|    |    |      |      |     |    |    | Ab  |     |    |    |

**Ut queant laxis**

| BA | DC | 1940 | 1982 | LBW | LW | PH | RCV | UCC | UM | WB |
|----|----|------|------|-----|----|----|-----|-----|----|----|
|    |    |      | m:d  |     |    |    |     |     |    |    |

**Uxbridge**

| BA | DC | 1940 | 1982 | LBW | LW | PH | RCV | UCC | UM | WB |
|----|----|------|------|-----|----|----|-----|-----|----|----|
|    | Eb |      |      |     | Eb | D  |     |     |    |    |

Polley, David  "This Child We Now Present to You"
**The Concordia Hymn Prelude Series**  Volume 16
Edited: Herbert Gotsch  Concordia Publishing House
97-5707  Key: Eb

# V

Valet will ich dir geben
(See also: St. Theodulph)
| BA | DC | 1940 | 1982 | LBW | LW | PH | RCV | UCC | UM | WB |
|----|----|------|------|-----|----|----|----|----|----|----|
|    |    |      | C    | Bb  | Bb |    | C  |    |    |    |

ORGAN COMPOSITIONS

Bender, Jan  **A Palm Sunday Processional on "All Glory
Laud, and Honor"**  Concordia Publishing House,
97-1396  Key: C

Bach, J. S.  **Organ Works**  Volume 3  "The Individually
Transmitted Organ Chorales"  Edited: Hans Klotz
Urtext of the New Bach Edition  Bärenreiter
5173  Key: Bb; Key: D

Bach, J.S.  **Organ Works**  Volume VI  Widor-Schweitzer
G. Schirmer  Key: Bb; Key: D

Bach, J.S.  **Orgelwerke**  Volume VII  #246  C.F. Peters
Corporation  (Two settings) Key Bb; Key: D

Bender, Jan  "All Glory, Laud, and Honor" **The Parish
Organist**  Part Seven  Music for Lent, Palm Sunday
and Holy Week  Edited: Erich Goldschmidt
Concordia Publishing House  97-1403  Key: C

Dupre, Marcel  **Seventy-Nine Chorales for Organ**
Opus 28  H. W. Gray  Key: D

Engel, James  "O Lord, How Shall I Meet You" **Preludes
on Six Hymn Tunes**  Augsburg Publishing House
11-9364  Key: Eb

Karg-Elert, Sigfrid "I Wish to Bid You Farewell"
**Choral Improvisations for Organ for Advent and
Christmastide**  Op. 65  Volume 1  Edited: Robert
Leech Bedell  Edward B. Marks Music Corp.  Key: C

Kaufman, Georg Friedrich  "All Glory, Laud, and Honor"
**The Parish Organist**  Part Three  Edited:
Heinrich Fleischer  Concordia Publishing House
97-1154  Key: C

Krapf, Gerhard  "O Jesus, King of Glory"  **The
Concordia Hymn Prelude Series**  Volume 6  Edited:
Herbert Gotsch  Concordia Publishing House
97-5612  Key: Bb

Manz, Paul "O Lord, How Shall I Meet Thee" **Ten Chorale
Improvisations** Set IV Op.10 Concordia Publishing
House 97-4951  Key: C

Manz, Paul "O Lord, How Shall I Meet Thee" **Ten Chorale
Improvisations** Set VII Op. 17 Concordia Publishing
House 97-5308  Key: Eb

Micheelsen, Hans Friedrich  "All Glory, Laud, and
Honor"  **The Concordia Hymn Prelude Series**
Volume 9  Edited: Herbert Gotsch  Concordia
Publishing House  97-5616  Key: Bb

FREE ACCOMPANIMENTS

Bender, Jan  **Hymn Preludes and Free Accompaniments**
Volume 1  Augsburg Publishing House  11-9397
Key: Bb

Bunjes, Paul  **New Organ Accompaniments for Hymns**
Concordia Publishing House  97-5348  Key: C

Noble, T. Tertius  **Free Organ Accompaniments to One
Hundred Well-Known Hymn Tunes**  J. Fischer & Bros.
#8175  Key: D

Valiant Hearts
       BA    DC    1940 1982 LBW  LW   PH   RCV  UCC  UM   WB
             G

Valley
       BA    DC    1940 1982 LBW  LW   PH   RCV  UCC  UM   WB
       F

Valour
       BA    DC    1940 1982 LBW  LW   PH   RCV  UCC  UM   WB
             G

Varndean
       BA    DC    1940 1982 LBW  LW   PH   RCV  UCC  UM   WB
       Db

<u>Vater unser im Himmelreich</u>
     BA    DC   1940 1982 LBW   LW    PH    RCV   UCC   UM    WB
                m:c  m:c  m:c   m:c   m:c         m:c   m:c

ORGAN COMPOSITIONS

Bach, J. S. **Organ Works** Volume 1 Edited: Heinz-
     Harald Löhlein Urtext of the New Bach Edition
     Bärenreiter 5171 Key: m:d

Bach, J. S. **Organ Works** Volume 3 "The Individually
     Transmitted Organ Chorales" Edited: Hans Klotz
     Urtext of the New Bach Edition Bärenreiter
     5173 Key: m:d

Bach, Johann Christoph "Our Father, Who Art in Heaven"
     **Short Classic Pieces for Organ from the 16th, 17th
     and 18th Centuries** Arr. Norris L. Stephens
     J. Fischer & Bros No. 9607 Key: m:d

Bach, J.S. **Organ Works** Volume VI Widor-Schweitzer
     G. Schirmer Key: (#56, 57, 74, 75) m:d

Bach, J.S. **Organ Works** Volume VII Widor-Schweitzer
     G. Schirmer (#37, 60 ) Key: m:d; Key: m:e

Bach, J.S. **Orgelwerke** Volume V C.F. Peters
     Corporation Nr. 244 #47, #48 Key: m:d

Bach, J.S. **Orgelwerke** Volume VII C.F. Peters
     Corporation Nr. 246 #60 Key: m:e; #66 Key: m:d

Bach, J.S. **The Liturgical Year** (Orgelbuchlein)
     Edited: Albert Reimenschneider Oliver Ditson Co.
     Key: m:d

Beck, Albert **76 Offertories on Hymns & Chorales**
     Concordia Publishing House 97-5207 Key: c

Dupre, Marcel **Seventy-Nine Chorales for Organ**
     Opus 28 H. W. Gray Key: d

Edmundson, Garth **A Galaxy of Hymn Tune Preludes**
     Galaxy Music Corp. GMC 2353 Key: c

Haan, Raymond H. "Our Father, Thou in Heaven Above"
     **The King of Love** The Sacred Music Press K-277
     Key: d

Krieger, Johann "Chorale Prelude on 'Vater unser im
     Himmelreich'" **For Manuals Only** Edited: John
     Christopher McAfee Music Corp. Key: m:d

Manz, Paul "Our Father, Thou in Heaven Above" **Ten Chorale Improvisations** Set II  Opus 7  Concordia Publishing House 97-4546  Key: c

Pachelbel, Johann  **Chorale Preludes by Masters of the 17th & 18th Centuries** Volume I  Edited: Walter Buszin  Concordia Publishing House  Key: m:c

Pepping, Ernst  **Praeludia Postludia I**  B. Schott's Sohne  Edition 6040  Key: m:c

Praetorius, Michael "Our Father, Thou in Heaven Above" **The Parish Organist** Part Three  Edited: Heinrich Fleischer  Concordia Publishing House 97-1154  Key:  m:c

Schneider, John "Our Father, Thou in Heaven Above" **Wedding Music** Part 2  Concordia Publishing House  97-1370  Key: c

## FREE ACCOMPANIMENTS

Cassler, G. Winston  **Organ Descants for Selected Hymn Tunes**  Augsburg Publishing House 11-9304  Key: c

Johnson, David N.  **Hymn Preludes and Free Accompaniments** Volume 14  Augsburg Publishing House  11-9410  Key: c

<u>Venerable</u>

| BA | DC | 1940 | 1982 | LBW | LW | PH | RCV | UCC | UM | WB |
|----|----|------|------|-----|----|----|-----|-----|----|----|
|    |    |      |      | m:g |    |    |     |     |    |    |

<u>Veni Creator</u>

| BA | DC | 1940 | 1982 | LBW | LW | PH | RCV | UCC | UM | WB |
|------|-----|------|------|-----|----|-----|-----|-----|-----|------|
| m:eb | m:e |      |      |     |    | m:f |     | m:f | m:f | m:eb |

## ORGAN COMPOSITIONS

Byrd, William  "Veni Creator Spiritus (1) **Tallis to Wesley** Number Eight  Edited: Philip Ledger Hinrichsen Edition Ltd.  No. 1543a  (Two settings) Key: g

Durufle, Maurice **Prelude, Adagio et Choral varie sur le theme du "Veni Creator"** Op. 4  Durand & Co. Key: E

Kreckel, Philip G. **Musica Divina** Volume I J. Fischer & Bros. No. 6623  Key: D

Sowerby, Leo "Come, Holy Ghost, our Souls Inspire"
**Advent to Whitsuntide** Hinrichsen No. 743b
Key: Bb

Wyton, Alec "Prelude on 'Come Holy Ghost'"
**Preludes, Fanfares and a March for the
Liturgical Year** Harold Flammer 3947  Key: Bb

<u>Veni Creator Spiritus</u>

| BA | DC | 1940 | 1982 | LBW | LW | PH | RCV | UCC | UM | WB |
|----|----|------|------|-----|-----|-----|-----|-----|-----|-----|
|    |    | m:e  | m:f  | m:f |    |    | m:e |    |    |    |

ORGAN COMPOSITIONS

Engel, James  "Come Holy Ghost, Our Souls Inspire"
**The Concordia Hymn Prelude Series** Volume 13
Edited: Herbert Gotsch  Concordia Publishing House
97-5620  Key: m:f

Held, Wilbur "Come Holy Ghost, Our Souls Inspire"
**Hymn Preludes for the Pentecost Season**
Concordia Publishing House 97-5517  Key: A

Manz, Paul "Come Holy Ghost, Creator Blest" **Ten
Chorale Improvisations** Op. 5  Concordia Publishing House 97-4554  Key: Bb/F

<u>Veni Emmanuel</u>

| BA | DC | 1940 | 1982 | LBW | LW | PH | RCV | UCC | UM | WB |
|----|----|------|------|-----|-----|-----|-----|-----|-----|-----|
| m:db | m:e | m:e | m:e | m:e | m:e | m:e | m:e | m:e | m:e | m:e |

ORGAN COMPOSITIONS

Bender, Jan  "Oh, Come, Emmanuel"  **The Concordia
Hymn Prelude Series** Volume 2  Edited: Herbert
Gotsch  Concordia Publishing House  97-5536
Key: m:e

Edmundson, Garth "Veni Emanuel" **Christus Advenit –
Christmas Suite No. 2** H.W. Gray  Key: d

Held, Wilbur "O Come, Emmanuel"  **Nativity Suite**
Concordia Publishing House  Key:e

Manz, Paul "Oh, Come, Oh, Come, Emmanuel" **Ten Chorale
Improvisations** Set IV Op. 10  Concordia Publishing House 97-4951  Key: e

Moser, Rudolf "Oh Come, Oh Come, Emmanuel" **The Parish Organist** Part Four Edited: Heinrich Fleischer Concordia Publishing House 97-1157 Key: e

Purvis, Richard "Prelude Solennel" **An American Organ Mass** Harold Flammer, Inc. Key: g

Reichel, Bernard "O Come, Oh, Come, Emmanuel" **The Parish Organist** Part Five Advent and Christmas Music Edited: Fleischer Goldschmidt Concordia Publishing House 97-1382 Key: e

Sowerby, Leo "O Come, O Come Emmanuel" **Advent to Whitsuntide** Volume Four Hinrichsen No. 743b Key: e

Wyton, Alec **Preludes, Fanfare and a March for the Liturgical Year** Harold Flammer 3967 Key: e

FREE ACCOMPANIMENTS

Cassler, G. Winston **Organ Descants for Selected Hymn Tunes** Augsburg Publishing House 11-9304 Key:e

Goode, Jack C. **Thirty-Four Changes on Hymn Tunes** H. W. Gray Co. GB 644 Key: e

Hancock, Gerre **Organ Improvisations for Hymn-Singing** Hinshaw Music Co. HMO-100 Key: e

Noble, T. Tertius **Fifty Free Organ Accompaniments to Well Known Hymn Tunes** J. Fischer & Bros. No. 8430 Key: e

Veni Jesu, Amor mi

| BA | DC | 1940 | 1982 | LBW | LW | PH | RCV | UCC | UM | WB |
|----|----|------|------|-----|----|----|-----|-----|----|----|
|    |    |      |      |     |    |    | Eb  |     |    |    |

Veni Redemptor gentium

| BA | DC | 1940 | 1982 | LBW | LW | PH | RCV | UCC | UM | WB |
|----|----|------|------|-----|----|----|-----|-----|----|----|
|    |    | m:f  |      |     |    |    |     |     |    |    |

Veni Sancte Spiritus

| BA | DC | 1940 | 1982 | LBW | LW | PH | RCV | UCC | UM | WB |
|----|----|------|------|-----|----|----|-----|-----|----|----|
|    |    | E    |      |     |    |    | F   |     |    |    |

ORGAN COMPOSITIONS

Kreckel, Philip G. **Musica Divina** Volume 2 J. Fischer & Bro. #6715 Key: d

Thalben-Ball, George **113 Variations on Hymn Tunes** Novello & Co., Ltd. Key: F

Noble, T. Tertius **Fifty Free Organ Accompaniments to
Well Known Hymn Tunes** J. Fischer & Bros.
No. 8430  Key: E

Veni Sancte Spiritus (Plainsong)

| BA | DC | 1940 | 1982 | LBW | LW | PH | RCV | UCC | UM | WB |
|---|---|---|---|---|---|---|---|---|---|---|
|  |  |  | m:d |  |  |  |  |  |  |  |

Veni, anima mea

| BA | DC | 1940 | 1982 | LBW | LW | PH | RCV | UCC | UM | WB |
|---|---|---|---|---|---|---|---|---|---|---|
|  |  |  |  |  |  | Ab |  |  |  |  |

Venice

| BA | DC | 1940 | 1982 | LBW | LW | PH | RCV | UCC | UM | WB |
|---|---|---|---|---|---|---|---|---|---|---|
|  | D |  |  |  |  |  |  |  | Eb |  |

Venite adoremus

| BA | DC | 1940 | 1982 | LBW | LW | PH | RCV | UCC | UM | WB |
|---|---|---|---|---|---|---|---|---|---|---|
|  |  | G | G |  |  |  | G |  |  |  |

ORGAN COMPOSITIONS

Elmore, Robert **Venite adoremus. Festival Prelude**
J. Fischer & Bros. 8662  Key: A

Verbum supernum

| BA | DC | 1940 | 1982 | LBW | LW | PH | RCV | UCC | UM | WB |
|---|---|---|---|---|---|---|---|---|---|---|
|  |  | m:b | m:a |  |  |  |  |  |  |  |

Verbum supernum prodiens (Einsiedeln

| BA | DC | 1940 | 1982 | LBW | LW | PH | RCV | UCC | UM | WB |
|---|---|---|---|---|---|---|---|---|---|---|
|  |  |  | m:a |  |  |  |  |  |  |  |

Verleich uns Frieden

| BA | DC | 1940 | 1982 | LBW | LW | PH | RCV | UCC | UM | WB |
|---|---|---|---|---|---|---|---|---|---|---|
|  |  |  |  | m:e | m:e |  |  |  |  |  |

Vermont (Miller)

| BA | DC | 1940 | 1982 | LBW | LW | PH | RCV | UCC | UM | WB |
|---|---|---|---|---|---|---|---|---|---|---|
|  |  | d |  |  |  |  |  |  |  |  |

Vermont (Williams)

| BA | DC | 1940 | 1982 | LBW | LW | PH | RCV | UCC | UM | WB |
|---|---|---|---|---|---|---|---|---|---|---|
| Db |  |  |  |  |  |  |  |  |  |  |

Vernon

| BA | DC | 1940 | 1982 | LBW | LW | PH | RCV | UCC | UM | WB |
|---|---|---|---|---|---|---|---|---|---|---|
|  |  | c |  |  |  |  |  |  |  |  |

## Vesper Hymn (Bortniansky)

| BA | DC | 1940 | 1982 | LBW | LW | PH | RCV | UCC | UM | WB |
|----|----|------|------|-----|----|----|-----|-----|----|----|
|    | Eb | 1940 | 1982 | LBW | LW | PH<br>D | RCV | UCC | UM<br>Eb | WB<br>Eb |

## Vesper Hymn (Rendle)

| BA | DC | 1940 | 1982 | LBW | LW | PH | RCV | UCC | UM | WB |
|----|----|------|------|-----|----|----|-----|-----|----|----|
|    | DC | 1940 | 1982 | LBW | LW | PH | RCV | UCC | UM<br>D | WB |

## Vetter

| BA | DC | 1940 | 1982 | LBW | LW | PH | RCV | UCC | UM | WB |
|----|----|------|------|-----|----|----|-----|-----|----|----|
|    | DC<br>D | 1940 | 1982 | LBW | LW | PH | RCV | UCC | UM | WB |

## Vexilla Regis

| BA | DC | 1940 | 1982 | LBW | LW | PH | RCV | UCC | UM | WB |
|----|----|------|------|-----|----|----|-----|-----|----|----|
|    | DC | 1940<br>m:e | 1982<br>m:e | LBW<br>m:e | LW<br>m:d | PH | RCV<br>m:e | UCC | UM | WB |

## ORGAN COMPOSITIONS

Held, Wilbur "The Royal Banners Forward Go" **A Suite of Passion Hymn Settings** Concordia Publishing House 97-4843 Key: f

Krapf, Gerhard "The Royal Banners Forward Go" **The Concordia Hymn Prelude Series** Volume 9 Edited: Herbert Gotsch Concordia Publishing House 97-5616 (Two settings) Key: d; Key: e

Krapf, Gerhard "The Royal Banners Forward Go" **The Concordia Hymn Prelude Series** Volume 9 Edited: Herbert Gotsch Concordia Publishing House 97-5616 Key: e

Lenel, Ludwig "The Royal Banners Forward Go" **The Parish Organist** Part Seven Music for Lent, Palm Sunday and Holy Week Edited: Erich Goldschmidt Concordia Publishing House 97-1403 Key: e

Purvis, Richard "Vexilla Regis" **Leeds' Organ Selections** Leeds Music Corp. Key: G/E

Shack, David "The Royal Banners Forward Go" **Preludes on Ten Hymntunes** Augsburg Publishing House 11-9363 Key: e

Willan, Healey "Vexilla Regis" **Six Chorale Preludes** Set II Concordia Publishing House 97-3905 Key: f

## Vicar

| BA | DC | 1940 | 1982 | LBW | LW | PH | RCV | UCC | UM | WB |
|----|----|------|------|-----|----|----|-----|-----|----|----|
|    | DC | 1940 | 1982 | LBW | LW | PH | RCV | UCC | UM<br>Eb | WB |

Victimae Paschali laudes
    BA   DC   1940 1982 LBW  LW     PH    RCV   UCC   UM     WB
              m:e  m:e  m:d

## ORGAN COMPOSITIONS

Held, Wilbur "The Easter Sequence" **Six Preludes on Easter Hymns** Concordia Publishing House 97-5330 Key: e

Kreckel, Philip G. **Musica Divina** Volume 1 J. Fischer & Bros. No. 6623 Key: m:d

Powell, Robert J. "Christians, to the Paschal Victim" **The Concordia Hymn Prelude Series** Volume 11 Edited: Herbert Gotsch Concordia Publishing House 97-5618 Key: m:d

Victory (Palestrina)
    BA   DC   1940 1982 LBW  LW     PH    RCV   UCC   UM     WB
             D     D    D     D     D     D     D     Eb    D

## ORGAN COMPOSITIONS

Held, Wilbur "The Strife is O'er" **Six Preludes on Easter Hymns** Concordia Publishing House 97-5330 Key: D

Wente, Stephen "The Strife is O'er, the Battle Done" **The Concordia Hymn Prelude Series** Volume 11 Edited: Herbert Gotsch Concordia Publishing House 97-5618 Key: D

Wyton, Alec Fanfare on "The Strife is O'er" **Preludes, Fanfares and a March for the Liturgical Year** Harold Flammer 3947 Key: D

## FREE ACCOMPANIMENTS

Wyton, Alec **New Shoots from Old Routes** Sacred Music Press KK 279 Key: D

Vienna
    BA   DC   1940 1982 LBW  LW     PH    RCV   UCC   UM     WB
             G            G     G

## ORGAN COMPOSITIONS

Canning, Thomas "Lord, We Come Before Thee Now" **The Parish Organist** Part Four Edited: Heinrich Fleischer Concordia Publishing House 97-1157 Key: G

Thalben-Ball, George **113 Variations on Hymn Tunes** Novello & Co., Ltd.  Key: G

## Vigil

| BA | DC | 1940 | 1982 | LBW | LW | PH | RCV | UCC | UM | WB |
|---|---|---|---|---|---|---|---|---|---|---|

## Vigiles et sancti
(See also: Lasst uns erfreuen)

| BA | DC | 1940 | 1982 | LBW | LW | PH | RCV | UCC | UM | WB |
|---|---|---|---|---|---|---|---|---|---|---|
|  |  | Eb |  |  |  |  | Eb |  |  |  |

### ORGAN COMPOSITIONS

Held, Wilbur "Ye Watchers and Ye Holy Ones" **Hymn Preludes for the Autumn Festivals** Concordia Publishing House  97-5360   Key: Eb

### FREE ACCOMPANIMENTS

Noble, T. Tertius **Free Organ Accompaniments to One Hundred Well-Known Hymn Tunes**  J. Fischer & Bros. #8175  Key: Eb

## Ville du Havre

| BA | DC | 1940 | 1982 | LBW | LW | PH | RCV | UCC | UM | WB |
|---|---|---|---|---|---|---|---|---|---|---|
| Db |  |  |  |  |  |  |  |  |  |  |

## Vineyard Haven

| BA | DC | 1940 | 1982 | LBW | LW | PH | RCV | UCC | UM | WB |
|---|---|---|---|---|---|---|---|---|---|---|
|  |  | c |  |  |  |  |  |  |  |  |

## Vi love dig, o store Gud

| BA | DC | 1940 | 1982 | LBW | LW | PH | RCV | UCC | UM | WB |
|---|---|---|---|---|---|---|---|---|---|---|
|  |  |  |  | m:e | m:e | m:e |  |  |  |  |

## Voller Wunder

| BA | DC | 1940 | 1982 | LBW | LW | PH | RCV | UCC | UM | WB |
|---|---|---|---|---|---|---|---|---|---|---|
|  |  |  |  |  | Bb |  |  |  |  |  |

### ORGAN COMPOSITIONS

Unkel, Rolf  "Safely Through Another Week" **The Parish Organist**  Part Four  Edited: Heinrich Fleischer Concordia Publishing House  97-1157  Key: Bb

### FREE ACCOMPANIMENTS

Bunjes, Paul  **New Organ Accompaniments for Hymns** Concordia Publishing House  97-5348  Key: F

<u>Vom Himmel hoch</u>
(See also: Erfurt)

| BA | DC | 1940 | 1982 | LBW | LW | PH | RCV | UCC | UM | WB |
|----|----|------|------|-----|----|----|----|----|----|----|
|    | C  |      | C    | C   | C  | C  | C  | C  | C  |    |

ORGAN COMPOSITIONS

Bach, J. S. **Organ Works** Volume 1  Edited: Heinz
    Harald Löhlein  Urtext of the New Bach Edition
    Bärenreiter  5171  Key: D

Bach, J.S. **Organ Works** Volume 2  Edited: Hans Klotz
    Urtext of the New Bach Edition  Bärenreiter  5172
    Key: C

Bach, J. S. **Organ Works** Volume 3  "The Individually
    Transmitted Organ Chorales"  Edited: Hans Klotz
    Urtext of the New Bach Edition  Bärenreiter
    5173  Key: C; Key: D; Key: C

Bach, J.S. **Organ Works** Volume VI Widor-Schweitzer
    G. Schirmer (#58, 59) Key: C; Key: D

Bach, J.S. **Organ Works** Volume VII  Widor-Schweitzer
    G. Schirmer  Key: D

Bach, J.S. **Organ Works** Volume VIII  Widor-Schweitzer
    G. Schirmer  Key: C

Bach, J.S. **Orgelwerke** Volume V  C.F. Peters
    Corporation  Nr. 244  Key: C; Key: D

Bach, J.S. **Orgelwerke** Volume VII C.F. Peters
    Corporation Nr. 246 #54 #55 Key: C

Bach, J.S. **The Liturgical Year** (Orgelbuchlein)
    Edited: Albert Reimenschneider  Oliver Ditson Co.
    Key: D

Boehm, Georg  "From Heaven Above to Earth I Come"
    **The Parish Organist** Christmas and Epiphany Music
    Part Six  Concordia Publishing House 97-1391
    Key: C

Briegel, Wolfgang C.  "From Heaven Above to Earth I
    Come" **Short Service Pieces for Organ**  Arr.
    Norris L. Stephens  J. Fischer & Bros.  FE 9797
    Key: D

Buttstedt, Johann Heinrich  "Vom Himmel hoch"
    **Organ Music for Christmas** Edited: C. H. Trevor
    Oxford University Press  Key: D

Dupre, Marcel **Seventy-Nine Chorales for Organ**
Opus 28  H. W. Gray  Key: D

Edmundson, Garth "Vom Himmel Hoch" **Christus Advenit –
Christmas Suite No. 2** H.W. Gray Key: D

Edmundson, Garth **A Galaxy of Hymn Tune Preludes for
Organ**  Galaxy Music Corp. GMC 2353  Key: D

Held, Wilbur "From Heaven Above" **Six Carol Settings**
Concordia Publishing House  Key:C

Karg-Elert, Sigfrid "From Heaven Above" **Choral
Improvisations for Advent and Christmastide** Op. 65
Volume 1  Edited: Robert Leech Bedell Edward B.
Marks Music Corp.  Key: D

Krieger, Johann  "From Heaven Above" **Short Classic
Pieces for Organ from the 16th, 17th and 18th
Centuries** Arr. Norris L. Stephens  J. Fischer
& Bros.  No. 9607  Key: D

Manz, Paul **Choral Partita on "From Heaven Above to
Earth I Come"** Op. 18  Concordia Publishing House
97-5343  Key: C

Marpurg, Friedrich Wilhelm **Twenty-One Chorale Preludes**
Edited: Robert M. Thompson  Augsburg Publishing
House  11-9506  Key: D

Pachelbel, Johann  "Chorale prelude 'Vom Himmel hoch
da komm' ich her'" **Organ Music for Christmas**
Volume 1  Edited: C. H. Trevor  Oxford University
Press  Key: D

Purvis, Richard "Elevation" **An American Organ Mass**
Harold Flammer, Inc.  Key: D

Walcha, Helmut  **Chorale Preludes** II  C.F. Peters
Nr. 4871  Key: D

Walther, Johann Gottfried "From Heaven Above to Earth
I Come" **The Parish Organist** Part Four  Edited:
Heinrich Fleischer  Concordia Publishing House
97-1157  Key: C

Walther, Johann Gottfried  "From Heaven Above to Earth
I Come" **The Concordia Hymn Prelude Series**
Volume 5  Edited: Herbert Gotsch  Concordia
Publishing House  97-5611  Key: C

Zachau, Friedrich Wilhelm "Chorale Prelude on 'Vom
    Himmel hoch, da komm' ich her'" **For Manuals Only**
    Edited: John Christopher  McAfee Music Corp.Key: D

Zachau, Friedrich Wilhelm "Hosanna to the Living Lord"
    **The Parish Organist**  Part Five  Advent and
    Christmas Music   Concordia Publishing House
    97-1382  Key: C

Zachau, Friedrich Wilhelm  "Vom Himmel Hoch"
    **Organ Music for Christmas**  Edited: C. H. Trevor
    Oxford University Press  Key: D

Zachau, Friedrich Wilhelm  "From Heaven Above to Earth
    I Come" **Short Service Pieces for Organ**  Arr:
    Norris L. Stephens  J. Fischer & Bros.  FE 9797
    Key: D

FREE ACCOMPANIMENTS

Arnatt, Ronald **Hymn Preludes and Free Accompaniments**
    Volume 9  Augsburg Publishing House  11-9405
    Key: C

Bender, Jan **Free Organ Accompaniments to Festival Hymns**
    Volume I  Augsburg Publishing House 11-9192  Key: C

Cassler, G. Winston  **Free Organ Accompaniments to Hymns**
    Augsburg Publishing House  11-9179  Key: C

<u>Vom Himmel kam der Engel Schar</u>
    BA   DC   1940 1982 LBW  LW    PH    RCV   UCC   UM    WB
                    m:a

ORGAN COMPOSITIONS

Bach, J. S.  **Organ Works**  Volume 1  Edited: Heinz
    Harald Löhlein  Urtext of the New Bach Edition
    Bärenreiter  5171  Key: m:g

<u>Von Gott will ich nicht lassen</u>
    BA   DC   1940 1982 LBW  LW    PH    RCV   UCC   UM    WB
                    g    g

ORGAN COMPOSITIONS

Bach, J.S.  **Organ Works**  Volume 2  Edited: Hans Klotz
    Urtext of the New Bach Edition  Bärenreiter 5172
    Key: f

Bach, J.S.  **Organ Works** Volume VIII  Widor-Schweitzer
    G. Schirmer  Key: f

Bach, J.S. **Orgelwerke** Volume VII   C.F. Peters
Corporation  #246   Key: f

Bach, Johann Christoph  **Chorale Preludes by Masters of
the 17th & 18th Centuries** Volume I   Edited: Walter
Buszin  Concordia Publishing House   Key: m:g

Buxtehude, Dietrich  "From God I Ne'er Will Turn Me"
**Anthologia Antiqua**  Book Five  **Six Chorale
Preludes**  Edited: Seth Bingham  J. Fischer & Bros.
No. 8090   Key: m:a

Dupre, Marcel  **Seventy-Nine Chorales for Organ**
Opus 28  H. W. Gray  Key: m:f

Marpurg, Friedrich Wilhelm  **Twenty-One Chorale Preludes**
Edited: Robert M. Thompson  Augsburg Publishing
House  11-9506  Key: a

Pepping, Ernst  **Fünfundzwanzig Orgelchorale**  Edition
Schott  4723  B. schott's Sohne  Key: m:g

Vox dilecti
| BA | DC | 1940 | 1982 | LBW | LW | PH | RCV | UCC | UM | WB |
|----|----|------|------|-----|----|----|-----|-----|----|-----|
|    |    | g    |      |     |    |    |     |     | G  |     |

Vruechten
| BA | DC | 1940 | 1982 | LBW | LW | PH | RCV | UCC | UM | WB |
|----|----|------|------|-----|----|----|-----|-----|----|-----|
| Eb |    |      | Eb   | Eb  | Eb |    |     |     |    |     |

ORGAN COMPOSITIONS

Shack, David  "This Joyful Eastertide"  **Preludes on Ten
Hymntunes**  Augsburg Publishing House   11-9363
Key: Eb

Thalben-Ball, George   **113 Variations on Hymn Tunes**
Novello & Co., Ltd.  Key: F

Weber, Paul D.  "This Joyful Eastertide"  **The Concordia
Hymn Prelude Series**  Volume 11  Edited: Herbert
Gotsch  Concordia Publishing House  97-5618
Key: Eb

Wyton, Alec  "Carol"  **Resurrection Suite**  Harold
Flammer, Inc.  HF 5014  Key: G

Vulpius
(See also: Mein Leben)

ORGAN COMPOSITIONS

Thalben-Ball, George **113 Variations in Hymn Tunes**
Novello & Co., Ltd. Key: C

FREE ACCOMPANIMENTS

Cassler, G. Winston **Organ Descants for Selected Hymn
Tunes** Augsburg Publishing House 11-9304 Key: C


# W

W zlobie lezy

| BA | DC | 1940 | 1982 | LBW | LW | PH | RCV | UCC | UM | WB |
|----|----|------|------|-----|----|----|-----|-----|----|----|
| G | Ab | | | F | | | | | Eb | |

ORGAN COMPOSITIONS

Bobb, Barry "Infant Holy, Infant Lowly" **The Concordia
Hymn Prelude Series** Volume 5 Edited: Herbert
Gotsch Concordia Publishing House 97-5611
Key: F

Haan, Raymond H. **Canonic Variations on "Infant Holy,
Infant Lowly"** Concordia Publishing House
97-5723 Key: A

Manz, Paul "Infant Holy, Infant Lowly" **Ten Chorale
Improvisations** Set X Op. 22 Concordia Publishing
House 97-5557 Key: F

Wachet auf
(See also: Sleepers, Wake)

| BA | DC | 1940 | 1982 | LBW | LW | PH | RCV | UCC | UM | WB |
|----|----|------|------|-----|----|----|-----|-----|----|----|
| | C | | C | C | C | C | | C | C | C |

ORGAN COMPOSITIONS

Bach, J. S. **Organ Works** Volume 1 Edited; Heinz-
Harald Löhlein Urtext of the New Bach Edition
Bärenreiter 5171 Key: Eb

Bach, J.S. **Six Organ Chorals** (Schubler)
Edited: Albert Riemenschneider Oliver Ditson
Distributed: Theodore Presser Co. Key: Eb

**Organ Works** VolumeVIII, Widor-Schweitzer
G. Schirmer Key: Eb

Bach, J.S. **Orgelwerke** Volume VII C.F. Peters
C.F. Peters Corporation #246 Key: Eb

Beck, Albert **76 Offertories on Hymns & Chorales**
Concordia Publishing House 97-5207 Key: C

Dupre, Marcel **Seventy-Nine Chorales for Organ**
Opus 28 H. W. Gray Key: Eb

Karg-Elert, Sigfrid "Sleepers Awake, A Voice Calleth"
**Choral Improvisations for Organ for New Year,
Easter and other Church Festivals** Op. 65, Volume 3
Edited: Robert Leech Bedell Edward B. Marks Music
Corporation Key: C

Manz, Paul "Wake, Awake, for Night is Flying" **Ten
Chorale Improvisations** Set IV Op. 10 Concordia
Publishing House 97-4951 Key: C

Manz, Paul "Wake, Awake, for Night is Flying" **Ten
Chorale Improvisations** Set X Op. 22 Concordia
Publishing House 97-5557 Key: C

Manz, Paul "Wake, Awake, for Night is Flying" **Ten
Chorale Improvisations** Op. 5 Concordia Publishing
House 97-4554 Key: C

Martin, Miles I'A. "Postlude on 'Sleepers Wake'"
**The Lutheran Organist** Compiled by John Holler
H. W. Gray Key: C

Peeters, Flor "Wake, Awake, for Night is Flying"
**30 Chorale Preludes** Op. 68 C. F. Peters
Corporation No. 6023 Key: Eb

Reger, Max **30 Short Chorale Preludes** Op. 135a
C. F. Peters Corporation Nr. 3980 Key: C

Walther, Johann Gottfried "Chorale Prelude on 'Wachet
auf, ruft uns die Stimme'" **For Manuals Only**
Edited: John Christopher McAfee Music Corp. Key: C

Walther, Johann Gottfried "Wake, Awake, for Night is
Flying" **The Parish Organist** Part Four Edited:
Heinrich Fleischer Concordia Publishing House
97-1157 Key: C

Walther, Johann Gottfried "Wake, Awake, for Night is
Flying" **The Concordia Hymn Prelude Series**
Volume 2 Edited: Herbert Gotsch Concordia
Publishing House 97-5536 Key: C

Walther, Johann G. **Short Service Pieces for Organ**
Arr. Norris L. Stephens J. Fischer & Bros.
FE 9797 Key: C

Zimmer, Dennis   "Awake, Awake, for Night is Flying"
**The Concordia Hymn Prelude Series**   Volume 14
Edited: Herbert Gotsch   Concordia Publishing House
97-5705   Key: C

FREE ACCOMPANIMENTS

Johnson, David N.   **Hymn Preludes and Free
Accompaniments**   Volume 14   Augsburg Publishing
House   11-9410   Key: C

Johnson, David N.   **Free Organ Accompaniments to Hymns**
Augsburg Publishing House 11-9179   Key: C

Johnson, David N.   **Free Harmonizations of Twelve Hymn
Tunes**   Augsburg Publishing House   11-9190   Key: C

Norris, Kevin   **Hymn Preludes and Free Accompaniments**
Volume 15   Augsburg Publishing House   11-9411
Key: C

## Wächterlied

| BA | DC | 1940 | 1982 | LBW | LW | PH | RCV | UCC | UM | WB |
|----|----|------|------|-----|----|----|-----|-----|-----|-----|
|    |    |      |      | G   |    |    |     |     |     |     |

ORGAN COMPOSITIONS

Krapf, Gerhard   "Rejoice, Angelic Choirs, Rejoice"
**The Concordia Hymn Prelude Series**   Volume 11
Edited: Herbert Gotsch   Concordia Publishing
House   97-5618   Key: F

## Wachusett

| BA | DC | 1940 | 1982 | LBW | LW | PH | RCV | UCC | UM | WB |
|----|----|------|------|-----|----|----|-----|-----|-----|-----|
|    |    |      |      |     |    |    |     |     | d   |     |

## Wainwright

| BA | DC | 1940 | 1982 | LBW | LW | PH | RCV | UCC | UM | WB |
|----|----|------|------|-----|----|----|-----|-----|-----|-----|
|    |    | Db   |      |     |    |    | Db  |     |     |     |

## Waits' Carol

| BA | DC | 1940 | 1982 | LBW | LW | PH | RCV | UCC | UM | WB |
|----|----|------|------|-----|----|----|-----|-----|-----|-----|
|    |    |      |      |     |    |    |     |     | Eb  |     |

## Walda

| BA | DC | 1940 | 1982 | LBW | LW | PH | RCV | UCC | UM | WB |
|----|----|------|------|-----|----|----|-----|-----|-----|-----|
|    |    |      |      |     |    |    |     |     | d   |     |

## Walden

| BA | DC | 1940 | 1982 | LBW | LW | PH | RCV | UCC | UM | WB |
|----|----|------|------|-----|----|----|-----|-----|-----|-----|
|    |    | D    |      |     |    |    |     |     |     |     |

## Walder

| | | | | | | | | | | |
|---|---|---|---|---|---|---|---|---|---|---|
| BA | DC | 1940 | 1982 | LBW | LW | PH | RCV | UCC | UM | WB |
| | | | | | G | | | | | |

## Walhof

| | | | | | | | | | | |
|---|---|---|---|---|---|---|---|---|---|---|
| BA | DC | 1940 | 1982 | LBW | LW | PH | RCV | UCC | UM | WB |
| | | | | C | C | | | | | |

## Walker

| | | | | | | | | | | |
|---|---|---|---|---|---|---|---|---|---|---|
| BA | DC | 1940 | 1982 | LBW | LW | PH | RCV | UCC | UM | WB |
| | | | | | | | | | | Ab |

## Walsall

| | | | | | | | | | | |
|---|---|---|---|---|---|---|---|---|---|---|
| BA | DC | 1940 | 1982 | LBW | LW | PH | RCV | UCC | UM | WB |
| | | f | | | | f | | | | |

ORGAN COMPOSITIONS

Willan, Healey **36 Short Preludes and Postludes on Well-Known Hymn Tunes** Set III  C. F. Peters Corporation  No. 6163  Key:  f

FREE ACCOMPANIMENTS

Noble, T. Tertius  **Free Organ Accompaniments to One Hundred Well-Known Hymn Tunes**  J. Fischer & Bros. #8175  Key: f

## Waltham

| | | | | | | | | | | |
|---|---|---|---|---|---|---|---|---|---|---|
| BA | DC | 1940 | 1982 | LBW | LW | PH | RCV | UCC | UM | WB |
| | D | | | | | Eb | | | | |

FREE ACCOMPANIMENTS

Noble, T. Tertius  **Free Organ Accompaniments to One Hundred Well-Known Hymn Tunes**  J. Fischer & Bros. #8175  Key: D

## Walther

| | | | | | | | | | | |
|---|---|---|---|---|---|---|---|---|---|---|
| BA | DC | 1940 | 1982 | LBW | LW | PH | RCV | UCC | UM | WB |
| | | | | | G | | | | | |

ORGAN COMPOSITIONS

Kosche, Kenneth T. "He's Risen, He's Risen"  **The Concordia Hymn Prelude Series**  Volume 11 Edited: Herbert Gotsch  Concordia Publishing House 97-5618  Key: G

## Walton
(See also: Germany)

| | | | | | | | | | | |
|---|---|---|---|---|---|---|---|---|---|---|
| BA | DC | 1940 | 1982 | LBW | LW | PH | RCV | UCC | UM | WB |
| | | | | Bb | | | | | | |

FREE ACCOMPANIMENTS

Cassler, G. Winston  **Organ Descants for Selected Hymn Tunes**  Augsburg Publishing House  11-9304
Key: Bb

Wareham

| BA | DC | 1940 | 1982 | LBW | LW | PH | RCV | UCC | UM | WB |
|----|----|------|------|-----|----|----|-----|-----|----|----|
| Bb | A  | A    | A    | A   | A  | A  |     | A   | Bb | A  |

ORGAN COMPOSITIONS

Coleman, Henry  "Come, Gracious Spirit, Heavenly Dove"  **The Concordia Hymn Prelude Series**  Volume 13
Edited: Herbert Gotsch  Concordia Publishing House
97-5620  Key: A

Lang, C. S.  **Twenty Hymn-Tune Preludes**  (First Set)
Oxford University Press  Key: Bb

Thalben-Ball, George  **113 Variations on Hymn Tunes**
Novello & Co., Ltd.  Key: Bb

Willan, Healey "Prelude on 'Wareham'"  **Ten Hymn Preludes**
Set II  C. F. Peters Corporation  6012 Key: A

FREE ACCOMPANIMENTS

Gehrke, Hugo  **Hymn Preludes and Free Accompaniments**
Volume 5  Augsburg Publishing House  11-9401
Key: A

Wyton, Alec  **New Shoots from Old Routes**  Sacred Music
Press  KK 279  Key: A

Warrenton

| BA | DC | 1940 | 1982 | LBW | LW | PH | RCV | UCC | UM | WB |
|----|----|------|------|-----|----|----|-----|-----|----|----|
| D  |    |      |      |     |    |    |     |     |    |    |

Warum sollt ich mich denn grämen
(See also: Ebeling)

| BA | DC | 1940 | 1982 | LBW | LW | PH | RCV | UCC | UM | WB |
|----|----|------|------|-----|----|----|-----|-----|----|----|
|    |    |      |      |     | F  | F  |     | F   | F  | F  |

ORGAN COMPOSITIONS

Pepping, Ernst  **Fünfundzwanzig Orgelchorale**  Edition
Schott  4723  B. Schott's Sohne  Key: m:f

415

# FREE ACCOMPANIMENTS

Krapf, Gerhard **Free Organ Accompaniments to Hymns**
Volume II Advent-Christmas-Epiphany Augsburg
Publishing House 11-9187 Key: F

Was <u>frag ich nach der Welt</u>

| BA | DC | 1940 | 1982 | LBW | LW | PH | RCV | UCC | UM | WB |
|----|----|------|------|-----|----|----|-----|-----|----|----|
|    |    |      |      | C   | D  |    |     |     |    |    |
|    |    |      |      |     | D  |    |     |     |    |    |

# ORGAN COMPOSITIONS

Beck, Albert **76 Offertories on Hymns & Chorales**
Concordia Publishing House 97-5207 Key: D

Gieschen, Thomas "When All the World Was Cursed" **The
Concordia Hymn Prelude Series** Volume 15 Edited:
Herbert Gotsch Concordia Publishing House
97-5706 Key: d

Was <u>Gott tut</u>

| BA | DC | 1940 | 1982 | LBW | LW | PH | RCV | UCC | UM | WB |
|----|----|------|------|-----|----|----|-----|-----|----|----|
|    |    |      |      |     | F  | F  |     |     |    | F  |

# ORGAN COMPOSITIONS

Bach, J. S. **Organ Chorales from the Neumeister
Collection** Edited: Christoph Wolff Yale
University Press/Bärenreiter 5181 Key: G

Beck, Albert **76 Offertories on Hymns & Chorales**
Concordia Publishing House 97-5207 Key: F

Karg-Elert, Sigfrid "What God Does, That is Indeed
Well Done" **Choral Improvisations for Organ for
Confirmation, Marriage, Christening and Harvest
Festival** Op. 65 , Volume 6 Edited: Robert Leech
Bedell Edward B. Marks Music Corp. Key: G

Manz, Paul "What God Ordains is Always Good" **Ten
Chorale Improvisations** Op. 5 Concordia Publishing House 97-4554 Key: F

Marpurg, Friedrich Wilhelm **Twenty-One Chorale Preludes**
Edited: Robert M. Thompson Augsburg Publishing
House 11-9506 Key: G

Reger, Max **30 Short Chorale Preludes** Op. 135a
C. F. Peters Corporation Nr. 3980 Key: G

Walther, Johann Gottfried  "Chorale Prelude on 'Was Gott tut, das ist wohlgetan'" **For Manuals Only** Edited: John Christopher  McAfee Music Corp. Key: F

<u>Was lebet</u>
| | | | | | | | | | | |
|---|---|---|---|---|---|---|---|---|---|---|
| BA | DC | 1940 | 1982 | LBW | LW | PH | RCV | UCC | UM | WB |
| | | | C | | | | | | | |

<u>Was mein Gott will</u>
| | | | | | | | | | | |
|---|---|---|---|---|---|---|---|---|---|---|
| BA | DC | 1940 | 1982 | LBW | LW | PH | RCV | UCC | UM | WB |
| | | | | m:a | m:g | m:a | | | | |

ORGAN COMPOSITIONS

Kindermann, Johann Erasmus  "Chorale Prelude on 'Was mein Gott will, gescheh allzeit'" **For Manuals Only** Edited: John Christopher  McAfee Music Corp. Key: m:a

Marpurg, Friedrich Wilhelm  **Twenty-One Chorale Preludes** Edited: Robert M. Thompson  Augsburg Publishing House  11-9506  Key: a

Pachelbel, Johann  **Chorale Preludes by Masters of the 17th & 18th Centuries**  Volume I  Edited: Walter Buszin  Concordia Publishing House  Key: g

Reger, Max  **30 Short Chorale Preludes**  Op. 135a C. F. Peters Corporation  Nr. 3980  Key: a

<u>ashburn</u>
| | | | | | | | | | | |
|---|---|---|---|---|---|---|---|---|---|---|
| BA | DC | 1940 | 1982 | LBW | LW | PH | RCV | UCC | UM | WB |
| G | | | | | | | | | | |

<u>ashed in the Blood</u>
| | | | | | | | | | | |
|---|---|---|---|---|---|---|---|---|---|---|
| BA | DC | 1940 | 1982 | LBW | LW | PH | RCV | UCC | UM | WB |
| Ab | | | | | | | | | | |

<u>atchman</u>
| | | | | | | | | | | |
|---|---|---|---|---|---|---|---|---|---|---|
| BA | DC | 1940 | 1982 | LBW | LW | PH | RCV | UCC | UM | WB |
| | | | D | | | | | | | |

Noble, T. Tertius  **Free Organ Accompaniments to One Hundred Well-Known Hymn Tunes**  J. Fischer & Bros. #8175  Key: D

<u>atermouth</u>
| | | | | | | | | | | |
|---|---|---|---|---|---|---|---|---|---|---|
| BA | DC | 1940 | 1982 | LBW | LW | PH | RCV | UCC | UM | WB |
| | | | F | | | | | | | |

# ORGAN COMPOSITIONS

Willan, Healey "O Savior, Precious Savior" **The Parish Organist** Part Twelve Edited: Willem Mudde Concordia Publishing House 97-4759 Key: F

**Way of the Cross**

| BA | DC | 1940 | 1982 | LBW | LW | PH | RCV | UCC | UM | WB |
|----|----|------|------|-----|----|----|-----|-----|----|----|
| G |  |  |  |  |  |  |  |  |  |  |

**We Are the Lord's**

| BA | DC | 1940 | 1982 | LBW | LW | PH | RCV | UCC | UM | WB |
|----|----|------|------|-----|----|----|-----|-----|----|----|
|  |  | d |  |  |  |  |  |  |  |  |

**We Shall Overcome**
(See also: Freedom Song)

| BA | DC | 1940 | 1982 | LBW | LW | PH | RCV | UCC | UM | WB |
|----|----|------|------|-----|----|----|-----|-----|----|----|
|  |  |  |  |  |  |  |  | C |  |  |

**Webb**
(See also: Morning Light)

| BA | DC | 1940 | 1982 | LBW | LW | PH | RCV | UCC | UM | WB |
|----|----|------|------|-----|----|----|-----|-----|----|----|
| Ab | Bb |  |  | Bb | Bb | Bb |  |  | Bb |  |

## ORGAN COMPOSITIONS

Arbatsky, Yury "Stand Up! Stand Up for Jesus" **The Parish Organist** Part Four Edited: Heinrich Fleischer Concordia Publishing House 97-1157 Key: Bb

Young, Gordon "Fanfare on 'Webb'" **Contemporary Hymn Preludes** Hope Publishing Co. No. 328 Key: Bb

## FREE ACCOMPANIMENTS

Lovelace, Austin C. **Hymn Preludes and Free Accompaniments** Volume 4 Augsburg Publishing House 11-9400 Key: Bb

Noble, T. Tertius **Free Organ Accompaniments to One Hundred Well-Known Hymn Tunes** J. Fischer & Bros. #8175 Key: A

**Webbe**

| BA | DC | 1940 | 1982 | LBW | LW | PH | RCV | UCC | UM | WB |
|----|----|------|------|-----|----|----|-----|-----|----|----|
|  | E |  |  |  |  |  |  |  |  |  |

**Wedlock**

| BA | DC | 1940 | 1982 | LBW | LW | PH | RCV | UCC | UM | WB |
|----|----|------|------|-----|----|----|-----|-----|----|----|
| e | f |  | f |  |  |  |  |  | f | f |

**Held, Wilbur  7 Settings of American Folk Hymns**
Concordia Publishing House  97-5829  Key: f

Weil ich Jesu Schäflein bin

| BA | DC | 1940 | 1982 | LBW | LW | PH | RCV | UCC | UM | WB |
|----|----|------|------|-----|----|----|-----|-----|----|----|
|    |    |      |      | D   |    |    |     |     |    |    |

ORGAN COMPOSITIONS

**Beck, Albert  76 Offertories on Hymns & Chorales**
Concordia Publishing House  97-5207  Key: Db

Weimar

| BA | DC | 1940 | 1982 | LBW | LW | PH | RCV | UCC | UM | WB |
|----|----|------|------|-----|----|----|-----|-----|----|----|
|    |    | F    |      |     |    |    |     |     |    |    |

Weisse Flaggen

| BA | DC | 1940 | 1982 | LBW | LW | PH | RCV | UCC | UM | WB |
|----|----|------|------|-----|----|----|-----|-----|----|----|
|    | G  |      |      |     |    | Bb |     | Bb  |    |    |

Welcome Voice

| BA | DC | 1940 | 1982 | LBW | LW | PH | RCV | UCC | UM | WB |
|----|----|------|------|-----|----|----|-----|-----|----|----|
| Eb |    |      |      |     |    |    |     |     |    |    |

Wellesley

| BA | DC | 1940 | 1982 | LB9 | LW | PH | RCV | UCC | UM | WB |
|----|----|------|------|-----|----|----|-----|-----|----|----|
| Bb | Bb |      |      |     |    | Bb | C   |     |    |    |

Wellington Square

| BA | DC | 1940 | 1982 | LBW | LW | PH | RCV | UCC | UM | WB |
|----|----|------|------|-----|----|----|-----|-----|----|----|
|    |    | f    |      | f   |    | f  |     | f   |    |    |

Welsh Melody

| BA | DC | 1940 | 1982 | LBW | LW | PH | RCV | UCC | UM | WB |
|----|----|------|------|-----|----|----|-----|-----|----|----|
|    | f# |      |      |     |    | f# |     |     |    |    |

Welwyn

| BA | DC | 1940 | 1982 | LBW | LW | PH | RCV | UCC | UM | WB |
|----|----|------|------|-----|----|----|-----|-----|----|----|
|    | F  | F    |      |     |    | F  |     | F   | F  | F  |

FREE ACCOMPANIMENTS

**Free Harmonizations to Hymn Tunes By Fifty American Composers**  Edited: D. DeWitt Wasson  Hinshaw Music, Inc.  HMO-145  Key: F

Wem in Leidenstagen

| BA | DC | 1940 | 1982 | LBW | LW | PH | RCV | UCC | UM | WB |
|----|----|------|------|-----|----|----|-----|-----|----|----|
|    |    |      | F    | F   | F  |    | F   |     |    |    |

ORGAN COMPOSITIONS

Beck, Albert  **76 Offertories on Hymns & Chorales**
Concordia Publishing House  97-5207  Key: F

Cassler, G. Winston  "Glory Be to Jesus" **The Concordia
Hymn Prelude Series**  Volume 9  Edited: Herbert
Gotsch  Concordia Publishing House  97-5616
Key: F

Gieschen, Thomas  **Four Quiet Hymn Settings**  Concordia
Publishing House  97-5839  Key: F

Powell, Newman W.  "Glory Be to Jesus"  **The Parish
Organist**  Part Four  Edited: Heinrich Fleischer
Concordia Publishing House  97-1157  Key: F

FREE ACCOMPANIMENTS

Gehrke, Hugo  **Hymn Preludes and Free Accompaniments**
Volume 5  Augsburg Publishing House  11-9401
Key: F

Weman

| BA | DC | 1940 | 1982 | LBW | LW | PH | RCV | UCC | UM | WB |
|----|----|------|------|-----|----|----|-----|-----|----|----|
|    | D  |      |      |     |    |    |     |     |    |    |

Wenn wir in höchsten Nöten sein

| BA | DC | 1940 | 1982 | LBW | LW | PH | RCV | UCC | UM | WB |
|----|----|------|------|-----|----|----|-----|-----|----|----|
|    |    |      |      | G   | G  |    |     |     |    |    |

ORGAN COMPOSITIONS

Bach, Johann Michael  "When in the Hour of Utmost Need"
**The Parish Organist**  Part Four  Edited: Heinrich
Fleischer  Concordia Publishing House  97-1157
Key: F

Bach, J. S.  **Organ Works**  Volume 1  Edited: Heinz-
Harald Löhlein  Urtext of the New Bach Edition
Bärenreiter  5171  Key: G

Bach, J.S. **Organ Works**  Volume VII  Widor-Schweitzer
G. Schirmer  Key: G

Bach, J.S.  **Organ Works** Volume VIII Widor-Schweitzer
G. Schirmer  Key: G

Bach, J.S. **Orgelwerke** Volume V  C. F. Peters
Corporation  Nr. 244  Key: G

Bach, J.S. **Orgelwerke** Volume VII  C. F. Peters
Corporation  Nr.246  Key: G

420

Bach, J.S. **The Liturgical Year** (Orgelbuchlein)
Edited: Albert Reimenschneider   Oliver Ditson Co.
Key: G

Bach, Johann Michael   **Chorale Preludes by Masters of
the 17th & 18th Centuries** Volume I   Edited:
Walter Buszin   Concordia Publishing House   Key: G

Scheidt, Samuel "Enslaved by Sin and Bound in Chains"
**The Parish Organist** Part Seven   Music for
Lent, Palm Sunday and Holy Week   Edited: Erich
Goldschmidt   Concordia Publishing House   97-1403
Key: F

Walcha, Helmut **Chorale Preludes** II   C. F. Peters
Corporation   Nr. 4871   Key: G

Wennerberg

| BA | DC | 1940 | 1982 | LBW | LW | PH | RCV | UCC | UM | WB |
|----|----|------|------|-----|----|----|-----|-----|----|----|
|    |    |      |      | C   |    |    |     |     |    |    |

Wentworth

| BA | DC | 1940 | 1982 | LBW | LW | PH | RCV | UCC | UM | WB |
|----|----|------|------|-----|----|----|-----|-----|----|----|
|    |    |      |      |     |    | PH |     |     | UM |    |
|    |    |      |      |     |    | C  |     |     | C  |    |

Wer nur den lieben Gott

| BA | DC | 1940 | 1982 | LBW | LW | PH | RCV | UCC | UM | WB |
|----|----|------|------|-----|----|----|-----|-----|----|----|
| g  |    | g    | g    | g   |    |    |     |     | g  |    |

ORGAN COMPOSITIONS

Bach, J. S.   **Organ Works** Volume 1   Edited: Heinz-
Harald Löhlein   Urtext of the New Bach Edition
Bärenreiter 5171 (Two settings) Key: m:c; Key: m:a

Bach, J. S.   **Organ Works** Volume 3   "The Individually
Transmitted Organ Chorales"   Edited: Hans Klotz
Urtext of the New Bach Edition   Bärenreiter
5173   Key: a

Bach, J.S. **Six Organ Chorals** (Schubler)
Edited: Albert Riemenschneider   Oliver Ditson
Distributed: Theodore Presser   Key: c

Bach, J.S. **Organ Works** Volume VI   Widor-Schweitzer
G. Schirmer (#60, 61) Key: a

Bach, J.S. **Organ Works** Volume VII   Widor-Schweitzer
G. Schirmer   Key: a

Bach, J.S. **Organ Works** Volume VIII Widor-Schweitzer
G. Schirmer Key: c

Bach, J.S. **Orgelwerke** Volume V   C.F. Peters
    Corporation   Nr. 244   #53, #54   Key: a

Bach, J.S. **Orgelwerke** Volume VII   C.F. Peters
    Corporation #246   Key: c

Bach, J.S. "If Thou But Suffer God to Guide Thee"
    **Wedding Music**   Part 2   Concordia Publishing
    House   97-1370   Key: a

Bach, J.S. **The Liturgical Year**   (Orgelbuchlein)
    Edited: Albert Reimenschneider   Oliver Ditson Co.
    Key: a

Bohm, George   "Chorale and Variation on "Wer nur den
    lieben Gott lasst walten"   **For Manuals Only**
    Edited: John Christopher   McAfee Music Corp. Key: a

Dupre, Marcel   **Seventy-Nine Chorales for Organ**
    Opus 28   H. W. Gray   Key: a

Karg-Elert, Sigfrid   "If Thou But Suffer God to Guide
    Thee"   **Choral Improvisations for Organ for Confir-
    mation, Marriage, Christening and Harvest Festival**
    Op. 65, Volume 6   Edited: Robert Leech Bedell
    Edward B. Marks Music Corp. #62 Key: A, #63 Key:a

Manz, Paul "If Thou But Suffer God" **Ten Chorale
    Improvisations** Set V Op. 14 Concordia Publishing
    House 97-5257   Key: g

Marpurg, Friedrich Wilhelm   **Twenty-One Chorale Preludes**
    Edited: Robert M. Thompson   Augsburg Publishing
    House   11-9506   Key: a

Pepping, Ernst   **Funfundzwanzig Orgelchorale**   Edition
    B. Schott   4723   B. Schott's Sohne   Key: m:g

Reger, Max **30 Short Chorale Preludes** Op. 135a
    C. F. Peters Corporation   Nr. 3980   Key: g

Reger, Max **Chorale Preludes for the Church Year from
    Max Reger, Op. 67** Edited: Alec Wyton   Carl
    Fischer, Inc.   0-4667   Key: a

Walcha, Helmut **25 Chorale Preludes** C. F. Peters
    Nr. 4850   Key: a

Walther, Johann Gottfried   "If Thou But Suffer God to
    Guide Thee"   **The Parish Organist**   Part Four
    Edited: Heinrich Fleischer   Concordia Publishing
    House   97-1157   Key: g

<u>Werde munter</u>

| BA | DC | 1940 | 1982 | LBW | LW | PH | RCV | UCC | UM | WB |
|----|----|------|------|-----|----|----|-----|-----|----|----|
|    |    | F    | F    | F   |    |    | F   | F   |    |    |

## ORGAN COMPOSITIONS

Bach, J. S. **Organ Chorales from the Neumeister Collection** Edited: Christoph Wolff Yale University Press/Bärenreiter 5181 Key: G

Karg-Elert, Sigfrid "Be Glad My Soul" **Choral Improvisations for Organ for Reformation Day, Fast Days, Communion and Funeral Rites** Op. 65, Volume 5 Edited: Robert Leech Bedell Edward B. Marks Music Corp. Key: G

Manz, Paul "Like the Golden Sun Ascending" **Ten Chorale Improvisations** Set IV Op. 10 Concordia Publishing House 97-4951 Key: F

Marpurg, Friedrich Wilhelm **Twenty-One Chorale Preludes** Edited: Robert M. Thompson Augsburg Publishing House 11-9506 Key: G

Pachelbel, Johann "Speak, O Lord, Thy Servant Heareth" **The Parish Organist** Part Four Edited: Heinrich Fleischer Concordia Publishing House 97-1157 Key: F

Pasquet, Jean "O My Soul, on Wings Ascending" **Nine Chorale Preludes** Augsburg Publishing House 11-9298 Key: F

## FREE ACCOMPANIMENTS

Cassler, G. Winston **Organ Descants for Selected Hymn Tunes** Augsburg Publishing House 11-9304 Key: F

<u>Were You There</u>

| BA | DC | 1940 | 1982 | LBW | LW | PH | RCV | UCC | UM | WB |
|----|----|------|------|-----|----|----|-----|-----|----|----|
| Eb | Eb | E    | E    | Eb  | Eb | Eb |     | Eb  | Eb |    |

## ORGAN COMPOSITIONS

Hancock, Eugene W. "Were You There" **The Concordia Hymn Prelude Series** Volume 9 Edited: Herbert Gotsch Concordia Publishing House 97-5616 Key: Eb

Stearns, Peter Pindar **Eight Hymn Preludes for Lent** Harold Flammer, Inc. HF-5133 Key: E

# FREE ACCOMPANIMENTS

Ferguson, John **Hymn Tune Harmonizations** Book III
  Ludwig Music Publishing Co.  Key: Eb

Wyton, Alec  **New Shoots from Old Routes**  Sacred
  Music Press  KK 279  Key: C

West Park

| BA | DC | 1940 | 1982 | LBW | LW | PH | RCV | UCC | UM | WB |
|----|----|------|------|-----|----|----|-----|-----|----|----|
|    |    | F    |      |     |    |    |     |     |    |    |

Westerly

| BA | DC | 1940 | 1982 | LBW | LW | PH | RCV | UCC | UM | WB |
|----|----|------|------|-----|----|----|-----|-----|----|----|
|    |    | D    |      |     |    |    |     |     |    |    |

Westminster Abbey

| BA | DC | 1940 | 1982 | LBW | LW | PH | RCV | UCC | UM | WB |
|----|----|------|------|-----|----|----|-----|-----|----|----|
|    |    | G    |      |     | G  |    |     |     |    |    |

# ORGAN COMPOSITIONS

Schultz, Ralph C.  "In His Temple Now Behold Him"
  **The Concordia Hymn Prelude Series**  Volume 15
  Edited: Herbert Gotsch  Concordia Publishing House
  97-5706  Key: D

Westridge

| BA | DC | 1940 | 1982 | LBW | LW | PH | RCV | UCC | UM | WB |
|----|----|------|------|-----|----|----|-----|-----|----|----|
|    |    | F    |      |     |    |    |     |     |    |    |

Wetherby

| BA | DC | 1940 | 1982 | LBW | LW | PH | RCV | UCC | UM | WB |
|----|----|------|------|-----|----|----|-----|-----|----|----|
|    |    | Db   |      |     |    |    |     |     |    |    |

Weymouth

| BA | DC | 1940 | 1982 | LBW | LW | PH | RCV | UCC | UM | WB |
|----|----|------|------|-----|----|----|-----|-----|----|----|
|    | F  | F    |      |     |    |    |     |     |    |    |

What a Friend
  (See also: Erie)

When Jesus Wept

| BA | DC | 1940 | 1982 | LBW | LW | PH | RCV | UCC | UM | WB |
|----|----|------|------|-----|----|----|-----|-----|----|----|
|    |    | F    |      |     |    |    |     |     |    |    |

While Shepherds Watched

| BA | DC | 1940 | 1982 | LBW | LW | PH | RCV | UCC | UM | WB |
|----|----|------|------|-----|----|----|-----|-----|----|----|
|    |    |      |      |     | F  |    |     |     |    |    |

# ORGAN COMPOSITIONS

Schack, David  "While Shepherds Watched" **The Concordia Hymn Prelude Series** Volume 5 Edited: Herbert Gotsch  Concordia Publishing House  97-5611  Key: F

## Whitfield

| BA | DC | 1940 | 1982 | LBW | LW | PH | RCV | UCC | UM | WB |
|----|----|------|------|-----|----|----|-----|-----|----|----|
| Eb |    |      |      |     |    |    |     |     |    |    |

## Whitford

| BA | DC | 1940 | 1982 | LBW | LW | PH | RCV | UCC | UM | WB |
|----|----|------|------|-----|----|----|-----|-----|----|----|
|    |    |      |      |     |    | g  |     |     |    | f  |

## Whittier
(See also: Rest)

| BA | DC | 1940 | 1982 | LBW | LW | PH | RCV | UCC | UM | WB |
|----|----|------|------|-----|----|----|-----|-----|----|----|
|    |    |      |      |     |    |    | C   |     |    |    |

## Whittle

| BA | DC | 1940 | 1982 | LBW | LW | PH | RCV | UCC | UM | WB |
|----|----|------|------|-----|----|----|-----|-----|----|----|
| Bb |    |      |      |     |    |    |     |     |    |    |

## Whosoever

| BA | DC | 1940 | 1982 | LBW | LW | PH | RCV | UCC | UM | WB |
|----|----|------|------|-----|----|----|-----|-----|----|----|
| C  |    |      |      |     |    |    |     |     |    |    |

## Wiant

| BA | DC | 1940 | 1982 | LBW | LW | PH | RCV | UCC | UM | WB |
|----|----|------|------|-----|----|----|-----|-----|----|----|
|    |    |      |      |     |    |    |     |     | F  |    |

## Wie lieblich ist der Maien

| BA | DC | 1940 | 1982 | LBW | LW | PH | RCV | UCC | UM | WB |
|----|----|------|------|-----|----|----|-----|-----|----|----|
|    |    |      |      | Bb  | Bb |    |     |     |    | Bb |

## Wie schön leuchtet der Morgenstern
(See also: Frankfurt)

| BA | DC | 1940 | 1982 | LBW | LW | PH | RCV | UCC | UM | WB |
|----|----|------|------|-----|----|----|-----|-----|----|----|
|    | D  |      | D    | D   | D  | D  | Eb  | D   | D  |    |

# INTONATIONS

Hermann, David  **11 Hymn Intonations, Free Accompaniments, Instrumental Descants for Organ** Volume I Advent, Christmas, Epiphany  G.I.A. Publications G-2378  Key: D

# ORGAN COMPOSITIONS

Bach, Johann Christoph  **Short Service Pieces for Organ** Arr. Norris L. Stephens  J. Fischer & Bros. FE 9797  Key: Eb

Bach, J.S. **Organ Works** Volume VI  Widor-Schweitzer
G. Schirmer  (#62,63)  Key: G

Bender, Jan  "O Holy Spirit, Enter In"  **The Concordia
Hymn Prelude Series**  Volume 13  Edited: Herbert
Gotsch  Concordia Publishing House  97-5620
Key: D

Buxtehude, Dietrich  **Short Classic Pieces for Organ
from the 17th and 18th Centuries**  Arr. Norris
Stephens  J. Fischer & Bros.  No. 9607  Key: G

Buxtehude, Dietrich  "How Brightly Shines the Morning
Star"  **Chorale Preludes** Volume II C.F. Peters
Corporation  No. 4457  Key: G

Distler, Hugo **Short Chorale Arrangements** Opus 8/3
Bärenreiter 1222  Key: D

Dupre, Marcel  **Seventy-Nine Chorales for Organ**
Opus 28  H. W. Gray  Key: G

Karg-Elert, Sigfrid "How Brightly Shines the Morning
Star"  **Choral Improvisations for Organ for
Ascensiontide and Pentecost** Op. 65 Volume 4 Edited:
Robert Leech Bedell  Edward B. Marks Music Corp.
Key: F

Karg-Elert, Sigfrid "How Brightly Shines the Morning
Star"  **Choral Improvisations for Organ for Con-
firmation, Marriage, Christening and Harvest
Festival** Op. 65, Volume 6 Edited: Robert Leech
Bedell  Edward B. Marks Music Corp.  Key: Eb

Manz, Paul "How Brightly Shines the Morning Star"
**Ten Chorale Improvisations** Set II  Op. 7
Concordia Publishing House 97-4656  Key: Eb

Manz, Paul "How Lovely Shines the Morning Star"
**Ten Chorale Improvisations** Set Op. 16  Set VI
Concordia Publishing House 97-5305  Key: D

Miles, George Th.  "How Bright Appears the Morning
Star"  **The Parish Organist** Christmas and Epiphany
Music  Part Six  Concordia Publishing House
97-1391  Key:  Eb

Pachelbel, Johann **Chorale Preludes by Masters of the
17th & 18th Centuries** Volume I  Edited:  Walter
Buszin  Concordia Publishing House  Key: Eb

Peeters, Flor  "How Lovely Shines the Morning Star"
    **30 Chorale Preludes** Op. 68  C. F. Peters
    Corporation  No. 6023  Key: D

Petzold, Johannes  "He is Arisen! Glorious Word!"
    **The Concordia Hymn Prelude Series** Volume 11
    Edited: Herbert Gotsch  Concordia Publishing House
    Key: D

Praetorius, Michael  "How Lovely Shines the Morning
    Star" **The Parish Organist** Part Four  Edited:
    Heinrich Fleischer  Concordia Publishing House
    97-1157  Key: Eb

Reger, Max **30 Short Chorale Preludes** Op. 135a
    C. F. Peters Corporation  Nr. 3980  Key: D

Reger, Max  **Chorale Preludes for the Church Year from
    Max Reger, Op. 67** Edited: Alec Wyton  Carl
    Fischer, Inc.  0-4667  Key: F

Telemann, Georg Philipp  "All Hail to You, O Blessed
    Morn!"  **The Concordia Hymn Prelude Series**
    Volume 5  Edited: Herbert Gotsch  Concordia
    Publishing House  97-5611  Key: D

Walcha, Helmut  **Chorale Preludes** II  C. F. Peters
    Corporation  Nr. 4871  Key: Eb

Wente, Steven  "O Morning Star, How Fair and Bright"
    **The Concordia Hymn Prelude Series** Volume 6
    Edited: Herbert Gotsch  Concordia Publishing
    House  97-5612  Key: D

## FREE ACCOMPANIMENTS

Bender, Jan **Free Organ Accompaniments to Festival
    Hymns** Volume I  Augsburg Publishing House
    11-9192  Key: D

Ferguson, John  **Hymn Tune Harmonzations** Book III
    Ludwig Music Publishing Co.  Key: D

Wie soll ich dich empfangen

| BA | DC | 1940 | 1982 | LBW | LW | PH | RCV | UCC | UM | WB |
|----|----|------|------|-----|----|----|-----|-----|----|----|
|    |    |      |      | D   | D  |    |     |     |    |    |

## ORGAN COMPOSITIONS

Manz, Paul "O Lord, How Shall I Meet You" **Ten Chorale
    Improvisations** Set X Op. 22  Concordia Publishing
    House 97-5557  Key: C

Manz, Paul "Rejoice, Rejoice, Believers" **Ten Chorale Improvisations** Set X Op. 22 Concordia Publishing House 97-5557 Key: C

Patterson, Kim Kondal "O Lord, How Shall I Meet You" **The Concordia Hymn Prelude Series** Volume 2 Edited: Herbert Gotsch Concordia Publishing House 97-5536 Key: D

## Wigan

| BA | DC | 1940 | 1982 | LBW | LW | PH | RCV | UCC | UM | WB |
|----|----|------|------|-----|----|----|-----|-----|----|----|
|    |    | f    |      |     |    |    |     |     |    | f  |

## Wigtown

| BA | DC | 1940 | 1982 | LBW | LW | PH | RCV | UCC | UM | WB |
|----|----|------|------|-----|----|----|-----|-----|----|----|
|    |    |      |      |     |    | F  |     |     |    |    |

ORGAN COMPOSITIONS

Thalben-Ball, George **113 Variations on Hymn Tunes** Novello & Co., Ltd. Key: F

## Wilcox

| BA | DC | 1940 | 1982 | LBW | LW | PH | RCV | UCC | UM | WB |
|----|----|------|------|-----|----|----|-----|-----|----|----|
|    |    |      |      |     |    |    |     | m:d |    |    |

## Wilderness

| BA | DC | 1940 | 1982 | LBW | LW | PH | RCV | UCC | UM | WB |
|----|----|------|------|-----|----|----|-----|-----|----|----|
|    |    | e    | e    |     |    |    |     |     |    |    |

## Williams Bay

| BA | DC | 1940 | 1982 | LBW | LW | PH | RCV | UCC | UM | WB |
|----|----|------|------|-----|----|----|-----|-----|----|----|
|    |    |      |      | F   |    |    |     |     |    |    |

## Wilton

| BA | DC | 1940 | 1982 | LBW | LW | PH | RCV | UCC | UM | WB |
|----|----|------|------|-----|----|----|-----|-----|----|----|
|    | A  |      |      |     |    |    |     |     |    |    |

## Wiltshire

| BA | DC | 1940 | 1982 | LBW | LW | PH | RCV | UCC | UM | WB |
|----|----|------|------|-----|----|----|-----|-----|----|----|
|    |    | Ab   |      |     |    | Ab |     |     |    |    |

ORGAN COMPOSITIONS

Thalben-Ball, George **113 Variations on Hymn Tunes** Novello & Co., Ltd. Key: A

FREE ACCOMPANIMENTS

Coleman, Henry **Varied Hymn Accompaniments** Oxford University Press Key: Bb

## Wimbledon

| BA | DC | 1940 | 1982 | LBW | LW | PH | RCV | UCC | UM | WB |
|---|---|---|---|---|---|---|---|---|---|---|
|  | D |  |  |  |  |  |  |  |  |  |

## Winchester New
(See also: Crasselius)

| BA | DC | 1940 | 1982 | LBW | LW | PH | RCV | UCC | UM | WB |
|---|---|---|---|---|---|---|---|---|---|---|
| Bb | Bb | Bb |  |  |  | Bb | Bb | Bb | Bb | Bb |

### ORGAN COMPOSITIONS

Bassett, Anita Denniston **Nine Hymn-Tune Preludes**
Ludwig Music Publishing Co.  0-08  Key: Bb

### FREE ACCOMPANIMENTS

Ferguson, John **Ten Hymn Tune Harmonizations** Book I
Ludwig Music Publishing Co.  0-05  Key: Bb

Noble, T. Tertius  **Free Organ Accompaniments to One
Hundred Well-Known Hymn Tunes**  J. Fischer & Bros.
#8175  Key: Bb

Wyton, Alec  **New Shoots from Old Routes**  Sacred
Music Press  KK  279  Key: Bb

## Winchester Old

| BA | DC | 1940 | 1982 | LBW | LW | PH | RCV | UCC | UM | WB |
|---|---|---|---|---|---|---|---|---|---|---|
| F | F | F | F | F | F | F | F | F | F |  |

### ORGAN COMPOSITIONS

Bichsel, M. Alfred  "When All Thy Mercies, O My God"
**The Parish Organist**  Part Four  Edited:
Heinrich Fleischer  Concordia Publishing House
97-1157  Key: F

### FREE ACCOMPANIMENTS

Bender, Jan  "O Jesus, King most wonderful" **Free
Organ Accompaniments to Hymns**  Volume III
General- Palm Sunday- Easter  Augsburg
Publishing House  11-9189  Key: F

Noble, T. Tertius **Fifty Free Organ Accompaniments to
Well Known Hymn Tunes**  J. Fischer & Bros.
No. 8430  Key: F

## Windham

| BA | DC | 1940 | 1982 | LBW | LW | PH | RCV | UCC | UM | WB |
|---|---|---|---|---|---|---|---|---|---|---|
|  | d |  |  | d | d |  |  |  | d |  |

ORGAN COMPOSITIONS

Gotsch, Herbert "We Sing the Praise of Him Who Died"
**The Concordia Hymn Prelude Series** Volume 9
Edited: Herbert Gotsch Concordia Publishing House
97-5616 Key: d

FREE ACCOMPANIMENTS

Lovelace, Austin C. **Hymn Preludes and Free
Accompaniments** Volume 4 Augsburg Publishing
House 11-9400 Key: d

Windsor

| BA | DC | 1940 | 1982 | LBW | LW | PH | RCV | UCC | UM | WB |
|----|----|------|------|-----|----|----|-----|-----|----|----|
|    |    | g    | g    | g   |    | g  | g   |     | g  |    |

ORGAN COMPOSITIONS

Coleman, Henry "There is a Green Hill Far Away" **The
Concordia Hymn Prelude Series** Volume 9 Edited:
Herbert Gotsch Concordia Publishing House
97-5616 Key: g

Thalben-Ball, George **113 Variations on Hymn Tunes**
Novello & Co., Ltd. Key: g

Willan, Healey "Jesus, the Very Thought of Thee" **The
Parish Organist** Part Twelve Edited: Willem
Mudde Concordia Publishing House 97-4759 Key: g

FREE ACCOMPANIMENTS

Johnson, David N. **Hymn Preludes and Free
Accompaniments** Volume 14 Augsburg Publishing
House 11-9410 Key: g

Noble, T. Tertius **Free Organ Accompaniments to One
Hundred Well-Known Hymn Tunes** J. Fischer & Bros.
#8175 Key: g

Winkworth

| BA | DC | 1940 | 1982 | LBW | LW | PH | RCV | UCC | UM | WB |
|----|----|------|------|-----|----|----|-----|-----|----|----|
|    |    | g    |      |     |    |    | g   |     |    |    |

Winter

| BA | DC | 1940 | 1982 | LBW | LW | PH | RCV | UCC | UM | WB |
|----|----|------|------|-----|----|----|-----|-----|----|----|
|    | Db |      |      |     |    |    |     |     |    |    |

Winterton

| BA | DC | 1940 | 1982 | LBW | LW | PH | RCV | UCC | UM | WB |
|----|----|------|------|-----|----|----|-----|-----|----|----|
|    |    |      |      |     | D  |    |     |     |    |    |

Beck, Albert **76 Offertories on Hymns & Chorales**
Concordia Publishing House  97-5207  Key: Eb

Wir dienen, Herr
  BA    DC    1940 1982 LBW   LW    PH    RCV   UCC   UM    WB
                    e

Rogers, Adrian  "Strengthen for Service, Lord"
  **The Concordia Hymn Prelude Series**  Volume 18
  Edited: Herbert Gotsch  Concordia Publishing House
  97-5709  Key: e

Wir glauben all
  BA    DC    1940 1982 LBW   LW    PH    RCV   UCC   UM    WB
                    m:d   m:d

Wir glauben all' an einen Gott, Schöpfer
  BA    DC    1940 1982 LBW   LW    PH    RCV   UCC   UM    WB
                          D     D

Bach, J. S.  **Organ Chorales from the Neumeister
  Collection**  Edited: Christoph Wolff  Yale
  University Press/Bärenreiter 5181  Key: m:d

Bach, J.S. **Organ Works** Volume VI  Widor-Schweitzer
  G. Schirmer  Key: F

Bach, J.S. **Organ Works** Volume VII  Widor-Schweitzer
  G. Schirmer  Key: d; Key: e

Bach, J.S. **Orgelwerke** Volume VII  C.F. Peters
  Corporation Nr. 246  #60 Key: d; #61 Key: e

Dupre, Marcel **Seventy-Nine Chorales for Organ**
  Opus 28  H. W. Gray  Key: d

Scheidt, Samuel **Chorale Preludes by Masters of the
  17th & 18th Centuries**  Volume I  Edited: Walter
  Buszin  Concordia Publishing House  Key: m:d

Zachau, Friedrich Wilhelm  "We All Believe in One True
  God" **The Parish Organist** Part Eight  Music for
  Easter, Ascension, Pentecost, and Trinity  Edited:
  Erich Goldschmidt  Concordia Publishing House
  97-1404  Key: m:d

<u>Wir hätten gebauet</u>

| BA | DC | 1940 | 1982 | LBW | LW | PH | RCV | UCC | UM | WB |
|----|----|------|------|-----|----|----|-----|-----|----|----|
|    |    |      | Eb   |     |    |    |     |     |    |    |

ORGAN COMPOSITIONS

Gieseke, Richard W.  "When Christmas Morn is Dawning"
**The Concordia Hymn Prelude Series** Volume 5
Edited: Herbert Gotsch  Concordia Publishing
House  97-5611  Key: Eb

<u>Wir pflügen</u> (Dresden)

| BA | DC | 1940 | 1982 | LBW | LW | PH | RCV | UCC | UM | WB |
|----|----|------|------|-----|----|----|-----|-----|----|----|
|    |    | A    | A    |     |    | Ab |     |     | A  |    |

FREE ACCOMPANIMENTS

Johnson, David N. **Hymn Preludes and Free
Accompaniments** Volume 14  Augsburg Publishing
House  11-9410  Key: A

<u>Wise Men, The</u>

| BA | DC | 1940 | 1982 | LBW | LW | PH | RCV | UCC | UM | WB |
|----|----|------|------|-----|----|----|-----|-----|----|----|
|    |    |      | Eb   |     |    |    |     |     |    |    |

<u>Without Him</u>

| BA | DC | 1940 | 1982 | LBW | LW | PH | RCV | UCC | UM | WB |
|----|----|------|------|-----|----|----|-----|-----|----|----|
| F  |    |      |      |     |    |    |     |     |    |    |

<u>Witmer</u>

| BA | DC | 1940 | 1982 | LBW | LW | PH | RCV | UCC | UM | WB |
|----|----|------|------|-----|----|----|-----|-----|----|----|
|    |    |      |      |     |    |    |     |     |    | WB |
|    |    |      |      |     |    |    |     |     |    | D  |

<u>Wittenberg New</u>

| BA | DC | 1940 | 1982 | LBW | LW | PH | RCV | UCC | UM | WB |
|----|----|------|------|-----|----|----|-----|-----|----|----|
|    |    |      |      | f   | f  |    |     |     |    |    |

ORGAN COMPOSITIONS

Manz, Paul "O God, O Lord of Heaven and Earth"
**Ten Chorale Improvisations** Set IX Op. 21
Concordia Publishing House 97-5556  Key: f

<u>Wo Gott zum Haus</u>

| BA | DC | 1940 | 1982 | LBW | LW | PH | RCV | UCC | UM | WB |
|----|----|------|------|-----|----|----|-----|-----|----|----|
|    |    |      | Eb   | Eb  |    |    | Eb  |     |    |    |

ORGAN COMPOSITIONS

Bach, Johann Christoph  "Oh, Blest the House, Whate'er
Befall" **The Parish Organist** Edited: Heinrich
Fleischer  Concordia Publishing House  97-1157
Key:  Eb

432

Distler, Hugo  "When Christ's Appearing Was Made Known"
**The Concordia Hymn Prelude Series**  Volume 6
Edited: Herbert Gotsch  Concordia Publishing House
97-5612  Key: Eb

Othmayr, Kaspar  "The Star Proclaims the King is Here"
**The Parish Organist**  Christmas and Epiphany
Music  Part Six  Concordia Publishing House
97-1391  Key: Eb

Pachelbel, Johann  "The Star Proclaims the King is Here"
**The Parish Organist**  Christmas and Epiphany
Music Concordia Publishing House 97-1391  Key: Eb

### FREE ACCOMPANIMENTS

Gehrke, Hugo  **Hymn Preludes and Free Accompaniments**
Volume 5  Augsburg Publishing House  11-9401
Key: Eb

Wo soll ich fliehen hin
(See also: Auf meinen lieben Gott)
BA    DC    1940 1982 LBW  LW    PH    RCV  UCC  UM   WB
D

### ORGAN COMPOSITIONS

Bach, J. S.  **Organ Works**  Volume 1  Edited: Heinz-
Harald Löhlein  Urtext of the New Bach Edition
Bärenreiter  5171  Key: e

Bach, J.S.  **Six Organ Chorals** (Schubler)
Edited: Albert Riemenschneider    Oliver Ditson
Distributed: Theodore Presser  Key: e

Bach, J.S. **Organ Works** Volume VI  Widor-Schweitzer
G. Schirmer  Key: g

Bach, J.S.  **Orgelwerke** Volume VII  C.F. Peters
Corporation  Nr. 246  Key: e

Walther, Johann Gottfried  "O Bride of Christ, Rejoice"
**The Concordia Hymn Prelude Series**  Volume 2
Edited: Herbert Gotsch  Concordia Publishing House
97-5536  Key: D

Wojtkiewiecz
BA    DC    1940 1982 LBW  LW    PH    RCV  UCC  UM   WB
F

Krapf, Gerhard **A New Song** The Sacred Music Press
Key: F

Woking

| BA | DC | 1940 | 1982 | LBW | LW | PH | RCV | UCC | UM | WB |
|----|----|------|------|-----|----|----|-----|-----|----|----|
|    |    | Bb   |      |     |    |    |     |     |    |    |

Wolvercote

| BA | DC | 1940 | 1982 | LBW | LW | PH | RCV | UCC | UM | WB |
|----|----|------|------|-----|----|----|-----|-----|----|----|
|    |    | A    |      |     |    |    |     |     |    |    |

Wondrous Love

| BA  | DC  | 1940 | 1982 | LBW | LW  | PH | RCV | UCC | UM  | WB |
|-----|-----|------|------|-----|-----|----|-----|-----|-----|----|
| m:d | m:e |      |      | m:d | m:d |    |     |     | m:d |    |

ORGAN COMPOSITIONS

Barber, Samuel **Wondrous Love - Variations on a Shape-note Hymn** New York: G. Schirmer Key: m:f

Johnson, David N. **Wondrous Love** Augsburg Publishing House 11-821 Key: e

McKinney, Mathilde "Chorale Prelude on 'Wondrous Love' **The Bristol Collection of Contemporary Hymn Tune Preludes for Organ** Volume 3 Edited: Lee Hastings Bristol Jr. Harold Flammer Key: m:d

Wood, Dale **Organ Book of American Folk Hymns** The Sacred Music Press Key: e

Wondrous Story

| BA | DC | 1940 | 1982 | LBW | LW | PH | RCV | UCC | UM | WB |
|----|----|------|------|-----|----|----|-----|-----|----|----|
| Eb |    |      |      |     |    |    |     |     |    |    |

ORGAN COMPOSITIONS

Held, Wilbur "I Will Sing the Wondrous Story" **Gospel Hymn Settings** Hinshaw Music Co., Inc. HMO-146 Key: Eb

Woodbird

(See also: Es flog ein kleins Waldvögelein)

| BA | DC | 1940 | 1982 | LBW | LW | PH | RCV | UCC | UM | WB |
|----|----|------|------|-----|----|----|-----|-----|----|----|
| G  | G  |      |      |     |    |    |     |     |    |    |

ORGAN COMPOSITIONS

Diercks, John "O Day of Rest and Gladness" **The Parish Organist** Part Twelve Edited: Willem Mudde Concordia Publishing House 97-4759 Key: G

Hancock, Gerre **Organ Improvisations for Hymn-Singing**
Hinshaw Music Co.   HMO-100   Key: G

**Woodbury**

| BA | DC | 1940 | 1982 | LBW | LW | PH | RCV | UCC | UM | WB |
|----|----|------|------|-----|----|----|-----|-----|----|----|
|    |    | g    |      |     |    |    |     |     |    |    |

**Woodlands**

| BA | DC | 1940 | 1982 | LBW | LW | PH | RCV | UCC | UM | WB |
|----|----|------|------|-----|----|----|-----|-----|----|----|
| Eb | D  |      | D    |     |    | D  |     | D   |    |    |

ORGAN COMPOSITIONS

Thalben-Ball, George   **113 Variations on Hymn Tunes**
Novello & Co., Ltd.   Key:  D

**Woodland Hills**

| BA | DC | 1940 | 1982 | LBW | LW | PH | RCV | UCC | UM | WB |
|----|----|------|------|-----|----|----|-----|-----|----|----|
| Bb |    |      |      |     |    |    |     |     |    |    |

**Woodworth**

| BA | DC | 1940 | 1982 | LBW | LW | PH | RCV | UCC | UM | WB |
|----|----|------|------|-----|----|----|-----|-----|----|----|
| Eb | Eb | D    | D    | Eb  | Eb | Eb |     | Eb  | D  |    |

ORGAN COMPOSITIONS

Beck, Albert   **76 Offertories on Hymns and Chorales**
Concordia Publishing House   97-5207   Key: Eb

FREE ACCOMPANIMENTS

**Free Harmonizations to Hymn Tunes By Fifty American Composers**   Edited: D. DeWitt Wasson   Hinshaw Music, Inc.   HMO-145   Key: Eb

Hancock, Gerre   **Organ Improvisations for Hymn-Singing**
Hinshaw Music Co.   HMO-100   Key: Eb

**Wooster**

| BA | DC | 1940 | 1982 | LBW | LW | PH | RCV | UCC | UM | WB |
|----|----|------|------|-----|----|----|-----|-----|----|----|
|    |    |      |      |     |    |    |     |     |    | D  |

**Worcester**

| BA | DC | 1940 | 1982 | LBW | LW | PH | RCV | UCC | UM | WB |
|----|----|------|------|-----|----|----|-----|-----|----|----|
|    |    |      |      |     | C  |    |     |     |    |    |

ORGAN COMPOSITIONS

Engel, James  "Glory be to God the Father"  **The
Concordia Hymn Prelude Series**  Volume 13
Edited: Herbert Gotsch  Concordia Publishing
House  97-5620  Key: C

Words of Life
BA   DC   1940 1982 LBW  LW    PH    RCV   UCC   UM   WB
F                                              G

ORGAN COMPOSITIONS

Held, Wilbur  "Wonderful Words of Life"  **Gospel Hymn
Settings**  Hinshaw Music Co., Inc.  Key: G

Worgan
(See also: Easter Hymn)

Worship
BA    DC   1940 1982 LBW  LW    PH    RCV   UCC   UM   WB
G                              G

Wulfrun
BA    DC   1940 1982 LBW  LW    PH    RCV   UCC   UM   WB
F                              F           F

Wunderbarer König
(See also: Arnsberg; Gröningen)
BA    DC   1940 1982 LBW  LW    PH    RCV   UCC   UM   WB
G    G                      G

ORGAN COMPOSITIONS

Cherwien, David  **Interpretations Based on Hymn-Tunes**
A.M.S.I.  OR-1  Key: G

Karg-Elert, Sigfrid "Mighty King of Miracles"
**Choral Improvisations for Organ for Confirmation
Marriage, Christening and Harvest Festival**
Op. 65, Volume 6  Edited: Robert Leech Bedell
Edward B. Marks Music Corp.  Key: C

Metzger, Hans Arnold  "Wondrous King, All-Glorious"
**The Parish Organist**  Part Four  Edited: Heinrich
Fleischer  Concordia Publishing House  97-1157
Key: G

Pepping, Ernst **Praeludia Postludia I**   B. Schott's
Sohne  Edition 6040  Key: m:e

Reger, Max **30 Short Chorale Preludes** Op. 135a
C. F. Peters Corporation Nr. 3980 Key: G

## FREE ACCOMPANIMENTS

Bunjes, Paul **New Organ Accompaniments for Hymns**
Concordia Publishing House 97-5348 Key: G

Wye Valley
BA  DC  1940 1982 LBW  LW  PH  RCV  UCC  UM  WB
F

Wylde Green
BA  DC  1940 1982 LBW  LW  PH  RCV  UCC  UM  WB
         F                                      F

Wyngate Canon
BA  DC  1940 1982 LBW  LW  PH  RCV  UCC  UM  WB
         F

# X

Xavier
BA  DC  1940 1982 LBW  LW  PH  RCV  UCC  UM  WB
f

# Y

Yarbrough
BA  DC  1940 1982 LBW  LW  PH  RCV  UCC  UM  WB
G

Yattendon
BA  DC  1940 1982 LBW  LW  PH  RCV  UCC  UM  WB
         F              F   F

## FREE ACCOMPANIMENTS

**Free Harmonizations to Hymn Tunes By Fifty American
Composers** Edited: D. DeWitt Wasson Hinshaw
Music, Inc. HMO-145 Key: F

Yigdal
(See also: Leoni)
BA  DC  1940 1982 LBW  LW  PH  RCV  UCC  UM  WB
              f   f                         f

437

Wyton, Alec **New Shoots from Old Routes** Sacred
Music Press KK 279 Key: f

## York

| BA | DC | 1940 | 1982 | LBW | LW | PH | RCV | UCC | UM | WB |
|----|----|------|------|-----|----|----|-----|-----|----|----|
|    |    | F    | F    |     |    | F  |     |     |    |    |

### ORGAN COMPOSITIONS

Wood, Charles "York Tune" **A Galaxy of Hymn Tune
Preludes for Organ** Galaxy Music Corp. GMC 2353
Key: Db

### FREE ACCOMPANIMENTS

**Free Harmonizations to Hymn Tunes By Fifty American
Composers** Edited: D. DeWitt Wasson Hinshaw
Music, Inc. HMO-145 Key: F

## Yorkshire

| BA | DC | 1940 | 1982 | LBW | LW | PH | RCV | UCC | UM | WB |
|----|----|------|------|-----|----|----|-----|-----|----|----|
|    |    | C    | C    |     |    | C  |     | C   |    |    |

### ORGAN COMPOSITIONS

Metzger, Hans Arnold "Christians, Awake, Salute the
Happy Morn" **The Parish Organist** Christmas and
Epiphany Music Part Six Concordia Publishing
House 97-1391 Key: C

### FREE ACCOMPANIMENTS

**Free Harmonizations to Hymn Tunes By Fifty American
Composers** Edited: D. DeWitt Wasson Hinshaw
Music, Inc. HMO-145 Key: C

# Z

## Zeuch mich, zeuch mich

| BA | DC | 1940 | 1982 | LBW | LW | PH | RCV | UCC | UM | WB |
|----|----|------|------|-----|----|----|-----|-----|----|----|
|    |    |      | Bb   |     |    |    |     |     |    |    |

## Zeuch uns nach Dir

| BA | DC | 1940 | 1982 | LBW | LW | PH | RCV | UCC | UM | WB |
|----|----|------|------|-----|----|----|-----|-----|----|----|
|    |    |      |      |     |    |    | C   |     |    |    |

## Známe to, Pane Bože náš

| BA | DC | 1940 | 1982 | LBW | LW | PH | RCV | UCC | UM | WB |
|----|----|------|------|-----|----|----|-----|-----|----|----|
|    |    |      | D    |     |    |    |     |     |    |    |

Beck, Theodore  "Your Heart, O God, Is Grieved"  **The Concordia Hymn Prelude Series**  Volume 9  Edited: Herbert Gotsch  Concordia Publishing House  97-5616  Key: D

<u>Zoan</u>

| BA | DC | 1940 | 1982 | LBW | LW | PH | RCV | UCC | UM | WB |
|----|----|------|------|-----|----|----|-----|-----|----|----|
|    | G  |      |      |     |    |    |     |     |    |    |

<u>Zpivejmež všickni vesele</u>

| BA | DC | 1940 | 1982 | LBW | LW | PH | RCV | UCC | UM | WB |
|----|----|------|------|-----|----|----|-----|-----|----|----|
|    |    |      |      | C   | C  |    |     |     |    |    |

Wienhorst, Richard  "Make Songs of Joy"  **The Concordia Hymn Prelude Series**  Volume 13  Edited: Herbert Gotsch  Concordia Publishing House  97-5618  Key: C

<u>Zu meinem Herrn</u>

| BA | DC | 1940 | 1982 | LBW | LW | PH | RCV | UCC | UM | WB |
|----|----|------|------|-----|----|----|-----|-----|----|----|
|    | Ab |      |      |     |    | Ab |     | Ab  |    | Ab |

439

# NOTES AND ADDITIONS

# NOTES AND ADDITIONS

# NOTES AND ADDITIONS

# NOTES AND ADDITIONS

# NOTES AND ADDITIONS

# NOTES AND ADDITIONS

# NOTES AND ADDITIONS

# NOTES AND ADDITIONS

# NOTES AND ADDITIONS